The
Constitution
in the
Supreme Court

The Constitution in the Supreme Court

The First Hundred Years

1789–1888

David P. Currie

University of Chicago Press • Chicago and London

DAVID P. CURRIE is Harry N. Wyatt Professor of Law
at the University of Chicago Law School.

The University of Chicago Press, Chicago 60637
The University of Chicago Press, Ltd., London
© 1985 by The University of Chicago
All rights reserved. Published 1985
Printed in the United States of America

94 93 92 91 90 89 88   5432

Library of Congress Cataloging in Publication Data

Currie, David P.
  The constitution in the Supreme Court

  Includes index.
    1. United States—Constitutional law—Interpretation
and construction.   2. United States.   Supreme Court.
3. United States—Constitutional history.   I. Title.
KF4550.C87   1985   342.73   85-1205
ISBN 0-226-13108-4   347.302

Contents

Introduction

Histories of the Supreme Court and of the Constitution abound, as do legal analyses of constitutional decisions. The histories, however, tend to eschew legal criticism, while the analyses tend to be organized by subject matter. My aim is to provide a critical history, analyzing from a lawyer's standpoint the entire constitutional work of the Court's first hundred years. My search is for methods of constitutional analysis, for techniques of opinion writing, for the quality of the performances of the Court and of its members.[1]

Standards of judicial performance not only change over time;[2] they are far from uniform today.[3] Accordingly, although my own criteria will appear clearly enough in

[1]Much of this book originally appeared in the form of articles in the *University of Chicago Law Review* and in the *Duke Law Journal*, to which thanks are extended for permission to reprint. See Currie, *The Constitution in the Supreme Court: 1789–1801*, 48 U. Chi. L. Rev. 819 (1981), ©1981 by The University of Chicago; *The Powers of the Federal Courts, 1801–1835*, 49 U. Chi. L. Rev. 646 (1982), ©1982 by The University of Chicago; *State and Congressional Powers, 1801–1835*, 49 U. Chi. L. Rev. 887 (1982), ©1982 by The University of Chicago; *Contracts and Commerce, 1836–1864*, 1983 Duke L. J. 471; *Article IV and Federal Powers 1836–1864*, 1983 Duke L. J. 695; *Civil War and Reconstruction, 1865–1873*, 51 U. Chi. L. Rev. 131 (1984), ©1984 by The University of Chicago; *Limitations on State Power, 1865–1873*, 51 U. Chi. L. Rev. 329 (1984), ©1984 by The University of Chicago. I should also like to express my appreciation to Richard S. Arnold, Douglas G. Baird, Gerhard Casper, Barbara Flynn Currie, Frank Easterbrook, Richard A. Epstein, Henry J. Friendly, Charles M. Gray, Richard H. Helmholz, Dennis J. Hutchinson, Stanton Krauss, Philip B. Kurland, John H. Langbein, Paul Mishkin, Henry Monaghan, Phil C. Neal, Michael E. Smith, Rayman Solomon, Geoffrey Stone, Cass R. Sunstein, and James B. White for unfailing help and encouragement; to Locke Bowman, Mark Holmes, Karla Kraus, Richard Levy, Paul Strella, and Roy Underhill for valuable research assistance; to the University of Chicago's computer, and to Robert L. Ashenhurst and Roland J. Bailey, respectively, for assistance in understanding and in feeding it; to Mary Goldman and Lorrie Shaw, who tirelessly typed the manuscript; to the Duke University School of Law, where portions of the book were delivered as the Brainerd Currie Memorial Lecture in 1982; to Ruth Wyatt Rosenson, whose generosity helped make this study possible; and to John E. Ultmann, without whom there would have been no book at all.

[2]*See* White, *The Working Life of the Marshall Court, 1815–1835*, 70 Va. L. Rev. 1, 52 (1984).

[3]*See* J. Ely, Democracy and Distrust, chs. 1-2 (1980).

the course of discussing the opinions, it may be well to state some of them explicitly at the start.

I begin with the conviction that the Constitution is a law binding the judges no less than the other officials whose actions the courts undertake to review. That is what the Constitution itself says,[4] and the Constitution is the source from which federal courts derive their powers. It is also the express basis on which the Supreme Court has claimed the power of judicial review.[5]

Since the Constitution is law, the judges have no right to ignore constitutional limitations with which they disagree. Moreover, the same clause that makes the Constitution the "Law of the Land" gives identical status to federal statutes enacted "in Pursuance thereof." Whatever this may signify as to the status of laws that contradict the Constitution,[6] it lends added strength to the unmistakable inference that when Congress has acted within the powers granted by that instrument, it is not for the courts to interfere.[7] The tenth amendment makes the same point with respect to state laws that do not offend the Constitution.[8] It follows that the judges have no more right to invent limitations not found in the Constitution than to disregard those put there by the Framers. In short, when a judge swears to uphold the Constitution,[9] he promises obedience to a set of rules laid down by someone else.[10]

This is not to say that either the text of the Constitution or the limited additional evidence we have of the Framers' intentions answers every question of constitutional interpretation. It is not to pretend that the Framers either thought out all the ramifications of their terminology or would have agreed in all particulars if they had. Nor is it to deny the possibility that one provision or another may have been meant to

---

[4]U.S. CONST. art. VI: "This Constitution, and the Laws of the United States which shall be made in Pursuance thereof; and all Treaties made, or which shall be made, under the Authority of the United States, shall be the supreme Law of the Land . . . ."

[5]See infra chapter 3, discussing Marbury v. Madison. The pedigree of the Constitution itself contains a significant blemish, for it took effect upon the approval of conventions in nine states despite an express provision of existing law that the "perpetual" Articles of Confederation could be altered only with the consent of the legislatures of all thirteen. Compare U.S. CONST. art. VII with Articles of Confederation, art. 13, Act of July 9, 1778, 1 Stat. 4, 8–9. The interesting question why one should treat as law an act arguably illegal in its inception is fortunately beyond the scope of the present inquiry. One rather formalistic response is that judges and other officials have sworn to do so, U.S. CONST. art. VI. Functional claims of repose and stability are also as relevant here as in the case of erroneous judicial precedents. See Madzimbamuto v. Lardner-Burke, [1969] 1 A.C. 645 (P. C.), refusing to recognize acts of the revolutionary government of Southern Rhodesia because of continued British efforts to regain control but quoting favorably from Ugandan and Pakistani decisions upholding acts of established revolutionary governments illegal in their inception. And perhaps it is not inconsistent with an ultimate right of revolution either to reserve it for truly pressing occasions (see J. LOCKE, SECOND TREATISE OF CIVIL GOVERNMENT chs. 18, 19 (C. Sherman ed. 1937)) or to insist that until we decide to take the ball home we ought to play by the rules. Cf. infra chapter 9, discussing the significance of the Supremacy Clause for the secession question.

[6]See infra chapter 3.

[7]E.g., U.S. CONST. art. I, § 8: "The Congress shall have Power to lay and collect Taxes . . . ."

[8]Id., amend. X: "The powers not delegated to the United States by the Constitution, nor prohibited by it to the States, are reserved to the States respectively, or to the people."

[9]Id., art. VI.

[10]The practical power of the Court to annul the applicable law does not detract from this conclusion. As H. L. A. Hart said, we may tell the umpire in a sporting match that we will accept his decision, but we also tell him his duty is to apply the rules. H. HART, THE CONCEPT OF LAW 138–41 (1961).

leave a broad range of judgment to the interpreter: a ban on "excessive fines,"[11] for example, on its face is less confining than a requirement that a President "have . . . attained to the Age of thirty-five Years."[12] The point is only that it is just as inappropriate for a judge as it is for a legislator or an executive to substitute his judgment for that of the "People of the United States"[13] in any case in which the latter can fairly be ascertained.

Beyond this, I share the conventional views that judges have an obligation to explain the reasons for their decisions as concisely and persuasively as practicable, and that they should strive for consistency, reserving the right to correct egregious and important errors on relatively rare occasions. I shall not stop to justify these convictions. As a colleague of mine recently remarked, "[s]cholars who spend too much time debating how to conduct a discourse may never be able to say anything" at all.[14] My aim is not to defend the rule of law but to apply its methodology to the cases.

[11]U.S. CONST. amend. VIII.

[12]*Id.*, art. II, § 1.

[13]*Id.*, preamble: "We, the People of the United States, . . . do ordain and establish this Constitution for the United States of America."

[14]Easterbrook, *Substance and Due Process*, 1982 SUP. CT. REV. 85, 91.

Part One

Chief Justices Jay and Ellsworth
1789–1801

Introduction to Part One

The accomplishments of the Supreme Court during the long period when John Marshall was Chief Justice were so great that the modest record of his predecessors tends to be overlooked. The relative paucity of early federal legislation, the absence of a general grant of original federal jurisdiction over cases arising under federal law, and the fact that the Court's jurisdiction was largely appellate contributed to a low starting caseload. Yet for all this the twelve years before Marshall's appointment proved to be a significant formative period during which the Justices established traditions of constitutional interpretation that were to influence the entire future course of decision.[1]

The first Chief Justice was John Jay; his associates were John Rutledge, William Cushing, James Wilson, John Blair, and James Iredell. Of the original appointees only Cushing remained in 1801. Jay was replaced by Oliver Ellsworth, his brethren by Thomas Johnson, Samuel Chase, Bushrod Washington, and Alfred Moore. Johnson in turn was replaced by William Paterson.[2] Twelve men in all sat before Marshall.[3]

[1] The most comprehensive legal history of the Court's work during this period is J. GOEBEL, 1 HISTORY OF THE SUPREME COURT OF THE UNITED STATES (1971). Also particularly useful in placing the decisions in historical context is 1 C. WARREN, THE SUPREME COURT IN UNITED STATES HISTORY (2d ed. 1926). See also the biographies cited in note 3 infra.

[2]

JUSTICES OF THE SUPREME COURT, 1789–1801

		1789	91	93	95	97	99	1801
*John Jay	(1789–1795)	├────────────────┤						
*John Rutledge	(1789–1791)(1795)	├──────┤		+				
James Wilson	(1789–1798)	├──────────────────────────┤						
John Blair	(1789–1796)	├────────────────────┤						
William Cushing	(1789–1810)	├───────────────────────────────────						
James Iredell	(1790–1799)	├───────────────────────────┤						
Thomas Johnson	(1791–1793)	├──────┤						

3

Several of these Justices, however, played no visible part in the decisions here considered. Rutledge, although he did some circuit duty, resigned without ever sitting on the Supreme Court. When reappointed as Chief Justice in 1795, he served only until the next session of Congress, for he was not confirmed.[4] Johnson departed before any significant opinions were written; Ellsworth sat in none of the cases that produced real opinions; Washington and Moore belong to the Marshall period. As far as the written word is concerned, we therefore are studying seven men: Jay, Cushing, Wilson, Blair, Iredell, Paterson, and Chase.

The Supreme Court published full-scale opinions construing the Constitution in only three cases before 1801. *Chisholm v. Georgia*[5] held that a state could be sued in federal court without its consent; *Hylton v. United States,*[6] that a federal tax on carriages was not a "direct" tax required to be apportioned among the states according to the census; *Calder v. Bull,*[7] that a state legislature had not passed a forbidden ex post facto law when it set aside a judicial decree in a will contest.

These three controversies, however, do not exhaust the pre–Marshall Court's encounters with matters constitutional. In *Ware v. Hylton,*[8] the Court invalidated a state law under the supremacy clause because it contradicted a treaty. *Penhallow v. Doane's Administrators*[9] produced opinions on federal powers before 1789; *Cooper v. Telfair,*[10] on questions under a state constitution. On at least nine other occasions, the Court faced questions with constitutional overtones respecting the powers of the federal courts. In *Hayburn's Case,*[11] the Court was asked to pass upon a statute subjecting certain circuit court decisions to revision by the Secretary of War; in

---

JUSTICES OF THE SUPREME COURT, 1789–1801 (*cont.*)

		1789	91	93	95	97	99	1801
William Paterson	(1793–1806)			├──	────	────	────	──────
*Oliver Ellsworth	(1796–1800)				├──	────	──┤	
Samuel Chase	(1796–1811)				├──	────	────	──────
Bushrod Washington	(1798–1829)					├─	────	──────
Alfred Moore	(1799–1804)						├──	──────

*Denotes Chief Justice.
See G. GUNTHER, CASES AND MATERIALS ON CONSTITUTIONAL LAW, app. A at A-1 to A-2 (10th ed. 1980). Five of the six vacancies in this short period were caused by resignations. This remarkably high turnover reflected the uncertain status of the new federal government and the arduous duty of riding circuit. Rutledge preferred to be Chief Justice of South Carolina, 1 C. WARREN, *supra* note 1, at 56–57, and Johnson refused to remain, as Iredell called the Justices, a "traveling postboy." *Id.* at 86.

[3]Biographies of the first Justices include R. MORRIS, JOHN JAY, THE NATION AND THE COURT (1967); G. MCREE, LIFE AND CORRESPONDENCE OF JAMES IREDELL (1857); W. BROWN, THE LIFE OF OLIVER ELLSWORTH (1905); J. CUSHING, A REVOLUTIONARY CONSERVATIVE: THE PUBLIC LIFE OF WILLIAM CUSHING, 1732–1810 (1959); J. ELSMERE, JUSTICE SAMUEL CHASE (1980); and J. O'CONNOR, WILLIAM PATERSON, LAWYER AND STATESMAN (1979).

[4]G. GUNTHER, *supra* note 2, app. A, at A-1; 1 C. WARREN, *supra* note 2, at 56–57, 128–37.

[5]2 U.S. (2 Dall.) 419 (1793).

[6]3 U.S. (3 Dall.) 171 (1796).

[7]3 U.S. (3 Dall.) 386 (1798).

[8]3 U.S. (3 Dall.) 199 (1796).

[9]3 U.S. (3 Dall.) 54 (1795).

[10]4 U.S. (4 Dall.) 14 (1800).

[11]2 U.S. (2 Dall.) 409 (1792).

Chandler's Case[12] and *United States v. Todd*,[13] upon the authority of circuit judges to act extrajudicially as "commissioners" under the same statute; and in *La Vengeance*,[14] upon the scope of the admiralty jurisdiction. In *Hollingsworth v. Virginia*,[15] the Court held that the eleventh amendment limited pending as well as future suits against states, and resolved a major issue as to the process of constitutional amendment. In *Wiscart v. D'Auchy*,[16] it respected a statutory limitation on its appellate jurisdiction, and in *Turner v. Bank of North America*,[17] it enforced a congressional restriction on the diversity jurisdiction, despite arguments that both restrictions offended article III. In *Mossman v. Higginson*,[18] it read restrictively a statute providing federal jurisdiction when an alien was a party in order to avoid finding the law unconstitutional. Finally, the Court invoked constitutional support in its refusal to honor an executive request for an advisory opinion in the so-called Correspondence of the Justices.[19] Not all these matters were clearly disposed of on constitutional grounds, and in none did the Court publish substantial opinions. But these facts are themselves of interest to the student of constitutional litigation.[20]

---

[12]The decision in *Chandler's Case* was not published and is known only from a speech in Congress, 11 ANNALS OF CONG. 903-04 (1802) (remarks of Rep. Dana), and from a discussion in Marbury v. Madison, 5 U.S. (1 Cranch) 137, 171-72 (1803).

[13]*Todd* also was unpublished. We know of the case from a report by Secretary of War Henry Knox to Congress (Feb. 21, 1794), *reprinted in* 1 AM. STATE PAPERS (MISCELLANEOUS) No. 47, at 78 (W. Lowrie & W. Franklin eds., Wash., D.C. 1834), and from Chief Justice Roger Taney's account in United States v. Ferreira, 54 U.S. (13 How.) 40, 52-53 (1851 Term) (Note by the Chief Justice, Inserted by Order of the Court). The entire record was published subsequently in Ritz, *United States v. Yale Todd (U.S. 1794)*, 15 WASH. & LEE L. REV. 220, 227-31 (1958).

[14]3 U.S. (3 Dall.) 297 (1796).

[15]3 U.S. (3 Dall.) 378 (1798).

[16]3 U.S. (3 Dall.) 321 (1796).

[17]4 U.S. (4 Dall.) 8 (1799).

[18]4 U.S. (4 Dall.) 12 (1800).

[19]*Reprinted in* P. BATOR, P. MISHKIN, D. SHAPIRO & H. WECHSLER, HART & WECHSLER'S THE FEDERAL COURTS AND THE FEDERAL SYSTEM 64-66 (2d ed. 1973) [hereinafter cited as HART & WECHSLER].

[20]A thorough understanding of the early development of constitutional doctrine must take account of the decisions of the Justices on circuit, but that is a project for another time.

1

Outlines of Federal Jurisdiction

Because jurisdiction is a threshold issue in every federal case, the Court would settle in its first forty years many of the fundamental issues surrounding the federal judicial power. A significant start was made in the cases decided before Marshall. These decisions are the subject of this chapter; the remaining pre-Marshall decisions are considered in the next.

I. "Cases" and "Controversies"

A. *Hayburn's Case*

In 1792, Congress authorized pensions for disabled war veterans. The statute required applicants to file proofs with "the circuit court," which, if it found the applicant eligible, was to certify its finding to "the Secretary at War."[1] The Secretary in turn could place the name of the certified applicant on the pension list, or he could withhold the name and report the matter to Congress if he had "cause to suspect imposition or mistake."[2]

William Hayburn filed for a pension under this statute, and the Circuit Court for the District of Pennsylvania refused to entertain his application. Although the judges apparently wrote no opinion, they took the unusual step of explaining their refusal in a letter to President Washington. Two other circuits[3] also addressed their views to the President, though one[4] conceded that no application was pending before it. All three courts concluded that the statute was unconstitutional because it attempted to

---

[1]Act of Mar. 23, 1792, ch. 11, § 2, 1 Stat. 243, 244 (repealed by Act of Feb. 28, 1793, ch. 17, § 1, 1 Stat. 324, 324).

[2]*Id*. § 4, 1 Stat. at 244.

[3]The Circuit Courts for the Districts of New York and North Carolina.

[4]The Circuit Court for the District of North Carolina.

subject court decisions to revision by the Secretary of War.[5] Five Supreme Court Justices sitting on circuit[6] joined in these declarations of unwillingness to carry out an act of Congress they deemed unconstitutional—eleven years before *Marbury v. Madison.*[7]

Attorney General Edmund Randolph then asked the Supreme Court for a writ of mandamus compelling the circuit court to pass upon Hayburn's petition. An examination on the merits would have required the Court to decide whether the statute conferred either nonjudicial power on the courts or judicial power on the Secretary of War, and if so, whether negative implications should be drawn from the provision of article III stating that "the judicial Power . . . shall be vested in . . . Courts."[8] But the Court never reached these questions. The Attorney General, having neglected to secure Hayburn as his client, announced that he was acting "without an application from any particular person, but with a view to procure the execution of an act of congress."[9] Evidently on its own motion, the Court "declared, that they entertained great doubt" as to the right of the Attorney General "to proceed *ex officio.*" The latter attempted to justify this manner of proceeding, "[b]ut the Court being divided in opinion on that question, the motion, made *ex officio*, was not allowed."[10] The Attorney General then entered an appearance as counsel for Hayburn, but the case later was mooted by the adoption of a new statute providing "in another way, for the relief of the pensioners."[11]

The Court seems to have taken for granted, as it since has held,[12] that certain objections to subject matter jurisdiction might properly be raised by the Court on its own motion. Were it otherwise, jurisdictional limitations serving important institutional goals[13] might be evaded by the agreement of parties with no incentive to enforce them.[14] The point is not confined to constitutional limitations on jurisdiction, but it embraces them; it is an important part of the procedural framework for the enforcement of constitutional limitations. Dallas's report, however, does not indi-

---

[5]The letters are reprinted in Dallas's report of Hayburn's Case, 2 U.S. (2 Dall.) 409, 410-14 n.(a) (1792), and in 1 AM. STATE PAPERS (MISCELLANEOUS), *supra* introduction to part one, note 13, Nos. 30-32, at 49-53. For additional material on the case, see Farrand, *The First Hayburn Case, 1792,* 13 AM. HIST. REV. 281 (1908). *See also* 2 ANNALS OF CONG. 556-57 (1792) (reporting Hayburn's memorial to Congress for relief following the circuit court's decision, and the appointment of a committee to inquire into Hayburn's allegations).

[6]Jay, Cushing, Wilson, Blair, and Iredell.

[7]5 U.S. (1 Cranch) 137 (1803).

[8]U.S. CONST. art. III, § 1. There was also a question whether there was, or needed to be under article III, a proper defendant. *Cf.* Tutun v. United States, 270 U.S. 568, 577 (1926) (holding naturalization petitions within the judicial power because the "United States is always a possible adverse party"); HART & WECHSLER, *supra* introduction to part one, note 19, at 90.

[9]2 U.S. (2 Dall.) at 408.

[10]*Id.* at 409.

[11]*Id.* at 409-10. *See* Act of Feb. 28, 1793, ch. 17, § 3, 1 Stat. 324, 324-25.

[12]*E.g.,* Mansfield, Coldwater & L. Mich. Ry. v. Swan, 111 U.S. 379, 382 (1884).

[13]*Contrast* Neirbo Co. v. Bethlehem Shipbuilding Corp., 308 U.S. 165, 167-68 (1939) (stating that an objection to venue may be "lost by failure to assert it seasonably" because venue, unlike subject matter jurisdiction, only "relates to the convenience of litigants").

[14]*Cf.* Currie, *Suitcase Divorce in the Conflict of Laws:* Simons, Rosenstiel *and* Borax, 34 U. CHI. L. REV. 26, 55-56 (1966) (collusive allegations of domicile by spouses traveling to liberal jurisdictions to obtain divorces).

cate that the Justices stopped to explain that they had the power or duty to raise such issues, or whence it was derived.

Nor does the report reveal the Justices' reasons for concluding that the Attorney General lacked authority to proceed *ex officio*. Indeed, we must turn to the newspapers to find that the vote was 3–3,[15] for Dallas reveals only that the Court was "divided."[16] Remembering the future, we can surmise that three Justices may have concluded that the Court could decide only "Cases" and "Controversies"—the terms employed in article III;[17] that there was no case or controversy unless the applicant for relief himself was injured by the disputed action;[18] and that the analogy of the Government's acknowledged authority to prosecute crimes[19] did not take the case outside this principle.[20]

None of these conclusions is obvious, and it is by no means clear that the Justices meant to invoke what we now know as the constitutional dimension of the law of standing to sue. It is conceivable that they gave a narrow reading to section 35 of the Judiciary Act,[21] which authorized the Attorney General only "to prosecute and conduct all suits in the Supreme Court in which the United States shall be concerned,"[22] or to section 13,[23] which gave the Supreme Court mandamus jurisdiction only "in cases warranted by the principles and usages of law"[24]—which in turn might have required an interested plaintiff. Either of these positions would have raised the further question whether, if the Attorney General's application *was* a case or controversy within article III, Congress had the power to deprive the Court of jurisdiction over it under its constitutional authority to make "Exceptions" to the Court's appellate jurisdiction.[25]

In short, the reported disposition of this first constitutional controversy in the Supreme Court was inconclusive. We know the Court left the validity of executive revision of court decisions for another day, but we cannot say whether the three

---

[15]*See* 1 C. WARREN, *supra* introduction to part one, note 2, at 77-78.

[16]2 U.S. (2 Dall.) at 409.

[17]U.S. CONST. art. III, § 2, para. 1.

[18]*See, e.g.*, Simon v. Eastern Ky. Welfare Rights Org., 426 U.S. 26, 38 (1976).

[19]Judiciary Act of 1789, ch. 20, § 35, 1 Stat. 73, 92.

[20]*See* HART & WECHSLER, *supra* introduction to part one, note 19, at 90, suggesting the analogies of the powers of English and state attorneys general "in relation to charities and in the enforcement of corporation laws." *Cf.* 28 U.S.C. § 2403(a) (1976) and 29 U.S.C. § 216(c) (Supp. III 1979) (respectively authorizing the United States to intervene in private actions to defend the constitutionality of statutes and to sue for damages on behalf of workers injured by violations of the Fair Labor Standards Act). Consider also the vexing precedents as to the authority of states to sue to vindicate sovereign or citizen concerns. D. CURRIE, FEDERAL COURTS: CASES AND MATERIALS 65–67 (3d ed. 1982). HART & WECHSLER, *supra* introduction to part one, note 19, at 90, calls attention to the problem that federal officials were on both sides of the *Hayburn* case.

[21]Julius Goebel seemed to believe this was the basis of the decision. J. GOEBEL, 1 HISTORY OF THE SUPREME COURT OF THE UNITED STATES 563 (1971). The scope of section 35 had been discussed by counsel, *see* 1 C. WARREN, *supra* introduction to part one, note 2, at 78.

[22]Judiciary Act of 1789, ch. 20, § 35, 1 Stat. 73, 93.

[23]*See* 1 C. WARREN, *supra* introduction to part one, note 2, at 81.

[24]Judiciary Act of 1789, ch. 20, § 13, 1 Stat. 73, 81 (current version in relevant part at 28 U.S.C. § 1651 (1976)).

[25]U.S. CONST. art. III, § 2, para. 2.

Justices who voted for this result did so on constitutional grounds.[26] It is tempting to criticize the Court for not explaining what it was doing, yet even today the Court usually does not write opinions when it is evenly divided and cannot resolve the questions presented. Moreover, we cannot be certain that the Justices did not reveal their reasons at the time, for there was no official reporter of decisions until 1816,[27] and until 1834, no requirement that opinions be filed.[28] Indeed, a later reporter of decisions who attempted to make a complete collection of early opinions concluded that before 1800 the written opinion was the exception, not the rule.[29] What got reported in the earliest days was what Alexander Dallas for his own purposes could gather and elected to divulge.[30]

B. *Chandler's Case* and *United States v. Todd*

The 1793 statute that mooted *Hayburn's Case* did not end litigation over the earlier pension law. Some of the judges, despite their conclusion that they could not certify pension claims in their judicial capacity, had been willing to do so "in the capacity of commissioners."[31] The 1793 act preserved "rights founded upon legal adjudications" under the prior law and directed the Secretary and the Attorney General "to take such measures as may be necessary to obtain an adjudication of the Supreme Court of the United States, on the validity of any such rights claimed under the act aforesaid, by the determination of certain persons styling themselves commissioners."[32]

Once again proceeding *ex officio*, the Attorney General first asked the Supreme Court for a writ of mandamus directing the Secretary to place on the pension list a certified claimant who had not been paid. As he reported, however, "two of the judges . . . expressed their disinclination," despite the new statute, "to hear a motion in behalf of a man who had not employed me for that purpose," and the motion prudently was withdrawn.[33] Once again we cannot be sure the Justices' qualms were of constitutional dimension; the statutory reference to "such measures

[26]A modern court probably would have refused to reach the constitutional question in the absence of a more explicit statutory right to sue.

[27]*See* Dunne, *The Early Court Reporters*, 1976 SUP. CT. HIST. SOC'Y Y.B. 61, 64.

[28]*Id.* at 62; Davis, *Appendix to the Reports of the Decisions of the Supreme Court of the United States*, 131 U.S. app. at xvi (1889).

[29]Davis, *supra* note 28, at xv-xvi. In *Calder v. Bull*, 3 U.S. (3 Dall.) 386, 398 (1798), Justice Iredell observed that he had "not had an opportunity to reduce [his] opinion to writing." By 1804, however, unofficial reporter William Cranch was able to describe "the practice which the court has adopted of reducing their opinion to writing, in all cases of difficulty or importance . . . ." 5 U.S. (1 Cranch) at pp. iv-v.

[30]*See* Dunne, *supra* note 27, at 62-63. Professor Goebel said that Dallas reported only about half the cases decided and reported them tardily: his fourth volume, containing Supreme Court cases decided in 1799 and 1800, appeared in 1807. J. GOEBEL, *supra* note 21, at 665.

[31]*See* Hayburn's Case, 2 U.S. (2 Dall.) 409, 410 n.(a).

[32]Act of Feb. 28, 1793, ch. 17, § 3, 1 Stat. 324, 325.

[33]Letter from Attorney General Edmund Randolph to Secretary of War Henry Knox (Aug. 9, 1793), *reprinted in* 1 AM. STATE PAPERS (MISCELLANEOUS), *supra* introduction to part one, note 13, No. 47, at 78; Ritz, *supra* introduction to part one, note 13, at 225.

as may be necessary" may have meant finding a case that met preexisting jurisdictional requirements.

The standing problem was cured when a similar request was made by an attorney representing an unpaid certified claimant named John Chandler. Nevertheless the Court denied relief: "having considered the two acts of Congress" relating to pensions, it was "of opinion that a *mandamus* cannot issue to the Secretary of War for the purpose expressed."[34] In *Todd*, the United States sued to recover money from a veteran already on the pension list, on the ground that the "commissioners" who had certified his claim had been without authority to pass upon the application. The Supreme Court held for the United States.[35]

Thus, *Todd* clearly established, and *Chandler* may have held, that the judges had lacked power to sit as commissioners. Like *Hayburn*, both *Chandler* and *Todd* can be justified on constitutional grounds: arguably article III forbids judges to do nonjudicial tasks; arguably the processing of claims subject to executive revision was not judicial; and arguably it made no difference that the judges had removed their robes.

It is improper to conclude, however, as occasional commentators have done, that the Supreme Court in *Chandler* or *Todd* held the 1792 pension statute unconstitutional.[36] As in *Hayburn*, no opinion was published in either case; indeed, not even the judgments were published.[37] We therefore do not know the Court's reasons for holding against Chandler and Todd, and in both cases there was a plausible statutory basis for decision. Because the statute required application to "the circuit court," it appeared, as the North Carolina circuit judges suggested in *Hayburn*, to authorize judges to act only as a court, not as commissioners.[38]

Both cases presented an additional constitutional problem. Neither *Chandler* nor

---

[34]11 ANNALS OF CONG. 904 (1802), *quoted in* Sherman, *The Case of John Chandler v. The Secretary of War*, 14 YALE L.J. 431, 435 (1905). The decision in *Chandler's Case* was not reported and is known only from other sources. *See* introduction to part one, note 12 *supra*.

[35]Like *Chandler's Case, United States v. Todd* was unreported and is known only from other sources. *See* introduction to part one, note 12 *supra*.

[36]Gordon Sherman so concluded as to *Chandler*, and Wilfred Ritz and John Bancroft Davis, a Supreme Court reporter, so concluded as to *Todd*. Sherman, *supra* note 34, at 437-38; Ritz, *supra* introduction to part one, note 13, at 227; Davis, *supra note 28, at ccxxxv. See also* Dianisopoulous & Peterson, *Rediscovering the American Origins of Judicial Review*, 18 JOHN MARSHALL L. REV. 49 (1984). To the contrary as to *Todd* are J. GOEBEL, *supra* note 21, at 564 n.57, and Farrand, *supra* note 5, at 282-83 & n.4 (citing J. THAYER, CASES ON CONSTITUTIONAL LAW pt. 1, at 105 n.1 (1894)).

[37]*See* introduction to part one, notes 12 and 13 *supra*.

[38]2 U.S. (2 Dall.) at 413 n.(a). In Chief Justice Taney's view, *Todd* had determined that the statute could not be construed to authorize the judges to act "out of court as commissioners." United States v. Ferreira, 54 U.S. (13 How.) 40, 53 (1851 Term) (Note of the Chief Justice, Inserted by Order of the Court). Modern theory tells us that the Justices *should* have chosen the statutory ground in preference to the constitutional. But this does not prove that that was what the Court in fact did.

In *Chandler*, the Court's cryptic reference to its consideration of "the two acts of Congress," 11 ANNALS OF CONG. 904 (1802), lends credence to the conclusion that the Constitution was not the basis of decision in that case. Moreover, it is not even clear that the ground for decision in *Chandler* was that the judges lacked authority to act as commissioners: the decision rather may have been that mandamus was unavailable. Marshall was later at pains to argue, without proof, that *Chandler* had not decided that mandamus was unavailable against a Cabinet officer. Marbury v. Madison, 5 U.S. (1 Cranch) 137, 171-72 (1803). But even if Marshall was right, *Marbury* itself would say that mandamus lay only to enforce a plain ministerial duty, *id.* at 165-73, while the pension statute directed the Secretary to exercise judgment in determining which certified applicants to place on the pension list.

Todd sought review of a lower court decision; each was filed as an original action in the Supreme Court.[39] If the statutory authorization of "measures . . . necessary to obtain an adjudication of the Supreme Court"[40] purported to give the Court original jurisdiction,[41] it was of doubtful constitutionality. Neither *Chandler* nor *Todd* was within those categories of cases over which article III specifies "the Supreme Court shall have original Jurisdiction,"[42] and *Marbury v. Madison* soon was to establish that Congress could not confer original jurisdiction in other cases.[43] The dismissal of *Chandler* may have been on this ground.[44] Chief Justice Taney, on the other hand, thought that by entertaining *Todd* the Court had held to the contrary.[45] The failure of the Court to leave any significant traces of its reasoning makes it equally plausible to surmise that in both cases the Justices simply overlooked the problem.

We are left with two precedents that fail to reveal whether a constitutional question was decided and that were not even made available to the bar for such guidance as the unadorned results might afford. *Chandler* and *Todd* tell us nothing about the Constitution, but they say much about the early Court's attitude toward explanation and dissemination of its decisions. One cannot but wonder how many other possibly significant decisions may yet turn up in somebody's attic, and how many more may never be found.[46] The chances may not be great, but *Chandler* and *Todd* are sobering admonitions for those who seek to know the complete history of constitutional adjudication.

C.   The Correspondence of the Justices

In July 1793, Secretary of State Thomas Jefferson wrote to the Justices on behalf of President Washington seeking their advice on a number of legal questions arising from the ongoing hostilities between England and France: whether, for example, existing treaties gave France the right "to fit out originally in and from the ports of the United States vessels armed for war," and whether the neutrality laws permitted France to establish prize courts in this country. Jefferson prefaced the specific inquiries with the general question "whether the public may, with propriety, be availed of [the Justices'] *advice on these questions?*"[47]

---

[39]*See* Ritz, *supra* introduction to part one, note 13, at 227-28; Sherman, *supra* note 34, at 435. Even if the collateral attack on the commissioners' action in *Todd* was the equivalent of an appeal, what it sought to review was a nonjudicial decision.

[40]Act of Feb. 28, 1793, ch. 17, § 3, 1 Stat. 324, 325.

[41]Whether it did is an open question.

[42]U.S. Const. art. III, § 2, para. 2 ("Cases affecting Ambassadors, other public Ministers and Consuls, and those in which a State shall be Party").

[43]5 U.S. (1 Cranch) 137, 174-76 (1803). *See infra* chapter 3.

[44]Once again, however, the Court's reference to its consideration of "the two acts of Congress," 11 Annals of Cong. 904 (1802), suggests the contrary.

[45]United States v. Ferreira, 54 U.S. (13 How.) 40, 53 (1851 Term) (Note by the Chief Justice, Inserted by Order of the Court). Taney added that "in the early days of the Government," this view of the Constitution "was maintained by many jurists." *Id.*

[46]*See* text and notes at notes 27-30 *supra.*

[47]Letter from Thomas Jefferson to the Justices (July 18, 1793) (emphasis in original). Jefferson's letter and several of the questions are reprinted in Hart & Wechsler, *supra* introduction to part one, note 19, at 64-65.

The Justices answered the prefatory question in the negative and refused to give the President advice:

> We have considered the previous question . . . [regarding] the lines of separation drawn by the Constitution between the three departments of the government. These being in certain respects checks upon each other, and our being judges of a court in the last resort, are considerations which afford strong arguments against the propriety of our extrajudicially deciding the questions alluded to, especially as the power given by the Constitution to the President, of calling on the heads of departments for opinions, seems to have been *purposely* as well as expressly united to the *executive* departments.[48]

This brief response has been an important precedent; with a few notable lapses,[49] it generally has been understood ever since that the federal courts are not to give advisory opinions.[50]

Today we are likely to explain that this rule is derived from article III, which defines the "judicial Power" to include specified categories of "Cases" and "Controversies."[51] This line of reasoning parallels the modern constitutional explanation of the Court's refusal to hear the Attorney General *ex officio* in *Hayburn's Case*.[52] Both involve the same two less-than-obvious steps: that by permitting judges to decide cases and controversies, the Framers implicitly forbade them to do anything else, and that a request for an advisory opinion does not present a case or controversy.[53]

Today we might shore up these conclusions by reference to the debates in the constitutional convention. One of the reasons given for rejecting judicial participation in the proposed Council of Revision was the danger that the judges might prejudge issues that later could be litigated before them,[54] a danger equally apparent if the judges gave advisory opinions.[55] Moreover, when James Madison objected to

---

[48]Letter from the Justices to George Washington (Aug. 8, 1793), *reprinted in* HART & WECHSLER, *supra* introduction to part one, note 19, at 65-66 (emphasis in original).

[49]*See* HART & WECHSLER, *supra* introduction to part one, note 19, at 68-69 (citing, *inter alia*, extrajudicial opinions by Justice William Johnson on the constitutionality of federally financed internal improvements, *see* 1 C. WARREN, *supra* introduction to part one, note 2, at 596-97, and by Chief Justice Taney on the constitutionality of taxing judges' salaries, 157 U.S. at 701).

[50]*See, e.g.,* Frankfurter, *Note on Advisory Opinions*, 37 HARV. L. REV. 1002 (1924); HART & WECHSLER, *supra* introduction to part one, note 19, at 66-70; 3 J. STORY, COMMENTARIES ON THE CONSTITUTION OF THE UNITED STATES § 1771, at 651 (1833).

[51]U.S. CONST. art. III, § 2, para. 1.

[52]*See* text and notes at notes 17-19 *supra*.

[53]For the opinion that British judicial practice sanctioned advisory opinions, see 1 C. HAINES, THE ROLE OF THE SUPREME COURT IN AMERICAN GOVERNMENT AND POLITICS 144 & n.110 (1944) (citing J. THAYER, LEGAL ESSAYS 46-48 (1908)).

[54]2 THE RECORDS OF THE FEDERAL CONVENTION OF 1787, at 75 (rev. ed. M. Farrand 1937) [hereinafter cited as CONVENTION RECORDS] (remarks of Caleb Strong) (the judges "in exercising the function of expositors might be influenced by the part they had taken, in framing the laws"); *id.* at 79 (remarks of Nathaniel Gorham) (the judges "ought to carry into the exposition of the laws no prepossessions with regard to them").

[55]But see Wheeler, *The Extrajudicial Activities of the Early Supreme Court*, 1973 SUP. CT. REV. 123, 125-31, showing that Pinckney thought the two situations different and that many of the Framers believed

jurisdiction over cases arising under the Constitution on the ground that courts should expound the law only in cases of a judicial nature, he recorded in his notes of the debates that it was "generally supposed" that the power given in article III would be so limited as a matter of construction.[56] The official journal of the convention, however, was withheld from public scrutiny until 1819, and Madison's notes were unavailable until after his death in 1836.[57] Thus the Justices were deprived of a valuable aid to construction during the critical formative years.[58]

The Justices may have intended to suggest the case-or-controversy argument in their response to Jefferson with their one-word reference to decisions made "extrajudicially." If so, they fell far short of the kind of explanation we have come to expect of major constitutional opinions. Moreover, a negative inference from article III's reference to "judicial Power" is one of no fewer than six constitutional arguments discernible within the two cryptic sentences of the Justices' response quoted above. In addition to characterizing the request as "extrajudicial," the Justices mentioned general structural principles both of separation of powers and of checks and balances. To readers of *Marbury v. Madison*, the "last resort" clause of the Justices' reply suggests that the Supreme Court, here resorted to in the first instance, has original jurisdiction under article III only if a state or a foreign diplomat is a party. The "last resort" reference also suggests the fear that to render advice the President was free to ignore would effectively permit him to review the actions of the tribunal that article III designated as "supreme." Finally, the letter suggested that requests for judicial advice might be precluded by negative inference from article II, which empowers the President to "require the Opinion, in writing, of the principal Officer in each of the executive Departments."[59]

None of these six suggestions was spelled out in any detail, and the Justices stopped short of actually declaring that the Constitution forbade advisory opinions. "Separation" appears in a restatement of Jefferson's question, not in the answer. "Extrajudicially" seems to have been used for purposes of description rather than argument. Article II merely "seems" to limit the President to seeking executive advice. "Checks" and "last resort" were cited not as conclusive, but only as "consid-

---

judges could be given certain extrajudicial duties; *id.* at 144-48, giving pre-1793 examples of judicial advice; *id.* at 156, arguing that the 1793 letter was meant not "to foreclose all extrajudicial advice-giving" but "to limit the contemporary view that extensive advice-giving was proper."

[56] 2 CONVENTION RECORDS, *supra* note 55, at 430.

[57] *See* 1 *id.* at xi-xii, xv.

[58] In his advice to Washington as to the constitutionality of a national bank, Hamilton had argued that the convention record was irrelevant:

> Whatever may have been the nature of the position or the reasons for rejecting it concludes nothing in respect to the real merits of the question . . . . [W]hatever may have been the intention of the framers of a constitution, or of a law, that intention is to be sought for in the instrument itself, according to the usual & established rules of construction.

Opinion of the Constitutionality of an Act to Establish a Bank, in 8 THE PAPERS OF ALEXANDER HAMILTON 111 (H. Synett ed. 1965).

[59] U.S. CONST. art. II, § 2, para. 1. See 2 CONVENTION RECORDS, *supra* note 54, at 80, reporting Rutledge's argument that "[t]he Judges ought never to give their opinions on a law until it comes before them," and that it was "unnecessary" for them to do so because "[t]he Executive could advise with the officers of State, as of war, finance, & c. and avail himself of their information and opinions."

erations which afford strong arguments," and the arguments they were said to
support were against the "propriety," not the constitutionality, of advisory opinions.

Should we lament that once again the Court failed in its obligation to provide an
adequate explanation for its decision? I think not. No one had attempted to require
the Justices to give advisory opinions; it was therefore entirely appropriate for them
to decline on policy grounds to do so, without reaching out to decide the constitutional question. The same considerations that made the Justices reluctant to give the
President substantive advice support their decision under these circumstances not to
give a definitive answer to the question of their constitutional power to advise.

II. Suits against States

A. *Chisholm v. Georgia*

Chisholm, a South Carolina citizen, brought an original action in assumpsit in the
Supreme Court against the State of Georgia.[60] The state argued there was no
jurisdiction; the Court disagreed.

This time there were opinions—real opinions—and this time a constitutional issue
clearly was resolved. There was no opinion for the Court; each Justice delivered his
own.[61] Four Justices wrote for the majority, and Iredell dissented alone. The majority opinions present interesting stylistic contrasts. Blair and Cushing were brief and
to the point, relying chiefly on the words of the Constitution.[62] Jay and Wilson wrote
far longer and more pretentious opinions in which the constitutional language played
a much smaller part; both have a very unfamiliar ring to the modern reader.

Jay's opinion is in three sections: "1st. In what sense, Georgia is a sovereign state.
2d. Whether suability is compatible with such sovereignty. 3d. Whether the constitution (to which Georgia is a party) authorizes such an action against her."[63] He thus
prefaced his discussion of what we would be inclined to view as the only issue with a
largely abstract discussion of the nature of sovereignty, including a paragraph on
"feudal principles."[64] He proceeded to a general commentary on each clause defining

---

[60]Chisholm v. Georgia, 2 U.S. (2 Dall.) 419 (1793). The official report is silent as to the basis of the
action. Charles Warren, relying on a newspaper account, described it as an action to recover on bonds
given by debtors whose property the state had confiscated. 1 C. WARREN, *supra* introduction to part one,
note 2, at 93 n.1. Later investigators have said it was an action for the price of goods furnished to the state.
J. GOEBEL, *supra* note 40, at 726; C. JACOBS, THE ELEVENTH AMENDMENT AND SOVEREIGN IMMUNITY 47
(1972).

[61]This practice of seriatim opinions would persist until the appointment of Marshall, who put an abrupt
end to it. The modern practice of writing one opinion speaking for the entire majority is likely to strike us
as both tidier and more powerful; it is difficult to say what a case stands for if those deciding it failed to
agree on a statement of reasons. *See, e.g.*, text and notes *infra* at chapter 2, notes 102-03. Yet seriatim
opinions actually may give us a better basis for predicting later decisions. We all have seen various Justices
give sharply different interpretations to opinions in which all joined. We can imagine how the press of
other business, the desire for ostensible consensus, and the unwillingness to antagonize a colleague might
lead a Justice to join an opinion he would not have written himself. The unity of reasoning reflected in
today's opinions "of the Court" thus may be more apparent than real.

[62]2 U.S. (2 Dall.) at 450–53 (Blair, J.), 466-69 (Cushing, J.).

[63]*Id.* at 470.

[64]*Id.* at 471-72.

the judicial power in article III,[65] devoting two of his ten pages to the relevant language[66] and concluding by patting the convention delegates on the back: "The extension of the judiciary power of the United States to [suits against a state by citizens of another state] appears to me to be wise, because it is honest, and because it is useful."[67]

Wilson also divided his opinion into three parts, examining the question of suability "1st. By the principles of general jurisprudence. 2d. By the laws and practice of particular states and kingdoms. . . . 3d. And chiefly, . . . by the constitution of the United States . . . ."[68] In the first section he declared, among other things, that "[m]an, fearfully and wonderfully made, is the workmanship of his all-perfect Creator: a state, useful and valuable as the contrivance is, is the inferior contrivance of man."[69] In the next section we encounter Bracton, Isocrates, Frederick the Great, an allegedly pre-Norman book called the *Mirror of Justice*, a work by "the famous Hottoman" describing the traditions of "the Spaniards of Arragon," and a successful proceeding by the son of Columbus against King Ferdinand.[70] Wilson's constitutional analysis begins with an "anecdote . . . concerning Louis XIV."[71] It continues through references to "the People of Athens"[72] to the unsurprising conclusion that the Constitution "*could* vest jurisdiction"[73] over states if the Framers wanted it to, and dedicates to article III a single paragraph at the end of the opinion.[74]

Today's observer is likely to dismiss the bulk of the Jay and Wilson opinions as persiflage.[75] Perhaps they should be taken rather as evidence that at least two prominent Justices at that time believed "general jurisprudence," sound policy, and the experience of other nations were more immediately relevant to the interpretation of our written Constitution than we are likely to think they should be.[76] The expansive notions of Wilson and Jay were not shared universally, however. Iredell insisted that it was not for the Court to consider questions of policy "unless the point in all other respects was very doubtful"[77] and that unless the Constitution conferred

[65]*Id.* at 475-76.
[66]*Id.* at 476-77.
[67]*Id.* at 479.
[68]*Id.* at 453.
[69]*Id.* at 455.
[70]*Id.* at 459-61.
[71]*Id.* at 461.
[72]*Id.* at 463.
[73]*Id.* at 464.
[74]*Id.* at 466.

[75]*See, e.g.,* J. GOEBEL, *supra* note 21, at 731-33; C. JACOBS, *supra* note 51, at 51-52. In Professor Goebel's view, Wilson's opinion shows him at his "fussiest," the "compulsive lecturer disposed to decorate his text with all the furbelows of learning, a great deal of which was dispensable"; Jay's was "considerably less than" a model of clarity and profundity, set "lamentable standards of American judicial historiography," and contained "digression" as well as "diversion." Clyde Jacobs, while terming the Wilson opinion "justly famed as a grandiloquent judicial exposition of general constitutional doctrines," adds that it was "rather weak in certain technical particulars" and, "as a state paper, . . . at least impolitic."

[76]The Supreme Court's own clerk praised the Wilson and Jay opinions effusively while giving short shrift to Cushing and Blair: Wilson's argument was "elegant, learned," and Jay "delivered one of the most clear, profound, and elegant arguments perhaps ever given in a Court of Judicature." *See* 1 C. WARREN, *supra* introduction to part 1, note 2, at 95.

[77]2 U.S. (2 Dall.) at 450.

the disputed authority, "ten thousand examples of similar powers would not warrant its assumption."[78] Blair dismissed European precedents as "utterly destitute of any binding authority here."[79]

The basic arguments of the majority can be summarized as follows. Article III extends the judicial power to "Controversies . . . between a State and Citizens of another State."[80] The provision that the Supreme Court's jurisdiction shall be original in cases "in which a State shall be Party" confirms that it is immaterial whether the state be plaintiff or defendant, for "Party" embraces both.[81] The inference is strengthened by the inclusion of controversies "between two or more States," for in such cases a state always must be defendant.[82] Cushing and Jay added an argument concerning the purpose of the jurisdictional grant: jurisdiction was conferred to prevent interstate friction that could arise if a state were left to judge its own cause, and the danger of friction was as great when the state was defendant as when it was plaintiff.[83] Jay invoked the preamble's goal to "establish justice" as a further aid to construction, arguing that it would be unjust if states could not be sued.[84] Wilson echoed this policy argument under the rubric of "general jurisprudence." He also noted that governments were suable in other countries and added that state suability was implicit in the clause forbidding states to impair contracts, which otherwise would be a dead letter.[85] Jay argued that article III was a "remedial"[86] provision that should be liberally construed and that the old-world notion of state sovereignty underlying immunity from suit was incompatible with the concept of popular sovereignty expressed in the preamble.[87]

These methods of constitutional interpretation are familiar to the modern reader. The words of the Constitution are parsed; inferences are drawn from the wording of other provisions; efforts are made to ascertain and achieve the purposes of the Framers; and arguments of policy and practice are advanced to establish that the conclusions we draw could have been intended. Taken by themselves, the arguments of the majority read very persuasively. The words of article III cover the case if given their ordinary meaning; the purpose imputed to the Framers, though not proved to

---

[78]*Id.* at 449.

[79]*Id.* at 450. See also the letter of William Davie to Iredell, *quoted in* J. GOEBEL, *supra* note 21, at 731 n.30, commenting on Wilson's opinion: "[P]erhaps, notwithstanding the tawdry ornament and poetical imagery with which it is loaded and bedizened, it may still be very 'profound.'" Wilson was a man of parts, "one of the best-educated men in America," a signer of the Declaration of Independence, "second only to Madison[]" in his contributions to the constitutional convention, father of the 1790 Pennsylvania constitution, and "the preeminent legal scholar of his generation." See the admiring biographical sketch in 1 R. McCloskey, The Works of James Wilson 1, 2, 9, 37 (1967). Wilson delivered a learned series of lectures on law at the College of Philadelphia, published in 1804 after his death (*id.*, vols. 1-2 at 53-707); *Chisholm* was his only significant constitutional opinion.

[80]2 U.S. (2 Dall.) at 450 (Blair, J.), 466 (Wilson, J.), 467 (Cushing, J.), 476 (Jay, C.J.).

[81]*Id.* at 451 (Blair, J.), 477 (Jay, C.J.).

[82]*Id.* at 451 (Blair, J.), 466 (Wilson, J.), 467 (Cushing, J.). Blair and Cushing made the same argument as to the provision for jurisdiction over controversies "between a State . . . and foreign States." The Court since has rejected the conclusion that a foreign state may sue an unconsenting state. Monaco v. Mississippi, 292 U.S. 313 (1934).

[83]2 U.S. (2 Dall.) at 467-68 (Cushing, J.), 475-76 (Jay, C.J.).

[84]*Id.* at 477.

[85]*Id.* at 456, 458-61, 465.

[86]*Id.* at 476.

[87]*Id.* at 470-72.

be authentic, seems a plausible deduction; and the result satisfies today's sense of good policy.

Justice Iredell found it unnecessary in his dissent to decide whether article III included suits against states, for he thought Congress had not conferred jurisdiction. The Court's original jurisdiction, he argued, was not self-executing; legislation was necessary even to determine the number of Justices.[88] Section 14 of the Judiciary Act authorized the Court to issue only those writs "agreeable to the principles and usages of law,"[89] and traditional legal principles, which Iredell derived largely from an extensive and learned investigation of English law, did not permit governments to be sued.[90] He added, without explaining why, that he thought this was just as well and that "nothing but express words, or an insurmountable implication (neither of which I consider, can be found in the case)" could justify holding suits against a state within article III.[91]

Although the majority unpardonably failed to respond,[92] Iredell was unconvincing. Article III is silent as to the number of Justices, but not as to the scope of original jurisdiction; legislation confirming the constitutional provision seems unnecessary. In any event, section 13 flatly provided that the Court should have original jurisdiction of suits "between a state and citizens of other states";[93] it should not have been necessary to seek an independent source of jurisdiction in section 14, which provided ancillary powers "necessary for the exercise of . . . jurisdiction[ ]" elsewhere conferred.[94]

Yet Iredell's argument from history and tradition, unpersuasive as he used it to interpret section 14, is much more troublesome if redirected to the meaning of section 13 and of article III itself. In England, the theory was that the King could not be sued in contract cases without his consent. In the states, apparently no suit lay against the government. Was it likely that, without specifically mentioning it, the convention meant to overthrow this established principle? An article III "Con-

[88]*Id.* at 432.

[89]Judiciary Act of 1789, ch. 20, § 14, 1 Stat. 73, 81-82 (current version in relevant part at 28 U.S.C. § 1651 (1976)).

[90]2 U.S. (2 Dall.) at 433-49.

[91]*Id.* at 449-50.

[92]The Justices did not always write out their opinions in those days, *see* note 30 *supra*, and Professor Goebel found evidence in two of the *Chisholm* opinions that the Justices had not conferred about the case before announcing their opinions. J. GOEBEL, *supra* note 21, at 728. Thus there might have been no opportunity to answer the Justice who spoke last. This does not explain the Justices' failure to respond to Iredell, however, for he was the first to deliver his opinion.

[93]Judiciary Act of 1789, ch. 20, § 13, 1 Stat. 73, 80 (current version in relevant part at 28 U.S.C. § 1251(b) (Supp. III 1979)). Iredell dismissed section 13 by construing the provision making the Supreme Court's jurisdiction "not exclusive" so as to limit it to cases over which state courts also had jurisdiction; more probably Congress meant only that state courts were not precluded from hearing such cases if they chose. The Court later accepted Iredell's argument, however, in holding a state not suable by its own citizen in Hans v. Louisiana, 134 U.S. 1, 18-19 (1890).

[94]Judiciary Act of 1789, ch. 20, § 14, 1 Stat. 73, 81-82 (current version in relevant part at 28 U.S.C. § 1651 (1976)). Presumably Iredell was concerned that without section 14 there would be no method of serving execution or other process on the state. But the immunity objection is one of jurisdiction; section 14 seemed to authorize whatever writs would traditionally be appropriate on the assumption that the Court had cognizance of the case. Yet one must acknowledge the danger of misunderstanding the relationship between jurisdiction and the writs across a gulf of 200 years.

troversy" arguably means one cognizable according to judicial traditions,[95] and if "Controversy" does not include advice to the executive, perhaps it does not include suits against unconsenting governments either.

This conclusion is supported by contemporaneous statements of several of the most prominent proponents of the Constitution. Madison and Marshall flatly told the Virginia ratifying convention that article III would not subject unwilling states to suits by individuals,[96] and Alexander Hamilton said the same thing in *The Federalist*.[97] Furthermore, the force of the majority's reliance on the plain constitutional language was weakened greatly by the admission of two Justices that, despite article III's inclusion of "Controversies to which the United States shall be a Party,"[98] the United States might not be suable without its consent. Jay thought the case of the United States was different because a judgment against the general government would be unenforceable.[99] Cushing thought the reason for jurisdiction was lacking because a suit against the United States presented no danger of interstate friction.[100] Thus half the majority Justices did not shrink from finding less in the words of article III than met the eye. For them, at least, the language was not so clear that tradition and legislative history should have been immaterial.[101]

Since *Chisholm*, the Court has found many implicit immunities in the Constitution. The United States cannot be sued,[102] and federal instrumentalities cannot be taxed or regulated,[103] without congressional consent. Even today the facially plenary

[95]*See* text and notes at notes 17-20, 51-53 *supra*.
[96]3 J. ELLIOT, THE DEBATES IN THE SEVERAL STATE CONVENTIONS ON THE ADOPTION OF THE FEDERAL CONSTITUTION 533 (2d ed. Wash., D.C. 1854) [hereinafter cited as ELLIOT'S DEBATES] ("It is not in the power of individuals to call any state into court. The only operation it can have, is that, if a state should wish to bring suit against a citizen, it must be brought before the federal court.") (Madison); *id.* at 555 (Marshall).
[97]THE FEDERALIST No. 81, at 487-88 (A. Hamilton) (C. Rossiter ed. 1961):

> It is inherent in the nature of sovereignty not to be amenable to the suit of an individual *without its consent* . . . . [T]here is no color to pretend that the State governments would, by the adoption of that plan, be divested of the privilege of paying their own debts in their own way, free from every constraint but that which flows from the obligations of good faith.

[98]U.S. CONST. art. III, § 2, para. 1.
[99]2 U.S. (2 Dall.) at 478. A similar fear of unenforceability later would inform Justice Felix Frankfurter's view of political questions. *See* Baker v. Carr, 369 U.S. 186, 266 (1962) (dissenting opinion). To the argument that even a judgment against a state would be unenforceable, Blair responded that jurisdiction and execution were independent questions: "Let us go as far as we can; and if, at the end of the business, . . . we meet difficulties insurmountable to us, we must leave it to those departments of government which have higher powers . . . ." 2 U.S. (2 Dall.) at 451-52.
[100]2 U.S. (2 Dall.) at 469. Cushing also saw some significance in "the different wording of the different clauses" of article III, section 2, paragraph 1: controversies "to which the United States shall be a Party" and "between a State and Citizens of another State." But this "Party" language parallels that respecting original jurisdiction over cases involving states, and other Justices plausibly took the latter as evidence that states could be made defendants. *See* text and note at note 82 *supra*.
[101]Charles Warren reported that the *Chisholm* decision produced a "profound shock." 1 C. WARREN, *supra* introduction to part one, note 2, at 96. Lopsided votes in Congress to overturn the decision (23–2 in the Senate and 81-9 in the House of Representatives, *id.* at 101) suggest either that the Court had not captured the original understanding or that the country had changed its collective mind most rapidly.
[102]Kansas v. United States, 204 U.S. 331, 341 (1907) (alternate holding).
[103]Johnson v. Maryland, 254 U.S. 51, 56-57 (1920) (regulation); McCulloch v. Maryland, 17 U.S. (4 Wheat.) 316, 436-37 (1819) (taxation). *See infra* chapter 6.

federal tax power is thought to be limited in application to the states themselves.[104] In addition, after the eleventh amendment reversed *Chisholm* itself by declaring that "[t]he Judicial power of the United States shall not be construed to extend to any suit in law or equity commenced or prosecuted against one of the United States by Citizens of another State, or by Citizens or Subjects of any Foreign State," the Court made up for the apparent carelessness of the amendment's draftsmen by construing other clauses of article III to respect the traditional sovereign immunity. Thus an unconsenting state also may not be sued by its own citizen,[105] or by a federal corporation,[106] or by a foreign state,[107] or in admiralty.[108] Although it is true that the adoption of the eleventh amendment helped the Court reach these latter decisions, they nevertheless support the conclusion that it would have been perfectly respectable if *Chisholm* had come out the other way.

This is not to say the decision was necessarily wrong. Madison, Marshall, and Hamilton notwithstanding, there was no unanimity among the Framers that immunity would exist. Edmund Randolph, who represented Chisholm in the Supreme Court, had praised the proposed Constitution in the Virginia ratifying convention because in his view it made states subject to suit: "whatever the law of nations may say, . . . any doubt respecting the construction that a state may be plaintiff, and not defendant, is taken away by the words *where a state shall be a party*."[109] Moreover, Wilson's survey of English law undercuts the accepted wisdom that the king could not be sued without his consent. Wilson asserted that the king was sued regularly through the mechanism of the petition of right.[110] Iredell responded by quoting Blackstone that the petition was "a matter of grace" and not of "compulsion."[111] But Wilson contended that "the difference is only in the form, not in the thing."[112] Professor Louis Jaffe, writing much later, agreed with Wilson: "when it was neces-

---

[104]*See* Massachusetts v. United States, 435 U.S. 444, 454-60 (1978); New York v. United States, 326 U.S. 572 (1946). The same was briefly true of the commerce power. *See* National League of Cities v. Usery, 426 U.S. 833, 840-52 (1976), *overruled*, Garcia v. San Antonio Metro. Transit Auth., 105 S. Ct. 1005 (1985).

[105]Hans v. Louisiana, 134 U.S. 1, 15 (1890).

[106]Smith v. Reeves, 178 U.S. 436, 446 (1900).

[107]Monaco v. Mississippi, 292 U.S. 313, 330 (1934).

[108]*Ex parte* New York, 256 U.S. 490, 497-98 (1921).

[109]3 ELLIOT'S DEBATES, *supra* note 96, at 573 (emphasis in original). That the statements of Madison, Marshall, and Hamilton were controverted by prominent opponents of the Constitution, *see, e.g., id.* at 319, 475 (Patrick Henry), 526-27 (George Mason), is not very important, because the question ought to be what those who voted *for* the Constitution meant by it. *See* Schwegmann Bros. v. Calvert Distillers Corp., 341 U.S. 384, 394-95 (1951) ("The fears and doubts of the opposition are no authoritative guide to the construction of legislation. It is the sponsors we look to when the meaning of the statutory words is in doubt."). *Cf.* Local 1545, United Bhd. of Carpenters v. Vincent, 286 F.2d 127, 132 (2d Cir. 1960) ("[D]issenting opinions are not always a reliable guide to the meaning of the majority; often their predictions partake of Cassandra's gloom more than of her accuracy."). For fuller accounts of contemporary statements in and out of the ratifying conventions, see C. JACOBS, *supra* note 60, at 27-40; Field, *The Eleventh Amendment and Other Sovereign Immunity Doctrines: Part One*, 126 U. PA. L. REV. 515, 522-36 (1978).

[110]2 U.S. (2 Dall.) at 460.

[111]*Id.* at 442, 444 (quoting 1 W. BLACKSTONE, COMMENTARIES ON THE LAWS OF ENGLAND 236 (Oxford 1765-69)).

[112]*Id.* at 460.

sary to sue the Crown eo nomine consent apparently was given as of course."[113] If Wilson and Jaffe were right, there was no meaningful tradition of sovereign immunity and thus no reason to strain the words of article III to respect it—and *Chisholm* may have been right after all.

What remains interesting is the general failure of the *Chisholm* opinions to come to grips with what we would think to be the real problem. Blair and Cushing confined themselves largely to the text of article III, without discussing either the tradition of immunity or the statements of the Framers, while Iredell made the right argument in the wrong context.[114] Nobody spoke, as Paterson later would,[115] of the unwritten understandings of those who were at the Philadelphia convention, and the first citation of *The Federalist* was still a few years away,[116] although Jay was one of Hamilton's fellow contributors to those essays. In the final analysis it was the discursive Jay and Wilson who made the most telling contributions for the majority: Jay argued that the tradition of immunity was based upon conditions not existent in America, Wilson that immunity was fictitious even in England and that the contract clause implied a judicial remedy.

Finally, Iredell in his dissent uttered a dictum that anticipated by ten years the decision in *Marbury v. Madison*. Judicial organization and procedure, he declared, were within the control of Congress, with

> but one limit; that is, "that they shall not exceed their authority." If they do, I have no hesitation to say, that any act to that effect would be utterly void, because it would be inconsistent with the constitution, which is a fundamental law, paramount to all others, which we are not only bound to consult, but sworn to observe; and therefore, where there is an interference, being superior in obligation to the other, we must unquestionably obey that in preference.[117]

B.   *Hollingsworth v. Virginia*

The eleventh amendment, overruling *Chisholm*, was adopted in January 1798.[118] One month later, in *Hollingsworth*, the Supreme Court, without dissent and again without published opinion, dismissed all pending suits filed by citizens of one state against another.[119]

It had been argued, largely on the ground that retroactivity was disfavored, that

[113]L. JAFFE, JUDICIAL CONTROL OF ADMINISTRATIVE ACTION 197 (student ed. 1965). *See also* C. JACOBS, *supra* note 60, at 6 ("The immunity doctrine by this time was largely a legal conception, which determined the forms of procedure in some cases but did not seriously impair the subject's right to recovery in accordance with the substantive law.").

[114]*See* text and notes at notes 88-95 *supra*.

[115]*See* text and notes *infra* at chapter 2, notes 24, 31.

[116]*See* text and note *infra* at chapter 2, note 86.

[117]2 U.S. (2 Dall.) at 433.

[118]*See* 1 C. WARREN, *supra* introduction to part one, note 2, at 101.

[119]3 U.S. (3 Dall.) 378 (1798). It may be significant that the Court did not dismiss, but only continued, a pending suit against a state by a foreign state. *See* C. JACOBS, *supra* note 60, at 62-63. But if the Court thought such a suit was still maintainable, it eventually would change its mind. *See* Monaco v. Mississippi, 292 U.S. 313 (1934).

the amendment did not apply to pending cases.[120] The Court demurred, saying only that it applied to "any case, past or future."[121] The amendment's text, though not unambiguous, is consistent with this conclusion: "The Judicial power . . . shall not be construed to extend to any suit . . . commenced or prosecuted" against one state by citizens of another.[122] "Shall not be construed" speaks to future acts of construction, but such acts of construction could occur in pending suits.[123] "Commenced" and "prosecuted" are indefinite as to time; the amendment does not say "to be commenced" or "which shall be commenced."[124] Moreover, the argument that the amendment's policy applied equally to pending cases[125] seems persuasive whether that policy was an abstract respect for sovereignty or the protection of state treasuries.[126]

More interesting still is an issue of continuing significance that the Court also resolved without giving any reasons, so far as the report reveals. The eleventh amendment, it was argued, had not been constitutionally adopted, because it had not been submitted to the President for approval under the veto clause of article I.[127] That provision applies not only to ordinary bills, but to "[e]very Order, Resolution, or Vote to which the concurrence of the Senate and House of Representatives may be necessary (except on a question of Adjournment)."[128] Article V in turn provides for submission of a proposed constitutional amendment to the states "whenever two thirds of both Houses shall deem it necessary."

The language of the veto clause thus seems to include constitutional amendments. Moreover, counsel argued, there was no reason to think the President ought to be excluded from the amending process, as his "concurrence . . . is required in matters of infinitely less importance."[129] It is no answer that article V already requires the same two-thirds vote that would override a President's veto; as counsel argued, "the reasons assigned for his disapprobation might be so satisfactory as to reduce the majority below the constitutional proportion."[130] Justice Chase's oral retort that "the negative of the president applies only to the ordinary cases of legislation"[131] is surely incorrect if taken literally because the veto clause on its face encompasses "[e]very Order, Resolution, or Vote" and extends the President's participation beyond "ordinary . . . legislation."

The feeling nevertheless lingers that the literal applicability of the veto clause to

[120]3 U.S. (3 Dall.) at 379-80 (argument of William Tilghman and William Rawle).

[121]*Id.* at 382.

[122]U.S. CONST. amend. XI.

[123]Moreover, future proceedings in pending suits are future exercises of the judicial power; they seem to be interdicted even if the amendment forbids only prospective action.

[124]Marshall later would say that "prosecuted" referred to the continuing process of cases previously commenced. Cohens v. Virginia, 19 U.S. (6 Wheat.) 264, 408-09 (1821).

[125]3 U.S. (3 Dall.) at 381.

[126]*See* C. JACOBS, *supra* note 60, at 67-74; 1 C. WARREN, *supra* introduction to part one, note 2, at 96-100. *See also Ex parte* McCardle, 74 U.S. (7 Wall.) 506, 514 (1869) (invoking what the Court termed the "general rule" that repeal of a jurisdictional provision requires dismissal of a pending appeal).

[127]3 U.S. (3 Dall.) at 379 (argument of Tilghman and Rawle).

[128]U.S. CONST. art. I, § 7, para. 3.

[129]3 U.S. (3 Dall.) at 379.

[130]*Id.* Cf. Powell v. McCormack, 395 U.S. 486, 506-10 & n.30 (1969) (exclusion versus expulsion of a member of Congress).

[131]3 U.S. (3 Dall.) at 381 n.(a).

amendments is the result of careless drafting. Unlike the property and full faith clauses of article IV,[132] article V does not simply confer additional substantive powers on Congress; it provides a separate procedure for the adoption of amendments, with the unique additional requirement of ratification by three-fourths of the states. Quite possibly this procedure was meant to be a self-contained whole, a substitute for the normal legislative process that included the President. This inference is strengthened by Madison's explanation, in offering to the convention the language found in the veto clause, that "if the negative of the President was confined to bills; it would be evaded by acts under the form and name of Resolutions, votes &c."[133] Another important consideration, as the Court was told, was that the first ten amendments had not been submitted to the President either.[134] Not only would the Court later defer to the construction adopted by other branches in the first days of the Constitution,[135] but in this instance rejection of the congressional reading would have upset°settled expectations by invalidating the Bill of Rights.

So far as the report shows, it did not occur to the Court to suggest that the question of the President's participation in the amending process was a political one beyond judicial competence, as the Court would say much later of some other issues of amendment procedure.[136] The Court simply decided, as Marshall's *Marbury* philosophy soon would suggest it should,[137] whether the amendment was law.

Finally, *Hollingsworth* may put to flight the conventional wisdom that *Marbury v. Madison* was the first case in which the Supreme Court held an act of Congress unconstitutional. Section 13 of the Judiciary Act, employing language that *Chisholm* had read to authorize suits by citizens of one state against other states, was still on the books.[138] In dismissing suits that fell within its provisions, the Court treated that construction as no longer law because of the supervening constitutional amendment. It is possible that the Court merely gave a narrow interpretation to section 13, either to avoid the constitutional question or in reliance on the amendment's command that the "Judicial power" be narrowly construed. On the other hand, "Judicial power" is a constitutional term, and the eleventh amendment was a constitutional amendment. It is thus possible that the Court in *Hollingsworth* invalidated section 13 as applied

---

[132]U.S. CONST. art. IV, § 1 (full faith and credit); *id.* § 3, para. 2 (Congressional control over property belonging to the United States).

[133]2 CONVENTION RECORDS, *supra* note 54, at 301. The amending power is discussed in THE FEDERALIST No. 43 (J. Madison) and the veto power in Nos. 51 (J. Madison) and 73 (A. Hamilton) without adverting to the question. Story gives only the holding of *Hollingsworth*, 3 J. STORY, COMMENTARIES ON THE CONSTITUTION § 1824, at 688 n.1 (Boston 1833), while referring in another connection to Madison's stated purpose. 2 *id.* at 355. See also J. POMEROY, AN INTRODUCTION TO CONSTITUTIONAL LAW 114-15 (1870), arguing that congressional action on a proposed amendment was outside the veto clause because it was "in no sense legislative" but "a mere proposal," and "the people, through their state legislatures or conventions, are the sole legislators."

[134]3 U.S. (3 Dall.) at 381.

[135]*See, e.g.*, Stuart v. Laird, 5 U.S. (1 Cranch) 299, 309 (1803), *discussed in infra* chapter 3 (upholding the power of Congress to impose circuit duties on Supreme Court Justices on the sole basis that the practice had existed since 1789).

[136]Coleman v. Miller, 307 U.S. 433, 450, 454 (1939) (effect of a state's previous rejection and time for ratification).

[137]5 U.S. (1 Cranch) at 177-78. *See infra* chapter 3.

[138]Judiciary Act of 1789, ch. 20, § 13, 1 Stat. 73, 80 (current version in relevant part at 28 U.S.C. § 1251(b) (Supp. III 1979)).

and construed in the light of *Chisholm*'s interpretation of the similar words of article III—without, so far as the record tells us, bothering to justify either the power of judicial review or its conclusion with respect to the statute in question.[139]

In short, the Court may well have been right on the merits of *Hollingsworth*. What is noteworthy is that once again either the Court did not offer an explanation of its conclusions or Dallas did not report it.

III. Other Cases

A. *La Vengeance*

The United States sought forfeiture of a vessel seized for exporting contraband "from Sandy Hook, in the state of New Jersey . . . to . . . the island of St. Domingo."[140] The district court, sitting without a jury, held for the United States. The circuit court reversed on the merits. The United States appealed, arguing that the district court's decision was not reviewable by the circuit court and that the case should have been tried by jury. The relevant statutes allowed appeals of certain causes "of admiralty and maritime jurisdiction"[141] and required a jury except in "civil causes of admiralty and maritime jurisdiction."[142] In the Government's view, the case was neither maritime nor civil. The Supreme Court in a single paragraph rejected both arguments: the case was maritime because "exportation is entirely a water transaction" and civil because as "a libel in rem," it "does not, in any degree, touch the person of the offender."[143] Thus it was proper to try the case without a jury, and the circuit court had jurisdiction over the appeal.

There were three possible objections to the existence of admiralty jurisdiction. It was argued at one time or another that in England the admiralty had no jurisdiction over acts "done part on land, and part on sea,"[144] or over acts done wholly on water but within the body of a county,[145] or over seizures for trade law violations, wherever they might occur.[146] Behind all three propositions lay the argument that the Court should follow British precedents in construing the terms "admiralty" and "maritime."[147]

Did the Court in *La Vengeance* reject any of these propositions? Marshall thought it had: twelve years later he cited *La Vengeance* as having held that trade law violations were within the admiralty jurisdiction.[148] Yet so far as the report of *La*

---

[139]Section 13 apparently was mentioned by neither Court nor counsel.

[140]3 U.S. (3 Dall.) 297, 298 (1796).

[141]Judiciary Act of 1789, ch. 20, § 21, 1 Stat. 73, 83-84 (repealed by Circuit Courts of Appeals Act, ch. 517, § 4, 26 Stat. 826, 827 (1891)).

[142]*Id.* § 9, 1 Stat. at 77 (current version in relevant part at 28 U.S.C. § 1873 (1976)).

[143]3 U.S. (3 Dall.) at 301.

[144]*Id.* at 300 (argument of Attorney General Charles Lee for the United States).

[145]*Id.* (citing 3 W. Blackstone, Commentaries on the Laws of England 106 (Oxford 1765-69)). *See* note 152 *infra*.

[146]The Betsey & Charlotte, 8 U.S. (4 Cranch) 443, 447-48 (1808) (argument of former Attorney General Lee for claimant).

[147]*See* Waring v. Clarke, 46 U.S. (5 How.) 441, 468-69 (1847 Term) (Woodbury, J., dissenting).

[148]The Betsey & Charlotte, 8 U.S. (4 Cranch) 443, 452 (1808).

Vengeance reveals, the contrary argument had not been made.[149] Nor did the case hold that the admiralty jurisdiction encompassed actions done partly on land; it flatly said the exportation in question was "entirely a water transaction" because alleged "to have commenced at Sandy Hook; which, certainly, must have been upon the water."[150] On the question whether Sandy Hook was within the body of a county, the Court seems to have been indifferent, but we have no way of knowing whether this was because it thought that British precedents did not govern,[151] that waters within counties were within the British admiralty jurisdiction, or that Sandy Hook was not within a county. Indeed, counsel's observation that local waters were excluded was so oblique that we cannot be confident the Court meant to address it at all.[152]

All the Court safely can be said to have held is that the particular transaction took place entirely on the water, a narrow factual determination of no great significance. But the cryptic nature of the opinion made it relatively easy for later observers to argue that the decision stood for more important propositions as well.

On its face this decision did not purport to resolve any constitutional questions: "civil" and "maritime" were statutory terms, and the Government's arguments were based on statute. Lurking in the background, however, were the constitutional provisions guaranteeing the right to a jury in "[t]he Trial of all Crimes,"[153] "all criminal prosecutions,"[154] and "Suits at common law."[155] The Court's holding that the case was "civil" and "maritime" for statutory purposes could be argued to mean it was neither a criminal prosecution[156] nor a suit at common law[157] for jury trial

[149]Former Attorney General Lee, arguing against jurisdiction in The Betsey & Charlotte, *id.* at 446 n.(a), was asked if he could distinguish *La Vengeance*, which he also had argued. He said he could and added that, in any event, "I know it was not so fully argued as it might have been; and some of the judges may recollect that it was rather a sudden decision." Chase retorted: "I recollect, that the argument was no great thing, but the *Ceurt* [*sic*] took time and *considered the case well*." *Id.* (emphasis in original).

[150]3 U.S. (3 Dall.) at 301. The Court also did not hold, as Marshall would hold in The Betsey & Charlotte, 8 U.S. (4 Cranch) 443, 452 (1808), that "[i]t is the place of seizure, and not the place of committing the offence, which decides the jurisdiction." Though its language was loose, *La Vengeance* clearly involved the business of water transportation—a maritime offense, not just a maritime seizure. Much later, persuasively citing the purposes of the admiralty clause, the Court would hold that federal admiralty jurisdiction could not be invoked in a plane crash case where the only maritime link was that the plane had crashed upon navigable water. Executive Jet Aviation, Inc. v. City of Cleveland, 409 U.S. 249, 268 (1972).

[151]*La Vengeance* would be cited in Waring v. Clarke, 46 U.S. (5 How.) 440, 457 (1847 Term) (*see infra* chapter 8), as an example of cases finding jurisdiction where a British court would not have. It should be clear that the Court in *La Vengeance* did not reveal that it did so consciously.

[152]Attorney General Lee, arguing for the United States, had quoted Blackstone for the proposition that admiralty jurisdiction was limited to "causes arising wholly upon the sea, and not within the precincts of any county," 3 U.S. (3 Dall.) at 300 (quoting 3 W. BLACKSTONE, COMMENTARIES ON THE LAWS OF ENGLAND 106 (Oxford 1765-69)), but he apparently did not mention whether Sandy Hook lay within a county.

[153]U.S. CONST. art. III, § 2, para. 3.

[154]*Id.* amend. VI.

[155]*Id.* amend. VII.

[156]Distinguishing criminal from noncriminal sanctions since has proved quite difficult for the Court. *See, e.g.*, Kennedy v. Mendoza-Martinez, 372 U.S. 144, 168-84 (Goldberg, J.), 202-10 (Stewart J., dissenting) (1963); *infra* chapters 9, 13, discussing *Cummings v. Missouri* and *Boyd v. United States*.

[157]That maritime cases were not "suits at common law" was stated in Parsons v. Bedford, 28 U.S. (3 Pet.) 443, 446-47 (1830 Term) (dictum), and held in Waring v. Clarke, 46 U.S. (5 How.) 441, 459-60 (1847 Term). *See infra* chapter 4.

purposes under the Constitution.[158] Moreover, the terms "admiralty" and "maritime," which in *La Vengeance* determined the statutory jury right, also appear in the delineation of federal judicial power in article III. The decision that the case was maritime within the statute implied that it was also a case the federal courts could constitutionally entertain. Thus the Court let fly in a most cavalier way two conclusions that later might prove highly influential in the interpretation of the Constitution.[159]

B.   *Wiscart v. D'Auchy*

The Circuit Court for the District of Virginia, sitting in equity, set aside a conveyance on the ground that it had been made to defraud creditors. On review the question arose whether the Supreme Court could reexamine the facts as well as the law.[160] An unreported companion case, evidently in admiralty, presented the same issue.[161] The question turned on the distinction between an appeal and a writ of error, for, as Ellsworth argued, facts could be reviewed only on appeal.[162]

The statutory provisions were confusing. Section 21 of the Judiciary Act authorized the circuit courts to review district court decisions in "admiralty and maritime" cases by "appeal,"[163] and section 22 authorized them to review "civil actions" by "writ of error."[164] Section 22 further provided that circuit court decisions "in civil actions, and suits in equity," whether brought there originally or "by appeal," were reviewable in the Supreme Court "upon a like process."[165]

Ellsworth said the statutory reference to civil and equity cases meant that all noncriminal judgments were to be reviewed in the Supreme Court by writ of error.[166] Wilson thought otherwise. To him, the distinction between admiralty and civil cases for purposes of circuit court review demonstrated that admiralty cases were not civil within the provision for Supreme Court review.[167] Thus Ellsworth concluded that Congress had forbidden the Supreme Court to review the facts in equity or maritime cases, and Wilson that Congress had made no provision for Supreme Court review of maritime cases at all.

[158]Marshall would make this argument soon in The Betsey & Charlotte, 8 U.S. (4 Cranch) 443, 452 (1808), where he would maintain, quite erroneously, that *La Vengeance* had held that the Constitution did not require jury trial under the circumstances.

[159]*See* The Belfast, 74 U.S. (7 Wall.) 624, 638 (1869) (citing *La Vengeance* and other cases for the proposition that Congress "intended by the ninth section of the Judiciary Act to invest the District Courts" with the "entire power of the Constitution"); *see also* Waring v. Clarke, 46 U.S. (5 How.) 441, 458 (1847 Term) (citing *La Vengeance* and other cases for the constitutional proposition that "the admiralty jurisdiction . . . is not confined to the cases of admiralty jurisdiction in England when the constitution was adopted").

[160]3 U.S. (3 Dall.) 321, 322 (1796).

[161]Ellsworth said the question had "been already argued in another cause." Dallas "believe[d] the chief justice referred to the case of Pintado v. Bernard, an admiralty case, which was argued a few days before, during my absence from the court." *Id.* at 324 & n.(a).

[162]*Id.* at 327.

[163]Judiciary Act of 1789, ch. 20, § 21, 1 Stat. 73, 83.

[164]*Id.* § 22, 1 Stat. at 84.

[165]*Id.*

[166]3 U.S. (3 Dall.) at 328.

[167]*Id.* at 325-26.

Both conclusions raise interesting constitutional questions. Article III extends the judicial power to cases like those considered in *Wiscart*. It places certain other cases within the Supreme Court's original jurisdiction. It also provides that "[i]n all the other Cases before mentioned, the supreme Court shall have appellate Jurisdiction, both as to Law and Fact, with such Exceptions, and under such Regulations as the Congress shall make."[168]

Wilson's thesis that Congress had made no provision for Supreme Court review raised the question whether the appellate jurisdiction was self-executing. Wilson thought it was: "an appeal is expressly sanctioned by the constitution; . . . and as there are not any words in the judicial act, restricting the power of proceeding by appeal, it must be regarded as still permitted and approved."[169] Ellsworth had no need to reach this question, for he found Congress *had* restricted the jurisdiction. Yet he disagreed with Wilson in dictum: "If congress has provided no rule to regulate our proceedings, we cannot exercise an appellate jurisdiction. . . ."[170] Iredell had made the same argument as to the original jurisdiction in *Chisholm*.[171]

The language of the Constitution is, as usual, ambiguous on this issue. If one focuses on the power to make "Exceptions," Wilson seems to have the better of the argument: the Court may review both fact and law until Congress otherwise provides. The "Regulations" clause, however, seems to support Ellsworth: the Court is authorized to exercise jurisdiction only under congressional regulations. Yet the latter is not the only possible reading; arguably, by analogy to the "Exceptions" provision, the clause means only that if there are "Regulations" the Court must obey them.

The Marshall Court would announce that the appellate jurisdiction was, as Wilson argued, self-executing: if Congress had established the Court without defining its jurisdiction, "in omitting to exercise the right of excepting from its constitutional powers, [Congress] would have necessarily left those powers undiminished."[172] But Wilson's belated victory was Pyrrhic, for in the same opinion Marshall would declare that by providing for jurisdiction in some cases, Congress implicitly had forbidden review of all others.[173] Thus, by a persuasive exercise in statutory construction, Marshall made it irrelevant that the appellate jurisdiction would have been self-executing in the face of congressional silence.

Ellsworth's conclusion that Congress had forbidden review of the facts, on the other hand, raised the question whether Congress had power thus to limit the Court's appellate jurisdiction. Article III seems to say it had: the Court has appellate jurisdiction "with such Exceptions, and under such Regulations as the Congress shall make." Ellsworth saw no difficulty: "if the rule [regarding jurisdiction] is provided, we cannot depart from it."[174] Wilson appeared at one point in his opinion to concede

[168]U.S. CONST. art. III, § 2, para. 2.

[169]3 U.S. (3 Dall.) at 325.

[170]*Id.* at 327.

[171]*See* text and note at note 88 *supra*.

[172]Durousseau v. United States, 10 U.S. (6 Cranch) 307, 313-14 (1810).

[173]*Id.* at 314. Not all this reasoning was necessary to the result, because the Court found Congress implicitly had contemplated Supreme Court review of the case before it. *See also* United States v. More, 7 U.S. (3 Cranch) 159, 173 (1805), *infra* chapter 3, where on the same reasoning jurisdiction had been denied.

[174]3 U.S. (3 Dall.) at 327.

that this was true,[175] but elsewhere he denied it: "Even, indeed, if a positive restriction existed by law, it would, in my judgment, be superseded by the superior authority of the constitutional provision."[176]

One might be tempted to dismiss Wilson's dictum as absurd on its face were it not that a host of later thinkers have agreed that the power to make exceptions to the Court's appellate jurisdiction is not so absolute as it appears. It has been argued that "Exceptions" may be made only as to issues of fact,[177] may not contradict the apparent command of article III that all cases there listed be cognizable by some federal court,[178] may not be used to deprive a litigant of a constitutional right,[179] and may not "destroy the essential role of the Supreme Court in the constitutional plan."[180]

Some of these arguments may reflect wishful thinking, and probably none would have supported Wilson's unexplained conclusion in *Wiscart*. Yet, contemplating later efforts in Congress to deprive the Supreme Court of jurisdiction to determine the constitutionality of important statutes,[181] one may conclude there is more to the question than the plain words of the exceptions provision. If *Marbury* was right that the Framers provided for judicial review to keep legislatures within constitutional bounds,[182] one reasonably may doubt that they meant to allow Congress to destroy that important check by the simple expedient of removing jurisdiction.[183]

The Court agreed with Ellsworth's conclusion that the facts could not be reviewed,[184] and the case remains as authority for the power of Congress to eliminate review of facts in ordinary equity or admiralty cases in the Supreme Court. No doubt it would be asking too much to expect the Court to have anticipated that more drastic limitations on jurisdiction could raise more serious questions, and it was proper for

[175]"The legislature might, indeed, have made exceptions, and introduced regulations upon the subject . . . ." *Id.* at 326.

[176]*Id.* at 325. Thus yet another Justice declared his readiness to ignore an act of Congress he deemed unconstitutional.

[177]Merry, *Scope of the Supreme Court's Appellate Jurisdiction: Historical Basis*, 47 MINN. L. REV. 53, 57-68 (1962).

[178]Martin v. Hunter's Lessee, 14 U.S. (1 Wheat.) 304, 328-31 (1816) (dictum); 1 W. CROSSKEY, POLITICS AND THE CONSTITUTION IN THE HISTORY OF THE UNITED STATES 610-18 (1953).

[179]*Cf.* Eisentrager v. Forrestal, 174 F.2d 961, 966 (D.C. Cir. 1949) (alternative holding) (habeas corpus), *rev'd on other grounds sub nom.* Johnson v. Eisentrager, 339 U.S. 763 (1950); Battaglia v. General Motors Corp., 169 F.2d 254, 257 (2d Cir.) (due process), *cert. denied*, 335 U.S. 887 (1948). Both cases discussed the analogous issue of district court jurisdiction.

[180]Hart, *The Power of Congress to Limit the Jurisdiction of Federal Courts: An Exercise in Dialectic*, 66 HARV. L. REV. 1362, 1365 (1953); *see also* Ratner, *Congressional Power Over the Appellate Jurisdiction of the Supreme Court*, 109 U. PA. L. REV. 157 (1960). For a critical review of these arguments, *see* Gunther, *Congressional Power to Curtail Federal Court Jurisdiction*, 36 STAN. L. REV. 895 (1984).

[181]*E.g.*, H.R. 11926, 88th Cong., 2d Sess. (1964) (bill to deprive the Supreme Court of jurisdiction to determine the constitutionality of reapportionment of state legislatures). *See also Ex parte* McCardle, 74 U.S. (7 Wall.) 506 (1869) (statute depriving the Supreme Court of jurisdiction over certain habeas corpus appeals); *infra* chapter 9.

[182]5 U.S. (1 Cranch) 137, 178 (1803). *See infra* chapter 3.

[183]Indeed, one statute limiting the Supreme Court's appellate jurisdiction has been struck down as an attempt to defeat substantive rights. United States v. Klein, 80 U.S. (13 Wall.) 128, 144-48 (1872) (congressional attempt to deprive Southern suitors in the Court of Claims of rights restored by presidential pardon). *See infra* chapter 9.

[184]Paterson later revealed that he had agreed with Wilson; the vote was thus 4-2. *See* The Perseverance, 3 U.S. (3 Dall.) 336, 337 (1797).

the Court not to comment on future cases. By purporting to perceive no difficulty at
all, however, the Court made it easier to cite *Wiscart* as establishing that the power to
make exceptions meant exactly what it said. In any case, the treatment of both
constitutional issues in *Wiscart* was cavalier in the extreme. Neither Ellsworth nor
Wilson bothered to state his reasons, and their contrary conclusions crossed unac-
knowledged like ships passing in the night.

C.   *Turner v. Bank of North America*

Officers of the bank, Pennsylvanians, sued a North Carolina citizen on a promissory
note that Biddle and Company had assigned to the bank. As to Biddle and Company,
the record showed only "'that they used trade and merchandise in partnership
together, at Philadelphia, or North Carolina.'"[185] Section 11 of the Judiciary Act
deprived the circuit courts of diversity jurisdiction over suits brought by the assignee
of any chose in action "unless a suit might have been prosecuted in such court . . . if
no assignment had been made";[186] because the citizenship of the assignor had not
been established, the Court ordered the action dismissed.[187]

The Question was important, however, and by no means free from doubt. Article
III declares that the judicial power "shall be vested"[192] in the courts and "shall extend
to" controversies "between citizens of different States,"[193] of which *Turner* was one.
This language looks mandatory. On the other hand, Congress is given power to make

Counsel for the bank argued that the assignee clause was unconstitutional: the
controversy before the Court was between "citizens of different States" and thus
within the article III "judicial Power,"[188] and "congress can no more limit, than
enlarge, the constitutional grant."[189] Ellsworth's one-page opinion for the Court, as
reported, ignored the constitutional question. From the bench during argument,
however, Ellsworth was incredulous: did counsel mean the courts could act without
legislative sanction "in every case, to which the judicial power of the *United States*
extends"?[190] Chase was more emphatic. First, he asserted, "the political truth is, that
the disposal of the judicial power (except in a few specified instances) belongs to
congress." Moreover, "congress is not bound . . . to enlarge the jurisdiction of the
federal courts, to every subject, in every form, which the constitution might
warrant."[191] Thus it hardly can be contended that the Court was unaware of the
argument that the assignee clause was unconstitutional. Rather, if the report is
complete, the Court seems to have rejected the constitutional challenge as unworthy
even of reply.

---

[185]4 U.S. (4 Dall.) 8, 8 (1799).
[186]Judiciary Act of 1789, ch. 20, § 11, 1 Stat. 73, 79 (repealed in the abolition of the circuit courts by the
Judicial Code of 1911, ch. 231, § 289, 36 Stat. 1087, 1167). For the analogous current limitation, see 28
U.S.C. § 1359 (1976).
[187]4 U.S. (4 Dall.) at 10-11.
[188]U.S. CONST. art. III, § 2, para. 2.
[189]4 U.S. (4 Dall.) at 9.
[190]*Id.* at 10 n.1 (emphasis in original).
[191]*Id.*
[192]U.S. CONST. art. III, § 1.
[193]*Id.* § 2, para. 1.

"Exceptions" to the Court's appellate jurisdiction,[194] and the convention records show that the constitutional reference to "such inferior Courts as the Congress may from time to time ordain and establish"[196] was meant to free Congress from the obligation to create any lower federal courts at all.[195] In addition, it would be unfortunate if Congress lacked authority to make such minor jurisdictional adjustments as the assignee clause and the jurisdictional amount to prevent imposition or overburden. None of this, however, conclusively refutes Justice Story's later position that the entire judicial power must be vested *somewhere*;[197] it establishes only that Congress has considerable leeway in determining where it shall be vested. Something might have been made of the fact that article III speaks of "all Cases" arising under federal law but only of "Controversies" between citizens of different states,[198] and much might have been said about deference to the interpretation of the First Congress. What is significant is that the Court settled this important and difficult issue without preserving the least hint of its reasoning.

D. *Mossman v. Higginson*

Higginson was a British subject suing to foreclose a mortgage on property in Georgia. The citizenship of the defendants was not stated, and once more the Court ordered the suit dismissed:[199] although section 11 of the Judiciary Act[200] gave the circuit court jurisdiction "where . . . an alien is a party," the statute "must receive a construction, consistent with the constitution," and "the legislative power of conferring jurisdiction on the federal courts, is in this respect, confined to suits between citizens and foreigners."[201]

Here the Court, in a one-paragraph unsigned opinion, for the first time expressly took liberties with a statute to avoid holding it unconstitutional. This has become familiar practice, praised by Professor Alexander Bickel as one of the "passive virtues" whereby the Court avoids ultimate confrontations with other branches.[202] The theoretical excuse for its use seems to be a presumption that Congress does not mean to exceed its powers, but in fact Congress may view its authority more generously than the Court does. In *Mossman*, one wonders whether the Court really thought the statute was meant to apply only if the other party was a state citizen; a holding of unconstitutionality might have been more candid.[203] At the very least, the practice of construing statutes down to constitutional size called for explanation,

[194]*Id.* § 2, para. 2.

[195]*Id.* § 1.

[196]*See* HART & WECHSLER, *supra* introduction to part one, note 19, at 11-12.

[197]Martin v. Hunter's Lessee, 14 U.S. (1 Wheat.) 304, 328-31 (1816) (dictum). *See* text and notes at notes 168-83 *supra.*; *infra* chapter 4.

[198]U.S. CONST. art. III, § 2, para. 1 (emphasis added). *But see* 1 W. CROSSKEY, POLITICS AND THE CONSTITUTION IN UNITED STATES HISTORY 610-18 (1953).

[199]4 U.S. (4 Dall.) 12, 14 (1800).

[200]Judiciary Act of 1789, ch. 20, § 11, 1 Stat. 73, 78. For the current version of the district courts' alienage jurisdiction, see 28 U.S.C. § 1332(a) (1976).

[201]4 U.S. (4 Dall.) at 14.

[202]*See* A. BICKEL, THE LEAST DANGEROUS BRANCH 113-27 (1962).

[203]*But see* Mahoney, *A Historical Note on Hodgson v. Bowerbank*, 49 U. CHI. L. REV. 725, 731-32 (1982) (quoting a letter from Oliver Ellsworth, who had drafted the provision, to Richard Law (Apr. 30,

especially because it approached in practical effect the not-yet-established power of judicial review.

That the case was not shown to be within article III is obvious: alienage is a basis for exercise of article III judicial power only if the controversy is "between a State, or the Citizens thereof, and foreign States, Citizens or Subjects."[204] The interesting problem, here resolved for the first time by the Supreme Court, was whether article III was the outer limit of federal judicial power. That it was had been assumed by counsel in *Turner*[205] and by all the Justices in *Chisholm*, who seemed to think it necessary to demonstrate that the case before them came within article III.[206] Several Justices on circuit in *Hayburn* had held that article III *was* the limit when they concluded that the courts could be given nothing but "judicial" power.[207] Later cases would confirm that article III was the sole source of judicial power,[208] and the point may seem obvious: Marshall soon would remind us that the federal government was one of enumerated powers,[209] and the tenth amendment drives the point home by reserving to the states or to the people "[t]he powers not delegated to the United States by the Constitution."

But the tenth amendment alone does not establish that Congress lacks power to give the courts jurisdiction over suits between two aliens. Such a statute arguably is "necessary and proper"[210] to Congress's power to regulate foreign commerce,[211] to the President's authority to recognize foreign governments,[212] or to some other federal foreign affairs function. The question that must be decided is whether article III's enumeration implicitly limits Congress's powers under the legislative grants of the Constitution. The inference that Congress's powers are so limited is plausible, but it has not gone unquestioned; as recently as 1949, three Justices asserted that Congress could give article III courts jurisdiction over lawsuits involving District of Columbia citizens by virtue of its power "[t]o exercise exclusive Legislation" over the District.[213] Thus, in *Mossman* the Court resolved two debatable issues fundamental to constitutional litigation, apparently without giving any reasons.

Mossman completes our survey of the Court's pre-Marshall decisions with implications for the constitutional scope of federal judicial power. Obviously some general observations are in order; but they can best be made after considering the substantive constitutional decisions of the same period, and that is the aim of the following chapter.

1789) (*reprinted in* W. BROWN, THE LIFE OF OLIVER ELLSWORTH 188-89 (1905)) to show that the Court's interpretation was consistent with Ellsworth's understanding).

[204]U.S. CONST. art. III, § 2, para. 1.

[205]Turner v. Bank of North America, 4 U.S. (4 Dall.) 8, 9 (1799) (argument of counsel for bank).

[206]*See* text and notes at notes 60-117 *supra*.

[207]*See* Hayburn's Case, 2 U.S. (2 Dall.) 409, 410-13 n.(a) (1792).

[208]*See* National Mut. Ins. Co. v. Tidewater Transfer Co., 337 U.S. 582, 607-15 (1949) (Rutledge & Murphy, JJ., concurring in the result); *id.* at 627-45 (Vinson, C.J., & Douglas, J., dissenting); *id.* at 647-52 (Frankfurter & Reed, JJ., dissenting); The Genesee Chief, 53 U.S. (12 How.) 443, 452 (1851 Term), *discussed in infra* chapter 8.

[209]McCulloch v. Maryland, 17 U.S. (4 Wheat.) 316, 405 (1819); *see infra* chapter 6.

[210]U.S. CONST. art. I, § 8, para. 18.

[211]*Id.* art. I, § 8, para. 3.

[212]*Id.* art. II, § 3. *See* United States v. Belmont, 301 U.S. 324, 330 (1937).

[213]U.S. CONST. art. I, § 8, para. 17. *See* National Mut. Ins. Co. v. Tidewater Transfer Co., 337 U.S. 582, 589 (1949) (Jackson, Black & Burton, JJ.).

2

Limitations on Congressional and State Powers

Most of the encounters between the Court and the Constitution in the days of Jay and Ellsworth had to do with the threshold questions of federal jurisdiction discussed in the preceding chapter. With the exception of *Chisholm v. Georgia*, however, none of these cases produced significant reported opinions. For further examination of the legal reasoning of the Court before Marshall, one must look at the handful of substantial opinions on substantive constitutional questions. Three important cases under the 1789 Constitution began to grapple with the meaning of provisions respecting direct taxes, federal supremacy, and ex post facto laws; two others construing pre-1789 federal powers and the Georgia constitution cast additional light on the early Court's approach to constitutional interpretation.

I. Taxes, Treaties, and Retroactivity

A. *Hylton v. United States*

Congress in 1794 laid a geographically uniform tax on carriages ranging from $1 to $10 according to the type of vehicle.[1] The United States sued Hylton, as the owner of "one hundred and twenty-five chariots . . . for the defendant's own private use,"[2] to collect the tax due. Hylton argued the tax was unconstitutional under article I, which provides that "direct Taxes shall be apportioned among the several States . . . according to their respective Numbers" and that "no Capitation, or other direct, Tax shall be laid, unless in Proportion to the Census or Enumeration herein before directed to be taken."[3] The Supreme Court in seriatim opinions unanimously upheld the tax, concluding that it was not "direct" and thus did not need to be apportioned.

---

[1]Act of June 5, 1794, ch. 45, § 1, 1 Stat. 373, 373-74 (repealed by Act of May 28, 1796, ch. 37, § 1, 1 Stat. 478, 478). The background of the tax and of the litigation are well told in 4 J. Goebel & J. Smith, The Law Practice of Alexander Hamilton 297-340 (1980).

[2]3 U.S. (3 Dall.) 171, 171 (1796).

[3]U.S. Const. art. I, § 2, para 3; *id.* § 9, para. 4.

That the Court was willing to decide this case was extraordinary, for the controversy bristled with procedural obstacles. The incredible stipulation that the
plaintiff owned 125 personal chariots was a transparent but clumsy effort to circumvent jurisdictional amount requirements:[4] the parties had agreed that a judgment for
the Government could be discharged by paying $16, the tax and penalty on a single
chariot,[5] and in any event, the statute respecting Supreme Court review required, if
applicable, that the amount not equal but *exceed* $2000.[6] Moreover, the court below,
equally divided, had not decided the case. Ignoring the statutory procedure for a
tie-breaking rehearing,[7] the defendant had "confessed judgment"[8] in an effort to
reach the Supreme Court. Thus there was arguably no "final judgment[ ]," as the
statute required for Supreme Court review.[9] Indeed, because there was no lower
court decision to review, it hardly could be said that the Court was exercising
"appellate" jurisdiction at all, as article III soon was held to require in such cases.[10]
One also would expect a party to be precluded from appealing a judgment to which
he had consented.[11] Further, although the Court may not have known this, the
Government paid the other side's attorneys,[12] destroying the adversary relationship
the Court since has found necessary[13] (and may have found necessary in *Hayburn*)[14]
for a case or controversy under article III. Finally, only three Justices participated in
the decision, and the statutory quorum was four.[15] The Court apparently did not bat
an eye; so far as the report reveals, each Justice went directly to the merits without
mentioning any of the procedural problems apparent from the reporter's summary.
The contrast with *Hayburn* and the *Correspondence*, in which the Court had gone
out of its way to avoid reaching difficult substantive questions, is striking.

Chase, Paterson, and Iredell wrote full opinions in *Hylton*. Wilson noted that he
was not voting because he had sat below, but added that he remained of the

---

[4]Judiciary Act of 1789, ch. 20, § 22, 1 Stat. 73, 84 (Supreme Court review of "final judgments and
decrees in civil actions, and suits in equity in a circuit court, brought there by original process, or removed
there from courts of the several States, or removed there by appeal from a district court where the matter
in dispute exceeds the sum or value of two thousand dollars"); *id.* § 11, 1 Stat. at 78 (circuit court
jurisdiction over suits "where the matter in dispute exceeds . . . the sum or value of five hundred dollars,
and the United States are plaintiffs, or petitioners"). See 4 J. GOBEL & J. SMITH, *supra* note 1, at 313, 341.

[5]3 U.S. (3 Dall.) at 172. *See* Act of June 5, 1794, ch. 45, §§ 1, 3, 1 Stat. 373, 373, 374.

[6]*See* note 4 *supra*. Although the absence of a comma following the term "district court" suggests
according to modern usage that the amount requirement may have applied only to cases in which the
circuit court had reviewed a district court decision, the parties in *Hylton* seem to have assumed otherwise.

[7] Act of Mar. 2, 1793, ch. 22, § 2, 1 Stat. 333, 334 (superseded by Act of Apr. 29, 1802, ch. 31, § 6, 2 Stat.
156, 159-61).

[8]3 U.S. (3 Dall.) at 172.

[9]*See* note 4 *supra*.

[10]Marbury v. Madison, 5 U.S. (1 Cranch) 137, 175 (1803). *See infra* chapter 3.

[11]*Cf.* Donovan v. Penn Shipping Co., 429 U.S. 648, 649-50 (1977) (no appeal from remittitur by party
who had accepted it "under protest").

[12]*See* 1 C. WARREN, *supra* introduction to part one, note 2, at 147; J. GOEBEL, *supra* chapter 1, note 21,
at 779 & n.64.

[13]*See, e.g.,* Lord v. Veazie, 49 U.S. (8 How.) 251, 255 (1850 Term) (case must present "an actual
controversy, and adverse interests," otherwise judgment is a "nullity").

[14]*See* text and notes at chapter 1, notes 17-20 *supra*.

[15]Judiciary Act of 1789, ch. 20, § 1, 1 Stat. 73, 73 (current version in relevant part at 28 U.S.C. § 1
(1976)).

unexplained opinion that the tax was valid.[16] None of the Justices bothered to resolve what we would view as the threshold question whether the Court had power to declare an act of Congress unconstitutional. Chase adverted to the question, saying he did not need to reach it because he found the statute constitutional;[17] the others said nothing about it at all. Thus the Court began to accustom the country to the fact of judicial review without proclaiming its power to exercise it. By the time *Marbury* claimed the power, its exercise was nothing new. Chase added, for the first time and without explanation, the important and now familiar reservation that if such power existed, he would "never exercise it, but in a very clear case."[18] How seriously the Court takes this soothing message is unclear. Equally uncertain is its consistency with *Marbury*'s conclusion that the judges are oath-bound to disregard a law that offends the Constitution.[19] But ever since Chase's unelaborated dictum, it has been an accepted part of our tradition of constitutional adjudication. Thus, in these early days, were many important principles forever settled.

On the merits, the Justices' methods of interpretation in *Hylton* contrast sharply with those in *Chisholm*. In *Chisholm*, the Justices focused largely on the words of the Constitution, essentially ignoring a troublesome contrary tradition. In *Hylton*, the Justices relied mostly on unverified tradition and their own conception of sound policy, paying little heed to the Constitution's words.

All three opinions in *Hylton* hazarded the suggestion that only capitation and land taxes were direct,[20] and for this unnecessarily broad conclusion (qualified in Paterson's opinion by additional possibilities) the decision was cited carelessly until 1895.[21] The basis for this conclusion is elusive. Chase stated it without reasons, following and perhaps resulting from his discussion of policy.[22] Iredell suggested that land taxes were direct because they could be apportioned fairly.[23] Paterson referred to "theory and practice" without expounding the one or illustrating the other, and he added without citation that the provision had been inserted during the convention to allay Southern fears regarding taxes on land and slaves.[24] But the opinions fall short of convincing the modern reader that contemporary understanding limited the term to land and poll taxes. That the Framers may have had land and poll taxes in mind does not prove that no others fall within the general term "direct"; even the *Slaughter-House Cases* conceded that the thirteenth amendment outlawed the enslavement of persons who were not black.[25]

[16]3 U.S. (3 Dall.) at 183-84.

[17]*Id.* at 175.

[18]*Id.*

[19]5 U.S. (1 Cranch) 137, 177-80 (1803). On this question see generally J. THAYER, *supra* chapter one, note 53, at 16-33, applauding the doctrine of deference enunciated by Chase in *Hylton* and reporting earlier statements by others outside the Supreme Court to the same effect.

[20]3 U.S. (3 Dall.) at 175 (Chase, J.), 177 (Paterson, J.), 183 (Iredell, J.).

[21]*See, e.g.*, Veazie Bank v. Fenno, 75 U.S. (8 Wall.) 533, 546 (1869); Pacific Ins. Co. v. Soule, 74 U.S. (7 Wall.) 433, 444-45 (1869); 1 J. KENT, COMMENTARIES ON AMERICAN LAW 241 (New York 1826). In Pollock v. Farmers' Loan & Trust Co., 158 U.S. 601 (1895), the Court adopted a broader view of direct taxes.

[22]3 U.S. (3 Dall.) at 175.

[23]*Id.* at 183.

[24]3 U.S. (3 Dall.) at 176-77.

[25]83 U.S. (16 Wall.) 36, 72 (1873). *See infra* chapter 10.

Policy considerations dominated all three opinions. Apportioning a carriage tax according to population would be unfair, the Justices argued, for if carriages were distributed unevenly, an owner in a state with few carriages would bear a heavier burden.[26] Paterson made no effort to relate this policy preference to the Constitution. On the contrary, he argued that the constitutional rule of apportionment was "radically wrong" and "ought not to be extended by construction"[27]—hardly the statement of a judge who views his task as implementing the commands of the people.

Chase and Iredell were nominally more deferential, reasoning that by direct taxes the Framers must have meant those that could be apportioned to the census fairly. This is a prevalent approach to the construction of documents, and it is not without appeal: surely the Framers were reasonable people, and it should not be concluded lightly that they meant to do something foolish.[28] This may be only a less candid way of saying that the judge's preferences govern when the drafters' intentions are undiscoverable. This result may be unavoidable, but it should not be a substitute, as it seems to have been in *Hylton*, for an honest attempt to give content to the constitutional text. The opinions should have begun by investigating what the word "direct" meant; on its face it does not begin to suggest taxes that may be apportioned fairly. Moreover, the Justices made no effort to show that carriages in fact were distributed unevenly per capita among the states,[29] which was the crucial question under the test they adopted. Unlike fur coats and cotton fields, carriages do not seem prima facie to be a regional commodity. Nor did the Justices stop to consider, beyond Iredell's bare conclusion,[30] whether the test of unequal distribution was consistent with their own admission that a land tax was direct, though a landowner in a state with few acres per capita would bear an unequal burden. Furthermore, Paterson's history casts considerable doubt on the Justices' conclusion that a direct tax was one on a subject that was distributed uniformly. He asserted that the reason the South insisted on apportionment was that, having more than its share of land and slaves, it feared that a *uniform* levy per acre or per head would burden it unfairly.[31] The

[26]*See* 3 U.S. (3 Dall.) at 174 (Chase, J.).

> For example: suppose, two states, equal in census, to pay $80,000 each, by a tax on carriages, of eight dollars on every carriage; and in one state, there are 100 carriages, and in the other 1000. The owners of carriages in one state, would pay ten times the tax of owners in the other.

See also id. at 179-80 (Paterson, J.), 181-83 (Iredell, J.).

[27]*Id.* at 178.

[28]*See, e.g.,* United States v. Fisher, 6 U.S. (2 Cranch) 358, 386, 390 (1805) (Marshall, C.J.):

> [W]here great inconvenience will result from a particular construction, that construction is to be avoided, unless the meaning of the legislature be plain . . . .
>
>   . . . .
>
> . . . Where rights are infringed, where fundamental principles are overthrown, where the general system of the laws is departed from, the legislative intention must be expressed with irresistible clearness to induce a court of justice to suppose a design to effect such objects.

Marshall added, however, that this was "a principle which must be applied with caution." *Id.* at 390.

[29]Paterson stated as a bare conclusion that "[i]n some states, there are many carriages, and in others, but few." 3 U.S. (3 Dall.) at 179.

[30]*Id.* at 183.

[31]*Id.* at 177.

inference to be drawn from this—that a direct tax is one on a subject that is *not* uniformly distributed—is the opposite of that drawn by the Justices.

Chase also argued that the carriage tax was not direct because it was a duty[32] and thus subject to the distinct constitutional requirement of uniformity.[33] This was a promising approach, for the constitutional categories seem mutually exclusive. But Chase dropped the ball. To justify his conclusion that the carriage tax was a duty, he told us only that the term in English usage included stamp taxes and tolls; he neglected to say why the carriage tax was more like these duties than it was like a land tax, which he conceded was direct.[34] Indeed, one easily might draw the opposite conclusion: unlike his English examples, carriage and land taxes are both laid upon property.

Finally, Chase declared that the carriage tax was a tax on expenditure and thus was indirect.[35] He did not add, as he should have, that this was what the carriage tax had in common with tolls and stamp taxes, bringing it within the principle underlying the English term "duty." He did not explain, as he should have, that a land tax was distinguishable because it was laid not upon a consumptive expense but upon productive capital, and he did not rely upon the carefully contrived stipulation, anticipating some such distinction, that Hylton's carriages were held "for the defendant's own private use, and not . . . to hire."[36] He did not say, as he should have, in what sense a tax on expenditures was "indirect"; that is, he made no attempt to relate his test to the constitutional language.

It was Paterson who advanced the most persuasive argument. He, too, concluded that "[a]ll taxes on expenses or consumption are indirect taxes," but he explained why: "Indirect taxes are circuitous modes of reaching the revenue of individuals, who generally live according to their income."[37] For this interpretation he quoted Adam Smith:

> "[T]he state, not knowing how to tax directly and proportionably the revenue of its subjects, endeavors to tax it indirectly, by taxing their expense, which it is supposed, in most cases, will be nearly in proportion to their revenue. . . .
>
> "Consumable commodities . . . may be taxed in two different ways; the consumer may either pay an annual sum, on account of his using or consuming goods of a certain kind, or the goods may be taxed, while they remain in the hands of the dealer . . . . [T]he coach-tax and plate-tax are examples of the former method of imposing; the greater part of the other duties of excise and customs of the latter."[38]

---

[32]*Id.* at 175.

[33]U.S. CONST. art. I, § 8, para. 1 (providing that "all Duties, Imposts and Excises shall be uniform throughout the United States").

[34]Hamilton had done better, arguing for the Government that "[i]f the meaning of the word *excise* is to be sought in the British Statutes, it will be found to include the duty on carriages . . . ." 4 J. GOEBEL & J. SMITH, *supra* note 1, at 355.

[35]3 U.S. (3 Dall.) at 175.

[36]*Id.* at 171.

[37]*Id.* at 180.

[38]*Id.* at 180-81 (quoting A. SMITH, AN INQUIRY INTO THE NATURE AND CAUSES OF THE WEALTH OF NATIONS bk. V, ch. II, pt. II, art. 4, at 482-83, 490-91 (London 1776)).

This at last is convincing. The Smith quotation at the same time gives an intelligible meaning to the term "direct," tells us specifically that a coach tax is not direct, and places the coach tax in the distinct category of "duties of excise," for which the Constitution prescribes not apportionment but uniformity.[39]

What is left unclear is whether the Framers had Smith's definition in mind. The convention debates, which as noted were still unavailable, would have suggested that the Framers had no clear idea of what they meant by direct taxes.[40] In addition, an alternative definition as current and linguistically plausible as Smith's but cutting the other way had also been pressed by counsel for Hylton: an indirect tax was one whose ultimate burden was not borne by the person who initially paid it, and only a tax on carriages for hire could be passed on to the passengers.[41] Paterson ought to have said

[39]The notes Hamilton prepared in anticipation of his oral argument suggest that he urged Smith's definition on the Court and that he reconciled it with the understanding that land as well as capitation taxes were direct by invoking Smith's own insistence that land and labor were the sources of income. See 4 J. GOEBEL & J. SMITH, supra note 1, at 344-48.

[40]See text and note supra, chapter 1, note 57. What little the debates reveal about direct taxes tends to support the Hylton decision. An initial proposal to apportion all taxes by the census was objected to on the ground that it might cause "embarrassments" and was restricted to "direct" taxes, 1 CONVENTION RECORDS, supra chapter 1, note 54, at 592, lending support to the Chase-Iredell position that the Framers thought of direct taxes as those susceptible of fair apportionment. Gouverneur Morris and Madison— despite the latter's argument in Congress that the carriage tax was direct, 4 ANNALS OF CONG. 730 (1794)—spoke of taxes on consumption as indirect, 1 CONVENTION RECORDS, supra chapter one, note 54, at 592 (Morris); 2 id. at 277 (Madison), thus supporting the Chase-Paterson conclusion as to taxes on expenditures. When "Mr. [Rufus] King asked what was the precise meaning of direct taxation?," however, "No one answd [sic]." 2 id. at 350 (emphasis in original). Fisher Ames would admit in the House debate over the carriage tax that it was not easy to define direct taxes; he thought this tax permissible for the cryptic reason that it "falls not on the possession, but the use." 4 ANNALS OF CONG. 730 (1794).

We fairly may conclude that the Framers could have been more informative in their terminology. Their inattention to detail seems explicable, however, on the ground that the apportionment scheme was in large part a method of bringing the North and South closer together on the question whether slaves should be included in the basis of representation. For the South would be less insistent on including the slaves, and the North less insistent on excluding them, if their inclusion would cause the South to bear a heavier share of federal taxes. See 2 CONVENTION RECORDS, supra chapter one, note 54, at 106. It is not clear that anyone at the Convention thought apportionment of any kind of taxes was desirable for its own sake.

[41]See 4 J. GOEBEL & J. SMITH, supra note 1, at 318, 326 (giving John Taylor's arguments in the Court below). For Hamilton's response that such a rule would have the absurd consequence of making an import duty both direct and indirect according to the intentions of the importer see id. at 351. See also J. S. MILL, PRINCIPLES OF POLITICAL ECONOMY bk. V, ch. III, § 1, at 367 (London 1848) ("indirect taxes are those which are demanded from one person in the expectation and intention that he shall indemnify himself at the expense of another . . . ."); ST. G. TUCKER, 1 APPENDIX TO BLACKSTONE'S COMMENTARIES 23, 24, in 1 BLACKSTONE'S COMMENTARIES: WITH NOTES OF REFERENCE TO THE CONSTITUTION AND LAWS OF THE FEDERAL GOVERNMENT OF THE UNITED STATES AND THE COMMONWEALTH OF VIRGINIA (St. G. Tucker ed. 1803), written before Hylton and citing "Stuart's Political Economy" for the same interpretation.

In Canada, the British North America Act permits the provinces to impose only "direct" taxes, 30 & 31 Vict., c.3, § 92(2) (1867) (reprinted at CAN. REV. STAT. app. II, No. 5, § 92(2) (1970)), and Canadian courts have adopted Mill's definition. See P. HOGG, CONSTITUTIONAL LAW OF CANADA 402 (1977) (citing Bank of Toronto v. Lambe, 9 App. Cas. 296, 302-03 (1887), and quoting Mill's definition, supra note 268). See also Whitney, The Income Tax and the Constitution, 20 HARV. L. REV. 280, 282-83 (1907). Cf. 1 W. BLACKSTONE, COMMENTARIES ON THE LAWS OF ENGLAND 306 (Oxford 1765-69) (describing customs duties without using the term "indirect" as "a tax immediately paid by the merchant, although ultimately by the consumer"). Ellsworth had suggested this theme in the Connecticut convention. See 2 ELLIOT'S DEBATES, supra chapter one, note 96, at 192.

why he rejected this interpretation, but he stood alone in addressing the right question.

In sum, the Chase and Iredell opinions demonstrate a total unconcern for making sense of the constitutional text, a tendency to equate law with their own policy preferences, and an inclination to lay down flat rules that went beyond what was necessary to the decision. Paterson was even more blatant in following his own preference, but in other respects his opinion is markedly superior. He was the most reluctant to jump to the unnecessary conclusion that only land or capitation taxes might be direct. He alone attempted to relate convention history to show what direct taxes the Framers had in mind and what purpose they had in requiring apportionment. Most important, he alone gave us in the Smith quotation both evidence of contemporary usage and an intelligible interpretation of the constitutional language. Yet although the various strands of Paterson's opinion—policy, history, and Smith's terminology—converge to support the constitutionality of the carriage tax, his position is internally contradictory in theory, and the contradiction would haunt the Court in the most important modern controversy surrounding the apportionment clauses.[42] In the first place, Paterson failed to recognize that his view of history contradicted his policy that only taxes on evenly distributed subjects should be apportioned. More important, both his history and the intimations that only land and poll taxes were direct suggested that income taxes need not be apportioned. Under Smith's definition, however, a tax on income is precisely what is meant by a direct tax.

B. *Ware v. Hylton*

The administrator of a British subject sued in federal court to recover on a bond. The debtor had paid the money to the Commonwealth of Virginia in 1780 under a statute making such payment a defense to a claim by an alien enemy. The 1783 Treaty of Peace, however, provided that "creditors . . . shall meet with no lawful impediment to the recovery . . . of all bona fide debts heretofore contracted."[43] The circuit court held the treaty did not resuscitate debts that previously had been discharged; the Supreme Court reversed.[44]

Chase, Paterson, Wilson, and Cushing wrote opinions. Iredell, who did not vote, published the contrary opinion he had delivered in the trial court. Paterson, Wilson, and Cushing issued forgettable opinions confined almost entirely to the interpretation of the treaty. Chase and Iredell, whose discussions of Virginia's initial power of confiscation sparkled with learned references to such authorities as Vattel and Bynkershoek,[45] addressed several interesting constitutional questions as well.

First, both Chase and Iredell agreed that it was immaterial whether Virginia's confiscation offended the law of nations: if it did, that was a matter for international

---

[42]*See* Pollock v. Farmers' Loan & Trust Co., 158 U.S. 601 (1895) (income tax).
[43]Treaty of Peace, Sept. 3, 1783, United States-Great Britain, art. IV, 8 Stat. 80, 82, T. S. No. 104.
[44]3 U.S. (3 Dall.) 199 (1796).
[45]*Id.* at 225-27, 230 (Chase, J.), 263 (Iredell, J.).

sanctions, but the courts were bound by Virginia law.[46] Second, Chase rejected the argument that the exclusive war power was in Congress as early as 1777 and that Virginia therefore had lacked power to confiscate debts.[47] Wilson's cursory opinion seems to have adopted this argument.[48] But to Chase the powers of Congress vis-à-vis the states before the Articles of Confederation were based more on custom than on ascertainable grants. He concluded that the only "safe rule" was

> that all the powers actually exercised by congress, before that period, were rightfully exercised, on the presumption not to be controverted, that they were so authorized by the people they represented, by an express or implied grant; and that all the powers exercised by the state conventions or state legislatures were also rightfully exercised, on the same presumption of authority from the people.[49]

Because Congress never had tried to confiscate British debts but states had, Chase found Virginia had acted within its power.[50] Wilson protested that this meant Virginia "must be equally empowered to pass a similar law, in any future war,"[51] but in fact that question would depend, as *Ware* did not, on the interpretation of the war provisions of the Constitution of 1789. Moreover, Chase's abnegation of the power to review pre-Articles of Confederation statutes ostensibly was attributable to the lack of any firm basis for determining what the authority of Congress then had been; he had not been so deferential to the fact of congressional action in the carriage tax case.[52] In any event, the war powers argument in *Ware* was a harbinger of many future arguments, some to be successful, that a grant of power to the federal government implicitly excluded concurrent state action.[53]

More important for the future was the Court's conclusion that Congress had had authority in 1783 to rescind the state confiscation. Cushing and Paterson merely stated this conclusion,[54] and Wilson and Iredell apparently assumed it. Chase gave

[46]*Id.* at 229 (Chase, J.), 265-66 (Iredell, J.). Iredell anticipated here the arguments he soon would turn against Chase in *Calder v. Bull*, 3 U.S. (3 Dall.) 386, 398-99 (1798); *see* text and notes at notes 117-18 *infra*, and he took the occasion to show that he embraced judicial review of both federal and state statutes:

> The power of the legislatures is limited; of the state legislatures, by their own state constitutions and that of the United States; of the legislature of the Union, by the constitution of the Union. Beyond these limitations, I have no doubt, their acts are void, because they are not warranted by the authority given. But within them, I think they are in all cases obligatory in the country subject to their own immediate jurisdiction, because, in such cases, the legislatures only exercise a discretion expressly confided to them by the constitution of their country . . . .

3 U.S. (3 Dall.) at 266. In all of this Iredell spoke for himself alone, while Chase's observations about the law of nations were unnecessary in light of his conclusion that the treaty overrode state law.

[47]3 U.S. (3 Dall.) at 231-33. This, too, was unnecessary in light of Chase's conclusion that the treaty overrode state law. *See also id.* at 219-20 (argument of counsel for Ware).

[48]*Id.* at 281.

[49]*Id.* at 232.

[50]*Id.* at 233.

[51]*Id.* at 281.

[52]*See* text and notes at notes 20-35 *supra*.

[53]*See, e.g.,* Chirac v. Chirac, 15 U.S. (2 Wheat.) 259, 269 (1817) ("That the power of naturalization is exclusively in Congress does not seem to be, and certainly ought not to be, controverted . . . ."); *infra* chapter 5.

[54]3 U.S. (3 Dall.) at 282 (Cushing, J.), 249 (Paterson, J.).

reasons. The 1778 Articles of Confederation, he said, gave Congress "the sole and exclusive right and power of determining on peace or war, . . . and of entering into treaties and alliances":[55]

> This grant has no restriction, nor is there any limitation on the power in any part of the confederation. A right to make peace, necessarily includes the power of determining on what terms peace shall be made. A power to make treaties must, of necessity, imply a power to decide the terms on which they shall be made . . . .[56]

Considering the narrow legislative powers granted to Congress by the Articles, this sweeping statement is remarkable. Counsel in discussing "the power of the commissioners" who negotiated the treaty had argued that "congress never was considered as a legislative body, except in relation to those subjects expressly assigned to the federal jurisdiction; and could, at no time, nor in any manner, repeal the laws of the several states, or sacrifice the rights of individuals."[57] Chase's sweeping statement rejected both contentions, and in so doing established that Congress could do by treaty what it might lack power to do by legislation and that it could disturb vested rights retroactively.[58] The latter conclusion may be qualified under the 1789 Constitution by the taking clause of the fifth amendment, but the former was as applicable to the new Constitution as to the old. As in *Hylton v. United States,* however, Chase went out of his way to say that because he found the treaty valid, he did not have to decide whether he had the power to hold treaties void; in any event, he said he would "never exercise it, but in a very clear case indeed."[59]

The most important constitutional holding of *Ware v. Hylton* was that the federal courts had the power to determine the constitutionality of state laws. This crucial point, so painstakingly established with respect to *federal* laws a few years later in *Marbury v. Madison,* passed almost unnoticed. Cushing, Wilson, and Paterson voted to strike down the state law without adverting to the question, and the report does not reveal that it was the subject of argument. Iredell, who thought the treaty initially only an unenforceable promise that the states would repeal inconsistent laws,[60] agreed that in 1789 it became under article VI the supreme law of the land, putting the case "upon the same footing, as if every act constituting an impediment to a creditor's recovery had been expressly repealed."[61] Chase also relied on the supremacy clause:

> A treaty cannot be the supreme law of the land . . . if any act of a state legislature can stand in its way . . . . [L]aws of any of the states, contrary to

[55]ARTICLES OF CONFEDERATION art. 9, § 1.

[56]3 U.S. (3 Dall.) at 236.

[57]*Id.* at 216 (argument of counsel for Hylton).

[58]In his unconcern for federalism in the exercise of the treaty power, *id.* at 235-37, Chase anticipated Missouri v. Holland, 252 U.S. 416, 432-35 (1920), where the Court upheld a migratory bird treaty and implementing statute against a claim that both invaded powers reserved to the states under the tenth amendment. On vested rights, Chase said simply with a citation to Vattel that "the sacrificing [of] public or private property, to obtain peace, cannot be the cases in which a treaty would be void." 3 U.S. (3 Dall.) at 236.

[59]3 U.S. (3 Dall.) at 237.

[60]*Id.* at 272, 277.

[61]*Id.* at 277. *See* U.S. CONST. art. VI, para. 2.

a treaty, shall be disregarded . . . . [I]t is the declared duty of the state
judges to determine any constitution or laws of any state, contrary to that
treaty . . . , null and void. National or federal judges are bound by duty
and oath to the same conduct.[62]

As the critics later were to complain of *Marbury,* the fact that the Constitution
restricts legislative powers does not prove that the courts have authority to determine whether the limits have been exceeded.[63] But in the case of state laws article VI
does just that. Not only is federal law (including the Constitution and treaties)
declared to be "supreme," suggesting it is to be applied by courts in preference to
conflicting laws that are not; but "the Judges in every State shall be bound thereby,
any Thing in the Constitution or Laws of any State to the Contrary notwithstanding."[64] As Chase said, state court judges are expressly directed to review the consistency of state law with federal.[65] Chase also seems correct that the reference to
state judges was inserted not to distinguish them from, but to assimilate them to,
federal judges: it would make no sense to require federal judges alone to enforce
unconstitutional state laws, and the mere declaration of supremacy might not have
sufficed to override the impression that a state court owed primary loyalty to its own
sovereign.[66]

Only Chase and Iredell made anything of the fact that the treaty in question had
been concluded before the Constitution was adopted. The former said simply that
the supremacy clause was "retrospective,"[67] the latter that it "extends to subsisting as
well as to future treaties."[68] The constitutional language supports them, giving
supremacy to "all Treaties *made, or which shall be made,* under the Authority of the
United States."[69] This language looks both forward and backward, in contrast to the
purely prospective language of the accompanying clause, "*[t]his* Constitution, and
the Laws of the United States which *shall be made* in Pursuance thereof."[70] This
contrast, and the nearly silent holding of the Court that pre-1789 treaties were
supreme, are important considerations against the half-hearted argument for judicial review of congressional acts that Marshall later was to extract from the supremacy clause.[71]

Finally, it was argued in *Ware* that the treaty had been broken by England and was
no longer in force.[72] The argument was ignored by the Supreme Court but deserved a
reply. Iredell had rejected it below on the ground that it was for Congress under the
war powers, or the President and Senate under the treaty power, to determine

[62]3 U.S. (3 Dall.) at 236-37.
[63]*See, e.g.,* Eakin v. Raub, 12 Serg. & Rawl. 330, 345-46 (Pa. 1825) (Gibson, J., dissenting). *See infra*
chapter 3.
[64]U.S. CONST. art. VI, para. 2.
[65]3 U.S. (3 Dall.) at 237.
[66]*Accord,* 2 W. CROSSKEY, *supra* chapter 1, note 178, at 988. It is even arguable that the reference to
judges "in every State" (according to Crosskey, a prior draft had said "of the several States") embraces
federal judges; Crosskey thought the change was meant to include local as well as state judges. *Id.*
[67]3 U.S. (3 Dall.) at 237.
[68]*Id.* at 277.
[69]U.S. CONST. art. VI, para. 2 (emphasis added).
[70]*Id.* (emphasis added).
[71]Marbury v. Madison, 5 U.S. (1 Cranch) 137, 180 (1803). *See infra* chapter 3.
[72]3 U.S. (3 Dall.) at 202 (defendant's plea in bar in the circuit court).

whether to declare a treaty abrogated by breach, because under the law of nations a broken treaty was not void but voidable.[73] Perhaps this can be characterized as an interpretation of international law, of no moment to the student of the Constitution. But perhaps Iredell meant to resolve a question of the constitutional separation of powers, to say in modern terms that the questions of treaty breach and its consequences were committed to other branches of government and were not within the "judicial Power" of article III. In this light, Iredell's disposition, and to a lesser extent the Court's silence, may be seen as early forerunners of the political question doctrine.[74]

In sum, although the *Ware* opinions are concerned largely with the transitory nonconstitutional issue of the meaning of a particular treaty, those of Chase and Iredell are also gold mines of interesting constitutional problems. Once more we find inadequate discussion of important issues: there was no opinion of the Court, Iredell wrote only for the circuit court, and most of the Justices had nothing meaningful to say. But in *Ware* the Court for the first time struck down a state law under the supremacy clause, establishing for all time its power of judicial review of state laws. At the same time, it established that pre-1789 treaties came within the supremacy clause and that the courts would not inquire whether a treaty had been broken, and it rendered an extremely broad interpretation of the Confederation treaty power that seemed equally applicable to the Constitution. The opinions also contain insights, though not holdings, concerning the exclusivity of congressional powers and whether legislative power is limited by international law. Yet all of this ferment was byplay to the Court and thus was considered poorly, for the Justices evidently viewed the constitutional issues as too easy to merit serious discussion. Thus once more were important constitutional questions settled in a most off-hand manner.

C.   *Calder v. Bull*

The Connecticut legislature ordered a new trial in a will contest, setting aside a judicial decree. Reviewing subsequent state court proceedings, the Supreme Court without dissent held that the legislature's action was not an "ex post facto Law" forbidden the states by article I, section 10.[75]

Again the Court exercised the power of judicial review, but only Iredell took the trouble to affirm the existence of that power. As in his opinion on circuit in *Ware*, he did so in words that drew no distinction between state and federal laws:

> If any act of congress, or of the legislature of a state, violates those constitutional provisions, it is unquestionably void . . . . If they transgress the boundaries of [their constitutionally delegated] authority, . . . they violate a fundamental law, which must be our guide whenever we are called upon, as judges, to determine the validity of a legislative act.[76]

[73]*Id.* at 258-61.

[74]*See infra* chapter 8, discussing *Luther v. Borden.*

[75]U.S. Const. art. I, § 10, para. 1; 3 U.S. (3 Dall.) 386, 392 (Chase, J.), 397 (Paterson, J.), 400 (Iredell & Cushing, JJ.) (1798).

[76]3 U.S. (3 Dall.) at 399. Chase explicitly left open the issue of judicial review of acts of Congress. *Id.* at 392.

Thus Iredell disposed in the same breath of the question already settled on the basis of the supremacy clause in *Ware v. Hylton* and the much harder question still to be determined in *Marbury*. Once more the Justices managed without actually so holding to imbed deeper the idea that they could review acts of Congress. Chase stated for the third time his dogma that he would not exercise the power to strike down legislation "but in a very clear case,"[77] and this time Iredell said it, too, giving as his reason only that the power "is of a delicate and awful nature."[78]

Chase refused, however, to decide whether the legislature's action was contrary to the constitution of Connecticut: "I am fully satisfied, that this court has no jurisdiction to determine that any law of any state legislature, contrary to the constitution of such state, is void."[79] This statement was unexceptionable in the context of *Calder* itself, for the case was on writ of error from a state court; under section 25 of the Judiciary Act, the Supreme Court had jurisdiction to review state courts only if federal rights had been denied and then only to review matters that "immediately respect[ed]" the federal question.[80] Chase's statement might be thought to mean the Court *never* could decide state constitutional questions, but that would have been erroneous. There was no limitation to issues of federal law in the provisions authorizing the circuit courts to hear diversity cases or the Supreme Court to review them,[81] and section 34 expressly directed federal courts in common circumstances to apply state law.[82] Indeed, in *Ware v. Hylton*, a diversity case, Chase himself had passed upon the question whether the law of nations limited Virginia's power of confiscation,[83] and the Court soon would decide state constitutional questions in *Cooper v. Telfair*.[84] Chase's remark therefore should be understood to apply only to cases coming from state courts.

On the merits of the ex post facto objection, opinions were written by Cushing, Iredell, Paterson and Chase. As junior Justice, Chase delivered the first and most extensive opinion, as he had in the carriage tax and treaty cases. The words "ex post facto law," he said, were "technical, they had been in use long before the revolution, and had acquired an appropriate meaning, by legislators, lawyers and authors."[85] Looking to Blackstone, to state constitutions, and for what may have been the first time to "the author of the *Federalist*,"[86] whom he praised for "his extensive and accurate knowledge of the true principles of government," Chase concluded that, according to settled usage, ex post facto laws were those that retroactively "create or aggravate the crime; or increase the punishment, or change the rules of evidence, for the purpose of conviction."[87] He added that this narrow construction was confirmed

[77]*Id.* at 395.
[78]*Id.* at 399.
[79]*Id.* at 392.
[80]Judiciary Act of 1789, ch. 20, § 25, 1 Stat. 73, 85-87 (current version at 28 U.S.C. § 1257 (1976)).
[81]*Id.* § 11, 1 Stat. at 78 (circuit court diversity jurisdiction); § 22, 1 Stat. at 84 (Supreme Court review). For the current version of the district courts' diversity jurisdiction, *see* 28 U.S.C. § 1332 (1976); for the current version of the Supreme Court's power to review decisions by the courts of appeals, *see* 28 U.S.C. § 1254 (1976).
[82]Judiciary Act of 1789, ch. 20, § 34, 1 Stat. 73, 92 (current version at 28 U.S.C. § 1652 (1976)).
[83]*See* text and note at note 46 *supra*.
[84]*See* text and notes at notes 152-172 *infra*.
[85]3 U.S. (3 Dall.) at 391.
[86]*See* Pierson, *The Federalist in the Supreme Court*, 33 YALE L. J. 728, 729 (1924).
[87]3 U.S. (3 Dall.) at 391-92.

by other clauses of the Constitution, for if the term "ex post facto" had included retroactive *civil* laws, it would have been unnecessary to forbid the states to impair contracts or the United States to take property without compensation.[88] Paterson reached the same conclusion for much the same reasons.[89] Iredell agreed that the prohibition applied only to criminal cases, but his assigned reason was naked policy: retroactive civil laws such as takings for public use were often justifiable; retroactive criminal sanctions were not.[90]

The techniques of constitutional interpretation employed by Chase and Paterson were straightforward and familiar to today's reader. Their conclusion that the term "ex post facto law" traditionally referred only to criminal matters, however, has been disputed vigorously. Chase did not bother to quote either Blackstone or *The Federalist,* on which he relied. Paterson did quote Blackstone,[91] but both sources have been argued by critics to have used criminal punishments only as an example and not as an exclusive definition of ex post facto legislation. Two of the state constitutions referred to by Chase and Paterson did not use the term "ex post facto" at all; two more used it without instructive amplification; and innumerable contemporary statements have been cited to show that the term commonly was used to refer to civil as well as to criminal matters.[92]

The critics have succeeded in demonstrating that the issue was not so one-sided as Chase and Paterson contended, but not, I think, that the decision was clearly wrong. The Maryland and North Carolina Constitutions provided "[t]hat retrospective laws, punishing facts committed before the existence of such laws, and by them only declared criminal, are oppressive, unjust, and incompatible with liberty; wherefore, no *ex post facto* law ought to be made."[93] Hamilton in *The Federalist* supported the federal prohibition on the ground that "[t]he creation of crimes after the commission

---

[88]*Id.* at 390, 394. *See* U.S. CONST. art. I, § 10, para. 1 (contracts clause); *id.* amend. V (compensation clause). In so doing, Chase implied without giving reasons that the contract clause was retrospective only, an assumption Marshall later would respectably dispute. *See* Ogden v. Saunders, 25 U.S. (12 Wheat.) 213, 332-58 (1827) (dissenting opinion); *infra* chapter 5. Chase made the same argument about the provision that the states not "make any Thing but gold and silver Coin a Tender in Payment of Debts," U.S. CONST. art. I, § 10, para. 1; 3 U.S. (3 Dall.) at 390, but Justice Washington later would concede in *Ogden* that the legal tender clause applied to subsequent as well as preexisting debts. 25 U.S. (12 Wheat.) at 269.

[89]3 U.S. (3 Dall.) at 396-97.

[90]*Id.* at 399-400.

[91]*Id.* at 396.

[92]*See* Satterlee v. Matthewson, 27 U.S. (2 Pet.) 380, 681-87 app. No. 1 (1829) (Johnson, J., concurring, Note on the Exposition of the Phrase, "Ex Post Facto," in the Constitution of the United States) (original ed. Phila. 1829); 1 W. CROSSKEY, *supra* chapter one, note 178, at 324-51; Field, *Ex Post Facto in the Constitution,* 20 MICH. L. REV. 315 (1922). Among the statements cited are an explicit one by Iredell in the North Carolina ratifying convention and an opinion on circuit in which Paterson seems to have assumed that the clause had civil application. *See* 1 W. CROSSKEY, *supra* chapter one, note 178, at 337-38, 341-42. Crosskey concluded that the Justices in *Calder* were attempting to clear the way for a retroactive federal bankruptcy law, which had been argued to be forbidden by the corresponding ex post facto clause of article I, section 9, paragraph 3. *Id.* at 346-49.

[93]MD. DECLARATION OF RIGHTS OF 1776 § 15 (current version at MD. CONST. declaration of rights, art. 17); N.C. DECLARATION OF RIGHTS OF 1776 § 24 (current version at N.C. CONST. art. I, § 16), *quoted in* 3 U.S. (3 Dall.) at 397. Crosskey argued that in these constitutions the "enacting part . . . went beyond the evil recited in its preamble." 1 W. CROSSKEY, *supra* note 195, at 345. This is a plausible but hardly a necessary conclusion.

of the fact" was a "favorite and most formidable instrument[ ]of tyranny."[94] Blackstone, after condemning Caligula for "ensnar[ing] the people" by giving inadequate notice of the law, had said there was "still a more unreasonable method than this, which is called making of laws, *ex post facto*; when *after* an action is committed, the legislator then for the first time declares it to have been a crime."[95] One reading these references might fairly conclude, though the inference is not inescapable, that their authors thought the term applied only to criminal punishments.

What this split of opinion seems to indicate is that, as in the case of direct taxes, there was no clear answer to what the Framers meant by ex post facto laws.[96] Yet two of the Justices told us only part of the story in an effort to persuade us that they modestly were following tradition, while the third, Iredell, told us the clause meant what he wanted it to mean without first showing that it had no established definition.

Later decisions basically have adhered to the conclusion that the ex post facto clauses apply only to retroactive punishment,[97] but the practice of seriatim opinions and the peculiar wording of the Paterson and Iredell opinions make it difficult to say that this was the holding of the Court in *Calder*. Paterson discussed the criminal issue only after declaring that "we may, in the present instance, consider the legislature of the state as having acted in their customary *judicial* capacity. If so, there is an end of the question."[98] He then proceeded to "consider the resolution . . . as the exercise of a legislative and not a judicial authority," "[f]or the sake of ascertaining the meaning" of the constitutional term.[99] Iredell was even more emphatic in resting his conclusion on the judicial ground. Like the House of Lords, he argued, the Connecticut legislature had judicial as well as legislative power: the power "to superintend the courts of justice . . . is judicial in nature; and whenever it is exercised, as in the present instance, it is an exercise of judicial, not of legislative, authority."[100] He then went on to discuss, hypothetically, the criminal issue. Cushing, the only other Justice to participate, wrote only one substantive sentence: "If the act is a judicial act, it is not touched by the federal constitution: and if it is a legislative act, it is

---

[94]THE FEDERALIST No. 84, *supra* chapter 1, note 97, at 511-12 (A. Hamilton). Johnson and Crosskey, in dismissing a passage in THE FEDERALIST that merely had condemned ex post facto laws without saying what they were, were referring to Madison's No. 44. Satterlee v. Matthewson, 27 U.S. (2 Pet.) 380, 685 app. No. 1 (1829) (Johnson, J., concurring, Note on the Exposition of the Phrase, "Ex Post Facto," in the Constitution of the United States) (original ed. Phila. 1829); 1 W. CROSSKEY, *supra* chapter 1, note 178, at 329.

[95]1 W. BLACKSTONE, *supra* note 41, at 46 (emphasis in original).

[96]The convention record itself contains conflicting evidence. Madison asked a question indicating that he thought ex post facto referred to civil as well as criminal matters, 2 CONVENTION RECORDS, *supra* chapter 1, note 54, at 440, and George Mason moved to strike the phrase because it might be held to reach civil cases. *Id.* at 617. John Dickinson, on the other hand, "mentioned to the House that on examining Blackstone's Commentaries, he found that the terms 'ex post facto' related to criminal cases only." *Id.* at 448. During the Virginia Ratifying Convention, Mr. Randolph also expressed this view. *See* ELLIOT'S DEBATES, *supra* note 113, at 477.

[97]*E.g.*, Watson v. Mercer, 33 U.S. (8 Pet.) 88, 109-10 (1834). *See* L. TRIBE, AMERICAN CONSTITUTIONAL LAW 479-82 (1978).

[98]3 U.S. (3 Dall.) at 395 (emphasis added).

[99]*Id.* at 396.

[100]*Id.* at 398.

maintained and justified by the ancient and uniform practice of the state of Connecticut."[101]

Thus it was possible thirty years later for Justice William Johnson to maintain with some plausibility that *Calder* had held only that the resolution was judicial: three Justices had so declared, and only Chase had limited the clause to criminal matters, for what Paterson and Iredell had said on that point was dictum.[102] It might be more accurate to call their comments on the criminal issue an alternative basis for their conclusion. In any event, *Calder* illustrates the uncertainty that can arise when each Justice writes separately[103] and half of them gratuitously give two independent reasons for their decisions.

None of the three Justices who concluded that the challenged action was judicial said why that was relevant to the constitutional question. The answer seems to be that the Constitution forbids only an "ex post facto Law," and that judicial action is not "Law."[104] It is hard to believe the Framers meant to outlaw the ordinary process of appellate review; they created an appellate federal court, and arguably it was of no concern to them how the states allocated governmental powers among their branches.[105] But there are reservations: if judicial action is not a law, a state might impose through a novel interpretation of the common law the same unfair punishment of the unsuspecting actor that the Justices thought the clause was designed to prevent.[106] Moreover, the separation of state powers was not a wholly improbable concern of the Framers: one common explanation for the prohibition of bills of attainder, which applies to the states as well as to Congress, is the unsuitability of

[101]*Id.* at 400-01. Cushing's second point left something to be desired, for Chase argued with some force that the whole point of the ex post facto clause was to outlaw previously accepted practice. *Id.* at 389.

[102]Satterlee v. Matthewson, 27 U.S. (2 Pet.) 380, 681-83 app. No. 1 (1829) (Johnson, J., concurring, Note on the Exposition of the Phrase, "Ex Post Facto," in the Constitution of the United States) (original ed. Phila. 1829).

[103]*See* chapter 1, note 61 *supra*.

[104]*See* Frank v. Mangum, 237 U.S. 309, 344 (1915); L. TRIBE, *supra* note 97, at 477-78. *Cf. infra* chapter 7, discussing the related question whether the adjacent provision that "No State shall . . . pass any . . . Law impairing the Obligation of Contracts" applied to judicial action.

[105]Article IV, section 4 of the Constitution, which guarantees each state "a Republican Form of Government," apparently was not invoked in *Calder*. It was touted in the convention as a safeguard against monarchy, 1 CONVENTION RECORDS, *supra* chapter 1, note 61, at 206 (remarks of George Mason and Edmund Randolph), and has since been held nonjusticiable, Pacific States Tel. Co. v. Oregon, 223 U.S. 118, 133, 151 (1912). See also 4 ELLIOT's DEBATES, *supra* chapter 1, note 96, at 195 (Mr. Iredell, asserting that article IV, section 4 was a protection against aristocracy and monarchy) and 2 *id.* at 482 (Mr. Wilson, arguing that a Republican form of government ". . . secures, in the strongest manner, the right of suffrage").

[106]More recently, such efforts have been struck down under the fourteenth amendment's due process clause, Bouie v. City of Columbia, 378 U.S. 347, 353-54 (1964), but until after the Civil War the Federal Constitution guaranteed due process only at the hands of the federal government. See Barron v. Baltimore, 32 U.S. (7 Pet.) 243, 249 (1834) (holding the fifth amendment's just compensation clause inapplicable to the states); *infra* chapter 6. In other contexts the term "laws" has come to include judicial decisions. Illinois v. City of Milwaukee, 406 U.S. 91, 100 (1972) (jurisdiction of cases arising under the laws of the United States): Erie R.R. v. Tompkins, 304 U.S. 64, 78 (1938) (state laws as rules of decision in the federal courts).

legislatures to conduct criminal trials.[107] In any case, plausible though the Justices' conclusion may have been, it deserved a fuller examination.

The most noteworthy aspect of the *Calder* opinions, however, had nothing to do with the ex post facto clause; it was the famous controversy between Chase and Iredell over the role of natural law in constitutional litigation. Chase's opinion started harmlessly enough by paraphrasing the tenth amendment: "It appears to me a self-evident proposition, that the several state legislatures retain all the powers of legislation, delegated to them by the state constitutions; which are not expressly taken away by the constitution of the United States."[108] He then asserted that the "sole inquiry" was whether the action of the Connecticut legislature offended the ex post facto clause of the Federal Constitution.[109] In the next paragraph, however, he stated:

> There are certain vital principles in our free republican governments, which will determine and overrule an apparent and flagrant abuse of legislative power . . . . An act of the legislature (for I cannot call it a law), contrary to the great first principles of the social compact, cannot be considered a rightful exercise of legislative authority.[110]

He gave as examples "a law that makes a man a judge in his own cause; or a law that takes property from A. and gives it to B."[111]

Did Chase mean to contradict himself and to assert power to strike down any law offending his sense of natural justice? John Hart Ely thinks not. If Chase had been of that view, Professor Ely argues, he would not have sustained the act before him, for he also declared that laws impairing rights vested under existing rules were unjust. To Ely, the "great first principles" Chase had in mind were those of the Federal Constitution.[112] Yet Chase cannot have meant that a law "that takes property from A. and gives it to B." offended the Federal Constitution, for he concluded that the ex post facto clause applied only to criminal cases. Moreover, Ely's interpretation does not account for the paragraph Chase devoted to demonstrating that the original decree had given Calder no vested right.[113] This paragraph is irrelevant to the ex post facto issue, and it seems to refute Ely's conclusion that Chase found the action of the Connecticut legislature offensive. It suggests that the reason Chase upheld the legislature's action was that it impaired no vested right and therefore was consistent with natural justice.[114]

---

[107]*See, e.g.,* United States v. Brown, 381 U.S. 437, 442-46 (1965); T. Cooley, Constitutional Limitations 260-61 (1868); L. Tribe, *supra* note 97, at 491-92.

[108]3 U.S. (3 Dall.) at 387.

[109]*Id.*

[110]*Id.* at 388.

[111]*Id.*

[112]J. Ely, Democracy and Distrust: A Theory of Judicial Review 210-11 (1980) (citing Chase's remarks in 3 U.S. (3 Dall.) at 391, and emphasizing his reference to limits on state authority beyond those imposed by state constitutions, *id.* at 387-88).

[113]3 U.S. (3 Dall.) at 395.

[114]Elsewhere in his opinion, Chase argued that "[t]o maintain that our federal, or state legislature possesses such powers, if they had not been expressly restrained; would, in my opinion, be a political heresy, altogether inadmissible in our free republican governments." *Id.* at 388-89. The reference to the

Iredell thought Chase was asserting the authority to measure laws against his own ideas of justice, and he protested vigorously. Despite the views of "some speculative jurists," Iredell argued, the Court could not pronounce state or federal legislation void "merely because it is, in their judgment, contrary to the principles of natural justice."[115] For one thing, "[t]he ideas of natural justice are regulated by no fixed standard" and would be a license for judges to set aside any law with which they disagreed.[116] Moreover, English judges could not disregard legislation on the basis of natural justice, and Americans had dealt with the problem of oppressive laws by adopting constitutions "to define with precision the objects of the legislative power, and to restrain its exercise within marked and settled boundaries."[117] The power of appointed judges to annul legislation on grounds of policy was thus not only undemocratic and contrary to the English legal tradition we had inherited; it was fundamentally inconsistent with the concept of a written constitution.[118] Iredell might have added the powerful language of the tenth amendment, which Chase himself had paraphrased:[119] "The powers not delegated to the United States by the Constitution, nor prohibited by it to the States, are reserved to the States respectively, or to the people."

The Chase-Iredell exchange was the opening salvo in a running battle that never

---

federal legislature shows that Chase was not speaking only of actions unrestrained by state constitutions; he seems to have been arguing that Congress, too, was subject to limits not found in any written document.

Other passages of the opinion suggest a third possible interpretation that would mean Chase was commenting on an issue he had said the Court lacked power to determine. The reason the legislature could not give A's property to B, Chase declared, was that "it is against all reason and justice, for a people to intrust a legislature with such powers, and therefore, it cannot be presumed that they have done it." *Id.* at 388. The next sentence attributed the "prohibition" of such laws to "[t]he genius, the nature and the spirit of our state governments." *Id.*

[115]*Id.* at 398-99.

[116]*Id.* at 399.

[117]*Id.* at 398-99.

[118]In other words, the adoption of a written constitution indicating the extent to which the courts were meant to interfere with legislative judgments had rendered the assertions of natural law in the Declaration of Independence and in other revolutionary writings obsolete. It had not, however, extinguished such assertions. Ellsworth, who did not sit in *Calder*, argued in the convention that it was unnecessary to prohibit ex post facto laws because "there was no lawyer, no civilian who would not say that ex post facto laws were void of themselves," and several others agreed with him. 2 CONVENTION RECORDS, *supra* chapter 1, note 61, at 376, 378-79. Obviously there was more to be said on the question than the countervailing assertions of Chase and Iredell, but the absence of a more complete discussion was understandable, for even Chase thought *Calder* was an inappropriate case for invoking natural law. For an examination of natural law ideas from Cicero to Coke to James Otis, see E. CORWIN, THE "HIGHER LAW" BACKGROUND OF AMERICAN CONSTITUTIONAL LAW (1955).

[119]3 U.S. (3 Dall.) at 387 (Chase, J.). A passage at the end of Paterson's opinion seems to suggest he shared Iredell's view that judges were limited by the Constitution:

> I had an ardent desire to have extended the [ex post facto] provision in the constitution to retrospective laws in general. . . . [T]hey neither accord with sound legislation, nor the fundamental principles of the social compact. But on full consideration, I am convinced, that *ex post facto* laws must be limited in the manner already expressed . . . .

Id. at 397. Crosskey construes this passage, however, to refer to a prior opinion Paterson held on circuit as to the meaning of the Constitution, not to his efforts at the convention, which he had left before the issue was discussed. 1 W. CROSSKEY, *supra* chapter 1, note 178, at 346.

has simmered down completely.[120] Chase's assertive position, trumpeted in a case in which in his own view it had no application, was elevated by Marshall in 1810 to what may have been an alternative holding in *Fletcher v. Peck*.[121] It was embraced in separate opinions by Marshall's colleague William Johnson[122] and was advanced as the Court's basis for striking down a state law in a famous opinion by Justice Samuel Miller after the Civil War.[123] More frequently the Court has formally renounced natural law.[124] In practice, however, some of the Court's more recent decisions under such rubrics as "substantive due process"[125] raise the question whether it is paying lip service to Iredell for the sake of appearances while effectively following Chase—a course of action that arguably compounds usurpation with deception.

Neither Chase, Marshall, Johnson, nor Miller invoked in support of this expansive view of judicial power the ninth amendment's provision that "[t]he enumeration in the Constitution, of certain rights, shall not be construed to deny or disparage others retained by the people." Overwhelmingly ignored for most of its history, this amendment recently has been exhumed by commentators[126] and has begun to appear modestly in Court opinions.[127] It is far from obvious that it empowers judges to define and enforce additional constitutional rights. Its history suggests it was meant merely to preclude any inference from the Bill of Rights that would lead to an unnaturally broad interpretation of the granted federal powers.[128] Whatever its meaning, a

---

[120]*See, e.g.,* J. ELY, *supra* note 112; Grey, *Do We Have an Unwritten Constitution?*, 27 STAN. L. REV. 703 (1975).

[121]10 U.S. (6 Cranch) 87, 139 (1810). *See infra* chapter 5.

[122]*E.g., id.* at 143.

[123]Loan Ass'n v. City of Topeka, 87 U.S. (20 Wall.) 655, 662-63 (1875). *See infra* chapter 11.

[124]*E.g.,* Nevada v. Hall, 440 U.S. 410, 426 (1979); Satterlee v. Matthewson, 27 U.S. (2 Pet.) 380, 413 (1829).

[125]*E.g.,* Roe v. Wade, 410 U.S. 113 (1973) (abortion); Lochner v. New York, 198 U.S. 45 (1905) (maximum working hours).

[126]*E.g.,* J. ELY, *supra* note 112, at 34-41.

[127]Richmond Newspapers, Inc. v. Virginia, 448 U.S. 555, 579 n.15 (1980) (Burger, C.J., announcing the judgment of the Court); Griswold v. Connecticut, 381 U.S. 479, 486-99 (1965) (Goldberg, J., concurring). Both opinions, however, fall short of saying that the ninth amendment *creates* constitutional rights. Chief Justice Burger noted only that the amendment "served to allay the fears of those who were concerned that expressing certain guarantees could be read as excluding others," 448 U.S. at 579 n.15, and Justice Goldberg cautioned that the ninth amendment does not leave judges "at large to decide cases in light of their personal and private notions," 381 U.S. at 493, or give them "unrestricted personal discretion," *id.* at 494 n.7.

[128]See the Federalist, No. 84 (Hamilton):

> [B]ills of rights . . . are not only unnecessary in the proposed constitution, but would even be dangerous. They would contain various exceptions to powers that were not granted; and on this very account, would afford a colourable pretext to claim more than were granted . . . . [M]en disposed to usurp . . . might urge with a semblance of reason, that the provision against restraining the liberty of the press afforded a clear implication, that a power to prescribe proper regulations concerning it, was intended to be vested in the national government.

Virginia, in ratifying the Constitution, had proposed an amendment to preclude any such implication: "That those clauses which declare that Congress shall not exercise certain powers, be not interpreted, in any manner whatsoever, to extend the powers of Congress . . . ." 3 ELLIOT'S DEBATES *supra* chapter 1, note 96, at 661. This was Madison's explanation in offering the amendment in the House, 1 Annals of Cong. 456 (1789):

sufficient explanation for the failure of early Justices to invoke the amendment in cases like *Calder* is the historically and structurally plausible inference, made law by the Marshall Court, that the Bill of Rights limited only federal and not state powers.[129]

In sum, the import of *Calder* was rendered obscure by the readiness of Paterson and Iredell to resolve two issues when one would have sufficed. Moreover, not all the opinions gave adequate explanations for their conclusions, and serious doubts have been raised as to the Justices' view of tradition. But the Paterson and Chase opinions are excellent examples of the weight that tradition and contemporary understanding can be given in interpreting the Constitution. If the same tools had been employed in *Chisholm*, that case might well have come out the other way.

II. State Constitutions and Congressional Power before 1789

The pre-Marshall Court's approach to constitutional adjudication may be illuminated further by its encounters with constitutions other than the present federal one. I have already discussed the Justices' treatment in *Calder* and in *Ware v. Hylton* of federal jurisdiction over state constitutional questions, of the relationship between state law and the law of nations, of the powers of the pre–Articles of Confederation Congress, and of the treaty power under the Articles.[130] Two other early cases presented the Court with similar constitutional problems.

A.   *Pennhallow v. Doane's Administrators*

In 1775 the Continental Congress passed a resolution calling on the colonies to establish prize courts for the condemnation of captured vessels employed to suppress the Revolution, providing that "in all cases, an appeal shall be allowed to the congress, or such person or persons as they shall appoint for the trial of appeals."[131] In 1777 a New Hampshire court condemned a captured vessel; in 1778 an appeal to Congress was filed; in 1780 Congress established a "Court of Appeals in cases of capture";[132] in 1783 that court reversed the state court decree. After the adoption of

---

It has been objected also against a Bill of Rights, that, by enumerating particular exceptions to the grant of power, it would disparage those rights which were not placed in the enumeration; and it might follow, by implication, that those rights which were not singled out, were intended to be assigned into the hands of the General Government, and were consequently insecure.

See generally Caplan, *The History and Meaning of the Ninth Amendment*, 69 Va. L. Rev. 223, 228, 256 (1983), concluding that "the amendment neither creates new rights" nor constitutionalizes existing ones and quoting Madison's statement that the amendment's formulation was the equivalent of what Virginia had requested: "'it would seem to be the same thing, whether [rights] be secured by declaring that they shall not be abridged, or that [powers] shall not be extended.'" Citing letter from James Madison to George Washington (Dec. 5, 1789), reprinted in 5 The Writings of James Madison 431, 432 (G. Hunt ed. 1904).

[129]Barron v. Baltimore, 32 U.S. (7 Pet.) 243, 249 (1833). *See infra* chapter 6.

[130]*See* text and notes at notes 46-73, 79-84 *supra.*

[131]1 J. Cong. 242 (1775) (Folwell's Press ed. Phila. 1800).

[132]The origins and work of this court are usefully described in H. Carson, History of the Supreme Court of the United States, chs. III-V (1902).

the new Constitution, a federal district court awarded damages for failure to respect a decision of the Court of Appeals. The Supreme Court essentially affirmed.[133]

The overriding constitutional question was the authority of Congress to establish a tribunal to review the state court decree. All four participating Justices said this issue had been settled by the decision of the Court of Appeals and could not be reopened collaterally.[134] Yet all four added comments on the merits of the question as well.

The Articles of Confederation expressly gave Congress the power of "establishing courts for receiving and determining finally appeals in all cases of captures."[135] Because Congress was not empowered to establish *trial* courts for capture cases, it was obvious that review of state court decisions was intended. The Court lost no sleep over the question, later so hotly disputed,[136] whether the tribunals of one sovereign could review those of another. Paterson, after paraphrasing the Articles, declared that the Court of Appeals had been "constitutionally established,"[137] and Blair said the authority of the court under the Confederation was "confessed."[138]

The difficulty was that the Articles had not been ratified until 1781, after the entry of the state court's decree and establishment of the Court of Appeals. Consequently it was argued that the jurisdiction of the Court of Appeals over the *Penhallow* case depended on Congress's power to provide for review of state capture cases prior to the Articles of Confederation. Iredell and Cushing, while commenting on Congress's pre-1781 authority, found it unnecessary to resolve the issue because it had been determined by the Court of Appeals.[139] Paterson and Blair upheld the pre-Articles of Confederation power on the merits. Paterson, like Chase in the later *Ware v. Hylton,*[140] sought the authority of Congress in the "powers they exercised": "in congress were vested, because by congress were exercised, with the approbation of the people, the rights and powers of war and peace," and the disposition of captured vessels was "incidental thereto."[141] Though Blair warned that "usurpation can give

---

[133]3 U.S. (3 Dall.) 54, 60-62 (1795). The Court also upheld the authority of the district court to entertain the action based on the earlier decree, reaffirming its decision in The Betsey, 3 U.S. (3 Dall.) 6 (1794), that prize cases were "civil causes of admiralty and maritime jurisdiction" within section 9 of the Judiciary Act of 1789, ch. 20, 1 Stat. 73, 77 (current version in relevant part at 28 U.S.C. § 1333 (1976)). Appellees' counsel in *The Betsey* had conceded that prize cases were "Cases of admiralty and maritime Jurisdiction" within article III, section 2, paragraph 1 of the Constitution, but had argued that they were not "civil causes" under the statute. 3 U.S. (3 Dall.) at 7. In *Penhallow,* 3 U.S. (3 Dall.) at 97, Iredell explained that the statutory and constitutional references to maritime as well as admiralty cases eliminated the British distinction between courts of prize and of instance.

[134]*Id.* at 85 (Paterson, J.), 95-96 (Iredell, J.), 113 (Blair, J.), 116-17 (Cushing, J.). This conclusion is of interest in light of the later understanding, prevalent until recently, that subject matter jurisdiction always could be examined in a suit on a sister-state judgment despite the full faith and credit clause. *See* Durfee v. Duke, 375 U.S. 106, 112 (1963); Thompson v. Whitman, 85 U.S. (18 Wall.) 457, 469 (1874), and cases cited therein.

[135]ARTICLES OF CONFEDERATION art. 9, § 1.

[136]*See* Martin v. Hunter's Lessee, 14 U.S. (1 Wheat.) 304 (1816), *discussed in infra* chapter 4.

[137]3 U.S. (3 Dall.) at 85.

[138]*Id.* at 113.

[139]*Id.* at 89-97 (Iredell, J.), 117 (Cushing, J.).

[140]*See* text and notes at notes 48-52 *supra.*

[141]3 U.S. (3 Dall.) at 80.

no right"[142] and sought to find authority in the states' written instructions to their delegates, he essentially agreed.[143]

It had been argued that any powers Congress might have had were merely "recommendatory" and that New Hampshire was thus free to disregard them.[144] Congress had rejected this contention in 1779, approving a committee declaration that "no act of any one state can or ought to destroy the right of appeals to Congress."[145] Paterson found this decision binding on New Hampshire and termed its reasoning "cogent and conclusive."[146] Blair was even more explicit: "those acts of New Hampshire which restrain the jurisdiction of congress, being contrary to the legitimate powers of congress, can have no binding force."[147]

The impact of *Penhallow* on later decisions was muted by the Justices' reliance upon res judicata and by the fact that the sources of authority they construed differed sharply from those of the present Constitution. Nevertheless the case is of significant interest. First, the jurisdiction it sustained was to become an important precedent for upholding Supreme Court review of state court judgments under the new Constitution.[148] Second, Paterson and Blair gave the idea of judicial review a boost by asserting, without benefit of an explicit supremacy clause, the power to disregard state laws contradicting a congressional resolution. The same two Justices also foreshadowed *McCulloch v. Maryland*[149] in their sweeping deduction of the power to provide for capture appeals from the congressional authority to make war. Finally, Paterson's gratuitous remark that "the states, individually, were not known nor recognised as sovereign, by foreign nations"[150] was to be echoed nearly 150 years later in support of an expansive view of federal authority over foreign affairs.[151]

B.   *Cooper v. Telfair*

This case was a diversity action on a debt. The defense was a 1782 Georgia statute attainting the plaintiff for adherence to the British and confiscating his property. Rejecting arguments that the attainder offended Georgia constitutional provisions declaring "trial by jury . . . inviolate" and legislative and judicial powers "separate

---

[142]*Id.* at 109.

[143]Congress's actions, Blair wrote, had afforded "an opportunity to their constituents to express their disapprobation, if they conceived congress to have usurped power, or, by their co-operation, to confirm the construction of congress; which would be as legitimate a source of authority, as if it had been given at first." He found in response to these actions "not the least symptom of discontent among all the confederated states, or the whole people of America." *Id.* at 111.

[144]*Id.* at 71 (argument of counsel for Penhallow).

[145]5 J. Cong. 65 (1779) (Folwell's Press ed. Phila. 1800), *quoted by* Justice Paterson in *Penhallow*, 3 U.S. (3 Dall.) at 83.

[146]3 U.S. (3 Dall.) at 82.

[147]*Id.* at 113.

[148]*See* Martin v. Hunter's Lessee, 14 U.S. (1 Wheat.) 304, 345-46 (1816).

[149]17 U.S. (4 Wheat.) 316 (1819). *See infra* chapter 6.

[150]3 U.S. (3 Dall.) at 81.

[151]United States v. Curtiss-Wright Export Corp., 299 U.S. 304, 315-17 (1936). *See* J. Goebel, *supra* chapter 1, note 21, at 768.

and distinct,"[152] the Court in 1800 unanimously affirmed the circuit court's decision for the defendant.[153]

Once again there was discussion of the propriety of judicial review. The parties conceded it,[154] and Cushing declared "that this court has the same power, that a court of the state of Georgia would possess, to declare the law void."[155] Chase noted quite unnecessarily that he concurred in the "general sentiment" that "the supreme court can declare an act of congress to be unconstitutional and therefore, invalid."[156] But he added a curious qualification: "whether the power, under the existing constitution, can be employed to invalidate laws previously enacted, is a very different question, turning upon very different principles." Chase did not resolve this question because he found the challenged law consistent with the Georgia Constitution.[157]

What the adoption of the 1789 Constitution has to do with the power to review state laws for consistency with *state* constitutions is not clear. Whether the Georgia Constitution is judicially enforceable is a question of Georgia law. But Chase's doubt as to the power to invalidate pre-1789 laws suggests a distinct issue not raised by the parties or considered in the opinions: why did not the Georgia law violate the *federal* ban on ex post facto laws, impairment of contracts, and bills of attainder? The answer must be that those prohibitions are prospective only, as their language suggests: "No State shall . . . pass"[158] those forbidden laws. The Court later would confirm that the contract clause did not apply to laws passed before the effective date of the Constitution.[159]

One should not conclude too hastily, however, that the Constitution grandfathers all preexisting laws. The fourteenth amendment expressly forbids any state either to "make or [to] enforce" certain kinds of laws, and a state probably can be said to "deprive" a person of property or to "deny" equal protection at the time it enforces a preexisting law.[160] Other clauses of article I are more ambiguous in this respect: no state shall "make any Thing but gold and silver Coin a Tender"[161] or "lay any Imposts or Duties on Imports or Exports."[162] These transitional issues are of little present significance, but the Framers seem not to have given them much attention.

On the merits, all four Justices seem to have concluded in *Cooper* that the state jury trial provision, read in conjunction with a separate requirement that criminal trials take place "in the county where the crime was committed,"[163] was inapplicable because the offense was not shown to have occurred in Georgia.[164] Indeed, three of them seem to have taken the venue provision to imply that the punishment of

[152]4 U.S. (4 Dall.) 14, 16 (1800) (assignments of error); *see* GA. CONST. OF 1777, art. LXI (jury trial); *id.* art. I (separation of powers).
[153]4 U.S. (4 Dall.) at 15.
[154]*Id.* at 16, 17.
[155]*Id.* at 20.
[156]*Id.* at 19.
[157]*Id.*
[158]U.S. CONST. art. I, § 10, para. 1.
[159]Owings v. Speed, 18 U.S. (5 Wheat.) 420 (1820).
[160]U.S. CONST. amend. XIV, § 1.
[161]*Id.* art. I, § 10, para. 1.
[162]*Id.* para. 2.
[163]GA. CONST. OF 1777, art. XXXIX.
[164]4 U.S. (4 Dall.) at 18 (Washington and Chase, JJ.), 19 (Paterson, J.), 20 (Cushing, J.).

offenses was a proper legislative function under Georgia's separation of powers: the power to punish must reside somewhere, and it did not reside in the courts.[165] Neither conclusion was obvious. As with legislative appeals in *Calder v. Bull*,[166] a little history might have shown a tradition of legislative punishments, but the question would have remained whether Georgia's separation of powers provision was meant to preserve or to alter that tradition.

Chase's opinion is the most interesting. After declaring the jury trial provision inapplicable, he added that the result would have been the same if the offense had been shown to have occurred in Georgia:

> The general principles contained in the constitution are not to be regarded as rules to fetter and controul; but as matter merely declaratory and directory: for, even in the constitution itself, we may trace repeated departures from the theoretical doctrine, that the legislative, executive, and judicial powers, should be kept separate and distinct.[167]

Was the aggressive advocate of judicial power to strike down laws that offended "natural justice"[168] here rejecting the principle of ordinary judicial review? Was he consistent in so doing, on the theory that judges can ignore constitutions as well as laws if they disagree with them? Because he endorsed judicial review in the next paragraph, I think his point was more modest: not everything in a constitution was to be regarded as "merely declaratory and directory," but only "general principles" such as Georgia's separation of powers provision, which was undercut elsewhere in the document. This was not a necessary conclusion either, however, for the provision was phrased in mandatory terms and the "departures" might have been exceptions to an enforceable rule. Moreover, Chase's thesis hardly explains why the jury provision would not apply to an offense committed within the state. That provision looks neither general nor declaratory in the sense of his opinion.

The particular Georgia issues resolved in *Cooper* are of no importance today. For us the case represents one more exercise of the increasingly familiar power of judicial review, explicitly endorsed as to federal statutes for the first time by Chase, and a recognition that, despite Chase's careless statement in *Calder*,[169] the Court could determine state constitutional questions in cases coming from lower federal courts. *Cooper* is noteworthy also for Chase's distinction between laws enacted before and after 1789 for purposes of judicial review and for his willingness to find some constitutional provisions judicially unenforceable. This approach suggests an exception to judicial review of undefinable scope, reminiscent of the later notion of political questions.[170] It is also interesting that Chase, who in *Calder* had unnecessarily declared that a law giving *A*'s property to *B* would be void because contrary to "natural justice,"[171] did not bother to explain why the same was not true of a naked

[165]*Id.* (Washington, Paterson, and Cushing, JJ.).
[166]*See* text and notes at notes 97-101 *supra.*
[167]4 U.S. (4 Dall.) at 19.
[168]*See* text and notes at notes 110-111 *supra.*
[169]*See* text and notes at notes 79-80 *supra.*
[170]*See, e.g.,* Baker v. Carr, 369 U.S. 186, 210-26 (1962) (discussing the scope of the political question doctrine).
[171]*See* text and notes at notes 110-111 *supra.*

bill of attainder. Perhaps he thought traitors were different, or maybe he had been bluffing in *Calder v. Bull.* Finally, in *Cooper* two more Justices—Washington and Paterson—echoed Chase's now familiar litany that laws would not be struck down except in clear cases.[172] The *Cooper* opinions suggest that the Justices took this admonition quite seriously: they seem to have identified possible interpretations of the Georgia Constitution that would uphold the bill of attainder and then resolved the ambiguities in favor of constitutionality.

[172] 4 U.S. (4 Dall.) at 18 (Washington, J.), 19 (Paterson, J.).

Conclusion to Part One

If one looks solely at the specific holdings of the Supreme Court before 1801, the achievements were modest. The *Chisholm* holding that states could be sued was overruled immediately by the eleventh amendment. *Hylton*'s narrow interpretation of the direct tax provisions was of more lasting significance, affording Congress a broad latitude for taxation for a hundred years. *Calder* gave a narrow reading to the ex post facto limitation, but the basis of the holding was unclear. *Ware* held that a particular treaty revived debts previously extinguished. *Mossman* held that an alien could not sue unless the defendant was a citizen of a state. In *Hollingsworth,* the Court without discussion excluded the President from the amending process.

The importance of this period lies in the extent to which the Court established an enduring framework for constitutional adjudication.[1] The practice of seriatim opinions, which weakened the force of the decisions, soon would be abandoned, but other aspects of the pre-Marshall Court's practice remained. Judicial review of state legislation was established in *Ware,* in which the Court struck down a state law contradicting a treaty. Judicial review of federal legislation was practiced in *Hylton,* in which the law was upheld. More than one Justice went on record in dictum declaring the power to exist, and a federal statute may have been struck down in *Hollingsworth v. Virginia.*

Moreover, two lasting principles of construction were established before 1801: doubtful cases were to be resolved in favor of constitutionality, and statutes were to be construed if possible in a manner consistent with the Constitution. There were intimations of the political question doctrine in the suggestions in *Ware* and *Cooper* that some issues, even of constitutional dimension, might be nonjusticiable. The informal *Correspondence* settled once and for all that the Court would decide legal questions only in the context of ordinary litigation. There were hints in *Ware* and in *Penhallow* of a coming tendency to construe federal grants of power extensively. In

[1] *See* A. McLaughlin, A Constitutional History of the United States 300-01 (1935).

55

Calder, Iredell and Chase began the debate over the power of judges to disregard laws not infringing particular constitutional provisions.

Furthermore, the basic tools of constitutional interpretation employed before 1801 are still in use today. The first Justices looked to the text of the governing constitutional provision, to inferences that could be drawn from other provisions, to contemporary usage, to the intentions or purposes of the Framers, and to their own conceptions of sound policy. The relative weight given to these various interpretive aids was, as it has remained, variable. The words were stressed in *Chisholm,* legal tradition in *Calder,* and policy in *Hylton.*

It is striking how difficult it is to say, even after nearly 200 years of opportunity for reflection, whether the Court was right or wrong in its early constitutional decisions. There seems to be no clear answer to the question whether the Framers meant to allow states to be sued, or to outlaw retroactive civil legislation, or to require apportionment of taxes on carriages. Perhaps this should not be surprising. No legislator can foresee and answer all questions that may arise, and the Framers consciously and properly limited themselves to the statement of a few general principles.[2] In any event, the small sample of decisions before 1801 dramatically illustrates the enormous latitude the Constitution has left to judicial judgment.

The Court's response to the Constitution's ambiguity is also interesting. Time and again the Justices pretended to find the answer in the language or history of the Constitution when the Framers apparently either had differed as to the meaning of the words (as in *Chisholm* and *Calder*) or had had no firm idea of what they were trying to say (as in *Hylton*). The Swiss Civil Code of 1907 appears to take the opposite tack, instructing the judge in the absence of authority to decide "according to the rules which he would establish if he were to assume the part of a legislator."[3] Perhaps there is a middle road. I would not vote as a legislator to institute sovereign immunity, and I do not think the Framers gave a clear answer to the immunity question, but I have difficulty believing that in the climate of 1789 they would have wanted to make states suable. Finally, there is another alternative: the Court might have taken Chase's deferential expressions seriously and upheld the challenged provisions in all three cases on the ground that they were not clearly unconstitutional. In any event, the *Chisholm* Court would not be the last to take refuge in the fiction that the Framers had answered a question that the judges actually may have resolved in a legislative manner.

The same decisions that reflect the foregoing tendency to cloak the exercise of real judgment in the trappings of deference also contain contrasting suggestions of judicial freedom from authority we would be likely to view as binding. In *Hylton,* all

---

[2]*See infra* chapter 6, discussing *McCulloch v. Maryland.*

[3]Schweizerisches Zivilgesetzbuch, Code Civil Suisse, Codice Civile Svizzero art. 1, para. 2 (codified at Systematische Sammlung des Bundesrechts ch. 210, art. 1 para. 2), quoted favorably in B. Cardozo, The Nature of the Judicial Process 140 (1921). Cardozo adds that even in such a case the judge is not "wholly free . . . in pursuit of his own ideal of beauty or of goodness. . . . He is to exercise a discretion informed by tradition, methodized by analogy, disciplined by system, and subordinated to 'the primordial necessity of order in the social life.' Wide enough in all conscience is the field of discretion that remains." *Id.* at 141 (footnote omitted) (translating and quoting 2 F. Gény, Méthode d'Interpretation et Sources en Droit Privé Positif 303 (2d ed. 1919). For a narrower view of the Swiss provision, *see* F. Wieacker, Privatrechtsgeschichte der Neuzeit 494 n.18 (2d ed. 1967).

three Justices leapt with what may appear unseemly haste to a discussion of the undesirability of apportioning carriage taxes, and Paterson made no effort to disguise the influence of his policy preference. The eclectic use of foreign precedents and general jurisprudence in Wilson's and Jay's *Chisholm* opinions suggests the kind of "pluralism of legal sources" that has been said to have been prevalent prior to the French Revolution, a kind of universality of legal principles transcending the commands of the particular sovereign.[4] Most of all, there is Chase's bold assertion in *Calder* of the power to disregard statutes contrary to "first principles."[5]

The symptoms of free-wheeling judicial discretion varied from Justice to Justice. Iredell and Blair protested Wilson's eclecticism in *Chisholm,* and Iredell flatly disagreed with Chase about natural justice. Most of the Justices spoke most of the time as if they conceived of their job as the important but limited one of attempting to understand and enforce the written Constitution. Most interesting of all, however, was the assertion of both fictitious deference and judicial license in one and the same opinion: Chase in his remarkable *Calder* pronouncement seemed to go out of his way to declare the right to nullify any legislation with which he disagreed, while in the same breath he pretended that in determining the meaning of the ambiguous ex post facto clause he exercised no independent judgment whatever.

Although it is not easy to say that any of the Court's earliest constitutional decisions was clearly wrong, it does appear to today's reader that too many important issues were decided without adequate consideration. That the President could not veto constitutional amendments comes down to us as a bare conclusion. That Congress could make exceptions to the diversity jurisdiction was not even stated in the reports. Long and learned opinions in *Chisholm, Ware,* and *Penhallow* refute the inference that eighteenth-century judges were not expected to explain what they were doing.[6] Yet the Justices did not feel the need to assure dissemination of their reasons for every constitutional decision.

Even the full opinions, moreover, often were flawed in their reasoning. In *Chisholm,* the Justices paid insufficient heed to tradition and to the statements of the Framers. In *Hylton,* they relied too heavily on policy before making a serious effort to explain the text. In *Calder,* they failed to explain why judicial action was not forbidden by the ex post facto clause, to acknowledge usage contrary to that which they invoked, and to make clear precisely on which ground they relied.

As far as the individual Justices are concerned, Paterson and Iredell seem the most impressive. In *Calder,* Paterson, like Chase, made effective—if selective—use of contemporary understanding. In *Hylton,* Paterson relied in part on his own policy preferences, but he alone attempted to interpret the constitutional language in light of current usage and the purposes of the Framers. Iredell receives favorable marks for his attention to history in *Chisholm* and for his opposition to limitless judicial

---

[4]Coing, *The Roman Law as Ius Commune on the Continent,* 89 Law Q. Rev. 505, 513 (1973) ("Pluralism of legal sources also means that a judge who has to decide a specific case, has to look for rules not only in the orders of the sovereign, but can apply rules which he finds in any book of authority, whether this has been expressly recognized by the sovereign or not.").

[5]3 U.S. (3 Dall.) at 388. *See* text and note at chapter 2, note 110 *supra.*

[6]*See* J. Dawson, The Oracles of the Law xii (1968) ("We now take this duty for granted but in its present form it came relatively late, not only to English legal tradition but still more in systems like the French and German that have derived continuous inspiration from Roman law.").

nullification in *Calder*. Chase could be thorough and persuasive, as in *Ware,* but he was unable to restrain himself from commenting on issues not presented, and his natural justice thesis showed him to be no respecter of the written Constitution.[7] Wilson displayed erudition in *Chisholm* but seemed pretentious and disorganized, hiding the majority's best points in a pile of verbiage. Jay's only opinion, also in *Chisholm,* seemed long-winded and off the point. Blair and Cushing wrote pedestrian opinions that added little.[8]

It was not a time of giant Justices or of great decisions. Yet in its first twelve years the Supreme Court set a pattern of constitutional adjudication that was to endure.

[7]*See* G. HASKINS & H. JOHNSON, 2 HISTORY OF THE SUPREME COURT OF THE UNITED STATES 93 (1981), citing Professor Corwin's judgment that Chase was the most notable Justice before Marshall; Presser & Hurley, *Saving God's Republic: The Jurisprudence of Samuel Chase,* 1984 U. ILL. L. REV. 771.

[8]*See* G. HASKINS & H. JOHNSON, *supra* note 7, at 87, noting John Dickinson's contemporaneous view that Cushing added nothing to his brethren's exposition of the law.

Part Two

Chief Justice Marshall
1801–1835

Introduction to Part Two

When John Marshall was appointed Chief Justice in 1801, as we have seen, the slate was by no means clean; his predecessors had established a number of important principles of constitutional jurisprudence. They had done so, however, in a tentative and unobtrusive manner, through suggestions in the seriatim opinions of individual Justices and through conclusory statements or even silences in brief *per curiam* announcements. Moreover, the Court had resolved remarkably few important substantive constitutional questions. It had essentially set the stage for John Marshall.

Marshall's long tenure divides naturally into three periods. From 1801 until 1810, notwithstanding the explosive decision in *Marbury v. Madison*,[1] the Court was if anything less active in the constitutional field than it had been before Marshall. Only a dozen or so cases with constitutional implications were decided; most of them concerned relatively minor matters of federal jurisdiction; most of the opinions were brief and unambitious. Moreover, the cast of characters was undergoing rather constant change. Of Marshall's five original colleagues, William Cushing, William Paterson, Samuel Chase, and Alfred Moore had all been replaced by 1811.[2]

From the decision in *Fletcher v. Peck*[3] in 1810 until about 1825, in contrast, the list of constitutional cases contains a succession of landmarks: *Martin v. Hunter's Lessee*,[4] *McCulloch v. Maryland*,[5] *Trustees of Dartmouth College v. Woodward*,[6]

---

[1] 5 U.S. (1 Cranch) 137 (1803).

[2] Only Bushrod Washington and Marshall himself remained. *See infra* note 25. The most comprehensive study of this part of the Marshall period is G. HASKINS & H. JOHNSON, 2 HISTORY OF THE SUPREME COURT OF THE UNITED STATES (1981). *See also* 1 C. WARREN, THE SUPREME COURT IN UNITED STATES HISTORY (rev. ed. 1926). Two further volumes of the HISTORY OF THE SUPREME COURT dealing with the remainder of Marshall's tenure had not been published when this volume went to the press.

[3] 10 U.S. (6 Cranch) 87 (1810).

[4] 14 U.S. (1 Wheat.) 304 (1816).

[5] 17 U.S. (4 Wheat.) 316 (1819).

[6] 17 U.S. (4 Wheat.) 518 (1819).

Cohens v. Virginia,[7] *Gibbons v. Ogden,*[8] *Osborn v. Bank of the United States,*[9] to name only a few. This was a time of vigorous affirmation of national authority and of vigorous enforcement of constitutional limitations on the states; a time of extensive opinions in the grand style we have come to associate with Marshall; a time, moreover, of remarkable stability and official unanimity. For most of the fifteen crucial years between 1810 and 1825, the Court comprised the same seven Justices: Marshall, Bushrod Washington, William Johnson, Brockholst Livingston, Thomas Todd, Joseph Story, and Gabriel Duvall.[10] Though all but Marshall and Washington had been appointed by the anti-Federalist Presidents Thomas Jefferson and James Madison,[11] the rarity of recorded dissent during this period was so great as to be almost incredible by modern standards. Some part of the apparent unanimity was doubtless due to Marshall's policy of keeping disagreements within the Court;[12] yet the opinions of William Johnson, his most independent colleague, suggest that all seven Justices shared a common view of the Constitution down to many matters of mere detail.

From the mid-1820s to Marshall's death in 1835, the Court continued to lay down decisions of lasting significance: *Ogden v. Saunders,*[13] *Brown v. Maryland,*[14] *Craig v. Missouri,*[15] *Worcester v. Georgia,*[16] *Barron v. Baltimore.*[17] Yet this period can be described as one of consolidation and transition. The Court increasingly refused to extend the limits it had found imposed on the states, and it increasingly revealed divisions as Marshall's longtime colleagues were gradually replaced by men of a new generation: Smith Thompson, Robert Trimble, John McLean, Henry Baldwin.[18]

Notwithstanding these divisions, the Marshall period as a whole has a coherent character of its own. The Court under Marshall had a unique opportunity to put meat

[7]19 U.S. (6 Wheat.) 264 (1821).

[8]22 U.S. (9 Wheat.) 1 (1824).

[9]22 U.S. (9 Wheat.) 738 (1824).

[10]*See infra* note 25. The seventh position had been authorized by the Act of Feb. 24, 1807, ch. 16, § 5, 2 Stat. 420, 421. Marshall's biographer insisted, without citation of authority, that the correct spelling of Justice Duvall's name was "Duval." 4 A. BEVERIDGE, LIFE OF JOHN MARSHALL 60 n.1 (1919). However, Cranch, Wheaton, and Peters, Supreme Court reporters while the Justice was on the bench, all spelled his name "Duvall." Irving Dilliard, who traced the family history, concluded that the original "DuVal" or "Duval" of the Justice's immigrant greatgrandfather had become "Duvall" by the time the future Justice was born. Dilliard, *Gabriel Duvall,* in 1 JUSTICES OF THE SUPREME COURT 419-21 (L. Friedman & F. Israel eds. 1969).

[11]*See infra* note 25.

[12]See D. MORGAN, JUSTICE WILLIAM JOHNSON: THE FIRST DISSENTER 168-86 (1954), and especially Johnson's letter to Thomas Jefferson (Dec. 10, 1822), *quoted in id.* at 182 ("[D]uring the rest of the session I heard nothing but lectures on the indecency of judges cutting each other . . . . At length I found that I must either submit to circumstances or become such a cypher in our consultations as to effect no good at all . . . ."). *See also* White, *The Working Life of the Marshall Court, 1815–1835,* 70 VA. L. REV. 1, 34-47 (1984); Roper, *Judicial Unanimity and the Marshall Court: A Road to Reappraisal,* 9 AM. J.L. HIST. 118 (1965).

[13]25 U.S. (12 Wheat.) 213 (1827).

[14]25 U.S. (12 Wheat.) 419 (1827).

[15]29 U.S. (4 Pet.) 410 (1830).

[16]31 U.S. (6 Pet.) 515 (1832).

[17]32 U.S. (7 Pet.) 243 (1833).

[18]McLean replaced Trimble, who died after two years on the bench. *See infra* note 25. James Wayne sat with Marshall during the latter's last Term, but no constitutional cases were then decided.

on the largely bare bones of the Constitution, and a great deal of what it put there has remained. One important factor in this durability was that the Court spoke with a remarkably uniform voice over a very long period of time. Only sixteen men sat on the Court during the entire Marshall period. Of the seven Justices who sat together between 1810 and 1823, four continued to sit until 1834;[19] a majority of the Court thus remained intact for twenty-three years. Even in the last years, moreover, when dissents became somewhat more frequent, the voice with which the Court spoke was almost exclusively that of John Marshall. Not only does there seem to have been but one constitutional case in thirty-five years in which the Chief Justice recorded a dissent;[20] there were only a handful in which he did not deliver the Court's opinion. Even the previously irrepressible Chase[21] was never heard from again after 1801.[22] Of most of Marshall's brethren, however great their backstage influence on the course of constitutional decision,[23] we know virtually nothing from the opinions beyond their concurrence in the results.[24] In stark contrast to our examination of the period before 1801, the present study is essentially of one man.[25]

[19]Marshall, Johnson, Duvall, and Story. *See id.*

[20]Ogden v. Sauders, 25 U.S. (12 Wheat.) 213, 332 (1827). *But see infra* chapter 4, note 132 and accompanying text (discussing *Houston v. Moore*).

[21]*See supra* chapter 2.

[22]Chase did, however, make additional headlines when the Republicans unsuccessfully impeached him in 1805. *See* 1 C. WARREN, THE SUPREME COURT IN UNITED STATES HISTORY 269-315 (rev. ed. 1926).

[23]That Marshall delivered the Court's opinion does not prove that he wrote it, or even that he agreed with it. *See* G. HASKINS & H. JOHNSON, 2 HISTORY OF THE SUPREME COURT OF THE UNITED STATES 384-86 (1981) (citing a case in which Marshall said he had been instructed to present the Court's reasons though he did not agree with them); Letter from Justice Johnson to Thomas Jefferson (Dec. 10, 1822) (complaining that it was Marshall's initial practice to "deliver[ ] all the opinions in cases in which he sat, even in some instances when contrary to his own judgment and vote"), *quoted in* D. MORGAN, *supra* note 12, at 181-82. *See also* Frankfurter, *John Marshall and the Judicial Function*, 69 HARV. L. REV. 217, 221 (1955) ("One may be confident in inferring that the novelty of the issues, the close social relations of the Justices, the ample opportunities they had for discussions among themselves, precluded Marshall's pathbreaking opinions from being exclusively solo performances.").

[24]Several of them made important contributions in the circuit courts, but that is material for another study.

[25]

JUSTICES OF THE SUPREME COURT DURING THE TIME OF CHIEF JUSTICE MARSHALL

		1800	05	10	15	20	25	30	35
William Cushing	(1789-1810)								
William Paterson	(1793-1806)								
Samuel Chase	(1796-1811)								
Bushrod Washington	(1798-1829)								
Alfred Moore	(1799-1804)								
John Marshall	(1801-1835)								
William Johnson	(1804-1834)								
Henry Brockholst Livingston	(1806-1823)								
Thomas Todd	(1807-1826)								
Gabriel Duvall	(1811-1835)								
Joseph Story	(1811-1845)								
Smith Thompson	(1823-1843)								
Robert Trimble	(1826-1828)								

Although my focus is chronological, my chief interest is in the Marshall period as a whole, and some grouping of cases by subject matter is necessary to avoid a totally disjointed presentation. I have therefore departed from a strictly chronological discussion. The first two chapters of this part deal with those constitutional decisions of Marshall's time respecting the powers of the federal courts;[26] the contemporaneous substantive decisions will be discussed in the chapters that follow.

JUSTICES OF THE SUPREME COURT DURING THE TIME OF CHIEF JUSTICE MARSHALL (*cont.*)

		1800	05	10	15	20	25	30	35
John McLean	(1829-1861)							┝━━━━	
Henry Baldwin	(1833-1844)								┝━━
James M. Wayne	(1835-1867)								┝━

SOURCE: Adapted from G. GUNTHER, CASES AND MATERIALS ON CONSTITUTIONAL LAW app. A, at A-1 to A-2 (10th ed. 1980).

Biographies of Justices of this period, in addition to those of Chase, Cushing, and Paterson listed in part one *supra*, include A. BEVERIDGE, THE LIFE OF JOHN MARSHALL (1919); L. BAKER, JOHN MARSHALL: A LIFE IN THE LAW (1974); D. MORGAN, JUSTICE WILLIAM JOHNSON: THE FIRST DISSENTER (1954); G. DUNNE, JOSEPH STORY AND THE RISE OF THE SUPREME COURT (1970); J. MCCLELLAN, JOSEPH STORY AND THE AMERICAN CONSTITUTION (1971); F. WEISENBURGER, THE LIFE OF JOHN MCLEAN (1937).

[26]Before Marshall's appointment to the Court, moreover, there were so few decisions that virtually every encounter with the Constitution told us something significant about the Court's developing approach to constitutional litigation. The relative profusion of cases during the Marshall era makes a comparable effort at completeness one of significantly diminishing returns. Thus I have reduced to brief references a number of decisions that afford little substantive or methodological illumination.

3

The Powers of the Federal Courts, 1801–1810

Issues of federal jurisdiction continued to dominate the Court's constitutional docket until 1810[1] and remained a significant part of it throughout Marshall's tenure.

Much of our current understanding of the federal judicial power dates from the Marshall period. *Marbury v. Madison*[2] confirmed the practice of judicial review of Acts of Congress and narrowly limited the Supreme Court's original jurisdiction. *Martin v. Hunter's Lessee*[3] and *Cohens v. Virginia*[4] affirmed the Court's authority to review state court decisions denying federal rights. *Osborn v. Bank of the United States*[5] opened the federal courts to suits against state officers and gave a broad interpretation to the power over cases "arising under" federal law. Numerous decisions, nominally interpreting the jurisdictional statutes, continued the process of giving content to the constitutional provisions for diversity and admiralty jurisdiction. *Wayman v. Southard*[6] affirmed the power of the courts, with statutory authorization, to regulate their own procedures. *Parsons v. Bedford*[7] and *Bank of Columbia v. Okely*[8] began to interpret the right to a civil jury. *American Insurance Co. v. Canter*[9] laid the foundation for the doctrine of "legislative" courts and thus for modern quasi-judicial agencies.

These are but the highlights of a rich collection, and most of them have withstood the test of time. It is significant that the Marshall Court took a rather broad view of the federal judicial power. It is also significant that the principal departure of

---

[1] As they had before Marshall's appointment. *See supra* chapter 1.
[2] 5 U.S. (1 Cranch) 137 (1803).
[3] 14 U.S. (1 Wheat.) 304 (1816).
[4] 19 U.S. (6 Wheat.) 264 (1821).
[5] 22 U.S. (9 Wheat.) 738 (1824).
[6] 23 U.S. (10 Wheat.) 1 (1825).
[7] 28 U.S. (3 Pet.) 433 (1830).
[8] 17 U.S. (4 Wheat.) 235 (1819).
[9] 26 U.S. (1 Pet.) 511 (1828).

Marshall's successors in this field would be to take a still broader view of federal jurisdiction in diversity[10] and admiralty[11] cases.

I. Marbury v. Madison

It seems entirely appropriate that the very first constitutional decision of the Court under Marshall was the most fundamental of them all. By establishing the power of judicial review, the *Marbury* opinion paved the way for great controversies to come. It was, moreover, in many respects highly representative of the style of Marshall's major opinions.

The facts are familiar. The commission of the Federalist William Marbury as justice of the peace had been signed and sealed just hours before the Federalists left office, and he asked the Supreme Court for a mandamus directing the new Republican Secretary of State to deliver it. The Court in an 1803 Marshall opinion dismissed for want of jurisdiction.[12]

En route to that disposition the Court did a number of interesting things. Of interest in respect to the mundane holding that the commission was effective without delivery[13] was the fact that the Court addressed the issue at all, for it held that it had no jurisdiction.[14] The same can be said of the famous conclusion that mandamus would lie against the Secretary of State,[15] which has had important implications for the overall doctrine of separation of powers.[16] This holding also bears examining for

[10]*E.g.*, Marshall v. Baltimore & O.R.R., 57 U.S. (16 How.) 314 (1854) (members of corporation deemed citizens of state of incorporation). See *infra* chapter 8.

[11]*E.g.*, The Propeller Genesee Chief v. Fitzhugh, 53 U.S. (12 How.) 443 (1852) (Great Lakes within admiralty jurisdiction). See *infra* chapter 8.

[12]5 U.S. (1 Cranch) 137, 173, 180 (1803). For the political background of this case, see R. Ellis, The Jeffersonian Crisis: Courts and Politics in the Young Republic 43-45, 58, 64-68 (1971).

[13]5 U.S. (1 Cranch) at 155-62.

[14]Some might call the Court's comments on this issue an advisory opinion, which the Justices ten years earlier had implied they had no power to give. *See* Letter from Thomas Jefferson to the Justices (July 18, 1793); Letter from the Justices to George Washington (Aug. 8, 1793) [hereinafter cited as Correspondence of the Justices], *reprinted in* P. Bator, P. Mishkin, D. Shapiro & H. Wechsler, Hart & Wechsler's The Federal Courts and the Federal System 64-66 (2d ed. 1973) [hereinafter cited as Hart & Wechsler]; J. Thayer, John Marshall 62-63 (P. Kurland ed. 1967) ("Unfortunately, instead of proceeding as courts usually do, the opinion began by passing upon all the points which the denial of its jurisdiction took from it the right to treat."); *supra* chapter 1. One must be cautious in evaluating early materials by modern standards; *Marbury* and other Marshall opinions suggest the important question whether attitudes about the propriety of judicial pronouncements going beyond the necessities of the case have remained constant over nearly two centuries. But Jefferson, at least, criticized Marshall for "traveling out of his case." Letter from Thomas Jefferson to Justice Johnson (June 12, 1823), *quoted in* 1 C. Warren, *supra* introduction to part two, note 22, at 245. *See also* 1 C. Warren, *supra* introduction to part two, note 22, at 249-51 (reporting similar contemporary views). G. Gunther, *supra* introduction to part two, note 25, at 12-13, raises the further question whether Marshall should have disqualified himself because he was the Secretary of State who had signed and sealed Marbury's commission and because his brother had submitted an evidentiary affidavit.

[15]5 U.S. (1 Cranch) at 162-73.

[16]In this connection we find in *Marbury* a constitutional explanation for the surviving rule limiting mandamus to matters outside the officer's "discretion." The Secretary is an "organ" of the President, in whom article II of the Constitution vests "certain important political powers," *id.* at 165-66; to interfere with the exercise of executive discretion would thus infringe on article II. The conclusion that the

its impact on the undiscussed issue of sovereign immunity,[17] and it has become fashionable to view *Marbury*'s references to unreviewable "political" actions of the executive[18] as the foundation of today's political question doctrine.[19]

On the jurisdictional issue the Court went out of its way to create a constitutional question. Standing alone, the statutory authorization of mandamus "to any . . . persons holding office, under the authority of the United States"[20] appeared to

Secretary could sometimes be sued, on the other hand, implicitly rejected the argument that every such proceeding would invade the constitutional domain of the executive. Sixty-odd years later the Court was to come close to holding the President could not be sued at all, Mississippi v. Johnson, 71 U.S. (4 Wall.) 475 (1867), *discussed in infra* chapter 9; *Marbury* reflects a strikingly different philosophy.

[17] In rejecting a state's immunity from suit in Chisholm v. Georgia, 2 U.S. (2 Dall.) 419 (1793), both Cushing and Jay had suggested it might not be possible to sue the United States, *id*. at 469, 478. *See supra* chapter 1. Mandamus against the Secretary would have had the same effect as if the government itself had been named defendant. Marshall's opinion, without mentioning the concept of sovereign immunity, foreshadowed the unsatisfying formalistic distinction the Court was later expressly to draw for this purpose, *see infra* chapter 4, notes 94-102 and accompanying text (discussing *Osborn v. Bank of the United States*), between governments and their officers: "If one of the heads of departments commits any illegal act, under color of his office, by which an individual sustains an injury, it cannot be pretended, that his office alone exempts him from being sued in the ordinary mode of proceeding . . . ." 5 U.S. (1 Cranch) at 170.

Marshall did not pause to investigate whether the British precedents treated mandamus actions as suits against the sovereign, though he did quote Blackstone suggestively. *Id*. at 165. To support his conclusion on the ground that there were no rights without remedies, as Marshall also did, *id*. at 163, raises doubt whether he believed the United States itself was immune. But the short answer to any suggestion of sovereign immunity in *Marbury* should have been that the statute expressly provided for mandamus "to any . . . persons holding office, under the United States." Judiciary Act of 1789, ch. 20, § 13, 1 Stat. 73, 81 (current version at 28 U.S.C. § 1651 (1976)). If consent to sue the government was needed, it had been given.

[18] See 5 U.S. (1 Cranch) at 165-67, 169-71, especially *id*. at 170 ("Questions in their nature political, or which are, by the constitution and laws, . . . submitted to the executive, can never be made in this court.").

[19] *See, e.g.*, C. HAINES, THE ROLE OF THE SUPREME COURT IN AMERICAN GOVERNMENT AND POLITICS 1789-1835, at 256 (1946); C. WRIGHT, THE LAW OF FEDERAL COURTS 52-56 (3d ed. 1976).

In the hands of proponents like Justice Frankfurter, this doctrine meant the courts would sometimes refuse to give a remedy for an assumed violation of the Constitution. *See* Baker v. Carr, 369 U.S. 186, 266-330 (1962) (Frankfurter, J., dissenting). It seems, however, that Marshall had nothing of the sort in mind in *Marbury*. It is true that the "political" discussion appears in a section of the opinion dealing with remedies, following the conclusion that Marbury had a "right" to his commission, 5 U.S. (1 Cranch) at 162, and that at one point Marshall spoke of certain executive "misconduct" for which the individual had no remedy, *id*. at 164. Elsewhere, however, the opinion appears to equate "political" matters with those in which the executive is entrusted by the Constitution or laws with "discretion," and if an officer has acted within his discretion, he has by definition offended no legal right. *See, e.g., id*. at 165-66:

> By the Constitution of the United States, the president is invested with certain important political powers, in the exercise of which he is to use his own discretion . . . . [W]here the heads of departments are the political or confidential agents of the executive, merely to execute the will of the president, or rather to act in cases in which the executive possesses a constitutional or legal discretion, nothing can be more perfectly clear, than that their acts are only politically examinable.

The sentence before the one quoted *supra* note 18 reads: "The province of the court is, solely to decide on the rights of individuals, not to inquire how the executive, or executive officers, perform duties at which they have a discretion." 5 U.S. (1 Cranch) at 170. Far from asserting that there might be rights without remedies, Marshall insisted that a government furnishing "no remedy for the violation of a vested legal right" would not deserve to be called one "of laws, and not of men." *id*. at 163.

[20] Judiciary Act of 1789, ch. 20, § 13, 1 Stat. 73, 81 (current version at 28 U.S.C. § 1651 (1976)).

authorize the Supreme Court to issue the writ as an original matter, and Marshall took it literally without suggesting there was any reason for doubt.[21] Significantly, he neglected to quote the entire provision, which read in context strongly suggests that mandamus against officers was to be issued only in appellate form or when ancillary to the exercise of jurisdiction independently existing.[22] In one of its last pre-Marshall decisions, the Court had performed major surgery on the statutory provision for jurisdiction when "an alien is a party" in order to avoid finding it unconstitutional;[23] the contrast with *Marbury* is striking.

The reason the Court declined jurisdiction in *Marbury* was of course its conclusion that Congress had no power to give the Court original jurisdiction over the controversy. Article III provides that the Supreme Court shall have "original Jurisdiction" in "Cases affecting Ambassadors, other public Ministers and Consuls, and those in which a State shall be Party."[24] *Marbury* was not such a case, and article III further provides that in all other cases within the judicial power the Court is to have "appellate Jurisdiction, both as to Law and Fact, with such Exceptions . . . as the Congress shall make."[25] To Marshall the words were clear: "If Congress remains at liberty to give this court appellate jurisdiction, where the constitution has declared their jurisdiction shall be original; and original jurisdiction where the constitution has declared it shall be appellate; the distribution of jurisdiction, made in the constitution, is form without substance."[26]

This reasoning is far from obvious. It would not have been idle for the Framers to make a provisional distribution of the Court's jurisdiction pending congressional revision;[27] that is precisely what they did with respect to the appellate jurisdiction by empowering Congress to make "Exceptions." Indeed, the exceptions clause itself arguably authorized the grant of original mandamus jurisdiction: Congress had made an "exception" to the appellate jurisdiction by providing original jurisdiction instead,[28] and it had made an "exception" to the otherwise applicable constitutional division. Nor would it have been irrational to read article III as defining a minimum

---

[21]5 U.S. (1 Cranch) at 173.

[22]The section in question consisted of four sentences. The first three confirmed the Supreme Court's original jurisdiction over cases involving states or foreign diplomats and provided for jury trial in original cases. The final sentence began by noting cases in which the Court has "*appellate jurisdiction*" and concluded with the quoted reference to the "*power*" to issue mandamus to federal courts as well as to other officers. Judiciary Act of 1789, ch. 20, § 13, 1 Stat. 73, 81 (current version at 28 U.S.C. § 1651 (1976)) (emphasis added). *See* Van Alstyne, *A Critical Guide to Marbury v. Madison*, 1969 Duke L. J. 1, 15. *See also* Corwin, *Marbury v. Madison and the Doctrine of Judicial Review*, 12 Mich. L. Rev. 538, 542 (1914) (emphasis in original):

> [I]n Common Law practice, in the light of which § 13 was framed, the writ of mandamus was not, ordinarily at least, an instrument of obtaining jurisdiction by a court, even upon appeal, but like the writs of habeas corpus and injunction, was a *remedy* available from a court in the exercise of its standing jurisdiction.

[23]Mossman v. Higginson, 4 U.S. (4 Dall.) 12, 14 (1800) (construing Judiciary Act of 1789, ch. 20, § 11, 1 Stat. 73, 78). *See supra* chapter 1.

[24]U.S. Const. art. III, § 2, para. 2.

[25]*Id.*

[26]5 U.S. (1 Cranch) at 174.

[27]*See* Van Alstyne, *supra* note 22, at 31 n.44.

[28]*See* 2 W. Crosskey, Politics and the Constitution in the History of the United States 1041 (1953); Corwin, *supra* note 22, at 540; Van Alstyne, *supra* note 22, at 32.

original jurisdiction to prevent Congress from excluding Supreme Court trial of the critical ambassador and state cases.[29] Marshall himself was to reject the implications of the *Marbury* reasoning in *Cohens v. Virginia*,[30] where he declared that Congress could grant appellate jurisdiction in cases where the Constitution provided for original.[31]

To dismiss the case, the Court had to conclude that its duty was to follow the Constitution in disregard of a contrary statute, and thus Marshall enunciated the doctrine of judicial review. As interesting as his conclusion is what these passages reveal about Marshall's approach to the writing of opinions.

The issue of judicial review was by no means new. The Privy Council had occasionally applied the ultra vires principle to set aside legislative acts contravening municipal or colonial charters.[32] State courts had set aside state statutes under constitutions no more explicit about judicial review than the federal.[33] The Supreme Court itself had measured a state law against a state constitution in *Cooper v. Telfair*[34] and had struck down another under the supremacy clause[35] in *Ware v. Hylton*;[36] in both cases the power of judicial review was expressly affirmed. Even Acts of Congress had been struck down by federal circuit courts,[37] and the Supreme Court, while purporting to reserve the question of its power to do so, had reviewed the constitutionality of a federal statute in *Hylton v. United States*.[38] Justice Iredell

[29]*See* 2 W. CROSSKEY, *supra* note 28, at 1041; Corwin, *supra* note 22, at 540; Van Alstyne, *supra* note 22, at 31. See also THE FEDERALIST No. 81, at 487 (A. Hamilton) (C. Rossiter ed. 1961), outlining reasons for the grant of original jurisdiction:

> All questions in which [public ministers] are concerned, are so directly connected with the public peace, that as well for the preservation of this, as out of respect to the sovereignties they represent, it is both expedient and proper, that such questions should be submitted in the first instance to the highest judicatory of the nation . . . . In cases in which a State might happen to be a party, it would ill suit its dignity to be turned over to an inferior tribunal.

But Hamilton also said, without squarely addressing the question of congressional power, that the "original jurisdiction of the Supreme Court would be confined to two classes of causes" and that in all others the Court "would have nothing more than an appellate jurisdiction" with such exceptions as Congress might make. *Id.*

[30]19 U.S. (6 Wheat.) 264 (1821). *See infra* chapter 4, notes 65–68 and accompanying text. *See also* Börs v. Preston, 111 U.S. 252, 260 (1884).

[31]19 U.S. (6 Wheat.) at 392-403 (alternative holding). Marshall failed to respond to the argument in *Marbury*, 5 U.S. (1 Cranch) at 148-49, that the Court had entertained original mandamus petitions before, though without addressing the constitutional issue. *See also* 2 W. CROSSKEY, *supra* note 28, at 1040. Albert Beveridge said Marshall's argument that section 13 was unconstitutional was "absolutely new, . . . the only original idea that Marshall contributed to the entire controversy." 3 A. BEVERIDGE, *supra* introduction to part two, note 10, at 128. The argument that the original jurisdiction could not be expanded, however, was not new. See the Justices' 1790 letter objecting to circuit duty and Justice Chase's 1802 letter on the same subject to Marshall, both cited *infra* notes 82, 101, and accompanying text.

[32]*See* J. GOEBEL, 1 HISTORY OF THE SUPREME COURT OF THE UNITED STATES 50-95 (1971).

[33]*See id.* at 96-142; A. MCLAUGHLIN, CONSTITUTIONAL HISTORY OF THE UNITED STATES 312-13 n.34 (1935).

[34]4 U.S. (4 Dall.) 14 (1800). *See supra* chapter 2.

[35]U.S. CONST. art VI, para. 2.

[36]3 U.S. (3 Dall.) 199 (1796). *See supra* chapter 2.

[37]*E.g.*, Hayburn's Case, 2 U.S. (2 Dall.) 409 (1792). *See* the opinions of the circuit courts for the districts of New York, Pennsylvania, and North Carolina, attached as a footnote in *id.* at 410-14 n.(a). *See supra* chapter 1.

[38]3 U.S. (3 Dall.) 171 (1796). *See supra* chapter 2.

had explicitly asserted this power both in *Chisholm v. Georgia*[39] and in *Calder v. Bull*,[40] and Chase had acknowledged it in *Cooper*.[41] In the Convention, moreover, both proponents and opponents of the proposed Council of Revision had recognized that the courts would review the validity of congressional legislation,[42] and Alexander Hamilton had proclaimed the same doctrine in *The Federalist*.[43] Yet though Marshall's principal arguments echoed those of Hamilton, he made no mention of any of this material, writing as if the question had never arisen before. Rare is the judge today who would disdain such support and rely wholly upon the force of his own argument, but his later opinions were to show that Marshall often paid little heed to precedents even when they squarely supported him.[44]

[39]2 U.S. (2 Dall.) 419, 433 (1793) (dissenting opinion). *See supra* chapter 1.

[40]3 U.S. (3 Dall.) 386, 399 (1798) (separate opinion). *See supra* chapter 2.

[41]4 U.S. (4 Dall.) at 19 (separate opinion). In Hollingsworth v. Virginia, 3 U.S. (3 Dall.) 378 (1798), the Court may actually have invalidated a federal statute, *see supra* chapter 1. On the other hand, the Justices did not refuse to sit on circuit even though they had apparently protested to President Washington that circuit duty was unconstitutional.

[42]*See, e.g.,* 1 THE RECORDS OF THE FEDERAL CONVENTION OF 1787, at 109 (M. Farrand rev. ed. 1937) [hereinafter cited as CONVENTION RECORDS] (Rufus King) (Council unnecessary "because the Judges will have the expounding of those Laws when they come before them; and they will no doubt stop the operation of such as shall appear repugnant to the constitution"); *id.* at 97 (Elbridge Gerry) ("they will have a sufficient check against encroachments on their own department by their exposition of the laws, which involved a power of deciding on their Constitutionality"); 2 *id,* at 73, 76, 78 (James Wilson, Luther Martin, and George Mason). James Mercer and John Dickinson went on record as disapproving of judicial review, but the latter saw no preferable alternative. *Id.* at 298-99. *See* Corwin, *supra* note 22, at 543 ("That the members of the Convention of 1787 thought the Constitution secured to courts in the United States the right to pass on the validity of acts of Congress under it cannot be reasonably doubted."). *Accord,* A. BICKEL, THE LEAST DANGEROUS BRANCH 15 (1962); HART & WECHSLER, *supra* note 14, at 9. *See also* 2 J. ELLIOT, THE DEBATES IN THE SEVERAL STATE CONVENTIONS ON THE ADOPTION OF THE FEDERAL CONSTITUTION 196 (2d ed. Wash., .C., 1836) (1st ed. Wash., D.C., 1827-30) [hereinafter cited as ELLIOT'S DEBATES] (Oliver Ellsworth); 3 *id.* at 553 (John Marshall).

[43]   If it be said that the legislative body are themselves the constitutional judges of their own powers, . . . this cannot be the natural presumption, where it is not to be recollected from any particular provisions in the Constitution. . . . It is far more rational to suppose that the courts were designed to be an intermediate body between the people and the legislature, in order, among other things, to keep the latter within the limits assigned to their authority.

THE FEDERALIST No. 78, *supra* note 29, at 467 (A. Hamilton). The First Congress had evidently contemplated that even state courts might hold federal statutes invalid: section 25 of the Judiciary Act gave the Supreme Court jurisdiction to review state court judgments "where is drawn in question the validity of a treaty or statute of . . . the United States, and the decision is against their validity." Judiciary Act of 1789, ch. 20, § 25, 1 Stat. 73, 85 (current version at 28 U.S.C. § 1257 (1976)). *But see* A. BICKEL, *supra* note 42, at 13 ("one may as easily conclude that the Supreme Court was meant only to enforce against state courts a rule that duly enacted federal statutes are constitutional by virtue of their due enactment"); 2 W. CROSSKEY, *supra* note 28, at 1029-33. *See also* 3 A. BEVERIDGE, *supra* introduction to part two, note 10, at 75, 116, 119 (observing that all of Marshall's arguments had been rehearsed in the congressional debate over the repeal of the Judiciary Act). *See* 11 ANNALS OF CONG. 23-186, 362-63, 475-78, 510-986, 1203-35 (1801).

[44]*See infra* notes 188-94, chapter 4, notes 42-46, 100-02 and accompanying text (discussing *Hodgson v. Bowerbank, Cohens v. Virginia,* and *Osborn v. Bank of the United States*); Trustees of Dartmouth College v. Woodward, 17 U.S. (4 Wheat.) 518 (1819), *infra* chapter 5. The Convention debates were not available to Marshall, but THE FEDERALIST had been cited as early as 1798. *See supra* chapter 2. *See also* 3 A. BEVERIDGE, *supra* introduction to part two, note 10, at 119 (noting that Marshall had read *The Federalist* and adding that "no case ever was decided in which a judge needed so much the support of judicial precedents" as in *Marbury*).

Marshall began his discussion of judicial review by making the reader *want* to find that the Court could strike down unconstitutional statutes. The reason for adopting a written constitution was to limit legislative power;[45] to require judges to enforce unconstitutional laws would give Congress "a practical and real omnipotence, with the same breath which professes to restrict their powers within narrow limits."[46] This rhetoric, borrowed from *The Federalist* without attribution,[47] was masterful. Surely the Framers were reasonable people, and surely they could not have meant to appoint the fox as guardian of the henhouse.[48]

It is noteworthy that the foregoing argument was derived from the nature of written constitutions in general, not from any particular provision of the Constitution Marshall was construing.[49] The same was true of his equally pivotal contention that judicial review was inherent in the process of deciding cases,[50] although the

[45]5 U.S. (1 Cranch) at 176.

[46]*Id.* at 178.

[47]*See* THE FEDERALIST No. 78, *supra* note 29, at 466 (A. Hamilton):

> By a limited constitution, I understand one which contains certain specified exceptions to the Legislative authority; such, for instance, as that it shall pass no bills of attainder, no ex post facto laws, and the like. Limitations of this kind can be preserved in practice no other way than through the medium of the courts of justice; whose duty it must be to declare all acts contrary to the manifest tenor of the Constitution void.

[48]Compare Marshall's own argument elsewhere in *Marbury* that for every right there is a remedy, 5 U.S. (1 Cranch) at 163, and the argument of Justice Wilson in Chisholm v. Georgia, 2 U.S. (2 Dall.) 419, 465 (1793) (separate opinion), *supra* chapter 1, that the contract clause implied that states could be sued to enforce their obligations: "What good purpose could this constitutional provision secure, if a state might pass a law, impairing the obligation of contracts; and be amenable, for such a violation of right, to no controlling judiciary power?" For a further example of Marshall's strategy of beginning by demonstrating the horrible consequences of not reaching his conclusion, see *infra* chapter 4, notes 40-42 and accompanying text (discussing *Cohens v. Virginia*).

[49]Indeed, Marshall overstated his case badly by asserting that judicial review was "essentially attached to a written constitution." 5 U.S. (1 Cranch) at 177. Not only is it possible to conceive of a written constitution that limits legislative power while precluding judicial review, but European experience has given us concrete examples. For example, FRENCH CONST. tit. 3, ch. 5, art. 3 (1789, repealed 1791), provided that "[t]he tribunals cannot interfere in the exercise of legislative power, nor suspend the execution of laws." *See* C. HAINES, THE AMERICAN DOCTRINE OF JUDICIAL SUPREMACY 6-9 (1932) (citing, among others, the constitutions of France (1875), Belgium (1830), and Switzerland (1874)); J. THAYER, *supra* note 14, at 78 (Marshall "assumes as an essential feature of a written constitution what does not exist in any one of the written constitutions of Europe."); J. THAYER, LEGAL ESSAYS 2-3 (1908); Cappelletti & Adams, *Judicial Review of Legislation: European Antecedents and Adaptations*, 79 HARV. L. REV. 1207, 1211-13 (1966). Hamilton's language of "presumption," *see supra* note 43, would have been more appropriate.

[50]　It is, emphatically, the province and duty of the judicial department, to say what the law is . . . . So, if a law be in opposition to the constitution; . . . the court must determine which of these conflicting rules governs the case . . . . If then, . . . the constitution is superior to any ordinary act of the legislature, the constitution, and not such ordinary act, must govern the case to which they both apply.

5 U.S. (1 Cranch) at 177-78. Hamilton had said this too:

> The interpretation of the laws is the proper and peculiar province of the courts. A Constitution is, in fact, and must be regarded by the Judges as a fundamental law . . . . If there should happen to be an irreconcilable variance between [it and a legislative act,] that which has the superior obligation and validity ought, of course, to be preferred: or in other words the Constitution ought to be preferred to the statute . . . .

THE FEDERALIST No. 78, *supra* note 29, at 467 (A. Hamilton). Of course these arguments beg the question;

supremacy clause would have lent substantial support to his crucial description of the Constitution as "the fundamental and paramount law of the nation."[51] For in declaring the Constitution the "supreme Law of the Land,"[52] that clause eliminated the possibility that the document should be regarded, as Chase had regarded Georgia's separation-of-powers provision,[53] as merely precatory;[54] and in declaring that state court judges were "bound thereby," it established that the Constitution was judicially enforceable.[55]

Like Chief Justice Jay and Justice Wilson in *Chisholm*,[56] Marshall turned to the words of the Constitution only as an afterthought: the "peculiar expressions of the constitution of the United States furnish additional arguments" for judicial review.[57] We might well have been tempted to begin with the constitutional language, as more recent opinions have admonished with regard to statutes;[58] in so doing we might well have written a less powerful opinion.

Marshall drew support from three specific constitutional provisions. The last he put forward with considerable hesitation: "It is . . . not entirely unworthy of observation" that not all federal laws are declared supreme, "but those only which shall be made in pursuance of the constitution."[59] A law contravening the Constitution, he implied, had not been made "in Pursuance" of it. Yet the same clause also gives supremacy to "all Treaties made, or which shall be made, under the Authority of the United States."[60] As the Court had held in *Ware v. Hylton*,[61] this provision embraces treaties made both before and after adoption of the Constitution; the contrast strongly suggests that the reference to laws made in pursuance of "*this* Constitution*" was meant to distinguish those made under the Articles of Con-

---

it would be quite consistent with a judicial duty to declare the law to find that the law commits to Congress the decision whether it has acted within its powers. *See* A. BICKEL, *supra* note 42, at 3; *cf.* G. GUNTHER, *supra* note 26, at 449. As Justice Gibson said in Eakin v. Raub, 12 Serg. & Rawle 330, 349 (Pa. 1825), "no one will pretend, that a judge would be justifiable in calling for the election returns, or scrutinizing the qualifications of those who composed the legislature," though legislative power is vested only in those qualified and elected.

[51]5 U.S. (1 Cranch) at 177 ("Certainly, all those who have framed written constitutions contemplate them as forming the fundamental and paramount law of the nation . . . .").

[52]U.S. CONST. art. VI, para. 2.

[53]Cooper v. Telfair, 4 U.S. (4 Dall.) 14, 18 (1800) (separate opinion) ("The general principles contained in the constitution are not to be regarded as rules to fetter and controul; but as matter merely declaratory and directory . . . ."). *See supra* chapter 2.

[54]See G. GUNTHER, *supra* introduction to part two, note 25, at 17, also invoking U.S. CONST. art. III, § 2, para. 2 ("Cases . . . arising under this Constitution").

[55]It did not, of course, answer the critical question whether the judges were to accept Congress's interpretation of the Constitution rather than adopting their own.

[56]*See supra*, chapter 1.

[57]5 U.S. (1 Cranch) at 178.

[58]*E.g.*, Watt v. Alaska, 451 U.S. 259, 265 (1981).

[59]5 U.S. (1 Cranch) at 180 (construing U.S. CONST. art. VI, para. 2). *Cf.* St. G. Tucker, 1 *Appendix to Blackstone's Commentaries* 369-70, in 1 BLACKSTONE'S COMMENTARIES: WITH NOTES OF REFERENCE TO THE CONSTITUTION AND LAWS OF THE FEDERAL GOVERNMENT OF THE UNITED STATES; AND OF THE COMMONWEALTH OF VIRGINIA (St. G. Tucker ed. 1803) [hereinafter cited as Tucker's Appendix to Blackstone].

[60]U.S. CONST. art. VI, para. 2.

[61]3 U.S. (3 Dall.) 199, 237 (1796) (separate opinion of Chase, J.). *See supra* chapter 2.

federation.[62] Indeed, if this interpretation is correct, the supremacy clause furnishes a powerful argument *against* judicial review of Acts of Congress. Although the clause plainly gives the Constitution the right of way over competing *state* law, it appears to equate federal statutes with the Constitution by declaring them both "supreme law."[63]

Marshall also invoked the provision of article VI that judges "shall be bound by Oath or Affirmation to support this Constitution":[64] "How immoral to impose it on them, if they were to be used as the instruments, and the knowing instruments, for violating what they swear to support!"[65] The response of Pennsylvania's Justice Gibson seems conclusive: the oath "must be understood in reference to supporting the constitution, *only as far as that may be involved in his official duty*; and consequently, if his official duty does not comprehend an inquiry into the authority of the legislature, neither does his oath."[66]

The strongest textual argument in *Marbury* was based upon article III, which extends the judicial power to "Cases . . . arising under this Constitution."[67] "Could it be the intention of those who gave this power, to say, that in using it, the constitution should not be looked into? That a case arising under the constitution should be decided, without examining the instrument under which it arises? This is too extravagant to be maintained."[68] On its face, however, the arising-under clause appears to be merely a jurisdictional provision; it need not be taken to dictate when the Constitution must be given precedence over other laws.[69] To that question the supremacy clause speaks directly, and that clause, as we have seen, seems to subordinate only state or executive action, not Acts of Congress, to the Constitution.

Thus we are left with no obvious peg on which to hang Marshall's conclusion. This is not to say he was wrong. The purpose of the supremacy clause seems to have been to declare the primacy of federal over state law; it need not be read to rebut the inference, based upon the Framers' statements and the presumption that they meant the limitations on Congress to be meaningful, that judicial review of federal statutes is implicit in the arising-under clause or in the limitations themselves.[70] What is

[62]*See* Reid v. Covert, 354 U.S. 1, 16-18 (1957) (opinion of Black, J., for four Justices) (repudiating Marshall's suggested interpretation of the "Pursuance" language in order to establish that treaties, as well as statutes, were subject to judicial review). *See also* 2 W. CROSSKEY, *supra* note 28, at 955-96. Others have suggested the "Pursuance" phrase might refer to statutes passed in conformity with the procedural requirements of the Constitution. *E.g.*, Van Alstyne, *supra* note 22, at 20.

[63]*See* 2 W. CROSSKEY, *supra* note 28, at 984-85. *But see* C. BLACK, THE PEOPLE AND THE COURT 8 (1960) ("If the conflict between the Constitution and the other kind of law is resolved in favor of the latter, then the Constitution is relegated not to an equal but to an inferior position.").

[64]U.S. CONST. art. VI, para. 3.

[65]5 U.S. (1 Cranch) at 180. *Cf.* 1 Tucker's Appendix to Blackstone, *supra* note 59, at 355.

[66]Eakin v. Raub, 12 Serg. & Rawle 330, 353 (Pa. 1825) (emphasis in original). *See also* 2 W. CROSSKEY, *supra* note 28, at 983-84.

[67]U.S. CONST art. III, § 2, para. 1.

[68]5 U.S. (1 Cranch) at 179.

[69]*See* A. BICKEL, *supra* note 42, at 5-6.

[70]Two basic counterarguments have been made to this part of Marshall's opinion: that it ignores the corresponding need for a check on the courts, A. BICKEL, *supra* note 42, at 3-4, and that if the Framers had meant the courts to restrain Congress they would not have given the latter so much power to frustrate review by such devices as restricting the appellate jurisdiction, 2 W. CROSSKEY, *supra* note 28, at 981-82.

interesting is that Marshall chose to make the question appear much easier than
it was.

There remains a crucial ambivalence in the *Marbury* opinion. Two disparate
principles impelled Marshall to find judicial review in the Constitution: that it is an
incidental byproduct of the task of deciding cases, and that it is the only means of
enforcing constitutional limitations. Although these two arguments converged to
support the result in *Marbury*, they suggest divergent answers to a number of
important related questions. If judicial review is merely incidental, the constitutional
plan is not endangered if Congress withdraws the Court's appellate jurisdiction in
constitutional cases,[71] or if it packs the Court with additional Justices of its own
persuasion,[72] or if no one has standing to challenge a spending program.[73] All of these
possibilities, however, raise serious problems if judicial review is an essential part of
our system of checks and balances.

In short, we find in *Marbury* a number of traits that were to characterize many
later Marshall opinions: great rhetorical power, invocation of the constitutional text
less as the basis of decision than as a peg on which to hang a result evidently reached
on other grounds, a marked disdain for reliance on precedent, extensive borrowing
of the ideas of others without attribution, an inclination to reach out for constitutional issues that did not have to be decided, a tendency to resolve difficult questions
by aggressive assertion of one side of the case, and an absolute certainty in the
correctness of his conclusions. We also see in *Marbury* the work of a masterful
tactician, for Marshall managed to lay the basis for enormous judicial power in the
future by sacrificing a trivial portion of the Court's jurisdiction in the immediate
case.[74]

II. Original and Appellate Jurisdiction

A. *Stuart v. Laird*

In 1801 the outgoing Federalist Congress finally abolished the arduous circuit-riding
duties of Supreme Court Justices, establishing a new set of circuit courts manned by
sixteen new Federalist judges.[75] The next year the Republican Congress did away
with the new courts and put the Justices back on circuit.[76]

These two objections contradict each other; the net result seems to be that no branch of government is free
from significant checks if there is judicial review.

[71]*See, e.g.*, H.R. 867, 97th Cong., 1st Sess., 127 Cong. Rec. H4116 (daily ed. Jan. 12, 1981)
("Notwithstanding the provisions of sections 1253, 1254, and 1257 of this chapter the Supreme Court shall
not have jurisdiction to review, by appeal, writ of certiorari or otherwise, any case arising out of any State
statute . . . relating to abortion."). *See infra* chapter 9, discussing *Ex parte McCardle*.

[72]*See* S. 1392, 75th Cong., 1st Sess., 81 Cong. Rec. 5639, 6787-6814, 7375-81, (1937); S. Rep. No. 711,
75th Cong., 1st Sess. (1937).

[73]*See* Massachusetts v. Mellon, 262 U.S. 447 (1923). *See also* 1 C. Warren, *supra* introduction to part
two, note 22, at 222-24 (describing the Jeffersonians' rearrangement of judicial terms so that the Supreme
Court could not meet for 14 months); *id.* at 269-315 (describing the impeachment of Justice Chase).

[74]*See* R. McCloskey, The American Supreme Court 41-42 (1960); Corwin, *supra* note 22, at 543.

[75]Act of Feb. 13, 1801, ch. 4, §§ 7, 27, 2 Stat. 89, 90, 98 (repealed 1802). *See* G. Haskins & H.
Johnson, *supra* introduction to part two, note 2, at 107-35; 1 C. Warren, *supra* introduction to part two,
note 2, at 185-89.

[76]Act of Mar. 8, 1802, ch. 8, §§ 1, 3, 2 Stat. 132, 132 (repealed 1911); Act of Apr. 29, 1802, ch. 31, § 4,

Having obtained a judgment from one of the courts created by the 1801 Act, Laird sought to enforce it in the court to which jurisdiction had been transferred by the 1802 Act. The defendant Stuart argued that this court had no jurisdiction because the statutes replacing the 1801 courts were unconstitutional. Chief Justice Marshall rejected Stuart's contentions at the circuit level and recused himself from reviewing his own decision. The Supreme Court affirmed in three brief paragraphs delivered by Justice Paterson, six days after *Marbury*.[76a]

The most fundamental objection to the 1802 Act was that, by abolishing the courts established in 1801, it had put out of their jobs sixteen judges who under article III were entitled to "hold their Offices during good Behaviour."[77] In support of the Act, counsel invoked the reference in the same section to "such inferior Courts as the Congress may from time to time ordain and establish":[78] "The tenure of office . . . cannot take away altogether the right to alter and modify existing courts."[79] Even Stuart's attorney, arguing against the statute, had to admit Congress could limit the jurisdiction of existing courts,[80] and it is not easy to determine where the line should be drawn. Later Justices were to assume that article III judges could not be discharged by abolishing their courts,[81] and Chase said so privately at the time,[82] but the Court avoided the question in *Stuart*. Counsel had contended that the various provisions of the statute were severable: it was admitted that Congress could transfer cases from one tribunal to another, and thus the tenure of the ousted judges "does not belong to this case."[83] The Court did not mention the circuit judges; it found no constitutional limit on the power "to transfer a cause from one . . . tribunal to another."[84]

---

2 Stat. 156, 157-58 (repealed 1911). For the political background of the repeal of 1801 Act, see R. ELLIS, *supra* note 12, at 36-52.

[76a]5 U.S. (1 Cranch) 299 (1803).

[77]U.S. CONST. art III, § 1. *See* 5 U.S. (1 Cranch) at 303-04 (Mr. Lee).

[78]U.S. CONST. art. III, § 1.

[79]5 U.S. (1 Cranch) at 307 (Mr. Gantt). Gantt might have added, as John Taylor of Caroline had argued, that the constitutional provisions (judges "shall hold their Offices," "during their continuance in Office") presupposed the continued existence of the office itself. *See* G. HASKINS & H. JOHNSON, *supra* introduction to part two, note 2, at 153-54.

[80]5 U.S. (1 Cranch) at 304-05 (Mr. Lee).

[81]See Glidden v. Zdanok, 370 U.S. 530, 544-47 (1962) (opinion of Harlan, J.), and O'Donoghue v. United States, 289 U.S. 516, 535-38 (1933), both explaining Congress's power to vest judicial power in "legislative" courts in the territories on the ground that, if article III governed, the government would be, as stated in *Glidden*, "left . . . with a significant number of territorial judges on its hands and no place to put them" when a territory became a state. 370 U.S. at 545-46.

[82]See Letter from Samuel Chase to John Marshall (Apr. 24, 1802), *reprinted in* G. HASKINS & H. JOHNSON, *supra* introduction to part two, note 2, at 172-77 n.182. Story was of the same opinion. *See* 3 J. STORY, COMMENTARIES ON THE CONSTITUTION OF THE UNITED STATES 494-95 (Boston 1833) (arguing that the repeal "prostrates in the dust the independence of all inferior judges, . . . and leaves the constitution a miserable and vain delusion"). St. George Tucker, whom Crosskey characterized as a "prominent Jeffersonian[]," 2 W. CROSSKEY, *supra* note 28, at 764, was less direct but seemed to reach the same conclusion in 1803. 3 Tucker's Appendix to Blackstone, *supra* note 59, at 25.

[83]5 U.S. (1 Cranch) at 306-07 (Mr. Gantt).

[84]*Id.* at 309. Chase did not note a dissent, though he had earlier written Marshall that any judge who held court under the new scheme "thereby, decides that the repealing was constitutional." G. HASKINS & H. JOHNSON, *supra* introduction to part two, note 2, at 172, 175.

Beveridge reported that the ousted judges did not, like Marbury, bring their own actions to recover their positions or their salaries: despite initial efforts, "their energies flagged, their hearts failed, and their only action was a futile and foolish protest to the very Congress that had wrested their judicial seats from

The Court did, however, decide a second constitutional question: whether Supreme Court Justices could constitutionally sit on circuit. There were three arguments that they could not. First, a litigant in the Supreme Court had a right to have his case determined by six unbiased Justices.[85] There were six Justices rather than four or five, however, only because Congress had said so.[86] The suggestion of bias is reminiscent of later decisions under the due process clause,[87] but those decisions reflect an interpretation that the Court would not embrace for many years,[88] and it is not certain that they would govern today.

Second, it was argued that the statute assigning circuit duties to the Justices effectively appointed them as circuit judges, in contravention of article II's provision that appointments were to be made by the President with Senate consent.[89] This contention was not at all frivolous. Although not every addition to a court's jurisdiction should be held to require a new appointment, some limit on congressional reassignment of the functions of incumbent officers seems implicit if the President's authority is not to be circumvented.[90]

The final argument drew strength from *Marbury v. Madison*: the Justices could not sit on circuit because the cases they would try there were outside the Supreme Court's original jurisdiction as defined by article III.[91] The immediate response to this argument is that it is not the Supreme Court but one of its members who exercises original jurisdiction; by the time the Court decides the case, it has the benefit of a decision below and is spared the collective burden of conducting a trial. The difficulty is that this response, by separating the Justice from the Court, strengthens the alternative objection that circuit riding is a distinct office requiring an additional appointment. To reject both contentions one must draw a delicate distinction: the new duties are a part of the existing office of Justice, but not a function of the Supreme Court as an institution.

---

under them." 3 A. BEVERIDGE, *supra* introduction to part two, note 10, at 123. Chase wrote that the law gave the judges no remedy. Letter from Samuel Chase to John Marshall (Apr. 24, 1802), *reprinted in* G. HASKINS & H. JOHNSON, *supra* introduction to part two, note 2, at 174-75. Warren stated that one of the judges did sue but said nothing of the outcome. 1 C. WARREN, *supra* introduction to part two, note 2, at 272 n.1.

[85]5 U.S. (1 Cranch) at 305-06 (Mr. Lee).

[86]*See* Chisholm v. Georgia, 2 U.S. (2 Dall.) 419, 432 (1793) (Iredell, J., dissenting).

[87]U.S. CONST. amend. V; *id.* amend. XIV, § 1. *See* Withrow v. Larkin, 421 U.S. 35, 58 n.25 (1975) (dictum) (speaking in the context of state administrative proceedings: "[W]hen review of an initial decision is mandated, the decisionmaker must be other than the one who made the decision under review.") (citing Gagnon v. Scarpelli, 411 U.S. 778, 785-86 (1973), and Morrissey v. Brewer, 408 U.S. 471, 485-86 (1972)).

[88]As late as 1856 the Court defined due process as conformity with "those settled usages and modes of proceeding existing in the common and statute law of England, before the emigration of our ancestors," Murray's Lessee v. Hoboken Land & Improv. Co., 59 U.S. (18 How.) 272, 277 (1856); in England judges habitually sat in review of their own decisions. The Justices were soon to abandon their early practice (now required by 28 U.S.C. § 47 (1976)) of refusing to review their own decisions. See Shirras v. Caig, 11 U.S. (7 Cranch) 34, 42n.(a) (1812), *cited* (with a minor inaccuracy) *in* T. SERGEANT, CONSTITUTIONAL LAW 102 (Philadelphia 1822).

[89]5 U.S. (1 Cranch) at 305 (Mr. Lee) (construing U.S. CONST. art. II, § 2, para. 2).

[90]For example, if Congress were to assign all the duties of the Secretary of State to his Assistant Secretary, or to the Secretary of the Treasury.

[91]5 U.S. (1 Cranch) at 305 (Mr. Lee).

The Court upheld the power of Congress to send the Justices out on circuit, but it did so without refuting any of the contrary arguments: "[P]ractice, and acquiescence under it, for a period of several years, commencing with the organization of the judicial system, affords an irresistible answer, and has indeed fixed the construction . . . . Of course, the question is at rest, and ought not now to be disturbed."[92]

Deference to legislative interpretation of the Constitution had been suggested by Chase and other Justices some time before, in repeated statements that legislation was not to be set aside except in a "clear" case.[93] Story was to make a particular point of the weight to be given the judgment of the First Congress, many of whose members had been at the Constitutional Convention, in *Martin v. Hunter's Lessee*.[94] But neither Chase nor Story ever contended that the Court was *bound* by Congress's interpretation; to hold that it was would overrule *Marbury v. Madison*.

The *Stuart* opinion did not rest upon the action of the First Congress alone; it invoked the Court's own "acquiescence" in circuit riding from 1789 until 1801.[95] Once again the contrast with *Marbury* is striking: counsel had there cited previous cases in which the Court had allegedly entertained original mandamus requests, and Marshall did not bother to respond.[96] Two years later, in *United States v. More*,[97] Marshall would expressly decline, as we would be likely to decline today,[98] to treat as binding precedent a decision in which the issue had been neither litigated nor decided.[99] Moreover, the Court's "acquiescence" had been less than absolute. The Justices had agitated repeatedly for relief from circuit duty[100] and had ostensibly protested to the President on constitutional grounds as early as 1790.[101] Finally, neither legislative practice nor judicial acquiescence should have been decisive of whether a presidential appointment was required. The Act of 1802 was the first to impose circuit duties upon Justices previously appointed.[102]

---

[92]*Id*. at 309.

[93]*See* Calder v. Bull, 3 U.S. (3 Dall.) 386, 395 (1798) (Chase, J.); *id*. at 399 (Iredell, J.); Hylton v. United States, 3 U.S. (3 Dall.) 171, 175 (1796) (Chase, J.). *See supra* chapter 2.

[94]*See infra* chapter 4, note 5 and accompanying text. *See also* McCulloch v. Maryland, 17 U.S. (4 Wheat.) 316, 400-01 (1819), *discussed in infra* chapter 6.

[95]5 U.S. (1 Cranch) at 309.

[96]*See supra* note 31.

[97]7 U.S. (1 Cranch) 159 (1805).

[98]See, e.g., Stone v. Powell, 428 U.S. 465, 481 n.15 (1976), and the contrary view expressed with respect to jurisdictional questions in the dissent, *id*. at 518-19 (Brennan, J., dissenting).

[99]7 U.S. (3 Cranch) at 172; *see infra* notes 103-17 and accompanying text. *But see* The Betsey & Charlotte, 8 U.S. (4 Cranch) 443, 452 (1808) (Marshall, C.J.), *discussed in supra* chapter 1.

[100]*See* 1 C. WARREN, *supra* introduction to part two, note 2, at 31-90.

[101]This letter from the Justices to George Washington (1790), with Washington's request for the Justices' remarks (Apr. 3, 1790), is reprinted in 3 J. STORY, *supra* note 82, at 438-41. The Justices made both of the principal arguments later advanced in *Stuart*. But see Wheeler, *Extrajudicial Activities of the Early Supreme Court*, 1973 SUP. CT. REV. 123, 148, doubting that the letter was ever sent. Contrast the well-known Correspondence of the Justices, *supra* chapter 1, three years after this letter, refusing to answer a similar request for advice respecting our neutrality in the war between England and France.

[102]The Justices had debated among themselves, in a series of letters, whether or not they should refuse on constitutional grounds to sit on circuit. Marshall, who had expressed "strong constitutional scruples," Letter from John Marshall to William Paterson (Apr. 6, 1802), *quoted in* G. HASKINS & H. JOHNSON, *supra* introduction to part two, note 2, at 168, suggested the possibility of distinguishing between "the

B. *United States v. More*

More, like Marbury, had been appointed to a five-year term as justice of the peace in the District of Columbia. At the time of his appointment the statute authorized him to collect fees for his services. The new Republican Congress repealed the fee provision in 1802, and More was prosecuted for taking a subsequent fee. He demurred on the ground that the statute abolishing his fees offended article III's guarantee that federal judges should receive "Compensation, which shall not be diminished during their Continuance in Office."[103] The trial court sustained the demurrer by a divided vote, and the government went to the Supreme Court.[104]

The dissenting judge below had argued that More had been appointed not under article III but under Congress's article I power of "exclusive Legislation" over the District of Columbia[105] and thus that he was not protected by the limitations of article III.[106] The difficulty was not with the premise of this argument but with its conclusion: why was not Congress's power to create District of Columbia courts, like its power to regulate commerce, subject to the explicit limits found elsewhere in the Constitution?[107] This was not the first case to present the difficult problem of fitting the District of Columbia and the territories into a constitutional scheme drafted essentially without thinking about them, and it was certainly not to be the last.[108]

In *More*, however, the Supreme Court managed to avoid deciding this question. For More's was a criminal case, and the Judiciary Act did not provide for Supreme Court review of criminal cases.[109] *More* itself was governed by a separate statute

original case of being appointed to duties marked out before their appointments, and of having the duties of administering justice in new Courts imposed after their appointments," but he thought it unconvincing and added that "[t]he law having been once executed will detract very much, in the public estimation, from the merit or opinion of the sincerity of a determination not now to act under it." Letters from John Marshall to William Paterson (Apr. 6 & 24, 1802), *quoted in* 1 C. WARREN, *supra* introduction to part two, note 2, at 269–71. Warren praised *Stuart* as a "striking example of the non-partisanship of the American Judiciary." 1 C. WARREN, *supra* introduction to part two, note 2, at 272. Given the Court's precarious position under the Jeffersonian siege, *see* G. HASKINS & H. JOHNSON, *supra* introduction to part two, note 2, at 136-181; 1 C. WARREN, *supra* introduction to part two, note 2, at 169-315, it may be more accurate to describe the decision as an exercise in self-preservation.

[103]U.S. CONST. art. III, § 1.

[104]7 U.S. (3 Cranch) 159 (1805).

[105]U.S. CONST. art. I, § 8, cl. 17.

[106]7 U.S. (3 Cranch) at 164-65 (footnote) (Kilty, J., dissenting).

[107]As Judge Cranch had written below: "The true consideration is, that Congress may legislate for us [in the District], in all cases where they are not prohibited by other parts of the constitution." *Id.* at 160. Judge Kilty did acknowledge in dissent that other constitutional limitations, such as the habeas corpus and ex post facto clauses and the first amendment, applied to the District; but article III's tenure provision, he concluded, was "evidently applicable [only] to the judicial power of the whole United States," and "not to a particular territory." *Id.* at 164–65. In the Supreme Court, counsel went further: "When legislating over the district of Columbia, congress are bound by no constitution." *Id.* at 171 (Mr. Mason). *Cf. infra* chapter 4, notes 194-214 and accompanying text (discussing *American Insurance Co. v. Canter*).

[108]*See, e.g.*, Loughborough v. Blake, 18 U.S. (5 Wheat.) 317 (1820), *discussed in* chapter 6 *infra*; *infra* notes 137-50, chapter 4, notes 38-76, 194-214, and accompanying text (discussing *Hepburn v. Ellzey, Cohens v. Virginia,* and *American Insurance Co. v. Canter*). In Palmore v. United States, 411 U.S. 389 (1973), the Court, after contrary suggestions in intervening opinions, adopted Judge Kilty's position that local judges in the District of Columbia need not be given article III tenure.

[109]*See* Judiciary Act of 1789, ch. 20, 1 Stat. 73.

authorizing review of "final judgment[s]" of the District of Columbia court,[110] but Marshall for the Court read the further provision for a minimum jurisdictional amount as indicating that only civil cases were included.[111] He repeated, without citation, Justice Wilson's earlier conclusion[112] that the Supreme Court's constitutional appellate jurisdiction would have been self-executing in the absence of congressional action.[113] He added, however, that by enacting statutes listing cases the Court could hear, Congress had implicitly exercised its article III authority to make "Exceptions" to the appellate jurisdiction: "[A]n affirmative description of [the Court's] powers must be understood as a regulation, under the constitution, prohibiting the exercise of other powers than those described."[114]

No one suggested in *More* that there might be any doubt of Congress's power to except criminal cases from the appellate jurisdiction. The words of article III are unqualified, but after *Marbury* it was not obvious that the power to make exceptions was absolute. *Marbury* had suggested that judicial review was implicit in constitutional provisions restricting congressional power;[115] arguably even the exceptions authority could not be used to deny a forum for the claim that Congress had offended the compensation clause of article III.[116] More himself had had his day in the court below, and he had won; the decision cannot be taken to mean there are no limits to Congress's power to curtail the appellate jurisdiction. Yet it is of some importance that no one seems to have doubted that Congress could close the Supreme Court itself to an important constitutional claim.[117]

C. *Ex parte Bollman*

Bollman and Swartwout, implicated in Aaron Burr's mysterious western adventures,[118] had been jailed by a District of Columbia court to await trial on charges of

---

[110]Act of Feb. 27, 1801, ch. 15, § 8, 2 Stat. 103, 106 (current version at 28 U.S.C. § 1257 (1976)).

[111]7 U.S. (3 Cranch) at 173-74.

[112]Wiscart v. D'Auchy, 3 U.S. (3 Dall.) 321, 325 (1796), *discussed in* chapter 1 *supra*.

[113]7 U.S. (3 Cranch) at 173. When Marshall reaffirmed this point and the one next discussed in Durousseau v. United States, 10 U.S. (6 Cranch) 307, 313-14 (1810), he cited neither *Wiscart* nor *More*.

[114]7 U.S. (3 Cranch) at 173. *See also id.* at 170-71. To the argument that the Court had exercised appellate jurisdiction in an earlier criminal case, Marshall responded that the question of jurisdiction had not there been raised: "It passed sub silentio, and the court does not consider itself as bound by that case." *Id.* at 172.

[115]*See supra* notes 45-46 and accompanying text.

[116]For additional considerations relevant to this point, see *supra* chapter 1 and *infra* chapter 9.

[117]In Durousseau v. United States, 10 U.S. (6 Cranch) 307 (1810), the Court similarly did not decide what limits there might be to Congress's power to make exceptions, and no argument to that effect is reported. After repeating the points made in *More*, the Court in *Durousseau* held that Congress had not implicitly forbidden review of decisions by the District Court for the territory of New Orleans. Constitutional scruples may, however, have underlain Marshall's expressed reluctance in *Durousseau* to find that Congress had intended the District Court of New Orleans to be, "in fact, . . . a Supreme Court." 10 U.S. (6 Cranch) at 318. Compare U.S. CONST. art. III § 1, which speaks of "one Supreme Court." Yet he had earlier referred to the Court's acceptance of a minimum-amount requirement for the exercise of its appellate jurisdiction, without suggesting it raised any constitutional problem. *Id.* at 314.

[118]For the historical setting of this case, see 3 A. BEVERIDGE, *supra* introduction to part two, note 10, at 274-397; G. HASKINS & H. JOHNSON, *supra* introduction to part two, note 2, at 248-62; 1 C. WARREN, *supra*

treason. They filed a petition for habeas corpus in the Supreme Court, which in 1807 ordered them discharged.[119]

The Court's jurisdiction to entertain the petition was challenged on both statutory and constitutional grounds. Section 14 of the Judiciary Act purported to give all federal courts "power to issue writs of *scire facias, habeas corpus*, and all other writs not specially provided for by statute, which may be necessary for the exercise of their respective jurisdictions."[120] Over Justice Johnson's dissent, the Court construed the clause limiting it to writs in aid of jurisdiction as applying only to "other writs" and not to habeas corpus;[121] it did not suggest that the statute should be read narrowly to avoid facing the constitutional question.

The constitutional question was that posed by *Marbury*:[122] if to issue the writ would be to exercise original jurisdiction, the Supreme Court could not do it, because neither a state nor a foreign diplomat was a party. Marshall's response was brief, invoking *Marbury*'s definition of the appellate power: the jurisdiction in *Bollman* was appellate because it involved "the revision of a decision of an inferior court, by which a citizen has been committed to gaol."[123]

Marshall made his task in *Bollman* much easier by not quoting the actual language of the decision on which he relied. In *Marbury* he had said that "the essential criterion of appellate jurisdiction" was "that it revises and corrects the proceedings in a cause already instituted and does not create that cause."[124] As applied to *Bollman*, this passage contains a crucial ambiguity. For though, as Marshall stressed, *Bollman* was an effort to "revise and correct" the decision of another judge,[125] it was not so clear that it was a part of the "cause already instituted." In later refusing to take jurisdiction of a habeas proceeding under a statute limited to criminal cases, for example, the Court would say that the writ was "not a proceeding in the [criminal] prosecution" but "a new suit brought . . . to enforce a civil right."[126] Yet it would be

---

introduction to part two, note 2, at 301-08. For the later adventures of the intrepid Sam Swartwout, see Murray's Lessee v. Hoboken Land Improvement Co., 57 U.S. (18 How.) 272 (1856); G. VIDAL, BURR 270-72, 363-69, 425 (1973).

[119]8 U.S. (4 Cranch) 75 (1807).

[120]Judiciary Act of 1789, ch. 20, § 14, 1 Stat. 73, 81-82 (current version at 28 U.S.C. § 1651 (1976)).

[121]8 U.S. (4 Cranch) at 95-100, 105. For discussion of the complicated statutory issues, see Oaks, *The "Original" Writ of Habeas Corpus*, 1962 SUP. CT. REV. 153, 173–76; Paschal, *The Constitution and Habeas Corpus*, 1970 DUKE L.J. 605, 623-25. Professor Paschal argues that Marshall made an error of constitutional proportion in concluding, 8 U.S. (4 Cranch) at 93-94, that statutory authority was necessary to enable the Court to issue the writ. Paschal contends that article I's provision that "[t]he Privilege of the Writ of Habeas Corpus shall not be suspended, unless when in Cases of Rebellion or Invasion the public Safety may require it," U.S.CONST. art. I, § 9, para. 2, "is a direction to all superior courts of record, state as well as federal, to make the habeas privilege routinely available"; the statement in *Bollman* means "that Congress can suspend the privilege in the federal courts at its pleasure, whether or not the public safety requires it," by withholding jurisdiction to grant the writ. Paschal, *supra*, at 605, 607. The thesis that article I requires that some court have habeas jurisdiction was accepted in Eisentrager v. Forrestal, 174 F.2d 961, 966-67 (D.C. Cir. 1949) (alternative holding), but because, so far as the report reveals, Paschal's argument was not squarely made in *Bollman*, the precedential value of Marshall's statement is less than complete.

[122]*See supra* notes 24-25 and accompanying text.

[123]8 U.S. (4 Cranch) at 101.

[124]5 U.S. (1 Cranch) at 175.

[125]8 U.S. (4 Cranch) at 101.

[126]*Ex parte* Tong, 108 U.S. 556, 559-60 (1883). *Cf.* Fay v. Noia, 372 U.S. 391, 428, 430 (1963)

a mistake to attribute to the Framers any purpose that would render the distinction between original and appellate power one of form rather than substance; the underlying policies of sparing the Supreme Court trial burdens and of affording it the benefit of lower court views were satisfied in *Bollman*.[127]

Marshall also invoked more specific precedents: in two earlier cases the Court had issued the writ under similar circumstances.[128] In the first, so far as the report reveals, the constitutional issue had not been raised; by the standard announced by Marshall two years earlier in *More*,[129] it was entitled to no precedential weight. Marshall had decided the second case in 1806 on the basis of the first—in disregard of his own statement in *More*. Johnson, naturally, invoked *More*.[130] He added, more generally, that the salutary doctrine of stare decisis was not an absolute command:

> I deny, that a court is precluded from the right, or exempted from the necessity, of examining into the correctness or consistency of its own decisions . . . . Strange indeed would be the doctrine, that an inadvertency once committed by a court shall ever after impose on it the necessity of persisting in its error.[131]

(describing the present statutes providing for district court habeas as furnishing "an independent, collateral remedy" and holding inapplicable to habeas proceedings the adequate state ground limitation applicable to direct Supreme Court review of state court judgments because, *inter alia*, the language of the habeas statute was "hardly characteristic of an appellate jurisdiction"). Compare also Paschal, *supra* note 121, at 626, discussing counsel's argument in *Ex parte* Burford, 7 U.S. (3 Cranch) 448, 449 (1806), that a case involving habeas corpus could be distinguished from *Marbury* because mandamus is a prerogative writ while the Constitution makes habeas a "writ of right," and therefore not subject to the restriction on the Supreme Court's original jurisdiction (*Burford* did not address this argument). Compare also *In re* Metzger, 46 U.S. (5 How.) 176, 191 (1847), holding that habeas review of a commitment made by a district judge in chambers was not appellate and casting aspersions on *Bollman* while distinguishing it:

> [T]here is some refinement in denominating that an appellate power which is exercised through the instrumentality of a writ of *habeas corpus*. In this from nothing more can be examined into than the legality of the commitment. However erroneous the judgment of the court may be, . . . if it had jurisdiction, and the defendant has been duly committed, under an execution or sentence, he cannot be discharged by this writ.

[127]Johnson dissented on the constitutional ground as well, arguing rather obscurely that any habeas jurisdiction conferred by section 14 was original because the Court's statutory power was identical to that of a district court. 8 U.S. (4 Cranch) at 106.

[128]*Id.* at 101 (citing United States v. Hamilton, 3 U.S. (3 Dall.) 17 (1795), and *Ex parte* Burford, 7 U.S. (3 Cranch) 448 (1806)).

[129]*See supra* note 114.

[130]8 U.S. (4 Cranch) at 104.

[131]*Id.* at 103-04. Johnson noted that he was "much relieved from the painful necessity of dissenting . . . , in being supported by the opinion of one of my brethren, who is prevented by indisposition from attending." *Id.* at 107. The reporter tells us, *id.* at 93 n.(a), that both Cushing and Chase were absent, and, *id.* at iii, that Cushing was absent for the entire Term. 3 A. BEVERIDGE, *supra* introduction to part two, note 10, at 349 & n.4, citing correspondence, said it was Chase who joined the dissent; T. SERGEANT, *supra* note 88, at 66, said flatly that it was Cushing.

Johnson added that he had objected to the issuance of the writ in *Ex parte* Burford, 7 U.S. (3 Cranch) 448 (1806), but had "submitted in silent deference to the decision of my brethren," 8 U.S. (4 Cranch) at 107. Later Justices seem to have felt a greater necessity to air publicly any disagreement with a majority opinion. Johnson's statement, taken with other evidence reported by Professor Morgan, *supra* introduction to part two, note 12, at 168-69, leads one to wonder how many other cases there were in which the Marshall Court was less unanimous than the report reveals.

The Court would have ample opportunities later on to agree with him.[132]

III. DIVERSITY JURISDICTION

Apart from the cases already considered, the Court's principal activity with constitutional overtones between 1801 and 1810 concerned the definition of federal jurisdiction in cases involving aliens or citizens of different states. Four decisions during this period dealt with this subject: *Hepburn v. Ellzey*,[133] *Strawbridge v. Curtiss*,[134] *Bank of the United States v. Deveaux*,[135] and *Hodgson v. Bowerbank*.[136]

A. *Hepburn v. Ellzey*

The defendant was a citizen of Virginia, the plaintiff of the District of Columbia. The Judiciary Act provided jurisdiction over suits "between a citizen of the State where the suit is brought [here Virginia], and a citizen of another State."[137] The circuit court certified the question of jurisdiction to the Supreme Court,[138] which in two pages by Marshall held in 1805 that there was no jurisdiction.[139]

Marbury v. Madison suggested a threshold problem[140] that apparently passed unobserved. The circuit court was sitting as a court of first instance, and it had not decided the certified question. Why wasn't the Supreme Court thus exercising a forbidden original jurisdiction? In 1838 the Court acknowledged that to decide the whole case on certified questions without a decision below would infringe the

---

[132]On the merits, and without recorded dissent, the Court proceeded in a second Marshall opinion to order the petitioners discharged for want of allegations sufficient to satisfy the constitutional definition of treason. *Ex parte* Bollman, 8 U.S. (4 Cranch) 126 (1807). Article III's provision that "Treason against the United States, shall consist only in levying War against them, or in adhering to their Enemies, giving them Aid and Comfort," U.S. CONST. art. III, § 3, para. 1, was said to require not a mere conspiracy but "an actual assembling of men . . . for the purpose of effecting by force a treasonable purpose," 8 U.S. (4 Cranch) at 126. The Justices divided as to whether evidence before the Court established that the expedition had been aimed at the United States, and all agreed there was no showing that an armed group had actually been assembled. *Id.* at 133, 135. For his interpretation of article III, Marshall relied not only on the constitutional text but on opinions of his brethren expressed on circuit. *Id.* at 127-28.

The treason decision in *Bollman* was an important precedent when Marshall on circuit presided over the trial of Burr himself, who was acquitted on the basis of Marshall's charge to the jury. United States v. Burr, 25 F. Cas. 55 (No. 14,693) (C.C.D. Va. 1807). For discussion of *Burr*, see, e.g., 3 A. BEVERIDGE, *supra* introduction to part two, note 10, at 274-545; G. HASKINS & H. JOHNSON, *supra* introduction to part two, note 23, at 612-46; 1 C. WARREN, *supra* introduction to part two, note 22, at 301-15.

[133]6 U.S. (2 Cranch) 445 (1805).

[134]7 U.S. (3 Cranch) 267 (1806).

[135]9 U.S. (5 Cranch) 61 (1809).

[136]9 U.S. (5 Cranch) 303 (1809).

[137]Judiciary Act of 1789, ch. 20, § 11, 1 Stat. 73, 78 (current version at 28 U.S.C. § 1332 (1976)).

[138]As authorized by Act of April 29, 1802, ch. 31, § 2, 2 Stat. 156, 159 ("whenever any question shall occur before a circuit court, upon which the opinions of the judges shall be opposed") (current version at 28 U.S.C. §§ 1254, 1255 (1976)).

[139]6 U.S. (2 Cranch) 445, 452-53 (1805).

[140]*See supra* notes 24-26 and accompanying text.

Marbury principle;[141] the objection seems equally valid when the Court decides a single issue.[142]

Marshall's disposition of the diversity question was brief and straightforward. The jurisdictional statute "obviously uses the word 'state' in reference to that term as used in the constitution," and the provisions of articles I and II respecting congressional and presidential elections demonstrated that "the members of the American confederacy only are the states contemplated in the constitution."[143]

This is vintage Marshall. It may well have been fair to presume that the statute used the term in the constitutional sense and that constitutional usage was consistent throughout. Marshall's dogmatic declarations, however, suggest no possibility that context or consequences might show the contrary. Later cases have generally construed statutes conferring jurisdiction of cases "arising under" federal law to be less comprehensive than the identically worded constitutional provision,[144] and corporations have come to be treated effectively as "citizens" under article III but not under article IV.[145] Moreover, powerful reasons had been urged in *Hepburn* for holding the District a "state" for diversity purposes. District citizens, it had persuasively been argued, were as much in need of an impartial forum as were citizens of Maryland;[146] Marshall acknowledged the term "state" was sometimes used to refer to any "distinct political society."[147] In addition, if the Court was right that "state" had a single meaning throughout the Constitution, Congress would be free after *Hepburn* to tax exports from the District or to channel all foreign commerce there, despite article I's

---

[141]White v. Turk, 37 U.S. (12 Pet.) 238, 239 (1838). *See* R. Stern & E. Gressman, Supreme Court Practice 597-98 (5th ed. 1978).

[142]*See* Wheeler Lumber Co. v. United States, 281 U.S. 572, 576 (1930) (reaffirming the holding of *White v. Turk* and adding that the power to decide single questions before decision below, while "rather exceptional in the appellate field," was "settled" by "[e]arly and long continued usage amounting to a practical construction of the constitutional provision").

[143]6 U.S. (2 Cranch) at 452. Marshall extended this reasoning to a citizen of a territory in New Orleans v. Winter, 14 U.S. (1 Wheat.) 91, 94 (1816):

> It has been attempted to distinguish a Territory from the District of Columbia; . . . but neither of them is a state, in the sense in which that term is used in the constitution. Every reason assigned for the opinion of the court, that a citizen of Columbia was not capable of suing in the courts of the United States, under the Judiciary Act, is equally applicable to a citizen of a territory.

[144]*Compare, e.g.,* Cohens v. Virginia, 19 U.S. (6 Wheat.) 264, 379 (1821) ("A case . . . consists of the right of the one party, as well as of the other, and may truly be said to arise under the constitution or a law of the United States [for the purposes of article III], whenever its correct decision depends on the construction of either.") *with* Gold-Washing & Water Co. v. Keyes, 96 U.S. 199 (1877) (disallowing removal based on a federal defense under the statutory provision for removal of cases "arising under the Constitution or laws of the United States"). *See* 1 Story, *supra* note 82, at 439-40 (arguing that a word used in two different parts of the Constitution might not necessarily have the same meaning in each).

[145]*Compare* Marshall v. Baltimore & O.R.R., 57 U.S. (18 How.) 314 (1854) (deeming members of corporation citizens of the state of incorporation for purposes of diversity jurisdiction) *with* Paul v. Virginia, 75 U.S. (8 Wall.) 168 (1869) (corporation not protected by the privileges and immunities clause). *See infra* chapter 8.

[146]6 U.S. (2 Cranch) at 448-49 (E.J. Lee).

[147]*Id.* at 452. *Cf. infra* chapter 4, notes 215-31 and accompanying text (discussing *Cherokee Nation v. Georgia*).

provisions forbidding Congress to tax articles "exported from any State"[148] or to give preferences "to the Ports of one State over those of another."[149] Marshall conceded it was "extraordinary" that federal courts should be closed to District citizens, "[b]ut this is a subject for legislative, not for judicial consideration."[150] The "other passages" cited to show that "state" was "sometimes used in its more enlarged sense," he added without explanation, "do not prove what was to be shown by them."[151]

B. *Strawbridge v. Curtiss*

The plaintiffs and several defendants were citizens of Massachusetts; one defendant was a citizen of Vermont. The year after *Hepburn*, in three brief Marshall paragraphs, the Court affirmed a dismissal for want of jurisdiction.[152]

[148]U.S. Const. art. I, § 9, cl. 5. *See also* the argument of Mr. Nicholas in the Virginia ratifying convention that the District of Columbia would remain a part of the state and would be so considered for purposes of general regulation. 3 Elliot's Debates *supra* note 42, at 434-35.

[149]*Id.* cl. 6. This provision was invoked by E.J. Lee in his argument for the District. 6 U.S. (2 Cranch) at 451.

[150]6 U.S. (2 Cranch) at 453. Only a few days before, Marshall had written that "the legislative intention must be expressed with irresistible clearness" to persuade a court that the drafters of a statute meant to reach "mischie[vous]" results "[w]here rights are infringed, where fundamental principles are overthrown, where the general system of the laws is departed from "; but otherwise "it would be going a great way, to say that a constrained interpretation must be put upon [the words], to avoid an inconvenience which ought to have been contemplated." United States v. Fisher, 6 U.S. (2 Cranch) 358, 389-90 (1805). Compare Marshall's argument from "mischie[vous] results" in *Marbury, supra* notes 45-48, and accompanying text.

The reference to "legislative" consideration suggests Marshall was inviting Congress to extend jurisdiction to cases involving District citizens, *see* T. Sergeant, *supra* note 115, at 110 n.(x); C. Wright, *supra* note 19, at 94; his equation of the statutory and constitutional language, however, suggests he would have thought any such statute unconstitutional. He seems rather to have been referring to the "legislative" process of constitutional amendment. A century and a half later, after Congress had taken up Marshall's suggestion, *see* 28 U.S.C. § 1332(d) (1976) ("The word 'States,' as used in this Section, includes the Territories, the District of Columbia, and the Commonwealth of Puerto Rico."), only two Justices would decline to follow *Hepburn* as an interpretation of the Constitution. National Mut. Ins. Co. v. Tidewater Transfer Co., 337 U.S. 582, 604, 617-26 (1949) (Rutledge & Murphy, J.J., concurring). Three others concluded, however, that Congress could confer jurisdiction on the basis of its article I power to legislate for the District of Columbia, *id.* at 588-604 (Jackson, Black & Burton, JJ.), despite precedents treating article III as a limitation on the powers Congress could give a federal court, *see, e.g.,* Mossman v. Higginson, 4 U.S. (4 Dall.) 12 (1800) (alien a party); Hayburn's Case, 2 U.S. (2 Dall.) 409, 410-14 n.(a) (C.C.D.N.Y., C.C.D. Pa. 1792) (nonjudicial authority); *see also supra* chapter 1. Because Marshall found Congress had not attempted to extend jurisdiction to District citizens, he had no need in *Hepburn* to face the constitutional argument.

[151]6 U.S. (2 Cranch) at 453. As to certain of the provisions that had been invoked, Marshall had a point. Counsel had argued that statutes extending full faith and credit and extradition duties to the District and to the territories could be sustained only by giving a broad interpretation to the term "State" in article VI, while an oblique reference to "privileges and immunities" suggested that otherwise the states could treat the District citizen as an outcast. *Id.* at 450-52. All of these problems, however, Congress could deal with without stretching the word "state," under its power to exercise "exclusive Legislation" for the District of Columbia. U.S. Const. art I, § 8, cl. 17. See Embrey v. Palmer, 107 U.S. 3 (1883) (full faith to District judgments). Marshall might have done better to explain all this, and none of it seems to answer the arguments respecting port preferences and export taxes, which are phrased in terms of "State[s]." *Id.* art. I, § 9, cls. 5 & 6.

[152]7 U.S. (3 Cranch) 267 (1806).

The statute, as noted above, gave jurisdiction of suits "between a citizen of the State where the suit is brought, and a citizen of another State."[153] Marshall's reasoning consisted of a bald conclusion: "The court understands these expressions to mean, that each distinct interest could be represented by persons, all of whom are entitled to sue, or may be sued, in the federal courts."[154] That is, all plaintiffs must be diverse from all defendants.

This interpretation was certainly not compelled by the statutory language, and the purpose of the clause might be thought to require a federal forum whenever an out-of-stater was a party. Marshall could have helped his case by invoking the latter-day explanation that the presence of a local codefendant insulates the outsider from prejudice;[155] perhaps it was some such consideration, rather than a simple disinclination to comment on a case not before the Court, that led him to reserve the question whether complete diversity was also required where the interests were not "joint" but "distinct."[156]

As in *Hepburn*, Marshall in *Strawbridge* purported only to construe the statute, but to judge by his *Hepburn* opinion equating statute and Constitution, he would have given the same construction to the Constitution. Later cases, however, have both extended the statutory *Strawbridge* rule to situations in which the interests are not joint[157] and held that Congress may abolish it, at least in certain cases.[158] If complete diversity was ever a constitutional requirement,[159] it seems not to be any more.

C.   Bank of the United States v. Deveaux

The "President, Directors and Company" of the first National Bank, alleging themselves to be citizens of Pennsylvania, filed a federal trespass action against Georgia citizens for carting silver away from the Bank's Savannah branch to satisfy

[153]Judiciary Act of 1789, ch. 20, § 11, 1 Stat. 73, 78 (current version at 28 U.S.C. § 1332 (1976)).
[154]7 U.S. (3 Cranch) at 267.
[155]See the argument of counsel in Case of the Sewing Mach. Cos., 85 U.S. (18 Wall.) 553, 572 (1874) ("When citizens of the State where the suit is, are on both sides in the suit, the local prejudice or influence is destroyed, or balanced. It favors one side as much as the other."). For the opposing view, see the concurring opinion of Justice Bradley in Removal Cases (Meyer v. Construction Co.), 100 U.S. 457, 479-80 (1879), arguing that *Strawbridge* should not be followed in construing a similarly worded removal provision:

> [T]hose terms include as well the case when only a part of the contestants opposed to each other are citizens of different States . . . . [The purpose] to establish a common and impartial tribunal . . . would be defeated in many cases if the fact that a single one of many contestants on one side of a controversy being a citizen of the same State with one or more of the contestants on the other side, should have the effect of depriving the federal courts of jurisdiction.

[156]7 U.S. (3 Cranch) at 267-68.
[157]*E.g.*, Owen Equip. & Erection Co. v. Kroger, 437 U.S. 365, 374-75 (1978) (joint tortfeasors).
[158]*E.g.*, State Farm Fire & Casualty Co. v. Tashire, 386 U.S. 523, 530-31 (1967) (interpleader).
[159]As it was asserted to be, for example, in Shields v. Barrow, 58 U.S. (17 How.) 130, 145 (1855) (Curtis, J.).

an unpaid state tax.[160] The circuit court dismissed for want of jurisdiction; the Supreme Court reversed in an 1809 Marshall opinion.[161]

This case was an early preview of the great controversies over state taxation of the second National Bank that the Court was to resolve ten and fifteen years later in *McCulloch v. Maryland*[162] and *Osborn v. Bank of the United States*.[163] In *Deveaux*, however, the Court found it unnecessary to determine the constitutional scope of federal question jurisdiction or to pass upon the merits; it remanded for further proceedings on finding the suit was one between citizens of different states.[164]

Deveaux is commonly viewed today as having severely *limited* diversity jurisdiction, for Marshall expressly stated that a corporation was not a "citizen" of a state for diversity purposes: "That invisible, intangible, and artificial being, that mere legal entity, a corporation aggregate, is certainly not a citizen; and consequently, cannot sue or be sued in the courts of the United States, unless the rights of the members, in this respect, can be exercised in their corporate name."[165] This meant, when taken with the complete diversity requirement just announced in *Strawbridge*,[166] that a corporation could not sue if any of its "members" was a cocitizen of the defendant[167]—a circumstance that became increasingly likely with the growth of nationwide businesses.[168]

For this important conclusion Marshall gave neither precedent nor argument, and a later Court would argue that a corporation *was* a "citizen" in the relevant respects: it had power to contract and to sue, and it could be the victim or beneficiary of state court bias.[169] Moreover, elsewhere in the same opinion Marshall himself cited British

[160]9 U.S. (5 Cranch) 61, 61 (1809).

[161]*Id.*

[162]17 U.S. (4 Wheat.) 316 (1819). *See infra* chapter 6.

[163]22 U.S. (9 Wheat.) 737 (1824). *See infra* chapter 6.

[164]9 U.S. (5 Cranch) at 91.

[165]*Id.* at 86.

[166]*See supra* notes 154-56 and accompanying text.

[167]It had been so argued at 9 U.S. (5 Cranch) at 77, 83.

[168]It is not clear whether "members" referred to the shareholders, the officers, the directors, or all of them. *See* Comment, *Limited Partnerships and Federal Diversity Jurisdiction*, 45 U. CHI. L. REV. 384, 405-06 (1978); *see also* Rundle v. Delaware & Raritan Canal Co., 55 U.S. (14 How.) 79, 94 (1852 Term) (separate opinion of Catron, J.). Justice Washington read "members" to include all "corporators," and he lamented that *Deveaux* meant that

> very few corporations can enjoy the privilege of suing, or being sued, in the Courts of the United States, . . . since it can seldom happen, we presume, but that some of their members reside in other states than that in which the business of the corporate body is transacted, and in which the suit is brought.

Kirkpatrick v. White, 4 Wash. C.C. 595, 599-600 (C.C.D. Pa. 1826). Charles Warren, agreeing that *Deveaux* referred to shareholders, argued that "Marshall and everybody else knew" the allegation that the Bank's "company" were Pennsylvanians was " a pure fiction": "a majority of the stockholders of the Bank of the United States were British citizens and aliens or else citizens of other States than Pennsylvania . . . ." Warren, *Corporations and Diversity of Citizenship*, 19 VA. L. REV. 661, 666 (1933).

[169]Marshall v. Baltimore & O.R.R., 57 U.S. (16 How.) 314, 329 (1854); Louisville, C. & C.R.R. v. Letson, 43 U.S. (2 How.) 497, 558 (1844). See also the argument of counsel in a companion case to *Deveaux*:

> If there was a probability that an individual citizen of a state could influence the state courts in his favor, how much stronger is the probability that they could be influenced in favor of a

examples holding corporations to be "inhabitants" for assessment purposes without regard to the residence of their members.[170] Perhaps he thought the term "Citizen" required flesh and blood as a simple dictionary matter,[171] though later cases were to hold that corporations were "citizens" for a variety of statutory purposes[172] as well as "Person[s]" within such provisions as the due process clause.[173] Perhaps he was thinking ahead in light of his conclusion in *Hepburn v. Ellzey* that the Framers had used words consistently throughout the Constitution:[174] if a corporation was a "citizen" within article III, the privileges and immunities clause[175] might give foreign corporations an advantage by placing them "on a parity with individual citizens,"[176] "free of such supervision and control as the state might think it requisite to exercise over its own corporations."[177] In any event *Deveaux* did not long survive as a limit on

---

> powerful moneyed institution, which might be composed of the most influential characters in the state.

Hope Ins. Co. v. Boardman, 9 U.S. (5 Cranch) 57, 60 (1809) (Mr. Adams).

[170]9 U.S. (5 Cranch) at 88-90.

[171]*See* Marshall v. Baltimore & O.R.R., 57 U.S. (16 How.) 314, 351 (1854) (Campbell, J., dissenting); Rundle v. Delaware & Raritan Canal Co., 55 U.S. (14 How.) 79, 97-98 (1852 Term) (Daniel, J., dissenting); McGovney, *A Supreme Court Fiction*, 56 HARV. L. REV. 853, 874 (1943).

[172]*E.g.*, United States v. Northwestern Express Co., 164 U.S. 686 (1897) (compensation for property of "citizens" taken or destroyed by Indians).

[173]*E.g.*, Kentucky Fin. Corp. v. Paramount Auto Exch. Corp., 262 U.S. 544, 550 (1923) (construing U.S. CONST. amend. XIV, § 1).

[174]*See supra* note 143 and accompanying text. *But see* Green, *Corporations as Persons, Citizens, and Possessors of Liberty*, 94 U. PA. L. REV. 202, 205-06 (1946):

> As to each grant of power the question is whether corporations possess the characteristics that bring them within the purposes which the terms of the grant manifest intent to accomplish. That a corporation is neither a person nor a citizen within the meaning of a statute about making wills, voting at elections, or being naturalized, has little bearing on the question whether it is a person or a citizen within the meaning of a provision prescribing the jurisdiction of courts for the enforcement of rights which the corporation possesses and of duties which it owes.

[175]U.S. CONST. art. IV, § 2, para. 1.

[176]G. HENDERSON, THE POSITION OF FOREIGN CORPORATIONS IN AMERICAN CONSTITUTIONAL LAW 56-57 (1918).

[177]Green, *supra* note 174, at 228. *See* Bank of Augusta v. Earle, 38 U.S. (13 Pet.) 519, 586 (1839), *infra* chapter 7 (refusing to apply *Deveaux* to the privileges and immunities clause); Paul v. Virginia, 75 U.S. (8 Wall.) 168, 177-82 (1869) (holding a corporation not a "Citizen" within article IV). See also McGovney, *supra* note 171, at 888, arguing on the basis of *Bank of Augusta* that if, as the Court declared in Marshall v. Baltimore & O.R.R., 57 U.S. (16 How.) 314, 326 (1854), "the reason for diverse citizenship jurisdiction was to protect privileges given by Article IV . . . the conclusion should have been that it was not intended to include suits by or against corporations." Compare Chief Justice Taney's use of arguments based on the privileges and immunities clause to support the conclusion that blacks could not be "Citizens" for diversity purposes. Scott v. Sandford, 60 U.S. (19 How.) 393, 417-18, 422-23 (1857), *infra* chapter 8.

Counsel in a companion case to *Deveaux* had anticipated this problem and asserted that the term "Citizen" "has different meanings in different parts of the constitution." Hope Ins. Co. v. Boardman, 9 U.S. (5 Cranch) 57, 59 (1809) (Mr. Adams). In *Bank of Augusta* itself, the Court would in fact refuse to apply to the privileges and immunities clause *Deveaux*'s other conclusion that the transaction could be viewed as one by persons comprising the corporation: "[I]n that case, the court confined its decision, in express terms, to a question of jurisdiction . . . ." 38 U.S. (13 Pet.) at 585. *See also* G. HENDERSON, *supra* note 176, at 180-81; Green, *supra* note 174, at 230.

jurisdiction; within less than fifty years Marshall's successors were to treat the state of incorporation as decisive.[178]

What is often overlooked is that the limiting language of *Deveaux* was unnecessary to the result, because the Court *upheld* jurisdiction. Indeed in *Deveaux* itself no one had argued that the Bank was a citizen of any state, and it would have been difficult to do so because it was a federal corporation. As counsel had said, the issue was "whether, by becoming members of the corporation, the individuals who compose it lose, in their corporate affairs, those privileges which as individuals they possessed before?"[179] Marshall's answer, once again equating the statutory and the constitutional language, was persuasive: the reason for diversity jurisdiction was the apprehension that state courts might not "administer justice as impartially as those of the nation" to parties from outside the state,[180] and outsiders "are not less susceptible of these apprehensions . . . because they are allowed to sue by a corporate name."[181] The methodological contrast with cases like *Strawbridge* is noteworthy. Instead of stating his bare conclusion, Marshall reasoned convincingly from the assumed purpose of the diversity clause.[182]

Deveaux is interesting as well for the further insight it affords into Marshall's view of precedent. The Court had entertained diversity cases involving corporations in the past, and that fact was entitled to "much weight, as they show that this point neither

---

[178]*See* cases cited *supra* note 169; *infra* chapter 8. In Louisville, C. & C.R.R. v. Letson, 43 U.S. (2 How.) 497, 555 (1844), Justice Wayne said that Marshall himself had "repeatedly expressed regret" at the restrictive interpretations he had rendered in *Deveaux* and *Strawbridge*. Story wrote in 1844 that Marshall had come to think a corporation was a citizen and that "[t]his was always Judge Washington's opinion." Letter from Joseph Story to James Kent (Aug. 31, 1844), *reprinted in* 2 LIFE & LETTERS OF JOSEPH STORY 469 (W. Story ed. 1851). For doubts as to the accuracy of these reports, see McGovney, *supra* note 171, at 877-78 ("In another instance—and why not in this one?—Mr. Justice Story was a false reporter of the 'real opinion' of the deceased Chief Justice.") (citing New York v. Miln, 36 U.S. (11 Pet.) 102, 161 (1837), *infra* chapter 7). It is clear enough that Justice Washington "regret[ted]" that a corporation was not itself treated as a citizen, Kirkpatrick v. White, 4 Wash. C.C. 595, 599 (C.C.D. Pa. 1826), but it is less clear that he thought *Deveaux* had misinterpreted the law.

[179]9 U.S. (5 Cranch) at 79 (Mr. Harper). A companion case in which the defendant was described simply as a Rhode Island corporation was ordered dismissed on the authority of *Deveaux*. Hope Ins. Co. v. Boardman, 9 U.S. (5 Cranch) 57, 61 (1809).

[180]9 U.S. (5 Cranch) at 87. Marshall cited no authority to support this conclusion, but the possibility of local bias had been given as a reason for diversity jurisdiction both in THE FEDERALIST No. 80, *supra* note 29, at 476-78 (A. Hamilton), and in the ratifying conventions, *e.g.*, 3 ELLIOT'S DEBATES, *supra* note 42, at 533 (Mr. Madison), 4 *id.* at 167 (Mr. Davie of North Carolina). *See generally* Friendly, *The Historic Basis of Diversity Jurisdiction*, 41 HARV. L. REV. 483 (1928).

[181]9 U.S. (5 Cranch) at 87. This line of argument seems to suggest one reason he thought the corporation itself was not a citizen: the members were real parties in interest, and it was their citizenship rather than the place of incorporation that determined whether there was a risk of bias.

Justice Daniel was later to criticize this part of the *Deveaux* opinion on the ground that it ignored the legal personality of the corporation; the individual members were not parties. Rundle v. Delaware & Raritan Canal Co., 55 U.S. (14 How.) 79, 99-100 (1852 Term) (dissenting opinion). *But see* McGovney, *supra* note 171, at 867-69 (concluding that instances in which courts had pierced the corporate veil were "too numerous to permit anyone to say that resort by the Court to this way of thinking in solving the jurisdictional problem in the *Deveaux* case was wrong").

[182]9 U.S. (5 Cranch) at 89. The report reveals no dissent, but Justice Johnson, sitting on circuit below, had ruled there was no jurisdiction: "As a suit in right of a corporation can never be maintained by the individuals who compose it, . . . how is the citizenship of the individuals of the corporate body even to be brought into question . . . ?" 2 F. Cas. 692, 693 (No. 916) (C.C.D. Ga. 1808).

occurred to the bar or the bench."[183] Nevertheless, despite the argument that the Court had had a duty in those cases to raise jurisdictional problems on its own motion,[184] Marshall declined to treat them "as authority; for they were made without considering this particular point."[185] This seems to strike an appropriate middle course between his earlier contradictory treatment of similar precedents as either binding[186] or irrelevant.[187]

D. *Hodgson v. Bowerbank*

The plaintiffs were British citizens; the defendants were described as "late of the district of Maryland,"[188] but their present citizenship was not averred. Jurisdiction was challenged in the Supreme Court, and Marshall found it wanting: "Turn to the article of the constitution of the United States, for the statute cannot extend the jurisdiction beyond the limits of the constitution."[189]

The statute purported to give jurisdiction of "all" civil suits in which "an alien is a party,"[190] but article III mentions only those "between a state, or the citizens thereof, and foreign states, citizens or subjects."[191] To read *Hodgson* one might think the issue was one of first impression, but the Court had already cut the statute down to constitutional size nine years earlier in *Mossman v. Higginson*.[192] Today we would expect the Court to strengthen its conclusion by citing such a square precedent. But precedent, while not wholly foreign to Marshall's opinions, was seldom prominent there. Very likely the explanation for the omission is that the point was obvious and Marshall's resolution extemporaneous; it is not even labelled an opinion of the Court.[193] An alternative possibility is that he did not know the issue had previously been resolved, for he was not on the Court when *Mossman* was decided, and the indexing of decisions seems to have been considerably less thorough than it is today.[194]

The cases so far considered not only are related by subject matter; they also constitute nearly the entire constitutional output of the Court between 1801 and

---

[183]9 U.S. (5 Cranch) at 88.

[184]*Id*. at 70 (Mr. Binney).

[185]*Id*. at 88.

[186]*E.g., Ex parte* Bollman, 7 U.S. (3 Cranch) 159 (1805). *See supra* note 128 and accompanying text.

[187]*E.g.,* United States v. More, 8 U.S. (4 Cranch) 75 (1807). *See supra* notes 103-17 and accompanying text.

[188]9 U.S. (5 Cranch) 303, 303 (1809).

[189]*Id*. at 304.

[190]Judiciary Act of 1789, ch. 20, § 11, 1 Stat. 73, 78 (current version at 28 U.S.C. § 1332 (1976)).

[191]U.S. Const. art. III, § 2, para. 1.

[192]4 U.S. (4 Dall.) 12 (1800). *See supra* chapter 1 for discussion of the merits of the issue. Both Hart & Wechsler, *supra* note 41, at 417, and C. Wright, *supra* note 19, at 93 & n.10, declare that *Hodgson* held the alien-a-party provision unconstitutional. For the contrary view, see Mahoney, *A Historical Note on Hodgson v. Bowerbank*, 49 U. Chi. L. Rev. 725 (1982). It is clear that *Mossman*, at least, was based upon a narrow interpretation of the statute.

[193]*See* Mahoney, *supra* note 192, at 739.

[194]A perusal of J.G. Marvin, Legal Bibliography (Philadelphia 1847), discloses publication of digests of Supreme Court decisions by John Anthon in 1813-1816, by Supreme Court Reporter Henry Wheaton in

1810.[195] Only in *Marbury* and in *Deveaux* were there opinions of any length on the constitutional questions. *Deveaux* shows that Marshall could argue persuasively from constitutional purposes; *Marbury* illustrates among other things his tendency to conclude that the Constitution means what he would like it to mean. The other opinions demonstrate that during this period Marshall, like his predecessors, considered it unnecessary to devote much effort to explaining every constitutional decision. Several of his pronouncements can be characterized as cavalier. *Strawbridge* is conclusory; *Hepburn* is highly literalistic; *Bollman* resolved a critical ambiguity in the governing standard without acknowledging its existence. In some cases this nonchalance may have been related to the relative unimportance of the issue, but the immediate controversy in *Bollman* was of considerable political significance; one might have expected the Court to be more careful. Finally, these early cases are of considerable interest for their efforts to establish a doctrine of precedent, and in that regard they run the gamut from unquestioning adherence to legislative practice and judicial "acquiescence" in *Stuart* to Marshall's failure to invoke precedential support in *Marbury* or *Hodgson* and Johnson's frank avowal in *Bollman* that no judicial precedent is beyond correction.

1821 and 1829, and by Richard S. Coxe in 1829. All of these compilations appeared after *Hodgson*. I am indebted for this information to Richard L. Bowler, former reference librarian at the University of Chicago Law School. See also the complaint of William Cranch, in offering the first volume of his Reports, that "[m]uch of th[e] uncertainty of the law . . . may be attributed to the want of American reports." 5 U.S. (1 Cranch) i, iii (1803). The volume containing *Mossman* had finally been published in 1807.

[195]Four other decisions of this period deserve brief mention for the sake of completeness. Two dealt with federal jurisdiction. In Owings v. Norwood's Lessee, 9 U.S. (5 Cranch) 344, 344 (1809), Marshall reaffirmed that article III was a limitation on Congress's power by observing in dictum that section 25 of the Judiciary Act of 1789, ch. 20, § 25, 1 Stat. 73, 83-87 (current version at 28 U.S.C. § 1257 (1976)), could not extend jurisdiction beyond the cases enumerated in that article. He also held, without invoking the Constitution, that a litigant could not assert the rights of third parties. 9 U.S. (5 Cranch) at 348.

The second jurisdictional decision was United States v. Peters, 9 U.S. (5 Cranch) 115 (1809), a highly confusing opinion allowing an action against administrators of a state treasurer despite the eleventh amendment. This case was later relied on as establishing an important point with respect to sovereign immunity, but because of its cryptic obscurity it seems preferable to discuss it below in connection with the more comprehensible opinion in Osborn v. Bank of the United States, 22 U.S. (9 Wheat.) 738, 795 (1824). *See infra* chapter 4, note 1 and accompanying text.

Finally, there were two substantive decisions of considerable innate interest, though of little lasting significance, perhaps because of their cryptic style. United States v. Fisher, 6 U.S. (2 Cranch) 358, 395 (1805), prefigured McCulloch v. Maryland, 17 U.S. (4 Wheat.) 316 (1819), by giving a broad interpretation to the necessary and proper clause, U.S. CONST. art. I, § 1, cl. 18; this case is discussed with *McCulloch* in chapter 6 *infra*. The Flying Fish, 6 U.S. (2 Cranch) 170 (1804), anticipated the famous *Steel Seizure Case* (Youngstown Sheet & Tube Co. v. Sawyer, 343 U.S. 579 (1952)), in its bare conclusion that Congress might forbid the President to seize vessels as a means of law enforcement, notwithstanding the command in U.S. CONST. art. II, § 3, that he "take Care that the Laws be faithfully executed."

4

Later Jurisdictional Decisions

As shown in the preceding chapter, most of the constitutional work of the first decade of Marshall's tenure dealt with the powers of the federal courts. In the remaining years of this period the Court continued to define the limits of those powers; and three of its further decisions rank almost with *Marbury* as landmarks of federal jurisdiction.

I. REVIEW OF STATE COURTS

A. *Martin v. Hunter's Lessee*

Virginia claimed to have escheated land owned by an enemy alien. In an earlier opinion, the Supreme Court had held the land had not been taken before a 1794 treaty confirming British titles.[1] The state court refused to obey the Supreme Court's mandate, arguing that Congress had no power to authorize federal review of state decisions.[2] The Supreme Court, in 1816, reversed.[3]

Marshall, who had once appeared as counsel in the controversy and whose family had an interest in the lands,[4] did not sit; Story wrote the Court's lengthy opinion. He relied in part upon established practice, and with considerable force: review of state courts had been authorized by the First Congress, which contained "men who had acted a principal part in framing, supporting or opposing [the] constitution";[5] it had

[1]Fairfax's Devisee v. Hunter's Lessee, 11 U.S. (7 Cranch) 603, 625-27 (1813).
[2]Hunter v. Martin, 18 Va. (4 Munf.) 1, 7 (1813).
[3]14 U.S. (1 Wheat.) 304 (1816).
[4]For the background of the controversy, see 4 A. BEVERIDGE, *supra* introduction to part two, note 10, at 145-67; 2 W. CROSSKEY, *supra* chapter 3, note 28, at 785-817; G. HASKINS & H. JOHNSON, *supra* introduction to part two, note 23, at 357-65; 1 C. WARREN, *supra* introduction to part 2, note 22, at 442-53.
[5]14 U.S. (1 Wheat.) at 351. But see the opinion of Justice Roane in the court below:

> I had not expected that they would have been quoted, to prove it constitutional. Their opinion was already manifest, in the act itself, and it required the opinions of others, at least

been exercised for nearly thirty years without objection;[6] it had been avowed by friends and admitted by enemies of the proposed Constitution "both in and out of the state conventions"; it had even been unmistakably authorized by the relatively feeble Articles of Confederation.[7] In contrast to the opinion in *Stuart v. Laird*,[8] however, Story's opinion did not treat practice as decisive; in accord with the opinion in *Marbury v. Madison*,[9] he recognized the Court's obligation to decide the question on its merits.[10]

Story attempted to make hay out of the language of article III: federal judicial power extends to "all" cases arising under federal law and therefore includes those decided by state courts.[11] The Virginia court had anticipated this ploy and destroyed it: no one would hold the Supreme Court could review judgments of foreign courts interpreting federal law.[12]

More compelling was Story's argument that the purposes of article III required that its terms be read to permit Supreme Court review of state judgments. In the first place, "[t]he constitution has presumed . . . that state attachments, state prejudices, state jealousies, and state interests, might sometimes obstruct, or control, or be supposed to obstruct or control, the regular administration of justice."[13] Moreover,

> [j]udges of equal learning and integrity, in different states, might dif-
> ferently interpret the statute, or a treaty of the United States, or even the
> constitution itself: If there were no revising authority to control these
> jarring and discordant judgments, . . . the laws, the treaties and the

----

to corroborate and support it. . . . [L]ittle credit is certainly due to the construction of those, who were parties to the conflict . . . .

18 Va. (4 Munf.) at 28-29.

[6]14 U.S. (1 Wheat.) at 351-52. It had also, though Story did not say so, been acknowledged by the Virginia Republican and judge St. George Tucker in 1803. *See* 1 Tucker's Appendix to Blackstone, *supra* chapter 3, note 59, at 183-84.

[7]See 14 U.S. (1 Wheat.) at 345, invoking the provision in ARTICLES OF CONFEDERATION art. 9, para. 1, establishing "courts for receiving and determining, finally, appeals in all cases of captures": "It is remarkable, that no power was given to entertain *original* jurisdiction in such cases; and consequently, the appellate power (although not so expressed in terms) was altogether to be exercised in revising the decisions of state tribunals" (emphasis added). Not cited by Story was Penhallow v. Doane's Administrators, 3 U.S. (3 Dall.) 54, 107, 115-16 (1795), where the Court ordered enforcement of a decree of the capture court and individual Justices affirmed the constitutionality of its power over state court judgments. *Id.* at 119-20 (Cushing, J.). *See supra* chapter 2.

[8]5 U.S. (1 Cranch) 299 (1803); *see supra* chapter 3, notes 75-102 and accompanying text.

[9]5 U.S. (1 Cranch) 137, 154 (1803); *see supra* chapter 3, notes 12-74 and accompanying text.

[10]14 U.S. (1 Wheat.) at 323.

[11]*Id.* at 338-39 ("The appellate power is not limited by the terms of the third article to any particular courts. . . . It is the *case*, then, and not *the court*, that gives the jurisdiction.") (emphasis added). Hamilton had made the same point in THE FEDERALIST No. 82, *supra* chapter 3, note 29, at 493-94. Story did not cite him, though counsel had done so. 14 U.S. (1 Wheat.) at 313 (Mr. Jones). Spencer Roane in the court below had dismissed *The Federalist* as "a mere newspaper publication, written in the heat and hurry of the battle, . . . and with a view to ensure [the proposed Constitution's] ratification." 18 Va. (4 Munf.) at 27.

[12]18 Va. (4 Munf.) at 14 (Cabell, J.) ("But this argument proves too much, and what is utterly inadmissible. It would give appellate jurisdiction, as well over the courts of England or France, as over the state courts . . . .").

[13]14 U.S. (1 Wheat.) at 347.

constitution of the United States would be different, in different states.
. . . [T]he appellate jurisdiction must continue to be the only adequate
remedy for such evils.[14]

It was not enough, he continued, that plaintiffs with federal claims could be
authorized to sue in federal trial courts. Defendants had federal rights, too, which
the Constitution meant to protect.[15] Removal[16] was no answer because (contrary to
common sense and to Marshall's definition in *Marbury*[17]) it too was an exercise in
"appellate" jurisdiction.[18] Further, removal was an inadequate safeguard. "If state
courts should deny the constitutionality of the authority to remove suits from their
cognizance, in what manner could they be compelled to relinquish the jurisdiction?"[19] Perhaps there would be ways,[20] but the Court had long since rejected the
notion that the necessary and proper clause authorized only those means of carrying
out federal powers that were indispensable;[21] it should have sufficed that Supreme
Court review was, in the words Marshall was soon to use in *McCulloch v. Maryland*,[22]
an "appropriate" means "plainly adapted" to the assertion of federal judicial power
over federal question cases, and entirely in accord with the "spirit" of the
Constitution.[23]

This reasoning was fully adequate to sustain the Court's jurisdiction.[24] Yet Story

---

[14]*Id.* at 348. Rutledge had expressly stated these purposes in discussing the arising-under jurisdiction
during the Convention. *See infra* note 24. *See also* 4 ELLIOT's DEBATES, *supra* chapter 3, note 42, at 166
(Mr. Davie): "A government would be *felo de se* to put the execution of its laws under the command of any
other body."

[15]14 U.S. (1 Wheat.) at 348-49.

[16]Removal had been invoked by the Virginia court in answer to the argument based on article III's
purposes. *See* 18 Va. (4 Munf.) at 15-16 (Cabell, J.).

[17]5 U.S. (1 Cranch) 137, 175 (1803) ("It is the essential criterion of appellate jurisdiction, that it revises
and corrects the proceedings in a cause already instituted, and does not create that cause."). In line with
Marshall's reference to causes "already instituted" elsewhere, Story (without citing *Marbury*) noted that
removal "presupposes an exercise of original jurisdiction to have attached elsewhere." 14 U.S. (1 Wheat.)
at 349. Yet removal before state court decision would not appear to "revise" or "correct" anything the
state court had done, and earlier decisions had emphasized that this was the governing consideration. *See
Ex parte* Bollman, 8 U.S. (4 Cranch) 75, 93, 101 (1807); *supra* chapter 3, notes 118-32 and accompanying
text.

[18]14 U.S. (1 Wheat.) at 349-50.

[19]*Id.* at 350.

[20]One is tempted to say by enjoining the state court plaintiff from proceeding. By the time the state
court had exhibited its defiance of the removal order by asserting its jurisdiction, however, the federal
injunctive proceeding might well be deemed appellate under Ex parte *Bollman* on the ground that it
entailed review of the State's jurisdictional decision. *See supra* chapter 3, notes 118-32 and accompanying
text.

[21]United States v. Fisher, 6 U.S. (2 Cranch) 358 (1805). *See supra* chapter 3, note 195.

[22]17 U.S. (4 Wheat.) 316 (1819). *See infra* chapter 6.

[23]*Id.* at 421. Justice Johnson, who had dissented on the merits when *Martin* was first before the Court,
11 U.S. (7 Cranch) at 628-32, this time wrote a long concurrence that emphasized that the Court was not
issuing a mandatory order to the state court, but added little to Story's reasoning, 14 U.S. (1 Wheat.) at
362-82.

[24]Moreover, as Professor Gunther has noted, "an expectation of Supreme Court review of state court
judgments runs through the Constitutional Convention debates." G. GUNTHER, *supra* introduction to part
two, note 25, at 36. When Rutledge moved to eliminate a provision establishing inferior federal courts, he
did so with the argument that "the right of appeal to the supreme national tribunal" was "sufficient to

began his opinion with the gratuitous contention that Congress was not only permitted but *required* to authorize Supreme Court review of state courts. Article III, he
argued, was mandatory, for it provided that the judicial power *"shall* extend to *all*
Cases"* arising under federal law and that it *"shall* be vested" in federal courts.[25] The
power to make "Exceptions" to the Supreme Court's appellate jurisdiction, he
acknowledged, gave Congress considerable discretion as to *which* federal courts
should be given jurisdiction; but "the whole judicial power of the United States
should be, at all times, vested, either in an original or appellate form, in some courts
created under its authority."[26] Federal questions were bound to arise in state court
proceedings, and the supremacy clause required state courts to decide them; the
federal power could reach these cases only by appellate review.[27] In addition, he
argued, Congress was required to create inferior federal courts to hear any article III
cases over which neither the Supreme Court nor a state court had original jurisdiction, for the federal judicial power would otherwise not reach these cases at all.[28]

None of this was necessary to the result, for Congress *had* conferred appellate
jurisdiction on the Supreme Court, and the necessity of creating district courts had
nothing to do with the case at all. Story's thesis that the entire judicial power must be
vested somewhere has not been very popular, though it was picked up as an
alternative holding by one modern court of appeals.[29] It does have the virtue of
reconciling all the apparently inconsistent words of article III, but it was contrary to
Supreme Court precedent,[30] which Story did not cite, as well as to consistent

secure the national rights & uniformity of Judgmts''; Madison, opposing the motion, did not dispute the
availability of Supreme Court review, but argued it was an inadequate remedy. 1 CONVENTION RECORDS,
supra chapter 3, note 42, at 124.

[25]14 U.S. (1 Wheat.) at 331 (quoting U.S. CONST. art. III, § 2, para. 1) (emphasis added).

[26]*Id.*

[27]*Id.* at 341-42.

[28]*Id.* at 330-31. Story spoke in particular of "that jurisdiction which, under the constitution, is
exclusively vested in the United States," *id.* at 331, and elsewhere he suggested that Congress could not
allow criminal cases or some maritime cases to be decided by state courts, *id.* at 336-37. *The Federalist* had
flatly taken the position that the Constitution did not make federal jurisdiction exclusive, THE FEDERALIST
No. 82, *supra* chapter 3, note 29, at 492 (A. Hamilton), and Congress had acted on that assumption in
1789, Judiciary Act of 1789, ch. 20, § 11, 1 Stat. 73, 78 (current version at 28 U.S.C § 1332(a) (1976)). With
respect to criminal cases, Story's dictum was repudiated by Justice Washington's opinion in Houston v.
Moore, 18 U.S. (5 Wheat.) 1, 12 (1820); *see infra* notes 115-32 and accompanying text. For elaboration of
Story's views on the exclusivity of federal admiralty power, see 3 J. STORY, *supra* chapter 3, note 82, at
533-34 n.3 (rejecting contemporary views that federal jurisdiction was exclusive even in cases over which
common law courts had previously exercised concurrent authority).

[29]Eisentrager v. Forrestal, 174 F.2d 961, 966 (D.C. Cir. 1949). *See also* 1 W. CROSSKEY, *supra* chapter 3,
note 28, at 610-18.

[30]Turner v. Bank of N. Am., 4 U.S. (4 Dall.) 8 (1799) (upholding the assignee clause described *infra*
note 31). *See supra* chapter 1.

See also United States v. Hudson, 11 U.S. (7 Cranch) 32, 33 (1812) (Johnson, J.) (denying the power of
federal courts to punish common law crimes: "[T]he power which Congress possess to create courts of
inferior jurisdiction, necessarily implies the power to limit the jurisdiction of those courts to particular
objects . . . ."). Whether there was really an absence of jurisdiction in *Hudson* is not so clear, for the
Judiciary Act of 1789 gave the circuit courts "cognizance of all crimes and offences cognizable under the
authority of the United States." Ch. 20, § 11, 1 Stat. 73, 79 (repealed 1911). Justice Story was to argue even
after *Hudson* that this provision both gave the courts jurisdiction over nonstatutory crimes and empowered them to define those crimes according to the common law. United States v. Coolidge, 25 F. Cas. 619
(No. 14,857) (C.C.D. Mass. 1813). *Hudson*, not mentioning section 11, had appeared to deny both

congressional practice,[31] which in the same opinion he insisted was entitled to considerable deference.[32] Finally, the strongest argument against giving a natural reading to the ostensibly unlimited discretion of Congress to limit federal jurisdiction is *Marbury*'s principle that the courts were intended to enforce constitutional limits on legislative power.[33] Story's interpretation poorly comports with that principle, for it outlaws such minor caseload adjustments as the jurisdictional amount while allowing Congress to evade any substantial check by vesting sole power over important constitutional questions in a single lower court selected for the complaisance of its judges.[34]

The contrast between the lengthy and intricate *Martin* opinion and the numerous

---

jurisdiction and lawmaking authority. *See* 11 U.S. (7 Cranch) at 34 ("The legislative authority of the Union must First make an act a crime, affix a punishment to it, and declare the court that shall have jurisdiction of the offence.").

Although *Hudson* was a libel case, *Coolidge* was maritime, and Story distinguished *Hudson* by arguing that in admiralty cases it was clear that judge-made law had always been acceptable. 25 F. Cas. at 621. In the Supreme Court, however, the government declined to make this argument, and the Court held that under the circumstances it would follow *Hudson*. United States v. Coolidge, 14 U:S. (1 Wheat.) 415, 416-17 (1816) (Johnson, J.). For approval of Story's distinction, see P. DuPonceau, A Dissertation on the Nature and Extent of the Jurisdiction of the Courts of the United States 9-11 (Philadelphia 1824 & reprint 1972).

Although *Hudson* and *Coolidge* seem to have been based upon a lack of jurisdiction, Johnson's additional suggestion that only Congress may create substantive offenses was an important precursor of Erie R.R v. Tompkins, 304 U.S. 64 (1938), which held the creation of federal common law in diversity cases in the absence of statutory authorization an invasion of "rights . . . reserved by the Constitution to the several states," *id*. at 80. It is interesting that Johnson stated in *Hudson* that he spoke for "the majority of this court," 11 U.S. (7 Cranch) at 33, for no dissent was recorded.

[31]The Supreme Court has never had appellate power over state court judgments in diversity cases, yet the Judiciary Act of 1789 excluded many such cases from inferior federal courts as well by the assignee clause, the jurisdictional amount, and the requirement that one party be a citizen of the forum state. Ch. 20, § 11, 1 Stat. 73, 78-79 (current provisions at 28 U.S.C. §§ 1332, 1359 (1976)). Story did suggest that diversity cases might be distingushable, despite the mandatory "shall," because in extending judicial power to them article III omitted the word "all." 14 U.S. (1 Wheat.) at 333-36. *Contra*, 1 W. Crosskey, *supra* chapter 3, note 28, at 614-15. Yet even with respect to federal question cases the Judiciary Act of 1789 failed this test, for it created no federal question jurisdiction in federal trial courts, and Supreme Court review was limited among other things to cases in which the state court had denied a federal right. Ch. 20, § 25, 1 Stat. 73, 85 (current provisions at 28 U.S.C. §§ 1257, 1331 (1976)).

[32]*See supra* note 5 and accompanying text.

[33]*See supra* chapter 3, notes 68-73 and accompanying text.

[34]The final question confronted in *Martin* was whether the Court had jurisdiction not only to construe the treaty but also to determine whether escheat had been accomplished before the treaty took effect. It held it had: the statute gave it power to decide upon the "title" claimed under federal law, and a "preliminary inquiry" into the title was unavoidable before the Court could decide whether it was protected by the treaty. 14 U.S. (1 Wheat.) at 358. This argument seems disingenuous. As a matter of logic, the state court's threshold determination of its own law could certainly have been accepted, and the Court was later to hold that the purposes of uniformity and protection of federal rights, which *Martin* had identified as underlying article III, did not generally require the Supreme Court to review state law questions in state court cases. Murdock v. City of Memphis, 87 U.S. (20 Wall.) 590, 621 (1875). Yet Story identified a pressing reason why those purposes did so require whenever a state law finding was a precondition to upholding a federal right: absent the power to review such determinations, the appellate jurisdiction could be "evaded at pleasure." 14 U.S. (1 Wheat.) at 357. *See* 1 W. Crosskey, *supra* chapter 3, note 28, at 615; 2 *id*. at 809-12 (arguing that as a matter of statutory construction Story's interpretation was questionable but that Congress's attempt to limit the Court to the decision of federal questions was unconstitutional).

curt and conclusory Marshall pronouncements previously considered is striking, and it may lead us to wish Story had been allowed to write more constitutional opinions. For apart from Story's strained excursion into the question whether Congress could *refuse* to grant jurisdiction (which is reminiscent of Marshall's excesses in *Marbury*), *Martin* is in many respects both a model opinion and a very modern one. It takes the constitutional question seriously, even though the answer may not be difficult; it marshalls convincing arguments based upon the purposes of the provision it is construing; and it supports them with a balanced and persuasive use of historical practice.

Differences in style between Marshall and Story are confirmed by opinions in other cases,[35] but they do not provide a complete explanation of the contrast between *Martin* and the early Marshall opinions. For one thing, Story could be cavalier and conclusory himself, as we shall soon see.[36] For another, *Martin*, like *Marbury*, was a case of considerable political significance; it was important for the Court to write a real explanation. Finally, constitutional opinion writing in general had undergone a marked change since Marshall's early opinions. The extensive *Martin* opinion, while more persuasive than many, was characteristic of a new style that Marshall himself had adopted in the contract clause cases beginning in 1810.[37]

B. *Cohens v. Virginia*

Convicted in state court for selling lottery tickets in Virginia, the brothers Cohen defended on the basis of an Act of Congress authorizing the local government of the District of Columbia to establish a lottery. Affirming on the ground that the law did not purport to authorize ticket sales outside the District,[38] Marshall in 1821 sustained the Court's appellate jurisdiction over a variety of interesting constitutional objections.[39]

[35]Compare the opinions of the two Justices in Trustees of Dartmouth College v. Woodward, 17 U.S. (4 Wheat.) 518, 624-54 (1819) (Marshall, C.J.), *id.* at 661-713 (Story, J.), *discussed in infra* chapter 5.

[36]*See, e.g., infra* notes 152-74 and accompanying text (discussing *The Thomas Jefferson*).

[37]*See infra* chapter 5. No doubt this change in style had something to do with the increased importance of the cases that reached the Court after 1810. Although there were to be sure continuing examples of perfunctory disposition of constitutional questions, that was no longer the prevailing mode after 1810.

For the suggestion that Marshall may not have been "as remote from the [*Martin*] cases as his self-disqualification suggests," see G. DUNNE, JUSTICE JOSEPH STORY AND THE RISE OF THE SUPREME COURT 135-36 (1970) (concluding that "the authorship seems a joint one"); White, *The Working Life of the Marshall Court, 1815-1835*, 70 VA. L. REV. 1, 11-20 (1984).

[38]19 U.S. (6 Wheat.) 264, 440-48 (1821). In reaching this conclusion Marshall announced an important rule of statutory construction based on concerns of federalism: "To interfere with the penal laws of a state, where they are not levelled against the legitimate powers of the Union, but have for their sole object the internal government of the country, is a very serious measure, which congress cannot be supposed to adopt lightly or inconsiderately." *Id.* at 443. *Cf.* United States v. Bass, 404 U.S. 336, 349 (1971) ("Unless Congress conveys its purpose clearly, it will not be deemed to have significantly changed the federal-state balance.").

[39]In passing on its jurisdiction the Court also held, essentially on the basis of the constitutional text alone, that an Act of Congress passed pursuant to the power "to exercise exclusive Legislation" over the District of Columbia, U.S. CONST. art. I, § 8, cl. 17, was a "law[ ] of the United States" for purposes of both section 25 of the Judiciary Act of 1789, ch. 20, § 25, 1 Stat. 73, 85 (current version at 28 U.S.C. § 1257

Marshall began, as in *Marbury v. Madison*, by predisposing the reader to his result. Assuming that the state court had denied a federal right, Marshall argued that Virginia was claiming that "it is not in the power of the government to apply a corrective . . . [;] that the nation does not possess a department capable of restraining, peaceably, and by authority of law, any attempts which may be made, by a part, against the legitimate powers of the whole."[40] Surely the Constitution was not so defective as to provide no remedy for its own violation.[41] It remained only to find pegs in the constitutional text on which to hang the foregoing conclusion.

(1976)), and the supremacy clause, U.S. CONST. art. VI, para. 2. Neither point was obvious. Indeed, the Court was to hold the contrary in the context of the appealability of the judgment of a District of Columbia court in Key v. Doyle, 434 U.S. 59, 67-68 (1977); and Marshall chose not to refer to earlier authority on the status of the District, *see supra* chapter 3, notes 103-17, 137-51, and accompanying text (discussing *United States v. More* and *Hepburn v. Ellzey*); Loughborough v. Blake, 18 U.S. (5 Wheat.) 317 (1820), *infra* chapter 6. Marshall ignored completely the further argument that the case arose not under the statute authorizing the local legislature to create a lottery but under the local legislation actually doing so. 19 U.S. (6 Wheat.) at 292-93 (Mr. Barbour). *Cf. Ex parte* Bransford, 310 U.S. 354, 359 (1940) (attack on administrative action taken pursuant to statute not attack on "statute" for purposes of three-judge court requirement).

It was in the context of whether laws passed under the District power were "laws of the United States" that Marshall chose to declare, largely on the basis of examples derived from statute, that a law passed under that power could be made to "operate without the district" if that was "necessary to its complete and effectual execution." 19 U.S. (6 Wheat.) at 426-29. The relevance of this conclusion to the jurisdictional issue was tangential (counsel had argued that a law applicable only to the District was not a "law[ ] of the United States," *id.* at 297), and the Court's finding on the merits that Congress had not attempted to authorize ticket sales in Virginia made it unnecessary to decide whether it could constitutionally have done so. The question of the extraterritorial reach of the District of Columbia power was to be debated again in National Mut. Ins. Co. v. Tidewater Transfer Co., 337 U.S. 582 (1949).

[40]19 U.S. (6 Wheat.) at 377.

[41]Marshall also argued that Virginia's position "would prostrate . . . the government and its laws at the feet of every state in the Union," *id.* at 385, and that "[n]o government ought to be so defective in its organization, as not to contain within itself, the means of securing the execution of its own laws," *id.* at 387. Marshall's remarks about the relevance of what he termed the "mischievous consequences" of Virginia's position are of interest:

> We do not mean to say, that the jurisdiction of the courts of the Union should be construed to be co-extensive with the legislative, merely because it is fit that it should be so; but we mean to say, that this fitness furnishes an argument in construing the constitution, which ought never to be overlooked, and which is most especially entitled to consideration, when we are inquiring, whether the words of the instrument which purport to establish this principle, shall be contracted for the purpose of destroying it.

Id. at 384-85. Compare the treatment of a similar argument from mischievous consequences in Hepburn v. Ellzey, 6 U.S. (2 Cranch) 445, 453 (1805), *discussed supra in* chapter 3, notes 146-50 and accompanying text.

The importance of the question in *Cohens* for the balance of federal-state power was recognized by John C. Calhoun, the high priest of states' rights, who placed a high priority on the repeal of section 25: "If the appellate power from the State courts to the United States court provided for by the 25th Sec. did not exist, the practical consequence would be, that each government would have a negative on the other . . . ." Letter from John C. Calhoun to Littleton W. Tazewell (Aug. 25, 1827), *quoted in* G. GÜNTHER, *supra* introduction to part two, note 25, at 46 n.t. Although this observation supports Marshall's conclusion that a contrary result in *Cohens* would have imperiled the vitality of the central government, it does not prove he was right in upholding jurisdiction. For as Spencer Roane had said in the *Martin* controversy, "there is a Charybdis to be avoided, as well as a Scylla; . . . a centripetal, as well as a centrifugal principle, exists in the government." Hunter v. Martin, 18 Va. (4 Munf.) 1, 26 (1815). Indeed

One of Virginia's principal arguments was that the appellate jurisdiction extended only to cases coming from lower federal courts.[42] This contention had been rejected five years earlier after exhaustive discussion in *Martin v. Hunter's Lessee.*[43] It was remarkable that the state was prepared to devote substantial efforts to rearguing the issue,[44] and more remarkable still that Marshall took it seriously. Rather than rejecting the argument summarily with a reference to *Martin*, he wrote ten pages retracing *Martin's* reasoning, without attribution or noticeable improvement, adding in the last sentence of the section that further observations were unnecessary "because the subject was fully discussed and exhausted in the case of *Martin v. Hunter.*"[45] This might look like a slap at the faithful Story, whose masterwork was reduced to an offhand reference; but, as Marshall was wont to treat his own precedents the same way,[46] it seems rather a commentary on his general disdain for reliance on authority.

One significant respect in which *Cohens* differed from *Martin*, however, was that it was a criminal proceeding, and Virginia had argued that the article III grant of power over "cases, in Law and Equity"[47] limited the jurisdiction to civil matters.[48] The words certainly did not compel this conclusion, and, as Marshall showed in responding to a different argument, the article's purpose of protecting federal rights was equally applicable to criminal and civil cases.[49] It is noteworthy, however, that while Marshall devoted ten pages to an issue foreclosed by precedent, he did not respond at all to the new argument that criminal cases were outside the federal question power.

---

events have proved him dead right, and there is as much reason to think the Framers would have been distressed by the destruction of state rights as by the crippling of federal power. For the view that the *Cohens* opinion was a response to the secession threat raised in debates over the Missouri Compromise, see 4 A. BEVERIDGE, *supra* introduction to part two, note 10, at 340-66, quoting, among other things, a letter from Marshall to Story (July 13, 1821): "'The attack upon the judiciary is in fact an attack upon the union.'" *Id.* at 365.

[42]19 U.S. (6 Wheat.) at 312-29 (Mr. Smyth). Barbour, also arguing for the state, noted his continuing disagreement with *Martin* but forbore to discuss it because "that question had been solemnly decided . . . by this Court . . . ." *Id.* at 310 n.(a).

[43]14 U.S. (1 Wheat.) 304, 323-52 (1816); *see supra* notes 3-23 and accompanying text.

[44]For a description of the vociferous political agitation in Virginia against the assertion of jurisdiction in *Cohens*, see 1 C. WARREN, *supra* introduction to part two, note 22, at 547-52.

[45]19 U.S. (6 Wheat.) at 413-23.

[46]See, e.g., Trustees of Dartmouth College v. Woodward, 17 U.S. (4 Wheat.) 518 (1819), and McCulloch v. Maryland, 17 U.S. (4 Wheat.) 316 (1819), *discussed in infra* chapters 5 and 6.

[47]U.S. CONST. art. III, § 2, para. 1.

[48]19 U.S. (6 Wheat.) at 321-23 (Mr. Smyth). The Court was later to hold, as Justice Iredell had already suggested in Chisholm v. Georgia, 2 U.S. (2 Dall.) 419, 431-32 (1793), that its original jurisdiction over "Controversies . . . between a State and Citizens of another State," U.S. CONST. art. III, § 2, para. 1, was limited to civil cases, in reliance on the tradition that "'[t]he courts of no country execute the penal laws of another,'" Wisconsin v. Pelican Ins. Co, 127 U.S. 265, 290 (1888) (quoting Marshall's opinion in The Antelope, 23 U.S. (10 Wheat.) 66, 123 (1825)). Indeed, Marshall hinted at this conclusion in *Cohens*, 19 U.S. (6 Wheat.) at 398-99; he did not explain why it was not equally true of "Cases . . . arising under" federal law. St. George Tucker had suggested in 1803 a textual basis for the distinction: although "[t]he word *cases* . . . comprehends . . . all cases, whether civil or criminal, . . . I do not recollect ever to have heard the expression, *criminal controversy.*" 1 Tucker's Appendix to Blackstone, *supra* chapter 3, note 59, at 420 (emphasis in original).

[49]*See infra* notes 54-55 and accompanying text.

Marshall did address at great length new arguments based upon the fact that in *Cohens*, in contrast to *Martin*, the state was a party. The first contention was that this fact deprived the federal courts of jurisdiction altogether because "a sovereign independent state is not suable, except by its own consent."[50] The simple answer would have been that nobody was suing Virginia; Virginia was suing the Cohens, and sovereign immunity had never meant that persons charged with crime could not defend themselves by appealing.[51] Never one to take the easy road if he could establish a broad principle instead, Marshall gave a much more controversial answer with implications far transcending the case: "[T]he judicial power, as originally given, extends to all cases arising under the constitution or a law of the United States, whoever may be the parties."[52] Far from excepting cases to which a state was a party, Marshall argued, the words of article III included "all" federal question cases.[53] Other clauses of the same article explicitly extended the judicial power to many controversies to which a state was a party;[54] review of "cases where a state shall prosecute an individual who claims the protection of an act of congress" was necessary to "the preservation of the constitution and laws of the United States."[55]

Marshall's broad conclusion that article III embraced "all" federal question cases and his characterization of the issue as one of sovereign immunity suggest he may have been taking a case in which a state was plaintiff as the occasion for asserting that a state could be made a defendant as well.[56] His reasoning paralleled that employed in *Chisholm v. Georgia*,[57] which typically he did not cite, where the Court had held that article III's provision for jurisdiction over "controversies . . . between a State and Citizens of another State"[58] included those in which the state was the defendant.[59] One might have thought the nation's outraged reversal of *Chisholm* by constitutional amendment would have made for greater caution in extending its repudiated principles to a clause that did not expressly refer to cases in which a state was a party,[60] or at

[50]19 U.S. (6 Wheat.) at 380. Marshall was accurately restating the argument of counsel. *See id.* at 302-09 (Mr. Barbour); *id.* at 315 (Mr. Smyth).

[51]*See* Governor of Georgia v. Madrazo, 26 U.S. (1 Pet.) 110, 131 (1828) (Johnson, J., dissenting) ("In England, the king cannot be sued, yet he is daily brought before the appellate court, as a defendant in error. . . . The thing is unavoidable—it is incident to the right of appeal."). Counsel had so argued in *Cohens*. 19 U.S. (6 Wheat.) at 350 (Mr. Ogden); *id.* at 366-67 (Mr. Pinkney). *See also infra* note 98.

[52]19 U.S. (6 Wheat.) at 392.

[53]*Id.* at 382.

[54]*Id.* at 383. This fact, of course, had been used by Virginia as an argument against jurisdiction: when the Framers meant to extend judicial power to cases involving states, they did so expressly. *Id.* at 303 (Mr. Barbour).

[55]*Id.* at 387, 391.

[56]At another point, Marshall seemed to concede that a citizen could not sue his own state to recover a tax unconstitutionally levied on exports, but his evident reason was that such a case might arise under an implied assumpsit rather than under the Constitution. *Id.* at 402-03. See *infra* chapter 12, discussing the *Virginia Coupon Cases*. He did not seem to say that the state was immune from suit.

[57]2 U.S. (2 Dall.) 419 (1793).

[58]U.S. CONST. art. III, § 2, para. 1.

[59]2 U.S. (2 Dall.) 450-51 (Blair, J.); *id.* at 465-66 (Wilson, J.); *id.* at 467-68 (Cushing, J.); *id.* at 475-77 (Jay, C.J.). Like *Chisholm*, *Cohens* ignored both the tradition of sovereign immunity that formed the backdrop of the Constitution and the explicit assurances of several prominent Framers that the Constitution respected that tradition. *See supra* chapter 1.

[60]*See* 19 U.S. (6 Wheat.) at 306-07 (Mr. Barbour) (arguing that the reason the eleventh amendment applied only to suits by aliens or citizens of other states was "that it was only to them that the privilege of

least would have restrained the Court from applying those principles gratuitously to a case in which the state was not a defendant.[61]

Having found the case within article III, Marshall held it was not forbidden by the eleventh amendment, which excluded from the judicial power "any suit in law or equity, commenced or prosecuted against one of the United States by Citizens of another State." Once again there was an obvious answer, and this time Marshall gave it: there was no allegation that the Cohens were citizens of another state, domestic or foreign.[62] But Marshall gave this answer only after he had devoted six pages to an alternative ground that, while convincing, was somewhat less obvious. This time the unnecessarily broad ground was the one that Marshall had disdained in connection with article III: the eleventh amendment did not apply because the Cohens had been defendants, not plaintiffs, below.[63] The writ of error was not an independent "suit" but "a continuation of the same suit, . . . not for the purpose of asserting any claim against the state, but for the purpose of asserting a constitutional defence against a claim made by a state."[64]

It was further contended that, if the Supreme Court could exercise jurisdiction at all, that jurisdiction must be original rather than appellate, for article III provides that the Court's jurisdiction shall be original in "all Cases affecting Ambassadors . . . and those in which a State shall be Party."[65] Marshall had two answers for this argument as well, though one would have sufficed. The first required the embarrassment of retracting much of the reasoning he had used in *Marbury v. Madison*; as noted in connection with that case,[66] he demonstrated in *Cohens* that the Framers

---

being parties in a controversy with a state, had been extended in the text of the Constitution"). The explicit reference to states in the applicable provision of article III had been a principal basis of the *Chisholm* decision.

[61]The implication in *Cohens* that an unconsenting state could be sued in a federal question case was repudiated in Hans v. Louisiana, 134 U.S. 1 (1890).

At one point in the *Cohens* opinion Marshall announced the "universally received opinion . . . that no suit can be commenced or prosecuted against the United States." 19 U.S. (6 Wheat.) at 411-12. This dictum was cited as establishing the sovereign immunity of the United States by both 3 J. STORY, *supra* chapter 3, note 82, at 538, and 1 J. KENT, COMMENTARIES ON AMERICAN LAW 297 n.d (4th ed. New York 1840) (1st ed. New York 1826). Yet Marshall seems to have meant only that there was no statutory basis for jurisdiction, because he followed the quoted language with the statement "that the judiciary act does not authorize such suits." 19 U.S. (6 Wheat.) at 412. *See* HART & WECHSLER, *supra* chapter 3, note 14, at 1340. On the immunity question, conflicting inferences can be drawn from the statements elsewhere in *Cohens* that "a sovereign independent state is not suable, except by its own consent," *id.* at 380, and that federal question cases are cognizable "whoever may be the parties," *id.* at 383. Federal immunity had earlier been suggested by two Justices in Chisholm v. Georgia, 2 U.S. (2 Dall.) 419, 469 (Cushing, J.); *id.* at 478 (Jay, C.J.). *See supra* chapter 1.

[62]19 U.S. (6 Wheat.) at 412. Marshall treated the case as one between the state and its own citizens, *e.g., id.* at 378, and counsel for the state declared that the Cohens were Virginia citizens, *id.* at 303.

[63]*Id.* at 406-12.

[64]*Id.* at 408-09. Rejecting the argument that the amendment's reference to cases "prosecuted" as well as "commenced" included proceedings to review suits brought by states, Marshall construed it to embrace original complaints against states already pending when the amendment took effect, *id.* at 408, as effectively held in Hollingsworth v. Virginia, 3 U.S. (3 Dall.) 378, 381 (1798), which he did not cite. *See supra* chapter 1.

[65]U.S. CONST. art. III, § 2, para. 2.

[66]*See supra* chapter 3, notes 24-31 and accompanying text.

could hardly have meant to prohibit Congress from giving appellate jurisdiction where the Constitution provided for original, and he left the *Marbury* holding essentially bereft of support.[67] His second basis for rejecting the original jurisdiction argument was that the case was not within the original jurisdiction at all. Jurisdiction was original not whenever a state was a party, but only in "those cases in which jurisdiction is given, because a state is a party"—that is, when the opposing party was another state, a foreign state, or one of its citizens.[68]

This is not the most natural reading of the original jurisdiction clause, but it is not implausible. Marshall buttressed it with a rather persuasive argument based upon the practicalities of litigation. Federal questions often arise, as in *Cohens* itself, only after commencement of suits over which the Supreme Court had no jurisdiction at the outset. To deny appellate jurisdiction in such a case would be to deny the Court's jurisdiction altogether; it "would be to construe a clause, dividing the power of the supreme court, in such a manner, as in a considerable degree to defeat the power itself."[69]

Implicit in this line of argument was yet another important interpretation of article III, which Marshall expressly affirmed elsewhere in the opinion in response to a vague suggestion of counsel: because a case "consists of the right of the one party, as well as of the other," a case "arise[s] under the constitution or a law of the United States, whenever its correct decision depends on the construction of either."[70] Because the point had not been challenged directly, perhaps Marshall may be forgiven for stating only the bald conclusion. That the point was not obvious is illustrated by the flatly contrary rule the Court has long followed in interpreting the same language in the statute providing for district court jurisdiction.[71] The purposes of article III to unify and enforce federal law, emphasized both in *Martin*[72] and

---

[67]19 U.S. (6 Wheat.) at 394-402. If Congress could not give the Court appellate jurisdiction of cases termed original by article III, he argued, the Court could not prevent a state court from exercising jurisdiction of suits against ambassadors, which were within its exclusive original jurisdiction; and "a clause inserted for the purpose of excluding the jurisdiction of all other courts than this, in a particular case, would have the effect of excluding the jurisdiction of this court, in that very case . . . ." *Id.* at 397.

Marshall's observations on the weight to be given dicta are instructive: "[G]eneral expressions" that "go beyond the case . . . may be respected, but ought not to control the judgment in a subsequent suit" because, although "[t]he question actually before the court is investigated with care," the bearing on other cases of "[o]ther principles which may serve to illustrate it . . . is seldom completely investigated." *Id.* at 399-400.

[68]*Id.* at 393-94. The Court's later decision to entertain original jurisdiction in a controversy between the United States and a state, United States v. Texas, 143 U.S. 621, 643-45 (1892), is inconsistent with this reasoning.

[69]19 U.S. (6 Wheat.) at 394. In part this argument seems to rest upon Justice Story's questionable position that removal before state court decision would be an exercise of appellate jurisdiction, *see supra* notes 16-18 and accompanying text, but it has force at least whenever federal questions arise for the first time in a state appellate court.

[70]19 U.S. (6 Wheat.) at 379.

[71]*E.g.*, Louisville & N.R.R. v. Mottley, 211 U.S. 149, 152 (1908) ("[A] suit arises under the Constitution and laws of the United States only when the plaintiff's statement of his own cause of action shows that it is based upon those laws or that Constitution.").

[72]*See supra* notes 13-14 and accompanying text.

elsewhere in *Cohens*,[73] certainly support Marshall's result,[74] but one wishes the Framers had adopted a more descriptive reference.[75]

Cohens showed that the new trend toward long opinions was not confined to Story. It also displayed many of the same qualities Marshall had exhibited in *Marbury*, his most extensive previous jurisdictional opinion: inattention to precedent, heavy emphasis on the intolerable consequences of a contrary decision, and insistence on reaching out for issues not necessarily presented. The strength of *Cohens*, like that of *Marbury*, lies in convincing the reader that the Framers were too wise and too patriotic to have created an imperfect Constitution.[76]

II. Osborn v. Bank of the United States

In defiance of square Supreme Court precedent,[77] Ohio assessed a whopping $50,000 tax against the Bank of the United States and collected it by force. The circuit court, having first enjoined the collection of the tax, ordered the seized money returned. The Supreme Court, per Marshall, affirmed in 1824.[78]

The interesting questions once more were jurisdictional.[79] Congress, Marshall rather debatably concluded, had attempted to give the federal circuit courts jurisdiction over all suits by or against the Bank.[80] The next issue was whether Congress had power to do so.

---

[73]*See* 19 U.S. (6 Wheat.) at 391-92.

[74]*See* 3 J. Story, *supra* chapter 3, note 82, at 509-10 (praising this aspect of *Cohens*: "Indeed, the main object of this clause would be defeated by any narrower construction; since the power was conferred for the purpose, in an especial manner, of producing a uniformity of construction of the constitution, laws, and treaties of the United States.").

[75]The language recommended by a committee proposing amendments to the Articles of Confederation for appellate jurisdiction of cases "wherein questions shall arise on the meaning and construction of" federal law, 31 Journals of the Continental Congress 497 (1786), would clearly have embraced defendants' rights; it would, however, have exacerbated an additional problem discussed *infra in* notes 81-93 and accompanying text.

[76]*Cf.* Monaghan, *Our Perfect Constitution*, 56 N.Y.U.L. Rev. 351 (1981).

[77]McCulloch v. Maryland, 17 U.S. (4 Wheat.) 316 (1819); *see infra* chapter 6.

[78]22 U.S. (9 Wheat.) 738 (1824).

[79]On the merits Marshall relied heavily on *McCulloch*, but typically he felt it necessary to retrace much of its reasoning, concluding with the unambiguous statement that Ohio's tax offended an implicit immunity found not in the Constitution itself but in the statute establishing the Bank. *Id.* at 865-68. Indeed on the merits *Osborn* was a stronger case for immunity than was *McCulloch*, for the Ohio tax looked prohibitive; Marshall said it was "much more objectionable than that of the state of Maryland." *Id.* at 868.

[80]The statute establishing the Bank made it "able and capable . . . to sue and be sued . . . in all state courts having competent jurisdiction, and in any circuit court in the United States." Bank of the United States Act, ch. 44, § 7, 3 Stat. 266, 269 (1816) (expired 1836). A few years earlier the Court had concluded that a similar provision conferred only capacity, not federal jurisdiction. Bank of the United States v. Deveaux, 9 U.S. (5 Cranch) 61, 85-86 (1809). In distinguishing this precedent, 22 U.S. (9 Wheat.) at 817-18, Marshall noted that the earlier statute had not specifically mentioned federal courts. He did not add, as he might have, that in view of the absence of a statute providing general federal question jurisdiction and the narrow construction of the diversity clause rendered in *Deveaux*, *see supra* chapter 3, notes 160-87 and accompanying text, it was difficult to see what the federal suability clause would have accomplished if read solely as a grant of capacity. Citing *Deveaux*, Johnson dissented on the statutory issue. 22 U.S. (9 Wheat.) at 876-84.

In *Osborn* itself this question seemed relatively easy, for the Bank claimed that its federal charter gave it immunity from state taxation; the basic issue in the case was one of federal law.[81] In the companion *Planters' Bank* case,[82] however, the bank sued on a note it had acquired by assignment, and no one suggested that the law governing the validity or interpretation of the note was federal. Marshall's *Osborn* opinion was broad enough to embrace both cases. Because there was "scarcely any case, every part of which depends on the constitution, laws or treaties of the United States,"[83] the mere fact that "the case involves questions depending on general principles" could . not exclude it from the jurisdiction;[84] it was enough that the Bank's ability to contract, which was based on federal law, "forms an original ingredient in every cause."[85]

Dissenting, Justice Johnson protested that the Bank's existence and its contractual capacity had not been questioned and were not likely to be questioned at this late date; he contended that the case could not be said to arise under federal law until the federal question was actually raised.[86] Johnson seems to have misinterpreted Marshall's opinion,[87] for Marshall relied not on the potential controversy over the Bank's capacity but on the fact that that capacity was an essential part of the Bank's claim. In holding that no disagreement over the meaning of federal law was needed, Marshall was plainly right; because a central purpose of the arising-under provision is to vindicate federal rights, a defendant cannot defeat jurisdiction by conceding liability.[88]

The real difficulty with Marshall's opinion was not that the Bank's capacity was uncontested but that it was so remote from the central issues actually involved in the litigation. As Johnson demonstrated, the potential jurisdiction embraced by the Court's thesis was enormous: any action on paper subject to a federal stamp tax or any action respecting land once acquired from the United States could be brought

[81]As an original matter the Court might have held the case did not arise under federal law because the charter was entered only as a reply to a defense based on the state's tax law; Marshall's suggestion in *Cohens* that a suit to recover an unconstitutional tax arose upon an "assumpsit," *see supra* note 56, may look in that direction. Compare Gully v. First National Bank, 299 U.S. 109 (1936), effectively so holding in interpreting a jurisdictional statute essentially identical to the Constitution. As a constitutional matter, however, Marshall had gone some distance toward rejecting this interpretation with his statement elsewhere in *Cohens* that a case "consists of the right of one party, as well as of the other." 19 U.S. (6 Wheat.) at 379. A distinction between the original and appellate jurisdictions in this regard would have been respectable despite the fact that both depended upon the same words; but Marshall was at pains in *Osborn* to affirm that the original jurisdiction was as broad as the appellate. 22 U.S. (9 Wheat.) at 821.

[82]Bank of the United States v. Planters' Bank, 22 U.S. (9 Wheat.) 904 (1824).

[83]22 U.S. (9 Wheat.) at 820.

[84]*Id.* at 821.

[85]*Id.* at 824.

[86]*Id.* at 884-89. "[A] constitutional question," he added, "may be raised, in any conceivable suit that may be instituted; but that would be a very insufficient ground for assuming universal jurisdiction . . . ." *Id.* at 886-87.

[87]As did Justice Frankfurter. *See* Textile Workers Union v. Lincoln Mills, 353 U.S. 448, 471, 481 (1957) (dissenting opinion).

[88]This example helps to explain why, as Professor Mishkin has pointed out, "the term 'federal *question*'" as applied to trial court jurisdiction is a "misnomer" that might better be replaced "by some such term as 'federal *claim.*'" Mishkin, *The Federal "Question" in the District Courts*, 53 COLUM. L. REV. 157, 170-71 (1953) (emphasis in original).

within the jurisdiction.[89] When Congress came to grant general arising-under jurisdiction,[90] the Court was to hold that it could not have intended to include cases in which the federal element was so remote.[91] Moreover, Marshall's argument seems incomplete; rejection of the extreme position that *all* questions in the case must be federal did not compel the conclusion that a single federal ingredient would suffice. Yet the purpose of the arising-under clause seems to support Marshall's conclusion. Absent federal jurisdiction, a state might undermine the Bank's authority indirectly by improperly finding against it on some issue of state law;[92] and, as Marshall noted, Supreme Court review would afford "the insecure remedy of an appeal, upon an insulated point, after it has received that shape which may be given to it by another tribunal, into which [a litigant] is forced against his will."[93]

The second great jurisdictional controversy in *Osborn* was one of sovereign immunity. The eleventh amendment forbids suits against one state by citizens of another; it was argued that the attempt to enjoin or to obtain restitution from a state officer in the course of his duties was "substantially, though not in form," a suit against the state.[94] Stressing that such a conclusion would impede the enforcement of federal law, Marshall contrasted the amendment's reference to suits "against a State" with article III's provision for suits "affecting" ambassadors,[95] analogized to the understanding that an executor's citizenship rather than that of the beneficiaries was determinative for diversity purposes, and concluded that the amendment was "limited to those suits in which a state is a party on the record."[96]

---

[89]22 U.S. (9 Wheat.) at 874-86. This example had been anticipated by Mr. Spencer during the North Carolina ratifying convention. *See* ELLIOT'S DEBATES, *supra* chapter 3, note 42, at 148.

[90]Act of March 3, 1875, ch. 137, § 1, 18 Stat. 470, 470 (current version at 28 U.S.C. § 1331 (1976 & Supp. IV 1980).

[91]*E.g.*, Shulthis v. McDougal, 225 U.S. 561, 570 (1912) ("[A] controversy in respect of lands has never been regarded as presenting a Federal question merely because one of the parties to it has derived his title under an Act of Congress."). *Cf.* T.B. Harms Co. v. Eliscu, 339 F.2d 823 (2d Cir. 1964) (dispute over assignment of copyright).

[92]*See* Mishkin, *supra* note 88, at 162:

> The potential judicial power of the United States over federal question cases must necessarily be extremely broad. The situations in which a sympathetic forum may be required for the vindication of national rights cannot always be foreseen, and there must be power under the Constitution to provide for those eventualities.

Johnson conceded in dissent that "a state of things has grown up, in some of the States, which renders all protection necessary, that the general government can give to this bank. The policy of the decision is obvious, that is, if the Bank is to be sustained . . . ." 22 U.S. (9 Wheat.) at 871-72.

[93]22 U.S. (9 Wheat.) at 822-23. Compare England v. Louisiana State Bd. of Medical Examiners, 375 U.S. 411, 416 (1964), reaffirming, as Madison had insisted in the Convention, *see* supra note 24, that Supreme Court review was "an inadequate substitute" for an initial federal determination, especially with respect to "issues of fact": "Limiting the litigant to review here would deny him the benefit of a federal trial court's role in constructing a record and making fact findings. How the facts are found will often dictate the decision of federal claims." *See* 1 C. WARREN, *supra* introduction to part two, note 22, at 629 ("Had the point been successfully maintained and the Bank excluded from the Federal Courts and obliged to trust its fate to local juries, its fortunes would have been highly insecure.").

[94]22 U.S. (9 Wheat.) at 846. *See id.* at 803-04 (Mr. Wright).

[95]*But see* United States v. Ortega, 24 U.S. (11 Wheat.) 467 (1826) (Washington, J.), holding that a prosecution of one who *attacked* a public minister was not one "affecting" the minister within article III.

[96]22 U.S. (9 Wheat.) at 847-58. It is noteworthy that Marshall did not contend that the amendment was inapplicable on the ground that the suit had been brought not by citizens of other states but by a federal

The trouble with this reasoning is that it reduces the amendment to an empty shell; it is not easy to imagine any policy that might have prompted the country to go to the length of amending the Constitution to forbid suing states by name while allowing suits with identical effects against their officers. Thus while Marshall invoked his pet argument of intolerable consequences,[97] *Osborn* seems to have been a case in which that argument cut more strongly against him. Indeed, Marshall himself would soon retract the more extreme implications of *Osborn* in disallowing a suit against state officers to obtain possession of slaves seized when allegedly imported in violation of federal law;[98] the Court has been searching for a rationale to distinguish these two cases ever since.[99] Marshall might have helped his cause by

corporation. An adequate explanation would be that he had already held in *Deveaux* that a suit by a corporation was to be treated as a suit by its members. Bank of the United States v. Deveaux, 9 U.S. (5 Cranch) 61, 91-92 (1809); *see supra* chapter 3, notes 165-68, 178, and accompanying text. There was some tension between this position and the flat statement in *Osborn* that "in all cases where jurisdiction depends on the party, it is the party named in the record." 22 U.S. (9 Wheat.) at 857. Perhaps the results can be reconciled on the ground that the eleventh amendment speaks explicitly of "State[s]," while neither it nor article III mentions corporations.

[97]22 U.S. (9 Wheat.) at 847-48 ("it may not be time misapplied, if we pause for a moment, and reflect on the relative situation of the Union with its members, should the objection prevail"). *See also* 1 J. KENT, *supra* note 61, at 350-51 (discussing *Osborn*: "[T]he objection, if it were valid, would go, in its consequences, completely to destroy the powers of the Union.").

[98]Governor of Georgia v. Madrazo, 26 U.S. (1 Pet.) 110 (1828). *Osborn* was distinguished on the grounds that in *Madrazo* the Governor was sued "not by his name, but by his title," and that "no case is made which justifies a decree against him personally." *Id.* at 123-24. Johnson, who had entertained the case below, dissented, but not from this reasoning; he argued that by initiating a proceeding to condemn the slaves the state had effectively been plaintiff rather than defendant in the case. *Id.* at 124-35.

Madrazo's claim had been filed in admiralty, because it related to cargo sold after capture at sea, and it was plausibly argued that the eleventh amendment did not apply because the case was not one "in law or equity." *Id.* at 116-17; *cf.* Parsons v. Bedford, 28 U.S. (3 Pet.) 433, 446-47 (1830) (neither admiralty nor equity cases were "Suits at common Law" within the seventh amendment jury provision), *discussed infra* in notes 137-41 and accompanying text. Marshall avoided the issue: "[I]f the 11th amendment . . . does not extend to proceedings in admiralty, it was a case for the original jurisdiction of the supreme court" because it was a suit between a state and a foreign national. 26 U.S. (1 Pet.) at 124. Yet under section 13 of the Judiciary Act of 1789 the Supreme Court's jurisdiction was "original but not exclusive" in such cases, ch. 20, § 13, 1 Stat. 73, 80 (current version at 28 U.S.C. § 1251 (1976)); *Cohens* seemed to support the conclusion that the Constitution itself did not make the original jurisdiction exclusive, *see supra* notes 38-76 and accompanying text, and the district court had jurisdiction in admiralty under section 9, 1 Stat. at 76-77 (current version at 28 U.S.C. § 1333 (1976)).

Educated by Marshall's advice, Madrazo next filed a libel against Georgia herself directly in the Supreme Court. Once more Marshall avoided the question of the effect of the eleventh amendment on admiralty cases, concluding, despite the assumption of all concerned, that the case was not maritime: "It is a mere personal suit against a state, to recover proceeds in its possession . . . ." *Ex parte* Madrazzo [*sic*], 32 U.S. (7 Pet.) 627, 632 (1833).

Much later the Court was to hold an unconsenting state could not be sued in admiralty. *Ex parte* New York, 256 U.S. 490, 498 (1911). *Cf.* Hans v. Louisiana, 134 U.S. 1 (1890), *discussed supra in* note 61.

[99]*See, e.g.,* Edelman v. Jordan, 415 U.S. 651 (1974); Pennoyer v. McConnaughy, 140 U.S. 1, 9-10 (1891). *See* D. CURRIE, FEDERAL COURTS—CASES AND MATERIALS 557-67 (3d ed. 1982); C. JACOBS, THE ELEVENTH AMENDMENT AND SOVEREIGN IMMUNITY 106-49 (1972). Marshall suggested a basis of distinction when he argued in *Osborn*, 22 U.S. (9 Wheat.) at 858, that the "true question" was "not one of jurisdiction, but whether [the defendants] are to be considered as having a real interest, or as being only nominal parties." 3 J. STORY, *supra* chapter 3, note 82, at 539-40, pursued this theme by invoking common law principles making an agent or servant generally liable for torts committed but not for contracts made on behalf of his employer. *See infra* chapter 12.

arguing that virtually automatic permission to file petitions of right rendered purely
symbolic the English immunity tradition on which the amendment was based,[100] but
in typical fashion he disdained reliance on British precedents,[101] just as he ignored
relevant previous pronouncements of his own.[102]

The companion *Planters' Bank* case[103] raised a somewhat different eleventh
amendment problem, for in that case the defendant was not a state officer but a bank
in which the state itself was a shareholder. Marshall was brief in upholding jurisdiction. The suit was "no more a suit against the state of Georgia, than against any other
individual corporator"; it was a suit "against a corporation."[104] Moreover,

> when a government becomes a partner in any trading company, it divests
> itself, so far as concerns the transactions of that company, of its sovereign
> character . . . . The State of Georgia, by giving to the bank the capacity to
> sue and be sued, voluntarily strips itself of its sovereign character, . . . and
> waives all the privileges of that character . . . .[105]

No fewer than three distinct bases for the decision are imbedded in this reasoning:
the state was not a party, the amendment does not forbid suits against a state in its
proprietary capacity, and the state had waived its immunity by consenting to suits
against the bank. Each was stated as a bare conclusion, and each was subject to
significant objections.

Johnson in dissent pointed out two of the problems. First, the holding that the

---

[100]*See* Chisholm v. Georgia, 2 U.S. (2 Dall.) 419, 460 (Wilson, J.), *discussed supra in* chapter 1. *See also*
United States v. Lee, 106 U.S. 196, 208 (1883), *infra* chapter 12, explaining the paucity of British
precedents in which officers had been sued: "There has been, therefore, no necessity for suing the officers
or servants of the King . . . , when the issue could be made with the King himself as defendant.").

[101] If this question were to be determined on the authority of English decisions, it is believed,
that no case can be adduced, where any person has been considered a party, who is not so
made in the record. But the court will not review those decisions, because it is thought, a
question growing out of the constitution of the United States, requires rather an attentive
consideration of the words of that instrument, than of the decisions of analogous questions
by the courts of any other country.

22 U.S. (9 Wheat.) at 851. Indeed, it is more than arguable that, however symbolic the English doctrine
may have been, the country must have meant to do something beyond symbolism when it took the trouble
to amend the Constitution.

[102]Marshall cited neither his statement in *Marbury*, 5 U.S. (1 Cranch) at 170 ("If one of the heads of
departments commits any illegal act, under color of his office, by which an individual sustains an injury, it
cannot be pretended, that his office alone exempts him from being sued in the ordinary mode of
proceeding . . . ."), nor his decision in United States v. Peters, 9 U.S. (5 Cranch) 115, 139-41 (1809)
(enforcing over eleventh amendment objections a decree against representatives of a deceased state
treasurer respecting "the proceeds of a vessel condemned in the court of admiralty": "[T]he suit was not
instituted against the state, or its treasurer, but against the executrices of David Rittenhouse"; the state
"had neither possession of, nor right to, the property"; and "a mere suggestion of title in a state, to
property in possession of an individual," could not destroy jurisdiction.).

Later Justices, rightly or wrongly, were to rely on *Peters* as the substantial equivalent of *Osborn*, *see,
e.g.*, United States v. Lee, 106 U.S. 196, 209-14 (1883), though in *Osborn* the treasurer had asserted no
personal rights. Both *Peters* and an English case alleged to have involved the recovery of illegally collected
taxes had been invoked by counsel. 22 U.S. (9 Wheat.) at 797 (Mr. Clay).

[103]Bank of the United States v. Planters' Bank, 22 U.S. (9 Wheat.) 904 (1824).

[104]*Id.* at 906-07.

[105]*Id.* at 907-08.

state was not a party was difficult to reconcile with *Bank of the United States v. Deveaux*,[106] in which a diversity suit by a corporation had been considered a suit by its members.[107] Second, Johnson argued, every suit against a state was in its "sovereign capacity"; "in what other capacity can a state appear, or even exist?"[108] We might be inclined to put this point somewhat differently by saying that the eleventh amendment bars *all* suits in law or equity against a state by citizens of another, with no exception for proprietary activities.[109]

Johnson did not advert to the waiver question. Later Justices have questioned whether waivability is consistent with the absolute language of the amendment;[110] the answer, if there is one, must be based upon the perception that the immunity, like a venue statute, exists for the protection of the defendant.[111] Apart from this, later cases have construed waivers of state immunity strictly,[112] and Marshall did not say the statute expressly made the bank suable in federal court. Johnson's objections were at the least sufficient to give pause as to the soundness of the Court's conclusions, yet Marshall did not stop to answer them.[113]

Thus *Osborn* and its companion case show Marshall at his most dogmatic and impervious to argument. His broad construction of the arising-under clause could have been made more persuasive by borrowing a page out of Story's use of the constitutional purpose in *Martin v. Hunter's Lessee*;[114] it was based instead on the demolition of a straw man. Marshall's conclusions with regard to sovereign immunity

---

[106]9 U.S. (5 Cranch) 61 (1809).

[107]22 U.S. (9 Wheat.) at 911-12; *see supra* chapter 3, notes 165-68, 178, and accompanying text. *See* Louisville R.R. v. Letson, 43 U.S. (2 How.) 497, 554 (1844) (arguing that *Planters'* had essentially overruled *Deveaux*). As in *Osborn*, *see supra* notes 95-102 and accompanying text, Marshall made no attempt in *Planters'* to argue that the eleventh amendment was inapplicable because the suit had been brought *by* a corporation.

[108]22 U.S. (9 Wheat.) at 912.

[109]Later decisions seem basically to have rejected Marshall's governmental/proprietary distinction. *E.g., Ex parte* New York, 256 U.S. 490, 500-03 (1921) (upholding without discussion a state's immunity to suit arising out of a collision with its tugboat); *cf.* Berizzi Bros. Co. v. Steamship Pesaro, 271 U.S. 562 (1926) (merchant ship owned by foreign sovereign). Yet considerations of the proprietary nature of the state's activity have reappeared in more recent years in connection with the question whether the state has consented to be sued. *Compare* Parden v. Terminal Ry., 377 U.S. 184 (1964) (allowing suit against state-owned railroad) *with* Employees v. Department of Public Health & Welfare, 411 U.S. 279, 284 (1973) (distinguishing *Parden* on the ground that "[s]tate mental hospitals, state cancer hospitals, and training schools for delinquent girls which are not operated for profit, are not proprietary."). The Foreign Sovereign Immunities Act, 28 U.S.C. §§ 1604, 1605(a)(2) (1976), whose constitutionality remains to be tested, adopts a similar distinction.

[110]*See, e.g.,* Employees v. Department of Public Health & Welfare, 411 U.S. 279, 321 (1973) (Brennan, J., dissenting).

[111]*See* Clark v. Barnard, 108 U.S. 436, 447 (1883) ("The immunity from suit belonging to a State . . . is a personal privilege which it may waive at pleasure.").

[112]*E.g.,* Kennecott Copper Co. v. State Tax Comm'n, 327 U.S. 573, 577 (1946).

[113]*Planters'* was extended to a case where the state was *sole* owner of stock in the defendant bank in Bank of Kentucky v. Wister, 27 U.S. (2 Pet.) 318 (1829). Johnson, who had dissented in *Planters'*, wrote the brief opinion, quoting Marshall's language about the state "divest[ing] itself" of sovereignty when it engages in trade. *Id.* at 323. He added that the case was easier than *Planters'*, for in *Wister* the state was merely a shareholder, not a "corporator"; only the president and directors constituted the body corporate. *Id.* Thus while Johnson appeared in *Wister* to bow to adverse precedent, he was in one sense consistent with his own prior position.

[114]*See supra* notes 13-14 and accompanying text.

were enough to destroy the eleventh amendment. His conclusory opinion in *Planters' Bank*, with its conspicuous failure to respond at all to a dissent responsibly invoking precedent, is the statement of a lawgiver confident of his power and sensitive to no compelling obligation to persuade.

III. Other Cases

A. *Houston v. Moore*

Among the more interesting jurisdictional cases not yet noted is the Court's 1820 decision upholding Pennsylvania's right to try a militiaman for failure to report for duty when his unit was called into federal service.[115] Here we encounter for the first time Justice Bushrod Washington, who had been on the Court for over twenty years; we shall meet him only very occasionally later on. After deciding that a federal statute punished the same offense and thus implicitly occupied the field,[116] Washington concluded that the state could assert jurisdiction to enforce the *federal* law: when Congress meant federal jurisdiction to be exclusive, it said so expressly.[117]

Two constitutional principles, which Washington found confirmed by congressional understanding and by *The Federalist*, underlay this conclusion: that the constitutional power over federal question cases was not itself exclusive and that

---

[115]18 U.S. (5 Wheat.) 1 (1820).

[116]"If . . . one [government] imposes a certain punishment, for a certain offence, the presumption is, that this was deemed sufficient, and, in all circumstances, the only proper one." *Id.* at 23. *Cf.* Pennsylvania v. Nelson, 350 U.S. 497 (1956) (federal ban on activities subverting federal government precludes similar state law). Yet examples of state and federal punishment for the same act are not uncommon, *see, e.g.*, Moore v. Illinois, 55 U.S. (14 How.) 13 (1852 Term) (concealment of fugitive slave), and examples cited *id.* at 19-20; Congress may have meant only to make certain that the offending act was punished, and indeed parallel state action might have been viewed as reinforcing federal policy. Justice Johnson, citing examples, expressly disagreed with Washington's conclusion on this point. 18 U.S. (5 Wheat.) at 33-36 (Johnson, J., concurring). Compare Marshall's statement in Cohens v. Virginia, 19 U.S. (5 Wheat.) at 443 ("To interfere with the penal laws of a State, where they . . . have for their sole object the internal government of the country, is a very serious measure, which Congress cannot be supposed to adopt lightly . . . ."). Shortly after *Houston*, Congress enacted an ambiguous law providing that nothing in the new federal criminal code should be construed "to deprive the courts of the individual states, of jurisdiction, under the laws of the several states, over offences made punishable by this act." Act of March 3, 1825, ch. 65, § 26, 4 Stat. 115, 122-23 (current version at 18 U.S.C. § 3231 (1976)). For varying judicial interpretations of this provision, see Grant, *The Scope and Nature of Concurrent Power*, 34 COLUM. L. REV. 995, 1013 (1934). Compare the question of preclusion of state law by federal action permitting, rather than prohibiting, an activity. *E.g.*, Gibbons v. Ogden, 22 U.S. (9 Wheat.) 1 (1824), *infra* chapter 6.

Washington's conclusion that the federal statute precluded a parallel state enactment followed two unnecessary but interesting conclusions respecting the arguable exclusivity of article I's grant of authority over the militia. It had correctly been conceded, he declared, that Congress's power was exclusive after the militia had been federalized, but not before. 18 U.S. (5 Wheat.) at 16-17. Story's dissent reinforced the former point: "[T]o suppose each state could have an authority to govern its own militia in such cases, . . . seems utterly inconsistent with that unity of command and action, on which the success of all military operations must essentially depend." *Id.* at 53. *Cf.* Wayman v. Southard, 23 U.S. (10 Wheat.) 1 (1825); Gibbons v. Ogden, 22 U.S. (9 Wheat.) 1 (1824); Sturges v. Crowninshield, 17 U.S. (4 Wheat.) 122 (1819). *See infra* text and accompanying notes 175-93 and chapters 5, 6.

[117]18 U.S. (5 Wheat.) at 25-32. *See* Arnold, *The Power of State Courts to Enjoin Federal Officers*, 73 YALE L.J. 1385, 1399-1400 (1964).

Congress had power to exclude concurrent state court jurisdiction.[118] Dissenting on the ground that the statute made federal jurisdiction exclusive,[119] Story appeared also to conclude, as he had unnecessarily suggested in *Martin v. Hunter's Lessee*,[120] that the constitutional grant itself was exclusive in criminal cases.[121] The compromise by which the Framers made the creation of inferior federal courts discretionary[122] seems to imply, Story to the contrary, that the trial of all article III cases might be left to state courts.[123] However, in light of Story's opinion, the *Martin* dictum, and occasional state court decisions embracing Story's position,[124] Washington would have been better advised to address the issue in greater detail. For the very passage of *The Federalist* on which he so heavily relied was based on the tradition that "[t]he judiciary power of every government looks beyond its own local or municipal laws,

---

[118]*See id.* at 25-26 (citing THE FEDERALIST No. 82 (A. Hamilton)). *Compare* Judiciary Act of 1789, ch. 20, § 9, 1 Stat. 73, 76 (repealed 1911) (current version at 18 U.S.C. § 3231 (1976)) (criminal jurisdiction of the federal trial courts "exclusive") *with id.* § 11, 1 Stat. at 78 (repealed 1911) (current version at 28 U.S.C. § 1332 (1976)) (diversity jurisdiction "concurrent"). *See also* 3 ELLIOT'S DEBATES, *supra* chapter 3, note 42, at 553-54; 4 *id.* at 171 (Messrs. Marshall and Maclaine).

[119]18 U.S. (5 Wheat.) at 71-72.

[120]14 U.S. (1 Wheat.) 34 (1816).

[121] It cannot be pretended, that the states have retained any power to enforce fines and penalties created by the laws of the United States, in virtue of their general sovereignty, for that sovereignty did not originally attach on such subjects. They sprang from the Union, and had no previous existence. . . .

. . . It has been expressly held by this court, that no part of the criminal jurisdiction of the United States can, consistently with the constitution, be delegated by congress to state tribunals.

18 U.S. (5 Wheat.) at 68-69, citing Martin v. Hunter's Lessee, 14 U.S. (1 Wheat.) 304, 336-37 (1816) (dictum), where the same nondelegation statement had followed the declaration that "the judicial power of the United States is unavoidably, in some cases, exclusive of all state authority, and in all others may be made so at the election of congress." Yet Story in *Houston* also distinguished examples of state court jurisdiction to enforce federal penal laws on the ground that in those instances Congress had expressly provided that it did not mean to deprive state courts of jurisdiction. 18 U.S. (5 Wheat.) at 74. In his treatise he conceded that although Congress could not vest jurisdiction over any cases in state courts, it could "permit the state courts to exercise a concurrent jurisdiction in many cases," and he followed that statement with a reference to criminal examples. 3 J. STORY, *supra* chapter 3, note 82, at 622-24. Story reminded the reader, however, that *Martin* had also "held" the constitutional grant of admiralty jurisdiction partly exclusive because there was "a direct repugnancy or incompatibility in the exercise of it by the states." 18 U.S. (5 Wheat.) at 49, citing *Martin*, 14 U.S. (1 Wheat.) at 337 ("it can only be in those cases where, previous to the constitution, state tribunals possessed jurisdiction independent of national authority, that they can now constitutionally exercise a concurrent jurisdiction"). *See also* 3 J. STORY, *supra* chapter 3, note 82, at 534 n.3 (explaining that the Constitution conferred admiralty jurisdiction "exactly according to the nature and extent and modifications, in which it existed in the jurisprudence of the common law. Where the jurisdiction was exclusive, it remained so."). To today's reader the alleged "repugnancy" between state and federal admiralty powers seems hard to find, and the alleged exclusivity of the constitutional admiralty grant is not easy to reconcile with the broad statements of *The Federalist* relied on by Washington in *Houston*, 18 U.S. (5 Wheat.) at 25-26 (1820). *See supra* note 118.

[122]*See supra* note 24.

[123]This consideration appears to refute the possibility that the tenure provisions of U.S. CONST. art. III, § 1, which forbid the creation of federal judges lacking independence, also forbid state court jurisdiction over cases within federal authority. *See infra* note 129. *See also* Warren, *Federal Criminal Laws and the State Courts*, 38 HARV. L. REV. 545 (1925) (arguing exhaustively that the criminal jurisdiction need not be exclusive).

[124]*See, e.g.*, Jackson v. Row, 2 Va. Cas. 34, 35-38 (1815); Warren, *supra* note 123, at 577-80 (and cases discussed therein).

and in *civil* cases, lays hold of all subjects of litigation between parties within its jurisdiction . . . ."¹²⁵ The implicit traditional corollary that "'[t]he courts of no country execute the penal laws of another,'"¹²⁶ which Story recited in his dissent,¹²⁷ cried aloud for an answer. This would not be the last time the notion that states were forbidden to exercise certain heads of article III jurisdiction would crop up,¹²⁸ but in general Washington's views have prevailed: the states may hear article III cases unless Congress otherwise provides.¹²⁹

Washington, however, cannot be said to have spoken for the Court in *Houston*; he noted that while all but two Justices agreed that the judgment should stand, "they do not concur in all respects in the reasons which influence my opinion."¹³⁰ What is peculiar is that except for Johnson, who wrote a long concurrence,¹³¹ we do not know the grounds on which the other Justices voted. Nor can we be certain who the second dissenter was; Story revealed only that his opinion had "the concurrence of one of my brethren."¹³²

¹²⁵THE FEDERALIST No. 82, *supra* chapter 3, note 29, at 493 (A. Hamilton) (emphasis added). Washington's paraphrase omitted the important word "civil."

¹²⁶Wisconsin v. Pelican Ins. Co., 127 U.S. 265, 290 (1888) (quoting Marshall in The Antelope, 23 U.S. (10 Wheat.) 66, 123 (1825)); *see supra* note 48, (discussing *Cohens*).

¹²⁷18 U.S. (5 Wheat.) at 69.

¹²⁸See, e.g., United States v. Bailey, 34 U.S. (9 Pet.) 238, 259 (1835) (McLean, J., dissenting), and the peculiar opinion of Justice Johnson in Ogden v. Saunders, 25 U.S. (12 Wheat.) 213, 271 (1827), *infra* chapter 5. Both 1 Tucker's Appendix to Blackstone, *supra* chapter 3, note 59, at 181-82, and W. RAWLE, A VIEW OF THE CONSTITUTION OF THE UNITED STATES OF AMERICA 202-08 (2d ed. Philadelphia 1829) (1st ed. Philadelphia 1825), took the position that in some cases the Constitution made federal jurisdiction exclusive.

¹²⁹*See, e.g.,* Charles Dowd Box Co. v. Courtney, 368 U.S. 502 (1962) (federal jurisdiction to enforce collective bargaining contracts affecting commerce not exclusive). Compare Tennessee v. Davis, 100 U.S. 257 (1880) (denying constitutional status to Story's doctrine against enforcing foreign penal laws by upholding a statute authorizing removal to federal court of state prosecutions of federal officers), *discussed in* Warren, *supra* note 123, at 592-94. The power to make federal jurisdiction exclusive, which was not directly involved in *Houston*, was confirmed without significant discussion in The Moses Taylor, 71 U.S. (4 Wall.) 411, 429-30 (1867), which by basing the exclusivity of federal jurisdiction over a maritime in rem proceeding on the statute avoided embracing Story's argument that the Constitution itself made jurisdiction exclusive. Without giving reasons, and despite the broad dictum in *Houston*, Rawle argued state courts could not be deprived of jurisdiction over diversity cases, or over "many other[s]." W. RAWLE, *supra* note 128, at 205 n.t.

Washington added in *Houston*, quite unnecessarily, that "congress cannot confer jurisdiction" on state courts. 18 U.S. (5 Wheat.) at 27. In agreeing with Washington on this point Story took a narrow view of the necessary and proper clause, U.S. CONST. art. I, § 8, cl. 18: "The nation may organize its own tribunals for this purpose; and it has no necessity to resort to other tribunals to enforce its rights." 18 U.S. (5 Wheat.) at 67. *Cf.* McCulloch v. Maryland, 17 U.S. (4 Wheat.) 316 (1819), *infra* chapter 6. *See also* 1 J. KENT, *supra* note 61, at 402 ("The doctrine seems to be admitted, that congress cannot compel a state court to entertain jurisdiction in any case."). The Court was to repudiate this position in part many years later. *See* Testa v. Katt, 330 U.S. 386, 394 (1947) (holding a state court required to entertain a treble-damage action under the Emergency Price Control Act).

¹³⁰18 U.S. (5 Wheat.) at 32. Johnson was still more emphatic: "[T]here is no point whatever decided, except that the fine was constitutionally imposed . . . . The course of reasoning by which the judges have reached this conclusion are [*sic*] various . . . ." *Id.* at 47.

¹³¹*Id.* at 32-47 (arguing that the defendant had not violated federal law and that the state could make the same act a crime even if he had).

¹³²*Id.* at 76. One suspects it may have been Marshall; the disintegration of the majority in *Houston* was paralleled during the Marshall years only in Ogden v. Saunders, 25 U.S. (12 Wheat.) 213 (1827), *infra*

B.   Judicial Provisions of the Bill of Rights

One of the arguments against permitting state court jurisdiction in *Houston* was, as Washington put it, that the determination of the state court "would either oust the jurisdiction of the United States court-martial, or might subject the accused to be twice tried for the same offence";[133] Story, in applying the Court's holding to a hypothetical case of treason, expressly invoked the double jeopardy clause of the fifth amendment.[134] Washington did not address the double jeopardy question,[135] and indeed Bill-of-Rights issues, even those respecting judicial procedure, rarely reached the Court during the Marshall period. The seventh amendment's civil jury guarantee was at stake, however, in cases defining the scope of the admiralty jurisdiction, because the Judiciary Act exempted admiralty cases from the jury requirement.[136] In an important dictum in *Parsons v. Bedford*,[137] Story confirmed in 1830 the validity of this exception, declaring that the constitutional guarantee in suits at common law "may well be construed to embrace all suits, which are not of equity and admiralty jurisdiction, whatever may be the peculiar form which they may assume to settle legal rights."[138] For this conclusion he relied convincingly on the language of article III, which distinguishes between "Cases, in Law and Equity," and "Cases of Admiralty and maritime Jurisdiction,"[139] and on the historical observation

---

chapter 5, the one constitutional case in which the Chief Justice openly dissented. Johnson's biographer, citing a letter of the Chief Justice and one of his opinions on circuit, Meade v. Deputy Marshall, 16 F. Cas. 1291 (No. 9372) (C.C.D. Va. 1815), neither of which appears conclusive, says the other dissenter "was doubtless Marshall." D. MORGAN, *supra* introduction to part 2, note 12, at 244 n.48.

[133]18 U.S. (5 Wheat.) at 31.

[134]*Id.* at 75.

[135]Washington said the state judgment would be as binding as one in a civil case, presumably under the statute requiring "every court within the United States" to give "faith and credit" to state court judgments, Act of May 26, 1790, ch. 11, 1 Stat. 122, 122 (1790) (current provision at 28 U.S.C. § 1738 (1976)), or under the common law doctrine of res judicata. *See* 18 U.S. (5 Wheat.) at 31. Story argued that to allow a second trial would offend legislative intent, common law principles, and "the genius of our free government." *Id.* at 72. The lack of reliance in either opinion on the fifth amendment seems attributable to the fact that the sentence in question was a mere fine, while the amendment speaks only of "jeopardy of life or limb." *See id.* at 34 (Johnson, J., concurring).

A related problem was presented in United States v. Perez, 22 U.S. (9 Wheat.) 579, 580 (1824), a brief Story opinion allowing a criminal defendant to be retried after discharge of a hung jury, on the ground that the law allowed a judge to abort the trial in cases of "manifest necessity" or when "the ends of public justice would otherwise be defeated." Later Justices have tended to read this case as implying that a declaration of mistrial without "manifest necessity" would offend the fifth amendment, *e.g.*, United States v. Dinitz, 424 U.S. 600, 606-07 (1976), but the interesting feature of the case is that the Constitution was not mentioned; evidently the Court thought the double jeopardy clause had nothing to do with the question. Story reveals why in his treatise: if the jury is discharged before verdict, the defendant "cannot judicially be said to have been put in jeopardy." 3 J. STORY, *supra* chapter 3, note 82, at 659-60 (citing *Perez*). See Crist v. Bretz, 437 U.S. 28, 34 n.10 (1978), enforcing a contrary rule while acknowledging that *Perez* had been misunderstood: though in *Perez* "the Court was not purporting to decide a constitutional question, . . . to cast such a new light on Perez at this late date would be of academic interest only" in view of intervening decisions.

[136]Judiciary Act of 1789, ch. 20, § § 9, 12, 1 Stat. 73, 77, 80 (current version at 28 U.S.C. § 1873 (1976)). *See infra* note 154 and accompanying text (discussing *The Thomas Jefferson*).

[137]28 U.S. (3 Pet.) 433 (1830).

[138]*Id.* at 447.

[139]U.S. CONST. art. III, § 2, para. 1.

that juries had been used in new proceedings involving "legal rights" but usually not in admiralty or in equity.[140] Thus at the same time that Story left equity and admiralty cases outside the jury provision, he read into the amendment a capacity for growth: it covered not only proceedings known to the common law when the amendment was adopted, but nonequity, nonmaritime proceedings later created by statute as well.[141]

The seventh amendment had come up once before, in the 1819 case *Bank of Columbia v. Okely*,[142] which, apart from undercurrents in the admiralty cases, may have been the first Bill-of-Rights case in the Supreme Court. A Maryland statute, incorporated by Congress in establishing the District of Columbia, authorized summary collection without trial of any notes expressly made negotiable at the bank; the Court upheld it over objections based on the seventh amendment and the jury and "law of the land" clauses of the Maryland constitution.[143] The seventh amendment

[140]This historical test requires the courts to engage in much esoteric research irrelevant to the underlying policies respecting the desirability of jury trials, *see, e.g.*, Damsky v. Zavatt, 289 F.2d 46, 48 (2d Cir. 1961), and there has been a tendency to reevaluate the availability of equitable remedies in light of modern procedure, *see, e.g.*, Ross v. Bernhard, 396 U.S. 531, 540 (1970); Beacon Theatres, Inc. v. Westover, 359 U.S. 500, 506-10 (1959). Yet some such irrelevant digging seems scarcely avoidable in light of Congress's debatable decision to phrase its proposed amendment in terms of distinctions that had developed for reasons not always related to the desirability of jury trial. For discussions of this problem, see, e.g., F. JAMES & G. HAZARD, CIVIL PROCEDURE 347-91 (2d ed. 1970); Redish, *Seventh Amendment Right to Jury Trial: A Study in the Irrationality of Rational Decision Making*, 70 Nw. U.L. REV. 486 (1975); Wolfram, *The Constitutional History of the Seventh Amendment*, 57 MINN. L. REV. 639 (1973), especially *id.* at 710-22 and 731-47, urging a "dynamic" rather than a strictly historical test and noting that throughout their history "the jurisdictions of the law courts and the chancellor . . . were subject to an unstatic process of accretion and erosion."

[141]*See, e.g.*, Curtis v. Loether, 415 U.S. 189, 193 (1974) (statutory damage action for housing discrimination). In interesting contrast was the actual holding in *Parsons*, refusing to reverse a judgment for failure to transcribe the evidence taken before the jury, as Louisiana law prescribed, despite a federal statute conforming practice in the Louisiana federal court to state law. The second clause of the seventh amendment precluded reexamination of facts found by a jury "otherwise . . . than according to the rule of the common law." Because at common law an appellate court had no power to investigate the facts found by a jury, said the Court, the statute should be construed not to authorize broader appellate review, so as to avoid "the most serious doubts, whether it would not be unconstitutional." 28 U.S. (3 Pet.) at 448. Any error in failing to record the evidence was therefore harmless. *Id.* In short, the Court seems to have viewed the reference to "common law" methods of reviewing juries as confining it rather strictly to 1791 practice, while interpreting the identical term in the preceding clause to require juries in new actions analogous to those already recognized at common law. For later developments in this area, see, e.g., Baltimore & Carolina Line v. Redman, 295 U.S. 654, 659 & n.5 (1935) (upholding the validity of a judgment notwithstanding the verdict and invoking pre-1791 precedent in cases in which the issue of sufficient evidence had been reserved).

[142]17 U.S. (4 Wheat.) 235 (1819).

[143]The peculiar hybrid nature of the law made the basis of Johnson's brief opinion somewhat obscure. He began by observing plausibly enough that because Congress had adopted only "existing" Maryland laws, state constitutional objections could not be avoided by reference to Congress's power to legislate for the District. *Id.* at 242. He went on to find it therefore "unnecessary to examine the question, whether the powers of Congress be despotic in this district, or whether there are any, and what, restrictions imposed upon it, by natural reason, the principles of the social compact, or constitutional provisions." *Id.* As we shall see in Fletcher v. Peck, 10 U.S. (6 Cranch) 87 (1810), *infra* chapter 5, Johnson was at this time a follower of Chase's views as to the invalidity of unjust statutes. *See supra* chapter 2. Johnson's conclusion that Maryland's law-of-the-land clause was "intended to secure the individual from the arbitrary exercise of the powers of government, unrestrained by the established principles of private rights and distributive justice," 17 U.S. (1 Wheat.) at 244, prefigured the later treatment of its federal due process cousin in such

jury guarantee, wrote Justice Johnson for the court, was waivable and had been waived. By preserving the "right" of trial by jury, the Constitution gave the party a "benefit" that might be "relinquished," and by signing the note the debtor had "voluntarily relinquished his claims to the ordinary administration of justice."[144] On the general point of waivability the language certainly cuts in Johnson's favor,[145] and though later decisions suggest caution in relying on the words alone without consideration of their antecedents or purposes,[146] counsel apparently did not contend that the jury could never be waived.[147] To classify a right as a personal privilege, however, is not necessarily to prove that it can be surrendered in advance of any dispute by signing a form contract.[148] Indeed, Johnson recognized that the words of the Constitution might not afford an answer to all questions respecting waiver. He prudently reserved the question whether the Court would uphold an act that "produced a total prostration of the trial by jury, or even involved the defendant in circumstances which rendered that right unavailing for his protection," noting that "cases may be supposed, in which the policy of a country may set bounds to the relinquishment of

---

cases as Lochner v. New York, 198 U.S. 45 (1905). *See generally infra* chapter 11. See also Livingston v. Moore, 32 U.S. (7 Pet.) 469, 551 (1833) (Johnson, J.).

Johnson seems to have been wrong in concluding that the reference to "existing" Maryland law made consideration of limits on Congress unnecessary. Even if Maryland was free to enact the law, Congress might have lacked power to adopt it. More surprisingly still, Johnson proceeded to consider on its merits the question whether the original Maryland law had offended the seventh amendment, 17 U.S. (4 Wheat.) at 242-44; he seems to have thought, contrary to the Court's later conclusion in Barron v. Baltimore, 32 U.S. (7 Pet.) 243 (1833), *infra* chapter 6, that the Bill of Rights applied to the states, though he neglected to address this portentous issue. *See* D. MORGAN, *supra* introduction to part two, note 12, at 135. Thus *Okely* did not face the question, though it should have, whether the seventh amendment applied to the District of Columbia. *Cf. supra* chapter 3, notes 103-17, 138-51, chapter 4, notes 38-76, *infra* notes 194-214, and accompanying text (discussing *United States v. More, Hepburn v. Ellzey, Cohens v. Virginia,* and *American Insurance Co. v. Canter*).

[144]17 U.S. (4 Wheat.) at 243-44.

[145]Compare Gannett Co. v. DePasquale, 443 U.S. 368, 382-87 (1979); Adams v. United States *ex rel.* McGann, 317 U.S. 269, 275 (1942); and Patton v. United States, 281 U.S. 276, 307-13 (1930), allowing criminal defendants to waive the similarly phrased sixth amendment "right[s]" to a public trial, to the assistance of counsel, and to trial by jury, respectively.

[146]See, e.g., Gannett v. DePasquale, 443 U.S. 368, 415-33 (1979) (Blackmun, J., dissenting in part), concluding that the sixth amendment gives the public a right to attend criminal trials over the objection of the defendant. Conversely, despite their apparently absolute language, both U.S. CONST. art. III, § 2, para. 3 ("The Trial of all Crimes . . . shall be by Jury"), and the eleventh amendment ("The judicial Power . . . shall not be construed to extend to any suit . . . against one of the United States"), have been construed to confer waivable privileges on defendants. Patton v. United States, 281 U.S. 276, 298 (1930) (article III); Clark v. Barnard, 108 U.S. 436, 447 (1883) (eleventh amendment).

[147]*See* 17 U.S. (4 Wheat.) at 239-40 (Mr. Jones).

[148] *See id.* (invoking the traditional common law antipathy to advance agreements to arbitrate disputes); *cf.* Atlas Credit Corp. v. Ezrine, 25 N.Y.2d 219, 250 N.E.2d 474, 303 N.Y.S.2d 382 (1969) (holding that a cognovit note waiving personal jurisdiction objections to suit anywhere offended due process); Von Mehren & Trautman, *Jurisdiction to Adjudicate: A Suggested Analysis,* 79 HARV. L. REV. 1121, 1138 (1966) ("Consent obtained before the action is brought—indeed, before any dispute has arisen—differs in several ways from consent given after an action has been initiated . . . ."). Recent choice-of-forum decisions have tended to allow advance waivers as well. *E.g.,* The Bremen v. Zapata Off-Shore Co., 407 U.S. 1 (1972) (commercial agreement to litigate in particular court); D.H. Overmyer Co. v. Frick Co., 405 U.S. 174 (1972) (cognovit note in commercial context); National Equipment Rental, Ltd. v. Szukhent, 375 U.S. 311 (1964) (appointment of agent for service of process in particular state).

private rights."[149] Johnson was right not to go too deeply into this vexing problem, and perhaps he had already said too much about it. As he pointed out, the statute allowed the debtor to claim a jury trial at the time of execution, and to require that he assert his right at that time may not have been inconsistent with the right.[150] Today, however, one might be less likely to agree that the defendant had consented to this limitation, even if it was otherwise acceptable; so far as the report shows, the note he signed revealed only the place of negotiation, not the statutory provision for summary execution.[151]

C. *The Thomas Jefferson*

Apart from diversity cases, the principal head of jurisdiction given to the lower federal courts by the Judiciary Act of 1789 was admiralty.[152] Maritime cases reaching the Supreme Court were common enough in the early days, and, although most of the interesting problems as to the scope of the jurisdiction were to be faced only after Marshall's departure, one of the Court's last pronouncements in this area during his tenure was of considerable though temporary significance.

The ship Thomas Jefferson was libeled for wages earned on a voyage from Kentucky up the Missouri River and back. It took Story but two pages to hold there was no admiralty jurisdiction. The answer was all history and unsupported assertion: "In the great struggles between the courts of common law and the admiralty, the latter never attempted to assert any jurisdiction . . . except in cases where the service was substantially performed . . . upon the sea, or upon waters within the ebb and flow of the tide."[153]

The year was 1825 and the Justice was Story, but this opinion was a reversion to the high-handed style Marshall had employed before 1810. The Court had never before decided the critical question whether admiralty jurisdiction was to be defined according to English precedents; the scattered and poorly explained Supreme Court precedents might have been taken to suggest that it was not.[154] Examination of the

---

[149]17 U.S. (4 Wheat.) at 243. It was the related statement that the law "must be subjected to a strict construction" because "in derogation of the ordinary principles of private rights," *id.* at 241-42, that led one admirer of Johnson to the surprising conclusion that the *Okely* opinion was protective of the right to jury trial. D. MORGAN, *supra* introduction to part two, note 12, at 134-35.

[150]17 U.S. (4 Wheat.) at 243. See the statute itself. *Id.* at 235-37. *Cf.* Fed. R. Civ. P. 38(b), (d) (requiring a party desiring a jury trial to request it within 10 days after service of the last relevant pleading). But contrast the various decisions culminating in Mitchell v. W.T. Grant Co., 416 U.S. 600 (1974), respecting the validity under the due process clause of pretrial attachment or garnishment of assets.

[151]*Cf.* Johnson v. Zerbst, 304 U.S. 458, 464 (1938) (defining waiver in the context of right to criminal defense counsel as "an intentional relinquishment or abandonment of a known right or privilege").

[152]Ch. 20, § § 9, 11, 1 Stat. 73, 76-77, 78 (current version at 28 U.S.C. § 1333 (1976)).

[153]23 U.S. (10 Wheat.) 428, 429 (1825).

[154]*See* The Betsey & Charlotte, 8 U.S. (4 Cranch) 443, 452 (1808) (holding the place of seizure rather than the place of the offense determined jurisdiction to condemn a vessel); La Vengeance, 3 U.S. (3 Dall.) 297 (1796) (holding maritime an action to condemn a vessel seized for exporting contraband, despite arguments based on British precedents). *See also* Waring v. Clarke, 46 U.S. (5 How.) 441, 458 (1847) (suggesting an English court would not have upheld maritime jurisdiction in *La Vengeance*); *supra* chapter 1. 1 J. KENT, *supra* note 61, at 376-77, expressed doubt whether *La Vengeance* "was sufficiently

purposes of the admiralty clause[155] might have suggested, as it later would to the Taney Court, that the English definition was too narrow to achieve what the Framers had in mind.[156] Yet Story did not even bother to state affirmatively his conclusion on this issue, much less to give reasons for it, and we are expected to take his word for what the precedents established without any supporting evidence whatever.[157]

The denial of jurisdiction in *The Thomas Jefferson* was all the more striking because Story, above all Justices, had acquired a reputation for an expansive view of the admiralty power. Ten years earlier, sitting on circuit, he had written a scholarly and controversial[158] opinion asserting jurisdiction over marine insurance, and in doing so he had expressly declared a certain degree of freedom from confining English precedents.[159] Thus while the opinion was heavy-handed, it can hardly have

---

considered," and doubted also whether the jurisdiction included "any thing more than that jurisdiction which was settled and in practice in this country under the English jurisprudence, when the constitution was made . . . ." Justice Washington on circuit, United States v. McGill, 4 U.S. (4 Dall.) 426, 429-30 (C.C.D. Pa. 1806), had said the Constitution "must be taken to refer to the admiralty and maritime jurisdiction of England." Because admiralty cases were not tried by jury, any expansion of admiralty beyond 1791 precedent would arguably have denied a jury in cases where it would have been required when the seventh amendment was adopted. Thus the historical approach the Court was soon to take to the seventh amendment in Parsons v. Bedford, 28 U.S. (3 Pet.) 443 (1830), *see supra* notes 137-41 and accompanying text, furnished a possible additional argument for adhering to historical limits on the admiralty jurisdiction.

[155]U.S. CONST. art. III, § 2, para. 1.

[156]The Propeller Genesee Chief v. Fitzhugh, 53 U.S. (12 How.) 443 (1852), *discussed infra in* chapter 8. Hamilton had argued that maritime causes "so generally depend upon the law of nations, and so commonly affect the rights of foreigners, that they fall within the considerations which are relative to the public peace." THE FEDERALIST No. 80, *supra* chapter 3, note 29, at 478 (A. Hamilton). Later Justices have said one purpose of the jurisdiction was to provide the basis for a uniform law governing transportation by water. *E.g.*, Knickerbocker Ice Co. v. Stewart, 253 U.S. 149, 160 (1920). *See* 3 J. STORY, *supra* chapter 3, note 82, at 532-33 (mentioning both the interests of "foreigners" and "uniform adjudication," and tying the jurisdiction to "the great interests of navigation and commerce" as well as to "our diplomatic relations and duties to foreign nations").

[157]In declaring that the English admiralty court "never pretended to claim, nor could it rightfully exercise any jurisdiction" except over cases involving services "substantially performed . . . upon waters within the ebb and flow of the tide," 23 U.S. (10 Wheat.) at 427, Story appeared to reject by obiter implication two serious arguments for further limits that had been made in earlier cases and that were to be made again: that the English jurisdiction had extended neither to tidewaters within the body of a county nor to transactions consummated only "substantially" at sea. *See, e.g.*, Waring v. Clarke, 46 U.S. (5 How.) 441, 468-69 (1847) (Woodbury, J., dissenting); La Vengeance, 3 U.S. (3 Dall.) 297, 300 (1796) (argument of Mr. Lee). Story himself had exhaustively refuted both arguments 10 years before on circuit. *See* DeLovio v. Boit, 7 F. Cas. 418 (No. 3776) (C.C.D. Mass. 1815). Possibly all he meant to do in *The Thomas Jefferson* was to say that not even the broadest claims for English admiralty power would support jurisdiction in the case before him. Nevertheless it is not surprising that, when the Court first squarely faced the question of internal tidewaters, Story's opinion was cited as a precedent for upholding jurisdiction. Waring v. Clarke, 46 U.S. (6 How.) 441, 463 (1847). Moreover, Story had added in *The Thomas Jefferson* that there was "no doubt that the jurisdiction exists, although the commencement or termination of the voyage may happen to be at some point beyond the reach of the tide." 23 U.S. (10 Wheat.) at 429. Thus he seems to have attempted to resolve by mere fiat at least one controversial issue that was not before him.

[158]*See, e.g.*, J. LUCAS, ADMIRALTY—CASES AND MATERIALS 31-32 (2d ed. 1978).

[159]DeLovio v. Boit, 7 F. Cas. 418, 441, 443 (No. 3776) (C.C.D. Mass. 1815). *See also* Note, 37 AM. L. REV. 911, 916 (1903) ("It was said of the late Justice Story, that if a bucket of water were brought into his court with a corn cob floating in it, he would at once extend the admiralty jurisdiction of the United States

been result-oriented; Story seems to have bowed to what he viewed as the unfortu-nate but inevitable limitations of the language.[160] Indeed, at the end of the opinion he went out of his way to suggest a legislative remedy. The Judiciary Act already provided for jurisdiction over seizures on navigable waters above the tide;[161] whether Congress might not also extend federal jurisdiction to include suits for seamen's wages on such waters "is unnecessary for us to consider."[162] This does not mean that Story thought the constitutional definition of admiralty broader than the identically worded statutory provision then in effect;[163] he explicitly referred instead to "the power to regulate commerce between the states."[164]

This suggestion raises troublesome constitutional questions of its own. Was Story suggesting that a case might arise under federal law within article III even though the only federal "ingredient" of the case was the statute giving jurisdiction? This would seem to be a significant step beyond the expansive *Osborn* definition.[165] Was he suggesting that the judge-made contract law that would be applied in such a case was a "law of the United States" for jurisdictional purposes? That idea has an interesting

---

over it."); Note, *From Judicial Grant to Legislative Power: The Admiralty Clause in the Nineteenth Century*, 67 HARV. L. REV. 1214, 1217 (1954) [hereinafter cited as Harvard Note] (*The Thomas Jefferson* "stands virtually alone, a curious landmark of admiralty abnegation in a judicial career marked otherwise by determined support of a broadened scope for the American maritime courts."). For lower-court cases before *The Thomas Jefferson* upholding nontidal jurisdiction, see T. SERGEANT, *supra* chapter 3, note 88, at 201-02; Harvard Note, *supra*, at 1218 n.28. There is some evidence that Marshall thought the case had been wrongly decided. Harvard Note, *supra*, at 1220 n.47. Story himself, however, wrote in 1835 that there was "nothing in that opinion, which I can, or desire to take back, if I could." Letter from Joseph Story to Joseph Hopkinson (Jan. 3, 1835), *quoted in* J. McCLELLAN, JOSEPH STORY AND THE AMERICAN CONSTITUTION 225 n.68 (1971).

[160]But see 1 E. JHIRAD & A. SAHN, BENEDICT ON ADMIRALTY 7-6 (7th ed. 1981), arguing that the "classical and scriptural equivalents" of the word "maritime"

> are applied to all sorts of navigable waters. It is not restricted, even in common speech, to waters where the tide ebbs and flows, for the Baltic Sea, the Black Sea, and the Sea of Azof, the Sea of Marmora, the Mediterranean Sea, the great scenes of early maritime enterprise have no visible tide.

The author of the Harvard Note, *supra* note 159, at 1218-20, suggests the Court may have trimmed its sails to deflect mounting criticism from Kentucky, noting that three brothers of a powerful Kentucky Senator were part owners of the vessel in question. The Kentucky controversy is also discussed in 1 C. WARREN, *supra* introduction to part two, note 22, at 633-35. But see G. DUNNE, *supra* note 37, at 239, discounting this view as that of a "cynic" and arguing that "the very historical exegesis which had sustained [Story] in *DeLovio* explicitly foreclosed an inland jurisdiction which English admiralty never had." This interpreta-tion is not inconsistent with *DeLovio*'s rejection of "English statutes, or decisions or common law founded on those statutes," 7 F. Cas. at 443, for in the same breath Story had equated the American jurisdiction with that "which originally and inherently belonged to the admiralty, before any statutable restric-tion," *id.*

[161]Judiciary Act of 1789, ch. 20, § 9, 1 Stat. 73, 77 (current version at 28 U.S.C. § 1333 (1976)).

[162]23 U.S. (10 Wheat.) at 430.

[163]Story never said whether he was dealing with the statutory or the constitutional question in deciding *The Thomas Jefferson*, and Marshall had flatly equated statute and Constitution in the diversity context. *See* Hepburn v. Ellzey, 6 U.S. (2 Cranch) 445 (1805), *discussed supra in* chapter 3, notes 137-51 and accompanying text.

[164]23 U.S. (10 Wheat.) at 430.

[165]*See supra* notes 77-93 and accompanying text. See also the interesting arguments about "protective jurisdiction" made by HART & WECHSLER, *supra* chapter 3, note 14, at 416-17, and rejected by Justice Frankfurter in Textile Workers Union v. Lincoln Mills, 353 U.S. 448, 473-75 (1957) (dissenting opinion).

later history,[166] but it is hard to square with Story's famous opinion in *Swift v. Tyson*,[167] in which he held that much judge-made law was not "law" within the statute requiring federal courts in many cases to apply state "laws" as rules of decision.[168] Was he suggesting that it was not necessary to fit the case within article III at all, because the enumeration of cases in that article did not limit the power of Congress to create additional jurisdiction necessary and proper to the exercise of its legislative powers?[169] Such a position would have contradicted earlier decisions.[170] Perhaps Story meant only that Congress could create federal question jurisdiction to enforce whatever substantive rights it created by statute under the commerce clause,[171] for his suggestion followed the conclusion that the existing statute governing the rights and duties of seamen did not extend the jurisdiction.[172] Yet it was reportedly Story himself who was so moved by the "public inconvenience" caused by his own decision that he dubiously stepped outside the judicial role to draft for Congress a statute extending the jurisdiction to cases arising from shipping on the Great Lakes and their connecting waters—without regard to whether the rights asserted were based on federal statute.[173] Of course it was appropriate for the Court not to be too specific about what Congress might have power to do in the future;[174] it might have been more appropriate still to say nothing on the subject at all.

D. *Wayman v. Southard*

A marshal had enforced a federal judgment pursuant to a Kentucky statute regulating the practice of execution; the Supreme Court in 1825 held the state law inapplicable.[175] The Conformity Act adopted only those state laws in force in 1789;[176]

[166]*See* Illinois v. City of Milwaukee, 406 U.S. 91, 99-100 (1972) (federal common law a law of the United States within 28 U.S.C. § 1331); Romero v. International Terminal Operating Co., 358 U.S. 354, 359-80 (1959) (general maritime law not within section 1331); Textile Workers Union v. Lincoln Mills, 353 U.S. 448, 456-57 (1957) (statute construed to authorize federal courts to develop common law).

[167]41 U.S. (16 Pet.) 1 (1842).

[168]Judiciary Act of 1789, ch. 20, § 34, 1 Stat. 73, 92 (current version at 28 U.S.C. § 1652 (1976)).

[169]*Cf.* National Mut. Ins. Co. v. Tidewater Transfer Co., 337 U.S. 582 (1949) (opinion of Jackson, J., for three Justices).

[170]*E.g.*, Hodgson v. Bowerbank, 9 U.S. (5 Cranch) 303 (1809) (no jurisdiction when alien a party unless other party citizen of a state); Mossman v. Higginson, 4 U.S. (4 Dall.) 12 (1800) (same); Hayburn's Case, 2 U.S. (2 Dall.) 409, 410-14 n.(a) (1792) (Justices on circuit refused to carry out statutory duties that were not "judicial"). *See supra* chapter 1.

In The Propeller Genesee Chief v. Fitzhugh, 53 U.S. (12 How.) 443, 451-53 (1852), *infra* chapter 8, the Court rejected the argument that the commerce clause empowered Congress to extend jurisdiction beyond article III.

[171]U.S. CONST. art. 1, § 8, cl. 3.

[172]23 U.S. (10 Wheat.) at 430.

[173]Act of Feb. 26, 1845, ch. 20, 5 Stat. 726. In deference to the constitutional qualms suggested by the seventh amendment, *see supra* notes 136-41 and accompanying text, this statute anomalously provided for jury trial. For Story's part in the drafting of the statute, see Harvard Note, *supra* note 159, at 1222 & n.66, and authorities cited therein.

[174]Compare the refusal of the Justices to give President Washington an advisory opinion about the legality of belligerent French activities in the United States, discussed *supra* in chapter 1.

[175]23 U.S. (10 Wheat.) 1 (1825).

[176]*Id.* at 32, 41-49. *See* Act of Sept. 29, 1789, ch. 21, § 1, 1 Stat. 93, 93; Act of May 8, 1792, ch. 36, § 2, 1 Stat. 275, 276.

the Rules of Decision Act required the application of state law only "to guide the court in the formation of its judgment";[177] and the state had no power to regulate the procedure of the federal courts directly.[178] Marshall's reasoning on this important constitutional principle consisted of a succession of expletives: it was "one of those political axioms, an attempt to demonstrate which, would be a waste of argument"; the argument "has not been advanced . . . and will, probably, never be advanced"; its "utter inadmissibility will at once present itself to the mind"; it was too "extravagant" to be maintained.[179] Congress, he had said earlier,[180] had power to provide for execution under the necessary and proper clause;[181] he might have argued that this power was implicitly exclusive. In contrast to the question of concurrent state jurisdiction in *Houston v. Moore*,[182] it does seem unlikely that the states were meant to have any such authority.[183] Marshall's conclusion, despite its lack of supporting reasons, is an important datum to which we shall return in considering the question whether other grants of congressional power should be interpreted as exclusive though they are not expressly made so.[184]

Of equal significance were the explicit dicta in *Wayman* upholding provisions of the Conformity Act that authorized the courts to adopt additional rules to govern their own process and procedure.[185] As applied to matters such as the definition of property to be seized, it was argued that these provisions constituted "a delegation of legislative authority which congress . . . has not the power to make."[186] This was the second time this interesting proposition had been argued to the Supreme Court,[187] and this time the Court conceded, without saying why, that Congress could not delegate to the courts or to other tribunals "powers which are strictly and exclusively

[177]23 U.S. (10 Wheat.) at 24. *See* Judiciary Act of 1789, ch. 20, § 34, 1 Stat. 73, 92 (current version at 28 U.S.C. § 1652 (1976)).

[178]23 U.S. (10 Wheat.) at 49-50.

[179]*Id.* at 49.

[180]23 U.S. (10 Wheat.) at 22.

[181]U.S. CONST. art. I, § 8, cl. 18. This conclusion does not seem hard to reach, as Congress's authority extends to laws necessary and proper for executing not only its own powers (which include the power to "constitute tribunals and inferior to the Supreme Court," U.S. CONST. art. I, § 8, cl. 9), but also "all other Powers vested by this Constitution in the Government of the United States, or in any Department or Officer thereof," U.S. CONST. art. I, § 8, cl. 18. Nevertheless, anticipating the later decision in Erie R.R. v. Tompkins, 304 U.S. 64 (1938), that the grant of diversity jurisdiction does not empower the courts to create substantive common law, counsel argued in *Wayman* that it was no more necessary and proper to provide execution rules for diversity cases than to enact a "civil code" for them; in either case state law applied. 23 U.S. (10 Wheat.) at 11-12. For confirmation of the power to regulate diversity procedure after *Erie*, see Hanna v. Plumer, 380 U.S. 460 (1965). See the suggestion in D. CURRIE, *supra* note 99, at 413, that the distinction can be supported by decisions indicating that a forum disinterested in the merits may have a legitimate stake in the administration of its courts.

[182]*See supra* notes 115-29 and accompanying text.

[183]1 Tucker's Appendix to Blackstone, *supra* chapter 3, note 59, at 180, had acknowledged in 1803 that Congress's power to establish inferior federal courts was exclusive, and it might be thought to follow that the same was true of regulating their procedures.

[184]*See* Gibbons v. Ogden, 22 U.S. (9 Wheat.) 1 (1823); Sturges v. Crowninshield, 17 U.S. (4 Wheat.) 122 (1819); *infra* chapters 5, 6.

[185]Act of May 8, 1792, ch. 36, § 2, 1 Stat. 275, 276 (current version at 28 U.S.C. § § 2071-2072 (1976)).

[186]23 U.S. (10 Wheat.) at 15-16 (argument for the defendants); *id.* at 42 (opinion of Marshall, C.J.) (quoted in text).

[187]*See* The Aurora, 11 U.S. (7 Cranch) 382, 386 (1813).

legislative."[188] Nevertheless, and again without giving reasons, Marshall concluded that no clear line separated legislative from other powers: "[C]ongress may certainly delegate to others, powers which the legislative may rightfully exercise itself"—such as "the mere regulation of practice in the court."[189] Thus, as in *The Aurora*,[190] where Johnson had flatly held that an embargo law could be made conditional on a presidential finding that Britain or France was no longer violating our neutrality,[191] Marshall laid down constitutional principles of first importance as a matter of mere fiat.[192] Nor in *Wayman* did he bother citing *The Aurora*; moreover, because the question in the case was the applicability of state law, the power of the court to make its own rule was not in issue at all.[193]

E. *American Insurance Co. v. Canter*

Bales of cotton salvaged from a shipwreck had been purchased at a judicial sale ordered by a court established by the legislature of the Territory of Florida. A federal district court held the Florida decree invalid; the circuit court disagreed; and the Supreme Court, in an 1828 Marshall opinion, upheld the circuit court.[194]

The constitutional objection to the Florida judgment was that the case was within the admiralty jurisdiction vested by article III in the Supreme Court and in "such

[188]23 U.S. (10 Wheat.) at 42. The most convincing reasons would be that the Constitution vests all its granted "legislative Powers" in Congress, U.S. CONST. art. I, § 1, *see* 23 U.S. (10 Wheat.) at 13 (argument of defendants), and that the courts are given only "judicial Power," U.S. CONST. art. III, § 1. On the first argument, see, e.g., Schechter Poultry Corp. v. United States, 295 U.S. 495 (1935); on the second, see Hayburn's Case, 2 U.S. (2 Dall.) 409, 410-14 n.(a) (C.C.D.N.Y. & C.C.D. Pa. 1792), and the Correspondence of the Justices, *supra* chapter 1.

[189]23 U.S. (10 Wheat.) at 42-43.

[190]11 U.S. (7 Cranch) 382 (1813).

[191]*Id.* at 388 ("[W]e can see no sufficient reason, why the legislature should not exercise its discretion in reviving the act of March 1st, 1809, either expressly or conditionally, as their judgment should direct.").

[192]Marshall could have avoided the broad conclusion that some legislative power could be delegated by finding that the judicial authority to try cases carried with it the power to determine how they should be tried. He had made such a suggestion with respect to the contempt power in *Ex parte* Bollman 8 U.S. (4 Cranch) 75, 94 (1807) (dictum); *cf.* Anderson v. Dunn, 19 U.S. (6 Wheat.) 204 (1821), *infra* chapter 6 (upholding the implicit power of the House of Representatives to punish contempts by nonmembers). Possibly that is what was meant by Marshall's statement in *Wayman* that "[a] general superintendence of this subject seems to be properly within the judicial province," 23 U.S. (10 Wheat.) at 45, but that would have been a significant decision too.

Again without relying on precedent or argument, Marshall suggested criteria relevant to drawing the line between permissible and impermissible delegations, a problem that continued to vex the Court for a great many years:

> The line has not been exactly drawn which separates those important subjects, which must be entirely regulated by the legislature itself, from those of less interest, in which a general provision may be made, and power given to those who are to act under such general provisions, to fill up the details.

Id. at 43.

[193]Marshall said as much himself, 23 U.S. (10 Wheat.) at 48; he was discussing the question in answer to the argument that Congress must have meant for new state laws to apply because otherwise federal courts in the newer states would be without an execution law, *id.* at 17.

[194]26 U.S. (1 Pet.) 511 (1828).

inferior Courts as the Congress may . . . ordain and establish,"[195] and therefore that it could be decided only by a court created by Congress.[196] Arguments in support of the jurisdiction included the contention that Congress had delegated its power to the territorial legislature;[197] opposing counsel responded that *"delegatus non potest delegare"*[198]—another foretaste of controversies to come.[199] It was also suggested that the entire Constitution was inapplicable in Florida[200]—a self-defeating argument that would appear to destroy the basis on which the territorial court had been established.[201]

Marshall's response was that article III did not limit the powers of the territorial courts because they had not been created under article III. "They are legislative courts, created in virtue of the general right of sovereignty which exists in the government, or in virtue of that clause which enables congress to make all needful rules and regulations, respecting the territory belonging to the United States."[202] The ambiguity of this passage as to the source of congressional authority over the territories was to haunt the Court in the *Dred Scott* case thirty years later.[203] For present purposes the significance of Marshall's opinion lies in his conclusion that jurisdiction of article III cases could be vested in tribunals not established in accordance with that article. Indeed, Marshall viewed the fact that the territorial judges did not hold their offices during "good Behaviour" as a factor *supporting* the constitutionality of their jurisdiction: article III did not apply *because* the judges had only four-year terms.[204]

But why was it that the Constitution vested the judicial power in courts whose judges enjoyed life tenure and irreducible salary? Hamilton made clear in *The*

[195]U.S. CONST. art. III, § 1.
[196]26 U.S. (1 Pet.) at 529 (Mr. Ogden).
[197]*Id.* at 534-35 (Mr. Whipple).
[198]*Id.* at 540 (Mr. Ogden).
[199]*See, e.g.*, Schechter Poultry Corp. v. United States, 295 U.S. 495 (1935). *See also supra* notes 185-93 and accompanying text (discussing *Wayman v. Southard* and *The Aurora*).
[200]26 U.S. (1 Pet.) at 533 (Mr. Whipple); *id.* at 538 (Mr. Webster).
[201]In the debate over a provisional government for the Louisiana Territory, the Jeffersonians had argued for an inherent power to acquire and govern territory wholly without reference to the Constitution. *See* 2 H. ADAMS, HISTORY OF THE UNITED STATES DURING THE ADMINISTRATIONS OF JEFFERSON AND MADISON 94-134 (1889). Webster seems to have embraced this position in his argument in *Canter*, 26 U.S. (1 Pet.) at 538, but Whipple's argument based the power to govern Florida on the Constitution, *id.* at 533.
[202]26 U.S. (1 Pet.) at 546. The clause in question appears in U.S. CONST. art. IV, § 3, para. 3 ("The Congress shall have Power to dispose of and Make all needful Rules and Regulations respecting the Territory or other Property belonging to the United States . . . .").
Earlier in the opinion Marshall had disposed by *ipse dixit* of the great constitutional question that had prompted Jefferson to agitate vainly for a constitutional amendment before buying Louisiana (*see* 2 H. ADAMS, *supra* note 201, at 74-93): "The constitution confers absolutely on the government of the Union, the powers of making war, and of making treaties; consequently, that government possesses the power of acquiring territory, either by conquest or by treaty." 26 U.S. (1 Pet.) at 542. Because no litigant had challenged the power to acquire Florida, there was no need to say anything on the subject.
[203]Scott v. Sandford, 60 U.S. (19 How.) 393 (1857), *infra* chapter 8. *See also* 1 C. Warren, *supra*, introduction to part two, note 22, at 700. (*Canter* "became the foundation of much of the discussion, thirty years later, in the debates on the power of Congress over slavery in the Territories"). Justice Johnson, in the circuit court opinion in *Canter*, had explicitly denied the applicability of article IV to territory acquired by cession, finding the power to acquire and govern territory "incidental to the treaty-making power, and perhaps to the power of admitting new states into the Union." 26 U.S. (1 Pet.) at 519 n.(a).
[204]26 U.S. (1 Pet.) at 546.

Federalist that this was a means of assuring the judiciary's independence: "That inflexible and uniform adherence to the rights of the Constitution, and of individuals, which we perceive to be indispensable in the courts of justice, can certainly not be expected from Judges who hold their offices by a temporary commission."[205] The Pennsylvania circuit court had reached the same conclusion in refusing to carry out the pension law in *Hayburn's Case* because the law subjected the court's decision to executive revision;[206] the North Carolina circuit in the same instance had concluded that the law was unconstitutional because it gave judicial power to the Secretary of War.[207] The tenure and salary provisions of article III can accomplish their evident purpose only if they are read to forbid the vesting of the functions within its purview in persons not enjoying those protections. Marshall cannot have been right that the violation of article III is its own justification.[208]

In any event, Marshall drew back from the extreme implications of his argument: "Although admiralty jurisdiction can be exercised in the states, in those courts only which are established in pursuance of the third article of the constitution; the same limitation does not extend to the territories."[209] Thus he acknowledged in general the negative implication of article III, but found this limitation inapplicable to the power to govern the territories.[210] *Canter*, as we have seen, was not the first case to raise the question of the constitutional status of those peculiar American areas that are not

---

[205]THE FEDERALIST No. 78, *supra* chapter 3, note 29, at 470-71 (A. Hamilton). *See also* 3 J. STORY, *supra* chapter 3, note 82, at 457-97 (quoting and expanding on *The Federalist*); 1 Tucker's Appendix to Blackstone, *supra* chapter 3, note 59, at 268 (praising the good-behavior requirement as placing judges "beyond the reach of hope or fear, where they might hold the balance of justice steadily in their hands").

[206]2 U.S. (2 Dall.) 409, 411-12 n.(a) (1792).

[207]*Id.* at 413:

> [F]or though congress may certainly establish . . . courts of appellate jurisdiction, yet such courts must consist of judges appointed in the manner the constitution requires, and holding their offices by no other tenure than that of their good behavior, by which tenure the office of secretary at war is not held.

[208]Justice Washington had already said in Houston v. Moore, 18 U.S. (5 Wheat.) 1, 25-26 (1820), that article III cases could be decided in state courts unless Congress otherwise provided, though Justice Johnson's peculiar opinion in Ogden v. Saunders, 25 U.S. (12 Wheat.) 213, 271 (1827), *infra* chapter 5, and some dicta of Story's about admiralty itself, *see supra* note 121, pointed the other way. Marshall might have cited the power of state courts over article III cases, as Brandeis was later to do in Crowell v. Benson, 285 U.S. 22, 86-87 & n.22 (1932) (dissenting opinion), as precedent that jurisdiction over such cases was not limited to article III courts. But *The Federalist* saw no inconsistency in arguing both that state courts could decide article III cases, THE FEDERALIST No. 82, *supra* chapter 3, note 29, at 492-93 (A. Hamilton), and that federal judges must have tenure, *id.* No. 78, at 469-72 (A. Hamilton). There are obvious grounds for deference to state interests that distinguish state courts from federal courts outside article III, and state courts, whatever their weaknesses, at least are independent of the President and of Congress. *See* Krattenmaker, *Article III and Judicial Independence: Why the New Bankruptcy Courts are Unconstitutional*, 70 GEO. L.J. 297, 304 (1981) (arguing that the central concern of the tenure and salary requirements was "the separation of powers at the *federal* level") (emphasis in original).

[209]26 U.S. (1 Pet.) at 456. Story, who had gone along in *Canter* despite his firm attachment to the tenure provisions, *see supra* note 205, explained in his treatise that territorial courts were a special case. 3 J. STORY, *supra* chapter 3, note 82, at 498-99.

[210]United States v. More, 7 U.S. (3 Cranch) 159 (1805), had presented the same question in the context of the District of Columbia, and the Court had not decided it. The lower court decision in *More*, which Marshall did not cite, held the salary provision of article III applicable within the District. United States v. More, *reprinted in* 7 U.S. (3 Cranch) at 160 n.(b) (inserted by Judge Cranch). See chapter 3 *supra*.

states,[211] yet Marshall referred to no prior decisions. Nor did he give any reason worthy of the name for his essentially bald conclusion; from his irreproachable statement that in legislating for a territory Congress has both general and local powers[212] it does not follow that the Framers were unconcerned about the independence of territorial judges.[213]

Thus even as to the territories themselves, the poorly explained *Canter* holding is difficult to reconcile with the purposes of article III. Moreover, despite its express disclaimer, the opinion has since been taken as authority for vesting powers over certain article III cases within the states in federal officers who do not enjoy the independence that article provides.[214] The first small step down the road to perdition may prove to be irreversible.

F. *Cherokee Nation v. Georgia*

The Cherokee Nation sued in the Supreme Court to enjoin the state from enforcing Georgia law within the territory reserved to the Cherokees by treaty. Jurisdiction was denied in 1831.[215] The Cherokees lived within the boundaries of the United States and their rights were subject to congressional restriction; the separate treatment of "foreign nations" and "Indian tribes" in the commerce clause[216] confirmed the conclusion that, although the Cherokees were a "State," they were not a "foreign State" within the article III provision extending the judicial power to controversies between "a State . . . and foreign states."[217]

This reasoning harks back to *Hepburn v. Ellzey*,[217] where Marshall had used a similar analogy to show the District of Columbia was not a "state" within article

---

[211]*See supra* chapter 3, notes 137-51 and accompanying text.

[212]26 U.S. (1 Pet.) at 546.

[213]*See* C. WRIGHT, *supra* chapter 3, note 19, at 31, 37 (terming *Canter* "a doctrine of doubtful soundness": "If judicial independence is of vital importance in the states, it is hard to see why it is not equally valuable in territories."). The latter-day rationalization that the Framers could not have intended to leave the country with a flock of judges with nothing to do but collect their salaries after a territory became a state, *see* O'Donoghue v. United States, 289 U.S. 516, 536-38 (1933), had to be abandoned when the *Canter* doctrine was extended to the District of Columbia, which was not meant to be transitory. *See* Palmore v. United States, 411 U.S. 389, 405-07 (1973). Moreover, this was a dangerous argument, because the reference to "such inferior Courts as the Congress *may from time to time* ordain and establish," U.S. CONST. art. III, § 1 (emphasis added), suggests that any grant of jurisdiction may be temporary—as was amply demonstrated by the repeal of the Judiciary Act of 1801. *See supra* chapter 3, notes 75-76 and accompanying text.

[214]*See Ex parte* Bakelite Corp., 279 U.S. 438, 448-51 (1929) (Court of Customs Appeals). *See generally* Currie, *Bankruptcy Judges and the Independent Judiciary*, 16 CREIGHTON L. REV. 441 (1983).

[215]30 U.S. (5 Pet.) 1, 29-30 (1831). The background of the litigation, including the execution of a Cherokee in defiance of a Supreme Court stay, *see id.* at 12-13, is discussed in 4 A. BEVERIDGE, *supra* introduction to part two, note 10, at 539-46, and 1 C. WARREN, *supra* introduction to part two, note 22, at 729-79.

[216]U.S. CONST. art. I, § 8, cl. 3 (granting Congress power "[t]o regulate Commerce with foreign Nations, and among the several States, and with the Indian Tribes").

[217]30 U.S. (5 Pet.) at 16-20 (construing U.S. CONST. art III, § 2, para. 1). Johnson, concurring, also doubted the Cherokees were a "State" at all, because "[t]hey never have been recognized as holding sovereignty over the territory they occupy." 30 U.S. (5 Pet.) at 22.

[218]6 U.S. (2 Cranch) 445 (1805).

III.[219] This time he acknowledged that "the same words have not necessarily the same meaning . . . in different parts of the same instrument," but he found "nothing in the context, and nothing in the subject of the article," to suggest "an intention to desert" the "former meaning" of the term "foreign state."[220] He did not refer to the purpose of the clause, which might have cut against him.[221]

This resolution made it unnecessary to decide whether Georgia was immune to suit by an Indian tribe, and Marshall said nothing on that subject. Thompson, joined in dissent by Story, said there was no immunity because the suit was outside the terms of the eleventh amendment.[222] The latter statement was true enough, but later cases would show it was not a complete answer,[223] and Thompson did not bother to invoke the authority of *Chisholm v. Georgia.*[224]

Marshall suggested an additional difficulty that he found it unnecessary to resolve:

> The bill requires us to control the legislature of Georgia, and to restrain the exertion of its physical force. The propriety of such an interposition by the court may be well questioned; it savors too much of the exercise of political power, to be within the proper province of the judicial department.[225]

Indeed as to some matters, such as "the laws making it criminal [for the Cherokees] to exercise the usual power of self-government in their own country," Marshall squarely said "this court cannot interpose; at least, in the form in which those matters are presented."[226] Just what Marshall meant by these passages is less than clear; obviously they lend some support to the later political question doctrine.[227] It does

[219] *See supra* chapter 3, notes 137-51 and accompanying text.
[220] 30 U.S. (5 Pet.) at 19-20. Thompson suggested in dissent that Indians had been specially mentioned in the commerce clause to counteract any negative inference that might otherwise have arisen from the separate powers of Congress respecting Indians in article 9 of the Articles of Confederation. *Id.* at 63-64. Moreover, he argued, the executive in negotiating treaties with Indian nations had consistently regarded them as "foreign." *Id.* at 59-62.
[221] *See, e.g.,* Chisholm v. Georgia, 2 U.S. (2 Dall.) 419, 467 (1792) (separate opinion of Cushing, J.) ("for preventing controversies between foreign powers or citizens from rising to extremities and to an appeal to the sword, a national tribunal was necessary"); THE FEDERALIST No. 80, *supra* chapter 3, note 29, at 475-76 (A. Hamilton) (assimilating controversies involving foreign states to "those which involve the PEACE of the CONFEDERACY" and arguing that "the peace of the WHOLE ought not to be left at the disposal of a PART"). For a thoughtfully reasoned contemporaneous criticism of the opinion on this and other grounds, see Everett, *The Cherokee Case,* 33 N. AM. L. REV. 136, 142-50 (1831).
[222] 30 U.S. (5 Pet.) at 52.
[223] *E.g.,* Monaco v. Mississippi, 292 U.S. 313 (1934) (foreign state cannot sue unconsenting state); Hans v. Louisiana, 134 U.S. 1 (1890) (citizen cannot bring federal question case against his own state without consent).
[224] 2 U.S. (2 Dall.) 419 (1793) (holding, before adoption of the eleventh amendment, that one state could be sued by a citizen of another). *See supra* chapter 1. In the same Term in which *Cherokee* was decided, the Court upheld its jurisdiction in a suit by one state against another without discussing immunity. New Jersey v. New York, 30 U.S. (5 Pet.) 283 (1831).
[225] 30 U.S. (5 Pet.) at 20.
[226] *Id.*
[227] *See* Baker v. Carr, 369 U.S. 186, 208-37 (1962). Marshall did not cite in *Cherokee* his earlier reference to "political" issues in Marbury v. Madison, 5 U.S. (1 Cranch) 137, 165-67, 169-71 (1803). *See supra* chapter 3, note 18.

seem, however, that Marshall did not mean the question of Georgia's legislative jurisdiction over the reservation was inherently nonjusticiable, for the next year the Court was to resolve that very question in *Worcester v. Georgia.*[228] If one has a legitimate complaint about Marshall's cryptic comments about "political" issues, it is that he once again felt called upon to discuss an issue not properly before him. Johnson, who made the "political" nature of the claim an alternative ground of his concurrence,[229] was even more willing to decide the larger question.[230]

Johnson's concurrence, together with the two dissents and another concurring opinion by Baldwin,[231] left Marshall speaking in the strict sense for only three of the seven members of the Court; the reporter's statement that the Chief Justice "delivered the opinion of the court" must be taken subject to qualification.

With the *Cherokee Nation* case in 1831 we approach the end of an era. Only four of the seven Justices who had constituted the Marshall Court for so many years remained. Two of the newcomers, Thompson and Baldwin, were striking out on their own, while both Johnson and Story, the most assertive of the old-timers, also expressed independent views. Marshall's iron grip, as other contemporaneous cases will confirm, was loosening; *Cherokee* was a long way both from the brief and unanimous Marshall pronouncements of the first decade and from the grandiloquent and largely unchallenged essays of the period around 1820, when Marshall's power was at its height. In another four years Johnson and Duvall, as well as Marshall, would be gone, leaving only Story of the central seven; a nine-member Court with seven Jackson and Van Buren appointees would be sitting by 1837.[232]

The most striking feature of the Court's decisions respecting the federal courts until almost the end of Marshall's tenure was the rarity of expressed differences of

---

[228]31 U.S. (6 Pet.) 515 (1832). Maybe Marshall was talking of limits on the traditional equity jurisdiction; maybe he was foreshadowing the limited view of state standing taken in Massachusetts v. Mellon, 262 U.S. 447 (1923); maybe he was relying implicitly on article III's "Case" or "Controversy" language or its reference to the "judicial" power.

[229]30 U.S. (5 Pet.) at 28-29. Even Thompson in dissent, *id.* at 75, conceded the Court should not enforce all treaty rights or exercise "political power." He insisted, however, that the Cherokees claimed invasions of "rights of person or property" that equity could protect—such as the seizure of their mines and the threatened survey and redistribution of their lands. *Id.* at 75-77.

[230]This, as we shall see, was characteristic of Johnson. *Cf.* Gibbons v. Ogden, 22 U.S. (9 Wheat.) 1 (1823); Fletcher v. Peck, 10 U.S. (16 Cranch) 87 (1810); *infra* chapters 5, 6.

[231]Justice Henry Baldwin, whom we here meet for the first time, was an 1830 Jackson appointee who belongs chiefly to the Taney period. In *Cherokee* he concurred "in the opinion of the Court, . . . but not for the reasons assigned." 30 U.S. (5 Pet.) at 31. He stressed the history of our Indian relations, drew inferences not only from the commerce clause but also from article I's apportionment of representatives and direct taxes according to population "excluding Indians not taxed," U.S. Const. art. I, § 2, para. 3, and lectured his dissenting colleagues as to the "sacrilege" of departing from the "plain" terms of the Constitution "according to any fancied use, object, purpose or motive, which, by an ingenious train of reasoning I might bring my mind to believe was the reason for its adoption." 30 U.S. (5 Pet.) at 41-43. "We can thus expound the constitution," he said snappishly, "without a reference to the definitions of a state or nation by any foreign writer, hypothetical reasoning, or the dissertations of the Federalist." *Id.* at 40-41.

[232]*See* G. Gunther, *supra* introduction to part two, note 25, app. A, at A-2, A-3. The eighth and ninth positions were created by the Act of March 3, 1837, ch. 32, § 1, 5 Stat. 176, 176 (current version at 28 U.S.C. § 1 (1976)).

opinion. Johnson was the most likely to dissent[233] or to concur specially,[234] and at the end he went so far as to say it was his "practice" to give his own opinion "on all constitutional questions."[235] Though sometimes less favorable to federal jurisdiction than Marshall,[236] even Johnson usually went along, most notably with the crucial decisions in *Martin v. Hunter's Lessee* and *Cohens v. Virginia*, and his concurring opinion in the former case indicates he did so there out of conviction, not from a mere respect for the principle of unanimity. Story was more nationalistic than the Court in *Houston* and in *Cherokee*, and in the latter case Thompson was with him. Apart from these, Baldwin's concurrence in *Cherokee*, and Story's unidentified compatriot in *Houston*, no Justice uttered a divergent word in any of the cases considered in this or the preceding chapter.

The overwhelming preponderance of opinions for the Court in this field during this period, moreover, bore the name of Marshall. Story spoke for the Court in *Martin*, and Paterson in *Stuart v. Laird*, where the Chief Justice could not participate; Story was also the spokesman in the much later cases of *The Thomas Jefferson* and *Parsons v. Bedford*. Johnson wrote for the Court in *Bank of Columbia v. Okely*, and Washington spoke for himself in *Houston*, where there was no majority opinion. The other eight Justices—Cushing, Chase, Moore, Livingston, Todd, Duvall, Trimble, and McLean—were not heard from at all.

In terms of results, the Court in the Marshall years was friendly toward the powers of federal courts but, with the possible exception of the sovereign immunity cases involving the national bank, not immoderately so.[237] Both the diversity and admiralty powers were construed with what later cases have shown to be considerable restraint,[238] as was the original jurisdiction in *Cherokee*; concurrent state authority even over criminal cases was recognized in Washington's opinion in *Houston v. Moore*. The most memorable cases, *Marbury* and *Martin*, which established the Court's effective power to determine the constitutionality of federal and state legislation, merely confirmed what seems to have been understood at the Philadelphia Convention.

With regard to the crafting of opinions, we have inconsistent glimpses of Story, careful and convincing in *Martin* and conclusory in *The Thomas Jefferson*. Johnson was strong in his use of precedent in *Planters' Bank*, confused in *Osborn* and in *Bank of Columbia v. Okely*, and eager to decide more than was necessary in *Cherokee*. The rest is almost all Marshall: rhetorical flourish, bare assertion, plentiful dicta, multiple holdings, inattention to favorable precedent, and emphasis on the undesir-

---

[233]*See supra* chapter 3, notes 118-32, chapter 4, notes 77-102, 103-14 and accompanying text, and *supra* note 98 (discussing Ex parte *Bollman, Osborn v. Bank of the United States, Bank of the United States v. Planters' Bank*, and *Governor of Georgia v. Madrazo*).

[234]*See supra* notes 1-37, 115-32, 215-31, and accompanying text (discussing *Martin v. Hunter's Lessee, Houston v. Moore*, and *Cherokee Nation v. Georgia*).

[235]Cherokee Nation v. Georgia, 30 U.S. (5 Pet.) 1, 21 (1831).

[236]In three of the four cases cited *supra* in note 234, Johnson dissented from the upholding of jurisdiction; in *Madrazo*, however, he dissented from its denial.

[237]*See* G. HASKINS & H. JOHNSON, *supra* introduction to part two, note 23, at 399 ("Self-restraint and extreme caution in asserting jurisdiction characterized the Supreme Court from 1801 to 1815 . . . .").

[238]*See supra* chapter 3, notes 10-11 and accompanying text.

able consequences of an interpretation at variance with his own. We shall see these same characteristics confirmed in the Court's contemporaneous decisions respecting the powers of Congress and of the states, which are the subject of the next two chapters.

5

The Contract Clause
and Natural Law

In the twelve years of its existence before the appointment of John Marshall as Chief Justice, the Supreme Court had decided few significant constitutional questions.[1] In the first decade of Marshall's tenure, apart from *Marbury v. Madison*,[2] the Court's constitutional docket consisted almost entirely of relatively minor matters respecting the powers of the federal courts.[3] Although important issues of federal jurisdiction confronted the Justices until Marshall's death in 1835,[4] after 1810 the constitutional docket was dominated for the first time by cases raising important substantive issues respecting state and congressional powers: *Fletcher v. Peck*,[5] *McCulloch v. Maryland*,[6] *Gibbons v. Ogden*,[7] *Brown v. Maryland*,[8] *Trustees of Dartmouth College v. Woodward*,[9] and many others. These decisions are the subject of the present chapter and of the one that follows.

With the replacement of the old Federalists William Cushing and Samuel Chase by Gabriel Duvall and Joseph Story in 1811, the Court consisted of two Justices appointed by President Adams—Marshall and Bushrod Washington—and five appointed by Presidents Jefferson and Madison—William Johnson, Brockholst Livingston, Thomas Todd, Duvall, and Story. These seven men were to sit together until 1823.[10] As on jurisdictional issues,[11] they were to speak with remarkable

[1]*See supra* chapters 1, 2.
[2]5 U.S. (1 Cranch) 137 (1803).
[3]*See supra* chapter 3.
[4]*See supra* chapter 4.
[5]10 U.S. (6 Cranch) 87 (1810).
[6]17 U.S. (4 Wheat.) 316 (1819).
[7]22 U.S. (9 Wheat.) 1 (1824).
[8]25 U.S. (12 Wheat.) 419 (1827).
[9]17 U.S. (4 Wheat.) 518 (1819).
[10]The terms of the Justices as well as their political party affiliations and the Presidents who appointed them are given in G. GUNTHER, CASES AND MATERIALS ON CONSTITUTIONAL LAW app. A, at A-1 to A-2

unanimity on other constitutional questions, and usually through the medium of Marshall himself. Major differences of opinion first surfaced in *Ogden v. Saunders*[12] in 1827; they became increasingly frequent as Marshall's earlier colleagues were supplanted by Smith Thompson, Robert Trimble, John McLean, and Henry Baldwin,[13] and at the end of the Marshall period three important constitutional cases had to be put off until the Taney period[14] because the illness of Duvall and Johnson prevented any decision from commanding a majority of the whole Court.[15]

The first set of substantive constitutional questions to command the serious attention of the Marshall Court, and the largest single group of cases presenting such questions during the entire Marshall period, were those under the clause of article I, section 10, forbidding the states to pass any "Law impairing the Obligation of Contracts."[16] While various Justices had made earlier suggestions about the meaning of this clause as an aid in construing other constitutional provisions,[17] the first case to confront the Court with the clause itself was *Fletcher v. Peck*[18] in 1810.

I. FLETCHER V. PECK

In 1795 the Georgia legislature evidently was bribed to enact a statute directing the Governor to convey most of what is now Alabama and Mississippi for less than two cents an acre. The next year a new legislature irately repealed the grant. Peck later

---

(10th ed. 1980). The terms of the Justices of the Marshall era are presented graphically in chapter 3 *supra* at 649 n.26.

[11]*See generally supra* chapters 3, 4.

[12]25 U.S. (12 Wheat.) 213 (1827).

[13]For a chronology of the Justices, see sources cited *supra* note 10. James Wayne sat with Marshall during the Chief Justice's last term in 1835, *see* 34 U.S. (9 Pet.) v (1835), but the Court was shorthanded that year and decided no constitutional cases, *see infra* note 15.

[14]Appointed by President Jackson in 1836, Roger Taney remained Chief Justice until his death in 1864. *See* G. GUNTHER, *supra* note 10, app. A, at A-2.

[15]Briscoe v. Commonwealth's Bank, 33 U.S. (8 Pet.) 118, 122 (1834) (also withholding judgment in *Mayor of New York v. Miln*) ("The practice of this court is, not (except in cases of absolute necessity) to deliver any judgment in cases where constitutional questions are involved, unless four judges concur in opinion, thus making the decision that of a majority of the whole court." *Id.*). Story and Charles Warren reported, without citation, that the same was true of the *Charles River Bridge* case. Charles River Bridge v. Warren Bridge, 36 U.S. (11 Pet.) 420, 583-84 (1837) (Story, J., dissenting); 1 C. WARREN, THE SUPREME COURT IN UNITED STATES HISTORY 790 (rev. ed. 1926).

According to Marshall's biographer, "Thompson, McLean, and Baldwin thought the [*Briscoe*] and [*Miln*] laws Constitutional; Marshall, Story, Duval [*sic*] and Johnson believed them invalid." 4 A. BEVERIDGE, LIFE OF JOHN MARSHALL 583 (1919) (citing no authority). Marshall optimistically directed reargument at the 1835 Term "under the expectation that a larger number of the judges may then be present," *Briscoe*, 33 U.S. (8 Pet.) at 122, but Johnson died and Duvall resigned, *see* 34 U.S. (9 Pet.) v (1835). Though the former was replaced by James Wayne, the Court refused to decide the cases until the second vacancy was filled. 34 U.S. (9 Pet.) 85 (1835). The cases were finally decided in 1837. Briscoe v. Bank of Kentucky, 36 U.S. (11 Pet.) 257 (1837); New York v. Miln, 36 U.S. (11 Pet.) 102 (1837); Charles River Bridge v. Warren Bridge, 36 U.S. (11 Pet.) 420 (1837). See *infra* chapter 7.

[16]U.S. CONST. art. I, § 10, para. 1.

[17]Calder v. Bull, 3 U.S. (3 Dall.) 386, 390 (1798) (separate opinion of Chase, J.) (construing the ex post facto clause of U.S. CONST. art. I, § 10, para. 1); Chisholm v. Georgia, 2 U.S. (2 Dall.) 419, 465-66 (1793) (separate opinion of Wilson, J.) (interpreting U.S. CONST. art. III, § 2). See *supra* chapters 1, 2.

[18]10 U.S. (6 Cranch) 87 (1810).

acquired some of these so-called "Yazoo" lands and deeded them to Fletcher with covenants of good title. Fletcher sued in federal court for breach of covenant, arguing that the original sale was invalid or had been lawfully rescinded. The Supreme Court rejected both contentions.[19]

The interesting objection to the initial grant was that it was vitiated by the alleged bribery.[20] Whether a court could ever set aside a law on this ground, Marshall wrote, "may well be doubted," and there would be "much difficulty" in administering any such rule: "Must it be direct corruption? or would interest or undue influence of any kind be sufficient? Must the vitiating cause operate on a majority? or on what number of the members?"[21] The question "how far the validity of a law depends upon the motives of its framers,"[22] as Marshall put it, was to be a pervasive one for the Court, transcending the bribery question and not susceptible to a simple answer.[23] It seems clear in *Fletcher* that there was nothing in the *federal* Constitution to make birbery a basis for striking down state legislation. Although such a limit might conceivably have been implicit in the *Georgia* constitution, Marshall made no attempt to tie the argument to that document, and he already had said the conveyance satisfied the state constitution.[24]

Marshall found it unnecessary to decide, however, whether bribery might invalidate the law; the state was not a party, and to decide "collaterally and incidentally" a "solemn question . . . respecting the corruption of the sovereign power of a state" would be "indecent, in the extreme."[25] The Court did not use the modern term "standing," but in effect it denied standing to assert the right of a third party.[26]

---

[19]*Id.* at 134, 139. For the interesting background of the litigation, see 3 A. BEVERIDGE, *supra* note 15, at 546-602; G. HASKINS & H. JOHNSON, 2 HISTORY OF THE SUPREME COURT OF THE UNITED STATES 336-53 (1981); 1 C. WARREN, *supra* note 15, at 392-99; and especially C. MACGRATH, YAZOO *passim* (1966).

[20]*Fletcher*, 10 U.S. (6 Cranch) at 129.

[21]*Id.* at 130. Justice Johnson in his separate opinion was even more emphatic, not only pointing to "insuperable difficulties" but terming the suggested inquiry an "absurdity" and concluding in circular fashion that legislative acts "must be considered pure . . . because there is no power that can declare them otherwise." *Id.* at 144.

[22]*Id.* at 130.

[23]*See, e.g.*, Washington v. Davis, 426 U.S. 229, 239-45 (1976) (equal protection violation requires a showing of racially discriminatory purpose); United States v. Darby, 312 U.S. 100, 114 (1941) (regulation of interstate commerce "not a forbidden invasion of state power merely because . . . its motive . . . is to restrict the use of articles of commerce within the states of destination"). *See generally* Ely, *Legislative and Administrative Motivation in Constitutional Law*, 79 YALE L. J. 1205 (1970); *see also infra* chapter 6, notes 39-46 and accompanying text (discussing the "pretext" passage in *McCulloch v. Maryland*).

[24]*Fletcher*, 10 U.S. (6 Cranch) at 128-29. He concluded, moreover, by holding that Georgia had owned the disputed lands despite their reservation for the use of the Indians in a royal proclamation of 1763. *Id.* at 139-43. Justice Johnson dissented from this conclusion. *Id.* at 145-47.

[25]*Id.* at 130-31. Elsewhere the Court suggested that bribery or fraud would be no basis for invalidating the claim of a later bona fide purchaser at common law, *id.* at 133-34, but this was not the expressed reason for refusing to determine whether the sale was invalid.

[26]*Cf.* Warth v. Seldin, 422 U.S. 490, 502 (1975) (taxpayers may not assert rights of victims of exclusionary zoning); Tileston v. Ullman, 318 U.S. 44, 46 (1943) (physician lacks standing to assert patient's due process claims). Indeed, just the year before *Fletcher*, the Court had refused to allow a litigant to argue the treaty rights of others. Owings v. Norwood's Lessee, 9 U.S. (5 Cranch) 344, 347 (1809). Nevertheless, *Fletcher* did decide on the merits that Georgia had no power to rescind the grant. *Fletcher*, 10 U.S. (6 Cranch) at 139; *see infra* notes 30-36 and accompanying text. Its reluctance to pass on the rights of the absent state was, without much explanation, confined to the bribery question.

130

Possibly in so doing the Court was influenced by the fear that this was, as Justice Johnson suggested, "a mere feigned case."[27] Today the Court would dismiss a collusive suit for want of a case or controversy,[28] but collusion is hard to establish. The danger that it may pass undetected may support the prophylactic decision not to allow litigation of the rights of third parties, though that is not an inflexible rule today.[29]

At the constitutional level the more interesting issue was whether the legislature had power to revoke the grant after it had been made. On this question Marshall's opinion bristles with references suggesting unwritten limitations derived from natural law. He began invoking "certain great principles of justice, whose authority is universally acknowledged,"[30] without relating them to any particular document. After adverting to the traditional equitable rights of bona fide purchasers,[31] he stated flatly that "when absolute rights have vested" under a statutory contract, "a repeal of

[27]*Fletcher*, 10 U.S. (6 Cranch) at 147. John Quincy Adams, who had argued for Peck, reported that both Marshall and Livingston had privately expressed "the reluctance of the Court to decide the case at all, as it appeared manifestly made up for the purpose of getting the Court's judgment." 1 MEMOIRS OF JOHN QUINCY ADAMS 546 (C. Adams ed. 1874), *quoted in* 1 C. WARREN, *supra* note 15, at 395. Marshall reportedly said from the bench that the pleadings revealed "that at the time when the covenants were made the parties had notice of the acts covenanted against." 1 MEMOIRS OF JOHN QUINCY ADAMS, *supra*, at 547, *quoted in* C. MAGRATH, *supra* note 19, at 66. If Cranch's report is anywhere near complete, Luther Martin's argument for Fletcher overlooked the two most important issues in the case. *See* 10 U.S. (6 Cranch) at 115, 124-25; C. MAGRATH, *supra* note 19, at 69 (explaining that Martin "was so drunk during its presentation that Marshall had the Court adjourn until the counsel regained his sobriety"). After the defendant lost in the Supreme Court on a technicality, *Fletcher*, 10 U.S. (6 Cranch) at 125-27, the plaintiff agreed to allow him to amend his pleadings, *id.* at 127, and the case was reconsidered. See also G. HASKINS & H. JOHNSON, *supra* note 19, at 344-45, adding that the amount in controversy originally stated in the complaint had been subsequently altered to conform with statutory minima, but arguing that the suit was not improper because such actions were and still are "an appropriate method of removing clouds on land titles."

With what has been variously characterized as naiveté, *id.* at 344, and as sarcasm, G. DUNNE, JUSTICE JOSEPH STORY AND THE RISE OF THE SUPREME COURT 75 (1970), Justice Johnson consented to decide the case because of his confidence that "the respectable gentlemen . . . engaged for the parties . . . would never consent to impose a mere feigned case upon this court," *Fletcher*, 10 U.S. (6 Cranch) at 147-48. Marshall's opinion did not mention the problem at all. Beveridge praised the Court for reaching the merits because the times demanded that a message be sent to the states about their federal obligations. He also judged it improper for Johnson to shift responsibility to the attorneys: if not prepared to denounce the case "for what everybody believed it to be, and what it really was," he should have said nothing at all. 3 A. BEVERIDGE, *supra* note 15, at 592-93. Compare the Court's earlier willingness to entertain an apparently collusive controversy over the validity of the federal carriage tax in Hylton v. United States, 3 U.S. (3 Dall.) 171 (1796), *discussed supra in* chapter 2.

[28]*See, e.g.*, United States v. Johnson, 319 U.S. 302, 305 (1943).

[29]*See, e.g.*, Barrows v. Jackson, 346 U.S. 249, 257 (1953) (seller of home may assert buyer's right to freedom from racial discrimination). Professor Warren viewed the Court's refusal to pass on the bribery question as a significant victory for state rights despite the ultimate invalidation of the repealing act: had the Court ruled otherwise, "a wide door would have been opened for the attack upon State legislation in countless instances." 1 C. WARREN, *supra* note 15, at 397. See also G. HASKINS & H. JOHNSON, *supra* note 19, at 348, calling the decision on the bribery issue "an important and far-reaching limitation on the power of the judiciary insofar as the separation of powers was concerned" and relating it to an attempt by Marshall "to dissociate law and the Court from politics."

[30]*Fletcher*, 10 U.S. (6 Cranch) at 133.

[31]*Id.* at 133-35.

the law cannot devest those rights."[32] He went on to say that "[i]t may well be doubted, whether the nature of society and of government does not prescribe some limits to the legislative power; and, if any be prescribed, where are they to be found, if the property of an individual, fairly and honestly acquired, may be seized without compensation."[33] This led him to add that the validity of the repeal "might well be doubted, were Georgia a single sovereign power."[34] He concluded that it was the Court's unanimous opinion that "Georgia was restrained, either by general principles which are common to our free institutions, or by the particular provisions of the constitution of the United States," from revoking its grant.[35] Johnson, concurring specially with respect to the invalidity of the repeal, flatly renounced reliance on the Constitution: "I do it, on a general principle, on the reason and nature of things: a principle which will impose laws even on the Deity."[36]

All of this is reminiscent of Justice Chase's famous dictum in *Calder v. Bull*[37] that "[t]here are certain vital principles in our free republican governments, which will determine and overrule an apparent and flagrant abuse of legislative power."[38] Just what Chase meant by that has been disputed.[39] Similarly, it is not clear that Marshall meant in *Fletcher* to say the courts could set aside legislation that they found contrary to natural law. The statement that repeal cannot "devest" rights seems to be one of fact rather than of law, for it follows a declaration that legislatures "cannot undo" an act . . . done" and is followed by the statement that "the act of annulling them, *if legitimate*, is rendered so by a power applicable to the case of every individual in the community."[40] For the suggestion that the repeal was of doubtful validity even apart from the federal Constitution, Marshall offered a positivistic explanation:

> To the legislature, all legislative power is granted; but the question, whether the act of transferring the property of an individual to the public, be in the nature of the legislative power, is well worthy of serious reflection.
>
> It is the peculiar province of the legislature, to prescribe general rules for the government of society; the application of those rules to individuals in society would seem to be the duty of other departments.[41]

---

[32]*Id.* at 135. On the question whether there were any bona fide purchasers, see C. MAGRATH, *supra* note 19, at 16-19. The validity of the repeal was decided on demurrer, however, which assumed such purchasers existed.

[33]10 U.S. (6 Cranch) at 135.

[34]*Id.* at 136.

[35]*Id.* at 139.

[36]*Id.* at 143.

[37]3 U.S. (3 Dall.) 386 (1798).

[38]*Id.* at 388. See E. CORWIN, LIBERTY AGAINST GOVERNMENT 66 (1948), arguing that the notion of natural law limits on legislative power was embraced "at one time or other by all of the leading judges and advocates of the initial period of our constitutional history, an era which closes about 1830."

[39]*See supra* chapter 1.

[40]10 U.S. (6 Cranch) at 135 (emphasis added).

[41]*Id.* at 136. He had already analogized the legislature's action to a judgment setting aside a fraudulent conveyance and described it as "judging in its own case." *Id.* at 133. This was a sweeping enough suggestion; one of the grounds of decision in *Calder* had been based upon the recognition that in Connecticut, at least, the legislature *did* have authority to perform judicial functions. 3 U.S. (3 Dall.) at

Thus he seems to have been suggesting not that the repeal offended natural law, but that it was not authorized by the grant of legislative power in the Georgia constitution.[42] Finally, even the ultimate declaration of invalidity under "either" the Constitution or "general principles" need not reflect an alternative holding based on natural law. Not only might these "general principles" be those Marshall had suggested should be read into the state constitutional delegation of legislative power; this was also his statement of the "unanimous" opinion of the Court. The reference to "general principles" was necessary to make this statement true of Justice Johnson; it need not imply that other Justices agreed with him.[43]

In any event, one clear basis of the *Fletcher* decision, if not the sole basis,[44] was that the repealing act violated the provision of article I, section 10, that "[n]o State shall . . . pass any . . . Law impairing the Obligation of Contracts."[45] One problem with this conclusion was that Marshall had just suggested that the act in question was not "legislation," and one ground of decision in *Calder v. Bull* had been that the comparable reference in the same clause to ex post facto "Law[s]"[46] applied only to "legislative" acts.[47] The *Fletcher* opinion did not advert to this difficulty.

Marshall did, however, address two important arguments against the applicability of the contract clause. The first question, as he saw it, was whether a "grant" was a "contract."[48] He concluded that it was: Blackstone had said not all contracts were executory, and the grant "implies a contract" by the grantor "not to reassert" the right conveyed.[49] Moreover, "[i]t would be strange if a contract to convey was

395 (Paterson, J.), 398 (Iredell, J.), 400-01 (Cushing, J.). Marshall made no effort to distinguish the Georgia and Connecticut constitutions. Moreover, it is not clear that the revocation was any less legislative an act than the original grant; it was certainly as "general," and one wonders whether Marshall meant to outlaw all private bills. Yet Marshall put his finger on a limitation of potential significance for the federal Constitution as well: the separate grant of "judicial power" to the courts may imply that there are certain things Congress may not do under its "legislative powers" even though they otherwise constitute, for example, regulations of commerce. See also E. CORWIN, JOHN MARSHALL AND THE CONSTITUTION 148 (1919), arguing that a remark of Madison's at the Constitutional Convention indicated an intention to protect against special legislation by Congress.

[42]Despite a disclaimer of authority in *Calder* to pass on state law questions in reviewing state court decisions, 3 U.S. (3 Dall.) at 392, Chase may have been suggesting the same thing: "it is against all reason and justice, for a people to intrust a legislature with such powers; and therefore, it cannot be presumed that they have done it," *id.* at 388. *See also* 3 J. STORY, COMMENTARIES ON THE CONSTITUTION OF THE UNITED STATES §§ 1393-1394, at 268-69 (Boston 1833); L. TRIBE, AMERICAN CONSTITUTIONAL LAW § 8-1, at 428 (1978).

[43]See G. DUNNE, *supra* note 27, at 75, terming this sentence evidence of "Marshall's skill in welding essentially divergent views into the 'unanimous opinion of the court'" in light of Johnson's opinion.

[44]Both Professors Warren and Hale said flatly the repeal act was held unconstitutional on the basis of the contract clause. 1 C. WARREN, *supra* note 15, at 396; Hale, *The Supreme Court and The Contract Clause* (pt. 2), 57 HARV. L. REV. 621, 633-34 (1944). *But see* L. TRIBE, *supra* note 40, § 8-1, at 429 ("Marshall straddled the fence between pure natural law, implied limitations, and formal interpretation of explicit constitutional commands . . . .").

[45]U.S. CONST. art. I, § 10, para. 1.

[46]*Id.*

[47]*Calder*, 3 U.S. (3 Dall.) at 395 (Paterson, J.), 398 (Iredell, J.), 400-01 (Cushing, J.). *See supra* chapter 2.

[48]*Fletcher*, 10 U.S. (6 Cranch) at 136.

[49]*Id.* at 136-37. Counsel had so argued, *id.* at 123, and so had Hamilton in a legal opinion relating to the same grant fifteen years before, *see* C. MAGRATH, *supra* note 19, at 22; Marshall did not cite Hamilton. For

secured by the constitution, while an absolute conveyance remained unprotected."[50] Justice Johnson agreed that a grant was a contract but could not agree that it imposed any continuing "obligation":[51] a conveyance "is most generally but the consummation of a contract, is *functus officio* the moment it is executed, and continues afterwards to be nothing more than the evidence that a certain act was done."[52]

Johnson's position is tempting. One dispossessed by his grantor might be expected to sue for ejectment, not for breach of contract.[53] In essence the repealing statute took property from its owners without compensation; Marshall himself had so characterized it in his discussion of limits derived from "the nature of society."[54] Uncompensated takings were separately prohibited by the fifth amendment,[55] which applied only to the federal government, as the Court was soon to hold.[56] One might infer from this separate treatment that the Framers had embraced the traditional distinction between contract and property,[57] and that the repealing act in *Fletcher* had not impaired a contractual obligation.[58]

Nevertheless Marshall's conclusion is not without plausibility. Though Marshall cited nothing for his crucial statement that a grantor implicitly promised not to retake the property, Coke had said long before that the ordinary words of conveyance implied a warranty of title,[59] ahd later commentators have affirmed that such a

---

an effort to evaluate Marshall's conclusion in terms of common law and continental use of the terms "contract" and "obligation," see W. HUNTING, THE OBLIGATION OF CONTRACTS CLAUSE OF THE UNITED STATES CONSTITUTION 19-39 (1919).

[50]*Fletcher*, 10 U.S. (6 Cranch) at 137.

[51]*Id.* at 144.

[52]*Id.* at 145. Johnson added that he feared the Court's interpretation might preclude the exercise of the power of eminent domain, *id.*, a plausible concern that the Court would later allay, *see, e.g.*, West River Bridge Co. v. Dix, 47 U.S. (6 How.) 507, 531-34 (1848), *infra* chapter 7. Johnson also expressed a more general fear that the decision might unduly interfere with the traditional and "beneficent" powers of the states to "affect[ ] existing contracts." *Fletcher*, 10 U.S. (6 Cranch) at 145. This concern seems essentially independent of the questions resolved in *Fletcher*; whether or not state grants were protected by the clause, later cases would confirm Johnson's lament, *id.*, that "where to draw the line, or how to define and limit the words, 'obligation of contracts,' will be found a subject of extreme difficulty." *See infra* notes 156-79 and accompanying text (discussing *Sturges v. Crowninshield*).

[53]See Trickett, *Is a Grant a Contract?*, 54 AM. L. REV. 718, 729 (1920), arguing that when A conveys a horse to B "B has no right *in personam* against A, but only the right *in rem*, which is precisely the same as to A, as it is to any other human being." It is noteworthy in light of later decisions that Marshall did not ask whether Georgia law either recognized such a promise or characterized a grant as a contract. *See infra* notes 205-60 and accompanying text (discussing *Ogden v. Saunders*).

[54]*Fletcher*, 10 U.S. (6 Cranch) at 135-36, *quoted supra* at text accompanying note 33.

[55]U.S. CONST. amend. V ("[n]or shall private property be taken for public use, without just compensation").

[56]Barron v. Mayor of Baltimore, 32 U.S. (7 Pet.) 243 (1833), *discussed infra* chapter 6, notes 191-217 and accompanying text.

[57]*See, e.g.*, 2 J. AUSTIN, LECTURES ON JURISPRUDENCE 1006 (3d ed. London 1869) (1st ed. London 1861-63) ("The confusion of *contract* and *conveyance*, by elliptical or improper expression, is one of the greatest obstacles in the way of the student" (emphasis in original)).

[58]See, e.g., J. SHIRLEY, THE DARTMOUTH COLLEGE CAUSES AND THE SUPREME COURT OF THE UNITED STATES 312-13, 404-10 (1895); Hutchinson, *Laws Impairing the Obligation of Contracts*, 1 S.L. REV. (n.s.) 401, 414-16 (1875), both criticizing this portion of the *Fletcher* decision. To Beveridge, however, the Court followed the Constitution's "plain command." 3 A. BEVERIDGE, *supra* note 15, at 594.

[59]E. COKE, FIRST PART OF THE INSTITUTES OF THE LAWES OF ENGLAND; OR A COMMENTARY UPON LITTLETON § 733, at 384a (2d ed. London 1629) (1st ed. London 1628).

warranty barred a claim by the grantor himself.[60] That *Fletcher* makes *some* takings also contract impairments does not mean the taking clause has no independent field of operation; the same authorities tell us the normal warranty in a private deed does not protect against the wrongful act of a third party.[61] Moreover, Marshall buttressed his conclusion with a strong argument of improbability: the Framers were not fools, and it would make no sense to allow states to undermine the purpose of the clause by requiring restitution after a contract was performed.[62] This is a respectable means of argument if not carried too far;[63] Marshall had used it most effectively before in *Marbury v. Madison.*[64] But the application of this reasoning in *Fletcher* contrasts strikingly with the treatment of the same theme in *Hepburn v. Ellzey,*[65] where Marshall had conceded it was "extraordinary" that District of Columbia citizens appeared to be excluded from the diversity jurisdiction and yet refused to give a broad reading to the term "State" in article III,[66] calling the apparent absurdity "a subject for legislative, not for judicial consideration."[67]

Finally, the Court said, the clause applied to the state's own contracts as well as to private ones. The words of the Constitution drew no distinction between public and private obligations;[68] other provisions such as the ex post facto clause[69] clearly limited the activity of the state itself,[70] and the original provision of article III allowing states

[60]*See, e.g.*, S. MILSOM, HISTORICAL FOUNDATIONS OF THE COMMON LAW 148 (1969); A. SIMPSON, AN INTRODUCTION TO THE HISTORY OF THE LAND LAW 118-19 (1969); H. TIFFANY, REAL PROPERTY § 681, at 705 (abr. ed. 1940).

[61]*See, e.g.*, H. TIFFANY, *supra* note 60, § 681, at 705. *See also* R. POWELL, REAL PROPERTY ¶ 908 (abr. ed. 1968).

[62]*Fletcher*, 10 U.S. (6 Cranch) at 137, *quoted supra* text accompanying note 50. *But see* Trickett, *supra* note 53, at 729 ("[I]s it not as strange, that the property rights of a vendee were protected against a vendor, and the property rights of others not protected at all?").

[63]It had been carried too far in the carriage-tax case of Hylton v. United States, 3 U.S. (3 Dall.) 171 (1796). *See supra* chapter 2. Marshall might have made the result more literally plausible had he argued in addition that revocation effectively impaired the obligation of the previous contract to sell.

[64]5 U.S. (1 Cranch) 137 (1803). Marshall argued that to require courts to enforce unconstitutional laws "would be to overthrow, in fact, what was established in theory; . . . would seem, at first view, an absurdity too gross to be insisted on," *id.* at 177; and "would be giving to the legislature a practical and real omnipotence, with the same breath which professes to restrict their powers within narrow limits," *id.* at 178. *See supra* chapter 3. For a prominent later example, see Cohens v. Virginia, 19 U.S. (6 Wheat.) 264, 377 (1821), *discussed supra in* chapter 4.

[65]6 U.S. (2 Cranch) 445 (1805).

[66]U.S. CONST. art. III, § 2, para. 2.

[67]*Hepburn*, 6 U.S. (2 Cranch) at 453. *See supra* chapter 3.

[68]*Fletcher*, 10 U.S. (6 Cranch) at 137.

[69]U.S. CONST. art. I, § 10, para. 1.

[70]*Fletcher*, 10 U.S. (6 Cranch) at 138. The analogy is flawed. No one disputed that the contract clause limited state legislative action; the question went to the scope of that limitation. At one point Marshall came close to suggesting that the rescinding act violated the ex post facto clause itself: "This . . . act would have the effect of an *ex post facto* law. It forfeits the estate of Fletcher for a crime not committed by himself, but by those from whom he purchased." *Id.* One leading student of the contract clause thought this passage showed Marshall "was uncertain as to precisely why the repeal act was invalid, although he was very sure that it was invalid." B. WRIGHT, THE CONTRACT CLAUSE OF THE CONSTITUTION 34 (1938). Because the legislature did not declare anything Peck had done a crime, application of the ex post facto clause in *Fletcher* would have been difficult to square with Calder v. Bull, 3 U.S. (3 Dall.) 386 (1798), which Marshall did not cite. *See supra* chapter 2. Moreover, the sentence following that passage suggests that he was merely using the ex post facto clause as the basis for another absurdity argument directed to the interpretation of the contract clause: "This cannot be effected in the form of an *ex post facto* law, or bill of

to be sued[71] implied that the state could not avoid liability by the simple act of legislatively repudiating its own contracts.[72] We might add that the purpose of protecting creditor expectations seems as applicable to public as to private contracts.

Later statutory cases were to invoke the maxim that provisions limiting preexisting powers should not be construed to include governments unless they specifically say so.[73] Marshall himself was to suggest in *Sturges v. Crowninshield*[74] that the Framers may have had certain types of private contracts particularly in mind.[75] Moreover, in proposing adoption of the clause in the Constitutional Convention, Rufus King had advocated "in the words used in the Ordinance of Congs [sic] establishing new States a prohibition on the States to interfere in *private* contracts,"[76] to which the provision of the Northwest Ordinance on which he drew was expressly limited.[77] On the other hand, the Convention ultimately used more general terms; it is unclear whether it meant to reject the Ordinance's limitation or to express the same idea in different words.[78]

Thus, as in many of his jurisdictional opinions,[79] it is difficult to say whether Marshall was right or wrong in *Fletcher*; he managed without very much explanation and without referring to available authority[80] to resolve both doubtful issues in favor

------

attainder; why, then, is it allowable in the form of a law annulling the original grant?" *Fletcher*, 10 U.S. (6 Cranch) at 139. *See* Hale, *supra* note 44, at 635 (Marshall "did not assert . . . that the rescinding act was in fact an *ex post facto* law, but only that it had the same effect and that therefore the contract clause should be construed to cover it.").

[71]That is, U.S. CONST. art. III, para. 1, as construed by the Court in Chisholm v. Georgia, 2 U.S. (2 Dall.) 419 (1793), before the adoption of the eleventh amendment. *See supra* chapter 1.

[72]*Fletcher*, 10 U.S. (6 Cranch) at 139. The argument could be turned around: if, as the adoption of the eleventh amendment suggests, the Court was wrong in holding article III made the states suable, *see supra* chapter 1, Marshall's own principle that for every right there is a remedy, Marbury v. Madison, 5 U.S. (1 Cranch) 137, 163 (1803), implies that the state was not forbidden to impair its own obligations.

[73]*E.g.*, Leiter Minerals, Inc. v. United States, 352 U.S. 220, 225 (1957) (anti-injunction provision of 28 U.S.C. § 2283 (1976)); United States v. United Mine Workers, 330 U.S. 258, 270 (1947) (Norris-LaGuardia Act, 29 U.S.C §§ 101-110, 113-115 (1976)).

[74]17 U.S. (4 Wheat.) 122 (1819).

[75]*Id.* at 204. *See infra* notes 156-204 and accompanying text.

[76]2 THE RECORDS OF THE FEDERAL CONVENTION OF 1787, at 439 (rev. ed. M. Farrand 1937) (emphasis added) [hereinafter cited as CONVENTION RECORDS].

[77]Northwest Territory Ordinance and Act of 1787, art. II, ch. 8, § 1, 1 Stat. 51, 52 n.(a) (1789).

[78]*See* E. CORWIN, *supra* note 41, at 167-68, arguing on the basis of a general reference to the Philadelphia Debates that only private contracts were meant to be included, and B. WRIGHT, *supra* note 70, at 3-16, tracing the occasional references to the clause both at Philadelphia and in the state ratifying conventions. Wright reported that two Anti-Federalist assertions that the clause embraced public contracts "were denied by members of the Convention, and their denials were not challenged." *Id.* at 16; *see id.* at 15-16 (citing 3 J. ELLIOT, THE DEBATES IN THE SEVERAL STATE CONVENTIONS ON THE ADOPTION OF THE FEDERAL CONSTITUTION 474 (statement of Patrick Henry), 477-78 (Governor Randolph's reply that the clause had been included because of "frequent interferences of the state legislatures with private contracts") (2d ed. Philadelphia 1861) (1st ed. Washington, D.C. 1827-30); 4 J. ELLIOT, *supra* at 190 (statement of James Galloway), 191 (W.R. Davie's answer that "[t]he clause refers merely to contracts between individuals")).

[79]*See generally supra* chapters 3, 4.

[80]*See* G. DUNNE, *supra* note 27, at 75, terming *Fletcher* an example of "characteristic soldier's prose—terse, lucid, persuasive, and free of a single legal citation." To one leading student of the case, Marshall's opinion contained "little that was original." C. MAGRATH, *supra* note 17, at 82. Not only had Hamilton said it all before, *see supra* note 49, but both Justice Paterson on circuit, Van Horne's Lessee

of an expansive meaning of the contract clause. This feat he accomplished in an apparently feigned case, largely on the basis of policy, notwithstanding his invocation of the already familiar shibboleth that a law ought "seldom, if ever" to be held unconstitutional "in a doubtful case."[81]

II. Other Public Contracts

A. *New Jersey v. Wilson*

In return for a surrender of other land claims, New Jersey had conveyed a tract in trust for the Delaware Indians pursuant to a statute providing that "'the lands to be purchased for the Indians aforesaid, shall not hereafter be subject to any tax'" and could not be conveyed.[82] Some years later, at the request of the Delawares, the legislature authorized the land to be sold. New Jersey proceeded to repeal the tax exemption and impose a tax on the purchasers; the Supreme Court in 1812 held without dissent that the state had impaired the obligation of contract.[83]

Marshall treated the case as an easy one: *Fletcher v. Peck* had settled that the contract clause included state contracts;[84] there was consideration for the promise; the exemption was attached to the land, and the state had not demanded its surrender as the price of consent to the resale.[85] None of this was particularly surprising, though a later Court might have agreed with the state court that the exemption was personal[86] or had been extinguished with the restraint on alienation.[87]

---

v. Dorrance, 28 F. Cas. 1012 (C.C.D. Pa. 1795) (No. 16,857), and the Supreme Court of Massachusetts, Derby v. Blake, decided in 1799 and belatedly reported at 226 Mass. 618 (1917), had reached similar conclusions. *See also* C. Magrath, *supra* note 19, at 52-53, 82-83. The same position had also been taken in congressional debates over compensation of the Yazoo claimants, *see* B. Wright, *supra* note 70, at 23-24, and Justice Wilson had assumed in Chisholm v. Georgia, 2 U.S. (2 Dall.) 419, 465 (1793), that the clause applied to public obligations. These earlier views may help to explain the fact that although some Republicans condemned the decision, it came as no surprise to the Bar. G. Haskins & H. Johnson, *supra* note 19, at 348, 351; 1 C. Warren, *supra* note 15, at 396.

[81]*Fletcher*, 10 U.S. (6 Cranch) at 128 (discussing the validity of the original grant under the Georgia constitution). The first Supreme Court appearance of this maxim seems to have been in Justice Chase's opinion in Hylton v. United States, 3 U.S. (3 Dall.) 171, 175 (1796), where it may have played some part in sustaining the challenged law. *See supra* chapter 2.

It has been said that *Fletcher* was "the first case in which the Court had held a State law unconstitutional." 1 C. Warren, *supra* note 15, at 392. Yet the Court had struck down a state law under the supremacy clause for conflict with a treaty as early as 1796, Ware v. Hylton, 3 U.S. (3 Dall.) 199 (1796), and Justice Chase's opinion in that case explicitly endorsed federal judicial review of state legislation, *id.* at 236-37. *See supra* chapter 2.

[82]New Jersey v. Wilson, 11 U.S. (7 Cranch) 164, 165 (1812) (quoting Act of Aug. 12, 1758 (colony of New Jersey)).

[83]*Id.* at 166-67.

[84]*See supra* notes 68-78 and accompanying text.

[85]*Wilson*, 11 U.S. (7 Cranch) at 166-67.

[86]*Cf., e.g.*, Chesapeake & O. Ry. v. Miller, 114 U.S. 176, 183-84 (1885) (so construing a promise of "no taxation upon the property of the said company" until its profits reached a certain level).

[87]State v. Wilson, 2 N.J.L. 282, 286-87 (Sup. Ct. 1807 term) (Rossell, J.), 291 (Pennington, J.), *rev'd*, 11 U.S. (7 Cranch) 164 (1812). See also Given v. Wright, 117 U.S. 648, 655 (1886), where taxation of land in the same tract was allowed on the basis of "long acquiescence" by the owners: "If the question [decided

As in *Fletcher*, Marshall did not stop to inquire whether his characterization of the transaction conformed to state law; in contrast to later Justices,[88] he seems to have thought the existence and interpretation of agreements for contract clause purposes entirely a matter of federal law. Nor did he suggest that it might be relevant that the tax exemption had been granted by the colonial government in the King's name in 1758,[89] long before the contract clause was adopted. As we shall see, however, such temporal questions posed interesting problems in the application of the clause.[90]

What was the most striking about *Wilson* was that no doubt was suggested as to the validity of the tax exemption in the first place. In *Fletcher*, while affirming that a legislature had authority to convey land,[91] Marshall had conceded that, "so far as respects general legislation," "one legislature cannot abridge the powers of" the next,[92] and Johnson had acknowledged that a sovereign could not part with its "right of jurisdiction."[93]

Neither Justice identified the source of this limit; perhaps they viewed it as implicit in the state constitution,[94] or perhaps it was another manifestation of natural law.[95] Their suggestion was to be picked up by later Justices who would use it to hold that the state could not validly promise that future legislators would not outlaw a lottery.[96] A promise not to tax is hard to distinguish in this respect from a promise not to regulate, and an occasional Justice was to argue after Marshall was gone that tax exemptions were also invalid.[97] But neither Marshall nor Johnson seems to have thought *Wilson* was affected by their principle that sovereignty could not be surrendered, and the decision was to survive.[98]

---

in *Wilson*] were a new one we might regard the reasoning of the New Jersey judges as entitled to a great deal of weight . . . ."

[88]*See, e.g.*, Indiana *ex rel.* Anderson v. Brand, 303 US. 95, 100 (1938) (whether the state had bound itself by contract is a question "primarily of state law" which the Supreme Court should review only with deference "in order that the constitutional mandate may not become a dead letter"). *See also infra* notes 205-60 and accompanying text (discussing Ogden v. Saunders); *infra* chapter 7, discussing *Piqua Branch of State Bank v. Knoop*. For general discussion of the relation of state law to the contract clause, see Hale, *The Supreme Court and the Contract Clause* (pt. 3), 57 HARV. L. REV. 852, 852-72 (1944).

[89]*See Wilson*, 11 U.S. (7 Cranch) at 165.

[90]*See infra* notes 126-55 and accompanying text (discussing *Trustees of Dartmouth College*); G. HASKINS & H. JOHNSON, *supra* note 8, at 599-600 (suggesting the problem).

[91]Fletcher v. Peck, 10 U.S. (6 Cranch) 87, 132 (1810).

[92]*Id.* at 135.

[93]*Id.* at 143 (Johnson, J., concurring).

[94]*See* Piqua Branch of State Bank v. Knoop, 57 U.S. (16 How.) 369, 392-405 (1853 Term) (Catron, J., dissenting), *infra* chapter 7.

[95]*See* Stone v. Mississippi, 101 U.S. 814, 819-20 (1880), *infra* chapter 11.

[96]*Id.* at 821.

[97]*E.g., Piqua Branch of State Bank*, 57 U.S. (16 How.) at 404-05 (Catron, J., dissenting). Justice Catron asserted that the point had not been litigated in *New Jersey v. Wilson. Id.* at 401. In this he was partly right; while counsel had plainly contended in the state court that the legislature could not grant a perpetual exemption, State v. Wilson, 2 N.J.L. at 285, the case was submitted in the Supreme Court "upon a statement of facts, without argument," 11 U.S. (7 Cranch) at 164. For later instances of the Court's wrestling with the tax exemption issue, see B. WRIGHT, *supra* note 70, at 73-75. See also Hale, *supra* note 44, at 654, who defends the Court: "[W]hen a state grants a tax exemption, it unquestionably surrenders . . . part of its sovereign power—the power to tax the exempted property. But to deny its power to grant the exemption by contract would be to take from it a sovereign power of perhaps greater moment."

[98]*See* B. WRIGHT, *supra* note 70, at 73-75; Hale, *supra* note 44, at 640-53.

B.   *Terrett v. Taylor*

The Episcopal Church had acquired land in Virginia before the Revolution. In 1776
the state legislature had confirmed the Church's title to the land; in 1784 it had
incorporated the Church; in 1786 it had repealed the act of incorporation while
reserving the Church's property rights.[99] In 1798, however, the legislature repealed
the 1776 and 1784 statutes as "inconsistent with the principles of the constitution and
of religious freedom,"[100] and in 1801 it asserted the right to all Church property.[101]
The Supreme Court, in an 1815 opinion by Justice Story, held the property still
belonged to the Church.[102]

The Court gave straightforward reasons for this conclusion. The 1786 statute
revoking the Church's charter had not purported to disturb its property rights, and
the 1798 repeal of confirmatory statutes had left intact the Church's preexisting
title.[103] The 1801 statute had been passed after the land in question became a part of
the District of Columbia "under the exclusive jurisdiction of congress."[104] Therefore,
"as to . . . property within that district, the right of Virginia to legislate no longer
existed."[105] One is tempted to interpret this last passage as a questionable constitu-
tionalization of Story's well-known views concerning the territorial limits of government power in general,[106] but with respect to the District of Columbia it was a
paraphrase of the explicit terms of article I, section 8.[107]

Story's gratuitous additional observations, however, are of special interest. The
1798 and 1801 statutes, he wrote, were ineffective to divest the Church of property
for another reason:

> That the legislature can repeal statutes creating private corporations, or
> confirming to them property already acquired under the faith of previous
> laws, and by such repeal can vest the property of such corporations
> exclusively in the state . . . we are not prepared to admit; and we think
> ourselves standing upon the principles of natural justice, upon the fun-
> damental laws of every free government, upon the spirit and letter of the
> constitution of the United States, and upon the decisions of most respect-
> able judicial tribunals, in resisting such a doctrine.[108]

---

[99]Terrett v. Taylor, 13 U.S. (9 Cranch) 43, 44 (1815).

[100]Act of Jan. 24, 1799, ch. 246, 1 Va. Acts 388 (S. Pleasants Jr. & H. Pace 1803).

[101]*Terrett*, 13 U.S. (9 Cranch) at 48.

[102]*Id.* at 55. Justices Johnson and Todd did not participate. *See id.* at 45.

[103]*Id.* at 51.

[104]*Id.* at 52.

[105]*Id.*

[106]*See* J. Story, Commentaries on the Conflict of Laws § 18, at 20 (2d ed. Boston 1841) (1st ed.
Boston 1834). *See also* Allgeyer v. Louisiana, 165 U.S. 578 (1897) (holding that the fourteenth amendment's due process clause forbade application of Louisiana law to a contract made outside its borders); *see
generally* R. Cramton, D. Currie & H. Kay, Conflict of Laws: Cases—Comments—Questions 403-519
(3d ed. 1981).

[107]U.S. Const. art. I, § 8, cl. 17 (empowering Congress to "exercise exclusive Legislation in all Cases
whatsoever, over such District . . . as may . . . become the Seat of the Government of the United
States").

[108]*Terrett*, 13 U.S. (9 Cranch) at 52.

There it is again: the principles of "natural justice" seem to have been invoked, as perhaps they had been in *Calder* and in *Fletcher*, as a basis for disregarding acts of a state legislature.[109] This time Story was speaking for the whole Court. At most, however, his reliance on natural justice was an alternative holding; possibly he only meant to express his moral outrage along the way to his clear conclusion that the Virginia statutes offended "the constitution of the United States."[110]

But why did the statutes offend the federal Constitution? Story referred to no specific provision; he gave no reasons; he cited none of those "decisions of most respectable judicial tribunals" to which he adverted. The provision most nearly applicable was the contract clause, which had just been read in *Fletcher v. Peck* to include grants of land by the state.[111] The difficulty was that in *Terrett* the Church's land had not been acquired from the state; it had been "purchased of a certain Daniel Jennings" in 1770.[112] Thus the attempted confiscation seems to have been a garden variety taking of private property uncomplicated by the contractual implications of an original state grant. If Story was suggesting that *every* taking of property was an impairment of contract, he was significantly extending *Fletcher*, and he owed us an explanation.[113]

To the extent that the Court relied upon the statutes incorporating the Church and confirming its title as contracts not to disturb the Church's property,[114] it was

[109]*See supra* notes 30-43 and accompanying text; *supra* chapter 2.

[110]*Terrett*, 13 U.S. (9 Cranch) at 52.

[111]*See supra* notes 44-72 and accompanying text. Chancellor Kent viewed this as the basis of *Terrett* as well. 1 J. KENT, COMMENTARIES ON AMERICAN LAW 415 (4th ed. New York 1840) (1st ed. New York 1826).

[112]*Terrett*, 13 U.S. (9 Cranch) at 43.

[113]One might argue that the expropriation impaired the *private* contracts by which the Church had obtained the property. In his treatise Story was later to say without explanation or authority that a state law "annulling conveyances between individuals, and declaring, that the grantors should stand seized of their former estates, . . . would be as repugnant to the constitution, as a state law discharging the vendors from the obligation of executing their contracts of sale." 3 J. STORY, *supra* note 42, § 1370, at 242. *Cf. supra* notes 44-72 and accompanying text (discussing Marshall's argument about public grants in *Fletcher*). It seems harder to infer a warranty against state action in a private deed than in a public one; at common law a warrantor was not responsible for the tortious act of a third party. *See* R. POWELL, *supra* note 61, ¶ 908; H. TIFFANY, *supra* note 60, § 681, at 705. Further, the state in *Terrett*, in contrast to the example given in Story's treatise, had not attempted to undo a private transaction by giving the Church's property back to its original owners.

[114]At one point in the opinion Story treated the 1776 act confirming the Church's interest as a "new grant" on the assumption that the Revolution had destroyed the Church's original title. *Terrett*, 13 U.S. (9 Cranch) at 50. Even on this assumption, however, it was not clear that this "grant" was a contract, since, unlike that in *Fletcher*, there was nothing to indicate it had been made for consideration. Moreover, the crucial assumption that the Revolution had divested the Church was expressly repudiated on the same page of the opinion. *Id.* Nevertheless, Story expressly referred to the repeal of the confirming statute in his statement of unconstitutionality, *quoted supra* at text accompanying note 108; perhaps he viewed that law as a contract in which the state promised (for what consideration?) to respect the Church's interest.

Story added that the state had no power to deprive the Church of its property by repealing its corporate charter, *see Terrett*, 13 U.S. (9 Cranch) at 50, and he accompanied this pronouncement with a general discourse on the inviolability of corporate charters. Forfeiture of a franchise for "*misuser*" or "*nonuser*" would be all right, as the common law to that effect was "a tacit condition" in every charter; new governments might abolish "such exclusive privileges . . . as are inconsistent with the new government"; and there might be extensive powers to modify the charters of "public corporations which exist only for public purposes, such as counties, towns, cities, &c." *Id.* at 51-52 (emphasis in original). The implication

necessary to reject the argument that those statutes had been invalid at the outset under the religion clauses of the Virginia constitution;[115] if the alleged contract was invalid, there was no obligation to impair. This reconstruction may explain the relevance of the apparently gratuitous remarks Story made about those clauses in the course of the *Terrett* opinion.[116] Direct Supreme Court encounters with the comparable provisions of the first amendment were far in the future;[117] Story's observations are therefore of some significance for first amendment law despite the somewhat different wording of the state and federal provisions.[118]

The legislature had been mistaken, Story said, in thinking that either the existence of religious corporations or the grant of property for church purposes offended the guarantee of " 'free exercise' " or the declaration that " 'religion can be directed only by the reason and conviction, not by force and violence.' "[119] The legislature "could not create or continue a religious establishment which should have exclusive rights and prerogatives, or compel the citizens to worship under a stipulated form or discipline, or to pay taxes to those whose creed they could not conscientiously believe."[120] However,

> the free exercise of religion cannot be justly deemed to be restrained by aiding with equal attention the votaries of every sect to perform their own religious duties, or by establishing funds for the support of ministers, for public charities, for the endowment of churches, or for the sepulture of the dead.[121]

Modern establishment clause doctrine has departed from the dicta endorsing state subsidies to all religions,[122] but today it might well offend the free exercise clause[123] to deny churches alone the benefits of the corporate form.[124]

---

seemed to be that otherwise the charter itself was protected, as the Court was soon to hold only after appropriate explanation. *See infra* notes 126-55 and accompanying text (discussing *Trustees of Dartmouth College*). But the conclusion in *Terrett* was only that a repeal of the charter could not operate to vest property in the state—a conclusion that was itself unnecessary since, as Story stressed, the statute revoking the charter had expressly declined to interfere with the Church's property rights. *See supra* note 103 and accompanying text.

[115]*Cf. supra* note 100 and accompanying text (quoting the repealing statute, which cited the religion clauses as the reason for the repeal).

[116]The statement in J. McClellan, Joseph Story and the American Constitution 198 (1971), that "Story struck down the rescinding statute as violating the free exercise of religion and the rights of property guaranteed by the Virginia constitution and bill of rights" seems to be in error.

[117]*See, e.g.*, Reynolds v. United States, 98 U.S. 145 (1878), discussed *infra* in chapter 13.

[118]*Compare* U.S. Const. amend. I ("Congress shall make no law respecting an establishment of religion, or prohibiting the free exercise thereof") *with* Va. Const. art. I, § 16 ("[t]hat religion . . . and the manner of discharging it, can be directed only by reason and conviction . . . and . . . all men are equally entitled to the free exercise of religion according to the dictates of conscience").

[119]*Terrett*, 13 U.S. (9 Cranch) at 48-49 (quoting the Virginia Bill of Rights).

[120]*Id.* at 49.

[121]*Id.*

[122]*See, e.g.*, Lemon v. Kurtzman, 403 U.S. 602 (1971) (striking down grants to church-related primary and secondary schools). *But cf.* Walz v. Tax Comm'n, 397 U.S. 664 (1970) (upholding tax exemptions for church property). For the view that Story had history on his side, see Corwin, *The Supreme Court as National School Board*, 14 Law & Contemp. Probs. 3, 9-16 (1949).

[123]U.S. Const. amend. I. *See supra* note 118.

[124]*Cf.* McDaniel v. Paty, 435 U.S. 618 (1978) (state may not exclude clergymen from legislature). *See generally* Kurland, *Of Church and State and the Supreme Court*, 29 U. Chi. L. Rev. 1 (1961).

Thus Story in his first constitutional opinion for the Court revealed several of Marshall's less attractive traits: unwillingness to confine himself to narrow grounds of decision, vague and conclusory resolution of important new constitutional questions,[125] failure to deal with the applicable precedents, and a strong suggestion of willingness to set aside legislation incompatible with his conception of "natural justice."

C. *Trustees of Dartmouth College v. Woodward*

Dartmouth College was established by royal charter in 1769. The charter appointed twelve trustees, gave them authority to govern the college, and empowered them to choose their successors. In 1816 the New Hampshire legislature passed a series of statutes increasing the number of trustees to twenty-one, authorizing the Governor to appoint the nine new members, and subjecting important decisions of the trustees to a new Board of Overseers largely chosen by the Governor. In an action by the old trustees to reclaim corporate books from an officer appointed under the new law, the state court upheld the statutory changes;[126] the Supreme Court in 1819 reversed.[127]

Though it evidently attracted little notice at the time outside New England,[128] this case later became a cause célèbre, and the Court made much of it. Marshall's opinion consumes thirty pages;[129] Washington and Story uncharacteristically felt obliged to

---

[125]*See* B. WRIGHT, *supra* note 70, at 39 ("[E]ven the Marshall court was hesitant to call [the 1776 act] a contract. But if it was not a contract, where in the national Constitution does one find an applicable clause?"); *see also* G. HASKINS & H. JOHNSON, *supra* note 19, at 404 (stating that both *Fletcher* and *Terrett* were based on "the contract clause and the doctrine of vested property rights"). In Town of Pawlet v. Clark, 13 U.S. (9 Cranch) 292 (1815), which Story's treatise cites in the same breath with *Terrett*, 3 J. STORY, *supra* note 42, § 1385, at 258 & n.1, he was even more vague about the basis of his conclusion; the unexplained statement that a statute "could not afterwards be repealed" "so far as it granted the glebes to the towns," 13 U.S. (9 Cranch) at 336, followed a discussion of the inability of the Crown at common law to resell granted lands without the consent of their owner. *Id.* at 334. The Court and Story himself were later to suggest that *Terrett* had been based on the contract clause. *See* Piqua Branch of State Bank v. Knoop, 57 U.S. (16 How.) 369, 389 (1853 Term); 3 J. STORY, *supra* note 42, § 1358, at 258 & n.1.

[126]Trustees of Dartmouth College v. Woodward, 1 N.H. 111 (1817), *rev'd*, 17 U.S. (4 Wheat.) 518 (1819). This opinion is interesting for its rejection of the argument that the repeal offended the law-of-the-land clause of the state constitution, *see* N.H. CONST. pt. 1, art. XV, a first cousin of due process:

> [H]ow a privilege can be protected from the operation of a law of the land, by a clause in the constitution declaring that it shall not be taken away, but by the law of the land, is not very easily understood. . . . It is evident, from all the commentaries upon it by *English* writers, that it was intended to limit the powers of the crown, and not of parliament.

1 N.H. at 129 (emphasis in original). Webster responded by quoting Blackstone's statement that "laws of the land" meant general legislation, not an act "'to confiscate the goods of Titius'" alone. 17 U.S. (4 Wheat.) at 580-81 (quoting 1 W. BLACKSTONE, COMMENTARIES *44).

[127]Trustees of Dartmouth College v. Woodward, 17 U.S. (4 Wheat.) 518 (1819). For the background of the case see 4 A. BEVERIDGE, *supra* note 15, at 220-81; 1 C. WARREN, *supra* note 15, at 475-92, and see generally the disorganized but detailed J. SHIRLEY, *supra* note 58, as to which Beveridge's cautionary evaluation rings true to at least the "harried reader," 4 A. BEVERIDGE, *supra* note 15, at 258 n.2. The legal arguments and other relevant materials have been collected by Timothy Farrar. T. FARRAR, REPORT OF THE CASE OF THE TRUSTEES OF DARTMOUTH COLLEGE AGAINST WILLIAM H. WOODWARD (Boston 1819).

[128]*See* 4 A. BEVERIDGE, *supra* note 15, at 237, 275-76.

[129]*Trustees of Dartmouth College*, 17 U.S. (4 Wheat.) at 624-54.

add lengthy explanations of their own;[130] Duvall, who after eight years of silence may have lost the ability to express himself, unpardonably dissented without opinion.[131] Yet the arguments the Justices were at most pains to refute seem today to have bordered on the frivolous. Marshall directed the bulk of his ammunition[132] against the lower court's suggestion that because Dartmouth had been established for the "public" purpose of education it was really a "public" corporation that could be abolished as readily as cities and towns;[133] Washington and Story plowed the same ground twice again,[134] the latter embellishing Marshall's first principles with extensive citation. For the rest, the opinions busied themselves largely with additional lightweight objections: that the trustees had no personal interest in the charter,[135] that the corporation did not exist until the charter was issued and hence could not be party to it,[136] and that state control did not significantly alter the charter.[137]

The essence of the transaction, it seems, was an uncompensated taking. As Marshall said, the statutes appear to have transferred "[t]he whole power of

---

[130]*See id.* at 654 (Washington, J.), 666 (Story, J.). Livingston concurred "for the reasons stated by the Chief Justice, and Justices Washington and Story," *id.* at 666; Johnson concurred for the reasons stated by Marshall, *id.* (despite his dissent from the contract clause reasoning of *Fletcher, see supra* note 22 and accompanying text). Todd was absent the whole Term "on account of indisposition." 17 U.S. (4 Wheat.) at iii n.1. Todd has been reported as opposing the trustees when the case was first argued. *See, e.g.,* 4 A. BEVERIDGE, *supra* note 15, at 225. This report evidently is based upon Webster's uncertain surmise. *See* 1 C. WARREN, *supra* note 15, at 480.

[131]*See Trustees of Dartmouth College,* 17 U.S. (4 Wheat.) at 713. Irving Dilliard rejects as "manifestly unfair" the allegation that Duvall was "'probably the most insignificant of all Supreme Court judges.'" Dilliard, *Gabriel Duvall,* in 1 THE JUSTICES OF THE UNITED STATES SUPREME COURT 1789-1969, at 428 (H. Friedman & F. Israel eds. 1969) (quoting E. BATES, THE STORY OF THE SUPREME COURT 109 (1936)). Indeed, Dilliard affects to give Duvall extra points for declining to reveal his reasons, suggesting that by his "blunt entry" Duvall "showed what he thought of Webster's long oratorical plea before the bench and of Chief Justice Marshall's pioneering decision." *Id.* at 420. Dilliard does not suggest which Justice or Justices he thinks more insignificant than Duvall. See Currie, *The Most Insignificant Justice,* 50 U. CHI. L. REV. 466 (1983); Easterbrook, *The Most Insignificant Justice: A Reply,* 50 U. CHI. L. REV. 481 (1983).

[132]*See Trustees of Dartmouth College,* 17 U.S. (4 Wheat.) at 627-41.

[133]*Trustees of Dartmouth College,* 1 N.H. at 132-34. Story had conceded in Terrett v. Taylor, 13 U.S. (9 Cranch) 43, 52 (1815), that a legislature might have power to alter "*public* corporations which exist only for public purposes, such as counties, towns, cities, &c. . . . securing however, the property for the uses of those for whom, and at whose expense, it was originally purchased" (emphasis added). To suggest that the state's relationship with a private school was analogous to that with its own political subdivisions, however, seems little more than a play on the word "public." Among other things, as Washington said of a law creating a governmental body, "there is in reality but one party to it." *Trustees of Dartmouth College,* 17 U.S. (4 Wheat.) at 661. For an interesting exploration of doubts as to Marshall's simple distinction engendered by much later decisions on the responsibility of states for private acts under the fourteenth amendment, see H. FRIENDLY, THE DARTMOUTH COLLEGE CASE AND THE PUBLIC-PRIVATE PENUMBRA (1968).

To the interesting analogy of the marriage "contract," also employed by the court below, *see Trustees of Dartmouth College,* 1 N.H. at 132-33, both Marshall and Story responded that divorce was no impairment but a remedy for breach; the latter strongly suggested that a unilateral divorce without fault would be unconstitutional, while the former reserved the question. *Trustees of Dartmouth College,* 17 U.S. (4 Wheat.) at 629 (Marshall, C.J.), 696-97 (Story, J.).

[134]17 U.S. (4 Wheat.) at 659-62 (Washington, J.), 668-82, 693-95 (Story, J.).

[135]*See id.* at 641-50, 653-54 (Marshall, C.J.), 697-98 (Story, J.).

[136]*See id.* at 690-706 (Story, J.).

[137]*See id.* at 650-53 (Marshall, C.J.), 662-65 (Washington, J.), 707-12 (Story, J.), answering the arguments of John Holmes, *id.* at 604-05, and of William Wirt, *id.* at 613-14.

governing the college" from the charter trustees "to the executive of New Hampshire";[138] they had turned a private school into a public one.[139] As an original matter one might have doubted that takings of property could be fitted into the contract clause.[140] The same objection, however, could have been made both in *Fletcher v. Peck*[141] and in *Terrett v. Taylor*.[142] Moreover, by invalidating an expropriation of property that had not been acquired from the state, *Terrett* had seemed to approach the position that every taking was an impairment of contract.[143] In relying instead upon the charter as a contract, Marshall without discussion may have rejected this broad reading of *Terrett*, but, because he did not cite that case, it is difficult to say what he thought it held. He did not cite *Fletcher* either, though its holding that a completed grant from the state was a contract resolved two of the most potent difficulties with his similar characterization of a corporate charter.[144]

Yet there were significant differences between *Fletcher* and *Dartmouth College*, scarcely adverted to in the opinions, that seem to have prevented the result from being a foregone conclusion.[145] In the first place, despite Justice Washington's bare

---

[138]*Id.* at 652.

[139]Webster repeatedly stressed in his argument for the trustees that they had been effectively deprived of their property, *id.* at 556, 558, 567, 573, 577-80, 587-88; Justice Washington said the same thing, *id.* at 664-65. The state court had protested that to invalidate the statutes in question would mean the state could not impose any new duties on existing corporations or "legislate at all, on the subject of corporations, without their consent." *Trustees of Dartmouth College*, 1 N.H. at 127. The Supreme Court was later to uphold public-utility regulation although it interfered with the freedom of the owners to manage their property. *See, e.g.*, Railroad Comm'n Cases, 116 U.S. 307 (1886); Munn v. Illinois, 94 U.S. 113 (1877), discussed *infra* in chapter 11; *cf.* Pruneyard Shopping Center v. Robins, 447 U.S. 74, 83-84 (1980) (state may require shopping center to allow distribution of pamphlets). Yet even the modern decisions recognize that no formal assertion of government title is necessary to constitute a taking. *E.g., id.* at 82-83 (dictum); *cf.* Kaiser Aetna v. United States, 444 U.S. 164 (1979) (government may not require that private marina be open to public without charge). Justice Washington recognized this point: "Would the difference have been greater in principle, if the law had appropriated the funds of the college to the making of turnpike roads . . . ?" *Trustees of Dartmouth College*, 17 U.S. (4 Wheat.) at 665.

[140]See generally Doe, *A New View of the Dartmouth College Case*, 6 HARV. L. REV. 161 (1892), in which a later New Hampshire Chief Justice contended that the vice of the state's action lay in transferring control of college property, not in repealing the charter.

[141]*See supra* notes 19-81 and accompanying text.

[142]*See supra* notes 100-125 and accompanying text.

[143]*See supra* notes 111-13 and accompanying text.

[144]Marshall's failure to cite *Fletcher* may help to explain why Washington and Story broke their silence, as both remedied the omission. *See Trustees of Dartmouth College*, 17 U.S. (4 Wheat.) at 656-57 (Washington, J.), 682-83 (Story, J.). Webster, who had unaccountably been permitted to devote the greater part of his long-winded argument to questions of state law he conceded were not before the Court, *see id.* at 557-88, had invoked not only *Fletcher* and *Terrett*, but *New Jersey v. Wilson* as well, *id.* at 590-91. Echoed by Washington, *see id.* at 663-64, he had particularly stressed Story's *Terrett* dicta implying that a corporate charter was a contract that normally could not be revoked, *see supra* note 114. Marshall ignored these too. In Marshall's defense it should be said that neither counsel nor the court below had denied that state grants could constitute contracts in appropriate cases. *See Trustees of Dartmouth College*, 1 N.H. at 132 (distinguishing *Fletcher* and *Wilson* as having involved "express contract[s]").

[145]Massachusetts Chief Justice Isaac Parker, writing to Webster after the argument, was unable to see how the college could lose, "considering the principles already adopted by the court." Letter from Isaac Parker to Daniel Webster (April 28, 1818), *quoted in* J. SHIRLEY, *supra* note 58, at 251. *See also* 4 A. BEVERIDGE, *supra* note 15, at 223 ("After . . . Fletcher . . . and . . . Wilson, nobody could have expected from John Marshall any other action than the one he took in the Dartmouth College case."); Hagan, *Fletcher vs. Peck*, 16 GEO. L.J. 1, 2-3 (1927) ("The Dartmouth College case simply applied the rule

assertion,[146] it seems less obvious in the case of a charter than in that of a land transfer that the grant is implicitly irrevocable; to the modern reader a charter may look rather more like a temporary permit or license. Dartmouth's charter, however, seemed to preclude that inference, for it provided not only that the trustees should constitute the corporation "'forever hereafter,'" but that their number should "'hereafter and forever'" be "'twelve and no more.'"[147] Yet the charter was a royal one antedating the contract clause, and the state court had persuasively held that the King could not have precluded the charter's legislative repeal.[148] If the extent of a contractual obligation is defined by the law in force at the time of its creation, as the Court was soon to hold over Marshall's partial objection,[149] then it could be argued strongly that there had no more been an obligation not to alter the college charter than there would have been if the document had expressly provided for its own repeal.[150]

The second serious problem was consideration, which Story alone addressed in detail. Unlike a sale of land, the grant of a charter seems likely prima facie to be a one-sided transaction. Story's assertions to the contrary notwithstanding,[151] there seems to be little in the language of the college's charter to indicate the King had bargained for anything in return, be it the donation of private assets to the corpora-

---

of *Fletcher v. Peck* to a corporate charter."). Beveridge also reported, however, that Webster thought little of the contract clause argument and saw to the institution of related federal court actions in hopes of getting the state law questions to the Supreme Court. 4 A. BEVERIDGE, *supra* note 15, at 251-52. The "belief was general," he added, that review of the state court decision was "a feeble and forlorn hope." *Id.* at 238-239. Despite *Fletcher* and *Terrett,* Webster did not ask the Court to strike down the repeal on grounds of natural justice, presumably because those cases had originated in lower federal courts, and the Court's jurisdiction therefore had been broader.

[146]*Trustees of Dartmouth College*, 17 U.S. (4 Wheat.) at 658 (Washington, J.).

[147]*Id.* at 525 (quoting charter of Dartmouth College). *But see* J. SHIRLEY, *supra* note 58, at 433 (terming these expressions merely "formal").

[148]*Trustees of Dartmouth College*, 1 N.H. at 134.

[149]*See infra* notes 205-60 and accompanying text (discussing *Ogden v. Saunders*).

[150]*See* J. SHIRLEY, *supra* note 58, at 398; Hagan, *The Dartmouth College Case*, 19 GEO. L.J. 411, 420 (1931). Webster argued that the applicability of the clause to a pre-Revolution grant had already been decided. *Trustees of Dartmouth College*, 17 U.S. (4 Wheat.) at 591 (citing as authority *New Jersey v. Wilson*, where the point had not been addressed). He also contended (as a matter of state law, which should have been irrelevant) that the legislature had not inherited Parliament's power to annul charters, which he describes as "sovereign" rather than "legislative." *Id.* at 558-61. *See also* Doe, *supra* note 140, at 213-16 (arguing that even after adoption of the contract clause New Hampshire's legislature lacked authority to promise not to exercise its regulatory power); *cf. supra* notes 82-98 and accompanying text (discussing *New Jersey v. Wilson*).

To be distinguished from the problem in *Trustees of Dartmouth College* is the Marshall decision in Owings v. Speed, 18 U.S. (5 Wheat.) 420 (1820), that the contract clause did not invalidate contractual impairments enacted before the Constitution took effect. Though the language of the clause clearly speaks only to future *impairments* ("No State shall . . . pass any . . . Law impairing the Obligation of Contracts . . . ," U.S. CONST. art. I, § 10, para. 1), it is not expressly limited to future *contracts*. Contrast U.S. CONST. amend. XIV, § 1 ("No State shall make *or enforce* any law which shall abridge the privileges or immunities of citizens of the United States . . . ." (emphasis added)). *See also supra* chapter 2 (discussing applicability of the ex post facto clause to statutes enacted before the Constitution); comments of Messrs. Davie and Maclaine, 4 ELLIOT'S DEBATES, *supra* note at 194, 179-80.

[151]*Trustees of Dartmouth College*, 17 U.S. (4 Wheat.) at 685-87 (paraphrasing the charter's statement "'considering the premises,'" *id.* at 524, as "*in consideration of the premises* in the introductory recitals," *id.* at 685 (emphasis added)).

tion or the implicit undertaking, confected by all three opinions,[152] to administer the college according to its stated purposes. Story further argued, unnecessarily in light of his conclusion just stated, that no consideration was necessary, but in so doing he seems to have leapt from the undeniable premise that a gift was irrevocable to the dubious conclusion that it was for that reason a contract within the meaning of the Constitution.[153]

The issues of consideration and duration thus seem to have been the principal stumbling blocks after *Fletcher* to the conclusion that corporate charters were protected by the contract clause; but Marshall basically ignored them, perhaps because counsel for the state had never clearly made the appropriate arguments.[154] Indeed, the court below, basing its decision on its characterization of the college as a "public" institution and on the pre-1789 charter date, had strongly hinted that the charter of a corporation for private profit could not be altered.[155] Thus, as in so many earlier cases, the Court in *Dartmouth College* settled important and difficult questions of constitutional law with hardly any discussion, and this time it simultaneously made mountains out of constitutional molehills.

III. Bankruptcy and Later Cases

A. *Sturges v. Crowninshield*

Sturges sued to collect on promissory notes; Crowninshield's defense was a discharge granted by a New York court under a state law, enacted after the notes had been given, "'for the benefit of insolvent debtors and their creditors.'"[156] On questions certified by the federal circuit court, the Supreme Court in an 1819 Marshall opinion held the purported discharge unconstitutional.[157]

The basis of the decision was once again the contract clause, and this time it seemed to fit like a glove. The notes were contracts between private parties; they had created obligations to pay specified sums of money; the discharge released the obligations and thus impaired them.[158] Perhaps, as Justice Livingston had said in

---

[152]*See id.* at 642 (Marshall, C.J.), 658-59 (Washington, J.), 688-90 (Story, J.).

[153] [T]he constitution did intend to preserve all the obligatory force of contracts, which they have by the general principles of law. . . . [W]hen a contract has once passed, *bona fide*, into grant, neither the king nor any private person, who may be the grantor, can recal [*sic*] the grant of the property, although the conveyance may have been purely voluntary.

Id. at 683. For an argument that there was no consideration in *Dartmouth College* and that the contract clause did not forbid the rescission of a gift, see Thompson, *Abuses of Corporate Privileges*, 26 Am. L. Rev. 169 (1892).

[154]*See Trustees of Dartmouth College*, 17 U.S. (4 Wheat.) at 600-15 (Messrs. Holmes and Wirt).

[155]*See Trustees of Dartmouth College*, 1 N.H. at 118-20 (discussing the matter evidently as one of state law).

[156]Sturges v. Crowninshield, 17 U.S. (4 Wheat.) 122, 122 (1819) (quoting Act of April 3, 1811, ch. 248, 1813 N.Y. Laws 468 (Southwick 1813)).

[157]*Id.* The court reached the same conclusion in Farmers & Mechanics' Bank v. Smith, 19 U.S. (6 Wheat.) 131 (1821), a case involving a Pennsylvania statute.

[158]*Sturges*, 17 U.S. (4 Wheat.) at 197-98 (adding that the obligation was not impliedly limited to payment out of property in possession when the contract was made). Justice Washington had reached the same conclusion on circuit in Golden v. Prince, 10 F. Cas. 542 (C.C.D. Pa. 1814) (No. 5509); Marshall did not cite him.

upholding the New York law on circuit,[159] the Framers had been motivated in drafting the clause by laws authorizing the issuance of paper money, allowing the tender of worthless property, and extending the time for payment; but, as Marshall responded, they had employed more general terms in the Constitution.[160]

> [I]f, in any case, the plain meaning of a provision, not contradicted by any other provision in the same instrument, is to be disregarded, because we believe the framers of that instrument could not intend what they say, it must be one in which the absurdity and injustice of applying the provision to the case, would be so monstrous, that all mankind would, without hesitation, unite in rejecting the application.[161]

Livingston had also concluded that it was too late to challenge state insolvency laws because they had been universally accepted since the adoption of the Constitution,[162] and in this connection counsel[163] properly invoked the opinion sustaining the circuit duties of the Justices in *Stuart v. Laird*.[164] Marshall replied that most of the insolvency laws cited merely released the debtor from prison, while the provision before him discharged the obligation itself.[165] Significantly, however, he elected not to base the validity of laws of the former description upon mere acquiescence. Misstating the unambiguous argument of counsel, he declared practice *before* 1789 irrelevant[166] and relied on original intent: "To punish honest insolvency by imprisonment for life, and to make this a constitutional principle, would be an excess of inhumanity which will not readily be imputed to the illustrious patriots who framed our constitution, nor to the people who adopted it."[167] Moreover, imprisonment was "no part of the contract" but at most "a means of inducing [the debtor] to perform it," and [w]ithout impairing the obligation of the contract, the remedy may certainly be modified as the wisdom of the nation shall direct."[168]

---

[159]Adams v. Storey, 1 F. Cas. 141, 145-46 (C.C.D.N.Y. 1817) (No. 66) (praising insolvency laws as universal and just). Marshall did not advert to this decision.

[160]*Sturges*, 17 U.S. (4 Wheat.) at 204-05.

[161]*Id.* at 202-03. Marshall employed similar language in *Dartmouth College*, prefaced by the statement:

> It is not enough to say, that this particular case was not in the mind of the Convention, when the article was framed, nor of the American people, when it was adopted. It is necessary to go farther, and to say that, had the particular case been suggested, the language would have been so varied, as to exclude it, or it would have been made a special exception.

Trustees of Dartmouth College v. Woodward, 17 U.S. (4 Wheat.) at 644. *See supra* notes 98-125 and accompanying text.

[162]Adams v. Storey, 1 F. Case. at 146-47.

[163]*Sturges*, 17 U.S. (4 Wheat.) at 162, 165-66; *see also id.* at 165 (quoting the maxim *"communis error facit jus"*).

[164]5 U.S. (1 Cranch) 299, 309 (1803) ("[P]ractice, and acquiescence under it, for a period of several years, commencing with the organization of the judicial system, affords an irresistible answer, and has indeed fixed the construction."). *See supra* chapter 3.

[165]*Sturges*, 17 U.S. (4 Wheat.) at 203.

[166]"If the long exercise of the power to emit bills of credit did not restrain the convention from prohibiting its future exercise, neither can it be said that the long exercise of the power to impair the obligation of contracts, should prevent a similar prohibition." *Id.*

[167]*Id.* at 200.

[168]*Id.* at 200-01.

The dictum endorsing retroactive laws releasing debtors from prison became an alternative holding in Justice Thompson's 1827 opinion in *Mason v. Haile*,[169] on the ground that they "act merely upon the remedy, and that in part only."[170] Marshall himself was later to come close to making the extraordinary concession in a desperate dissent that the state could abolish all remedies for preexisting contracts.[171] Yet any sharp distinction between obligation and remedy was difficult to square with Marshall's insistence in *Marbury v. Madison*[172] on the intimate relationship between rights and remedies,[173] and, in striking down laws restricting the rights of landowners to recover against squatters in *Green v. Biddle*,[174] Justice Washington went to the opposite extreme: "If the remedy afforded be qualified and restrained by conditions of any kind, the right of the owner . . . is impaired . . . ."[175]

No one seriously contended, however, that the clause forbade changes in the minutiae of court procedure for enforcing existing agreements; the Court therefore was unable to avoid drawing lines to determine which remedial modifications had such a significant impact as to impair the obligation itself.[176] Marshall's concession in

[169]25 U.S. (12 Wheat.) 370 (1827).

[170]*Id.* at 378 (citing *Sturges*). Justice Washington, dissenting, did not dispute the Court's reasoning as a general principle. He argued that the debtor's release from prison impaired the obligation and not merely the remedy because the contract in suit was a bond conditioned on his remaining in custody. *Id.* at 380-81 ("*restraint of the person* is the sole object of the contract" (emphasis in original)). Thompson responded that the statutory release satisfied the bond's condition that the prisoner remain until "lawfully discharged." *Id.* at 375, 377.

[171]Ogden v. Saunders, 25 U.S. (12 Wheat.) 213, 351 (1827) (Marshall, C.J., dissenting):

> [T]he constitution . . . prohibits the States from passing any law impairing the obligation of contracts; it does not enjoin them to enforce contracts. Should a State be sufficiently insane to shut up or abolish its Courts, and thereby withhold all remedy, would this annihilation of remedy annihilate the obligation also of contracts? We know it would not.

He appeared to take it back in the next breath, suggesting it would be unconstitutional "if a State shall not merely modify, or withhold a particular remedy, but shall apply it in such a manner as to extinguish the obligation, without performance." *Id.* at 352; *see infra* notes 217-39 and accompanying text.

[172]5 U.S. (1 Cranch) 137 (1803).

[173]*See id.* at 163, 177-78 *supra* chapter 3.

[174]21 U.S. (8 Wheat.) 1 (1823).

[175]*Id.* at 76. The case was decided twice. Story had put the point more modestly in reaching the same result in 1821, before the rehearing: "If those acts so change the nature and extent of existing remedies, as materially to impair the rights and interests of the owner, they are just as much a violation of the compact, as if they directly overturned his rights and interests." *Id.* at 17.

Green was significant also for its conclusion that a compact between Virginia and Kentucky was protected by the contract clause, *id.* at 92 (citing *Fletcher*); the contrary argument, Washington said, "was not much pressed," *id.* Counsel had argued that the clause was "intended merely for the protection of private rights," *id.* at 37, as it had been applied in all prior cases. Madison had described the sentence containing it as a "bulwark in favor of personal security and private rights." THE FEDERALIST No. 44, at 282 (J. Madison) (C. Rossiter ed. 1961). As Marshall said in *Sturges*, however, the Framers had used broader words. See the argument in B. WRIGHT, *supra* note 70, at 46-47, 76, that it was "far-fetched" to hold a compact a contract but harmless because, as later cases were to hold, congressional approval made the compact a federal law entitled to precedence under the supremacy clause. Johnson concurred in *Green* on the basis of the state constitution, not of the contract clause. *Green* 2 U.S. (8 Wheat.) at 94-107 (Johnson, J., concurring).

[176]*See, e.g.*, Bronson v. Kinzie, 42 U.S. (1 How.) 311 (1843), *infra* chapter 7. *See also* B. WRIGHT, *supra* note 70, at 107-18; Hale, *The Supreme Court and the Contract Clause* (pt. 1), 57 HARV. L. REV. 512, 534-37 (1944). Compare this issue with the question of the extent to which the application of state procedural rules in state court actions based on federal statutes is precluded because of their effect on substantive

Sturges that laws opening the debtors' prisons were valid may have been inescapable in light of practice, but his explanation that they went merely to the remedy suggested that remedial changes might embrace far more than procedural details.[177] Later decisions would exploit this opening as an avenue for making substantial inroads upon the protection afforded by the clause.[178]

Before reaching the contract clause question in *Sturges*, the Court had unnecessarily resolved another issue of major importance. Sitting on circuit five years before, Justice Washington had held Congress's power to adopt "uniform Laws on the subject of Bankruptcies"[179] exclusive because state laws "would be dissimilar and frequently contradictory."[180] Hamilton had said the same of the similarly worded power to adopt "an uniform Rule of Naturalization,"[181] since otherwise "there could not be a UNIFORM RULE,"[182] and in *Chirac v. Chirac*[183] the Supreme Court itself had declared without explanation that the exclusivity of the naturalization power "ought not to be controverted."[184] Moreover, counsel argued, the tenth amendment implied that all federal powers were exclusive, for it reserved to the states only those powers "'not delegated to the United States by the Constitution.'"[185]

Marshall was unimpressed. Express provisions such as that forbidding state treaties, he began, showed "the sense of the Convention to have been, that the mere grant of a power to Congress, did not imply a prohibition on the States to exercise the same power."[186] Marshall conceded, however, as Hamilton had argued in *The Federalist*,[187] that such a grant was implicitly exclusive whenever its "terms" or its "nature" so required.[188] Although this was obvious enough in the case of government debts and the establishment of federal courts,[189] Marshall could readily have argued

federal rights. *E.g.*, Dice v. Akron, C. & Y.R.R., 342 U.S. 359 (1952) (requiring jury to decide question of fraud in release of FELA claim).

[177]Marshall might have limited the impact of his concession had he picked up counsel's suggestion that imprisonment was a purely nominal remedy that did not significantly improve the chances of collection. *Sturges*, 17 U.S. (4 Wheat.) at 155.

[178]*See, e.g.*, Ewell v. Daggs, 108 U.S. 143 (1883) (allowing retroactive repeal of a usury law).

[179]U.S. CONST. art. I, § 8, cl. 4.

[180]Golden v. Prince, 10 F. Cas. 542, 545 (C.C.D. Pa. 1814) (No. 5509). The suggestion that Story had reached the same conclusion in 1812, G. DUNNE, *supra* note 27, at 9 (citing Babcock v. Weston, 2 F. Cas. 306 (C.C.D.R.I. 1812) (No. 704)), seems erroneous; Story merely refused to respect a legislative stay pending final decision whether to grant a discharge and questioned a state's power to bind an outsider suing in federal court. Despite the reporter's interpolated citation in *Babcock* to decisions rendered as late as 1827, the original report shows the case was actually decided in 1812. *See* Babcock v. Weston, 1 Gall. 168 (C.C.D.R.I. 1812).

[181]U.S. CONST. art. I, § 8, cl. 4.

[182]THE FEDERALIST No. 32, at 199 (A. Hamilton) (C. Rossiter ed. 1961) (emphasis in original).

[183]15 U.S. (2 Wheat.) 259 (1817).

[184]*Id.* at 269 (Marshall, C.J.).

[185]*Sturges*, 17 U.S. (4 Wheat.) at 124 (Mr. Daggett) (quoting U.S. CONST. amend. X).

[186]*Id.* at 193 (Marshall, C.J.).

[187]Cited by neither the Court nor counsel, Hamilton had argued for exclusivity when the Constitution "granted an authority to the Union to which a similar authority in the States would be absolutely and totally *contradictory* and *repugnant*." THE FEDERALIST No. 32, at 198 (A. Hamilton) (C. Rossiter ed. 1961) (emphasis in original).

[188]*Sturges*, 17 U.S. (4 Wheat.) at 193.

[189]Counsel conceded the exclusivity of Congress's powers in these areas and in the more controversial area of regulating commerce. *Id.* at 167-78 (Mr. Ogden). *See infra* chapter 6, notes 74-126 and accompanying text (discussing *Gibbons v. Ogden*). *See also* Wayman v. Southard, 23 U.S. (10 Wheat.) 1, 49-50 (1825) (dictum) (states cannot directly regulate procedure of federal courts), *discussed in supra* chapter 4.

that concurrent bankruptcy powers were not so absurd as to overcome the presumption that when the Framers meant federal power to be exclusive they said so. Instead he took a narrower view based apparently on his familiar precept that the Framers had done nothing undesirable.[190] It was admitted, he said, that states might enact "insolvent" laws; the distinction between these and "bankrupt" laws was so indistinct that "much inconvenience would result" from holding the bankruptcy power exclusive.[191]

That was all. Marshall could have demolished the tenth amendment contention by noting the incongruity of holding that a provision designed to protect state authority had actually impaired it.[192] He could have countered Washington's textual argument by invoking counsel's analogy[193] of the provision for "uniform" federal taxes,[194] which obviously was a limit only on Congress and not on the states. He also could have argued, with counsel and with Livingston's circuit opinion upholding the law involved in *Sturges*,[195] that the Court's recognition of the exclusivity of naturalization had been based solely on statute,[196] that Justices Wilson and Blair had upheld state naturalization in 1792 before the enactment of a prohibitory federal law,[197] and that the alleged exclusivity of the naturalization clause was based upon an argument, inapplicable to bankruptcy,[198] that the power to confer citizenship would enable one state to foist undesirables onto another by virtue of the privileges and immunities clause of article IV.[199] Not only were Marshall's arguments a good deal less than

[190]*See supra* notes 62-67 and accompanying text (discussing *Fletcher v. Peck*).

[191]*Sturges*, 17 U.S. (4 Wheat.) at 194-96. In reaching this conclusion, Marshall incidentally proclaimed that the bankruptcy power would enable Congress to pass laws discharging only the person of the debtor, or operating at the debtor's instance, though both were said to be "insolvent" rather than "bankrupt" laws in contemporary parlance. *Id.* at 194. Livingston, in contrast, had doubted Congress had power to pass laws discharging anyone but "traders," and he had declared that "a bare inspection of the act," also involved in *Sturges*, "will leave no doubt in the mind of any one to which class it belongs." Adams v. Storey, 1 F. Cas. 141, 142 (C.C.D.N.Y. 1817) (No. 66).

[192]*See* 1 ANNALS OF CONG. 449-50, 458-59, 790 (J. Gales ed. 1789); *infra* chapter 6, notes 1-73 and accompanying text (discussing *McCulloch v. Maryland*).

[193]*Sturges*, 17 U.S. (4 Wheat.) at 174 (Mr. Ogden).

[194]U.S. CONST. art. I, § 8, cl. 1 (Congress's power "To Lay . . . Duties, Imposts and Excises" subject to limitation that they "be uniform throughout the United States").

[195]Adams v. Storey, 1 F. Cas 141, 143-44 (C.C.D.N.Y. 1817) (No. 66).

[196]The act in force at the time of the state's attempted naturalization in *Chirac* provided that an alien could become a citizen "on the following conditions, and not otherwise." Act of Jan. 29, 1795, ch. 20, § 1, 1 Stat. 414, 414 (codified as amended in scattered sections of 8 U.S.C. (1976); *see Sturges*, 17 U.S. (4 Wheat.) at 169-72 (Mr. Ogden). Marshall had said in *Chirac* that it was argued that the state law had been "virtually repealed by the constitution of the United States, and the act of naturalization passed by Congress." Chirac v. Chirac, 15 U.S. (2 Wheat.) at 269. Moreover, as Marshall noted, the exclusivity of federal authority had not been denied by counsel in *Chirac, id.*, and the entire passage was unnecessary to the result since the party asserting state power to confer citizenship prevailed on another ground.

[197]Collet v. Collet, 6 F. Cas. 105, 106-07 (C.C.D. Pa. 1792) (No. 3001) (Wilson and Blair, Circuit Justices; Peters, District Judge) (invoking the uniform-tax analogy), *cited in* Adams v. Storey, 1 F. Cas. at 141, 143. See also United States v. Villato, 28 F. Cas. 377 (C.C.D. Pa. 1797) (No. 16,622), where Justice Iredell suggested that "if the question had not previously occurred, [he] should be disposed to think, that the power of naturalization operated exclusively, *as soon as it was exercised by congress*," *id.* at 379 (dictum) (emphasis added).

[198]*Sturges*, 17 U.S. (4 Wheat.) at 148 (Mr. Hunter); Adams v. Storey, 1 F. Cas. at 143.

[199]*See* U.S. CONST. art. IV, § 2, cl. 1 ("The Citizens of each State shall be entitled to all Privileges and Immunities of Citizens in the several States."). This was Madison's argument, THE FEDERALIST No. 42, at 269-71 (J. Madison) (C. Rossiter ed. 1961), echoed by counsel in *Chirac*, 15 U.S. (2 Wheat.) at 264

complete, but the narrow basis of his conclusion left the door open for his later dictum that the commerce power might be exclusive,[200] and thus to a whole raft of decisions striking down state laws on the ground that they encroached on congressional authority.

Perhaps most interesting is what *Sturges* tells us about the internal practices of the Marshall Court. As we have seen, Livingston had disagreed on circuit with the conclusion that the New York law offended the contract clause, and Washington had rejected the conclusion that the bankruptcy power was concurrent.[201] Neither registered a dissent in *Sturges*, but there is extrinsic evidence that neither was persuaded to abandon his position.[202] Moreover, later statements by Johnson have led observers to conclude that he agreed with Livingston.[203] Thus what the reports tell us was just another pronouncement of the Harmonious Seven turns out to have reflected the thinking of only three or four of their number, and we are left wondering on how many other occasions the Justices elected to suppress fundamental differences of view.[204]

B.   *Ogden v. Saunders*

In *Sturges* the Court had held without recorded dissent that the contract clause prohibited the discharge of debts contracted before enactment of an insolvency law.[205] Eight years later it held by a vote of four to three that a state was free to discharge obligations incurred to its own citizens after the law was passed.[206]

(Mr. Harper), and by Chancellor Kent in his treatise, 1 J. KENT, *supra* note 109, at 424. This argument was to play a significant role in the Dred Scott decision, Scott v. Sandford, 60 U.S. (19 How.) 393, 405-07, 417-18, 422-23 (1857), discussed *infra* in chapter 8. Its validity had been denied by Blair and Wilson in *Collet*: "[T]he state which communicates the infection must herself be first infected; and in this, as in all other cases . . . the principle of self-preservation will inculcate every reasonable precaution." 6 F. Cas. at 106-07.

[200]*See infra* chapter 6, notes 74-126 and accompanying text (discussing *Gibbons v. Ogden*).

[201]*See also* 3 J. STORY, *supra* note 42, at 14: "It is well known that Mr. Justice Washington was not alone in the Court in this opinion."

[202]*See infra* note 211 and accompanying text (discussing *Ogden v. Saunders*); 1 LIFE AND LETTERS OF JOSEPH STORY 326 (W. Story ed. 1851) ("All the Judges, except judge Livingston, concurred in this opinion").

[203]*See, e.g.*, D. MORGAN, JUSTICE WILLIAM JOHNSON 117 n.33, 216 (1954) (citing Ogden v. Saunders, 25 U.S. (12 Wheat.) 213 (1827)). In *Ogden*, Justice Johnson denied the federal power was exclusive and said *Sturges* "partakes as much of a compromise, as of a legal adjudication." *Ogden*, 25 U.S. (12 Wheat.) at 272-73. He said the "minority" in that case had surrendered their position that retroactive laws were permissible rather than "risk the whole." *Id.* at 273. In addition, he described insolvency laws as just and said it was "no objection" to the "correctness" of his argument that it was said to be "as applicable to contracts prior to the law, as to those posterior to it" and thus inconsistent with *Sturges*: "I entertained this opinion then, and have seen no reason to doubt it since." *Id.* at 284.

[204]Washington also revealed in Mason v. Haile, 25 U.S. (12 Wheat.) at 370, that it had "never been my habit to deliver dissenting opinions in cases where it has been my misfortune to differ from those which have been pronounced by a majority of this Court," and that he did so in that case only out of "regard for my own consistency" in light of the perceived conflict between *Sturges* and the case before him. *Id.* at 379. Washington added that he had "prepared no written opinion" in *Mason*. *Id.* at 382. His saying so may suggest that by 1827 this had become a departure from the norm.

[205]*See supra* notes 156-204 and accompanying text.

[206]Ogden v. Saunders, 25 U.S. (12 Wheat.) 213 (1827). The case is discussed briefly in 1 C. WARREN, *supra* note 15, at 686-93, and in 4 A. BEVERIDGE, *supra* note 15, at 480-82.

Ogden was the only constitutional case in thirty-four years in which Marshall signed a dissent, and he took Story and Duvall with him.[207] Headless for the first time, the majority reverted to the pre-Marshall practice of seriatim opinions. Washington, who had never before broken publicly with the Chief,[208] delivered a solid opinion[209] whose becoming modesty[210] contrasted sharply with Marshall's habitual certainty. In revealing that he had always thought the federal bankruptcy power exclusive,[211] Washington also exhibited admirable self-restraint; for by respecting the precedential effect of what was really only a dictum in *Sturges*, he cast the deciding vote to uphold a law he believed invalid. The relatively independent Johnson was the most discursive,[212] pausing to tell us not only his views on issues already resolved in *Sturges*,[213] but also that his predecessors had been wrong to limit the ex post facto clause to criminal matters.[214] The newcomers Thompson[215] and Trimble,[216] whose disagreement with Marshall was an omen, added important refinements to Washington's arguments at various points; but basically all four opinions said much the same things.

The Constitution protected not contracts as such, the majority observed, but only their "Obligation." The existence and extent of the obligation were determined by the law in force at the time of the agreement; that law was state law, and it included the insolvency provision. It was as if the contract itself had provided that insolvency would discharge the debt. It would be "something of a solecism," said Washington, to hold that the law creating an obligation impaired it at the same time.[217] The vice the Framers had meant to attack was retroactive legislation, which was "oppressive, unjust, and tyrannical";[218] there was nothing unjust about affording relief in accordance with rules accessible to the parties at the time of their agreement.[219]

---

[207] *Ogden*, 25 U.S. (12 Wheat.) at 332.

[208] In a letter to Jefferson, Johnson had said that Marshall and Washington were "commonly estimated as one judge." Letter from William Johnson to Thomas Jefferson (Dec. 10, 1822), *quoted in* D. MORGAN, *supra* note 203, at 182.

[209] *See Ogden*, 25 U.S. (12 Wheat.) at 254.

[210] "[M]y labors . . . have led me to the only conclusion by which I can stand with any degree of confidence; and yet, I should be disingenuous were I to declare . . . that I embrace it, without . . . a doubt of its correctness." *Id.* at 256.

[211] *Id.* at 264.

[212] *See id.* at 271. For an earlier prominent difference of opinion between Johnson and Marshall, see *supra* notes 8-62 and accompanying text (discussing *Fletcher v. Peck*).

[213] *Ogden*, 25 U.S. (12 Wheat.) at 272-81, 284; *see supra* note 203.

[214] *Ogden*, 25 U.S. (12 Wheat.) at 286.

[215] *Id.* at 292. Thompson had replaced the deceased Livingston in 1823.

[216] *Id.* at 313. Trimble, whose opinion in *Ogden* was perhaps the most convincing, had been appointed after Todd's death in 1826.

[217] *Id.* at 260 (Washington, J.).

[218] *Id.* at 266 (Washington, J.).

[219] *Id.* at 256-60, 266-67 (Washington, J.). *See also id.* at 283-85 (Johnson, J.), 297-303, 308-10 (Thompson, J.), 316-21, 324-27 (Trimble, J.). Webster had argued that the parties to a contract made before the insolvency law might equally have expected that such a law might be passed, *id.* at 245-46, but the ex post facto provision showed that at least in the criminal context the Framers had not found his equation convincing. Washington's policy argument also enabled him to explain why the Framers had, as he concluded, permitted prospective bankruptcy laws while forbidding those allowing tender other than in gold or silver: while the former merely afforded a person "by misfortunes . . . reduced to poverty" the chance "to become once more a useful member of society," the latter were "always unjust" because,

Through much of his dissenting opinion Marshall seemed to flirt with the idea that the Constitution protected agreements whether or not they were recognized by state law: "[I]ndividuals do not derive from government their right to contract, but bring that right with them into society; that obligation is not conferred on contracts by positive law, but is intrinsic, and is conferred by the act of the parties."[220] The implication, supported by Webster's argument that the Framers' purpose had been not simply to protect vested rights but "to establish confidence, credit, and commerce,"[221] seemed to be that the contract clause guaranteed a freedom of contract resembling that which later Justices were to discover in the due process clause:[222] a state impaired the obligation of contract not only when it destroyed a pre-existing contractual duty, but whenever it denied legal effect to the parties' intentions.[223]

Although the words of the clause seem capable of bearing this interpretation,[224] and although no one provided direct evidence to refute Webster's assertions respecting the Framers' intentions,[225] this aspect of Marshall's opinion proved to be nothing

"unsupported . . . by the plea of necessity," they relieved "the opulent debtor" as well. *Id.* at 269-70 (Washington, J.); *see also id.* at 288-89 (Johnson, J.).

[220]*Id.* at 346 (Marshall, C.J., dissenting).

[221]*Id.* at 247-48 (Mr. Webster); *see also id.* at 335-36 (Marshall, C.J., dissenting) (while the ex post facto clause is "in its very terms, confined to pre-existing cases," the contract clause "is expressed in more general terms . . . which comprehend, in their ordinary signification, cases which occur after, as well as those which occur before, the passage of the act.").

[222]*E.g.*, Lochner v. New York, 198 U.S. 45 (1905). *See* B. Wright, *supra* note 70, at 50, 52; Isaacs, *John Marshall on Contracts: A Study in Early American Juristic Theory*, 7 Va. L. Rev. 413, 426 (1921) (finding it ironic that "although Marshall was overruled in his attempt to find [liberty of contract] in the Constitution where it *was* written, a juristic tendency of a later day . . . succeeded in finding it in clauses where it had *not* been written" (emphasis in original).

[223]If this was true, the case was not the same as if the parties had stipulated for discharge in the event of insolvency, for only in the latter instance would a discharge accomplish the intentions of the parties.

[224]Each side attempted, without much success, to derive support from the relation of the clause to other arguably similar provisions. *See, e.g., Ogden*, 25 U.S. (12 Wheat.) at 265-66 (Washington, J.) (noting that a single clause proscribed both contractual impairments and the retroactive ex post facto laws and bills of attainder, while prospective bans on coinage, bills of credit, and legal tender were lumped together elsewhere); *id.* at 335-36 (Marshall, C.J., dissenting) (observing that the retrospective ex post facto and bill of attainder provisions were both applicable only to criminal matters, while the other civil prohibitions all had prospective force). Justice Washington maintained that the text had been "so maturely considered" that the placement of each clause gave an important clue to its meaning. *Id.* at 268. Yet the document of which he was speaking contains two distinct requirements that direct taxes be apportioned and places the power to govern the District of Columbia and the territories in entirely separate articles.

[225]The Convention debates, still unavailable at the time, are less than conclusive. Rufus King had moved "to add, in the words used in the Ordinance of Congs [sic] establishing new States, a prohibition on the states to interfere in private contracts." 2 Convention Records, *supra* note 76, at 439. To Mason's objection that "[t]his is carrying the restraint too far," *id.* at 440, Wilson replied that "*retrospective interferences only are to be prohibited,*" *id.* (emphasis in original). But the Northwest Ordinance provision that King had proposed to copy, and that Wilson was discussing, expressly referred to "private contracts or engagements . . . *previously formed.*" Northwest Territory Ordinance and Act of 1787, art. II, ch. 8, § 1, 1 Stat. 51, 52 n.(a) (1789) (emphasis added). As with the question of public contracts, *see supra* notes 68-78 and accompanying text (discussing *Fletcher v. Peck*), we do not know whether the Convention later dropped the explicit limitation because it was undesirable or because it was understood. Justice Chase had used the assumed retrospection of the contract clause to show that the ex post facto provision must be limited to criminal matters to avoid redundancy. Calder v. Bull, 3 U.S. (3 Dall.) 386, 390 (1798), *discussed supra* in chapter 2. Nobody cited Chase in *Ogden*.

but a distraction, for he ended by abandoning it in the face of its insupportable consequences. As the majority pointed out, no one had ever doubted that the states could pass prospective statutes of frauds or of limitations, or outlaw usury or penalty clauses in future contracts.[226] If the whole "power to pass prospective laws, *affecting contracts*, was denied to the states," said Washington, "it is most wonderful, that not one voice was raised against the provision . . . by the jealous advocates of state rights,"[227]—especially because, as Thompson added, Congress did not seem to have been given power to do it either.[228]

Unwilling, as in the case of debtor's prison,[229] to overthrow so much accepted practice, Marshall conceded the majority's basic premise: acknowledging state power "to regulate contracts" and "to prohibit such as may be deemed mischievous,"[230] he attempted instead to distinguish the Court's analogies. Statutes of limitations, he urged, extinguished merely the remedy and not the right; even *Sturges* had recognized that the law of remedies was subject to modification.[231] The Court had already held, however, that the remedial label was no talisman permitting indirect destruction of the obligation;[232] both Washington and Trimble pointed out that Marshall himself had expressly denied in *Sturges* that statutes of limitation could be applied retroactively.[233] Moreover, some of the Court's examples could not fairly be characterized as remedial. Marshall had another explanation for them: usury laws and statutes of frauds "precede the obligation of the contract" and "declare the contract to be void in the beginning"; and "obligation must exist before it can be impaired,"[234] but a discharge in bankruptcy "defeat[s] a contract once obligatory."[235] As Trimble argued, however, "a power competent to declare a contract shall have no obligation, must necessarily be competent to declare it shall have only a conditional

---

[226]*Ogden*, 25 U.S. (12 Wheat.) at 257, 259, 261 (Washington, J.), 286-87 (Johnson, J.), 299 (Thompson, J.), 326 (Trimble, J.).

[227]*Id.* at 268 (Washington, J.); *see also id.* at 258 (Washington, J.), 305 (Thompson, J.).

[228]*See id.* at 308 (Thompson, J.). Counsel had made this point as well. *Id.* at 236-37. We do not know exactly who made the argument; although Wheaton reported at length his and his colleague Webster's arguments against the law, *id.* at 214-26, 237-54, he impartially reduced the combined arguments of his seven distinguished adversaries to an amalgam of ten pages without individual attribution, *see id.* at 227. Unlike Thompson, Professor Crosskey, who believed the commerce clause gave Congress general authority over contract law, *see infra* chapter 6, note 86, found it not at all absurd to think the states had been ousted from the field entirely; in his view, *Ogden v. Saunders* was wrongly decided, 1 W. CROSSKEY, POLITICS AND THE CONSTITUTION IN THE HISTORY OF THE UNITED STATES 359 (1953).

[229]*See supra* notes 166-68 and accompanying text.

[230]*Ogden*, 25 U.S. (12 Wheat.) at 347 (Marshall, C.J., dissenting).

[231]*Id.* at 348-54 (Marshall, C.J., dissenting). It was in this connection that he was to make the sweeping suggestion that the Constitution did not require the states "to enforce contracts." *Id.* at 351; *see supra* notes 156-78 and accompanying text (discussing *Sturges v. Crowninshield*). Washington argued that a bankruptcy discharge was equally "remedial" in that, like a time limitation, it must be pleaded and could be defeated by a subsequent promise unsupported by consideration. *Ogden*, 25 U.S. (12 Wheat.) at 262-63 (Washington, J.); *see also id.* at 287 (Johnson, J.).

[232]*See supra* notes 174-75 and accompanying text (discussing *Green v. Biddle*).

[233]*Ogden*, 25 U.S. (12 Wheat.) at 262 (Washington, J.) (citing *Sturges*, 17 U.S. (4 Wheat.) at 207), 326-27 (Trimble, J.).

[234]*Id.* at 348 (Marshall, C.J., dissenting).

[235]*Id. See also id.* at 337 (Marshall, C.J., dissenting) (arguing that an insolvency law had "no effect whatever" on a contract "until an insolvency should take place, and a certificate of discharge be granted").

or qualified obligation";[236] the law effectively made continued solvency a condition of the original obligation, and the discharge therefore took nothing from the creditor.[237]

At this point Marshall was on the ropes, but he came up with a startling analogy of his own that must give pause to those who share my sense that the majority was right. If the clause merely protected existing expectations, said Marshall, the state could make it inapplicable to all future agreements by enacting that agreements "should be discharged as the legislature might prescribe."[238] Principled grounds for distinguishing the prospective bankruptcy law are not easy to find; and thus the contending Justices seem to have demonstrated that either to uphold the law or not to uphold it would lead to consequences so absurd that they could not have been intended.[239]

Having furnished the one-vote margin for upholding the state's power to provide for the discharge of future debts owing to its own residents,[240] Justice Johnson composed a mysterious cadenza in which he cast the decisive vote *against* applying

[236]*Id.* at 323 (Trimble, J.).

[237]*Id.* at 323-24 (Trimble, J.); *see also id.* at 308 (Trimble, J.). *Compare* Hale, *supra* note 176, at 521-22, 528-31 (criticizing Marshall's efforts) *with* 4 A. Beveridge, *supra* note 15, at 481 (terming the *Ogden* dissent one of Marshall's "most powerful" opinions).

[238]*Ogden*, 25 U.S. (12 Wheat.) at 339 (Marshall, C.J., dissenting); *see also id.* at 338 (less shocking argument that if the bankruptcy law determined the obligation of contracts made after its enactment, it could not be repealed as applied to them). Washington conceded this latter point. *Id.* at 260-61 (Washington, J.). For an argument that Marshall was right, *see* Epstein, *Toward a Revitalization of the Contract Clause*, 51 U. Chi. L. Rev. 703, 723-30 (1984).

[239]Marshall commendably conceded that the question had been settled neither by *Sturges* nor by its companion case of McMillan v. McNeill, 17 U.S. (4 Wheat.) 209 (1819), despite the statement in the latter case that it was immaterial that the law had been "passed before the debt was contracted," *id.* at 213. In *McMillan* the contract had been "made in a different state, by persons residing in that state, and consequently without any view to" the insolvency law in question. *Ogden*, 25 U.S. (12 Wheat.) at 333 (Marshall, C.J., dissenting). Thus the application of the law in *McMillan* had had retrospective effect after all; the case fell within the purpose of protecting vested rights even though it was hard to say the state had "passed" a law impairing the obligation of contracts. *Cf.* Owings v. Speed, 18 U.S. (5 Wheat.) 420 (1820) (holding the clause inapplicable to an impairment occurring before 1789). In any event, *McMillan* affords support for the argument that retroactive application of the law of even an interested state may be unconstitutional, despite the Court's later holding to the contrary in Clay v. Sun Ins. Office, Ltd., 377 U.S. 179 (1964). *See* B. Currie, Selected Essays on the Conflict of Laws 625-26 (1963) (arguing that it was "just as unreasonable, and just as much an impairment of the obligation of contracts, to apply the law for the protection of the new resident with an out-of-state contract as to apply it for the protection of an old resident with a contract antedating the statute"). *But see* Currie, *Full Faith and Credit, Chiefly to Judgments: A Role for Congress*, 1964 Sup. Ct. Rev. 89, 93-94 (taking it back).

Washington and Thompson argued with some force that the issue in *Ogden* was at least doubtful, and, therefore, in light of the Court's many previous statements about doubtful cases, the statute ought to be upheld. *Ogden*, 25 U.S. (12 Wheat.) at 270 (Washington, J.), 294 (Thompson, J.). Thompson further suggested that, since the words did not forbid it, the Court should do what sound policy required. *Id.* at 310 (Thompson, J.). Marshall ventured a general approach to constitutional interpretation:

> To say that the intention of the instrument must prevail; that this intention must be collected from its words; that its words are to be understood in that sense in which they are generally used by those for whom the instrument was intended; that its provisions are neither to be restricted into insignificance, nor extended to objects not comprehended in them, nor contemplated by its framers;—is to repeat what has been already said more at large, and is all that can be necessary.

Id. at 332 (Marshall, C.J., dissenting).

[240]This holding disposed of a number of cases argued together with *Ogden*. *See* 25 U.S. (12 Wheat.) at 357.

the law even prospectively against a creditor from another state.[241] It seems certain that this opinion was not based upon the contract clause; to determine what it *was* based on is appreciably more difficult.

Johnson devoted a good deal of attention to demonstrating that American courts rejected the English conflict-of-laws principle that a discharge by the place of contracting was binding on foreign creditors,[242] but he had declared at the outset that the question was whether the discharge had been valid when rendered.[243] Because the Court had made clear much earlier that state authority was not limited[244] by what Johnson kept referring to as "international" law,[245] it seemed incumbent on him to suggest that there was something in the Constitution to impose on New York the Court's conclusions as to the proper choice of law. Later passages seemed to suggest he saw deficiencies of notice[246] and possibly of personal jurisdiction over an out-of-state creditor,[247] as well as interference with federal court judgments that Johnson did not say existed.[248] Yet the due process clause, on which we would rely for notice and personal jurisdiction today,[249] apparently applied at the time only to federal action.[250] The further possibility that in these allusions Johnson was anticipating the natural law notions later suggested in *Pennoyer v. Neff*[251] seems to yield on closer reading to the conclusion that notice problems merely illustrated that there was "good reason" for limiting state power over foreign creditors.[252]

Johnson's one concrete constitutional reference was to "the provision . . . which gives the power to the general government to establish tribunals of its own in every State, in order that the citizens of other states or sovereignties might therein prosecute their rights under the jurisdiction of the United States."[253] The purpose of this clause, he thought, was "to confine the States, in the exercise of their judicial sovereignty, to cases between their own citizens" to prevent "jealousy, irritation, and national complaint or retaliation."[254] Johnson seems to have been suggesting, in other words, that article III gave the federal courts *exclusive* jurisdiction of diversity cases.[255] This remarkable and unsupported suggestion was contrary to the explicit

[241]*Id.* at 358 (Johnson, J.) (disposing of *Ogden* itself); *see id.* at 213-14.

[242]*Id.* at 359-66 (Johnson, J.).

[243]*Id.* at 358. Johnson expressly declined to consider whether a valid discharge could be disregarded in another forum: "The question . . . steers clear of that provision in the constitution which purports to give validity in every state to the records, judicial proceedings, and so forth, of each state." *Id.*

[244]Ware v. Hylton, 3 U.S. (3 Dall.) 199, 299 (1796) (Chase, J.), *discussed in* chapter 2 *supra*.

[245]*E.g., Ogden*, 25 U.S. (12 Wheat.) at 359 (Johnson, J.) ("The question is one partly international, partly constitutional.").

[246]*Id.* at 365-66 (Johnson, J.).

[247]*Id.* at 366 (Johnson, J.) ("on what principles can a citizen of another State be forced into the Courts of a State"). *See* Denny v. Bennett, 128 U.S. 489, 497-98 (1888), explaining *Ogden* on this ground.

[248]*Id.* at 367 (Johnson, J.).

[249]*See, e.g.*, Mullane v. Central Hanover Bank & Trust Co., 339 U.S. 306 (1950) (notice); International Shoe Co. v. Washington, 326 U.S. 310 (1945) (jurisdiction).

[250]*See infra* chapter 6, notes 234-61 and accompanying text (discussing *Barron v. Mayor of Baltimore*).

[251]95 U.S. 714 (1878) *See infra* chapter 11.

[252]*Ogden*, 25 U.S. (12 Wheat.) at 365 (Johnson, J.).

[253]*Id.* at 359 (Johnson, J.) (referring to U.S. Const. art. III, § 1).

[254]*Id.* (Johnson, J.).

[255]*See also id.* at 368-69 (Johnson, J.) (describing the discharge as contrary to "the judicial powers granted to the United States"); Hale, *supra* note 176, at 524 (Johnson's reasoning may imply that the discharge was limited by "the constitutional grant of federal judicial power").

assurances of *The Federalist*,[256] to thirty-eight years of uninterrupted practice based
upon the laws enacted by the First Congress,[257] and to Justice Washington's conclusion in *Houston v. Moore*[258] that the constitutional grant of federal-question jurisdiction was not exclusive.[259] So far as I am aware it has never surfaced in any other
context since.[260]

C. *Coda*

Ogden v. Saunders represents a watershed in contract clause litigation, for it finally
set a limit to expansive construction of the clause. Before *Ogden*, the Court had only
once rejected a contract clause claim, holding the clause inapplicable to a law passed
before the Constitution took effect.[261] Meanwhile the Court not only had invoked the
clause to invalidate retroactive bankruptcy laws[262] and changes in the law of remedies
that seriously obstructed contractual obligations,[263] but had stretched it to cover land
grants,[264] corporate charters,[265] and interstate compacts.[266] The contract clause remained a potent limitation throughout the nineteenth century,[267] but *Ogden* established the important principle that it did not apply to prospective laws, and other
decisions beginning the same year increasingly upheld even retroactive legislation
respecting contracts.[268]

One method of upholding such legislation was to take advantage of the *Sturges*
dicta allowing "remedial" changes that did not go to the essence of the obligation; on

[256]THE FEDERALIST No. 82 (A. Hamilton).

[257]Judiciary Act of 1789, ch. 20, § 11, 1 Stat. 73, 78 (current version in relevant part at 28 U.S.C. § 1332
(1976)) (diversity jurisdiction "concurrent with the courts of the several States").

[258]18 U.S. (5 Wheat.) 1 (1820), *discussed supra in* chapter 4.

[259]18 U.S. (5 Wheat.) at 32 (Washington, J.).

[260]One would have thought Johnson spoke only for himself; for although he said he had been
"instructed by the majority finally to dispose of this cause," *Ogden*, 25 U.S. (12 Wheat.) at 358 (Johnson,
J.), Marshall and the others agreeing with Johnson's result had already given ample grounds for their vote,
and Johnson did not say they agreed with his reasons. Story later said, however, in an opinion for the
Court, that Johnson had spoken for all four of them. Boyle v. Zacharie, 31 U.S. (6 Pet.) 635, 643 (1832);
see also id. at 348 (Marshall's response to counsel). The holding of Johnson's coda to *Ogden* was
reaffirmed in Baldwin v. Hale, 68 U.S. (1 Wall.) 223 (1864); although the Court reported Johnson's
reasoning, it added:

> Insolvent laws of one State cannot discharge the contracts of citizens of other States,
> because they have no extra-territorial operation, and consequently the tribunal sitting
> under them, unless in cases where a citizen of such other State voluntarily becomes a party
> to the proceeding, has no jurisdiction in the case.

Id. at 234.

[261]Owings v. Speed, 18 U.S. (5 Wheat.) 420 (1820); *see supra* note 150.

[262]Sturges v. Crowninshield, 17 U.S. (4 Wheat.) 122 (1819); *see supra* notes 156-204 and accompanying
text.

[263]Green v. Biddle, 21 U.S. (8 Wheat.) 1 (1823); *see supra* notes 174-76 and accompanying text.

[264]Fletcher v. Peck, 10 U.S. (6 Cranch) 87 (1810); *see supra* notes 19-81 and accompanying text.

[265]Trustees of Dartmouth College v. Woodward, 17 U.S. (4 Wheat.) 518 (1819); *see supra* notes 126-55
and accompanying text.

[266]Green v. Biddle, 21 U.S. (8 Wheat.) 1 (1823); *see supra* notes 174-76 and accompanying text.

[267]*See* B. WRIGHT, *supra* note 70, at 91-93.

[268]*See infra* notes 269-80 and accompanying text.

this ground the Court allowed relief for imprisoned debtors in *Mason v. Haile*.[269] A second method was narrow construction of the contract: the Kentucky-Virginia compact that had been held impaired by anti-squatter legislation in *Green v. Biddle*[270] was held in *Hawkins v. Barney's Lessee*[271] unimpaired by such "reasonable" regulation of the land titles it protected as the enactment of a new seven-year statute of limitation; a state land grant was held in *Jackson v. Lamphire*[272] not to imply a promise that the state would not enact a statute imposing a limit on the time during which persons might challenge recorded decisions respecting land titles; and, despite *McCulloch v. Maryland*'s famous aphorism about the power to tax and the power to destroy,[273] a state bank charter was held not to imply an immunity from state taxation in *Providence Bank v. Billings*.[274] Marshall relied in the latter case on the common practice of taxing corporations,[275] noted that the bank's argument would also exempt land granted by the state from taxation,[276] and laid down the general principle that because of the "vital importance" of the taxing power "its abandonment ought not to be presumed."[277] Finally, in *Satterlee v. Matthewson*[278] and in *Watson v. Mercer*,[279] the Court relied on the language of the contract clause itself in holding that it did not forbid laws retroactively *creating* contracts, though the purpose of the clause might apply; only "impair[ment]" of contractual obligations was prohibited.[280]

Justice Johnson's separate opinion in *Satterlee* warrants brief attention. Finding unrelated grounds upon which to concur, he protested that, although

> [t]o give efficacy to a void contract, is not . . . violating a contract, . . . it is doing infinitely worse; it is advancing to the very extreme of that class of arbitrary and despotic acts, which bear upon individual rights and liabilities, and against . . . which the Constitution most clearly intended to interpose a protection.[281]

He appended a lengthy note that concluded with a reference to the principle of "the equity of a statute," suggesting that the contract clause might apply because the

[269]25 U.S. (12 Wheat.) 370 (1827); *see supra* notes 169-70 and accompanying text.
[270]21 U.S. (8 Wheat.) 1 (1823); *see supra* notes 174-76 and accompanying text.
[271]30 U.S. (5 Pet.) 457, 465-66 (1831) (Johnson, J.).
[272]28 U.S. (3 Pet.) 280, 290 (1830) (Baldwin, J.).
[273]McCulloch v. Maryland, 17 U.S. (4 Wheat.) 316, 427 (1819); *see infra* notes 275-80 and accompanying text.
[274]29 U.S. (4 Pet.) 514, 563-64 (1830) (Marshall, C.J.), distinguishing *McCulloch* on the ground that it had relied on the supremacy clause and the absence of state power over the creatures of Congress. The contract clause, however, gives state charters the same priority over later state laws that the supremacy clause gives federal charters over state law.
[275]*Id.* at 561.
[276]*Id.* at 562.
[277]*Id.* at 561.
[278]27 U.S. (2 Pet.) 380 (1829) (Washington, J.).
[279]33 U.S. (8 Pet.) 88 (1834) (Story, J.).
[280]*See Satterlee*, 27 U.S. (2 Pet.) at 413 (Washington, J.) ("it surely cannot be contended, that to create a contract, or to destroy or impair one, mean the same thing"). But see Allied Structural Steel Co. v. Spannaus, 438 U.S. 234 (1978), holding it an impairment of contract to *increase* the obligations of an employer under a pension plan: "[I]n any bilateral contract the diminution of duties on one side effectively increases the duties on the other." *Id.* at 245 n.16. *See also* Hale, *supra* note 176, at 515-17 & n.24.
[281]*Satterlee*, 27 U.S. (2 Pet.) at 414-15 (Johnson, J.).

retroactive creation of a contract, while "out of the letter" of the clause, was "within the same mischief" it was designed to prevent.[282] Despite the freewheeling natural law views he had expressed in *Fletcher v. Peck*,[283] however, Johnson acknowledged he had "serious doubt" whether the "equity of a statute" idea could be applied to the Constitution.[284] Instead he rested his case on the ex post facto clause, attacking "that unhappy idea, that the phrase 'ex post facto,' in the Constitution of the United States was confined to criminal cases exclusively,'"[285] and arguing that *Calder v. Bull* had not, as commonly supposed, so decided.[286] Because the opening quotation from his opinion suggests he had decided to strike down the law before he discovered the clause of the Constitution upon which he could pin the result,[287] this retreat from earlier natural law pronouncements may indicate that he had acquired not modesty but dissimulation.

Washington, writing for the majority, did not respond directly to the ex post facto argument; he said, however, that the Constitution did not forbid the divesting of vested rights as such,[288] adding that nothing in *Fletcher* was to the contrary. After quoting one of Marshall's more florid natural law passages, Washington emphasized that *Fletcher* had reviewed a federal rather than a state court decision; he seems to have read Marshall as talking about the state constitution.[289] Thus by 1829 the Justices seem to have become more reluctant than in the early days of contract clause litigation to look outside the Constitution for limits on state power.[290] The new attitude is reflected in *Watson v. Mercer*,[291] where, in upholding retroactive validation of a conveyance against both ex post facto and contract clause objections, Story was to repeat, despite *Terrett v. Taylor*,[292] that "the mere fact that it divests antecedent rights of property" did not bring a statute into conflict with the federal Constitution.[293]

[282]*Id.* at 687 app. No. 1 (original ed. Philadelphia 1829).

[283]10 U.S. (6 Cranch) 87, 143-48 (1810) (Johnson, J., concurring); *see supra* note 36 and accompanying text. Arguing that *Fletcher* was Johnson's "one notable appeal . . . to natural law," Professor Morgan pointed to Johnson's earlier acknowledgment that "'[t]here are certain eternal principles of justice which never ought to be dispensed with, and which courts . . . never can dispense with but when compelled by positive statute,'" D. MORGAN, *supra* note 203, at 211 & n.25 (quoting Mills v. Duryee, 11 U.S. (7 Cranch) 481, 486 (1813) (Johnson, J., dissenting), and to Johnson's later statement that he had once given "'too much weight to natural law and the suggestions of reason and justice in a case which ought to be disposed of upon the principles of political and positive law, and the law of nations,'" *id.* at 227 (quoting Shanks v. Dupont, 28 U.S. (3 Pet.) 242, 258 (1830) (Johnson, J., dissenting)).

[284]27 U.S. (2 Pet.) at 687 app. No. 1 (original ed. Philadelphia 1829).

[285]*Satterlee*, 27 U.S (2 Pet.) at 416 (Johnson, J.) (quoting U.S. CONST. art. I, § 10, cl. 1).

[286]*Id.* at 681, 682 app. No. 1 (original ed. Philadelphia 1829). *See supra* chapter 2 (discussing *Calder*).

[287]*See supra* text accompanying note 281.

[288]*Satterlee*, 27 U.S. (2 Pet.) at 413 (Washington, J.).

[289]*Id.* at 413-14.

[290]Later in the same Term, however, Story was to say without pointing to anything in the Constitution that New Hampshire could not authorize an executrix to sell land in Rhode Island because "[t]he legislative and judicial authority of New Hampshire were bounded by the territory of the state." Wilkinson v. Leland, 27 U.S. (2 Pet.) 627, 655 (1829).

[291]33 U.S. (8 Pet.) 88 (1834).

[292]13 U.S. (9 Cranch) 43 (1815); *see supra* notes 79-97 and accompanying text.

[293]33 U.S. (8 Pet.) at 110-11. Johnson, nearing the end of his time, was absent. *Id.* at iii. Story did not mention his contrary, unsuccessful efforts in *Satterlee* but relied on supporting precedent. *See id.* at 110-11. *See also* 3 J. STORY, *supra* note 42, § 1392, at 266-68 (reaffirming that the Constitution did not invalidate all retroactive legislation).

In short, after leaping to give the contract clause a debatably broad reading in *Fletcher v. Peck* and the next few cases, the Court, largely with Marshall's acquiescence, declined to undertake further extensions of its underlying principle beyond the ordinary meaning of particular contracts or of the clause itself.

6

Congressional Authority and Other Limits on State Power

The contract clause, as the preceding chapter shows, played a dominant role in the substantive constitutional adjudication of the Marshall era. Of even greater lasting significance, however, were the contemporaneous decisions respecting the powers of Congress and other limitations on the states, some of them not expressly mentioned in the Constitution. These decisions will complete our examination of the Marshall period.

I. McCulloch v. Maryland

Maryland imposed a tax of one to two percent on the issuance of notes by banks established "'without authority from the state.'"[1] The Bank of the United States, chartered by Act of Congress and owned in part by the United States,[2] issued notes without paying the tax. The state court penalized the Bank's cashier; the Supreme Court in the famous 1819 Marshall opinion unanimously reversed.[3]

Since McCulloch claimed federal incorporation as his defense, Congress's authority to establish the Bank was in issue, and the Court sustained it. As in *Martin v. Hunter's Lessee*,[4] practice was invoked to illustrate contemporary understanding: "The principle now contested was introduced at a very early period of our history, has been recognised by many successive legislatures, and has been acted upon by the

---

[1]McCulloch v. Maryland, 17 U.S. (4 Wheat.) 316, 321 (1819) (quoting Act of Feb. 11, 1818, ch. 156, § 1, 1 Md. Laws 679, 679 (Dorsey 1840)). The obligation could be discharged by an annual payment of $15,000. Act of Feb. 11, 1818, ch. 156, § 1, 1 Md. Laws 679, 679 (Dorsey 1840).

[2] See Act of Apr. 10, 1816, ch. 44, § 1, 3 Stat. 266, 266 (expired by its terms in 1836), providing that twenty percent of the shares should belong to the United States.

[3]McCulloch v. Maryland, 17 U.S. (4 Wheat.) 316 (1819). The case is set in context by 4 A. Beveridge, *supra* chapter 5, note 15, at 282-339, and by 1 C. Warren, *supra* chapter 5, note 15, at 499-500.

[4]14 U.S. (1 Wheat.) 304, 351-52 (1816); *see supra* chapter 4.

judicial department, in cases of peculiar delicacy, as a law of undoubted obligation";[5] Congress had created a similar bank as early as 1791.[6] Thus the issue could "scarcely be considered as an open question, entirely unprejudiced by the former proceedings of the nation . . . . An exposition of the constitution, deliberately established by legislative acts, on the faith of which an immense property has been advanced, ought not to be lightly disregarded."[7] As in *Martin*, however, and in contrast to *Stuart v. Laird*,[8] practice was not asserted to be conclusive. Even long acquiescence, Marshall acknowledged, would not justify "a bold and daring usurpation," but "a doubtful question . . . in the decision of which the great principles of liberty are not concerned, . . . if not put at rest by the practice of the government, ought to receive a considerable impression from that practice."[9] He went on to find constitutional support for the Bank as an original matter.

Marshall began his discussion by conceding that the federal government was one of "enumerated powers," which could "exercise only the powers granted to it."[10] The tenth amendment, reserving to the states "[t]he powers not delegated to the United States by the Constitution,"[11] simply confirmed this conclusion in order to "quiet[] the excessive jealousies which had been excited";[12] it did not, unlike the provision in the Articles of Confederation reserving powers not "expressly" given Congress,[13] preclude finding that Congress had "incidental or implied powers."[14] To avoid prolixity, the Constitution contained only "its great outlines" and designated only "its important objects."[15] It was "not denied, that the powers given to the government imply the ordinary means of execution."[16] A federal corporation was

[5]*McCulloch*, 17 U.S. (4 Wheat.) at 401.
[6]Act of Feb. 25, 1791, ch. 10, 1 Stat. 191 (expired by its terms in 1811).
[7]*McCulloch*, 17 U.S. (4 Wheat.) at 401.
[8]5 U.S. (1 Cranch) 299, 308 (1803), *discussed supra in* chapter 3.
[9]*McCulloch*, 17 U.S. (4 Wheat.) at 401.
[10]*Id.* at 405. Speaker after speaker favoring the Constitution had confirmed this in the state ratifying conventions. See, e.g., 2 ELLIOT'S DEBATES, *supra* chapter 5, note 78, at 435-36, 454, 540 (Messrs. Wilson and McKean), 3 *id.* at 95, 246, 444, 553 (Messrs. Madison, Nicholas, and Marshall); 4 *id.* at 149, 259-60 (Messrs. Iredell and Pinckney).
[11]U.S. CONST. amend. X.
[12]*McCulloch*, 17 U.S. (4 Wheat.) at 406.
[13]ARTICLES OF CONFEDERATION art. 2.
[14]*McCulloch*, 17 U.S. (4 Wheat.) at 406. *See also* 1 ANNALS OF CONG. 790 (J. Gales ed. 1789) (Madison, opposing a motion to add the word "expressly" to what became the tenth amendment, argued "there must necessarily be admitted powers by implication, unless the constitution descended to recount every minutia").
[15]*McCulloch*, 17 U.S. (4 Wheat.) at 407. It was in this context that Marshall uttered that greatly admired and essentially vacuous bon mot: "we must never forget that it is a *constitution* we are expounding." *Id.* (emphasis in original). See Kurland, *Curia Regis: Some Comments on the Divine Right of Kings and Courts to Say What the Law Is*, 23 ARIZ. L. REV. 582, 591 (1981), arguing that whenever an opinion quotes this passage, "you can be sure that the court will be throwing the constitutional text, its history, and its structure to the winds in reaching its conclusion." One might have thought, as a later Justice has written, that "precisely *because* 'it is a *constitution* we are expounding,' we ought not to take liberties with it." National Mut. Ins. Co. v. Tidewater Transfer Co., 337 U.S. 582, 647 (1949) (Frankfurter, J., dissenting) (quoting McCulloch v. Maryland, 17 U.S. (4 Wheat.) 316, 407 (1819) (first emphasis added, second emphasis in original).
[16]*McCulloch*, 17 U.S. (4 Wheat.) at 409.

permissible, therefore, if it was an "essential," "appropriate," "direct" means of carrying out powers explicitly given to Congress.[17]

This view of incidental powers Marshall found confirmed by the authorization to make "'all laws which shall be necessary and proper, for carrying into execution'" powers elsewhere granted the United States.[18] This clause was not a limitation on the power that would otherwise have existed, but a grant; a sufficient motive for its inclusion was "to remove all doubts respecting the right to legislate on that vast mass of incidental powers which must be involved in the constitution, if that instrument be not a splendid bauble."[19] Nor was the clause itself limited to "those single means, without which the end would be entirely unattainable";[20] "necessary" was a term admitting "of all degrees of comparison," in contrast to the prohibition of state import duties not "'*absolutely* necessary'" for executing inspection laws.[21] In summary: "Let the end be legitimate, let it be within the scope of the constitution, and all means which are appropriate, which are plainly adapted to that end, which are not prohibited, but consist with the letter and spirit of the constitution, are constitutional."[22]

In all of this I find Marshall at his most persuasive. The natural inference of incidental powers was confirmed in *The Federalist*;[23] the necessary and proper clause removes any doubt; a requirement of indispensable necessity would have been so confining that it could hardly have been intended. Marshall's examples of unquestioned laws inconsistent with that strict reading were compelling: surely if Congress may establish courts and executive departments it may punish perjury and prescribe oaths of office; surely the power to tax to pay the debts includes the power to transport money from place to place.[24] Marshall's final statement regarding the extent of incidental powers is remarkably careful and hard to improve upon in the light of a century and a half of experience.

What is surprising is that Marshall treated all this as an open question. The issue had arisen fourteen years before in *United States v. Fisher*,[25] where the Court had upheld Congress's power to give claims of the United States priority in the distribution of insolvent estates. Marshall had disposed of the issue in two quick paragraphs. There too he had acknowledged that the federal government had limited powers.[26] There too he had rejected the argument that indispensable necessity was required: "Where various systems might be adopted for that purpose, it might be said, with respect to each, that it was not necessary, because the end might be obtained by other means."[27] It followed that Congress "must be empowered to use any means which

---

[17]*Id.* at 409-11.

[18]*Id.* at 411-12 (quoting U.S. Const. art. I, § 8, cl. 18).

[19]*Id.* at 420-21.

[20]*Id.* at 414.

[21]*Id.* (quoting U.S. Const. art. I, § 10, para. 2) (emphasis in original).

[22]*Id.* at 421.

[23]The Federalist No. 33 (A. Hamilton); *id.* No. 44 (J. Madison).

[24]*McCulloch*, 17 U.S. (4 Wheat.) at 409, 416-17.

[25]6 U.S. (2 Cranch) 358 (1805).

[26]*Id.* at 396.

[27]*Id.* See also Marshall's second "Friend of the Union" letter, The Philadelphia Union, April 28, 1819, *reprinted in* G. Gunther, John Marshall's Defense of *McCulloch v. Maryland* 95 (1969), giving illustrations including the raising of armies: "A bounty . . . is unconstitutional, because the power may be executed by a draft; and a draft is unconstitutional, because the power may be executed by a bounty."

are in fact conducive to the exercise of a power granted by the constitution."[28] Because "the government is to pay the debt of the Union," it has "a right to make remittances, by bills or otherwise, and to take those precautions which will render the transaction safe."[29]

It was typical of Marshall not to cite even his own opinions although they squarely supported him; witness the omission of any reference to *Fletcher* in *Dartmouth College*.[30] In *Dartmouth* two of his brethren stepped in to remind the public that the question was not new;[31] in *McCulloch* they stood by while he threw away his trump card. So far as the report reveals, counsel had not invoked *Fisher*, and maybe nobody remembered it. That decision had not raised much dust in 1805;[32] that was a long time before *McCulloch*, and the indexing of cases was not what it is today.[33]

In fact the *Fisher* test is subject to serious criticism. Marshall's rejection of a straw man had led him unjustifiably to the opposite extreme: that Congress has some latitude in the choice of means need not mean it may employ any "which are in fact conducive to the exercise of a power granted by the constitution."[34] Virtually anything Congress might want to do could meet that criterion; among other things, it would authorize whatever might bring the government additional money to pay its debts or to support armies. It was on this basis that Congress not long ago was permitted to escheat the estates of veterans who die without heirs;[35] the same argument would seem to support escheat of everyone else's property, or the operation of any enterprise for profit.[36] Not only is such a lax standard difficult to square with the language authorizing laws that are both "necessary and proper,"[37] but, more fundamentally, it contradicts *Fisher*'s simultaneous acknowledgement of the basic principle that the subjects of federal legislation are limited.

In this critical respect, despite superficial similarities, the *McCulloch* formulation is a vast improvement upon *Fisher*.[38] The means chosen must be "plainly" adapted to

[28]*Fisher*, 6 U.S. (2 Cranch) at 396.

[29]*Id. See* U.S. CONST. art. I, § 8, cl. 1.

[30]*See supra* chapter 5, note 144 and accompanying text.

[31]*Id.*

[32]*See* 1 C. WARREN, *supra* chapter 5, note 15, at 503-04. It had, however, provoked one congressman to propose a constitutional amendment limiting Congress to the passage of laws bearing a "rational connection with and immediate relation to the powers enumerated." *Id.* at 502.

[33]*See supra* chapter 3.

[34]*Fisher*, 6 U.S. (2 Cranch) at 396.

[35]United States v. Oregon, 366 U.S. 643, 645-47 (1961).

[36]See also Jefferson's famous argument:

> Congress are authorized to defend the nation. Ships are necessary for defence; copper is necessary for ships; mines necessary for copper; a company necessary to work the mines; and who can doubt this reasoning who has ever played at "This is the House that Jack Built"? Under such a process of filiation of necessities the sweeping clause makes clean work.

Letter from Thomas Jefferson to Edward Livingston (April 30, 1800), *reprinted in* 9 THE WORKS OF THOMAS JEFFERSON 132-33 (P. Ford ed. 1905).

[37]In *McCulloch* Marshall argued that the effect of adding the word "proper" was if anything "to qualify" the "strict and rigorous meaning" that might otherwise have been suggested by "necessary," 17 U.S. (4 Wheat.) at 418-19, but the use of "and" rather than "or" seems to imply, as counsel had argued, that it is not enough that a law be merely "proper," *id.* at 367 (Mr. Jones).

[38]Although Marshall had dropped less guarded references to means that were "convenient," *id.* at 413, "conducive," or "appropriate," *id.* at 415, elsewhere in *McCulloch*, the famous passage, *supra* text accompanying note 22, was the summation of his argument.

the end, not merely conducive to it; tenuous connections to granted powers will not pass muster. It must in addition be "appropriate," which implies some supervision of the reasonableness of the means. It must not, Marshall added in a later paragraph, be a mere "pretext . . . for the accomplishment of objects not entrusted to the government."[39] Finally, and most important, it must consist with the "spirit" as well as the letter of the Constitution. In light of earlier statements in his opinion, the implication seems unmistakable: incidental authority must not be so broadly construed as to subvert the basic principle that Congress has limited powers.

Though much sweat is often shed over general principles, as it was in *McCulloch*, it is not news that they seldom decide actual cases,[40] and Marshall's formula for determining the necessity and propriety of incidental legislation left even more than every standard must to the judgment of those who were to apply it. Marshall's effort succeeded, nevertheless, in setting a mood in which the problem should be approached, and it seems to me he set one that precisely captured the constitutional spirit. While respecting the limited nature of federal power, he managed to avoid a construction that would have crippled the ability of Congress to carry out the purposes for which it had been established.

Marshall was far weaker, however, in applying his exemplary criteria to the case before him. He mentioned in passing various enumerated powers to which the creation of a bank might be incidental: "to lay and collect taxes; to borrow money; to regulate commerce; to declare and conduct a war; and to raise and support armies and navies."[41] What is striking is that he made no serious effort to demonstrate how the bank was necessary and proper, or even conducive, to any one of them. Indeed all he said on this score was that the bank's utility in "fiscal operations" of the government was "not now a subject of controversy."[42] Hamilton had done somewhat better in his defense of the first Bank of the United States: it would facilitate tax collection and commerce by creating a medium of payment or exchange and by increasing the money supply; it was a "usual, and in sudden emergencies, an

[39]17 U.S. (4 Wheat.) at 423. This is an interesting contrast to Marshall's refusal to investigate the motive for the Yazoo land grant in *Fletcher*. *See supra* chapter 5, notes 20-29 and accompanying text. The "pretext" concept has since had a checkered career. *Compare* United States v. Kahriger, 345 U.S. 22, 28-32 (1953) (rejecting pretext argument), *and* United States v. Darby, 312 U.S. 100, 114 (1941) (same) *with* United States v. Butler, 297 U.S. 1 (1936) (congressional power denied as pretext).

[40]*See, e.g.*, Associated Indus. v. Department of Labor, 487 F.2d 342, 349-50 (2d Cir. 1973) (doubting whether it made any practical difference whether regulations of the Occupational Safety and Health Administration were reviewed under the "arbitrary and capricious" standard or the "substantial evidence" rule). *See also* Industrial Union Dep't v. Hodgson, 499 F.2d 467, 473 (D.C. Cir. 1974) ("rigorousness" of court's review of Occupational Safety and Health Administration regulation would not be affected by applying a combined standard of substantial evidence and rationality); Currie, *OSHA*, 1976 Am. B. Found. Research J. 1107, 1127 n.112.

[41]*McCulloch*, 17 U.S. (4 Wheat.) at 407. *See* U.S. Const. art. I, § 8. Hamilton in his well-known defense of the first national bank had also relied on article IV's authority to "make all needful Rules and Regulations respecting the . . . Property belonging to the United States," U.S. Const. art. IV, § 3, para. 2, i.e., its money. 1 The Works of Alexander Hamilton 138 (New York 1810), *quoted in* 3 J. Story, *supra* chapter 5, note 42, § 1261, at 137 n.4.

[42]*McCulloch*, 17 U.S. (4 Wheat.) at 422. *See also* 3 J. Story, *supra* chapter 5, note 42, § 1261, at 135 (concluding that to reveal why the Bank was a useful and appropriate governmental institution "would be a waste of time").

essential instrument, in the obtaining of loans to government."[43] Even this proved only that some of the Bank's functions were, in *Fisher*'s terms, "conducive to the exercise of . . . power[s]" given to Congress; it did not seem to establish that even these functions were consistent with the federative spirit of the Constitution or to justify the Bank as a whole.[44]

I do not mean to suggest that Marshall was wrong to uphold either the Bank in *McCulloch* or the government priority in *Fisher*. I do suggest that to reach those conclusions on the basis of the test stated in *McCulloch* would have required a careful examination of the powers actually granted the Bank, of their relationship to the explicit powers of Congress, and of the degree to which they undermined the principle of limited federal powers. In short, Marshall devoted most of his effort to demolishing the straw man of indispensable necessity and slid over the real question of the propriety of the Bank itself.[45] Moreover, in so doing he seems to have undermined the exemplary test he had just laid down. His cavalier application of the test to the case before him, reinforced by his explicit refusal to examine the "degree of . . . necessity" of any law "really calculated to effect any of the objects entrusted to the government,"[46] seemed to mean that the limits he had laid down should not be taken seriously.

Having upheld the existence of the Bank, the Court went on to hold Maryland could not tax it. The policy basis for this conclusion was plainly stated in the famous aphorism that "the power to tax involves the power to destroy";[47] to allow the states to tax or to regulate the activities of the federal government would make it "dependent on the States."[48] As to the legal basis of his conclusion Marshall was a good deal more obscure. It is not even clear whether he meant to find tax immunity in the Constitution itself or in the Bank's statutory charter.[49] He phrased the question as a constitutional one, asserted that the relevant principle "pervades the constitution," and said a power to destroy the Bank was incompatible with Congress's "power" to

[43]*See* 1 THE WORKS OF ALEXANDER HAMILTON, *supra* note 41, at 138-41. Some of Hamilton's arguments were repeated by counsel. *McCulloch*, 17 U.S. (4 Wheat.) at 388-90 (Mr. Pinkney).

[44]*See McCulloch*, 17 U.S. (4 Wheat.) at 334-37 (Mr. Hopkinson) (arguing that the Bank's *branches* served merely a profit-making function and could not be sustained). But see 3 J. STORY, *supra* chapter 5, note 42, § 1264, at 146-47, implying that anything that made the Bank more effective was permissible: "All the powers given to the bank are to give efficacy to its functions of trade and business." For details concerning the Bank's functions and its utility in carrying out congressional powers, see B. HAMMOND, BANKS AND POLITICS IN AMERICA 251-85 (1957); W. SMITH, ECONOMIC ASPECTS OF THE SECOND BANK OF UNITED STATES 99-230 (1953).

[45]It was, however, the abstract test Marshall laid down that attracted the most vehement criticism. *See* G. GUNTHER, *supra* note 27, at 18-19.

[46]*McCulloch*, 17 U.S. (4 Wheat.) at 423.

[47]*Id.* at 431.

[48]*Id.* at 432; *see id.* ("They may tax the mail; they may tax the mint; . . . they may tax judicial process . . . .").

[49]The distinction may be important, for although Congress may repeal any immunity it has created, there have been decisions against the power of Congress to confer on states powers withdrawn from them by the Constitution. *See, e.g.*, Cooley v. Board of Wardens, 53 U.S. (12 How.) 299, 317 (1851), *infra* chapter 7. More recent commerce clause cases tend to be less exacting. *E.g.*, Prudential Ins. Co. v. Benjamin, 328 U.S. 408, 421-27 (1946). *Cf.* Clark v. Barnard, 108 U.S. 436, 447 (1883) (allowing a state to waive the immunity from federal suit afforded by the eleventh amendment).

.create it.[50] However, the "principle" to which he referred was federal supremacy; he expressly invoked the supremacy clause,[51] which merely subordinates state law in the event it conflicts with other federal provisions; and at several points he adverted to the invalidity of state action incompatible with federal "laws."[52] In fact, a few years later, in *Osborn v. Bank of the United States*,[53] he would decide a similar case squarely on the ground of conflict with the Bank's federal charter.[54]

Whether based upon Constitution or statute, the Bank's immunity was implicit only. The charter law was silent on the question. While a confiscatory tax or one that placed the Bank at a fatal competitive disadvantage would have contradicted the statute by destroying what Congress had created,[55] Marshall expressly declined to investigate whether the Maryland tax was confiscatory,[56] and he did not rely on its discriminatory nature. Moreover, a few years later, despite an argument invoking *McCulloch*, Marshall was to hold that a *state* bank charter did not imply immunity from state taxation—though the power to tax was the power to destroy a state corporation no less than a federal one.[57]

To the extent that Marshall relied on the Constitution itself, the argument was once again that the Framers were reasonable people who could not have meant to place federal operations at the mercy of state laws.[58] But a similar argument for implicit immunity had been made in *Chisholm v. Georgia*,[59] and the Court had

[50]*McCulloch*, 17 U.S. (4 Wheat.) at 425-26. Here he paraphrased Pinkney's argument for the Bank. *See id.* at 391 (Mr. Pinkney). Pinkney had also said both that the power to tax was the power "to repeal the law, by which the bank was created," *id.* at 394 (Mr. Pinkney), and that, like the immunity of a foreign vessel from judicial process, The Schooner Exchange v. McFaddon, 11 U.S. (7 Cranch) 116 (1812), the Bank's immunity arose "out of general considerations" "independent of the letter of the constitution, or of any other written law," *McCulloch*, 17 U.S. (4 Wheat.) at 395 (Mr. Pinkney). Marshall expressly declined to hold the federal tax power exclusive, *id.* at 424; obviously the Framers had not meant to deprive the states of all revenue. *See also* THE FEDERALIST No. 32 (A. Hamilton).

[51]U.S. CONST. art. VI, para. 2.

[52]*McCulloch*, 17 U.S. (4 Wheat.) at 425-27; *see also id.* at 436: "[T]he States have no power . . . to retard . . . the operations of the constitutional laws enacted by Congress." Webster had said that the "only inquiry" was whether the state law "be consistent with the free operation of the law establishing the bank, and the full enjoyment of the privileges conferred by it." *Id.* at 327.

[53]22 U.S. (9 Wheat.) 738 (1824).

[54]*Id.* at 865-68. *See supra* chapter 4. Justice Stone was later to say that *McCulloch* itself had been based on the charter. Helvering v. Gerhardt, 304 U.S. 405, 411 (1938).

[55]*See* 1 C. WARREN, *supra* chapter 5, note 15, at 505 (giving examples of state legislation actually outlawing the Bank).

[56]   We are not driven to the perplexing inquiry, so unfit for the judicial department, what degree of taxation is the legitimate use, and what degree may amount to the abuse of the power. The attempt to use it on the means employed by the government of the Union, in pursuance of the constitution, is itself an abuse, because it is the usurpation of a power which the people of a single State cannot give.

McCulloch, 17 U.S. (4 Wheat.) at 430. See the celebrated riposte of Justice Holmes, in arguing to sustain a state sales tax on sales to the United States: in the days of *McCulloch* "it was not recognized as it is today that most of the distinctions of the law are distinctions of degree. . . . The power to tax is not the power to destroy while this Court sits." Panhandle Oil Co. v. Mississippi *ex rel.* Knox, 277 U.S. 218, 233 (1928) (Holmes, J., dissenting).

[57]Providence Bank v. Billings, 29 U.S. (4 Pet.) 514, 560 (1830); *see supra* notes 47-52 and accompanying text.

[58]*Cf. supra* chapter 5, notes 62-67 and accompanying text (discussing *Fletcher v. Peck*).

[59]2 U.S. (2 Dall.) 419 (1793); *see supra* chapter 1.

rejected it largely on the ground that the words of the Constitution did not except suits against states;[60] Marshall made no attempt to distinguish *Chisholm*. More basically, *McCulloch*'s argument positing absurd consequences did not hold up on its merits. As another Justice Marshall has pointed out, no implicit immunity is necessary to protect federal operations;[61] Congress can immunize them at any time by statute under the necessary and proper clause.[62]

In interesting dicta, Marshall attempted to limit the scope of *McCulloch*'s immunity decision. First, he denied that *state* banks would be free of *federal* taxation; although a state tax upon federal operations would fall largely upon outsiders with no voice in determining state policy, the representation of the states in Congress would prevent abuse of a federal power to tax them.[63] The enumeration of federal powers emphasized by Marshall elsewhere in the opinion,[64] however, demonstrates that the Framers were not content as a general matter to rely solely on political safeguards to protect the interests of the states. Indeed, Marshall's principal argument for implicit immunity seems far stronger in the converse case than in *McCulloch* itself: unlike the United States, the states cannot protect themselves by enacting an immunity statute; the supremacy clause is a one-way street.[65] It was not too long after *McCulloch* that the states were held immune from federal taxes as well.[66]

Marshall's second reservation was that the opinion did not preclude nondiscriminatory taxes on "real property of the bank" or on "the interest which the citizens of Maryland may hold in this institution."[67] This too derives support from his discussion of political checks, though not tied to it in the opinion; that the state cannot overburden federal activities without doing the same to those of its own citizens furnishes some degree of protection. If this was the reason for Marshall's

[60]*Chisholm*, 2 U.S. (2 Dall.) at 450-51 (Blair, J.), 466 (Wilson, J.), 467 (Cushing, J.), 476-77 (Jay, C.J.).
[61]First Agricultural Nat'l Bank v. State Tax Comm'n, 392 U.S. 339, 352 (1968) (Marshall, J., dissenting) ("Congress could provide . . . statutory immunity from state taxation for the federal instrumentalities it may establish."). The majority in that case illustrated his principle by finding national banks immune from the state tax in question under 12 U.S.C. § 548 (1976). *First Agricultural Nat'l Bank*, 392 U.S. at 345.
[62]In *McCulloch* Marshall essentially ignored counsel's strenuous argument that, if the government itself was immune from state taxes, the Bank was not because it was basically a private operation carried on for profit. *See McCulloch*, 17 U.S. (4 Wheat.) at 340-41 (Mr. Hopkinson); Plous & Baker, McCulloch v. Maryland: *Right Principle, Wrong Case*, 9 STAN. L. REV. 710, 720-23 (1957). In Bank of the United States v. Planters' Bank, 22 U.S. (9 Wheat.) 904, 906 (1824), Marshall was to insist that a suit against a corporation chartered and partly owned by a state was not a suit against the state barred by the eleventh amendment. *See supra* chapter 4. A parity of reasoning would suggest that a tax on the Bank was not a tax on the United States. *Cf.* New York v. United States, 326 U.S. 572, 582-83 (1946) (allowing a federal tax on the state's sale of mineral water while assuming that other state functions were immune).
[63]*McCulloch*, 17 U.S. (4 Wheat.) at 428, 435. *See* Veazie Bank v. Fenno, 75 U.S. (8 Wall.) 533, 547-48 (1869), *infra* chapter 9 (upholding a federal tax on the issuance of state bank notes). For an excellent explication of other examples of the same principle of political safeguards, see J. ELY, DEMOCRACY AND DISTRUST 82-87 (1980).
[64]*See supra* notes 41-42 and accompanying text.
[65]*See* Powell, *The Waning of Intergovernmental Tax Immunities*, 58 HARV. L. REV. 633, 652-64 (1945).
[66]Collector v. Day, 78 U.S. (11 Wall.) 113, 126-27 (1871), *infra* part four, *overruled in part*, Graves v. New York *ex rel.* O'Keefe, 306 U.S. 466, 486 (1939) (holding salaries of government officials subject to income taxation).
[67]*McCulloch*, 17 U.S. (4 Wheat.) at 436.

concession concerning property and stock taxes, it should have permitted a nondiscriminatory tax on the issuance of banknotes as well; yet in the body of his opinion Marshall nowhere relied on the fact that the Maryland tax was discriminatory.[68] A property tax might be consistent with the notion, elsewhere found in the opinion, that the Constitution did not "deprive the States of any resources which they originally possessed,"[69] because the land had not been created by Congress. But shares of bank stock had been; like the notes taxed in *McCulloch* itself, they were "means employed by the government . . . for the execution of its powers."[70] Marshall nowhere explained why stock was not also governed by his earlier injunction that the state could not tax such means at all.[71] In fact, the concessions for property and stock did not sit well with the rest of the opinion; Marshall himself was to ignore them in *Weston v. City Council*,[72] where, over a pointed Johnson dissent, he struck down a tax on the holders of federal securities without even discussing whether it was discriminatory.[73]

II. Gibbons v. Ogden

Ogden, owner of a steamboat monopoly granted by New York, obtained a state court injunction restraining Gibbons from operating steamboats across the Hudson River between New York and New Jersey.[74] Gibbons's boats, however, were licensed and enrolled under federal statute;[75] the Supreme Court in 1824 held the federal license gave Gibbons a right to operate his boats notwithstanding the state law.[76]

---

[68]Moreover, his distinction of the property and stock cases was simply that the case before him concerned "a tax on the operations of the bank," *id.* at 436; and elsewhere he had flatly limited the state to taxing "every thing which exists by its own authority, or is introduced by its permission," finding "a total failure of this original power to tax the means employed by the government of the Union, for the execution of its powers." *id.* at 429-30. A nondiscriminatory tax on banknotes would be inconsistent with these passages.

For discussion of the nondiscrimination dictum in *McCulloch* and its application to a tax on occupiers of government property in United States v. County of Fresno, 429 U.S. 452 (1977), see Hellerstein, *State Taxation and the Supreme Court: Toward a More Unified Approach to Constitutional Adjudication?*, 75 Mich. L. Rev. 1426, 1434-41, 1446-54 (1977) (praising *Fresno* but concluding for "cogent policy reasons" that "the M'Culloch dictum concerning nondiscriminatory taxes on federal *property* may be best left unexhumed," *id.* at 1454 (emphasis added)).

[69]*McCulloch*, 17 U.S. (4 Wheat.) at 436.

[70]*Id.* at 430.

[71]*Id.*

[72]27 U.S. (2 Pet.) 449, 468-69 (1829).

[73]*Id.* at 472-73. Johnson argued that the tax was not discriminatory and therefore was valid. *Id.* Justice Thompson also dissented. *Id.* at 473. The tax applied to all interest-bearing obligations except bank stock and those of the state itself. *Id.* at 449-50. See T. Powell, Vagaries and Varieties in Constitutional Interpretation 92 (1956), suggesting that the tax was "to some extent" discriminatory "because it did not apply to all property."

[74]Ogden v. Gibbons, 4 Johns. Ch. 150 (N.Y. Chan. 1819), *aff'd*, 17 Johns. 488 (N.Y. 1820), *rev'd*, 22 U.S. (9 Wheat.) 1 (1824). New Jersey and Connecticut had enacted retaliatory legislation against the New York monopoly. *See* 4 A. Beveridge, *supra* chapter 5, note 15, at 404.

[75]Act of Feb. 18, 1793, ch. 8, 1 Stat. 305 (codified as amended in part at 46 U.S.C. §§ 251-252 (1976)).

[76]Gibbons v. Ogden, 22 U.S. (9 Wheat.) 1 (1824). *See generally* M. Baxter, The Steamboat Monopoly (1972) (providing useful and interesting background of the case); 4 A. Beveridge, *supra* chapter 5, note

The threshold question was whether Congress had power to license vessels traveling between two states. The answer seems easy today: interstate navigation was "Commerce . . . among the several states,"[77] for commerce necessarily involved not only the exchange of goods but all "commercial intercourse."[78] Congress had enacted navigation laws at its very first session.[79] Moreover, the constitutional provisions forbidding Congress to prefer one state's port over another's or to require ships bound for one port to clear at another[80] would have been unnecessary if navigation had not been included.[81] Marshall stressed that there was no reason to give the Constitution an unnaturally narrow construction:[82] the Framers "must be understood . . . to have intended what they have said . . . [;] [w]e know of no rule for construing the extent of such powers, other than is given by the language of the instrument which confers them, taken in connection with the purposes for which they were conferred."[83]

15, at 397-460 (recounting the litigation and Chief Justice Marshall's construction of the commerce clause). For the interesting observation that repeal of the increasingly unpopular monopoly by the state legislature was hindered by arguments based on the contract clause, see Mendelson, *New Light on Fletcher v. Peck and Gibbons v. Ogden*, 58 YALE L.J. 567 (1949). See also 28 NILES WEEKLY REGISTER 147 (1825), reporting the voyage of a new steamboat gratefully christened the "'Chief Justice Marshal' [*sic*]."

[77]U.S. CONST. art. I, § 8, cl. 3.

[78]*Gibbons*, 22 U.S. (9 Wheat.) at 189-90. Counsel had conceded that the transportation of goods was closely enough connected with their exchange to be considered a part of commerce. *Id.* at 76-77 (Mr. Oakley), 89-90 (Mr. Emmet). What Marshall did not clearly reveal in this connection was that the vessels in question were used for transporting passengers. *See* 4 Johns. Ch. at 152. Later Justices were to assert, as counsel had argued in *Gibbons*, that the distinction was important. *See, e.g.*, Edwards v. California, 314 U.S. 160, 182 (1941) (Jackson, J., concurring) ("the migrations of a human being . . . do not fit easily into my notions as to what is commerce"); Passenger Cases, 48 U.S. (7 How.) 283, 473-74, 493 (1849) (Taney, C.J., dissenting). See *infra* chapter 7. Marshall had already said on circuit that the commerce power authorized Congress to outlaw the importation of persons, The Wilson v. United States, 30 F. Cas. 239, 243 (C.C.D. Va. 1820) (No. 17,846), while holding that the case before him did not come within the law, *id.* at 244-45. As Beveridge said, the fact that counsel did not invoke this precedent seems to say much about the dissemination of opinions at the time. 4 A. BEVERIDGE, *supra* chapter 5, note 15, at 427-29. For a documented argument that the Framers had a narrow view of what Congress could do under the interstate commerce clause but that navigation acts were specifically contemplated, see Abel, *The Commerce Clause in the Constitutional Convention and in Contemporary Comment*, 25 MINN. L. REV. 432, 451-59, 478-80 (1941).

[79]*Gibbons*, 22 U.S. (9 Wheat.) at 190. *See, e.g.*, Act of Sept. 1, 1789, ch. 11, 1 Stat. 55, *amended by* Act of Dec. 31, 1792, ch. 1, 1 Stat. 287 (codified as amended at 46 U.S.C. § 11 (1976)).

[80]U.S. CONST. art. I, § 9, cl. 6.

[81]*Gibbons*, 22 U.S. (9 Wheat.) at 191. *But see* T. POWELL, *supra* note 73, at 52 ("Marshall . . . does not note that there is another maxim for interpretation, namely, *ex majore cautela*—out of an abundance of caution. . . . Obviously, . . . sometimes one [maxim] is appropriate and at other times the other.").

Justice Johnson, arguing that "[s]hip-building, the carrying trade, and propagation of seamen, are such vital agents of commercial prosperity, that the nation which could not legislate over these subjects, would not possess power to regulate commerce," *Gibbons*, 22 U.S. (9 Wheat.) at 230 (Johnson, J., concurring), added a similar inference from the twenty-year moratorium in the same section on federal statutes prohibiting "[t]he Migration or Importation of such Persons as any of the States now existing shall think proper to admit," *id.* at 230 (referring to U.S. CONST. art. I, § 9, cl. 1). As Marshall had said on circuit, The Wilson v. United States, 30 F. Cas. 239, 243 (C.C.D. Va. 1820) (No. 17,846), this inference was equally relevant to the question, adumbrated *supra* note 78, whether "Commerce" included the transportation of persons, and Johnson expressly referred in *Gibbons* to "the transportation of both men and their goods." *See Gibbons*, 22 U.S. (9 Wheat.) at 230-31 (Johnson, J., concurring).

[82]*Gibbons*, 22 U.S. (9 Wheat.) at 187-89.

[83]*Id.* at 188-89. St. George Tucker had argued that federal powers should be strictly construed because

At the same time Marshall emphasized that federal power extended only to commerce "with foreign Nations, and among the several States, and with the Indian Tribes";[84] "the enumeration of the particular classes of commerce to which the power was to be extended, would not have been made, had the intention been to extend the power to every description."[85] Commerce "among" the states thus was limited to that "commerce which concerns more states than one. . . . The completely internal commerce of a state, then, may be considered as reserved for the state itself."[86] It bears emphasizing that in *Gibbons*, as in *McCulloch v. Maryland*,[87] the great exponent of national power expressly acknowledged significant limitations on the reach of federal legislation;[88] it was Marshall's successors who were to expand the commerce power to cover virtually everything.[89]

"[o]therwise the gradual and sometimes imperceptible usurpations of power, will end in the total disregard of all its intended limitations." St. G. Tucker, 1 *Appendix to Blackstone's Commentaries* 153, in 1 BLACKSTONE'S COMMENTARIES: WITH NOTES OF REFERENCE, TO THE CONSTITUTION AND LAWS, OF THE FEDERAL GOVERNMENT OF THE UNITED STATES; AND OF THE COMMONWEALTH OF VIRGINIA (St. G. Tucker ed. 1803) [hereinafter cited as Tucker's Appendix to Blackstone]. It is well that Tucker's profession was law and not medicine; deliberate undernourishment is a costly safeguard against accidental overeating.

[84]U.S. CONST. art. I, § 8, cl. 3. *See Gibbons*, 22 U.S. (9 Wheat.) at 193.

[85]*Gibbons*, 22 U.S. (9 Wheat.) at 194-95.

[86]*Id.* Professor Crosskey devoted much of his professional life to attacking the traditional understanding that Congress's power was limited to "interstate" commerce. "Commerce," he urged, was not restricted to interchange; "States" meant the people of the States, not territorial units; and "among," as illustrated by such phrases as "marriage among the Indian tribes," did not mean from one community to another. *See* 1 W. CROSSKEY, *supra* chapter 5, note 228, at 50-83. *See also* B. POTTER, THE TALE OF PETER RABBIT 25 (1972) (1st ed. 1903) ("He lost one of his shoes among the cabbages and the other shoe amongst the potatoes."). Crosskey concluded that Congress was meant to have power to regulate all gainful activity within the United States, 1 W. CROSSKEY, *supra* chapter 5, note 228, at 83, that it was therefore not absurd after all to read the contract clause as depriving the states of all power to legislate with respect to contract, *id.* at 288-92, and that construing the ex post facto clause to include civil legislation would therefore not have made the contract clause redundant, *id.* at 324-51. Thus Crosskey disagreed not only with the limitations the Court found in the commerce clause but with *Ogden v. Saunders* and *Calder v. Bull* as well. *Id.* at 348-51. *See supra* chapter 5, notes 224-28 and accompanying text; *supra* chapter 2. Crosskey's work, after a barrage of devastating reviews, has been profoundly ignored. See, e.g., Brown, Book Review, 67 HARV. L. REV. 1439 (1954), pointing out among other things that Crosskey's arguments were almost entirely "lexicographical," *id.* at 1442, and eschewed any real effort to reconcile his conclusions with the "larger political and institutional forces which must have had some part in shaping the new government," *id.* at 1441. Brown gives numerous examples of eighteenth-century usage contradicting Crosskey, *id.* at 1446-55 ("'a league *among* twelve Grecian cities,'" *id.* at 1450 (quoting 1 THE WORKS OF JAMES WILSON 247 (R. McCloskey ed. 1967)); "'hostility among nations,'" *id.* at 1450 (quoting THE FEDERALIST No. 6, at 54 (A. Hamilton) (C. Rossiter ed. 1961))). In addition, leading Federalists such as Washington and Marshall had praised *The Federalist*, which, as virtually everyone else had, acknowledged that Congress was to have limited powers, *id.* at 1443-46. For the view taken in *The Federalist*, see, for example, THE FEDERALIST No. 42, at 235 (J. Madison) (C. Rossiter ed. 1961) (speaking of commerce "between State and State").

[87]*See supra* notes 10-40 and accompanying text.

[88]In defining "to regulate" as "to prescribe the rule by which commerce is to be governed," *Gibbons*, 22 U.S. (9 Wheat.) at 196, Marshall suggested a second limitation that seemed to cast doubt on whether the commerce clause supported expenditures for navigation aids or for internal improvements. President Monroe's interpretation had been narrower still, limiting Congress to outlawing state imposts on commerce. *See* 2 J. RICHARDSON, MESSAGES AND PAPERS OF THE PRESIDENTS 140, 161-62 (1900). See also Abel, *supra* note 78, at 465-81, arguing that Congress was not meant to have the general affirmative regulatory power that the words seem to convey.

[89]*See, e.g.*, Wickard v. Filburn, 317 U.S. 11 (1942) (upholding federal regulation of growing wheat for on-farm consumption). Marshall did not clearly say, however, as later Justices would argue, that

More questionable was Marshall's conclusion that the federal licenses were intended to give Gibbons an indefeasible right to navigate the Hudson River. He seemed to think it self-evident: "The word 'license,' means permission or authority; and a license to do any particular thing, is a permission or authority to do that thing . . . ."[90] It was immaterial that the particular waters in question were not mentioned in the licenses; it was enough that they authorized the boats to engage in "'the coasting trade.'"[91] Yet other licenses or permits have been construed merely as indicating the absence of federal objection to the proposed activity, not as affirmative authorizations.[92] The state court had plausibly held,[93] and Justice Johnson agreed,[94] that the licenses in *Gibbons* were merely a means of enforcing a discrimination against foreign vessels;[95] Marshall himself was to hold a few years later, quite

---

Congress's power was strictly limited to interstate commerce. *See* Passenger Cases, 48 U.S. (7 How.) 283, 400 (1849) (opinion of McLean, J.). Note the reference, quoted *supra* in text accompanying note 86, to commerce that "concerns" more than one state, the similar mention of that "which does not extend to or *affect* other states," *Gibbons*, 22 U.S. (9 Wheat.) at 194 (emphasis added), and the later statement in arguing against concurrent state power that "[i]f congress license vessels to sail from one port to another, in the same state, the act is supposed to be, necessarily, incidental to the power expressly granted to congress, and implies no claim of a direct power to regulate the purely internal commerce of a state," *id.* at 204. *See* F. FRANKFURTER, THE COMMERCE CLAUSE UNDER MARSHALL, TANEY AND WAITE 41-42, 60-61 (1937); T. POWELL, *supra* note 73, at 50 ("Commerce . . . 'which concerns more states than one' . . . is a much more expansive conception than 'interstate commerce'" (quoting *Gibbons*, 22 U.S. (9 Wheat.) at 194)). After *Gibbons*, the New York Court in a split decision held the federal license authorized intrastate as well as interstate navigation, and upheld its constitutionality in reliance on *Gibbons*, pointing out that the licensing statute, first enacted in 1789, *see supra* note 79 and accompanying text, contained regulations expressly applicable to intrastate voyages. North River Steamboat Co. v. Livingston, 3 Cow. 713 (N.Y. 1825). Beveridge misstates both the trial court's decision in this case and the effect of the affirmance. *See* 4 A. BEVERIDGE, *supra* chapter 5, note 15, at 447-50.

[90]*Gibbons*, 22 U.S. (9 Wheat.) at 213.

[91]*Id.* at 214 (quoting the language of the license).

[92]*E.g.*, Organized Village of Kake v. Egan, 369 U.S. 60, 62-64 (1962) (federal permits to anchor fish traps in National Forest land and to obstruct navigable waters with them do not prevent state from forbidding their use); Huron Portland Cement Co. v. City of Detroit, 362 U.S. 440, 446-48 (1960) (local smoke abatement code enforceable against federally licensed boiler).

[93]Ogden v. Gibbons, 17 Johns. at 509 ("[T]he only design of the federal government in regard to the enrolling and licensing of vessels, was to establish a criterion of *national character*, with a view to enforce the laws which impose *discriminating duties* on *American vessels*, and those of foreign countries." (emphasis in original)).

[94]*Gibbons*, 22 U.S. (9 Wheat.) at 232 (Johnson, J., concurring) ("[I]t is to confer on her American privileges, as contradistinguished from foreign; and to preserve the government from fraud by foreigners, in surreptitiously intruding themselves into the American commercial marine, as well as frauds upon the revenue, in the trade coastwise, that this whole system is projected.").

[95]From the outset foreign vessels had been subjected to grossly discriminatory duties. *See, e.g.*, Act of July 20, 1790, ch. 30, 1 Stat. 135 (codified as amended at 46 U.S.C. § 121 (1976)). Section 6 of the statute involved in *Gibbons* provided for payment of the higher foreign duties by ships not enrolled or licensed. Act of Feb. 18, 1793, ch. 8, § 6, 1 Stat. 305, 307-08 (codified as amended at 46 U.S.C. § 318 (1976)). In 1817 foreign ships were excluded from the coasting trade entirely. Act of March 1, 1817, ch. 31, 3 Stat. 351, *repealed in part by* Act of June 28, 1864, ch. 170, 13 Stat. 201, *remainder repealed by* Act of Mar. 3, 1933, ch. 202, 47 Stat. 1428.

Chancellor Kent, who had given the license a narrow reading in the state trial court, Ogden v. Gibbons, 4 Johns Ch. at 156-59, stuck to his guns after the Supreme Court's decision:

The great objects and policy of the coasting act were, to exclude foreign vessels from commerce between the states, in order to cherish the growth of our marine, and to provide that the coasting trade should be conducted with security to the revenue. The register and

without explanation, that an identical license did not prevent a state from obstructing the passage of the licensee by authorizing the damming of a navigable stream.[96]

More important than the holding that the New York monopoly contravened a federal statute were Marshall's dicta suggesting that in the absence of statute it might have offended the commerce clause itself. "It has been contended," said Marshall,

> that, as the word "to regulate" implies in its nature, full power over the thing to be regulated, it excludes, necessarily, the action of all others that would perform the same operation on the same thing. . . . There is great force in this argument, and the court is not satisfied that it has been refuted.[97]

Justice Johnson went further: rejecting the argument based upon the licenses,[98] he based his concurrence on the ground that the federal commerce power was exclusive.[99]

> enrolment of the vessel were to ascertain the national character; and the license was only evidence that the vessel had complied with the requisites of the law, and was qualified for the coasting trade under American privileges.

1 J. KENT, *supra* chapter 5, note 111, at 435. For approving views of Kent's conclusion, see, for example, F. FRANKFURTER, *supra* note 89, at 15-16; T. POWELL, *supra* note 73, at 53, 142; Campbell, *Chancellor Kent, Chief Justice Marshall and the Steamboat Cases*, 25 SYRACUSE L. REV. 497, 525-28 (1974).

[96]Willson v. Black Bird Creek Marsh Co., 27 U.S. (2 Pet.) 245 (1829); *see infra* notes 119-26 and accompanying text. See also Douglas v. Seacoast Prods., Inc., 431 U.S. 265, 275-77 (1977), casting aspersions on Marshall's interpretation in *Gibbons* and recasting the license's effect as a (still questionable) prohibition of discriminatory treatment.

[97]*Gibbons*, 22 U.S. (9 Wheat.) at 209 (Marshall, C.J.).

[98]*Id.* at 231-33 (Johnson, J., concurring).

[99]*Id.* at 226-29 (Johnson, J., concurring):

> The power of a sovereign state over commerce . . . amounts to nothing more than a power to limit and restrain it at pleasure. And since the power to prescribe the limits to its freedom, necessarily implies the power to determine what shall remain unrestrained, it follows, that the power must be exclusive . . . .

Id. at 227. But no one denied that Congress had *power* to insist that commerce be free; the argument was that the states retained concurrent authority until Congress insisted. Johnson on circuit had already held the commerce power exclusive in striking down a South Carolina law imprisoning and in many cases enslaving black seamen arriving in South Carolina ports, Elkison v. Deliesseline, 8 F. Cas. 493 (C.C.D.S.C. 1823) (No. 4366), partly in evident reliance on the unpromising text, *id.* at 495 ("the words of the grant sweep away the whole subject, and leave nothing for the states to act upon"), and partly because exclusivity was desirable, *id.* ("If this law were enforced . . . retaliation would follow; and the commerce of this city . . . might be fatally injured."). Johnson also found the black-sailor law contrary to federal law and a treaty, and added that the powers to fix the value of foreign coins and to set standards of weights and measures were also exclusive. *Id.*

William Rawle, writing shortly after *Gibbons*, quoted at length from Marshall's opinion. W. RAWLE, A VIEW OF THE CONSTITUTION OF THE UNITED STATES OF AMERICA 82-84 (2d ed. Philadelphia 1829) (1st ed. Philadelphia 1825), and argued that the risk of varying and obstructive state regulations, "mutual rivalries, and other obvious inconveniences" meant that only Congress could regulate foreign commerce or commerce "between the different states," *id.* at 82. More significantly, the Virginia Republican St. George Tucker had reached the same conclusion without explanation as early as 1803. 1 Tucker's Appendix to Blackstone, *supra* note 83, at 180. Story disingenuously professed that *Gibbons* had settled the question. 2 J. STORY, *supra* chapter 5, note 42, §§ 1067-1068, at 12-13. Professor Corwin agreed that the

This was the beginning of incessant litigation over the extent to which state legislation is precluded by the commerce clause.[100] The wording of the clause suggests no limitation on the states; it merely grants Congress the authority to "regulate Commerce."[101] This language contrasts vividly with Congress's power of "exclusive Legislation" over the District of Columbia[102] and with the various provisions of article I, section 10, expressly forbidding states to invade such federal preserves as the making of treaties or the coining of money.[103] Moreover, though Marshall did not say so, *Gibbons* was not the first case confronting the Court with a question of the exclusivity of a grant of federal power. Four years earlier the Court had allowed a state to punish failure to respond to a call-up of the federal militia, despite the argument that both federal legislative and judicial powers were exclusive.[104] In 1819 Marshall himself had written for the Court in holding the federal bankruptcy power not exclusive;[105] the unexplained contrary suggestion respecting naturalization in an earlier case could easily have been based upon a preemptive federal statute.[106] Chief Justice Taney was later to argue with great plausibility,[107] as had Chancellor Kent and his brethren in an earlier New York case,[108] that the commerce clause did not limit the

---

Framers had meant the commerce power to be exclusive, E. Corwin, *supra* chapter 5, note 38, at 142, but gave no reasons for the conclusion. *See also* Abel, *supra* note 78, at 484-94 (arguing for the same conclusion largely on the basis of scattered hints in the federal and state conventions). *But see* F. Frankfurter, *supra* note 89, at 12-13 ("[t]he conception that the mere grant of the commerce power to congress dislodged state power finds no expression" in either state or federal conventions); 2 J. Thayer, Cases on Constitutional Law 2190-91 (1895) (arguing the commerce power was not exclusive).

[100]For one more recent example, see Kassel v. Consolidated Freightways Corp., 450 U.S. 662 (1981) (invalidating an Iowa law limiting the length of trucks).

[101]U.S. Const. art. I, § 8, cl. 3.

[102]*Id.* § 8, cl. 17. *See supra* chapter 5, notes 103-07 and accompanying text (discussing *Terrett v. Taylor*).

[103]U.S. Const. art. I, § 10, para. 1 ("*No State shall* enter into any Treaty, Alliance, Confederation; . . . coin money" (emphasis added)).

[104]Houston v. Moore, 18 U.S. (5 Wheat.) 1 (1820), *discussed supra* chapter 4.

[105]Sturges v. Crowninshield, 17 U.S. (4 Wheat.) 122 (1819); *see supra* chapter 5, notes 156-204 and accompanying text. Both *Sturges* and Houston v. Moore, 18 U.S. (5 Wheat.) 1 (1820), had been urged on the Court in *Gibbons* by counsel as decisive. *Gibbons*, 22 U.S. (9 Wheat.) at 35 (Mr. Oakley), 86 (Mr. Emmet).

[106]*See supra* chapter 5, notes 195-96 and accompanying text (discussing *Chirac v. Chirac*). Later cases also have held the federal patent and copyright powers not to be exclusive. *E.g.*, Kewanee Oil Co. v. Bicron Corp., 416 U.S. 470 (1974); Goldstein v. California, 412 U.S. 546 (1973). The New York court had held the patent power not exclusive in Livingston v. Van Ingen, 9 Johns. 507 (N.Y. 1812), which also involved the steamboat monopoly. The question was litigated but not decided in *Gibbons*. See *Gibbons*, 22 U.S. (9 Wheat.) at 221. As he had in *McCulloch*, *see supra* note 50, Marshall conceded that the federal tax power was not exclusive, but he distinguished the taxing power from the commerce power, *Gibbons*, 22 U.S. (9 Wheat.) at 198-200. *See also id.* at 199 ("In imposing taxes for state purposes, [the states] are not doing what congress is empowered to do," for Congress may tax only "to pay the debts, and provide for the common defence and general welfare of the United States.").

[107]License Cases, 46 U.S. (5 How.) 504, 579 (1847) (Taney, C.J., concurring). *See infra* chapter 7.

[108]Livingston v. Van Ingen, 9 Johns. 507 (N.Y. 1812). See especially the argument of Judge (later Justice) Thompson that federal powers were impliedly exclusive only if, as with borrowing on federal credit and establishing federal courts, *id.* at 565-66, they "did not antecedently form a part of state sovereignty," *id.* at 565, or their objects "from their nature, are beyond the reach and control of the state governments," *id.* Though appointed to the Supreme Court in 1823, Thompson did not arrive in time to participate in *Gibbons v. Ogden. See* 22 U.S. (9 Wheat.) at iii. For his later views on the commerce clause, see *infra* notes 134-39 and accompanying text (discussing *Brown v. Maryland*); chapter 7 *infra*.

states.[109] What is most significant for present purposes, however, is Marshall's willingness once again to reach out and make one-sided suggestions about an issue that he conceded he did not have to resolve.

Both Marshall and Johnson took pains to emphasize that the states were not without all power to *impede* interstate or foreign commerce. Article I itself recognized, for example, that states might pass laws requiring inspection of goods to be exported,[110] but these, Marshall insisted, were not regulations of commerce. Their object was

> to improve the quality of articles produced by the labor of a country . . . .
> They act upon the subject, before it becomes an article of foreign commerce, or of commerce among the states . . . . They form a portion of that immense mass of legislation, which embraces everything within the territory of a state, not surrendered to the general government . . . .[111]

Similarly, state "quarantine and health laws," explicitly recognized by Congress,[112] "are considered as flowing from the acknowledged power of a state, to provide for the health of its citizens."[113] Johnson was of the same opinion:

[109]The Court seems right in its subsequent conclusion that one purpose of the commerce clause was to prevent untenable state obstructions to the free flow of goods. *See* H.P. Hood & Sons v. Du Mond, 336 U.S. 525, 534 (1949) (citing 3 CONVENTION RECORDS, *supra* chapter 5, note 76, at 547 (Madison's explanation)); THE FEDERALIST No. 22, at 144-45 (A. Hamilton) (C. Rossiter ed. 1961):

> The interfering and unneighborly regulations of some States, contrary to the true spirit of the Union, have, in different instances, given just cause of umbrage and complaint to others, and it is to be feared that examples of this nature, if not restrained by national control, would be multiplied and extended till they became not less serious sources of animosity and discord than injurious impediments to the intercourse between the different parts of the Confederacy.

See also 2 J. STORY, *supra* chapter 5, note 42, § 1066, at 11. But see Kitch, *Regulation and the American Common Market*, in REGULATION, FEDERALISM AND INTERSTATE COMMERCE 11-19 (A. Tarlock ed. 1981), arguing that the Framers' perceptions of substantial state interference lacked support in either theory or practice. In any event, the Constitution on its face suggests that the means of national control the Framers selected was to authorize Congress, not the Court, to keep open the channels of trade. *See* U.S. CONST. art I, § 8, cl. 3.

Justice Johnson declared in his concurrence that the entire panoply of state commercial regulations "dropped lifeless from their statute books" when the Constitution was adopted, implying a general agreement that federal power was exclusive. *Gibbons*, 22 U.S. (9 Wheat.) at 226 (Johnson, J., concurring). *Accord* B. WRIGHT, THE GROWTH OF AMERICAN CONSTITUTIONAL LAW 52 (1942). Others, however, have disputed Johnson's version of the facts. *See, e.g.*, F. FRANKFURTER, *supra* note 89, at 51 ("From the beginning of the Union, the states had woven a network of regulatory measures over foreign and interstate commerce."). Counsel in *Gibbons* cited these past state practices to the Court. *Gibbons*, 22 U.S. (9 Wheat.) at 63-64 (Mr. Oakley), 97 n.(a) (Mr. Emmet). Marshall attempted to distinguish some of them as police power regulations rather than regulations of commerce, *see infra* notes 110-13 and accompanying text, but he said nothing about counsel's examples relating to trade with the Indians, *Gibbons*, 22 U.S. (9 Wheat.) at 82-83 (Mr. Oakley), or regulation of stagecoach fares, *id.* at 97 n.(a)(2) (Mr. Emmet).

[110]U.S. CONST. art. I, § 10, para. 2 ("No State shall, without the Consent of the Congress, lay any Imposts or Duties on Imports or Exports, except what may be absolutely necessary for executing its inspection Laws . . . .").

[111]*Gibbons*, 22 U.S. (9 Wheat.) at 203 (Marshall, C.J.).

[112]Act of May 27, 1796, ch. 31, 1 Stat. 474, *repealed by* Act of Feb. 25, 1799, ch. 12, § 8, 1 Stat. 619, 621 (codified as amended at 42 U.S.C. §§ 88-91, 97, 112 (1976)).

[113]*Gibbons*, 22 U.S. (9 Wheat.) at 205 (Marshall, C.J.).

The same bale of goods, the same cask of provisions, or the same ship, that may be the subject of commercial regulation, may also be the vehicle of disease. And the health laws that require them to be stopped and ventilated, are no more intended as regulations on commerce, than the laws which permit their importation, are intended to innoculate the community with disease.[114]

The reader may well find the resulting "exclusivity" of congressional authority in the sphere of commerce a peculiar one. If the purpose of the Framers was to create a self-executing safeguard against state interference with commerce, one might expect them to have done so without regard to the name of the power the state purported to exercise.[115] Fifty years later the Court was to recognize that the federal interest that had led to Marshall's suggestion of exclusivity was threatened equally by state action under the police-power label[116] and to reject, at least for the time being,[117] the *Gibbons* distinction.[118]

Five years after *Gibbons*, in *Willson v. Black Bird Creek Marsh Co.*,[119] Marshall wrote for a unanimous Court in upholding a state law that authorized construction of a dam obstructing a small navigable creek. Stressing that Congress had passed no law affecting the question, Marshall concluded that the state law could not, "under all the circumstances of the case, be considered as repugnant to the power to regulate commerce in its dormant state."[120] That Congress had passed no relevant law was not clear after *Gibbons*, for Willson had a federal license to engage in the coasting trade.[121] Counsel had argued with some force that if, under *Gibbons*, "Delaware has

[114]*Id.* at 235 (Johnson, J., concurring).

[115]*Cf.* License Cases, 46 U.S. (5 How.) 504, 583 (1847) (Taney, C.J., separate opinion) (objecting that if the states are "absolutely prohibited . . . from making any regulations of foreign commerce . . . such regulations are null and void, whatever may have been the motive of the State"); F. FRANKFURTER, *supra* note 89, at 52-53 (concluding that "Taney's analysis destroys the illusive simplicity of Marshall's concession of a 'police' power to the states" (footnote omitted)); T. POWELL, *supra* note 73, at 51 (characterizing Marshall's distinction as an "exercise in verbalisms"), 150 (suggesting that Marshall's police-power exceptions were so sweeping that it hardly mattered whether the states could "regulate commerce").

[116]Henderson v. Mayor of New York, 92 U.S. 259, 271-72 (1876) ("Nothing is gained in the argument by calling it the police power. . . . [W]henever the statute of a State invades the domain of legislation which belongs exclusively to the Congress of the United States, it is void, no matter under what class of powers it may fall . . . ."). *See infra* chapter 10.

[117]Although a later Court was to note that over the years the Court had "consistently . . . rebuffed attempts of states to advance their own commercial interests by curtailing the movement of articles of commerce . . . while generally supporting their right to impose even burdensome regulations in the interest of local health and safety," H.P. Hood & Sons v. Du Mond, 336 U.S. 525, 535 (1949), the Court had stopped viewing the matter as one of simple labeling. In fact, the Court has struck down health and safety regulations whose burden on commerce it has found unjustified. *See, e.g.*, Raymond Motor Transp., Inc. v. Rice, 434 U.S. 429 (1978); Bibb v. Navajo Freight Lines, Inc., 359 U.S. 520 (1959); Southern Pac. Co. v. Arizona, 325 U.S. 761 (1945).

[118]Like Marshall's concession respecting the imprisonment of debtors in *Sturges, see supra* chapter 5, notes 165-78 and accompanying text, the distinction drawn in *Gibbons* seems an afterthought employed to avoid the many examples that seemed to contradict his theory. *See* F. FRANKFURTER, *supra* note 89, at 27 (Marshall's "doctrine of a completely exclusive commerce power could not be rigorously applied without changing the whole political character of the states").

[119]27 U.S. (2 Pet.) 245 (1829).

[120]*Id.* at 252.

[121]*Id.* at 246, 248 (Mr. Coxe). *See supra* note 96.

no right to restrain particular vessels from using her navigable streams, she cannot stop the navigation of those streams" altogether.[122]

The more interesting question was why, after *Gibbons*, the dam did not offend the commerce clause itself. Some of Marshall's contemporaries thought he meant to retract the feelers of exclusivity he had put out in *Gibbons*.[123] More likely, since Johnson did not dissent, the key lay in Marshall's statement that the "value of the property on [the creek's] banks must be enhanced by excluding the water from the marsh, and the health of the inhabitants probably improved."[124] "Measures calculated to produce these objects," he added in an evident reference to his discussion of inspection and quarantine laws in *Gibbons*,[125] were allowable—"provided," he added ambiguously, "they do not come into collision with the powers of the general government."[126] The important point is that he made no real effort to explain, though this was the first case in which he had to face the issue of the preemptive effect of the commerce clause itself; he left us to wonder what was the basis of the decision.[127]

III. Later Commerce Clause Cases

A. *Brown v. Maryland*

Brown had imported goods from abroad and sold them in the original package. Maryland convicted him for selling them without paying a fifty dollar license tax for the privilege of selling imported goods. In 1827 the Supreme Court reversed.[128]

Much of the opinion was devoted to showing that Maryland's law offended the provision of article I, section 10, forbidding a state, without congressional consent, "to lay any Imposts or Duties on Imports or Exports, except what may be absolutely necessary for executing its inspection Laws."[129] "[I]mports," said Marshall, invoking the "lexicons" and "usage," are "things imported"; a "'duty on imports' then, is not

---

[122]*Willson*, 27 U.S. (2 Pet.) at 249 (Mr. Coxe). Marshall did not answer this contention in his opinion. Frankfurter read *Willson* as holding that the license conveyed no right to navigate unimportant small streams. F. FRANKFURTER, *supra* note 89, at 20-21. Taney thought *Willson* meant the license gave a right to navigate only those streams which were not obstructed. Pennsylvania v. Wheeling & Belmont Bridge Co., 54 U.S. (13 How.) 518, 585-87 (1852) (Taney, C.J., dissenting), *infra* chapter 7.

[123]*See* New York v. Miln, 36 U.S. (11 Pet.) 102, 149-50 (1837) (Thompson, J., concurring). Thompson had participated in *Willson*. *See also* F. FRANKFURTER, *supra* note 89, at 28 (suggesting that *Willson* was a retreat from Marshall's earlier conception of an exclusive commerce power).

[124]*Willson*, 27 U.S. (2 Pet.) at 251.

[125]*See supra* notes 112-13 and accompanying text.

[126]*Willson*, 27 U.S. (2 Pet.) at 251. Story explained *Willson* as holding that the state's authority to act under "other powers, beside that of regulating commerce," was not destroyed by the commerce clause. 2 J. STORY, *supra* chapter 5, note 42, § 1069, at 517. *See also* F. FRANKFURTER, *supra* note 89, at 29 n.37 (citing Story with approval).

[127]Justice Frankfurter put the point somewhat less critically: Marshall "did little more than decide, stating hardly any doctrine but hinting enough to foreshadow, certainly in direction, the vitally important accommodation between national and state needs formulated more than 20 years later in *Cooley v. Board of Wardens*, 12 How. 299, 319 (1851)." Frankfurter, *John Marshall and the Judicial Function*, 69 HARV. L. REV. 217, 223 (1955).

[128]Brown v. Maryland, 25 U.S. (12 Wheat.) at 419 (1827). *See* 4 A. BEVERIDGE, *supra* chapter 5, note 15, at 454-60; 1 C. WARREN, *supra* chapter 5, note 15, at 693-96.

[129]U.S. CONST. art. I, § 10, para. 2.

merely a duty on the act of importation, but is a duty on the thing imported."[130] Whatever the purpose of the clause, a tax on the sale of imported goods would undermine it as effectively as a tax on the act of importation; for "[n]o goods would be imported if none could be sold."[131] Thus an import remained an import, immune from state taxation, "while remaining the property of the importer, in his warehouse, in the original form or package in which it was imported."[132] Finally, a tax on the business of selling imported goods was in effect a tax on the goods themselves: "It must add to the price of the article, and be paid by the consumer, or by the importer himself, in like manner as a direct duty on the article itself . . . ."[133]

All of this sounds very plausible. Surely the Framers had not meant to allow the free entry of goods to be sabotaged by nominally distinguishable taxes levied after importation. The trouble was, as pointed out by Justice Thompson's dissent, that Marshall's reasoning proved too much: a tax on a later resale of the goods at retail

> would equally increase the burden, and enhance the expense of the article . . . . [I]t will necessarily affect the importation. So that nothing short of a total exemption from State charges or taxes, under all circumstances, will answer the supposed object of the constitution. And to push the principle to such lengths, would be a restriction upon State authority, not warranted by the constitution.[134]

Thompson therefore would have restricted the prohibition to "foreign duties, and not to taxes imposed by the States, after the imports became articles of internal trade, and for domestic use and consumption."[135]

Marshall conceded that "there must be a point of time when the prohibition ceases."[136] He then stated:

> when the importer has so acted upon the thing imported, that it has become incorporated and mixed up with the mass of property in the country, it has, perhaps, lost its distinctive character as an import, and has become subject to the taxing power of the State; but while remaining the property of the importer, in his warehouse, in the original form or package in which it was imported, a tax upon it is too plainly a duty on imports, to escape the prohibition . . . .[137]

The arbitrariness of the line drawn is evident;[138] it can be derived neither from the words nor from the purpose of the import-export clause. Nevertheless, neither alternative seemed palatable: on the one hand it seems unlikely the Framers meant

[130]*Brown*, 25 U.S. (12 Wheat.) at 437-38 (quoting U.S. CONST. art. I, § 10, para. 2).
[131]*Id.* at 439.
[132]*Id.* at 442.
[133]*Id.* at 444.
[134]*Id.* at 455 (Thompson, J., dissenting).
[135]*Id.* at 456 (Thompson, J., dissenting).
[136]*Id.* at 441.
[137]*Id.* at 441-42.
[138]*See* T. POWELL, *supra* note 73, at 181 ("So far as I know, the removal of one pasteboard box from the wooden shipping case ends the immunity of other pasteboard boxes still left in the traveling container."); Trickett, *The Original Package Ineptitude*, 6 COLUM. L. REV. 161 (1906).

to give imported goods a perpetual tax exemption, and on the other Marshall seems right that Thompson's narrow interpretation would drain the clause of all meaning.

To the extent the clause was meant to protect citizens of inland states from tolls exacted by states through which their goods were imported,[139] the tax in *Brown* was arguably all right, for there was no suggestion that Brown had sold the goods for transport to another state. But the language of the clause forbids imposts and duties on *all* imports, whether or not destined for other states. To the extent this language reflects a policy "to maintain unimpaired our commercial connexions [*sic*] with foreign nations, or to confer this source of revenue on the government of the Union,"[140] the Maryland tax seems particularly offensive, because it placed imports at a disadvantage—it did not apply to sellers of local products. At a minimum, as the Court was to say with the hindsight of 150 more years, the import-export clause "prohibits state taxation based on the foreign origin of the imported goods"[141]— regardless, I should have thought, of whether they are singled out for taxation at the wholesale or the retail stage or in the hands of the ultimate consumer.[142] From this perspective, the original-package distinction not only was unnecessary as a means of keeping the clause from overly infringing the reserved powers of the states, but it also left the clause incapable of achieving its purposes and subjected it to patent evasion. Although the validity of a nondiscriminatory property tax on imported goods may not be as easy a question as the Court recently made it,[143] that is another reason why

---

[139]*See* THE FEDERALIST No. 42, at 267 (J. Madison) (C. Rossiter ed. 1961) (arguing that "[a] very material object" of the federal commerce power "was the relief of the States which import and export through other States, from the improper contributions levied on them by the latter"); *id.* No. 44, at 283 (J. Madison) ("The restraint on the power of the States over imports and exports is enforced by all the arguments which prove the necessity of submitting the regulation of trade to the federal councils."); *see also* Marshall's statement in *Brown*, 25 U.S. (12 Wheat.) at 440 ("The great importing states would thus levy a tax on the non-importing states . . . ."). *See also* the comments of Messrs. Hamilton and Nicholas during the New York and Virginia ratifying Conventions, 2 ELLIOT'S DEBATES, *supra* chapter 5, note 78, at 363 and 3 *id.* at 241.

[140]*Brown*, 25 U.S. (12 Wheat.) at 439. *See also* Michelin Tire Corp. v. Wages, 423 U.S. 276 (1976):

> The Framers of the Constitution thus sought to alleviate three main concerns by committing sole power to lay imposts and duties on imports in the Federal Government, with no concurrent state power: the Federal Government must speak with one voice when regulating commercial relations with foreign governments, and tariffs, which might affect foreign relations, could not be implemented by the States consistently with that exclusive power; import revenues were to be the major source of revenue of the Federal Government and should not be diverted to the States; and harmony among the States might be disturbed unless seaboard States, with their crucial ports of entry, were prohibited from levying taxes on citizens of other States by taxing goods merely flowing through their ports to the other States not situated as favorably geographically.

Id. at 285-86 (footnote omitted).

[141]*Michelin*, 423 U.S. at 287.

[142]*See* 1 W. CROSSKEY, *supra* chapter 5, note 228, at 296-97 (arguing that while "Imposts" were understood as restricted to "customs duties," which were "duties collected . . . *at the time and place of importation or exportation*," "Duties" included "excises" and "*all state taxes . . .* save property taxes only" (emphases in original)). Crosskey buttressed these conclusions with the persuasive example of Connecticut's 1790 repeal of a discriminatory excise on the retail sale of imported goods after arguments that it offended the import-export clause. *Id.* at 306-11.

[143]*See* Michelin Tire Corp. v. Wages, 423 U.S. 276 (1976). As the Court acknowledged in *Michelin Tire Corp.*, a nondiscriminatory tax on goods imported for shipment to another state at least arguably offends the avowed purpose of preventing coastal states from levying tolls on their inland neighbors, *id.* at 290;

Marshall would have done better to avoid deciding *Brown* on a basis that seemed to embrace it. It would have sufficed to hold that the state could not levy taxes that applied only to imported goods.

Typically, Marshall was not content to rest the invalidity of Maryland's license requirement on the import-export clause alone; he went on to add, unnecessarily, that it was unconstitutional on a second ground.[144] The commerce clause empowered Congress to authorize importation; since "[s]ale is the object of importation, and is an essential ingredient of that intercourse, of which importation constitutes a part," Congress may also "authorize the importer to sell."[145] The tariff act, which "offers the privilege" of importation "for sale at a fixed price," implicitly conveyed also the right to sell, without which the right to import was of no value.[146] Marshall concluded accordingly:

> Any penalty inflicted on the importer for selling the article in his charac-
> ter of importer, must be in opposition to the act of Congress which
> authorizes importation. Any charge on the introduction and incorpora-
> tion of the articles into and with the mass of property in the country, must
> be hostile to the power given to congress to regulate commerce . . . .[147]

Thus the case was governed by precedent:[148] *McCulloch v. Maryland.*

McCulloch v. Maryland?! As the dissent shouted,[149] *McCulloch* was not a commerce clause case; it had held a state could not tax the operations of the federal government.[150] One might have thought the proper starting point was *Gibbons v. Ogden*, in which Marshall had hinted but not decided that the commerce power was exclusive.[151] But one then would have encountered Marshall's explicit concession in *Gibbons* that this arguable exclusivity did not preclude the states from *affecting*

---

and there is a semantic difficulty in holding that nondiscriminatory property taxes are "Duties on Imports" only when applied to goods to be exported after arrival, *see* Hellerstein, *Michelin Tire Corp. v. Wages: Enhanced State Power to Tax Imports*, 1976 SUP. CT. REV. 99, 115-17. Furthermore, as Hellerstein also points out, it is not entirely clear that nondiscriminatory taxes even on those goods consumed in the importing state are consistent with the assumed purposes of freedom of foreign commerce and of protecting federal revenue. *See id.* at 108-09. On the other hand, it is not clear that the Framers meant to give foreign goods a competitive advantage or to free those dealing in them from bearing the cost of state services such as police and fire protection. *See Michelin*, 423 U.S. at 287; Early & Weitzman, *A Century of Dissent: The Immunity of Goods Imported for Resale from Nondiscriminatory State Personal Property Taxes*, 7 Sw. U.L. REV. 247, 247, 252 (1975).

[144]*See* T. POWELL, *supra* note 73, at 182 ("[I]t was an adventure in supererogation to wield the club of the commerce clause for a second lethal blow after the import clause had successfully committed legicide.").

[145]*Brown*, 25 U.S. (12 Wheat.) at 447. This was an interesting step beyond *Gibbons*, where Congress had been held to have power to regulate interstate movement. As Thompson observed in his *Brown* dissent, the resale of goods after importation was a wholly intrastate transaction if viewed in isolation. *Id.* at 453 (Thompson, J., dissenting). *Gibbons*, of course, had refused to view the New York and New Jersey portions of a single journey as separate transactions. *Gibbons*, 22 U.S. (9 Wheat.) at 195-96.

[146]*Brown*, 25 U.S. (12 Wheat.) at 447.

[147]*Id.* at 448.

[148]*Id.* at 449.

[149]*Id.* at 457-58 (Thompson, J., dissenting).

[150]*See supra* notes 1-73 and accompanying text.

[151]*See supra* notes 97-127 and accompanying text.

commerce by the exercise of distinct reserved powers.[152] Indeed, in rejecting the argument that the import-export clause itself implied that, apart from its strictures, the states were free to regulate commerce, *Gibbons* had as much as said that the commerce clause did not preclude state taxation: "This prohibition . . . is an exception from the acknowledged power of the states to levy taxes, not from the questionable power to regulate commerce";[153] it and the limitation of state tonnage duties[154] "presuppose the existence of that which they restrain, not of that which they do not purport to restrain."[155] *McCulloch*'s precept that the power to tax involved the power to destroy thus could not be applied to the commerce clause itself without undermining the basis of the *Gibbons* opinion.

What *Brown* had in common with *McCulloch* was that Congress had exercised its legislative power, in the one case by chartering a national bank, in the other by imposing a tariff. In both decisions Marshall obscured the basis of his holding by declaring alternately that the state law offended federal "law" and that it conflicted with congressional "power."[156] In *Brown*, at least, the inference seems strong that it was the federal statute that Marshall found decisive.[157] For, as recounted above, he went into some detail to show that the tariff act gave the importer a right to sell,[158] as he had held the steamboat license in *Gibbons* gave a right to navigate the Hudson.[159] That *McCulloch* was invoked in *Brown* adds strength to the conclusion that the immunity of the Bank also had been inferred from the statute.

As in *Gibbons* and *McCulloch*, the argument for a statutory immunity in *Brown* is weak; the tariff act seems rather a revenue measure than an affirmative grant of the privilege of importing the goods, let alone that of selling them.[160] And of course the fictitious statutory right, like the immunity under the import-export clause, had to be limited arbitrarily so that the states could exclude unhealthful products and tax the

[152]*See supra* notes 110-13 and accompanying text.

[153]*Gibbons*, 22 U.S. (9 Wheat.) at 201-02.

[154]U.S. CONST. art. I, § 10, para. 3 ("No State shall, without the Consent of Congress, lay any Duty of Tonnage . . . .").

[155]*Gibbons*, 22 U.S. (9 Wheat.) at 203. *See* THE FEDERALIST NO. 32, at 199 (A. Hamilton) (C. Rossiter ed. 1961) (arguing that the import-export clause "implies . . . that as to all other taxes, the authority of the States remains undiminished"); 1 W. CROSSKEY, *supra* chapter 5, note 228, at 320 (adding that powers to tax and to regulate had been considered distinct since colonial days).

[156]*See, e.g., supra* notes 129-33, 136-37, 146-48 and accompanying text (discussing *Brown v. Maryland*); *cf. supra* notes 49-52 and accompanying text (discussing *McCulloch v. Maryland*).

[157]*See* Sholley, *The Negative Implications of the Commerce Clause*, 3 U. CHI. L. REV. 556, 572 (1936) (adding, however, that dicta in *Brown* suggest that Marshall meant to recede from the distinction between regulation and taxation he had drawn in *Gibbons*). *But see* 1 W. CROSSKEY, *supra* chapter 5, note 228, at 311 (concluding *Brown* "rested solely on the Imports and Exports Clause"); T. POWELL, *supra* note 73, at 54, 181-82 (acknowledging the "uncertainty" of the opinion); B. WRIGHT, *supra* note 109, at 54 (concluding that "the dormant commerce power" was "insufficient" for Marshall in *Brown* "as in the Gibbons case").

Both Beveridge and Story seemed to think that the decision was based on the commerce clause itself. *See* 4 A. BEVERIDGE, *supra* chapter 5, note 15, at 457; 2 J. STORY, *supra* chapter 5, note 42, §§ 1068-1069, at 515-17. *See also* F. FRANKFURTER, *supra* note 89, at 50 & n.6 (concluding that although both *Gibbons* and *Brown* "rest on a finding of conflict between Congressional and state statutes . . . Marshall intended these opinions to develop a doctrine of limitations upon state authority implied from the commerce clause").

[158]*See supra* notes 145-48 and accompanying text.

[159]*See supra* notes 90-91 and accompanying text.

[160]*See* F. FRANKFURTER, *supra* note 89, at 20 (terming *Brown*'s statutory construction "esoteric"); T. POWELL, *supra* note 73, at 54 (describing it as "imaginative"), at 182 (calling it "as questionable as Marshall's invocation of the Coasting License in *Gibbons v. Ogden*" (footnote omitted)).

retailer.[161] In the last analysis, however, it does seem that the Court in *Brown* was taking liberties only with a statute and not with the commerce clause itself.[162]

B. *Worcester v. Georgia*

After the Cherokees' effort to enjoin the enforcement of Georgia laws regulating reservation affairs had failed on the ground that the tribe was not a "foreign State" entitled to sue under article III,[163] the state prosecuted and convicted Worcester for living on Cherokee land without a license. The Supreme Court reversed in 1832 in a famous Marshall opinion.[164]

Some later decisions determining the limits of state power over Indian affairs have spoken mystically about the inherent sovereignty of the Indian nations, as if that extra-constitutional thesis somehow limited state authority.[165] Though it is possible to pluck statements from *Worcester* that, separated from their context, appear to look in that direction,[166] Marshall explicitly rejected such a conclusion: "If the objection to [Georgia's] . . . legislation . . . was confined to its extra-territorial operation, the objection, though complete, so far as respected mere right, would give this court no power over the subject."[167] Instead, he flatly held the state law "in direct hostility with treaties [that] . . . recognise the pre-existing power of the

---

[161]*See Brown*, 25 U.S. (12 Wheat.) at 443-44.

[162]Marshall added, quite gratuitously, "that we suppose the principles laid down in this case, to apply equally to importations from a sister state." *Id.* at 449. Since the tariff statute did not apply to interstate shipments and the decision seems not to have been based on the commerce clause itself, this passage seems to mean the Court thought the imports clause applied to goods coming from the other states. The Supreme Court later denied this application in Woodruff v. Parham, 75 U.S. (8 Wall.) 123 (1869), *infra* chapter 10. Crosskey and Powell, however, argued that Marshall was right. *See* 1 W. CROSSKEY, *supra* chapter 5, note 228, at 297-301, 315; T. POWELL, *supra* note 73, at 281. *But see* F. FRANKFURTER, *supra* note 89, at 37 (disagreeing with Crosskey and Powell).

[163]Cherokee Nation v. Georgia, 30 U.S. (5 Pet.) 1, *supra* chapter 4.

[164]Worcester v. Georgia, 31 U.S. (6 Pet.) 515 (1832). *See* 4 A. BEVERIDGE, *supra* chapter 5, note 15, at 539-51 (reporting that "the mandate" in *Worcester* "was never obeyed," *id.* at 551); 2 C. WARREN, *supra* chapter 5, note 15, at 189-239 (pointing to serious procedural obstacles to the coercive enforcement of a Supreme Court mandate in a state criminal case and noting that after Jackson's stern reaction to South Carolina's Ordinance of Nullification, Worcester and his fellow defendants were pardoned by the Governor of Georgia). Warren also doubted that President Jackson ever said " 'John Marshall has made his decision, now let him enforce it.' " *Id.* at 219 (footnote omitted).

[165]*See, e.g.*, McClanahan v. Arizona State Tax Comm'n, 411 U.S. 164, 172 (1973) (adding that "the trend has been away from the idea of inherent Indian sovereignty as a bar to state jurisdiction and toward reliance on federal pre-emption"). That "inherent . . . sovereignty" remains a basis for upholding the governmental authority of Indian tribes was dramatically confirmed in United States v. Wheeler, 435 U.S. 313, 332 (1978), which concluded for this reason that the double jeopardy clause did not bar successive prosecutions by a tribe and by the United States; but Justice Rehnquist affirmed for the Court in Moe v. Confederated Salish & Kootenai Tribes, 425 U.S. 463, 481 n.17 (1976), that Indian immunities from state law derive from the supremacy clause alone, i.e., from conflicts between state law and federal statutes and treaties. *See also* F. COHEN, HANDBOOK OF FEDERAL INDIAN LAW 117 (1942) (noting the basis of the federal government's authority over Indian affairs rests in statutes and treaties).

[166]*E.g., Worcester*, 31 U.S. (6 Pet.) at 559 ("The Indian nations had always been considered as distinct, independent, political communities, retaining their original natural rights from time immemorial . . . ."), 561 ("The Cherokee nation, then, is a distinct community, occupying its own territory . . . in which the laws of Georgia can have no force . . . .").

[Cherokee] nation to govern itself"[168] and with "acts of congress"[169] that "manifestly consider the several Indian nations as distinct political communities, having territorial boundaries, within which their authority is exclusive,"[170] both of which he had earlier discussed in considerable detail.

Georgia had denied the power of the federal government to bind it by an Indian treaty.[171] Although the state did not appear in the Supreme Court, Marshall unambiguously posed the question[172] and rejected Georgia's answer: "The constitution, by declaring treaties already made, as well as those to be made, to be the supreme law of the land, has adopted and sanctioned the previous treaties with the Indian nations, and consequently, admits their rank among those powers who are capable of making treaties."[173]

This important constitutional question need not have been reached, since Marshall had found the state laws contrary to statutes as well as to treaties,[174] and since Congress had explicit authority "[t]o regulate Commerce . . . with the Indian Tribes."[175] Out of the blue, however, and wholly without amplification, Marshall added that Georgia's actions "interfere forcibly with the relations established between the United States and the Cherokee nation, the regulation of which, according to the settled principles of our constitution, are committed exclusively to the government of the Union."[176] Justice McLean's long-winded concurrence[177] expressly and unnecessarily[178] jumped to the essentially unexplained conclusion that Congress's power over Indian commerce was exclusive;[179] possibly that is what Marshall had in

[168]*Id.* at 561-62.

[169]*Id.* at 562.

[170]*Id.* at 557.

[171]*See* 2 C. WARREN, *supra* chapter 5, note 15, at 190.

[172]*Worcester*, 31 U.S. (6 Pet.) at 541, 557-58.

[173]*Id.* at 559. It was in this context that Marshall declared that Indian nations were "distinct, independent, political communities." *Id.*

[174]*Id.* at 561-62.

[175]U.S. CONST. art. I, § 8, cl. 3.

[176]*Worcester*, 31 U.S. (6 Pet.) at 561.

[177]*Id.* at 563-96 (McLean, J., concurring). McLean had been appointed by President Jackson in 1829. The *Worcester* opinion contains a rather complete statement of McLean's judicial philosophy, including his favorable opinions of such chestnuts as Marbury v. Madison, 5 U.S. (1 Cranch) 137 (1803), and Cohens v. Virginia, 19 U.S. (6 Wheat.) 264 (1821). Since Georgia had denied the Supreme Court's authority to review its criminal convictions, *see* 2 C. WARREN, *supra* chapter 5, note 15, at 213-14, the latter observation was not entirely out of place, *see supra* chapter 4 (discussing *Cohens*). Marshall may have been alluding to this situation when he wrote that the statute gave the Court both the "power" and the "duty" to decide the case: "This duty, however unpleasant, cannot be avoided." *Worcester*, 31 U.S. (6 Pet.) at 541.

Justice Baldwin dissented on procedural grounds, *id.* at 596 (Baldwin, J., dissenting), saying that his opinion on the merits was the same one he had expressed in the *Cherokee Nation* case, 30 U.S. (5 Pet.) at 31-50, where he had concluded that Georgia had full sovereignty over the Cherokee territory. Baldwin's conclusions are summarily reported, for the interesting reason that (as late as 1832) his opinion "was not delivered to the reporter." *Worcester*, 31 U.S. (6 Pet.) at 596.

[178]McLean, like Marshall, found the Georgia laws contrary to treaty and federal statute. *Worcester*, 31 U.S. (6 Pet.) at 578-79.

[179]*Id.* at 580-81. The reason given was simply that this power was "enumerated in the same section" with Congress's authority "to regulate commerce with foreign nations, to coin money, to establish post-offices, and to declare war" and "belongs to the same class of powers." *Id.* Coinage and war are easily distinguishable, because the Constitution expressly limits state power in these fields, U.S. CONST. art. I, § 10, paras. 1, 3, and the Court never had held either the postal power or that over foreign commerce to be

mind as well, though his well-documented conclusions regarding the statutes and treaties were quite ample to dispose of the case. If Marshall meant to reach still another important and avoidable constitutional question, to resolve a difficult issue without discussion, and to give three grounds where one would have sufficed, it would not be for the first time. If, more charitably, we read the exclusivity remark as an aside and the reference to interference with "the relations established" as relying on the statutes and treaties, then, despite its well-known hints, the Court seems never to have invalidated a state law on the basis of the unimplemented commerce clause during Marshall's tenure, and it would be a long time before his successors did so.[180]

IV. OTHER CASES ON CONGRESSIONAL POWER

The limits of federal power, apart from those of the judiciary, were not often litigated in the days of Marshall. *McCulloch* and *Gibbons* were of course the great cases; in upholding the Bank[181] and the power to license steamboats,[182] Marshall gave a liberal but restrained direction to the interpretation of grants of congressional authority. In the same tradition, *United States v. Fisher*[183] upheld priority for government claims against an insolvent estate; *Loughborough v. Blake*[184] held that direct

---

exclusive. The difficulties posed by an implied exclusion of state authority over interstate commerce are considered *supra* notes 97-126 and accompanying text (discussing *Gibbons v. Ogden*); they seem equally applicable to Indian commerce. Justice Story, citing *Worcester*, described the Indian-commerce power as exclusive, 2 J. STORY, *supra* chapter 5, note 42, §§ 1094-1095, at 540-42; Rawle had reached the same conclusion before *Worcester*, evidently on the basis of *Gibbons*, W. RAWLE, *supra* note 99, at 82, 84. For recent statements casting doubt on this notion without ruling out negative effects on state law entirely, see Washington v. Confederated Tribes, 447 U.S. 125, 150-62 (1980), and cases cited; Moe v. Confederated Salish & Kootenai Tribes, 425 U.S. 463, 481 n.17 (1976).

[180]The first unequivocal example seems to have been Case of the State Freight Tax, 82 U.S. (15 Wall.) 232 (1873), *infra* chapter 10. See also Southern S.S. Co. v. Portwardens, 73 U.S. (6 Wall.) 31 (1867) (alternative holding), also discussed in chapter 10.

[181]See *supra* notes 1-73 and accompanying text (discussing *McCulloch v. Maryland*).

[182]See *supra* notes 74-127 and accompanying text (discussing *Gibbons v. Ogden*).

[183]6 U.S. (2 Cranch) 358 (1805); *see supra* notes 25-37 and accompanying text.

[184]18 U.S. (5 Wheat.) 317 (1820). The power "'to lay and collect taxes, duties, imposts and excises,'" said Marshall, was "without limitation as to place." *Id.* at 318 (quoting U.S. CONST. art. I, § 8, cl. 1). The requirement that direct taxes be "apportioned among the several States . . . according to their respective Numbers," U.S. CONST. art. I, § 2, para. 3, was meant "to furnish a standard by which taxes are to be apportioned, not to exempt from their operation any part of our country," *Loughborough*, 18 U.S. (5 Wheat.) at 320. The further requirement of apportionment "in Proportion to the Census or Enumeration" of the states' respective populations, U.S. CONST. art. I, § 9, cl. 4, neither forbade nor required inclusion of the District of Columbia, *Loughborough*, 18 U.S. (5 Wheat.) at 321-22. The contrary implication derived from the well-known American aversion to taxation without representation was untenable, for it would deprive Congress of all power to tax residents of the District, contrary to the requirement that duties, imposts, and excises be "uniform throughout the United States," U.S. CONST. art. I, § 8, cl. 1, which admittedly "not only allows, but enjoins the government to extend the ordinary revenue system to this district," *Loughborough*, 18 U.S. (5 Wheat.) at 325. This last dictum may seem debatable, but the holding itself seems convincing.

More questionable seems Marshall's additional conclusion, apparently unnecessary to the decision, that if the District was included in a direct tax its share would have to be proportional to its own population, *id.* at 321-22, 325, because the census by which such a tax must be apportioned is the one

taxes could be extended to the District of Columbia; and *Martin v. Mott*[185] declared that congressional power "'to provide for calling forth the militia, to . . . repel invasions'" supported a statute empowering the President to do so when, in the Court's words, there was "imminent danger of invasion."[186]

The relationship between Congress and the other federal branches was inconclusively touched upon in three cases. *The Cargo of the Brig Aurora v. United States*[187] and *Wayman v. Southard*[188] conclusorily upheld statutes giving authority to the President and to the courts, respectively, over objections that they delegated legislative power. *The Flying Fish*[189] enforced a statute that the Court read to limit the President's right to seize vessels operated in violation of an embargo, despite Marshall's concession that the President might have had power to make such seizures in the absence of the statute under his constitutional duty to "'take care that the laws be faithfully executed.'"[190]

What most of these decisions save *McCulloch* and *Gibbons* have in common is a lack of serious attention to the constitutional issue. *Fisher* leapt to a broad interpretation of the necessary and proper clause simply because it rejected the straw man of indispensable necessity; *Wayman* and *The Cargo of the Brig Aurora* were purely conclusory, and *The Flying Fish* did not advert to any question of Congress's power to limit the methods by which the President executes the laws.

Of greater interest is Justice Johnson's opinion for a unanimous Court in *Anderson v. Dunn*,[191] upholding the implicit power of the House of Representatives to punish nonmembers for contempt. He began with a ringing endorsement of *McCulloch*'s principle of incidental powers:

> Had the faculties of man been competent to the framing of a system of government which would have left nothing to implication, it cannot be

---

"herein before directed to be taken," U.S. Const. art. I, § 9, cl. 4. Marshall correctly had emphasized that the latter clause need not include the District at all: "The census referred to is admitted to be a census exhibiting the numbers of the respective States." *Loughborough*, 18 U.S. (5 Wheat.) at 321.

    Marshall's resolution has much to commend it in policy, for it extended the Framers' ideas of tax equity to a case for which, as was generally true of the territories and the District of Columbia, they had failed adequately to provide. *Cf. supra* chapters 3, 4 (discussing United States v. More, 7 U.S. (3 Cranch) 159 (1805); Hepburn v. Ellzey, 6 U.S. (2 Cranch) 445 (1805); Cohens v. Virginia, 19 U.S. (6 Wheat.) 264 (1821); American Ins. Co. v. Canter, 26 U.S. (1 Pet.) 511 (1828)). For the Court's first encounter with the direct tax provisions, see *supra* chapter 2 (discussing Hylton v. United States, 3 U.S. (3 Dall.) 171 (1796)).

[185]25 U.S. (12 Wheat.) 19 (1827).

[186]*Id.* at 28-29 (Story, J.) (quoting U.S. Const. art. I, § 8, cl. 15). Story stated that "[o]ne of the best means to repel invasion is to provide the requisite force for action, before the invader himself has reached the soil." *Id.* at 29. The point had not been contested. Story added that the statute gave the President unreviewable discretion to determine whether there was an imminent danger, *id.* at 29-32; the latter passage was to be used to support the conclusion in Luther v. Borden, 48 U.S. (7 How.) 1, 44-45 (1849), denying judicial authority to determine which was the legitimate government of Rhode Island. See *infra* chapter 8.

[187]11 U.S. (7 Cranch) 382 (1813); *see supra* chapter 4.

[188]23 U.S. (10 Wheat.) 1 (1825); *see supra* chapter 4.

[189]6 U.S. (2 Cranch) 170 (1804).

[190]*Id.* at 177 (quoting U.S. Const. art. II, § 3).

[191]19 U.S. (6 Wheat.) 204 (1821). For a brief explanation of the facts see D. Morgan, *supra* chapter 5, note 203, at 119.

doubted, that the effort would have been made by the framers of the constitution. But what is the fact? There is not in the whole of that admirable instrument, a grant of power which does not draw after it others, not expressed, but vital to their exercise . . . .[192]

The principal basis for inferring a legislative contempt power was necessity:

[I]f there is one maxim which necessarily rides over all others, in the practical application of government, it is, that the public functionaries must be left at liberty to exercise the powers which the people have intrusted to them . . . .[193] That a deliberate [sic] assembly . . . should not possess the power to suppress rudeness, or repel insult is a supposition too wild to be suggested.[194]

Johnson invoked analogy as well: it was on the same principle that the courts were "universally acknowledged" to have inherent contempt power, though Congress had expressly confirmed that authority by statute out of "abundant caution."[195] The existence of an explicit provision enabling each House to "punish its Members for disorderly Behaviour,"[196] Johnson concluded, did not negate the power to punish others: no one thought the express authority to punish piracy meant that Congress could not create other criminal offenses, and "the exercise of the powers given over their own members, was of such a delicate nature, that a constitutional provision became necessary to assert or communicate it."[197] Arguments based upon the constitutional jury provisions and upon article III's vesting of the "judicial Power" in the courts[198] were simply ignored.[199]

---

[192]*Anderson*, 19 U.S. (6 Wheat.) at 225-26.

[193]*Id.* at 226.

[194]*Id.* at 228-29. For an approving view, see Landis, *Constitutional Limitations on the Congressional Power of Investigation*, 40 HARV. L. REV. 153, 158 (1926).

[195]*Id.* at 227-28. Marshall had proclaimed an inherent judicial contempt power in *Ex parte* Bollman, 8 U.S. (4 Cranch) 75, 94 (1807). *See supra* chapter 3. So had Johnson himself in the course of denying that federal courts had implicit authority to punish common law crimes. United States v. Hudson, 11 U.S. (7 Cranch) 32, 34 (1812). Johnson cited neither Marshall nor himself; indeed, he cited nothing in the entire *Anderson* opinion.

[196]U.S. CONST. art. I, § 5, para. 2.

[197]*Anderson*, 19 U.S. (6 Wheat.) at 233.

[198]*See id.* at 214, 218 (Mr. Hall). *See also* 1 Tucker's Appendix to Blackstone, *supra* note 83, at 200 (criticizing an earlier exercise by the House of the power to punish nonmembers on these grounds as well as for want of a grand jury and of due process, and arguing that the enumerated powers of each House, like those of Congress itself, were a barrier to the discovery of unlisted powers).

[199]For an approving view of *Anderson*, see 1 J. KENT, *supra* chapter 5, note 111, at 235-36 & 236 n.a., invoking not only "the principle of self-preservation," *id.* at 236, but also the practice of Parliament, *id.* at 235, which had been noted by counsel in *Anderson*, 19 U.S. (6 Wheat.) at 219-20, but not relied on in the opinion. *Anderson* was distinguished in Kilbourn v. Thompson, 103 U.S. 168, 196-97 (1881), *infra* chapter 13 (casting aspersions on the Parliamentary analogy while holding a particular contempt citation beyond the House's power). *But see* Potts, *Power of Legislative Bodies to Punish for Contempt* (pts. 1 & 2), 74 U. PA. L. REV. 691, 780 (1926) (criticizing *Kilbourn's* approach and endorsing *Anderson*). The Court relied on *Anderson* in McGrain v. Daugherty, 273 U.S. 135, 160-78 (1927), in upholding the implicit investigatory power of the Senate.

This was a remarkable performance in which Jefferson's first appointee, who was to acquire a reputation as dissenter and upholder of state rights,[200] proved himself the spittin' image of John Marshall.[201] What the Constitution ought to provide, it provides—even though, as with the tax immunity in *McCulloch*,[202] Congress's authority under the necessary and proper clause deprives the necessity argument of much of its force.[203] It is noteworthy that Johnson elected to announce a broad principle of inherent powers rather than more modestly to find contempt authority in the provision empowering each House to "determine the Rules of its Proceedings."[204] It is also notable that Johnson undertook in best Marshall fashion to lay down obiter limitations on the implicit power determined much as a legislature would have determined them: imprisonment was the only permissible sanction, because it was "'the least possible power adequate to the end proposed'";[205] even imprisonment "must terminate with . . . adjournment," since when it adjourns "the legislative body ceases to exist."[206] "[N]either analogy nor precedent would support the assertion of such powers in any other than a legislative or judicial body" since it would never "be necessary to the executive, or any other department, to hold a public deliberative assembly."[207]

V. Bills of Credit and the Bill of Rights

A. *Craig v. Missouri*

Two more great cases remain for consideration; both came near the end of Marshall's service, and in both, as usual, he wrote the opinion. The first ranks with *McCulloch* as one of the early landmarks in defining what Kenneth Dam has called our "fiscal constitution";[208] it involved the important but now forgotten clause of article I, section 10, forbidding the states to "emit Bills of Credit."[209]

Missouri had issued to Craig, in return for a promissory note, a certificate in the amount of $199.99 plus interest. The state had agreed to accept such certificates in payment of taxes and debts, had announced its intention of paying its officers' salaries with them, and had pledged for their redemption the proceeds of state

---

[200]*See generally* D. Morgan, *supra* chapter 5, note 203.

[201]See *id.* at 120, speaking of *Anderson*: "William Johnson had turned his back on strict construction."

[202]*See supra* notes 58-62 and accompanying text.

[203]See In re Chapman, 166 U.S. 661, 671-72 (1897) (upholding a statute punishing contempt of Congress). An argument can nevertheless be made that the Framers would not have intended to leave one House at the mercy of the other and of the President. Cf. U.S. Const. art. I, § 5, para. 2 (each House to adopt own rules); United States v. Nixon, 418 U.S. 683, 705-706 (1974) (recognizing implicit constitutional basis for executive privilege).

[204]U.S. Const. art. I, § 5, para. 2.

[205]*Anderson*, 19 U.S. (6 Wheat.) at 230-31.

[206]*Id.* at 231.

[207]*Id.* at 233-34. Examples of greater punishments by Parliament were brushed aside as merely "historical facts, not . . . precedents for imitation." *Id.* at 231.

[208]Dam, *The American Fiscal Constitution*, 44 U. Chi. L. Rev. 271 (1977).

[209]U.S. Const. art. I, § 10, para. 1. In the indexes to at least two modern treatises, the clause is not listed at all. J. Nowak, R. Rotunda & J. Young, Constitutional Law 967 (1978); L. Tribe, *supra* chapter 5, note 42, at 1176 (1978).

operations in the salt market, all debts owing to the state, and the faith of the state itself. The state sued Craig to collect on his promissory note and prevailed in state court. In 1830 the Supreme Court reversed, holding that the note had been issued for an illegal consideration: the certificate was a prohibited bill of credit.[210]

Craig is another typical Marshall opinion, devoted primarily to the dissection of a red herring. Counsel had argued that the certificates were not bills of credit because they were not legal tender.[211] Marshall spent some time giving historical examples of bills of credit issued before 1789 that were *not* legal tender but "were productive of the same effects."[212] Though he referred to particular issues of bills, he recited no evidence to prove his conclusory assertions as to their effects; and he had already disposed of the legal-tender argument by showing that it would render the bill-of-credit clause superfluous in light of the independent provision forbidding states to "make anything but gold or silver a legal tender."[213]

Establishing that bills of credit are forbidden even if not legal tender does not tell us what a bill of credit is; to answer that question Marshall resorted again to history. "The term has acquired an appropriate meaning"; there was a "sense in which the terms have been always understood."[214] Before 1789

> the attempt to supply the want of the precious metals by a paper medium was made to a considerable extent; and the bills emitted for this purpose have been frequently denominated bills of credit. . . . Such a medium has been always liable to considerable fluctuation. Its value is continually changing; and these changes, often great and sudden, expose individuals to immense loss, are the sources of ruinous speculations, and destroy all confidence between man and man.[215]

Thus the prohibition was directed toward paper money; "it must comprehend the emission of any paper medium, by a state government, for the purpose of common circulation."[216] The small denominations of the bills in question, he concluded, "fitted them for the purpose of ordinary circulation; and their reception in payment of taxes, and debts to the government and to corporations, and of salaries and fees, would give them currency."[217]

All this sounds, as Marshall usually did, very plausible.[218] One notices at once, however, that as usual his history was stated as a simple conclusion with virtually no reference to supporting materials.[219] We have essentially only his word for it either

---

[210]Craig v. Missouri, 29 U.S. (4 Pet.) 410, 437 (1830).

[211]*Id.* at 421-22 (Mr. Benton) ("Free to refuse them, the citizen may protect himself from loss by their depreciation, by rejecting them.").

[212]*Id.* at 435 (Marshall, C.J.); *see id.* at 434-36.

[213]*Id.* at 433-34. *See* U.S. CONST. art. I, § 10, para. 1.

[214]29 U.S. (4 Pet.) at 432. *Cf.* Calder v. Bull, 3 U.S. (3 Dall.) 386, 390-94 (1798), employing a similar argument in construing the ex post facto clause. *See supra* chapter 2.

[215]*Craig*, 29 U.S. (4 Pet.) at 432.

[216]*Id.*

[217]*Id.* at 433.

[218]See E. CORWIN, *supra* chapter 5, note 41, at 92, declaring without elaboration that the certificates in *Craig* were plainly unconstitutional.

[219]He did cite "Hutchinson's History of Massachusetts, vol. 1, p. 402," for his examples of early issues of bills of credit. *Craig*, 29 U.S. (4 Pet.) at 434.

that paper money was commonly known as a bill of credit or that its evils were the "mischief" the clause was designed to prevent.[220] Moreover, although rejection of tender as an essential ingredient makes attractive his conclusion that these certificates shared the relevant attributes of paper money, his concession that the state could issue an instrument promising "to pay money at a future day for services actually received, or for money borrowed"[221] raises serious questions as to whether he drew the line at the right place. Surely, as he admitted, the state was not forbidden to issue promissory notes when it borrowed money. The hard problem in the case was to define the difference between such a note and the forbidden bill, and Marshall made no real effort to wrestle with it.

The difficulty was highlighted by the interesting dissent of Justice Johnson,[222] which demonstrates the respect that he held for Marshall, despite occasional disagreement, after many years of joint labor. Entirely missing is the strident tone of today's dissents, which often characterize the majority as a band of unprincipled brigands; Johnson's is a measured, statesmanlike opinion. He agreed with Marshall that history furnished the guide to the meaning of the constitutional terms: since the terms were "vague and general, and, at the present day, almost dismissed from our language," it was "only by resorting to the nomenclature of the day of the constitution, that we can hope to get at the idea which the framers of the constitution attached to it."[223] He agreed that "'bill of credit'" meant "paper money" and that it was not limited to legal tender.[224] But he also agreed with Marshall that the clause did not forbid the state to borrow, and he thought that was what the state had done in *Craig:*[225] it had given its certificates in exchange for private notes, which could then be discounted to produce cash for state expenditures.[226] He added that the fact the certificates bore interest "disqualifies them for the uses and purposes of a circulating medium" by giving them a variable value, and that the state had promised not to pay certificate holders but to receive the certificates in satisfaction of taxes; "the objection to a mere paper medium is, that its value depends upon mere national faith," while the certificate holder "has a better dependence" in that he may tender it for paying his taxes.[227]

[220]THE FEDERALIST NO. 44 (J. Madison), which counsel had cited, *Craig*, 29 U.S. (4 Pet.) at 418-19, not only had confirmed that the bill-of-credit provision was aimed at "the pestilent effects of paper money," THE FEDERALIST No. 44, at 281 (J. Madison) (C. Rossiter ed. 1961), but was the evident source of Marshall's reference to "confidence between man and man," *Craig*, 29 U.S. (4 Pet.) at 432. St. George Tucker had equated bills of credit with "paper money" and had explained the clause as directed against its "depreciation." 1 Tucker's Appendix to Blackstone, *supra* note 83, at 312. Marshall cited neither. *See also* 3 ELLIOT's DEBATES, *supra* note 10, at 76 (comments of Mr. Randolph); 4 *id.* at 181, 183-84, 184, 185, 334 (comments of Messrs. Maclaine, Davie, Cabarrus, Iredell, and Pinckney).

[221]*Craig*, 29 U.S. (4 Pet.) at 431-32.

[222]*Id.* at 438-44 (Johnson, J., dissenting).

[223]*Id.* at 442.

[224]*Id.* Johnson added that the certificates in question *were* made "tender" for salaries of state officials, which might imply their invalidity under the legal tender clause, but he dropped the suggestion and voted to uphold them. *Id.* Counsel had argued that the requirement that the bills be accepted by state officers was "not before the court," *id.* at 422 (Mr. Benton), and Thompson in dissent agreed, *id.* at 446-47.

[225]Counsel had so argued. *Id.* at 421 (Mr. Benton).

[226]*Id.* at 443-44 (Johnson, J., dissenting) (terming the transaction an "amphibious" one and affording what seems to be a rather rare example of the application of Justice Chase's familiar maxim that a law is to be upheld if it is not clearly unconstitutional).

[227]*Id.* at 444.

This is not the place to determine whether Johnson was right in any of these distinctions; what is important for present purposes is that Marshall loftily ignored them all.[228] Thompson also dissented, arguing that there was a difference "between a bill drawn on a fund . . . constituted or pledged for . . . payment," as he said was the case in *Craig*, and one "resting merely upon the credit of the drawer."[229] He added that the decision appeared to outlaw all notes issued by state-chartered banks, since "the states cannot certainly do that indirectly which they cannot do directly";[230] Marshall ignored him too. Finally, the newcomer McLean added a wordy dissent in which he seemed to suggest, contrary to Johnson, that the state was essentially *lending* money to the certificate holders,[231] but he agreed with Johnson that the certificates were not bills of credit because they contained only a promise of acceptance in satisfaction of taxes, not a promise to pay.[232]

All this ferment suggests that *Craig* was a pretty difficult case; Marshall sailed right over the top of it without acknowledging any of the difficult problems.[233]

B.   *Barron v. Mayor of Baltimore*

Our final case was one of enormous significance. Barron argued that the city had taken his property without compensation by destroying the navigability of a stream and rendering his wharf unusable. Marshall's brief 1833 opinion declined to review the state court's denial of relief, holding despite the apparently all-embracing terminology of the fifth amendment provision ("nor shall private property be taken for public use, without just compensation")[234] that it did not apply to the states.[235]

[228]Marshall of course spoke first, and, in a day in which not all opinions were written out in advance, *see supra* chapter 5, note 204, there may have been less opportunity than there is today to respond to dissent; yet it is hard to believe Johnson had not revealed his views in the course of deliberation before decision.

[229]*Craig*, 29 U.S. (4 Pet.) at 447 (Thompson, J., dissenting). *See also id.* at 448 ("when a fund is pledged, or ample provision made for the redemption of a bill or voucher, . . . there is but little danger of a depreciation or loss").

[230]*Id.* at 449. This passage sheds interesting light on the modern question of the degree to which ostensibly private action is subject to constitutional provisions applicable in terms only to states. *See, e.g.,* Burton v. Wilmington Parking Auth., 365 U.S. 715 (1961).

[231]*Id.* at 456-57 (McLean, J., dissenting). McLean stated the object was "to furnish the citizens of Missouri with the means of paying to the state the taxes which it imposed, and other debts due to it," at a time when bank failures had destroyed the value of existing currency. *Id.* Thus he argued that Missouri was trying to alleviate the very dangers the clause was designed to prevent. This was a clever argument but rather disingenuous, for he had earlier said the same was true of early issues of paper money that the clause was designed to preclude. *Id.* at 452.

[232]*Id.* at 457-58 (McLean, J., dissenting). McLean also concluded that the Court's decision that the certificates were invalid did not justify a reversal of the state court's judgment: whether a contract was void because its consideration was illegal was a matter of state law. *Id.* at 459-63. For Justice Story's belated response that most of the allegedly distinguishing features pointed out by the dissenters had been shared by bills of credit issued before 1789, see 3 J. STORY, *supra* chapter 5, note 42, §§ 1362-1365, at 232-37 & 235 n.2.

[233]*Craig* was reaffirmed without dissent in Byrne v. Missouri, 33 U.S. (8 Pet.) 40 (1834), shortly before Marshall's death. But one of the first acts of the Court after his departure was to uphold state bank notes on the basis of narrow distinctions of *Craig*, Briscoe v. Bank of Kentucky, 36 U.S. (11 Pet.) 257 (1837), leading Story in dissent to complain that that case had been overruled, *id.* at 328-50 (Story, J., dissenting). *See infra* chapter 7. Marshall's cavalier treatment of the real issues in *Craig* made the task in *Briscoe* much easier.

[234]U.S. CONST. amend. V.

[235]Barron v. Mayor of Baltimore, 32 U.S. (7 Pet.) 243, 247 (1833). There were no dissents.

Marshall began by suggesting that the answer was inherent in the very nature of the document: "The constitution was ordained and established by the people of the United States for themselves, for their own government, and not for the government of the individual states."[236] This did not get him very far, for it proved too much: the entire tenth section of article I was explicitly devoted to limitations on state power. In attempting to explain these away he came perilously close to misrepresentation, suggesting that they "generally restrain state legislation on subjects intrusted to the general government, or in which the people of all the states feel an interest."[237] Neither the prohibition of ex post facto laws and bills of attainder nor the contract clause as it had been construed[238]—neither of which he bothered mentioning in this connection[239]—fit Marshall's description any better than did the taking clause itself.

Somewhat more appealing was his argument that when the Framers had meant to limit state power they had specifically said so: despite its general language, the provision in article I, section 9, that "'no bill of attainder or ex post facto law shall be passed'"[240] could not apply to the states because section 10 expressly provided that "[n]o State shall . . . pass any Bill of Attainder, [or] ex post facto Law."[241] That the original document did not limit states without mentioning them, however, does not prove the same was true of the amendments, which contained no separate provisions naming states; indeed the contrast between the taking clause and the first[242] and seventh amendments,[243] which spoke expressly of "Congress" and of "any Court of the United States," arguably suggested that when the amendments limited only federal action they said so.[244] But, as Marshall noted in passing,[245] although article I, section 9, similarly limited the powers of "Congress" over the "Migration or Importation of . . . Persons,"[246] that phraseology does not seem to rebut the inference that the more general provisions of that section apply only to the federal government. Though far from conclusive, the contrast between sections 9 and 10 helped to confirm Marshall's initial presumption that "limitations on power, if expressed in

---

[236]*Id.* at 247.

[237]*Id.* at 249 (instancing coinage, letters of marque and reprisal, and international and interstate treaties, the last of which "can scarcely fail to interfere with the general purpose of and intent of the constitution").

[238]*See supra* chapter 5, notes 205-60 and accompanying text (discussing *Ogden v. Saunders*); *supra* chapter 5, note 228; chapter 6, note 86, (discussing Professor Crosskey's dissenting view).

[239]"It would be tedious to recapitulate the several limitations on the powers of the states which are contained in this section." *Barron*, 32 U.S. (7 Pet.) at 249.

[240]*Id.* at 248 (quoting U.S. CONST. art. I, § 9, cl. 3).

[241]U.S. CONST. art. I, § 10, para. 1.

[242]*Id.* amend. I ("Congress shall make no Law respecting an Establishment of Religion . . . . ").

[243]*Id.* amend. VII ("no fact tried by a jury, shall be otherwise re-examined in any Court of the United States, than according to the rules of the common law").

[244]*See* W. RAWLE, *supra* note 99, at 124 (the first amendment "expressly refers to the powers of congress alone, but some of those which follow are to be more generally construed, and considered as applying to the state legislatures as well as that of the Union"), 127 (discussing the fourth amendment and stating "[h]ere again we find the general terms which prohibit *all* violations of these personal rights, and of course extend both to the state and the United States" (emphasis in original)). *See also* 2 W. CROSSKEY, *supra* chapter 5, note 228, at 1057-58 (arguing that because most of the amendments were to apply to the states, those that were to bind only the federal government were explicitly so limited).

[245]*Barron*, 32 U.S. (7 Pet.) at 248.

[246]U.S. CONST. art. I, § 9, cl. 1.

general terms, are naturally . . . applicable [only] to the government created by the instrument."[247]

Marshall put his best argument last, and it was based on history: the amendments had been adopted in response to a demand for "security against the apprehended encroachments of the general government—not against those of the local governments."[248] Typically, this crucial conclusion was essentially unsubstantiated. Marshall did refer generally to the recommendations of the various state ratifying conventions without quoting them,[249] and there is support in them for his position.[250] Moreover, it was clear that as originally proposed the amendments would have limited only federal action; for though none was expressly so restricted, they were offered as additions to article I, section 9, together with a separate provision that "[n]o State shall violate the equal rights of conscience, or the freedom of the press, or the trial by jury in criminal cases," which was to go with other limitations on state power in section 10.[251] The vagaries that befell this proposal during its odyssey through Congress obscured both its terminology and its structure with respect to the *Barron* question. Yet the most significant change—the decision to append the amendments at the end of the Constitution rather than inserting them more comprehensively in article I—was plainly motivated by purely formal or technical considerations quite divorced from the breadth of their application.[252] If either the addition of language making clear that certain of the new provisions did not apply to the states or the elimination of the only provision expressly naming them was meant to have the paradoxical effect of expanding the reach of other provisions whose language was not altered, one would expect to find some evidence of that intention. Professor Fairman has shown, however, that the subsequent actions of numerous members of

[247] *Barron*, 32 U.S. (7 Pet.) at 247.

[248] *Id.* at 250.

[249] *Id.*

[250] New Hampshire and Massachusetts, for example, had both asked for amendments to "more effectually guard against an undue administration of the federal Government"; some of their specific proposals spoke of "Congress," while others were phrased in general terms. 2 DOCUMENTARY HISTORY OF THE CONSTITUTION OF THE UNITED STATES OF AMERICA 93-96, 141-44 (U.S. Dep't of State comp. 1894). The Virginia proposals, cited by Professor Crosskey as asking for limitations on the states as well, were similar in phrasing but substituted for the preliminary references to the "federal Government" an unilluminating desire for provisions "'asserting and securing from encroachment the essential and unalienable Rights of the People.'" 2 W. CROSSKEY, *supra* chapter 5, note 228, at 1061; *see id.* at 1061-64. Crosskey did not cite the New Hampshire or Massachusetts recommendations, leading one respected reviewer to the conclusion that "Mr. Crosskey *suppressed* this important evidence." Fairman, *The Supreme Court and the Constitutional Limitations on State Governmental Authority*, 21 U. CHI. L. REV. 40, 51 (1953) (emphasis in original).

[251] 1 ANNALS OF CONG. 451-52 (J. Gales ed. 1789). Professor Crosskey conceded as much. 2 W. CROSSKEY, *supra* chapter 5, note 194, at 1066-67.

[252] In the House of Representatives Sherman argued that "to interweave our propositions into the work itself" would be "destructive of the whole fabric" and would go beyond the amending authority given by article V because it would "establish a new constitution." 1 ANNALS OF CONG. 734-35 (J. Gales ed. 1789). Clymer added that separate amendments would preserve the original text as "a monument to justify those who made it." *Id.* at 737. On the other side, Madison argued sensibly that discrete amendments would make the document harder to understand. *Id.* at 735. Gerry saw no advantage save "to give every one the trouble of erasing out of his copy of the constitution certain words and sentences, and inserting others." *Id.* at 738. A variety of speakers lamented the investment of so much time in what Gerry termed "matters of little consequence." *Id. See id.* at 735-44.

the Congress that had proposed the amendments were inconsistent with the notion that the Bill of Rights was applicable to the states.[253] Indeed the Senate attached to the proposal a preamble that seemed rather to confirm that its purpose was to limit federal power.[254] In addition, despite two equivocal hints by Justice Johnson,[255] a flat statement in an 1829 treatise,[256] and an "inclination" in one New York decision,[257] the

[253]For example, several of them participated actively in state constitutional conventions after 1791 in which, without apparent objection, grand jury provisions were drafted that did not measure up to those in the fifth amendment. *See generally* Fairman, *supra* note 250. Professor Crosskey, who believed that *Barron* was "without any warrant at all," mentioned none of these episodes and came up with no counterexamples of his own. 2 W. CROSSKEY, *supra* chapter 5, note 228, at 1067.

[254]The preamble recited that the amendments were proposed because "[t]he Conventions of a number of the States [had] at the time of their adopting the Constitution expressed a desire, in order to prevent misconstruction or abuse of its powers, that further declaratory and restrictive clauses should be added" and in hopes that "extending the ground of public confidence in the government [would] best insure the beneficent ends of its institution." 1 Stat. 97 (1789) (the preamble never became part of the Constitution). Crosskey argued that "*its* Powers" might mean state as well as federal powers, since the Constitution "was, in fact, a scheme of '*Government*' through state '*Powers*' as well as National 'Powers,'" and since state authority had been limited by the original instrument. 2 W. CROSSKEY, *supra* chapter 5, note 228, at 1065 (emphasis in original) (quoting 1 Stat. 97).

[255]*See* Bank of Columbia v. Okely, 17 U.S. (4 Wheat.) 235, 242-44 (1819), *discussed supra in* chapter 4, where Johnson for the Court held that a federal statute incorporating Maryland law did so only to the extent the state law was valid and proceeded to measure it, "as a law of Maryland," against the seventh amendment; Houston v. Moore, 18 U.S. (5 Wheat.) 1 (1820), where Johnson argued in a concurrence that the states had concurrent power to punish the failure to report when the militia was called into federal service:

> I cannot imagine a reason why the States may not also, if they feel themselves injured by the same offence, assert their right of inflicting punishment also. In cases affecting life or member, there is an express restraint upon the exercise of the punishing power. But it is a restriction which operates equally upon both governments; and according to a very familiar principle of construction, this exception would seem to establish the existence of the general right.

Id. at 34. For a possibly too skeptical dismissal of these passages, see Fairman, *supra* note 250, at 76-77. Johnson acceded to *Barron*, without naming it, in his opinion for the Court in Livingston v. Moore, 32 U.S. (7 Pet.) 469, 551-52 (1833), applying its reasoning to the requirement of a civil jury, U.S. CONST. amend. VII, and due process, *id.* amend. V: "As to the amendments of the constitution of the United States, they must be put out of the case; since it is now settled, that those amendments do not extend to the states . . . . " Morgan said that Johnson was absent from the "session of the Court" in which *Barron* was decided, D. MORGAN, *supra* chapter 5, note 203, at 135 n.33, but he misstated the date of *Barron* as 1832, and in fact *Livingston* and *Barron* were decided during the same Term. Later cases applying the *Barron* principle to additional Bill of Rights provisions include Smith v. Maryland, 59 U.S. (18 How.) 71, 76 (1855) (search and seizure) and Permoli v. New Orleans, 44 U.S. (3 How.) 589 (1845) (freedom of religion); *Barron* itself was reaffirmed in Withers v. Buckley, 61 U.S. (20 How.) 84, 90 (1858). Today it is understood to be the fourteenth amendment that makes much of the Bill of Rights applicable to the states. *See* Duncan v. Louisiana, 391 U.S. 145, 147-49 (1968).

[256]W. RAWLE, *supra* note 99, at 124, *quoted supra* note 244.

[257]People v. Goodwin, 18 Johns. 187, 201 (N.Y. 1820), where Chief Justice Spencer "inclined" to the view that, because of its "unrestricted . . . terms," the double jeopardy clause applied to the states, but found it unnecessary to resolve the question because the same principles governed under New York law. Although Professor Fairman argued that Spencer spoke for himself alone, Fairman, *supra* note 250, at 74, the opinion not only is titled that of the court but adds that the other judges "entirely concur," 18 Johns. at 200, 207. *But see infra* note 258 (later New York decisions rejecting Spencer's inclination in *Goodwin*).

result Marshall reached in *Barron* was supported by a respectable body of previous state-court authority[258]—which characteristically was not noted in Marshall's opinion.[259]

Thus Marshall's last great opinion brings us full circle to the strengths and weaknesses of his first one. As in *Marbury v. Madison*,[260] his instincts seem as usual to have led him to a sound result, and as in *Marbury* he began with an overstatement from the nature of the Constitution and disdained serious explication of supporting materials.[261]

---

[258]Maurin v. Martinez, 5 Mart. 432, 436 (La. 1818) (civil jury); Renthorp v. Bourg, 4 Mart. 97, 131-32 (La. 1816) (taking); Livingston v. Mayor of New York, 8 Wend. 85, 100-01 (N.Y. 1831) (opinion of Chancellor Walworth; not mentioned in parallel opinion of Senator Sherman) (due process, taking, and civil jury); Jackson v. Wood, 2 Cow. 819, 820-21 (N.Y. 1824) (grand jury and criminal jury); Murphy v. People, 2 Cow. 815, 818 (N.Y. 1824) (grand jury and criminal jury). *See also id.* at 818 (reporter's note that although the other members of the court did not discuss the case they "agreed clearly"); Huntington v. Bishop, 5 Vt. 186, 193-94 (1832) (terming it "very doubtful" that the civil jury requirement of the seventh amendment applied to the states). Professor Crosskey cited none of these cases.

[259]It also seems significant that in neither *Fletcher v. Peck, supra* chapter 5, notes 19-81 and accompanying text, nor *Trustees of Dartmouth College, supra* notes 126-55 and accompanying text, where the Court performed considerable surgical feats to prove that a taking of property was an impairment of contract, did it occur to the eminent attorneys to suggest the applicability of the fifth amendment. Furthermore, for what it is worth, the Constitution of the short-lived Confederate States of America, drafted after *Barron* and displaying a remarkable likeness to that of the United States, inserted the first eight amendments unambiguously in article I, section 9, with other limitations applicable (by contrast with section 10) only to the central government. CONFEDERATE STATES OF AMERICA CONST., art. I, §§ 9-10, *reprinted in* THE STATUTES AT LARGE OF THE PROVISIONAL GOVERNMENT OF THE CONFEDERATE STATES OF AMERICA 15-17 (J. Mathews ed. 1864).

[260]5 U.S. (1 Cranch) 137 (1803). *See supra* chapter 3.

[261]The Annals of Congress were not published until 1834; their title page reveals simply that they were "compiled from authentic materials." 1 ANNALS OF CONG. (J. Gales ed. 1789).

To be mentioned for the sake of completeness are Hampton v. McConnell, 16 U.S. (3 Wheat.) 234 (1818), and Mills v. Duryee, 11 U.S. (7 Cranch) 481 (1813). These decisions held that the 1790 statute requiring "every court within the United States" to give to records and judicial proceedings "such faith and credit as they have . . . in the court of the state from whence [they] . . . are . . . taken," Act of May 26, 1790, ch. 11, 1 Stat. 122, 122, *amended by* Act of Mar. 27, 1804, ch. 56, §§ 1, 2, 2 Stat. 298, 298-99 (current version at 28 U.S.C. § 1738 (1976)), gave judgments the same effect as in the state rendering them. Because the statutory terms "faith and credit" parrot those of U.S. CONST. art. IV, § 1, these decisions are of relevance in construing the Constitution itself; there are scholars who endorse Justice Johnson's dissenting view in *Mills* that "faith and credit" referred only to admissibility in evidence, 11 U.S. (7 Cranch) at 485-87; *see, e.g.*, Whitten, *The Constitutional Limitations on State-Court Jurisdiction: A Historical-Interpretative Reexamination of the Full Faith and Credit and Due Process Clauses* (pt. 1), 14 CREIGHTON L. REV. 499, 566-67 (1980). Yet as a constitutional question the issue seems unimportant, since article IV expressly authorizes Congress to prescribe not only "the Manner in which such Acts, Records, and Proceedings shall be proved," but also the "Effect thereof." U.S. CONST. art. IV, § 1; *see* Cook, *The Powers of Congress under the Full Faith and Credit Clause*, 28 YALE L.J. 421 (1919). The opinions in *Hampton* and *Mills* are brief and conclusory.

Conclusion to Part Two

We all knew beforehand that Marshall's time was a time of great decisions; to see them all together makes quite an impression. Substantively the cases tend to confirm the popular view that the Court under Marshall construed federal powers generously and put teeth into constitutional limits on the states. The Court may have pushed beyond the Framers in attempting to make the contract clause cover certain takings of private property, in finding an implicit immunity of federal instrumentalities from taxation, in circumventing the apparent purpose of the eleventh amendment, and in suggesting, without holding, that the commerce clause implicitly limited state power. Nevertheless, it is difficult to say with any certainty that the Marshall Court was ever clearly wrong. Nor was the Court unfailingly nationalistic. In its later years it held back from pushing the logic of the contract clause to extreme conclusions; it resolved a debatable issue against the exclusivity of the federal bankruptcy power; its interpretations of the diversity and admiralty clauses were quite modest; and in both *McCulloch* and in *Gibbons*, the two great decisions sustaining federal legislative power, Marshall emphasized the limited nature of Congress's authority. On the whole the Marshall Court seems to have steered a statesmanlike course between the competing centrifugal and centripetal forces; at Marshall's death it could still be said, as in 1789, that the federal government was neither feeble nor of unlimited powers.

When we attempt to analyze the work of individual Justices, the most striking fact is that most of Marshall's brethren were nearly invisible. The old Federalists appointed before Marshall (Cushing, Paterson, Chase, and Moore) spoke a total of three paragraphs in constitutional cases after he was appointed.[1] Todd, Livingston, and Duvall passed through without writing a single constitutional opinion, though together they sat for a total of sixty years. Washington wrote a handful of opinions in thirty years, nearly all of them about the contract clause and only two of them for the

---

[1] *See supra* chapter 3 (discussing *Stuart v. Laird*).

194

Court.[2] Trimble wrote once, for himself alone, to uphold the prospective bankruptcy law.[3] Thompson, another relative latecomer, dissented from several decisions striking down state laws[4] and joined the majority, also on behalf of state rights, in the one case in which Marshall openly dissented;[5] yet he also dissented from the denial of jurisdiction in the first Cherokee case.[6] McLean, appointed in 1829, showed signs of independence and strength in two important separate opinions, vigorously nationalist in arguing for exclusive powers concerning Indians but lenient toward the states on bills of credit.[7] Baldwin, appointed in 1830, took the opposite position from McLean on both these issues. Both Justices belonged essentially to the Taney period, as did James Wayne, who participated in none of the constitutional decisions under Marshall.

Of Marshall's fifteen colleagues only Story and Johnson wrote enough to demonstrate much in the way of individual style, and even they were minor figures. Story could write a more lawyerlike opinion than Marshall, as his opinions in *Martin v. Hunter's Lessee* and in *Trustees of Dartmouth College* showed, with more concern for precedent and for the purposes underlying the Constitution. *Terrett v. Taylor* and *The Thomas Jefferson*,[8] however, showed him equally capable of resolving critical issues by bald fiat and equally susceptible to the siren song of natural law. With the possible exception of *Houston v. Moore*, where Marshall's vote was not disclosed, Story seems to have disagreed only once with his Chief Justice in a constitutional case: he would have upheld jurisdiction in *Cherokee Nation*.[9]

Johnson was more interesting than Story because he was more independent, differing with Marshall more often than any of his colleagues,[10] though often only with respect to the reasons supporting the decision. Sometimes Johnson was less willing than the majority to extend federal judicial power: he voted against a broad view of the arising-under jurisdiction in *Osborn v. Bank of the United States*, in favor of state sovereign immunity in *Bank of the United States v. Planters' Bank*, against original habeas corpus jurisdiction in *Ex parte Bollman*, and he wrote separately in *Martin v. Hunter's Lessee* to say the state court could not be ordered to obey the Supreme Court's mandate. Moreover, sometimes he was less vigorous than Marshall

[2]*See supra* chapter 5, notes 170, 174-75, 205-39, 278-89, and accompanying text (discussing *Mason v. Haile, Green v. Biddle, Ogden v. Saunders,* and *Satterlee v. Mathewson*); *supra* chapter 4 (discussing *Houston v. Moore*).

[3]*See supra* chapter 5, notes 215-39 and accompanying text (discussing *Ogden v. Saunders*).

[4]*See supra* chapter 6, notes 72-73, 128-62, 229-30, and accompanying text (discussing *Weston v. City Council, Brown v. Maryland,* and *Craig v. Missouri*). Thompson also wrote for the Court in upholding a state law opening debtors' prisons in *Mason v. Haile. See supra* chapter 5, notes 169-70 and accompanying text.

[5]*See supra* chapter 5, notes 205-60 and accompanying text (discussing *Ogden v. Saunders*).

[6]*See supra* chapter 4 (discussing *Cherokee Nation v. Georgia*).

[7]*See supra* chapter 6, notes 177-79, 231-32, and accompanying text (discussing *Worcester v. Georgia* and *Craig v. Missouri*).

[8]23 U.S. (10 Wheat.) 428 (1825); *see supra* chapter 4.

[9]Story's 1833 treatise is largely a compendium of Marshall opinions and of excerpts from *The Federalist. See generally* J. STORY, *supra* chapter 5, note 42. But see J. McCLELLAN, *supra* chapter 5, note 116, at 307, arguing that Story was the "pillar of the Marshall Court" and that Marshall was "so unsure of himself that he must constantly exploit the mind of Mr. Justice Story."

[10]*See* D. MORGAN, *supra* chapter 5, note 203, at 178-79, 188.

in enforcing limitations on the states: he voted to uphold prospective bankruptcy laws in *Ogden*, taxation of federal securities in *Weston*, and the loan certificates in *Craig v. Missouri*.

Far more remarkable than these divergences, however, were the wide area of Johnson's agreement with Marshall and the respectful manner in which he usually couched his occasional dissentient views, as exemplified by *Craig*. Indeed, when it came to the protection of vested rights from state action he was more interventionist than Marshall, resting his concurrence in *Fletcher* squarely on natural law and fighting a futile rearguard action in *Satterlee*. He alone argued in *Ogden v. Saunders* that the diversity jurisdiction was exclusive, and it was he, not Marshall, who wanted to rest *Gibbons v. Ogden* on the exclusivity of the federal commerce power. Johnson could be as conclusory as Marshall (*The Aurora*), as inattentive to detail (*Bank of Columbia v. Okely*), as confused as any other Justice (*Ogden v. Saunders*); at times he could point out serious flaws in Marshall's reasoning (*Craig, Planters' Bank*). In general his opinions do not come across as high on the scale of legal craftsmanship; he seems to have been led less by his head than by his heart.[11]

This brings us to the man at center stage, who impressed thirty-four years of constitutional decision with his own personality as no one else has ever come close to doing. In later years the cognoscenti have rightly come to think of Chief Justices as essentially one voice among nine. But from 1801 to 1835 the Supreme Court was the Marshall Court; this utter domination is perhaps the greatest tribute to the force of John Marshall.

And his opinions? The sample is extensive and varied. Often, like his predecessors, he would toss off a constitutional issue in a single conclusory paragraph or less, as with the original jurisdiction in *Ex parte Bollman*, the complete-diversity rule in *Strawbridge v. Curtiss*,[12] the delegation issue in *Wayman v. Southard*, the exclusivity of the naturalization power in *Chirac*, and the legality of damming a navigable stream in *Willson*. At the opposite extreme he would write at great length on issues that seemed frivolous, as in *Dartmouth College*, or that were foreclosed by precedent, as in *Cohens v. Virginia*.

His disdain for precedent in general was extraordinary, even when it squarely supported him; neither *McCulloch*, nor *Cohens*, nor *Dartmouth*, nor *Hodgson v. Bowerbank*,[13] nor even *Marbury v. Madison* was, as Marshall led us to believe, essentially a case of first impression. In contrast, there were early cases such as *Bollman* and *The Charming Betsy*[14] in which he gave excessive weight to precedents in which the issue had not been argued—a position he seems to have soon outgrown.

In contrast to his predecessors, who had construed a statute narrowly to avoid holding it unconstitutional,[15] Marshall went out of his way in *Marbury* to create a

[11]For a fascinating account of the temporal variations in Johnson's pattern of expressing his own opinions, see *id.* at 168-89. Morgan attributed the marked increase in separate opinions after 1823 to a letter from Johnson's old mentor, Thomas Jefferson, urging that every judge "'prove by his reasoning that he had read the papers, that he has considered the case, and that in the application of the law to it, he uses his own judgment.'" *Id.* at 183 (quoting letter from Thomas Jefferson to William Johnson (Mar. 4, 1823)).

[12]7 U.S. (3 Cranch) 267 (1806); *see supra* chapter 3.

[13]9 U.S. (5 Cranch) 303 (1809); *see supra* chapter 3.

[14]Murray v. The Schooner Charming Betsy, 6 U.S. (2 Cranch) 64 (1804), discussed in chapter 1 *supra*. *See also supra* chapter 3 (discussing *Ex parte Bollman*).

[15]*See* Mossman v. Higginson, 4 U.S. (4 Dall.) 12 (1800); *supra* chapter 1.

conflict by statutory interpretation. Similarly, although in *Cohens* he felt impelled in
retracting some careless dicta to inveigh against the dangers of obiter comments, he
seldom missed the opportunity to rest a decision on two or three grounds when one
would have sufficed, as in *Planters' Bank*, or to pick the more difficult ground for
decision, as on the question of the state as a party in *Cohens*, or to pass on issues not
necessarily presented, like the merits in *Marbury*, the exclusivity of the commerce
clause in *Gibbons*, and the possible extra-constitutional limitations in *Fletcher v.
Peck*.

Sometimes Marshall was highly literal in his reliance on the constitutional text, as
in denying diversity jurisdiction for the District of Columbia in the face of powerful
arguments respecting the Framers' purposes; at other times, like Jay and Wilson in
the earlier *Chisholm* case, he reduced the applicable text to an afterthought, most
prominently in *Marbury v. Madison*. He succeeded in *Marbury* in persuading us not
so much that judicial review could be found in the Constitution, but that it ought to
have been put there; time and again he seems to have been writing a brief for a
conclusion reached independently of the Constitution. Repeatedly he ran oblivious
over obvious difficulties raised by dissenting opinions, as in the bill-of-credit case and
on the sovereign immunity question in *Planters' Bank*. At other times he endorsed
unsatisfying distinctions that would prove troublesome to his successors in order to
explain away embarrassing precedents: witness the concessions for state health laws
in *Gibbons*, for state taxation of bank stock in *McCulloch*, for retail taxes in *Brown*,
and for remedial laws affecting contracts in *Sturges*. In *McCulloch*, *Brown*, and
Worcester he failed to identify clearly just what it was that state law conflicted with:
the Constitution itself, a statute, or a treaty. When he relied on history he tended to
state it on his own authority without supporting citations. He had a strong tendency,
as seen in *McCulloch*, *Fisher*, and *Craig*, to devote his energies to straw men and to
shortchange the difficult issue. In short, though Marshall has been generally
admired,[16] it is difficult to find a single Marshall opinion that puts together the
relevant legal arguments in a convincing way.

Andrew McLaughlin once wrote that if Marshall had been a better lawyer, he
would not have been so great a judge.[17] Just what this means I am not certain; if the
suggestion is that the law is of marginal relevance to judges, I would have to dissent

---

[16]*See, e.g.*, J. THAYER, JOHN MARSHALL 57 (1901) (calling Marshall "preeminent" in the constitutional
field: "first, with no one second"); Esterline, *Acts of Congress Declared Unconstitutional*, 38 AM. L. REV.
21, 41 (1904):

> [I]f at this hour the world were called upon to close and render up its account to the Creator .
> . . and the United States of America were reached on the roll, and its inhabitants from the
> beginning were signaled to nominate one personage as their loftiest illustration of man who
> was created in His image, how well, oh, how well, they could stand unanimously agreed in
> awarding the glory, and sending up . . . the revered, magisterial and immortal name — John
> Marshall!

Justice Frankfurter echoed Holmes's view that Marshall was the "'one alone' to be chosen 'if American
law were to be represented by a single figure,'" Frankfurter, *supra* chapter 6, note 127, at 217 (quoting
O.W. HOLMES, *John Marshall*, in COLLECTED LEGAL PAPERS 270 (1920)).

[17]A. MCLAUGHLIN, A CONSTITUTIONAL HISTORY OF THE UNITED STATES 300 (1935) (adding that "his
duties called for the talent and insight of a statesman capable of looking beyond the confines of legal
learning"). *See also* E. CORWIN, *supra* chapter 5, note 41, at 42 (1919), arguing that Marshall's unstudious
habits contributed to his achievement: "he made more use of his brain than of his bookshelf."

on the basis of the supremacy clause. In any event, while it is always risky to judge the past by modern standards, it seems to me Marshall would have lost nothing in his eminence as a judge if he had refrained from such blatant overstatements as that written constitutions necessarily contemplate judicial review, strengthened *Cohens* and *Dartmouth* by invoking precedent, avoided reaching out for issues that did not need to be decided, as in *Gibbons*,[18] or told his audience in *McCulloch* whether the state tax offended the statute or the Constitution.

Marshall was a strong man with a fascinating style, a strong sense of where he was going, and wonderfully sound instincts in the building of a constitution. Whatever his technical shortcomings, one who reads many of Marshall's opinions seems likely to find merit in Thayer's verdict that Marshall was "one of the greatest, noblest and most engaging characters in American history."[19] Marshall's time was one of those in which it would be exciting to have lived; and Marshall was one of those people it would be nice to have been.

[18]*But see* Frankfurter, *supra* chapter 6, note 127, at 221 ("To slight these phases of his opinion as dicta, though such they were on a technical view, is to disregard significant aspects of his labors and the way in which constitutional law develops.") *But cf.* Frankfurter, *Note on Advisory Opinions*, 37 HARV. L. REV. 1002 (1924) (discussing the dangers of advisory opinions).

[19]J. THAYER, *supra* note 16, at 157.

Part Three

Chief Justice Taney
1836–1864

Introduction to Part Three

The appointment of Roger B. Taney as Chief Justice in 1836 marked a watershed in the membership of the Court.[1] President Jackson had appointed three new Justices in the seven years before Taney: John McLean, Henry Baldwin, and James M. Wayne. Within a year, Jackson and President Van Buren were to appoint three

[1]

JUSTICES OF THE SUPREME COURT DURING THE TIME OF CHIEF JUSTICE TANEY

		1835	40	45	50	55	60	65
Joseph Story	(1811-1845)	⊢————————————⊣						
Smith Thompson	(1823-1843)	⊢——————————⊣						
John McLean	(1829-1861)	⊢————————————————————————————⊣						
Henry Baldwin	(1830-1844)	⊢———————————⊣						
James M. Wayne	(1835-1867)	⊢——————————————————————————————⊣						
Roger B. Taney	(1836-1864)	⊢————————————————————————————⊣						
Philip P. Barbour	(1836-1841)	⊢——⊣						
John Catron	(1837-1865)	⊢——————————————————————————————⊣						
John McKinley	(1837-1852)	⊢————————————⊣						
Peter V. Daniel	(1841-1860)	⊢——————————————⊣						
Samuel Nelson	(1845-1872)	⊢————————————————————⊣						
Levi Woodbury	(1845-1851)	⊢———⊣						
Robert C. Grier	(1846-1870)	⊢——————————————⊣						
Benjamin R. Curtis	(1851-1857)	⊢———⊣						
John A. Campbell	(1853-1861)	⊢———⊣						
Nathan Clifford	(1858-1881)	⊢——————⊣						
Noah H. Swayne	(1862-1881)	⊢——⊣						
Samuel F. Miller	(1862-1890)	⊢——⊣						
David Davis	(1862-1877)	⊢——⊣						
Stephen J. Field	(1863-1897)	⊢——⊣						

SOURCE: (G. GUNTHER, CASES AND MATERIALS ON CONSTITUTIONAL LAW app. A, at A-2, A-3 (10th ed. 1980)).

more: Philip P. Barbour, John Catron, and John McKinley.[2] Of the Justices who sat with Marshall before 1829, only Joseph Story and Smith Thompson remained. Thus, from nearly the beginning of his tenure, Taney presided over an almost entirely new Court, one with seven members appointed by Jackson and Van Buren. It was an opportunity for a fresh start.

Taney's term stretched from the age of Jackson until almost the end of the Civil War. Twenty Justices sat during these twenty-eight years. Four of Taney's original brethren—Barbour, Baldwin, Thompson, and Story—left the Court between 1841 and 1845. During the next fifteen years, as in the middle days of Marshall,[3] the Court enjoyed a notable stability in membership. Seven Justices sat together from 1846 to 1860: Taney, McLean, Wayne, Catron, Peter V. Daniel, Samuel Nelson, and Robert C. Grier. McKinley, Levi Woodbury, Benjamin R. Curtis, and John A. Campbell effectively completed the roster during this period. The remaining five Justices—Nathan Clifford, Noah H. Swayne, Samuel F. Miller, David Davis, and Stephen J. Field—appeared only briefly at the end of Taney's Chief Justiceship, as forerunners of the next sea change in Court membership. Taney's tenure ended as it began, with a whole generation of Justices ending their careers at nearly the same time.

Accomplishments sometimes end before careers, however, and the Supreme Court had been in a somewhat suspended state before Taney appeared on the scene. The bulk of Marshall's architectural work—federal judicial power to protect federal rights, congressional authority to regulate navigation and establish a bank, and significant limitations on state legislative power—had been completed by about 1825.[4] New Justices like McLean, Baldwin, and Thompson broke more frequently with the Marshall consensus, taking a less restrictive view of limitations on state authority. As the absences of Justices Duvall and Johnson increased, three major constitutional cases were deferred due to inability to muster a majority of the full Court. In 1835 and 1836 three vacancies occurred, and the Court decided no important constitutional cases.[5] History was waiting for the new Chief Justice.

[2]Congress created two new seats on the Court by the Act of Mar. 3, 1837, ch. 34, § 1, 5 Stat. 176, 176 (current version at 28 U.S.C. § 1 (1976)). A number of new states had been without circuit justices and thus without circuit courts before this expansion. *See* 5 C. SWISHER, HISTORY OF THE SUPREME COURT OF THE UNITED STATES 58 (1974).

[3]*See supra* part two.

[4]*See generally id.*

[5]*See generally* G. GUNTHER, *supra* note 1, app. A, at A-2, A-3.

7

Contracts and Commerce

The new era opened with a bang in 1837, when the three big cases so long postponed were finally decided: *New York v. Miln*,[1] *Briscoe v. Bank of Kentucky*,[2] and *Charles River Bridge v. Warren Bridge*.[3] Each concerned limitations on state power; in each the Court upheld state authority; in each Story wrote an impassioned dissent lamenting the dismantling of all that Marshall had built. Despite a flock of Republican appointments, Jefferson and Madison had failed to dislodge the Federalist philosophy from its last citadel in the courts; Jackson and Van Buren now had apparently succeeded.

Overall, however, the 1837 decisions proved to have created a false impression. In certain respects the Court continued to be somewhat more solicitous of state authority under Taney than it had been under Marshall. Yet Taney and his brethren not only wielded the contract clause with considerable vigor to protect vested rights against state impairment, but also (with one notorious exception) forcefully extended the limits of federal legislative and judicial power. None of this was accomplished with the unanimity that had characterized the best days of Marshall; repeated dissents by true states'-righters like Campbell and Daniel highlighted just how far from that category Taney and most of his colleagues were. At the same time, Taney abandoned Marshall's insistence on writing nearly everything himself; accordingly, in this part we shall examine the judicial product of quite a number of Justices.[4]

---

[1]36 U.S. (11 Pet.) 102 (1837).

[2]36 U.S. (11 Pet.) 257 (1837).

[3]36 U.S. (11 Pet.) 420 (1837).

[4]The best general Court histories of the period as a whole are C. SWISHER, *supra* introduction to part 3, note 2, and 2 C. WARREN, THE SUPREME COURT IN UNITED STATES HISTORY (rev. ed. 1926). Biographies of Justices of the time include H. CONNOR, JOHN ARCHIBALD CAMPBELL (1920); Curtis, *Memoir of Benjamin Robbins Curtis*, in 1 A MEMOIR OF BENJAMIN ROBBINS CURTIS, LL. D. (B. R. Curtis, Jr. ed. 1879); G. DUNNE, JUSTICE JOSEPH STORY AND THE RISE OF THE SUPREME COURT (1970); J. FRANK, JUSTICE DANIEL DISSENTING (1964); A. LAWRENCE, JAMES MOORE WAYNE, SOUTHERN UNIONIST (1943); J. MCCLELLAN,

I. THE THREE BOMBSHELLS OF 1837

A. *New York v. Miln*

As part of a scheme for preventing immigrants from becoming public charges, a New York statute required ship captains to furnish local authorities with a list of all passengers they brought into the state.[5] Over Story's dissent, the Court held that this requirement did not conflict with Congress's power to regulate foreign commerce.[6]

Four Marshall decisions had touched on the negative effects of the commerce clause on state authority, but none had clearly struck down a state law on commerce clause grounds. *Gibbons v. Ogden*[7] had invalidated a state steamboat monopoly; *Brown v. Maryland*[8] had set aside a tax on the privilege of selling imported goods in their original package; *Worcester v. Georgia*[9] had held the state could not prohibit whites from living on the Cherokee Reservation; *Willson v. Black Bird Creek Marsh Co.*[10] had allowed the damming of a navigable stream. The first three cases variously intimated that the commerce clause might have a negative effect of its own, but each also recited alternative grounds of decision. In *Willson*, stressing that no federal statute forbade construction of the dam, Marshall concluded that the law in question could not, "under all the circumstances of the case, be considered as repugnant to the power to regulate commerce in its dormant state."[11]

All four Justices who wrote in *Miln* took these precedents quite seriously.[12] Justice Barbour, a "states-right's Virginian"[13] appointed just the year before *Miln*, wrote for the Court a relatively straightforward opinion leaving open the question whether Congress possessed exclusive authority to regulate commerce.[14] The Court had already acknowledged in *Gibbons* that the states could constitutionally affect commerce by such exercises of the police power as quarantine and inspection laws;[15] the law requiring a passenger list was similarly a police measure designed to protect the

---

JOSEPH STORY AND THE AMERICAN CONSTITUTION (1971); C. SWISHER, ROGER B. TANEY (1936); F. WIESENBURGER, THE LIFE OF JOHN MCLEAN (1937).

[5]Act of Feb. 11, 1824, ch. 37, 1824 N.Y. Laws 27.

[6]New York v. Miln, 36 U.S. (11 Pet.) 102 (1837). The statute also required the master to post a bond to cover expenditures if the immigrant became a public charge, and to remove him from the country in such event. Act of Feb. 11, 1824, ch. 37, §§ II, III, 1824 N. Y. Laws 27, 27-28. The suit in *Miln* did not involve these provisions, and the Court did not rule on them. *See Miln* 36 U.S. (11 Pet.) at 144-45 (Thompson, J., concurring).

[7]22 U.S. (9 Wheat.) 1 (1824).

[8]25 U.S. (12 Wheat.) 419 (1827).

[9]31 U.S. (6 Pet.) 515 (1832).

[10]27 U.S. (2 Pet.) 245 (1829).

[11]*Id.* at 252. For discussion of these cases, see *supra* chapter 6.

[12]The official report contains the opinions of Justices Barbour, Thompson, and Story. *Miln*, 36 U.S. (11 Pet.) at 130, 143, 153. Justice Baldwin later published a separate opinion. *See infra* note 19. For the Marshall Court's contrasting tendency to ignore precedent, see *supra* chapter 6.

[13]*See* C. SWISHER, *supra* note 4, at 139, 360; C. SWISHER, *supra*, introduction to part 3, note 2, at 56.

[14] *Miln*, 36 U.S. (11 Pet.) at 132.

[15]*Id.* at 133, 141-42 (citing *Gibbons*); *see Gibbons*, 22 U.S. (9 Wheat.) at 205 (Marshall, C.J.). For criticism of this distinction as an original matter, see *supra* chapter 6.

welfare of New Yorkers by keeping down the tax burden.[16] A state had as much right to guard against "the moral pestilence of paupers, vagabonds, and possibly convicts," Barbour added crudely, as against "the physical pestilence" of infected crews and cargo.[17] Thompson's literate concurrence added a citation to *Willson*, in which Marshall had apparently elevated his police power dictum into a holding.[18] Thompson also questionably took *Willson* as authority that Congress's power to regulate commerce itself was not exclusive.[19]

In dissent, Story agreed that the states could affect commerce by exercising their police powers and seemed to concede that therefore they could exclude paupers.[20] He argued, however, that the passenger list requirement did more than affect commerce: it regulated commerce itself, namely, "the conduct of masters, and owners and passengers, in foreign trade."[21] Though the states might pass health laws and other police power measures, said Story, they "cannot make a regulation of commerce, to enforce" them,[22] for *Gibbons* had settled that Congress had exclusive power to regulate commerce.[23]

Gibbons, of course, had settled no such thing. As Thompson pointed out in his concurrence,[24] *Gibbons* held only that state law must yield when it contradicted a federal statute—Marshall's suggestions about the exclusivity of the commerce power were obiter as well as inconclusive.[25] Moreover, Story's position seems inconsistent both with his own concessions about the exclusion of paupers and with Marshall's

[16] *Miln*, 36 U.S. (11 Pet.) at 141. New York had passed the law, wrote Barbour, "to prevent her citizens from being oppressed by the support of multitudes of poor persons . . . [without] the means of supporting themselves." *Id.*

[17] *Id.* at 142-43. In distinguishing *Brown v. Maryland*, Barbour added unnecessarily that, unlike goods, persons "are not the subject of commerce." *Id.* at 136. This remark was later to be the focus of serious controversy within the Court. *See infra* text accompanying notes 222-24 (discussing the *Passenger Cases*).

[18] *See Willson*, 27 U.S. (2 Pet.) at 149-50; *supra* chapter 6.

[19] *Miln*, 36 U.S. (11 Pet.) at 149-53. Thompson expressly refrained from deciding the extent of Congress's power over commerce, but at one point he seemed to suggest Congress might lack capacity to legislate with respect to passengers already landed. *Id.* at 146-47. Justice Baldwin later made the same point explicitly in a long and boring statement. *See* 36 U.S. (11 Pet.) at 152-53 (3d ed. 1884), *originally published in* H. BALDWIN, A GENERAL VIEW OF THE ORIGIN AND NATURE OF THE CONSTITUTION AND GOVERNMENT OF THE UNITED STATES 181 (1837), *reprinted in* 9 L. Ed. 961 (1883 ed.). Baldwin explained that later events had caused him to abandon his "intention" of "a silent concurrence," and that he had also abandoned a plan to publish the opinion "in an appendix" to the official reports. *See* 9 L. Ed. at 873, 928. It thus seems unclear that Baldwin ever considered the statement an actual concurring opinion. *Cf.* C. HAINES & F. SHERWOOD, THE ROLE OF THE SUPREME COURT IN AMERICAN POLITICS 1835-1864 46 n. 61 (1957) (statement "accidentally omitted").

Justice Wayne later asserted that Thompson, initially assigned to write for the Court, could not secure the needed majority "on account of some expressions . . . concerning the power of Congress to regulate commerce." *Passenger Cases*, 48 U.S. (7 How.) 283, 431 (1849) (separate opinion).

[20] *Miln*, 36 U.S. (11 Pet.) at 156.

[21] *Id.* at 157.

[22] *Id.* at 156.

[23] *Id.* at 158. Story also argued the state law was contrary to federal statutes he read as "authoriz[ing] . . . the introduction of passengers into the country." *Id.* at 158-59. As both Barbour and Thompson noted, however, these statutes seemed remote from the issue: they regulated shipboard safety and required delivery of passenger lists to federal authorities for customs and census purposes. *Id.* at 138, 146.

[24] *Id.* at 145.

[25] *See supra* chapter 6.

discussion of quarantine laws in *Gibbons.*[26] A law excluding paupers or quarantining vessels is no less a regulation of commerce than is a requirement that the master provide a passenger list. Indeed, as Barbour noted,[27] the statute in *Miln* required delivery of the list after the passengers landed, while the quarantine and exclusion laws interrupted transportation itself. If such interruptions are acceptable because they are enacted under the police power label, the list requirement should be too.[28]

Story stood alone in dissent, but he invoked his departed leader for support. Marshall had heard the arguments before he died and had agreed, said Story, that the New York law fell "directly within the principles established" by *Gibbons* and *Brown v. Maryland.*[29] This remarkable breach of the confidentiality of Court deliberations has led at least one commentator to accuse Story of misrepresenting Marshall's position.[30] None of Marshall's other former colleagues stepped up to dispute Story's account, however; more likely, the Chief Justice had begun to regret his broad concessions to the states' police power.

Even if Story was right that Marshall would have joined his dissent in *Miln*, the majority opinion does not seem to represent the sudden break with Marshall's earlier jurisprudence that Story claimed. On the contrary, the majority seems to have applied Marshall's own declared principles fairly and accurately to sustain state power in an easy case.[31]

B. *Briscoe v. Bank of Kentucky*

The Bank of Kentucky, a corporation owned and controlled by the state, issued a negotiable instrument payable to the bearer in exchange for Briscoe's promissory note. When the Bank sued to collect on the note, Briscoe defended on grounds of illegal consideration, arguing that the instrument issued by the bank had offended the provision of article I, section 10, that "[n]o State shall . . . emit Bills of Credit."[32] The state courts rejected this argument, and the Supreme Court affirmed, once again over Story's solitary dissent.[33]

---

[26]It also seems inconsistent with Story's own statement in his treatise, 2 J. Story, Commentaries on the Constitution of the United States 515 (Boston 1833), that the commerce and police powers might be carried out by the "same means."

[27]*Miln*, 36 U.S. (11 Pet.) at 142.

[28]*See* Greeley, *What Is the Test of a Regulation of Foreign or Interstate Commerce?*, 1 Harv. L. Rev. 159, 166 (1887). One of the weaknesses of Marshall's thesis was that the police power concept was hardly self-defining. The Court made no serious effort in *Miln* or elsewhere to define it, but even Story's dissent conceded that "poor laws" and the exclusion of paupers were police power measures. *Id.* at 156.

[29]*Id.* at 161. Confirming this account without citation, Marshall's biographer added that Johnson and Devall had taken the same position, but that the former's absence had prevented a decision. 4 A. Beveridge, The Life of John Marshall 583 (1919).

[30]*See* McGovney, *A Supreme Court Fiction*, 56 Harv. L. Rev. 853, 877-78 (1943).

[31]*See* J. Nowak, R. Rotunda & J. Young, Handbook on Constitutional Law 247 (1978); C. Warren, *supra* note 4, at 27. Chancellor Kent, however, agreed with Story. 1 J. Kent, Commentaries on American Law 439 n.b. (4th ed. 1840). *See also* R. Newmyer, The Supreme Court under Marshall and Taney 102 (1968), contending, among other things, that *Miln* "flatly contradicted the *Gibbons* opinion which gave federal law priority in case of conflict," but not identifying any conflicting federal law.

[32]U.S. Const. art. I § 10, cl. 1.

[33]Briscoe v. Bank of Kentucky, 36 U.S. (11 Pet.) 257 (1837).

As in *Miln*, the opinions dealt largely with precedent. Only seven years earlier, in *Craig v. Missouri*,[34] the Court had divided four to three in striking down certificates issued by Missouri under the bills of credit clause. Story's dissent focused on Marshall's broad interpretation of the clause in that case: "'it must comprehend the emission of any paper medium by a state government, for the purposes of common circulation.'"[35] In a sparkling display of scholarship, Story gave numerous examples of early issues of paper that had been denominated "bills of credit" even though they were not legal tender, even though special funds were established for their redemption, even though they were payable to bearer on demand, even though they involved no explicit pledge of government credit, and even though they were acceptable in payment of taxes.[36] Experience had shown, he argued, that none of these devices sufficed to prevent depreciation in value, the mischief the bills of credit clause was designed to prevent.[37] Finally, if the state could do through a wholly-owned corporation what it could not do directly, "the prohibition is a dead letter. It is worse than a mockery."[38] Marshall, he noted once again, had agreed that the law in *Briscoe* was unconstitutional.[39]

Responding for the majority, Justice McLean acknowledged that the bills to which the Framers objected had included those payable on demand, chargeable to a fund, or not made legal tender, and that a state could not issue bills of credit indirectly through a corporation.[40] However, he concluded, in contrast to *Craig*, the bank in *Briscoe* had issued the instrument on its own credit, not on that of the state. Unlike the state itself, the bank could be sued without its consent, and thus all its assets could be seized to satisfy the obligation.[41] Thompson, concurring again, put the same point clearly and concisely:

> The two great infirmities which attended the bills of credit which circulated as money, and come within the mischief intended to be guarded against by the constitutional prohibition, were the want of some real and substantial fund being provided for their payment and redemption, and no mode provided for enforcing payment . . . , [as the agent who signed the bills] could not . . . be made personally responsible . . . ; and the State was not suable . . . . [T]heir credit depended solely upon the faith and voluntary will of the State; and were therefore purely bills of credit. But that is not the situation or character of the bills of the bank in question.

[34] 29 U.S. (4 Pet.) 410 (1830); *see supra* chapter 6.
[35] *Briscoe*, 36 U.S. (11 Pet.) at 329 (Story, J., dissenting) (quoting *Craig*, 29 U.S. (4 Pet.) at 432 (Marshall, C.J.)). In contrast to *Craig*, the facts in *Briscoe* did not suggest the possibility that the state had, in effect, issued a promissory note for borrowed money, which all agreed it could do. *See Briscoe*, 36 U.S. (11 Pet.) at 327-28 (Thompson, J., concurring); *id.* at 331 (Story, J., dissenting) *Craig*, 29 U.S. (4 Pet.) at 431-32 (Marshall, C.J.); *id.* at 443 (Johnson, J., concurring); *id.* at 455-56 (McLean, J., dissenting).
[36] *Briscoe*, 36 U.S. (11 Pet.) at 333-39.
[37] *Id.* at 339.
[38] *Id.* at 348.
[39] *Id.* at 328; *see also* A. BEVERIDGE, *supra* note 29, at 583.
[40] *Briscoe*, 36 U.S. (11 Pet.) at 312-13, 318, 319.
[41] *Id.* at 321. In this connection it may be significant that the Framers forbade only states and not private bankers from issuing paper money. The state court had said only that *Craig* was "distinguishable in at least one important and essential particular" without saying what that particular was. Briscoe v. Bank of the Commonwealth, 30 Ky. (7 J.J. Marsh.) 349, 349 (1832).

There is an ample fund provided for their redemption, and they are
issued by a corporation which can be sued, and payment enforced in the
courts of justice.[42]

Story answered the majority by arguing that the opportunity to sue the bank was
an illusory safeguard because the state could abolish the bank, reclaim its assets, and
leave the holders of bank paper without remedy.[43] The conclusion that such a course
would have been constitutional seems hasty: although the bank could hardly object
to anything the state might do with its own property, destruction of the bank's ability
to pay might well have impaired its contractual obligation to the bill holder in
violation of an adjacent clause of article I, section 10.[44] Even so, Story might have
responded, the state could not be sued to undo its misdeed; whether the holder could
collect his due would depend upon whether any state officer was suable under the
uncertain criteria laid down by Marshall in *Osborn v. Bank of the United States*[45] and
Governor of Georgia v. Madrazo.[46]

The bills of credit clause is seldom heard of today; its function is now largely
supplanted in practice by federal statutes regulating the money supply.[47] Several
commentators have agreed with Story that *Briscoe* essentially overruled *Craig* and
cut the heart out of the clause,[48] but I think *Briscoe* was a hard case in which the
opposing opinions dealt intelligently with the competing considerations.[49]

---

[42]*Briscoe*, 36 U.S. (11 Pet.) at 327-28. As in *Miln, see supra* note 19, the third edition of the official
reports contains a long and boring concurring opinion by Baldwin that did not appear in the original. 36
U.S. (11 Pet.) at 327-28s (3d ed. 1884), *originally published in* H. BALDWIN, *supra note* 19, at 113-34,
reprinted in 9 L. Ed. 928 (1883 ed.). The only Justice to join both *Craig* and *Briscoe*, Baldwin explained
that he had disagreed with Marshall's broad definition at the time *Craig* was decided, but had been too
busy and too new on the job to express a separate opinion. 36 U.S. (11 Pet.) at 327-28 (3d ed. 1884). He
had gone along in striking down the Missouri paper because, unlike the one in *Briscoe*, it had been issued
on the credit of the state itself and had been made legal tender for certain debts. *Id.* at 328-28b. In contrast
to McLean and Thompson, Baldwin gave no reasons for his apparently paradoxical contention that it was
better if the state did not promise to redeem. The Court had already rejected his legal-tender argument in
Craig; quite apart from Story's impressive contradictory history in *Briscoe*, that argument made the bills of
credit clause entirely redundant.

[43]*Briscoe*, 36 U.S. (11 Pet.) at 344-45.

[44]U.S. CONST. art. I, § 10, cl. 1 ("No State shall . . . pass any . . . Law impairing the Obligation of
Contracts . . ."); *see* Curran v. Arkansas, 56 U.S. (15 How.) 304, 319-20 (1853) (removal of assets from
state-owned bank impaired obligations owed to its creditors).

[45]22 U.S. (9 Wheat.) 738 (1824).

[46]26 U.S. (1 Pet.) 110 (1828); *see supra* chapter 4. *See also* Beers v. Arkansas, 61 U.S. (20 How.) 527
(1858) (dictum) (state may withdraw consent to be sued in its own courts on obligations previously
incurred) (noted *infra* at note 91).

[47]*See, e.g.,* Veazie Bank v. Fenno, 75 U.S. (8 Wall.) 533 (1869) (upholding a prohibitive federal tax on
circulating paper issued by state-chartered banks), *infra* chapter 10; C. SWISHER, *supra* introduction to
part 3, note 2, at 109. The clause was hardly mentioned in a treatise published as early as 1868. *See*
T. COOLEY, CONSTITUTIONAL LIMITATIONS 15 (1868).

[48]*See, e.g.,* J. KENT, *supra* note 31, at 407 n.a.; J. MCCLELLAN, *supra* note 4, at 257-58;
A. MCLAUGHLIN, A CONSTITUTIONAL HISTORY OF THE UNITED STATES 463-64 (1935); R. NEWMYER, *supra*
note 31, at 101; F. WEISENBURGER, *supra* note 4, at 160.

[49]The Court reaffirmed *Briscoe* in Woodruff v. Trapnall, 51 U.S. (10 How.) 190, 205 (1850), and
Darrington v. Bank of Alabama, 54 U.S. (13 How.) 12, 16-17 (1852), both written by McLean.

C. *Charles River Bridge v. Warren Bridge*

In 1785 the Massachusetts legislature granted a corporate charter to the proprietors of the Charles River Bridge, authorizing them to construct a bridge between Boston and Charlestown and to collect tolls for a period later extended to seventy years. In 1828 the legislature authorized another company to build a second bridge adjacent to the first, providing that the new bridge would revert to the state and become toll-free after a maximum of six years. The proprietors of the first bridge argued that the act authorizing the second bridge impaired the obligation of their charter in violation of article I, section 10.[50] The state court held it did not, and a divided Supreme Court affirmed.[51]

Chief Justice Taney's opinion for the Court—his first in a constitutional case—was brief, lucid, and to the point. Rejecting the natural law notions appearing in such early cases as *Calder v. Bull*[52] and *Fletcher v. Peck*,[53] Taney refreshingly insisted the only question was whether the state had promised "not to establish a free bridge at the place where the Warren bridge is erected."[54] Common law precedents established a rule of strict construction for public grants: "'any ambiguity in the terms of the contract, must operate against the adventurers, and in favor of the public, and the plaintiffs can claim nothing that is not clearly given them by the act.'"[55] The charter did not say it granted an exclusive right;[56] legislatures had often authorized roads or railroads adjacent to previously chartered turnpikes without legal challenge;[57] and the same considerations of public interest that had led Marshall to hold in *Providence Bank v. Billings*[58] that a corporate charter did not imply a promise of tax immunity led to the conclusion that the mere right to charge tolls should not imply a promise of exclusivity.[59]

As in the other great cases of the first Taney term, Story dissented vehemently[60]—joined this time by Thompson,[61] whose record had been considerably less restrictive of state authority. Omitting any trace of his earlier flirtations with natural law,[62] Story argued with impressive historical support that the law had never required strict

---

[50]Charles River Bridge v. Warren Bridge, 36 U.S. (11 Pet.) 420, 423-28 (1837).

[51]Taney reported that the state judges had actually been equally divided and had dismissed the complaint to allow the case to be taken to the Supreme Court. *Id.* at 538; *see* Charles River Bridge v. Warren Bridge, 24 Mass (7 Pick.) 344 (1829). For a general discussion of the case, see S. KUTLER, PRIVILEGE AND CREATIVE DESTRUCTION: THE CHARLES RIVER BRIDGE CASE (1971); C. SWISHER, *supra* introduction to part 3, note 2, at 74-98.

[52]3 U.S. (3 Dall.) 386 (1798); *see supra* chapter 2.

[53]10 U.S. (6 Cranch) 87 (1810); *see supra* chapter 5.

[54]*Charles River Bridge,* 36 U.S. (11 Pet.) at 539-40.

[55]*Id.* at 544 (quoting Proprietors of the Stourbridge Canal v. Wheeley, 109 Eng. Rep. 1336, 1337 (K.B. 1831)).

[56]*Charles River Bridge*, 36 U.S. (11 Pet.) at 548-49.

[57]*Id.* at 551-52.

[58]29 U.S. (4 Pet.) 514 (1830); *see supra* chapter 5.

[59]*Charles River Bridge*, 36 U.S. (11 Pet.) at 546-48.

[60]*Id.* at 583.

[61]*Id.* at 650.

[62]*See supra* chapter 5. In this connection, it may well have been significant for Story that the case came from a state rather than a federal court.

construction of public grants that were supported by consideration—as in the case before him, where the proprietors had promised to keep the bridge in good repair.[63] As Coke and other authorities had established, a charter implied "that the legislature shall not do any act directly to prejudice its own grant, or to destroy its value."[64] The Court had so held in *Fletcher v. Peck*,[65] where it found that a conveyance of land contained an implicit promise not to retake the property; in the case at hand, construction of the second bridge had put an end to toll-paying traffic and destroyed the value of the franchise as effectively as an express revocation.[66]

Story seems right this time; finding an implied promise by the state not to destroy what it had given seems no harder in *Charles River Bridge* than in *Fletcher* itself, and Taney's competing precedent allowing a state to tax a corporation it had created[67] was easily distinguishable. As Justice McLean observed in his concurring opinion,[68] the ordinary tax does not in fact destroy; loose language in *McCulloch v. Maryland*[69] notwithstanding, *Fletcher* showed that even Marshall did not believe the state could destroy its own franchise just because it could tax it. Moreover, in interesting contrast to Marshall's bare assertion in *Fletcher* that a grant implied a promise not to reassert title,[70] Story provided an impressive array of common law authorities for his analogous conclusion in *Charles River Bridge*.[71] Taney was unable to refute him, alleging only that many owners of railroads and turnpikes had put up with competitors—he did not say with competitors who had charged nothing—without going to court. Unlike his *Miln* opinion, Story's *Charles River* dissent seems both admirable and convincing.[72]

II. Later Contract Clause Cases

Contract clause cases dominated the Supreme Court's docket in the Taney period even more than they had during that of Marshall. Despite the discouraging tone of

[63]*Charles River Bridge*, 36 U.S. (11 Pet.) at 589-611.

[64]*Id.* at 617.

[65]10 U.S. (6 Cranch) 87 (1810), *cited in Charles River Bridge*, 36 U.S. (11 Pet.) at 617; *see supra* chapter 5.

[66]*Charles River Bridge,* 36 U.S. (11 Pet.) at 615-16. At common law, Story added, the grant of a franchise to hold a market or fair or to operate a ferry was consistently held to be implicitly exclusive; bridges were indistinguishable, and Chancellor Kent had so held. *Id.* at 618-34.

[67]*Id.* at 546-48 (Taney, C.J.).

[68]*Id.* at 566-67. McLean agreed with Story that the franchise was exclusive, but he argued there had been no contractual impairment. The state, McLean argued, had taken the bridgeowners' property without compensation, which a Massachusetts court could give them under the state constitution; but the state had not promised it would not exercise the power of eminent domain. McLean added that, but for *Fletcher*, he would not have thought the contract clause applied to grants at all, but only to executory agreements.

The third edition of the reports also contains Baldwin's third consecutive long and boring concurrence, *see* 36 U.S. (11 Pet.) at 583-83ee (3d ed. 1884), of the same questionable origin as those in *Miln* and *Briscoe. See supra* notes 19, 42. Baldwin agreed with Taney's reasoning and recited prodigious numbers of ancient precedents about ferries in such an unfocused manner as to make Story's more professional use of authority all the more luminous.

[69]17 U.S. (4 Wheat.) 316, 427 (1819); *see supra* chapter 6.

[70]*Fletcher*, 10 U.S. (6 Cranch) at 136-37.

[71]*See supra* note 63.

[72]Webster and Kent thought Taney's decision had destroyed the contract clause. *See* C. Swisher, *supra* note 4, at 378. Later observers have tended to deny that the case represented a sharp break with Marshall's

the *Charles River Bridge* decision, thirty of the over one hundred constitutional decisions between 1837 and 1864 involved contract clause claims. Moreover, Taney and his colleagues enforced the clause vigorously in many cases; it remained the basis of more decisions striking down state legislation than any other clause of the Constitution. Many of the cases had no doctrinal significance, merely applying settled principles to yet another fact situation; the important cases can be discussed in rather short compass.

A.   *Bronson v. Kinzie*

After Kinzie had mortgaged land to Bronson, the Illinois legislature enacted statutes forbidding foreclosure sales for less than two-thirds of market value and giving a mortgagor and his judgment creditors a right to redeem within a year after sale. Over the lone dissent of Justice McLean, the Court held that both laws offended the contract clause.[73]

Decided in 1843, *Bronson* was the first major contract clause case since *Charles River Bridge*. Chief Justice Taney again wrote for the majority, and again the opinion displayed an economy and lucidity of style coupled with a tendency to rely on precedent. There, however, the resemblance ended: the earlier opinion had given a niggardly interpretation of a charter, but in *Bronson*, joined by five of his Democratic brethren,[74] Taney delivered a ringing affirmation of the contract clause.

In Taney's view, the earlier Illinois law giving the mortgagee an unrestricted right to foreclose "entered into the contract, and formed a part of it, without any express stipulation to that effect in the deed."[75] The later statute extending the right of redemption acted "directly upon the contract itself" by giving the mortgagor and his other creditors "an equitable estate in the premises, which neither of them would have been entitled to under the original contract," and thus impaired the initial obligation.[76] That the other provision requiring a sale price at least two-thirds of the land's value "apparently acts upon the remedy"[77] did not save it; although the clause often allowed remedial alterations "render[ing] the recovery of debts more tardy and difficult,"[78] Taney endorsed the Marshall Court's condemnation of acts that "'so

---

jurisprudence, pointing to *Providence Bank. See, e.g.,* B. WRIGHT, THE CONTRACT CLAUSE OF THE CONSTITUTION 63-65 (1938).

This time Story did not say Marshall had agreed with him; and while Swisher reported that he had, C. SWISHER, *supra* note 4, at 363; *see also* C. WARREN, *supra* note 4, at 28, one of the lawyers in the case said he had been "credibly informed" to the contrary. *See* G. DUNNE, *supra* note 4, at 364, & n.18 (1970); S. KUTLER, *supra* note 51, at 172-79; *see also* G. DUNNE, *supra* note 4, at 360 (questioning whether Story should have recused himself, in view of his teaching position at Harvard University, which was entitled to a share of the tolls).

[73]Bronson v. Kinzie, 42 U.S. (1 How.) 311 (1843).

[74]Thompson, Baldwin, Wayne, Catron, and Daniel joined Taney's opinion. Story and McKinley were absent. *Id.* at 322 n.*. As we shall see, in McKinley's case absences were not at all unusual. Story later expressed warm support for the opinion in a letter to Taney. *See* C. WARREN, *supra* note 4, at 103.

[75]*Bronson*, 42 U.S. (1 How.) at 319; *see also id.* at 321.

[76]*Id.* at 319-20. The Court reaffirmed this holding in Howard v. Bugbee, 65 U.S. (24 How.) 461 (1861) (Nelson, J.).

[77]*Bronson*, 42 U.S. (1 How.) at 320.

[78]*Id.* at 315-16. See Crawford v. Branch Bank, 48 U.S. (7 How.) 279, 282 (1849) (McLean, J.), upholding a law retroactively authorizing banks to sue in their own names on notes payable to their officers

change the nature and extent of existing remedies as materially to impair the rights and interests of the owner,'"[79] and commendably refused "to sanction a distinction between the right and the remedy, which would render the provision illusive and nugatory."[80] The two-thirds law in *Bronson* crossed this forbidden line because "its effect is to deprive the party of his pre-existing right to foreclose the mortgage by a sale of the premises, and to impose upon him conditions which would frequently render any sale altogether impossible."[81]

In *Charles River Bridge*, Taney had seized on Marshall's refusal to infer corporate tax immunity from a mere state charter as a lever to weaken the protections Marshall had afforded under the contract clause.[82] Notably, Taney did not attempt to do likewise in *Bronson*; but McLean, in dissent, showed how it could be done.[83] *Sturges v. Crowninshield*[84] had conceded the state's power over remedies; nobody doubted that a state might abolish imprisonment for past debts, though doing so "takes away a means, and often a principal means, of enforcing . . . payment," or shorten the period of suing on existing contracts, though doing so "bars the right of action."[85] "[S]urely," McLean reasoned, "the exercise of the lesser power, by modifying the remedy at discretion, must also be constitutional."[86] Indeed, though McLean did not

---

("The law is strictly remedial. . . . This is nothing more than carrying out the contract according to its original intendment."), and Beers v. Arkansas, 61 U.S. (20 How.) 527, 530 (1858), allowing a state to require holders to deposit previously-issued bonds in court before suing on them, in part because the state's requirement "merely regulated the proceedings in its own courts."

[79]Green v. Biddle, 21 U.S. (8 Wheat.) 1 (1823), *cited in Bronson*, 42 U.S. (1 How.) at 316; *see supra* chapter 5.

[80]*Bronson*, 42 U.S. (1 How.) at 318; *see also id.* at 317:

> [N]o one, we presume, would say that there is any substantial difference between a retrospective law declaring a particular contract or class of contracts to be abrogated and void, and one which took away all remedy to enforce them, or encumbered it with conditions that rendered it useless or impracticable to pursue it.

[81]*Id.* at 320. In saying all this, Taney, in best Marshall fashion, had gone further than the case required. As he acknowledged, the mortgage in question expressly authorized a foreclosure sale, so the case could have gone off on Justice Washington's narrower ground that when a contractual provision gave the right to a particular remedy, that remedy was a part of the obligation itself. *Id.* at 320-21; *see* Mason v. Haile, 25 U.S. (12 Wheat.) 370, 379 (1827) (dissenting opinion); *supra* chapter 5.

Bronson was later extended to a contract lacking an express foreclosure provision. McCracken v. Hayward, 43 U.S. (2 How.) 608 (1844). In what appears to be the only constitutional opinion he wrote for the Court in fourteen years, Justice Baldwin repeated much of what *Bronson* had said already, even though, as Catron protested in his concurring opinion, there seemed to be no occasion to reach the constitutional question. *Id.* at 617; *see also* Lessee of Gantly v. Ewing, 44 U.S. (3 How.) 707, 717 (1845) (Catron, J.) (striking down a similar law on the basis of *Bronson*).

[82]36 U.S. (11 Pet.) 420 (1837).

[83]McLean reached the merits reluctantly after arguing that the Court should not have reached the constitutional questions at all. The circuit court rule referring to state law seemed to have been superseded by equity rules later adopted by the Supreme Court; furthermore, the old rule by its own terms made the two-thirds law applicable only to legal and not to equitable proceedings. *Bronson*, 42 U.S. (1 How.) at 322-23. McLean's charge that the Court was reaching out to make an unnecessary constitutional pronouncement suggested yet another unfortunate parallel between Taney and Marshall; however, it received no reply.

[84]17 U.S. (4 Wheat.) 122 (1819); *see supra* chapter 5.

[85]*Bronson*, 42 U.S. (1 How.) at 328 (McLean, J., dissenting).

[86]*Id.* ; *see* C. SWISHER, *supra* note 4, at 387-88 (terming McLean's position "odd . . . in view of the conservative ideas on property rights which he was known to hold" and opining that his convictions may have yielded to his "perennial hopes of achieving the presidency").

say so, Marshall had conceded both of his examples in *Sturges*; and the Court had actually upheld the state's power to abolish debtors' prison retroactively in *Mason v. Haile*.[87]

McLean's attempt to distinguish the Court's best precedent was lame,[88] but Marshall had asked for trouble in *Sturges* by making such broad concessions about the power to alter remedies. Whether the measures endorsed in *Sturges* were less intrusive than Illinois's two-thirds rule, moreover, Taney did not bother to say.[89] Ninety years later his successors would uphold a law authorizing two-year extensions of a redemption period and suspension of the right to a deficiency judgment;[90] even without this glaring contrast, it is difficult to argue that *Bronson* was hostile to the contract clause.[91]

B.   *West River Bridge Co. v. Dix*

In 1795 Vermont granted an exclusive one-hundred-year franchise to build and operate a toll bridge. In 1843 a Vermont county court ordered the bridge taken for public use on payment of $4000. In an 1848 opinion by Justice Daniel,[92] over Justice Wayne's dissent, the Supreme Court held that the taking had not constituted an impairment of the bridge company's contract.[93]

This result may not seem surprising; not only the state courts cited by Daniel[94] but even the rigid Justice Story had acknowledged that a state could take bridge franchises, like any other property, on payment of just compensation.[95] Yet neither Daniel nor Story gave a satisfactory answer to the crucial question earlier posed by

[87]25 U.S. (12 Wheat.) 370 (1827).

[88]Green v. Biddle, 21 U.S. (8 Wheat.) 1 (1823), had struck down squatter laws impairing the rights of landowners although conceding that they went only to the remedy. McLean argued that *Green* involved an interstate compact and not the Constitution, *Bronson*, 42 U.S. (1 How.) at 327-28, but the Court had treated the compact as a contract protected against impairment by the contract clause.

McLean's analogy to the right of a court applying foreign law to employ its own procedures, *id.* at 329-30, was both instructive and restrictive; in theory the court was expected not to interfere with vested rights under the guise of procedure. *See* 3 J. BEALE, THE CONFLICT OF LAWS 1599-601 (1935).

[89]Taney conceded that a state could retroactively exempt tools or household furniture from execution, *Bronson*, 42 U.S. (1 How.) at 315, but did not say why such measures were less destructive of the right than the two-thirds rule. *See* B. WRIGHT, *supra* note 72, at 70 ("This opinion does little more than say that the change in the remedy must, in the opinion of the Court, be a reasonable one.").

[90]Home Bldg. & Loan Ass'n v. Blaisdell, 290 U.S. 398 (1934).

[91]*See* C. SWISHER, *supra* note 4, at 389 (*Bronson* "quieted the last of the fears that the court would eventually overthrow the major doctrines of Taney's predecessor."); C. WARREN, *supra* note 4, at 103 (*Bronson* "carried Marshall's view of obligation of contract even further than Marshall had himself."); Harris, *Chief Justice Taney: Prophet of Reform and Reaction*, 10 VAND. L. REV. 227, 237 (1957); *see also* Curran v. Arkansas, 56 U.S. (15 How.) 304, 319-20 (1853) (Curtis, J.) (relying on *Bronson* in holding that the withdrawal of all realty from a state-owned bank impaired its obligations to its creditors by leaving them without remedy). *But see* Beers v. Arkansas, 61 U.S. (20 How.) 527, 529-30, (1858) (Taney, C.J.) (dictum) (Court unanimously said a state would be free to withdraw its consent to be sued on bonds previously issued).

[92]Daniel had replaced Barbour in 1841. *See supra* introduction to part three, n. 1.

[93]West River Bridge Co. v. Dix, 47 U.S. (6 How.) 507 (1848).

[94]*Id.* at 534-35.

[95]Charles River Bridge v. Warren Bridge, 36 U.S. (11 Pet.) 420, 644 (1837) (dissenting opinion).

Justice Johnson in his concurrence to *Fletcher v. Peck*:[96] how could the exercise of
eminent domain be reconciled with the *Fletcher* holding that the state had implicitly
promised not to take back the property it had granted?

Vermont's counsel came up with a promising response: the grantor had agreed
only that it would not impair the grant, and compensation gave the grantee the
equivalent of his original right.[97] There was something to Webster's riposte that
compensation was not really the same as the franchise itself;[98] the owner might have
preferred not to sell his rights, and the traditional availability of specific performance
of land contracts suggests the inadequacy of damages in this area. The basis of
Fletcher's implied promise, however, was the reasonable expectations of the parties;
in these terms a promise not to steal property is much easier to infer than a promise
not to buy it at a fair price. In refusing to infer a promise not to tax a corporation,
Providence Bank v. Billings[99] had shown that a grant did not imply rights superior
to those of others similarly situated; and *Charles River Bridge*[100] had refused to
infer a promise not to undermine the value of a bridge franchise even *without*
compensation.

Justice Daniel, however, invoked neither these precedents nor the cogent arguments of counsel. After describing eminent domain (without citation) as an essential
attribute of "every sovereign political community,"[101] he insisted without further
explanation that the franchise implicitly provided for its exercise.[102] Thus Daniel
reached by pure fiat a conclusion he could easily have justified; and by finding an
implicit reservation of the taking power instead of simply declining to find an implied
promise not to exercise it, he made the issue look harder than it was.[103]

Moreover, the argument that *Fletcher's* implicit promise not to destroy a grant

[96]10 U.S. (6 Cranch) 87, 143 (1810) (concurring opinion); *see supra* chapter 5.

[97]*West River Bridge*, 47 U.S. (6 How.) at 525 (Mr. Phelps); *see* Hale, *The Supreme Court and the
Contract Clause; II*, 57 HARV. L. REV. 621, 638-39 (1944) (arguing that retaking a granted franchise might
"be regarded as a breach" rather than an impairment of the obligation and citing Hays v. Port of Seattle,
251 U.S. 233 (1920), as establishing that the state had the option under the contract clause of breaking its
agreement and paying damages).

[98]*West River Bridge*, 47 U.S. (6 How.) at 517 (Messrs. Webster & Collamer).

[99]29 U.S. (4 Pet.) 514 (1830); *see supra* chapter 5.

[100]*See supra* notes 50-72 and accompanying text.

[101]*West River Bridge*, 47 U.S. (6 How.) at 531.

[102]Despite a general statement that "all private rights" were held subject to the power of eminent
domain, *id.* at 532, Daniel did not say the state could not validly promise to waive the exercise of its power.
As he saw the case, the state had not attempted to make such a promise. Thus there seems no basis for the
apparent suggestion in B. WRIGHT, *supra* note 72, at 66-67, that the issue was "the inalienability of the right
of eminent domain," for the flat statement in J. NOWAK, R. ROTUNDA & J. YOUNG, *supra* note 31, at
423-44, that *West River Bridge* held the power inalienable, or for the conclusion in J. FRANK, *supra* note 4,
at 211-12, that the case established a "police-power limitation on the contract clause." *Cf. infra* text
accompanying notes 125-47 (discussion of contractual tax immunities).

[103]Woodbury, who had replaced Story in 1845, said much the same thing in a concurring opinion,
adding unnecessarily that he doubted any necessity could justify taking private property for uses such as
marine hospitals and jails. *West River Bridge*, 47 U.S. (6 How.) at 546. He also said, even less relevantly,
that he thought a state could modify at will a contract of employment of a public officer. *Id.* at 548; *see infra*
notes 106-24 and accompanying text (discussing *Butler v. Pennsylvania*, 51 U.S. (10 How.) 402 (1850)).
McLean, as in *Charles River Bridge*, concurred on the ground that a taking of property was not an
impairment of contract. *West River Bridge*, 47 U.S. (6 How.) at 536-39. Justice Wayne was reported to
have "delivered a dissenting opinion," but its contents were not revealed. *Id.* at 549.

does not prevent a compensated taking seemed to require an examination into the adequacy of the compensation. Nevertheless, though the franchisee's counsel had argued that the price paid was grossly insufficient,[104] Daniel expressly declined to undertake that inquiry.[105] Indeed he never clearly said, though *Fletcher* would seem to require it, that compensation had to be paid at all. Thus, although the general principle established in *West River Bridge* appears both reasonable as a matter of contract interpretation and in accord with precedent, the majority opinion gave the states an easy means of circumventing *Fletcher v. Peck* without even adverting to that decision.

C.   *Butler v. Pennsylvania*

Less than a year after appointing Butler a canal commissioner "for the term of one year" with "all the rights, powers, and emoluments of the said office" under a statute providing a compensation of four dollars per day, the state reduced his salary and then replaced him entirely.[106] The state courts rejected the argument that this conduct had impaired a contractual obligation.[107] In 1851 the Supreme Court affirmed, without dissent on the merits, in another opinion by Justice Daniel.[108]

Pennsylvania case law, which Daniel cited,[109] emphatically denied that public officers enjoyed a contractual relation with the state, and ever since *Ogden v. Saunders*[110] the Court had proceeded on the premise that the existence and extent of an obligation depended on the law in effect at the time the obligation allegedly arose. Thus, having checked that the Pennsylvania decisions were not latter-day concoctions to evade the contract clause,[111] the Court could easily have justified its decision on the ground that the governing state law created no obligation.

Daniel took a broader approach, however, concluding that appointments of state officers "do not come within the import of the term *contracts*" in the Constitution.[112] The contract clause, he said (again without citation), applied only to "contracts by which *perfect rights, certain definite, fixed private rights* of property, are vested";[113] "from the necessity of the case, and according to universal understanding," engagements "undertaken by the body politic or State government for the benefit of all" could be varied at will.[114] A contrary holding would be "reconcilable with neither

---

[104]*West River Bridge*, 47 U.S. (6 How.) at 513, 520 (placing the value of the franchise at $10,000).

[105]*Id.* at 535.

[106]Butler v. Pennsylvania, 51 U.S. (10 How.) 402, 403-05 (1850).

[107]*Id.* at 405-06.

[108]Justice McLean argued that there was no contract to be impaired and thus no jurisdiction; the logic of this position suggests that the Court never has jurisdiction to reject a constitutional claim on the merits. *Id.* at 419.

[109]*Id.* at 517-18.

[110]25 U.S. (12 Wheat.) 213 (1827); *see supra* chapter 5.

[111]*Cf.* Indiana *ex rel.* Anderson v. Brand, 303 U.S. 95, 100 (1938) (whether the state has bound itself by contract is a question "primarily of state law" which the Court should review only with deference "in order that the constitutional mandate may not become a dead letter"); *infra* notes 131-47 and accompanying text, discussing Piqua Branch of State Bank v. Knoop, 57 U.S. (16 How.) 369 (1854).

[112]*Butler*, 51 U.S. (10 How.) at 417.

[113]*Id.* at 416.

[114]*Id.*

common justice nor common sense"; it would either "arrest necessarily every thing like progress or improvement in government" or turn the state into "one great pension establishment on which to quarter a host of sinecures."[115] The regulation and appointment of state officers, he added, were "functions . . . which governments cannot be presumed to have surrendered, if indeed they can under any circumstances be justified in surrendering them."[116]

There is in these passages a strong echo of Marshall's habit of concluding that the Framers have done no wrong.[117] There is the bare assertion that foisting "sinecures" on the public payroll is worse than breaking faith with one's employees.[118] There is the unsupported attribution of this same set of values to those who wrote into the Constitution an explicit requirement that the states keep their promises. There is no attempt to reconcile the broad conclusion that the contract clause is inapplicable to engagements "for the benefit of all" with the *Dartmouth College* case, which had held that a charter granted to an eleemosynary institution for the public good was protected by the Constitution,[119] or to explain why the canal commissioners in *Butler* had rights any less "perfect," "definite," "fixed," "vested," or "private" than those of Dartmouth itself.

The Court could have made a respectable effort along this line; Marshall had conceded in *Dartmouth* that the contract clause did not "restrain the states in the regulation of their civil institutions, adopted for internal government,"[120] and even Story had acknowledged that states could abolish municipal corporations.[121] On the other hand, as Justice Washington had explained, in the case of a municipal corporation the state was essentially contracting with itself.[122] *Butler*, in contrast, also involved the interests of the officers themselves, and Story had admitted that an agreement to pay an officer a stipulated salary would fall within the contract clause.[123]

In short, as in *West River Bridge*, Daniel could have written a persuasive opinion

---

[115]*Id.*

[116]*Id.* at 417. These last passages confused the basis of the holding by suggesting two grounds distinct from the question of what constituted a "contract" within the meaning of the clause. Daniel's statement that the state's surrender of power to alter an officer's salary "cannot be presumed" seemed to suggest a narrow interpretation of the agreement itself, *id.*; his doubt whether the state *could* make such a surrender seemed to echo the undeveloped suggestion of both Marshall and Johnson in Fletcher v. Peck, 10 U.S. (6 Cranch) 87 (1810), that the state constitution might limit the authority of the state government to contract away its sovereign powers. *Cf. infra* notes 125-47 and accompanying text (discussing contractual tax exemptions).

[117]*See* Merrill, *Application of the Obligation of Contract Clause to State Promises*, 80 U. PA. L. REV. 639, 656 (1932) (arguing that the "considerations of policy set forth in [Butler] . . . seem unanswerable"). *See generally* part two *supra*.

[118]*Butler*, 51 U.S. (10 How.) at 416.

[119]Trustees of Dartmouth College v. Woodward, 17 U.S. (4 Wheat.) 518 (1819); *see supra* chapter 5.

[120]*Dartmouth*, 17 U.S. (4 Wheat.) at 629.

[21]*Id.* at 694 (concurring opinion); *see also* Terrett v. Taylor, 13 U.S. (9 Cranch) 43, 52 (1815); *supra* chapter 5.

[122]17 U.S. (4 Wheat.) at 661 (concurring opinion).

[123]*Id.* at 694. Story had left the Court before the *Butler* decision, and no Justice picked up his argument. Daniel's apparent view that no agreements of public employment were within the contract clause has not survived. *See, e.g.*, Indiana *ex rel.* Anderson v. Brand, 303 U.S. 95, 99-100 (1938); Hale, *supra* note 97 at 666-70.

to justify his decision sustaining state authority; but, as in *West River Bridge*, he elected to rely on bare assertions instead.[124]

D.   The Tax Exemption Cases

With the conspicuous exception of *Bronson v. Kinzie*,[125] all the opinions discussed so far display a marked hostility to the contract clause; and only *Bronson* involved a contract between private parties. The tempting inference that the Taney Court distinguished sharply between public and private contracts, however, is severely weakened by that Court's sympathetic approach to state promises not to impose taxes.

The Marshall Court had enforced a state promise not to impose taxes as early as 1812 in *New Jersey v. Wilson*.[126] In 1845, in *Gordon v. Appeal Tax Court*,[127] the Taney Court unanimously enforced another, construing a promise not to impose additional taxes on banks to forbid taxation of their shareholders.[128] Though perhaps correct,[129] this interpretation was hardly compelled by clear language; the decision seemed to show that, despite *Charles River Bridge*, the Taney Court would not always take a restrictive view of promises in public contracts.[130]

---

[124]Justice Woodbury's opinion the same term for a unanimous Court in Town of East Hartford v. Hartford Bridge Co., 51 U.S. (10 How.) 511 (1850), provides an interesting contrast to *Butler*. Woodbury invoked both Washington's and Story's *Dartmouth* opinions, to reach the less controversial conclusion that the state could rescind a ferry right it had granted to a municipal corporation. *Id.* at 536. However, the broad holding of *East Hartford* that arrangements between states and their subdivisions lay outside the contract clause was unnecessary in light of the alternative conclusion of estoppel: the city had earlier admitted it held the ferry at legislative pleasure. *Id.* at 537. Woodbury also added both that the legislature had no power to surrender the right to retract its franchises, *id.* at 534-35, and that it had implicitly reserved power to modify the arrangement as public need dictated. *Id.* at 536-37. Both these points seemed equally applicable to grants to private parties, and in that context they appeared to conflict with all the precedents refusing to allow alteration of public grants; but they were both quite unnecessary to the decision.

[125]*See supra* text accompanying notes 73-91.

[126]11 U.S. (7 Cranch) 164 (1812); *see supra* chapter 5.

[127]44 U.S. (3 How.) 133 (1845).

[128]The promise was found in a statute providing that if existing banks would invest in a proposed turnpike and pay an annual sum of twenty cents per hundred dollars of capital stock, "the faith of the state is hereby pledged not to impose any further tax or burden upon them during the continuation of their charters under this act." *See id.* at 146.

[129]Counsel had argued that the exemption would otherwise become worthless. *Gordon*, 44 U.S. (3 How.) at 139. Wayne said the condition that the exemption take effect on acceptance by "the bank" showed the legislature had equated the institution with its owners, since they alone could agree to the terms of the bargain. *Id.* at 147-48. Professor Wright termed Wayne's conclusion "very doubtful." B. WRIGHT, *supra* note 72, at 183.

[130]Indeed, Wayne rejected an argument that the exemption applied only to franchise taxes on the ground that the banking franchise itself, unlike land acquired from the state, would have been implicitly exempt in the absence of an express provision: the bank paid a price for the privilege, "and any tax upon it would substantially be an addition to the price." *Gordon*, 44 U.S. (3 How.) at 146. Despite Wayne's disclaimer, this argument would appear equally applicable to every sale of state land, or for that matter to every corporate charter for which there is consideration (though Wayne explicitly denied this application,

The major 1854 case of *Piqua Branch of State Bank v. Knoop*[131] demonstrated that the *Gordon* decision was no mere sport.[132] Ohio had passed a statute authorizing any group of five or more persons to form a banking corporation, requiring any bank so organized to pay the state six percent of its net profits semiannually, and providing that this amount "shall be in lieu of all taxes to which such company, or the stockholders thereof on account of stock owned therein, would otherwise be subject."[133] The Ohio courts upheld a later statute taxing the capital stock, surplus, and contingent fund of such banks. The Supreme Court, in an opinion by Justice McLean, reversed.

As Justice Campbell pointed out in a well-written and well-documented dissent joined by Catron and Daniel,[134] the state had not explicitly promised that the taxing arrangement in the 1845 statute would remain unaltered by subsequent legislation.[135] In contrast to the pledge in *Gordon* to impose no further tax on banks "during the continuation of their charters," the assurance in *Piqua*, by which the state had only declared that the semiannual payments should be "in lieu of all taxes," might as easily mean " 'till otherwise provided by law' " as " 'during the existence of the banks' ";[136] as Campbell said, *Charles River Bridge* seemed to require a resolution of the ambiguity in favor of the state.[137]

---

id. at 145-46). This incidental conclusion that bank franchises possessed implicit immunity from taxes seemed not only out of harmony with the principles of construction set forth and applied in *Charles River Bridge*, but also irreconcilable with Marshall's holding in *Providence Bank v. Billings* that the mere grant of a charter did not imply an exemption from state taxes. *Providence Bank*, 29 U.S. (4 Pet.) at 560-65. *See supra* chapter 5; *see also supra* text accompanying note 58.

[131]57 U.S. (16 How.) 369 (1854). For the background and aftermath of this controversy, see C. HAINES & F. SHERWOOD, *supra* note 19, at 370-89; C. WARREN, *supra* note 4, at 474-81.

[132]In 1842 the Court had held that a statute making the property of a state university "forever" tax free was implicitly repealed by a later law authorizing sale to private parties. Armstrong v. Treasurer of Athens County, 41 U.S. (16 Pet.) 281 (1842) (Catron, J.). Unlike the otherwise similar exemption in *New Jersey v. Wilson*, 11 U.S. (7 Cranch) at 166-67, the exemption in *Armstrong* had not been a part of the consideration for a private grant protected by the clause. *Cf.* Philadelphia & Wilmington R.R. v. Maryland, 51 U.S. (10 How.) 376, 382-83 (1850) (Taney, C.J.) (statute authorizing merger and continuing "all . . . privileges" of predecessor corporations did not extend tax immunity of one predecessor to all the property of the new firm).

[133]*Piqua*, 57 U.S. (16 How.) at 377.

[134]*Id.* at 395-405.

[135]*Id.* at 406.

[136]*Id.*

[137]*Id.* at 409-12. Taney concurred specially to say he did not agree with everything in the majority opinion but that "the words used are too plain" to avoid McLean's conclusion. *Id.* at 392-93. The companion case of Ohio Life Ins. & Trust Co. v. Debolt, 57 U.S. (16 How.) 416 (1854), involved the same statutes, but with a different twist and a different result. The company was not, strictly speaking, a bank, but its charter provided it should be taxed no more heavily than banks. Taney and Grier thought the state had agreed to give the company "the benefit of its general regulations and laws . . . but not of its special contracts" concerning bank taxes, *id.* at 441, and the 1845 provision involved in *Piqua* was a "special contract" applicable only to banks established under its other provisions. *Id.* at 439. As McLean and Curtis pointed out in separate dissents, *id.* at 444, 450, this seemed a peculiar construction because every bank in the state was subject to the 1845 rate at the time the statute was passed. Once the Court had answered the hard question in *Piqua* by favoring exemption, the same result should apparently have followed easily in *Debolt*, but with the votes of Catron, Daniel, and Campbell (who adhered to their position that the banks themselves were taxable at the 1851 rate), the vote in *Debolt* was five to four against immunity. For further discussion of *Debolt*, see also *infra* note 142.

In a separate dissent, Catron added a more fundamental objection: the Ohio courts had already held that irrepealable tax exemptions were an impermissible abandonment of sovereignty,[138] and the state courts were the ultimate arbiters of state law.[139] Conceding that federal courts normally deferred to state courts in the interpretation of state law, McLean persuasively responded that the contract clause demanded an exception: to make the state sole judge of whether it had given what the Constitution forbade it to revoke would "surrender one of the most important provisions in the federal Constitution."[140]

On the merits, McLean noted that state legislatures and prior decisions had long assumed the power to grant irrepealable exemptions[141] and argued that an agreement not to tax a particular corporation no more abrogated sovereignty than would an agreement to repay money borrowed or the issuance of a corporate charter itself.[142]

Absent some unusual provision in the Ohio constitution—and nobody pointed to one—McLean seemed to have the better of this argument.[143] Catron's view would reappear in dissents even on the tax issue,[144] and the Court would later adopt it with respect to alleged promises not to exercise the police[145] and eminent domain[146] powers. During Taney's term, however, the Court not only enforced tax exemptions; it also gave them, on the whole, a reasonably broad construction[147]— despite the contrary philosophy of *Charles River Bridge*.

E.   *Gelpcke v. Dubuque*

Pursuant to statutory authorization, the City of Dubuque issued bonds in exchange for shares of railroad stock. The Iowa Supreme Court had held before the bond issue that the authorizing statute was consistent with the state constitution; after the issue,

---

[138]*Piqua*, 57 U.S. (16 How.) at 404 (dissenting opinion).

[139]*Id.* at 403, 405.

[140]*Id.* at 391-92 (majority opinion); *accord*, Indiana *ex rel.* Anderson v. Brand, 303 U.S. 95 (1938); *cf.* Martin v. Hunter's Lessee, 14 U.S. (1 Wheat.) 304, 357 (1816) (investigating whether title had passed under state law before a treaty allegedly violated by expropriation); *supra* chapter 4 (discussing *Martin v. Hunter's Lessee*).

[141]*Piqua*, 57 U.S. (16 How.) at 389.

[142]*Id.* In the companion *Debolt* case, discussed *supra* at note 137, Justice Daniel joined Catron's rejection of what Daniel termed the "suicidal doctrine" that a legislature could "bind forever and irrevocably their creator," the "sovereign people." *Debolt*, 57 U.S. (16 How.) at 443 (Daniel, J., concurring in judgment). Whether this view was consistent with *any* legislative power to contract he did not say. Taney, joined by Grier, wrote separately to affirm both the power of Ohio's legislature to give irrepealable exemptions and the Court's duty to reexamine the state's interpretation of its original action, while finding no contractual exemption on the facts. *Id.* at 427, 432-33, 441. Campbell once again properly found it unnecessary to decide the broader question. *Id.* at 443-44 (separate opinion).

[143]*See also* Hale, *supra* note 97, at 654.

[144]*See, e.g.*, Washington Univ. v. Rouse, 75 U.S. (8 Wall.) 439, 443 (1869) (Miller, J., dissenting); B. Wright, *supra* note 72, at 75.

[145]*See, e.g.*, Stone v. Mississippi, 101 U.S. 814 (1880), *infra* chapter 11.

[146]*See, e.g.*, Contributors to Pennsylvania Hospital v. Philadelphia, 245 U.S. 20 (1917).

[147]*See* Jefferson Branch Bank v. Skelly, 66 U.S. (1 Black) 436 (1862); Rector of Christ Church v. County of Philadelphia, 65 U.S. (24 How.) 300 (1861); Dodge v. Woolsey, 59 U.S. (18 How.) 331 (1856).

the court reversed itself. In a federal diversity action to recover interest, the Supreme Court disregarded the latest state court decision and held for the bondholders.[148]

For the Court, Justice Swayne argued that the "settled rule" requiring respect for state court decisions "giving constructions to the laws and constitutions of their own States"[149] had been held inapplicable in "exceptional cases,"[150] none of which he had the grace to identify. The earlier Iowa decisions favoring the bonds were "sustained by reason and authority" and "in harmony with the adjudications of sixteen States," and, Swayne noted, "[i]t cannot be expected that this court will follow every . . . oscillation" in state decisions.[151] As Taney had said in earlier dicta, a contract valid according to contemporaneous state interpretation "cannot be impaired by any subsequent action of legislation, or decision of its courts altering the construction of the law."[152] "To hold otherwise," Swayne added, "would be as unjust as to hold that rights acquired under a statute may be lost by its repeal."[153]

Whatever else may be said about *Gelpcke*, Swayne can hardly be accused of having revealed the basis of his decision.[154] Professor Swisher has taken the Taney quotation as proof the case held that the contract clause precluded judicial as well as legislative impairment of agreements.[155] Swisher's interpretation is strengthened by the fact that Taney's remark was made in a case decided on contract clause grounds and by a later Swayne statement that, while still ambiguous, was somewhat more explicit.[156] This interpretation suffers, however, from the conspicuous failure of Swayne ever to *mention* the contract clause and from Justice Miller's emphatic and uncontradicted assertion in dissent that it was "not pretended" that the Iowa decision was "in conflict with the Constitution of the United States."[157] Indeed, the references to "exceptional cases," to "oscillation," and to the correctness of the repudiated Iowa holdings suggest the Court simply thought itself free to depart from a state court's interpretation of its own constitution. This conclusion, although not easy to reconcile with the many precedents cited by Miller[158] or with the underlying Rules of Decision Act,[159] indicates *Gelpcke* may well have been an extension of *Swift v. Tyson*[160] rather than an expansive reading of the contract clause.

---

[148]Gelpcke v. Dubuque, 68 U.S. (1 Wall.) 175 (1864). *See generally* 6 C. FAIRMAN, HISTORY OF THE SUPREME COURT OF THE UNITED STATES 935-44 (1971); C. FAIRMAN, MR. JUSTICE MILLER AND THE SUPREME COURT 213-21(1939).

[149]*Gelpcke*, 68 U.S. (1 Wall.) at 206.

[150]*Id.*

[151]*Id.* at 205-06.

[152]*Id.* at 206 (citing Ohio Life Ins. & Trust Co. v. Debolt, 57 U.S. (16 How.) 416, 432 (1854) (separate opinion) (discussed *supra* notes 137, 142). Taney was ill when *Gelpcke* was decided and did not sit. *See* 68 U.S. (1 Wall.) at vii.

[153]*Gelpcke,* 68 U.S. (1 Wall.) at 206.

[154]*See* B. WRIGHT, *supra* note 72, at 81 (the "constitutional justification for the [decision] . . . has never been entirely clear.")

[155]C. SWISHER, *supra* introduction to part 3, note 2; at 335.

[156]"The National Constitution forbids the States to pass laws impairing the obligation of contracts. In cases properly brought before us that end can be accomplished unwarrantably no more by judicial decisions than by legislation." Township of Pine Grove v. Talcott, 86 U.S. (19 Wall.) 666, 678 (1874); *see also* Douglass v. County of Pike, 101 U.S. 677, 687 (1879) (Waite, C.J.).

[157]*Gelpcke*, 68 U.S. (1 Wall.) at 209; *see also id.* at 210.

[158]*Id.* at 210-13.

[159]Act of Sept. 24, 1789, ch. 20, § 34, 1 Stat. 73, 92 (codified as amended at 28 U.S.C. § 1652 (1976)).

[160]41 U.S. (16 Pet.) 1, 18-19 (1842) (Rules of Decision Act limited to "laws strictly local"), *overruled,*

If Swayne did mean to hold that the Constitution forbade judicial impairment of contract, he had some explaining to do. The contract clause forbids only "Law[s]" impairing obligations;[161] the Court had held in *Calder v. Bull* that the similarly worded ex post facto clause[162] applied only to legislation.[163] Swayne might have invoked the purpose of the contract clause to protect legitimate expectations, along with a recognition that judges effectively make law by deciding cases.[164] Perhaps his failure to do any of this resulted from an inability to muster a majority for what at the time may have seemed an unwarranted extension; it may be rough justice, if hardly consolation, that the Court gave no better explanation when it later said the clause did not apply to judicial decisions.[165] In any event, though *Gelpcke* neither clearly expanded the contract clause nor contained any acceptable justification for its holding, it was certainly not unfriendly to contract rights.

F.   Summary

The cases considered above make it impossible to conclude that the Court consistently displayed toward the clause the kind of hostility that its crippling construction of the charter in *Charles River Bridge* appeared to represent. *Bronson v. Kinzie* showed that the new Justices had little inclination to use Marshall's right/remedy distinction to weaken the clause, and the tax exemption cases demonstrate they were

Erie R.R. v. Tompkins, 304 U.S. 64, 79-80 (1938) (state laws rules of decision in federal courts). The *Swift* doctrine was an explicit ground of decision in the *Pine Grove* case. *Pine Grove*, 86 U.S. (19 Wall.) at 678 (*see supra* note 156 for quotation); *see also* Tidal Oil Co. v. Flanagan, 263 U.S. 444, 451-52 (1924); 6 C. FAIRMAN, HISTORY OF THE SUPREME COURT OF THE UNITED STATES 937-38 (1971) (insisting that *Swift* was the sole basis for *Gelpcke*). For a defense of *Gelpcke* on this ground because of the diversity policy of protecting outsiders from state-court bias, see Thayer, *The Case of Gelpcke v. Dubuque*, 4 HARV. L. REV. 311 (1891).

[161]"No State shall . . . pass any . . . Law impairing the Obligation of Contracts . . . ." U.S. CONST. art. I §10, cl. 1.

[162]"No State shall . . . pass any . . . ex post facto Law . . . ." *Id.*

[163]3 U.S. (3 Dall.) 386, 392 (Chase, J.), 397 (Patterson, J.), 400 (Iredell & Cushing, JJ.) (1798) (alternative holding); *see supra* chapter 2.

[164]In other contexts the Court has since construed the term "laws" to include judge-made law. *See Erie*, 304 U.S. at 78 (state laws rules of decision in federal courts); Illinois v. City of Milwaukee, 406 U.S. 91, 100 (1972) (jurisdiction of cases arising under federal law.).

Swayne might also have added that *Calder's* contrary reading of the ex post facto clause had been assumed rather than explained, and that a limitation on the power to overrule prior contract decisions could more easily be attributed to the Framers than could a prohibition on appeals from inferior courts, which was all that had been involved in *Calder*. Swayne's later suggestion that to follow state decisions in cases like *Gelpcke* would be to "abdicate one of the most important duties with which this tribunal is charged," *Pine Grove*, 86 U.S. (19 Wall.) at 678, echoes McLean's correct conclusion in *Piqua* that to give binding effect to state decisions when legislation is attacked would emasculate the contract clause. In *Gelpcke*, however, no legislation was under attack; the issue was the threshold question of whether judicial action could ever offend the clause. Since the case providing Taney's dictum involved an attack on state legislation, and since Taney in the same breath reaffirmed the point made in *Piqua*, Miller seems correct in saying that Taney had not meant what Swayne appeared to cite him for in *Gelpcke*. *See Gelpcke*, 68 U.S. (1 Wall.) at 216-17.

[165]*See* New Orleans Waterworks Co. v. Louisiana Sugar Ref. Co., 125 U.S. 18, 30 (1888) ("The prohibition is aimed at the legislative power of the State, and not at the decisions of its courts, or the acts of administrative or executive boards or officers . . . ."). Since the action involved was not that of a court, the reference to decisions was dictum.

sometimes even generous in their interpretation of government promises. After Marshall's refusal to infer a promise not to tax, there was nothing radical about his successors' refusal in *West River Bridge* to infer a promise not to exercise the ordinary power of condemnation. Even the relatively extreme holding in *Butler* that contracts for the employment of state officers were not protected had roots in Marshall's dictum exempting purely governmental arrangements and could easily have been justified on the basis of state law. Though the additional decisions not discussed here may confirm a certain inclination toward narrow construction of public promises outside the tax exemption field, they do not seem to alter the picture very significantly.[166] In short, notwithstanding *Charles River Bridge* and occasional extreme statements by unrepresentative Justices like Daniel and Catron, the overall impression conveyed by the contract cases of the Taney years is one of continuity with the Marshall tradition.[167]

III. Later Commerce Clause Cases

A. *Groves v. Slaughter*

In 1835 and 1836, Slaughter brought slaves into Mississippi and sold them on credit.[168] Some of his customers failed to pay and defended themselves on grounds of illegality: the Mississippi constitution provided that the "introduction of slaves into

[166]*See, e.g.*, Bridge Proprietors v. Hoboken Land & Improvement Co., 68 U.S. (1 Wall.) 116 (1864) (Miller, J.) (imaginative opinion that exclusive bridge franchise did not preclude construction of railroad bridge that was said not to divert tollpaying foot and horse traffic); Gilman v. City of Sheboygan, 67 U.S. (2 Black) 510 (1863) (Swayne, J.) (authorization to impose certain taxes was not part of city's contract with its bondholders); Sherman v. Smith, 66 U.S. (1 Black) 587 (1862) (Nelson, J.) (charter provision revocable because state had expressly reserved power of repeal, as Story had said in *Dartmouth*); Aspinwall v. Commissioners of Daviess County, 63 U.S. (22 How.) 364 (1860) (Nelson, J.) (railroad charter provision authorizing county to buy railroad stock gave county no right protected by contract clause); Richmond, Fredericksburg, & Potomac R.R. v. Louisa R.R., 54 U.S. (13 How.) 71 (1852) (Grier, J.) (promise in one railroad franchise not to grant another diverting traffic between terminal points not impaired by chartering another railway over part of same distance); Baltimore & Susquehanna R.R. v. Nesbit, 51 U.S. (10 How.) 395 (1850) (Daniel, J.) (legislative new-trial order respecting particular condemnation did not impair contractual power of eminent domain); Paup v. Drew, 51 U.S. (10 How.) 218 (1850) (alternative holding) (McLean, J.) (promise to accept banknotes for state debts inapplicable to purchase of land the state held in trust); Phalen v. Virginia, 49 U.S. (8 How.) 163 (1850) (Grier, J.) (state may ban lottery five years after enacting statute authorizing turnpike commissioners to operate one in order to raise $30,000 to repair a small stretch of road); Woodruff v. Trapnall, 51 U.S. (10 How.) 190 (1850) (McLean, J.) (bank charter promising acceptance of banknotes in satisfaction of debts to the state created a contractual obligation to noteholders); Planters' Bank v. Sharp, 47 U.S. (6 How.) 301, 306 (1848) (Woodbury, J.) (charters empowering banks either to dispose of property or to exercise the "usual . . . powers" of banking institutions gave them a contractual right to transfer promissory notes); Maryland v. B & O.R.R., 44 U.S. (3 How.) 534 (1845) (Taney, C.J.) (charter provision requiring railroad to pay penalty to county if it did not build there gave no contractual right to the county). Many of these decisions were unanimous; but Catron, Daniel, Taney, Nelson, and Grier each dissented from at least one case striking down state action, and McLean, Wayne, and Curtis dissented from the upholding of state action in the *Richmond* case, 54 U.S. (13 How.) at 83.

[167]*See* B. WRIGHT, *supra* note 72, at 62-63, 245-46 (concluding that the contract clause was a "more secure and a broader base for the defense of property rights in 1864 than it had been in 1835").

[168]Groves v. Slaughter, 40 U.S. (15 Pet.) 449, 497 (1841).

this state, as merchandise, or for sale, shall be prohibited, from and after the first day of May, [1833]."[169] The trial court rejected this defense, and the Supreme Court, over two dissents, affirmed.[170]

Justice Thompson's opinion for the Court scrupulously avoided the ticklish question whether the commerce clause deprived Mississippi of power to prohibit the importation of slaves, concluding, in the absence of clear state decisions, that its slave importation clause was a mere direction to the legislature, not a self-executing prohibition.[171] McLean, Taney, and Baldwin each published concurring opinions expressing highly divergent views on the commerce clause issue, which all three conceded did not have to be decided.[172] Like Story in *Miln*, McLean began by inflating *Gibbons* into a holding that Congress had exclusive power over commerce but concluded that slaves were not articles of commerce[173] because the Constitution referred to them as "persons."[174] Responding persuasively that the clause of article I, section 9 forbidding Congress to outlaw the slave trade before 1808 demonstrated that slaves otherwise fell within the commerce power,[175] Baldwin admitted that a law forbidding the importation of *all* slaves could have been sustained under the police power on grounds either of morality or safety, but argued convincingly that the purpose of the Mississippi provision was purely commercial because it forbade only importation for sale.[176] Taney said only that

[169]*Id. See generally* C. SWISHER, *supra* introduction to part 3, note 2, at 366 ("the importation of slaves depressed the market value of those already held in the state" and the slave traders brought in slaves who were "troublemakers or in other respects undesirable"); C. WARREN, *supra* note 4, at 68 n.1, (this was "a financial rather than a slavery measure," designed "to check the drain of capital away from the state").

[170]*Groves v. Slaughter*, 40 U.S. (15 Pet.) 449 (1841).

[171]*Id.* at 496-503. Surprisingly, the Court adhered to this conclusion after the Mississippi courts decided to the contrary. *See* Rowan v. Runnels, 46 U.S. (5 How.) 134, 139 (1847) (Taney, C.J.) (arguing that to give state-court decisions retroactive effect might render the diversity clause "utterly useless and nugatory"). For cogent criticism of the *Rowan* decision as inconsistent with precedent, see C. HAINES & F. SHERWOOD, *supra* note 10, at 120-121 (invoking Green & Neal, 31 U.S. (6 Pet.) 291 (1832)).

[172]*Groves*, 40 U.S. (15 Pet.) at 504 (McLean, J.), 508 (Taney, C.J.), 510 (Baldwin, J.). McLean began by saying the question was "so intimately connected with" the case and had been "so elaborately argued" that it was "fit and proper" to discuss it. *Id.* at 504. Taney and Baldwin said that, once McLean had spoken, they dared not let their silence be misconstrued. *Id.* at 508 (Taney, C.J.), 510 (Baldwin, J.); *see* F. WEISENBURGER, *supra* note 4, at 165-66 ("McLean went far out of the usual judicial course" and "needlessly exposed . . . differences . . . on questions of crucial importance.").

[173]*Groves*, 40 U.S. (15 Pet.) at 504, 506-08.

[174]*Id.* at 506 (citing U.S. CONST. art. I, § 2 (apportionment of representatives and direct taxes); U.S. CONST. art. I, § 9 (Congressional power over slave trade); U.S. CONST. art. IV, § 3 (fugitive slaves)); *see* C. SWISHER, *supra* note 4, at 398 (explaining that despite his nationalist ("Whig") views McLean was "an abolitionist . . . deeply interested . . . in preserving the power of the state to do away with slavery").

[175]*Groves*, 40 U.S. (15 Pet.) at 513-14. McLean responded unconvincingly, suggesting that Congress's power over interstate commerce was narrower than its identically worded power over foreign trade, *id.* at 505-06, and that, given the exclusivity of the commerce clause, section nine's recognition of state authority over slave importation until 1808 showed that the subject fell outside the commerce clause altogether. *Id.* at 506. The latter contention overlooked the possibility that such state laws might fall within Marshall's conception of the police power (which McLean conceded gave the states some authority to affect the same subject as Congress's commercial regulations, *id.* at 505), as well as the Framers' explicit termination of the limitation as of 1808.

[176]*Groves*, 40 U.S. (15 Pet.) at 511-12, 516. This time, Baldwin seems to have captured the spirit of Marshall's distinction. *Cf. supra* notes 19, 42, 68 (discussing *New York v. Miln*, *Briscoe v. Kentucky*, and *Charles River Bridge v. Warren Bridge*). He was less successful, however, in suggesting a violation of the privileges and immunities clause of article IV, *see Groves*, 40 U.S. (15 Pet.) at 516-17, since Mississippi

the introduction of slaves was a state matter not subject to Congressional control; he did not say why.[177]

Between the opinions of Taney and Baldwin, the reporter added the following peculiar paragraph.

> Mr. Justice STORY, Mr. Justice THOMPSON, Mr. Justice WAYNE and Mr. Justice McKINLEY, concurred with the majority of the Court in opinion that the provision of the Constitution of the United States, which gives the regulation of commerce to Congress, did not interfere with the provision of the constitution of the state of Mississippi, which relates to the introduction of slaves as merchandise, or for sale.[178]

For Story and McKinley, who dissented from the decision that Mississippi's constitution was not self-executing,[179] the quoted paragraph meant the state had power to forbid the importation of slaves for sale. That Thompson and Wayne joined in this paragraph—rather than resting solely on the former's conclusion that the Mississippi provision had no legal effect—suggests that they could not resist adding their two-cents-worth on the issue Thompson had so carefully and properly avoided. None of the four, however, gave any inkling of a reason for their conclusion.[180]

Inconclusive as it was on the commerce clause issue, *Groves* did serve to repudiate Webster's astounding assurance during argument that "all questions" relating to the clause "are now fully settled."[181] Six of the seven participating Justices[182] apparently concluded that Mississippi could forbid the importation of slaves for sale; the seventh seemed to suggest it could have excluded slaves entirely. For all but two of them, however, this was only dicta. The three Justices who gave reasons for their decision took three distinct positions. The other four left us to wonder whether they thought such a law valid because the commerce power was not exclusive, because of the police power theory applied in *Miln*, or because the subject lay wholly outside the commerce clause.[183] For those counting heads in anticipation of the inevitable showdown, after *Groves* four Justices—Johnson, Story, McLean, and Baldwin—

---

appeared to disapprove of importation for sale by its own citizens as well as by outsiders. Unable to stay within the case, Baldwin also added (in anticipation of Scott v. Sandford, 60 U.S. (19 How.) 393 (1857), *infra* chapter 8), that slaveowners were "protected from any violations of rights of property by Congress, under the fifth amendment." *Groves*, 40 U.S. (15 Pet.) at 515.

[177]*Id.* at 508-09. Taney correctly noted that the exclusivity question remained open, but then made the "astonishingly inaccurate prediction," C. SWISHER, *supra* note 4, at 398, that the Court would never have to decide it. *Groves*, 40 U.S. (15 Pet.) at 509-10.

[178]*Groves*, 40 U.S. (15 Pet.) at 510.

[179]*Id.* at 517.

[180]McKinley apparently delivered an oral opinion whose contents are unknown; Story was absent when the decision was announced. C. SWISHER, *supra* introduction to part 3, note 2, at 367.

[181]*Groves*, 40 U.S. (15 Pet.) at 494.

[182]Catron was absent, and Barbour had died. *Id.* at 517.

[183]In a private letter Story said he had concluded that the commerce clause did not oust state power, "admitting it to be exclusive." C. SWISHER, *supra* introduction to part 3, note 2, at 367 (quoting Letter from Justice Story to Robert J. Walker 2 (May 22, 1841) (available in New York Historical Society Library). Professor Swisher took this to mean Story thought the state provision to be an exercise of the police power, in contradiction to his own dissent in *Miln*. C. SWISHER, *supra* introduction to part 3, note 2, at 370.

had gone on record that Congress had exclusive power, and only Thompson had yet indicated the contrary.

B. *The License Cases*

Convicted of selling imported liquor without licenses required by state law, the defendants in three separate cases attacked their convictions on constitutional grounds. The Supreme Court unanimously affirmed,[184] but it is difficult to say why. There was no opinion for the Court. Of the seven Justices whose vote was reported, six wrote separate opinions; two wrote more than one.[185]

McLean and Grier[186] took the easy line: earlier cases confirmed that the commerce clause did not forbid states to protect health and morals under their police powers.[187] This seemed to be the basis of Marshall's decision in *Willson v. Black Bird Creek Marsh Co.,*[188] of his quarantine example in *Gibbons,* and of the nearly unanimous *Miln* decision; the only Justices who gave reasons in support of the power to exclude slaves in *Groves v. Slaughter* had conceded it. Yet in the *License Cases* only Woodbury joined McLean and Grier in basing his vote on the police power,[189] and it was not the sole ground of his opinion.[190]

Woodbury also argued that the sale of imported liquor did not fall within the federal commerce power at all: the interstate transaction ended once the liquor entered the state, and the state had exclusive authority to regulate ensuing sales as a matter of local commerce.[191] This seemed a rather extreme position; after *McCulloch v. Maryland*[192] it could easily have been argued that some federal control over the sale

---

[184]*License Cases*, 46 U.S. (5 How.) 504 (1847).

[185]Two of the cases, concerning beverages imported from foreign countries, principally involved a statutory argument based on Brown v. Maryland, 25 U.S. (12 Wheat.) 419 (1827) (*supra* chapter 6): federal tariff acts authorized the importation and sale of the goods, and under the supremacy clause the state could not take away what Congress had given. See *License Cases*, 46 U.S. (5 How.) at 512-14 (Mr. Webster), 546 (Messrs. Ames and Whipple). Taney went out of his way to concede that *Brown* had been rightly decided, and Daniel did likewise to dispute Taney's view, *id.* at 575-76, 612-16; but neither case involved a prosecution of the importer, and nobody seemed willing to extend *Brown's* peculiar holding beyond the importer himself.

There was some discussion in the third case of whether the prohibition on state import taxes, U.S. Const. art. I, § 10, applied to interstate shipments. *See, e.g., License Cases*, 46 U.S. (5 How.) at 595 (McLean, J.) (denying application despite contrary dictum in *Brown*). As Catron said, however, the license requirement was not even clearly a tax, for it imposed only a nominal fee to cover administrative costs. *Id.* at 599. In the cases involving foreign liquor the imports clause argument met the same fate as that based on the tariff act: after leaving the hands of the importer, the liquor was no longer an "Import[ ]." *See, e.g., id.* at 577 (Taney, C.J.).

[186]Grier had replaced Baldwin in 1846. *See supra* introduction to part 3, note 1.

[187]*License Cases*, 46 U.S. (5 How.) at 595, 631-32. Chief Justice Shaw had taken this position in upholding the Massachusetts law. Commonwealth v. Kimball, 41 Mass. (24 Pick.) 359 (1837).

[188]27 U.S. (2 Pet.) 245 (1829); *see supra* introduction to part 3, notes 4-5, and accompanying text.

[189]*License Cases*, 46 U.S. (5 How.) at 627-32.

[190]Indeed, he appeared to have doubts that the police power could be used to interfere with interstate commerce itself, although that was what both *Groves* and the quarantine case seemed to mean. *Id.* at 630.

[191]*Id.* at 625. Justice Daniel echoed this point. *See id.* at 614-16. Compare this position with the arguments of Taney and McLean in *Groves. See supra* notes 172-75, 177 and accompanying text.

[192]17 U.S. (4 Wheat.) 316 (1819); *see supra* chapter 6.

of imported goods was necessary and proper to prevent the effective obstruction of commerce itself.

Most interesting and important was the argument of at least four Justices that Congress's power over commerce was not exclusive. As Taney and Catron convincingly explained,[193] the Court had never held it was; in contrast to the power to coin money, the Constitution did not say it was, and the Court had held that Congress's comparable powers over bankruptcy and the militia were not.[194] Furthermore, quarantine and pilotage laws showed that states had regulated commerce with congressional blessing ever since 1789, and not because they fell within the "police power"; if federal authority were exclusive, it would be irrelevant whether a state's motive was "to guard the citizens of the State from pestilence and disease" or to promote "the interests and convenience of trade."[195]

As usual, Taney's opinion was competent and straightforward.[196] Woodbury and Nelson, as well as Catron, agreed with him,[197] and an aside in Daniel's opinion also seems to suggest the same conclusion.[198] Only McLean, gratuitously repeating his *Groves* argument, disagreed.[199] Grier properly avoided the subject,[200] McKinley was absent, and Wayne apparently did not vote.[201] Thus four of the seven Justices who voted flatly and persuasively[202] declared that the commerce clause did not limit state power. It seems unfortunate that Daniel did not express more definitively the similar sentiments he was to utter two years later in a dissent to the *Passenger Cases*.[203] Although the Court in Taney's own time would demonstrate that constitutional precedents enjoyed no immunity from being overruled,[204] the *License Cases* were hardly a precedent at all.

[193]*License Cases*, 46 U.S. (5 How.) at 578-86 (Taney, C.J.), 601-08 (Catron, J.).

[194]*See supra* chapter 4 (discussing Houston v. Moore, 18 U.S. (5 Wheat.) 1 (1820)); *supra* chapter 5 (discussing Sturges v. Crowninshield, 17 U.S. (4 Wheat.) 122 (1819)). Taney persuasively explained that the arguably contrary naturalization decision of Chirac v. Chirac, 15 U.S. (2 Wheat.) 259 (1817), was based upon a conflict with federal law. *License Cases*, 46 U.S. (5 How.) at 585.

[195]*License Cases*, 46 U.S. (5 How.) at 583. Taney's flat denial that the laws requiring use of local pilots could be characterized as police power measures, *id.*, was unexplained and unconvincing; those laws seemed clearly designed to promote safety.

[196]See the admiring discussions in T. POWELL, VAGARIES AND VARIETIES IN CONSTITUTIONAL LITIGATION 148-51 (1956), and in F. FRANKFURTER, THE COMMERCE CLAUSE UNDER MARSHALL, TANEY, AND WAITE 51-53 (1937).

[197]*License Cases*, 46 U.S. (5 How.) at 618, 624. Nelson had replaced Thompson in 1845. *See supra* introduction to part 3, note 1.

[198]Daniel said state laws affecting commerce were void only if "essentially and directly in conflict with some power clearly invested in Congress by the constitution; and, I would add, with some regulation actually established by Congress in virtue of that power." *License Cases*, 46 U.S. (5 How.) at 615.

[199]*Id.* at 595.

[200]*Id.* at 631-32.

[201]*See* C. SWISHER, *supra* note 4, at 372 ("[U]nder pressure from circuit court litigants," McKinley "had notified . . . Taney that he was going to New Orleans for circuit work instead of coming to Washington."). Wayne, however, was present at least during the argument, for he interjected remarks from the bench. *License Cases*, 46 U.S. (5 How.) at 545. Professor Swisher claims, without citation, that Wayne agreed the laws were constitutional. C. SWISHER, *supra* note 4, at 372.

[202]*See supra* chapter 6.

[203]48 U.S. (7 How.) 283, 494 (1849) (Daniel, J., dissenting); *see infra* notes 220-21 and accompanying text; *see also* J. FRANK, *supra* note 4, at 191 ("for a fleeting and confused moment . . . the law . . . was that the commerce clause was *not* exclusive—and Daniel's position was the most extreme of all.").

[204]*See infra* chapter 8 (discussing the admiralty and diversity cases). See also Justice Daniel's view in the

C. The Passenger Cases

New York and Massachusetts charged ship captains a fee for every passenger they brought into the state. By a five to four vote in 1849 the Court held these levies invalid.[205]

Only two years had passed since laws limiting the sale of imported liquor had been upheld in the *License Cases*,[206] and the Court's personnel had not changed. Once again no one spoke for the Court: eight Justices felt called upon to write extensive opinions. As in *Groves* and the *License Cases*, McLean argued that only Congress could regulate commerce,[207] and this time Wayne and McKinley agreed.[208] Wayne asserted that all five members of the majority joined in this conclusion,[209] but there is room for doubt. Neither Grier[210] nor Catron[211] discussed the commerce clause; Catron, who had argued at some length in the *License Cases* against an exclusive federal commerce power,[212] merely said in the *Passenger Cases* that the issue was not presented.[213]

Separate dissents by Taney, Daniel, and Woodbury[214] offered three strong responses and one weak one to the exclusivity argument, and as in the *License Cases* Nelson mercifully joined Taney without explanation.[215] First, *Miln* and other cases had recognized that the states retained their police powers whether or not the commerce power itself was exclusive; because the passenger fees funded the treatment of diseased passengers and the support of indigent aliens, they served the acknowledged police purposes of avoiding the burden of supporting paupers and the

---

License Cases themselves, 46 U.S. (5 How.) at 611-12, that constitutional precedents were never binding, as well as the views of Justice Johnson, noted *supra* in chapter 3.

[205] *Passenger Cases*, 48 U.S. (7 How.) 283 (1849). For the context of the cases, see C. SWISHER, *supra* note 4, at 382-93; C. WARREN, *supra* introduction to part three, note 2. at 168-82.

[206] 46 U.S. (5 How.) 504 (1847).

[207] *Passenger Cases*, 48 U.S. (7 How.) at 393-400. In the course of this discussion McLean quoted, to no particular avail, from Madison's recently published notes of the Constitutional convention. This may have been the first time the Court cited the notes. *See id.* at 396.

[208] *Id.* at 410-11, 452. Protesting that "a majority" of those voting to strike down the laws "do not think it necessary . . . to reaffirm" the exclusivity of federal power, Wayne went right on to reaffirm that it had been established in *Gibbons* and was the "foundation" of his conclusion. *Id.* at 411. McKinley both endorsed McLean's opinion, *see id.* at 452, and restated its holding of exclusive power, *id.* at 454.

[209] *Id.* at 410-15; *see also* L. TRIBE, AMERICAN CONSTITUTIONAL LAW 324 n.2 (1978) (questionably describing the *Passenger Cases* as "the first to hold a state's action violative of the commerce clause in the absence of a relevant federal statute").

[210] *Passenger Cases*, 48 U.S. (7 How.) at 455-64.

[211] *Id.* at 437-52.

[212] *See supra* text accompanying notes 193-95.

[213] *Passenger Cases*, 48 U.S. (7 How.) at 446. Grier did join Catron's opinion, *id.* at 452, and in a separate paragraph Catron announced mysteriously that he joined McKinley's opinion (which did argue exclusivity) "so far as Mr. Justice McKinley's individual views are expressed, when taken in connection with Mr. Justice Catron's opinion," *id.* at 455. It is difficult to believe that by this oddly qualified endorsement of McKinley's views Catron meant to announce without explanation that he had completely reversed the position he had taken in the *License Cases* only two years before.

[214] *Id.* at 464 (Taney, C.J.), 494 (Daniel, J.), 518 (Woodbury, J.). Taney emphasized, *id.* at 492, that the passengers involved in the case had come from abroad, adding in anticipation of Crandall v. Nevada, 73 U.S. (6 Wall.) 35 (1868), that American citizens had a right to travel from one state to another derived by inference from a variety of constitutional provisions. *See infra* chapter 10.

[215] *Passenger Cases*, 48 U.S. (7 How.) at 518; *see also supra* text accompanying note 197.

introduction of disease.[216] McLean's response that these were revenue rather than police measures[217] recalls Story's losing contention in *Miln* that a state could not enforce its health laws by regulating commerce;[218] all the other Justices, including McLean, had concluded in *Miln* that purpose rather than form controlled. Second, the dissenters argued, if form was indeed the test, the passenger fees were taxes, not regulation, and Marshall had clearly stated in *Gibbons* that the states retained not only the police power but the tax power as well.[219] The third argument, joined this time by Daniel, was that the commerce power itself was not exclusive;[220] five of the nine Justices were now firmly on record against exclusivity, but unfortunately not all in the same case.[221]

The dissenters' final argument that the transportation of passengers fell entirely outside the commerce clause[222] contradicted the holding of *Gibbons*. It also demonstrated the inconsistency of McLean, who had said in *Groves* that Mississippi could exclude slaves because people were not articles of commerce,[223] and it served Marshall right for not clearly stating, when he had sustained federal power to license steamboats, that the vessels in question carried only passengers.[224]

[216]*Passenger Cases*, 48 U.S. (7 How.) at 465-70, 483-90 (Taney), 518-24, 546 (Woodbury); *cf.* New York v. Miln, 36 U.S. (11 Pet.) 102 (1837) (paupers); Gibbons v. Ogden, 22 U.S. (9 Wheat.) 1 (1824) (quarantine) (both discussed *supra* at text accompanying notes 5-31). Chief Justice Shaw had adopted this police power ground in upholding the Massachusetts law at the state level. Norris v. City of Boston, 45 Mass. (4 Met.) 282 (1842).

[217]*Passenger Cases*, 48 U.S. (7 How.) at 403-04.

[218]*See supra* text accompanying notes 21-23.

[219]*See Passenger Cases*, 48 U.S. (7 How.) at 479-80 (quoting Gibbons v. Ogden, 22 U.S. (9 Wheat.) 1, 201-02 (1824), *supra* chapter 6, where Marshall had rejected the contention that the Import-Export Clause implied a state power otherwise to regulate commerce ("This prohibition . . . is an exception from the acknowledged power of the States to levy taxes, not from the questionable power to regulate commerce.")); *see also Passenger Cases*, 48 U.S. (7 How.) at 545-49 (Woodbury, J.). McLean addressed this problem by vaguely invoking the unsatisfying argument of *McCulloch v. Maryland* that the power to tax was the power to forbid, which Marshall himself had rejected in contract clause cases, *see supra* text accompanying notes 58-59, 67-69 (discussing Providence Bank v. Billings, 29 U.S. (4 Pet.) 514 (1830)) as well as in the passage just quoted from *Gibbons*. *Passenger Cases*, 48 U.S. (7 How.) at 404 (McLean, J.).

[220]*Passenger Cases*, 48 U.S. (7 How.) at 470-71 (Taney, C.J.), 497-500 (Daniel, J.), 545, 554-61 (Woodbury, J.). Woodbury equivocated somewhat as to "matters of exterior, general, and uniform cognizance," *id.* at 559, anticipating the distinction later drawn by the Court in the *Cooley* case. *See infra* text accompanying notes 244-49. He considered the taxes in question to fall into the category of "details and local matters," where he found no exclusivity. *Passenger Cases*, 48 U.S. (7 How.) at 558-59.

[221]Despite the contention of Taney and Daniel that five Justices had voted against exclusivity in the *License Cases, see Passenger Cases*, 48 U.S. (7 How.) at 470, 497, Daniel's adherence to that position in the earlier case had been equivocal at best. *See supra* notes 198, 203 and accompanying text. Similarly, Catron not only failed to repeat his anti-exclusivity argument in the *Passenger Cases*; he arguably repudiated it by endorsing McKinley's opinion taking the opposite view. *See supra* note 208.

[222]*Passenger Cases*, 48 U.S. (7 How.) at 493-94 (Taney, C.J.), 509-11 (Daniel, J.), 541-44 (Woodbury, J.).

[223]*See supra* text accompanying notes 173-74. McLean had acknowledged in *Groves* that the navigation of ships transporting passengers was a commercial activity. *See Groves*, 40 U.S. (15 Pet.) at 505-06. He never explained how that squared with his conclusion that people were not articles of commerce.

[224]The question whether commerce included passenger service provoked a long exchange between Wayne and Taney over the genesis of a stray remark in *Miln* that seemed to say it did not. *See Passenger Cases*, 48 U.S. (7 How.) at 428-36, 487-90 (referring to *Miln*, 36 U.S. (11 Pet.) at 136). Because *Miln* had focused on the police power, and neither Wayne nor Taney suggested *Gibbons* had been overruled, the substantive controversy seems to have been blown out of all proportion.

Catron and Grier, the two members of the majority who did not invoke the commerce clause, found at least four other grounds for striking down the passenger taxes, and each joined the other's opinion.[225] Catron argued that the state laws conflicted both with federal statutes and with treaties: by exempting personal baggage from import duties Congress had effectively given its owners a right to enter for nothing, and a treaty explicitly guaranteed British subjects free entry.[226] As Daniel noted on behalf of the dissenters, the exemption seemed to prove only that Congress had decided to lay no federal tax on baggage, and both of Catron's arguments seemed to contradict the state's admitted power to exclude the indigent or diseased.[227] Nevertheless, Justice Wayne seemed correct that every Justice in the majority agreed that the statute and treaty superseded state power;[228] it was quite superfluous for three of them to add that the commerce clause did too.

More inventive and less contrived than any of the foregoing objections was Justice Grier's position that the passenger fees were in effect tonnage and import duties forbidden by article I, section 10.[229] In form the tax lay neither on the vessel nor on imported goods, and, as the dissenters pointed out, the term "imports" could hardly apply to passengers arriving of their own free will.[230] Grier's point, however, was that the state could not tax either the ship or the passengers' baggage by indirection: making the captain pay for each passenger was just another way of scaling his liability to the size of the ship. This seems to have been the majority's best argument, but the dissenters did not dignify it with a reply.[231]

Not content to have enunciated five distinct grounds for their conclusion, the majority Justices embellished their opinions with four others that were so transparently flimsy that I have relegated them to a footnote.[232] The upshot was almost

[225]*Passenger Cases*, 48 U.S. (7 How.) at 452, 464.

[226]*Id.* at 439-44.

[227]*Id.* at 508-09. Catron's conclusions followed easily from Brown v. Maryland, 25 U.S. (12 Wheat.) 419 (1827), where the court had overridden cogent objections similar to those of the *Passenger Cases* dissenters in holding that an importer had purchased immunity from state taxes by paying federal customs duties. *See supra* chapter 6.

[228]*Passenger Cases*, 48 U.S. (7 How.) at 406, 408 (McLean, J.), 411-13 (Wayne, J.), 439-44 (Catron, J.), 452 (Grier & McKinley, J.J.).

[229]*Id.* at 458-59; *see also id.* at 412 (Wayne, J.), 445-46, 452 (Catron and McKinley, J.J.).

[230]*Id.* at 477-78 (Taney, C.J.), 535 (Woodbury, J.). The dissenters could have strengthened this point by reference to the distinction between "Importation" and "Migration" of persons in the slave-trade clause of article I, section 9, but they had to deny that "Migration" in this clause applied to free persons, lest it imply that passenger traffic was commerce. U.S. CONST. art. I, § 9; *see, e.g., Passenger Cases*, 48 U.S. (7 How.) at 474-76 (Taney, C.J.), 511-14 (Daniel, J.). For the contrary view, see *id.* at 452-54 (McKinley, J.), supported by the uncited statements of Wilson and Iredell in the state ratifying conventions. 2 ELLIOT'S DEBATES, *supra* chapter 3, note 42, at 452; 4 *id.* at 102.

[231]Taney gave only his conclusion that the tonnage clause did not apply. *Passenger Cases*, 48 U.S. (7 How.) at 473. The other dissenters said nothing at all.

[232]*See id.* at 405 (McLean, J.), 419-21 (Wayne, J.) (suggesting that the states had offended the provisions of article I, sections 8 and 9, requiring uniform duties and forbidding preferences for the ports of one state over those of another). As the Court would later confirm in the case of port preferences (Morgan v. Louisiana, 118 U.S. 455, 467 (1886)), the context indicates both constitutional provisions limited only federal authority. *See also Passenger Cases*, 48 U.S. (7 How.) at 426 (Wayne, J.) (arguing that taxing immigration offended the naturalization clause because it might interfere with federal policy); *id.* at 447 (Catron, J.) (arguing that if the states do what Congress has power to do they are subject to the limitations applicable to Congress and thus cannot tax for purely local purposes).

total incoherence. Unlike its predecessors, the Taney Court certainly could not be accused of deciding major constitutional cases without writing sufficiently lengthy opinions. Rather, it submerged the unhappy reader in a torrent of verbiage: the Justices had written over one hundred pages of opinions in the *License Cases* and nearly two hundred in the *Passenger Cases* without providing any meaningful guidance for future controversies.[233]

D.   *Cooley v. Board of Wardens*

Help was badly needed, and it was not long in coming. Gathered to his ancestors after only six years of service, Justice Woodbury was replaced by Benjamin R. Curtis of Massachusetts,[234] the only Whig ever to ascend to the supreme bench and very likely the only sorcerer. Within a few months of his appointment Curtis would conjure up out of the morass a solid majority for a brand new commerce clause interpretation that would play a prominent part in decisions for nearly a century.[235]

The occasion was an action by the Wardens of the Port of Philadelphia to recover half the prescribed pilotage fee as a penalty for the departure of two ships without local pilots. The central argument was that the state law offended the commerce clause, but the Court held that it did not. Wayne and McLean dissented, McKinley was absent, and Daniel wrote a separate concurrence;[236] but Curtis, refreshingly, wrote an opinion for the Court.[237]

The result was predictable. Congress had provided in 1789 that state pilotage laws should govern,[238] and in decisions from *Gibbons* to the *Passenger Cases* Justices of all persuasions had branded them valid.[239] As safety measures[240] they seemed, as Daniel's concurrence argued,[241] classic exercises of the police power[242] and therefore easy to sustain on the basis of precedent.[243]

[233]For similar criticism, see also C. WARREN, *supra* note 4, at 179.

[234]*See supra* introduction to part 3, note 1.

[235]Even in reformulating the issue in Southern Pacific Co. v. Arizona, 325 U.S. 761 (1945), the Court paid obeisance to Curtis's test. *See* L. TRIBE, *supra* note 209, at 324 (*Cooley* "laid the groundwork for all that has come since.").

[236]Cooley v. Board of Wardens, 53 U.S. (12 How.) 299, 321, 325 (1852); *see* C. SWISHER, *supra* introduction to part 3, note 2, at 405 ("Justice McKinley being absent because of the illness that was soon to terminate in death").

[237]*Cooley*, 53 U.S. (12 How.) at 311.

[238]Act of Aug. 7, 1789, ch. 9, § 4, 1 Stat. 53, 54.

[239]*E.g.*, *Passenger Cases*, 48 U.S. (7 How.) 283, 401-02 (McLean, J.), 497 (Daniel, J.) (1849); Gibbons v. Ogden, 22 U.S. (9 Wheat.) 1, 207-08 (1824) (Marshall, C.J.).

[240]*See Cooley*, 53 U.S. (12 How.) at 312 (Curtis, J.) ("they rest upon the propriety of securing lives and property exposed to the perils of a dangerous navigation, by taking on board a person peculiarly skilled to encounter or avoid them").

[241]Daniel also argued—unnecessarily and unconvincingly, *cf.* United States v. Coombs, 37 U.S. (12 Pet.) 72 (1838) (Congress may punish theft of shipwrecked goods) (noted *infra* note 268 and accompanying text)—that the safety of interstate shipping was beyond congressional control. *Cooley*, 53 U.S. (12 How.) at 325-26.

[242]Marshall had equivocated; *see* Gibbons v. Ogden, 22 U.S. (9 Wheat.) at 208:

> The acknowledged power of a State to regulate its police, its domestic trade, and to govern its own citizens, may enable it to legislate on this subject, to a considerable extent; and the

Curtis's reasoning, however, was a bolt out of the blue. Ignoring Marshall's treatment of the analogous quarantine laws, Curtis frankly acknowledged that the pilotage law was a regulation of commerce: the Court had already held navigation was commerce,[244] and the pilots' job was navigation.[245] By calling the pilotage law a commercial regulation, Curtis appeared either to reject Marshall's metaphysical police power distinction altogether or to resuscitate Story's repudiated view that form rather than purpose was controlling;[246] yet he acknowledged neither that his approach was new nor that the police power had ever played a part in the Court's decisions.[247] Indeed, in best Marshall fashion, Curtis barely acknowledged that there had been any earlier decisions. Correctly observing that prior cases had not decided whether the federal commerce power was exclusive,[248] Curtis cited none of them and treated the question as one of first impression:

> Now the power to regulate commerce, embraces a vast field, containing not only many, but exceedingly various subjects, quite unlike in their nature; some imperatively demanding a single uniform rule, operating

---

adoption of its system by Congress, and the application of it to the whole subject of commerce, does not seem to the Court to imply a right in the States so to apply it of their own authority.

The offenders' counsel argued in *Cooley* that the fee supported "decayed" or "superannuated" pilots, making it not a police regulation but a tax analogous to that in the *Passenger Cases*. *Cooley*, 53 U.S. (12 How.) at 302, 308 (Messrs. Morris and Tyson). But the fees were assessed only on those who disobeyed the law, *see id.* at 311-12, thus clearly promoting safety by encouraging compliance; and surely the police power included, as in *Miln* and the *License Cases*, the authority to punish offenders.

[243]The holding that the measure was not a tax, *id.* at 313, provided a basis for the similarly correct holding that the fee did not violate the prohibition of article I, section 10 on state tonnage or export duties, the requirement of article I, section 8, that federal taxes be uniform, or the provision of article I, section 9 that ships going to one state not be required to pay duties in another. *Id.* at 313-14. Curtis rightly added that the fee requirement created "an objection" to Philadelphia rather than a preference forbidden by article I, section 9. See *Cooley*, 53 U.S. (12 How.) at 313-15. The Court could also have pointed out that the last three of these provisions applied only to federal measures. *Cf.* Barron v. Baltimore, 32 U.S. (7 Pet.) 243 (1833) (discussed in chapter 6 *supra*). Their invocation had been encouraged by the unrestrained opinions of Wayne and Catron in the *Passenger Cases*.

[244]*Gibbons v. Ogden*, 22 U.S. (9 Wheat.) at 193 (Curtis did not restate this holding); *see supra* chapter 6.

[245]*Cooley*, 53 U.S. (12 How.) at 315-16.

[246]New York v. Miln, 36 U.S. (11 Pet.) 102, 153-61 (1837) (dissenting opinion).

[247]None of Curtis's colleagues noted this apparent change of direction either. Both Grier and McLean had based their concurrence in the *License Cases* on the police power, see *supra* text accompanying notes 186-87; yet the former remained silent in *Cooley*, and McLean surprisingly dissented on the ground that the commerce power was exclusive, without mentioning the police power at all. See *Cooley*, 53 U.S. (12 How.) at 321-25. Wayne, who had joined the police power opinion in *Miln*, see *supra* note 12, dissented without opinion.

[248]The Marshall Court's decisions on the commerce clause were inconclusive, *see supra* chapter 6; *Miln* expressly left the issue open; *Groves* reflected no consensus as to the reason for its dictum that states could exclude slaves; the positions of Daniel in the *License Cases* and of Catron and Grier in the *Passenger Cases* were obscure enough to prevent any confident statement that a majority of the whole Court held in the former that states could regulate commerce or in the latter that they could not. See *supra* text accompanying notes 198-203, 210-13, 225-31. Surprisingly, Curtis's statement provoked no challenge by any of the three Justices (Wayne, Taney, and Daniel) who had stoutly maintained in the *Passenger Cases* only three years before that the issue was already settled. See *supra* notes 209, 221 and accompanying text.

equally on the commerce of the United States in every port; and some, like the subject now in question, as imperatively demanding that diversity, which alone can meet the local necessities of navigation. . . . Whatever subjects of this power are in their nature national, or admit only of one uniform system, or plan of regulation, may justly be said to be of such a nature as to require exclusive legislation by Congress. That this cannot be affirmed of laws for the regulation of pilots and pilotage is plain. The act of 1789 contains a clear and authoritative declaration by the first Congress, that the nature of this subject is such, that until Congress should find it necessary to exert its power, it should be left to the legislation of the States; that it is local and not national; that it is likely to be the best provided for, not by one system, or plan of regulations, but by as many as the legislative discretion of the several States should deem applicable to the local peculiarities of the ports within their limits.[249]

This was a revolution. Curtis's interpretation was contrary to that formally embraced in previous cases by every one of his brethren except Grier,[250] yet three of them acquiesced without a murmur.[251] Of course the result in *Cooley* did not conflict with the theory of fully concurrent authority that these three had earlier announced, and scholars have speculated that they joined the opinion either out of a lack of interest in Curtis's "incidental remarks"[252] or "as a barrier to the adoption of a more rigid formula."[253] The impression remains, however, of a statesmanlike compromise designed to bring order out of chaos, and of most remarkable leadership by a Justice who had barely had time to slip into his robe.

Whether Curtis's interpretation was convincing is another story. The words of the clause cut against him: the simple grant of authority to regulate commerce might or might not imply exclusivity, but it certainly seemed to treat the subject as unitary.[254] Moreover, though the degree of need for uniformity was obviously relevant to the Framers' ostensible purpose of preventing undue obstructions to commerce,[255] the clause appeared to empower Congress rather than the court to make the determination. Indeed, Curtis made no effort to reconcile his conclusion with either the text or the purpose of article I. Instead, borrowing another page from Marshall, he simply took it for granted that the Framers had done the right thing. Marshall had said the

---

[249]*Cooley*, 53 U.S. (12 How.) at 319.

[250]The only evidence of a similar view to be found in earlier opinions was a stray remark by Woodbury in the *Passenger Cases. See supra* note 220; *see also* J. FRANK, *supra* note 4, at 196-97 (tracing Curtis's conclusion to the argument of "his mentor Webster" in *Gibbons*, 22 U.S. (9 Wheat.) at 14:

> the words used in the constitution . . . are so very general and extensive, that they might be construed to cover a vast field of legislation, part of which has always been occupied by State laws; and, therefore, . . . the power should be considered as exclusively vested in congress, so far, and so far only, as the nature of the power requires).

[251]Taney, Catron, and Nelson silently joined Curtis's opinion. The formerly uncommited Grier was the fifth Justice to join the opinion.

[252]C. SWISHER, *supra* note 4, at 406.

[253]F. FRANKFURTER, *supra* note 196, at 56-58.

[254]In this respect Marshall's police power distinction was more satisfactory; there was a certain linguistic persuasiveness in arguing that the only power denied the states was that given to Congress.

[255]*See, e.g.*, THE FEDERALIST No. 22 (A. Hamilton).

Court could ignore unconstitutional legislation and review state court judgments because reasonable Framers would have so provided;[256] Curtis said the commerce power was exclusive only when it ought to be.

Curtis also failed to explain how the Court was supposed to determine whether or not a need for uniformity existed,[257] and his application of the new criterion to the case before him left something to be desired. The "local peculiarities" of various ports seemed to require only local pilots, not a plethora of different rules to confuse the traveler.[258] Curtis's only other argument was that Congress had thought diversity preferable, and he had already gone out of his way to argue that Congress's approval of state laws was not decisive:

> If the law of Pennsylvania, now in question, had been in existence at the date of this act of Congress, we might hold it to have been adopted by Congress, and thus made a law of the United States, and so valid.[259] . . .
>
> But the law on which these actions are founded was not enacted till 1803.
>
> If the constitution excluded the states from making any law regulating commerce, certainly Congress cannot re-grant, or in any manner re-convey to the states that power.[260]

Whether the commerce clause flatly "excluded the states from making any law" on the subject was, however, the very question in issue. That the clause might have an implicit restraining effect on the states did not compel the conclusion that the restraint was as absolute as the explicit bar on coining money.[261] The language of the clause made more persuasive an analogy to the clauses forbidding state imposts, wars, and compacts "without the Consent of [the] Congress"[262]: even if the Court must guard the federal interest in uniformity in the numerous cases Congress might have difficulty anticipating, the Framers still seem to have vested ultimate trust in Congress to determine the extent of free commerce.[263] In other words, a decision to

[256]See supra chapters 3,4 (discussing Marbury v. Madison, 5 U.S. (1 Cranch) 137 (1803), and Cohens v. Virginia, 19 U.S. (6 Wheat.) 264 (1821)).

[257]See R. Newmyer, supra note 31, at 107 ("the significant feature of the decision was not the formulation of a definitive doctrine but the court's tacit agreement to stop looking for one"). For a discussion of the ambiguity of the test, see T. Powell, supra note 196, at 153-55.

[258]Fifty years after Cooley, in holding that the admiralty clause of article III deprived a state of power to make a foreign vessel liable for supplies furnished to an independent contractor, the Court would stress the inability of the master "to acquaint himself with the laws of each individual State he may visit." The Roanoke, 189 U.S. 185, 195 (1903). For discussion of the negative effect of the admiralty clause on state laws, see Currie, Federalism and the Admiralty: "The Devil's Own Mess", 1960 Sup. Ct. Rev. 158.

[259]Cf. Act of Sept. 29, 1789, ch. 21, 1 Stat. 93; Act of May 8, 1792, ch. 36, § 2, 1 Stat. 275, 276 (adopting state procedures in force in 1789 to govern federal court proceedings); Wayman v. Southard, 23 U.S. (10 Wheat.) 1 (1825) (discussed in chapter 4 supra).

[260]Cooley, 53 U.S. (12 How.) at 317-18.

[261]U.S. Const. art. I, § 10. Indeed, Curtis had already held it was not, for he said federal power was exclusive only when uniformity was required.

[262]U.S. Const. art. I, § 10; see T. Powell, supra note 196, at 161.

[263]"The Congress shall have Power . . . [t]o regulate Commerce . . . among the several States . . . ." U.S. Const. art. I, § 8, cl. 3 (emphasis added).

allow state regulation of commerce may itself be a regulation of commerce, and the contrary view taken in *Cooley* has not survived.[264]

Taken by itself, *Cooley* may appear arbitrary, conclusory, and irreconcilable with the constitutional text. Nevertheless, anyone who has slogged through the Augean agglomeration preceding Curtis's labors must find them scarcely less impressive than those of the old stable-cleaner himself.

E.   Aftershocks

In doctrinal terms, *Cooley* began a new era, but practically speaking it concluded the Taney Court's pronouncements on the negative effect of the commerce clause. The Court decided a number of additional cases with commerce clause overtones during Taney's twelve remaining years, but not one of them squarely faced the question whether Congress's power was exclusive, and not one so much as cited *Cooley*.

Several of the decisions upholding state authority rested at least in part on the reasonable conclusion that the activity in question was not "commerce" at all. A tax on negotiable instruments or other property was not one on commerce even though the articles might later be sent outside the state;[265] navigation of a landlocked body of water was neither interstate nor foreign commerce.[266] On the other hand, the Court held that Congress could regulate a vessel that helped land interstate cargoes even though it never left Mobile harbor[267] and could punish those who stole shipwrecked goods.[268] From the conclusion that Congress could protect commerce from thieves not themselves operating interstate it seems only a small step to the notorious 1914 Shreveport decision, allowing federal regulation of local rates that drew business away from interstate railroads.[269] On balance, the Taney Court did not take a narrow view of Congress's commerce power.[270]

---

[264]*See, e.g.*, Prudential Ins. Co. v. Benjamin, 328 U.S. 408 (1946); Cohen, *Congressional Power to Validate Unconstitutional State Laws: A Forgotten Solution to an Old Enigma*, 35 STAN. L. REV. 387, 406-07 (1983) (arguing that Congress should be allowed to "consent to state laws where constitutional restrictions bind the states but not Congress": "it is difficult to understand why the federal interest that underlies a constitutional grant of 'exclusive' federal power needs to be protected from the very body to whose care it has been entrusted").

[265]Nathan v. Louisiana, 49 U.S. (8 How.) 73, 80-81 (1850) (McLean, J.). *Cf.* Mager v. Grima, 49 U.S. (8 How.) 490 (1850) (Taney, C.J.) (allowing taxation of a legacy left to an alien).

[266]Veazie v. Moor, 55 U.S. (14 How.) 568, 573-75 (1853) (Daniel, J.).

[267]Foster v. Davenport, 63 U.S. (22 How.) 244, 246 (1859) (Nelson, J.) ("The lightering or towing was but the prolongation of the voyage of the vessels assisted to their port of destination.").

[268]United States v. Coombs, 37 U.S. (12 Pet.) 72, 78 (1838) (Story, J.) (the power to regulate commerce "extends to such acts, done on land, which interfere with, obstruct, or prevent the due exercise of the power to regulate commerce and navigation").

[269]Houston E. & W. Texas Ry. v. United States, 234 U.S. 342 (1914).

[270]*See also* United States v. Marigold, 50 U.S. (9 How.) 560, 566-67 (1850) (resolving an old controversy by unanimously holding that Congress might prohibit the importation of counterfeit money: "it can scarcely, at this day, be open to doubt, that every subject falling within the legitimate sphere of commercial regulation may be partially or wholly excluded, when either measure shall be demanded by the safety or by the important interests of the entire nation."). Justice Daniel, the most extreme states'-righter on the Court, wrote this opinion. For a discussion of the earlier controversy over Jefferson's embargo *see* 3 J. STORY, *supra* note 26, at 161-63.

Moreover, despite its refusal to discuss the preclusive effect of the commerce clause after *Cooley*,[271] the Court was not reluctant to find other ways of protecting commerce against state interference. In ordering removal of the obstructive Wheeling bridge, for example,[272] the Court aggressively extended Marshall's interpretation of a federal coasting license[273] and invoked an interstate compact provision whose applicability was debatable.[274] A tax on gold shipped from California to New York was struck down on the basis of article I, section 10[275] without discussion of the crucial question whether the ban on export taxes in that section applied to interstate as well as to foreign shipments.[276] And in *Hays v. Pacific Mail Steamship Co.*[277] the Court invalidated a California property tax on out-of-state vessels without even identifying the provision on which it relied.[278]

[271]*See, e.g.*, Cushing v. Owners of Ship John Fraser, 62 U.S. (21 How.) 184, 187-88 (1858) (Taney, C.J.) (allowing state to restrict the time and place of anchorage and require lights on anchored ships because laws contained "nothing . . . in conflict with any law of Congress regulating commerce, or with the general admiralty jurisdiction conferred on the courts of the United States").

[272]Pennsylvania v. Wheeling & Belmont Bridge Co., 54 U.S. (13 How.) 518, 578 (1852) (McLean, J.) (over dissents by Taney and Daniel). *See generally* C. Swisher, *supra* introduction to part 3, note 2, at 408-18. Because this holding was entirely statutory, a second decision allowing Congress to permit the obstruction, Pennsylvania v. Wheeling & Belmont Bridge Co., 59 U.S. (18 How.) 421 (1856) (Nelson, J.), remained true to *Cooley*'s conclusion that Congress could not give the states powers denied them by the Constitution.

[273]Gibbons v. Ogden, 22 U.S. (9 Wheat.) 1 (1824); *see supra* chapter 6. *See also* Sinnot v. Davenport, 63 U.S. (22 How.) 227, 240-44 (1859) (Nelson, J.) (holding a similar license forbade application of a state law requiring registration of shipowners). At the end of his opinion in *Sinnot* Nelson conceded that quarantine laws had been upheld except when "in conflict . . . with the act of Congress." *Id.* at 244. He made no effort to show why the registration law conflicted with the license if a quarantine did not. Later decisions, however, upheld the application to federally licensed ships of state laws regulating oystering tools and granting a monopoly of interstate ferry service. *See, e.g.*, Smith v. Maryland, 59 U.S. (18 How.) 71, 74-76 (1855) (Curtis, J.); Conway v. Taylor's Executor, 66 U.S. (1 Black) 603, 633-35 (1862) (Swayne, J.). In the former case the Court explained only that the state owned the seabed and was attempting evenhandedly to conserve its resources; in the latter, only that a *Gibbons* dictum and long practice had confirmed state power over ferries. *See Smith*, 59 U.S. (18 How.) at 74-75; *Conway*, 66 U.S. (1 Black) at 633-35.

[274]Taney argued in dissent that such compacts have "always been construed to mean nothing more than the river shall be as free to the citizens or subjects for which the other party contracts, as it is to the citizens or subjects of the State in which it is situated." *Wheeling & Belmont Bridge Co.*, 54 U.S. (13 How.) at 583. Taney also argued that Willson v. Black Bird Creek Marsh Co., 27 U.S. (2 Pet.) 245 (1829), *supra* chapter 6, had shown the license gave only "the right to navigate the public waters wherever they find them navigable." *Wheeling & Belmont Bridge Co.*, 54 U.S. (13 How.) at 586. McLean, speaking for the Court, seemed to think *Willson* allowed the state to obstruct only small streams. *Id.* at 566.

[275]"No State shall . . . lay any imposts or duties on imports or exports, except what may be absolutely necessary for executing its inspection laws . . . ." U.S. Const. art. I, § 10, cl. 2.

[276]Almy v. California, 65 U.S. (24 How.) 169 (1861) (Taney, C.J.). Marshall had said that the ban applied to interstate shipments in dictum in Brown v. Maryland, 25 U.S. (12 Wheat.) 419, 449 (1827) ("[W]e suppose the principles laid down in this case, to apply equally to importations from a sister State."), *see generally supra* chapter 6, and though McLean had disagreed in the *Passenger Cases*, *see* 48 U.S. (7 How.) at 407 (McLean, J.), he remained silent in *Almy*. The Court destroyed this basis for *Almy*'s holding shortly after Taney left the bench. *See* Woodruff v. Parham, 75 U.S. (8 Wall.) 123 (1869), *infra* chapter 10.

[277]58 U.S. (17 How.) 596 (1855).

[278]Federal statutes, Nelson said, required registration of the vessels in their home port of New York. *Id.* at 598. The ships engaged in commerce between the states. They entered harbors and discharged

In sum, *Cooley*'s dictum finally established that the commerce clause sometimes limited state power. When Taney died in 1864, however, no one could yet say confidently that the Court had ever found an instance in which it did.

Despite the three 1837 bombshells, then, later decisions revealed that the Court under Taney was prepared to act vigorously to protect both contracts and commerce from state interference. They also showed that in Taney, Story, Curtis, and Thompson the period had its share of strong Justices. Both these strengths and the Court's general affinity for Marshall's nationalistic views were confirmed, moreover, by decisions in other areas. Those decisions are considered in the next chapter.

---

cargoes "independently of any control over them, except as it respects such municipal and sanitary regulations of the local authorities as are not inconsistent with the constitution and laws of the general government, to which belongs the regulation of commerce with foreign nations and between the States." *Id.* at 599. If California could tax these ships, he claimed, so could every other state they touched. Finally, "the admiralty law" recognized many distinctions between local and foreign vessels, and

> California had no jurisdiction over these vessels for the purpose of taxation; they were not, properly, abiding within its limits, so as to become incorporated with the other personal property of the State; they were there but temporarily, engaged in lawful trade and commerce with their *situs* at the home port, where the vessels belonged, and where the owners were liable to be taxed for the capital invested, and where the taxes had been paid.

Id. at 599-600. Daniel's dissent relied on an unexplained lack of jurisdiction to hear the case. *Id.* at 600.

8

Article IV and Federal Powers

Articles I–III of the Constitution, which define the powers of the three branches of the federal government, are familiar to every student. Article IV, which is less well known, contains a variety of provisions designed to require the states to be good neighbors: full faith and credit to one another's judgments, privileges and immunities for one another's citizens, extradition of criminals and of runaway slaves. It also guarantees to each state a republican form of government and empowers Congress both to admit new states and to adopt rules and regulations governing the territory or other property of the United States. Circumstances brought about an unusual concentration on various issues concerning the effect of article IV on both state and federal powers during the Taney period, and the Court's response to those issues is the centerpiece of this chapter.

Apart from article IV cases and the decisions already considered, one of the major accomplishments of the time was the extension of the admiralty and diversity jurisdictions of the federal courts. These developments are also treated here; the chapter concludes with the important questions of federal authority resolved in two decisions of great historical significance: the Civil War *Prize Cases* and *Dred Scott v. Sandford*.

I. OTHER LIMITS ON STATE POWER

A. The Privileges and Immunities Clause

Incorporated in Georgia, the Bank of Augusta sued in federal circuit court on a bill of exchange it had purchased in Alabama. The lower court held for the defendant on the ground that foreign corporations had no authority to buy bills in Alabama; in the 1839 Taney opinion in *Bank of Augusta v. Earle* the Supreme Court reversed.[1]

---

[1]38 U.S. (13 Pet.) 519 (1839). For a good background explanation, see G. HENDERSON, THE POSITION OF FOREIGN CORPORATIONS IN AMERICAN CONSTITUTIONAL LAW 42-59 (1918).

Dissenting alone, Justice McKinley adhered to the position he had taken on circuit:[2] it was up to Alabama to decide whether or not foreign corporations could do business there, and by imposing strict limits on the incorporation of banks the Alabama Constitution expressed a policy inconsistent with purchases by foreign banking corporations.[3] Taney, on the other hand, concluded that Alabama law allowed the Georgia bank to buy bills of exchange,[4] and that was all he needed to say.

Following Marshall's pattern, however, Taney began his opinion by deciding a fundamental constitutional question that proved purely hypothetical: he agreed with McKinley that Alabama could have forbidden the transaction.[5] Ignoring a plausible commerce clause argument,[6] Taney announced in two quick paragraphs that a prohibition on contracts by foreign corporations would not run afoul of article IV's provision that the "Citizens of each State shall be entitled to all Privileges and Immunities of Citizens in the several States." Though the Court had held in *Bank of the United States v. Deveaux*[7] that citizens of a state did not lose the right to invoke the diversity jurisdiction by assuming the corporate form,[8] that decision was "confined . . . to a question of jurisdiction": the privileges and immunities clause was not meant to give outsiders "greater privileges than are enjoyed by the citizens of the state itself," and the liability of those citizens—unlike that of members of a foreign corporation—was not limited to their investment.[9]

It may have been fear of such preferential treatment that led Marshall in *Deveaux* to deny that the corporation was a "citizen" for diversity purposes.[10] It is not clear, however, that the outsiders in *Bank of Augusta* would have enjoyed a preferential position if the Court had held either that the corporation itself was a citizen[11] or that

---

[2]Justice Johnson was absent. 38 U.S. (13 Pet.) at xv. Justice McKinley, it has been observed, "seldom wrote opinions of any kind." C. Swisher, 5 History of the Supreme Court of the United States 120 (1974).

[3]"Can it be believed, that [Alabama] intended to protect herself against the encroachments of her own legislature only, and to leave herself exposed to the encroachments of all her sister states?" *Bank of Augusta*, 38 U.S. (13 Pet.) at 605. McKinley also argued that the legislature itself could not have recognized the Georgia corporation because it did not meet the standards for an Alabama charter, and thus that a court could not recognize it either. *Id.* at 599-604.

[4]"[T]he state never intended by its constitution to interfere with the right of purchasing or selling bills of exchange," but only to limit "the power of the legislature, in relation to banking corporations"; otherwise "no individual citizen of Alabama could purchase such a bill." *Id.* at 595-96.

[5]Baldwin concurred in the judgment. *Id.* at 597. His opinion was unreported, but a newspaper account has been cited to show that he thought the privileges and immunities clause forbade exclusion of a foreign corporation. *See* 5 C. Swisher, *supra* note 2, at 120.

[6]*See Bank of Augusta*, 38 U.S. (13 Pet.) at 531-32 (Mr. Ogden) ("bills of exchange are one of the great means of carrying on the commerce of the world"). No one relied on the full faith and credit clause; the defendants noted that the clause "seems to be as yet confined to judicial acts" and thus did not require recognition of foreign corporate charters. *Id.* at 570 (Mr. Ingersoll). For later decisions indicating that the full faith and credit clause requires respect for state statutes as well as judicial decisions under certain circumstances, see generally B. Currie, Selected Essays on the Conflict of Laws 188-282, 318-19 (1963). Whether the circumstances would require Alabama to defer to Georgia law today under the full faith and credit clause is nevertheless highly doubtful. *See id.* at 188-282, 318-19.

[7]9 U.S. (5 Cranch) 61 (1809); *see supra* chapter 3.

[8]9 U.S. (5 Cranch) at 87-92.

[9]*Bank of Augusta*, 38 U.S. (13 Pet.) at 586.

[10]*See supra* chapter 3; G. Henderson, *supra* note 1, at 56-57.

[11]No doubt because of *Deveaux*, it was not even argued that the corporation was a citizen.

its contracts, like its suits, belonged to its members. As its language suggests, the privileges and immunities clause has since been held to forbid only discrimination against outsiders as such,[12] leaving Alabama free in any event to hold the members of a foreign banking corporation individually responsible for corporate debts or to limit the number of banks,[13] so long as it applied the same rules to both local and foreign bankers.[14] Thus Taney seems to have erred in believing a narrow definition of citizenship necessary to avoid preferences for outsiders, and if his decision meant that Alabama could deny the privilege of acting in corporate form to outsiders while allowing it to insiders, the decision contradicted the purpose of the privileges and immunities clause.

Even if the Alabama Constitution did forbid the purchase of bills by foreign banking corporations, however, it apparently did not disadvantage citizens of other states. Outsiders remained free to buy bills in their individual capacities;[15] Alabama citizens could do no more unless they met the stringent requirements necessary to obtain a charter. Furthermore, the limited privileges of incorporation in Alabama

[12]See, e.g., Toomer v. Witsell, 334 U.S. 385, 395 (1948); Paul v. Virginia, 75 U.S. (8 Wall.) 168, 180 (1869). Dissenting in the *Slaughterhouse Cases*, 83 U.S. (16 Wall.) 36, 118 (1873), *infra* chapter 10, Justice Bradley suggested that the clause might be more than "a guarantee of mere equality," and one commentator has argued that it would be "only . . . a small step" beyond Justice Washington's famous decision in Corfield v. Coryell, 6 F. Cas. 546, 551-52 (C.C.E.D. Pa. 1823) (No. 3230), to hold that article IV gave citizens fundamental rights against their own states as well. L. TRIBE, AMERICAN CONSTITUTIONAL LAW § 6-32, at 406 (1978). Justice Washington's solo performance in *Corfield*, however, concluded no more than that the clause allowed discrimination against an outsider if the right in question was not "fundamental." It seems more than a "small step" to convert this passage narrowing the clause into one expanding it, or to transform what Justice Washington termed a necessary condition into a sufficient one.

The privileges and immunities clause was not discussed in the Convention, but its placement among other provisions plainly concerned with interstate relations (full faith and credit, extradition, and fugitive slaves) and its origin in a provision of the Articles of Confederation expressly designed "to secure and perpetuate mutual friendship and intercourse among the people of the different States" suggest that the conventional interpretation is correct. ARTICLES OF CONFEDERATION art. 4, § 1.

Charles Pinckney, in a paper written at the time of the Convention, seemed to imply equality for outsiders when he spoke of the clause as "extending the rights of Citizens of each State, throughout the United States." *See* C. PINCKNEY, OBSERVATIONS ON THE PLAN OF GOVERNMENT SUBMITTED TO THE FEDERAL CONVENTION, *reprinted in* 3 THE RECORDS OF THE FEDERAL CONVENTION OF 1787 106, 113 (M. Farrand ed. 1966) [hereinafter cited as 3 CONVENTION RECORDS]. So did *Federalist No. 80*, in explaining that diversity jurisdiction (which requires that an outsider be a party) was meant to assure "that equality of privileges and immunities to which the citizens of the union will be entitled." THE FEDERALIST No. 80, at 537 (A. Hamilton) (J. Cooke ed. 1961). Story flatly said that the clause, removing the disabilities of alienage, gave outsiders "all the privileges and immunities, which the citizens of the same state would be entitled to under the same circumstances." 3 J. STORY, COMMENTARIES ON THE CONSTITUTION OF THE UNITED STATES § 1800, at 674-75 (Boston 1833).

[13]See the argument of the Court in Paul v. Virginia, 75 U.S. (8 Wall.) 168, 181-82 (1869), *infra* chapter 10, in holding that corporations were not "citizens."

[14]See *Bank of Augusta*, 38 U.S. (13 Pet.) at 593 (quoting with minor inaccuracy ALABAMA CONST. OF 1819 art. VI, *Establishment of Banks*, § 1, cl. 3 ("'[t]he state and individual stockholders shall be liable respectively for the debts of the bank, in proportion to their stock holden therein.'")); T. SERGEANT, CONSTITUTIONAL LAW 394 (2d ed. Philadelphia 1830) (1st ed. Philadelphia 1822) (citing the New York steamboat case of Livingston v. Van Ingen, 9 Johns. 506 (N.Y. 1812), as holding that the clause "means only, that citizens of other states shall have *equal* rights with the citizens of a particular state" and "does not therefore, affect the right of the legislature of a state, to grant to individuals an exclusive privilege of navigating the waters").

[15]See *Bank of Augusta*, 38 U.S. (13 Pet.) at 603 (McKinley, J., dissenting).

were evidently equally available to out-of-staters.[16] Thus not only did Taney insist on deciding a constitutional question he did not have to reach, but he could have achieved the same result without making the uncomfortable ruling that citizenship should be determined in inconsistent ways under adjacent articles of the Constitution.[17]

The Court faced the privileges and immunities clause again in 1856, when it unanimously held in *Conner v. Elliott*[18] that Louisiana did not have to give a Mississippi widow the same interest in her husband's Louisiana realty that a Louisiana widow would have enjoyed. Article IV, wrote Justice Curtis in his usual terse way, protected only those privileges "which belong to citizenship."[19] Community property in Louisiana was based not upon Louisiana citizenship but upon marriage or domicile there, in accord with the traditional choice-of-law rule referring contract questions to the local law of the place where the contract was made or performed:

> The laws of Louisiana affix certain incidents to a contract of marriage there made, or there partly or wholly executed, not because those who enter into such contracts are citizens of the State, but because they there make or perform the contract. . . . The law does not discriminate between citizens of the State and other persons. . . .[20]

Curtis seems correct that neutral choice-of-law rules such as those referring to the place of contracting do not discriminate against outsiders as such and thus do not violate the privileges and immunities clause. His conclusion that the place-of-performance rule was equally neutral, however, raises more interesting problems, because he equated the place a marriage agreement was performed with "the domicile of the marriage."[21] Because state citizenship depends not on official cer-

---

[16]The constitution spoke generally of "individual stockholders," requiring only that "[a]t least two-fifths of the capital stock shall be reserved for the state." *Id.* at 593.

[17]*See* F. FRANKFURTER, THE COMMERCE CLAUSE UNDER MARSHALL, TANEY AND WAITE 65 (1937) ("Taney rejected the applicability of this clause to the corporation, not because textual analysis or controlling precedents forbade. He did so because, having the power to choose, he chose to deny, by reason of his economic and political outlook, the enhancement of strength that such constitutional protection would give.").

[18]59 U.S. (18 How.) 591 (1856).

[19]*Id.* at 593.

[20]*Id.* at 594. The statement that community property was not among the "'privileges of a citizen'" in Louisiana, *id.* at 593, has reminded at least two commentators of Justice Washington's famous circuit court dictum in Corfield v. Coryell, 6 F. Cas. 546, 551-52 (C.C.E.D. Pa. 1823) (No. 3230), that the clause protects only those privileges which are "fundamental." *See* B. CURRIE, *supra* note 6, at 498. The Court itself later suggested that *Conner* had established that rights like community property and dower lay outside the clause entirely. *See* Ferry v. Spokane, P. & S. Ry., 258 U.S. 314, 318 (1922). One recent decision has resuscitated the limitation to "fundamental" privileges in the teeth of article IV's reference to "all," *see* Baldwin v. Fish & Game Comm'n, 436 U.S. 371, 388 (1978) (over three dissents), but I do not think Curtis meant to say community property was never protected. His reason for holding the right not one belonging to citizenship was that it was not defined in terms of citizenship; he seems to have upheld the law because it did not discriminate against citizens of other states. For an approving view of decisions before *Baldwin* that extended protection to "ordinary legal rights," see B. CURRIE, *supra* note 6, at 460-67.

[21]*Conner*, 59 U.S. (18 How.) at 593.

tification but on domicile,[22] this classification seems precisely what article IV forbids.[23] Thus Curtis seemed to be saying that, despite the language of the clause, a state could discriminate against citizens of other states under some circumstances. He also suggested why: surely a state may deem it "proper not to interfere . . . with the relations of married persons outside of that State."[24] Just how to reconcile this conclusion with the language of the clause is not clear, but once more Curtis's instincts were sound. A literal reading requiring a state with lenient marriage or divorce laws to provide a haven for those hoping to circumvent the more restrictive rules of their own states would convert a provision designed to forestall interstate friction into a tool for exacerbating it.[25] Curtis certainly did not get to the bottom of the perplexing relationship between the privileges and immunities clause and inter-state choice of law, but he does deserve credit for having doubted that the Framers meant to require one state to trample on the legitimate interests of another and for having been one of the first to perceive a problem for which we have yet to find a wholly satisfactory solution.

B.   Fugitive Slaves

Persons held in captivity had an understandable propensity to run away, and persons in areas without slavery had a similarly understandable tendency not to send them back. Consequently, article IV of the Constitution forbade any state to discharge

[22]*See, e.g.*, Williamson v. Osenton, 232 U.S. 619, 624 (1914) (for purposes of diversity jurisdiction). The fourteenth amendment, adopted after *Conner*, makes Americans citizens of "the State wherein they reside." U.S. CONST. amend. XIV, § 1.

[23]*See* Blake v. McClung, 172 U.S. 239, 247 (1898) (striking down a classification favoring local "residents" after holding it referred "to those whose residence in Tennessee was such as indicated that their permanent home or habitation was there, without any present intention of removing therefrom, and having the intention, when absent from that State, to return thereto; such residence as appertained to or inhered in citizenship"). For a discussion of inconsistent decisions on the question whether mere residence is the equivalent of domicile under article IV, see B. CURRIE, *supra* note 6, at 468-75, asserting that "[i]f it were possible to escape the constitutional restraint by the simple device of substituting residence for citizenship as the basis of classification, the clause would be rendered nearly meaningless." *Id.* at 470.

[24]*Conner*, 59 U.S. (18 How.) at 594. Later decisions have carried this idea to the point of holding that both the due process clause and the full faith and credit clause *preclude* one state from regulating matters wholly the concern of another. The decisions are discussed in Allstate Ins. Co. v. Hague, 449 U.S. 302 (1981), and in B. CURRIE, *supra* note 6, at 498-523. Obviously, one clause of the Constitution cannot be read to require what another forbids; but we have here the classic problem of the chicken and the egg.

[25]The Supreme Court has since managed to get around the problem by concluding that the privileges and immunities clause "does not preclude disparity of treatment in the many situations where there are perfectly valid independent reasons for it," thus evidently turning the clause into a prohibition on *unreasonable* discrimination against outsiders. Toomer v. Witsell, 334 U.S. 385, 396 (1948). *See also id.* at 398; Hicklin v. Orbeck, 437 U.S. 518, 525-26 (1978) (dictum); Chemung Canal Bank v. Lowery, 93 U.S. 72, 77 (1876) (upholding a provision tolling the statute of limitations only if the plaintiff's residence was local); L. TRIBE, *supra* note 12, §§ 6-32, 6-33, at 407-11. The tension between article IV and reasonable choice-of-law principles based upon domicile might have been resolved without taking such liberties: to refuse to apply local community property law to infringe rights created by the law of the state where the parties live is to classify people according to the laws of their own states, not on the basis that they are outsiders. Unfortunately this approach seems to prove too much, for it would allow exclusion of citizens of

fugitive slaves from their "Service or Labour," and required that they "be delivered up on Claim of the Party to whom such Service or Labour may be due."[26] Congress implemented this clause in 1793 by authorizing the owner to arrest a fugitive and bring him before any federal judge or local magistrate for a determination of status.[27] In 1826 Pennsylvania passed a statute empowering its judges to enforce the federal law and making it a crime to abduct "any negro or mulatto from the state."[28] Under this law a Pennsylvania jury convicted Edward Prigg of abducting a runaway slave. Reversing, the Supreme Court held the Pennsylvania law unconstitutional in the celebrated 1842 case of *Prigg v. Pennsylvania*.[29]

Justice Story unnecessarily gave three different reasons for this conclusion. First, article IV gave the slaveowner everywhere the same right of ownership that he enjoyed in his own state, including "the right to seize and repossess the slave," and any state law that "interrupts, limits, delays or postpones" the obligation of service "operates, pro tanto, a discharge of the slave therefrom."[30] Second, the federal statute "cover[ed] the whole ground" and thus excluded even "auxiliary" state laws because "the legislation of Congress, in what it does prescribe, manifestly indicates, that it does not intend that there shall be any farther legislation to act upon the subject-matter."[31] Third, the need for uniformity dictated that only Congress could legislate on the subject, and no state legislation would have been valid even if Congress had not spoken.[32]

None of Story's three arguments will bear close scrutiny. First, the state law appeared to satisfy both provisions of article IV: it liberated no slaves, and it provided for sending them back to slavery. Despite echoes in modern due process decisions of Story's argument that delay effected a pro tanto discharge,[33] suspension of someone's rights is unavoidable when there are conflicting claims.[34] By command-

---

some states from benefits even if no interest of their own state so required. *See* B. CURRIE, *supra* note 6, at 508 ("[W]hen the law of a state provides benefits for its residents generally, the same benefits should [under the privileges and immunities clause] be extended to citizens of other states . . . . [This is so,] provided it can [be done] . . . without trespassing upon the interests of other states.") For a more recent recognition of the seriousness of the problem see Ely, *Choice of Law and the State's Interest in Protecting its Own*, 23 WM. & MARY L. REV. 173, 181-91 (1981).

[26]U.S. CONST. art. IV, § 2.

[27]Act of Feb. 12, 1793, ch. 7, § 3, 1 Stat. 302, 302-05.

[28]Act of Mar. 25, 1826, ch. 50, 1826 Pa. Laws 150.

[29]41 U.S. (16 Pet.) 539 (1842). *See generally* C. SWISHER, *supra* note 2, at 535-47. Near the beginning of the Court's opinion Story made a classic statement about constitutional interpretation:

> [P]erhaps, the safest rule of interpretation after all will be found to be to look to the nature and objects of the particular powers, duties, and rights, with all the lights and aids of contemporary history; and to give to the words of each just such operation and force, consistent with their legitimate meaning, as may fairly secure and attain the ends proposed.

Prigg, 41 U.S. (16 Pet.) at 610-11.

[30]*Prigg*, 41 U.S. (16 Pet.) at 612-13.

[31]*Id.* at 617-18.

[32]*Id.* at 622-25. Baldwin concurred in the result but disagreed with the Court's reasons, without offering any of his own. *Id.* at 636. The other separate opinions are discussed *infra* notes 35-55 and accompanying text.

[33]*See, e.g.*, Fuentes v. Shevin, 407 U.S. 67 (1972) (invalidating some pretrial attachments).

[34]The logic of Story's decision would apparently require the Solomonic judgment that if two masters claimed a slave, the slave must be delivered to both at the same time. *Cf. In re* Booth, 3 Wis. 1, 103 (1854)

ing delivery only of a "Person held to Service or Labour" and only to "the Party to whom such Service or Labour may be due," article IV itself seemed to contemplate proceedings to determine the facts of slavery and ownership.[35] In short, as McLean argued in his separate opinion,[36] the Pennsylvania law seemed to be a conscientious effort to carry out the state's constitutional duties while protecting the rights of its free black population.[37]

Story's second and third arguments depended on a finding that Congress had power to legislate with respect to fugitive slaves. None of the Justices denied Story's presumption of congressional capacity. It was not at all clear, however, that Congress had such power, for the fugitive slave clause contained no express grant. In contrast, the explicit provisions for congressional enforcement of the full faith and credit clause of the same article and for the enactment of laws necessary and proper to the effectuation of powers elsewhere given to the federal government[38] arguably implied that when the Framers intended to give such authority they said so. As Marshall had noted, however, the necessary and proper clause does not seem to have been intended to limit the powers Congress would otherwise have had.[39] Similarly, though citation to the analogous holding that the House of Representatives had implied contempt powers[40] would have strengthened his case, Story made a reasonably convincing argument that legislative implementing power was implied in the vague requirement that the fugitive be "delivered" upon "claim" by his owner.[41] At one point he even attempted (with some success) to fit the statute into the necessary and proper clause itself: because the judges authorized by the federal law to determine ownership claims exercised judicial power, the entire legislation implemented the federal question jurisdiction conferred by article III.[42] Coupled with long ac-

---

(opinion of Smith, J.) (*Prigg* meant that "[i]f I replevy my horse, my title to him is *discharged* pending the litigation"), *rev'd.* Ableman v. Booth, 62 U.S. (21 How.) 506 (1859). Even today courts do not release a habeas corpus applicant before he has proved his claim. *See* 28 U.S.C. § 2243 (1976) (disposition after hearing).

[35]U.S. CONST. art. IV, § 2. Congress had held the same opinion, for it had provided for such determinations before the victim could be shipped across the state line. Act of Feb. 12, 1793, ch. 7, § 3, 1 Stat. 302, 303-05. Story's arguments seemed to imply that the federal act was also unconstitutional, though he relied on it elsewhere to preempt state law. *Prigg*, 41 U.S. (16 Pet.) at 622-25.

[36]*Prigg*, 41 U.S. (16 Pet.) at 667-72. McLean did not say whether he was concurring or dissenting, and Wayne, with his penchant for summing up, *cf. supra* chapter 7 (discussing the *Passenger Cases*), declared that all nine Justices found the Pennsylvania law unconstitutional. *Prigg*, 41 U.S. (16 Pet.) at 637. McLean did agree with Story that Congress possessed exclusive power to *enforce* the clause, but the only state provision actually in issue was that forbidding abduction, which McLean seemed to find valid. *Id.* at 661-63, 669. Thus McLean could have concurred only by finding that provisions not in issue were unconstitutional and that the kidnapping provision was inseparable. He did not say this, however, and separability should have been a question of state law to be resolved by the state court.

[37]*See* W. WIECEK, THE SOURCES OF ANTISLAVERY CONSTITUTIONALISM IN AMERICA, 1760-1848, at 159 (1977); D. FEHRENBACHER, THE DRED SCOTT CASE 42 (1978). *But see* 5 C. SWISHER, *supra* note 2, at 547 ("it is hard to conceive that the Court might have decided . . . that the states might enact legislation interfering with the recapture of known [sic] fugitives"). There was no significant discussion of the Fugitive Slave Clause in either the Philadelphia Convention or The Federalist.

[38]U.S. CONST. art. I, § 8; U.S. CONST. art. IV, § 1.

[39]McCulloch v. Maryland, 17 U.S. (4 Wheat.) 316, 411-21 (1819); *see supra* chapter 6.

[40]Anderson v. Dunn, 19 U.S. (6 Wheat.) 204 (1820); *see supra* chapter 6.

[41]*Prigg*, 41 U.S. (16 Pet.) at 615-16.

[42]*Id.* at 616.

quiescence in the construction given the clause by Congress as early as 1793,[43] these arguments made it relatively easy to sustain congressional authority. It is interesting, nonetheless, to see a states'-righter like Daniel, under the influence of the slavery question, swallow such a heavy dose of implied federal power.[44]

The constitutionality of the federal statute, however, did not prove that it precluded state legislation. In light of what Professors Hart and Wechsler perceptively called the "interstitial" nature of federal law,[45] it seems at least as likely that Congress meant to leave unregulated matters to the states as that it meant to leave them unregulated entirely. Story made no effort to show any actual inconsistency between the state and federal provisions. As McLean insisted, both required official approval of a claim of ownership before a slave could be taken away; the federal law did not authorize the self-help that Pennsylvania had attempted to punish.[46] Despite its reputation as a defender of state interests, the Taney Court had once again followed Marshall in reading more preemptive effect into federal statutes than Congress appeared to have put there.[47]

Similarly, that Congress could legislate on the subject of fugitive slaves by no means compelled the conclusion that the states could not. Taney, Thompson, and Daniel all deserted Story on this issue.[48] Taney persuasively argued that the apparent requirement that states deliver fugitives implied state implementing legislation;[49] Daniel properly observed that the Court had already held the explicit bankruptcy power was not exclusive.[50] Story neither responded to the bankruptcy analogy, nor came up with counterexamples of his own,[51] nor gave any convincing reason why

[43]*Id.* at 620-21.

[44]*Id.* at 651-52 ("These [powers] are not properly concurrent, but may be denominated dormant powers in the federal government; they may at any time be awakened into efficient action by Congress, and from that time so far as they are called into activity, will of course displace the powers of the states.")

[45]H. HART & H. WECHSLER, THE FEDERAL COURTS AND THE FEDERAL SYSTEM 470-71 (2d ed. 1973) ("Congress acts . . . against the background of the total *corpus juris* of the states in much the way that a state legislature acts against the background of the common law, assumed to govern unless changed by legislation.").

[46]*Prigg*, 41 U.S. (16 Pet.) at 667-72. Although the federal law arguably required only ex parte proof of ownership, Act of Feb. 12, 1793, ch. 7, § 3, 1 Stat. 302, 303-04 ("upon proof to the satisfaction of such judge or magistrate, either by oral testimony or affidavit"), Pennsylvania required a trial, Act of Mar. 25, 1826, ch. 50, § 6, 1826 Pa. Laws 150, 152-53; but Prigg was hardly in a position to complain since he also did not have a federal certificate.

[47]*Compare, e.g.*, Gibbons v. Ogden, 22 U.S. (9 Wheat.) 1 (1824) (federal coasting license bars state steamboat monopoly) *and* Brown v. Maryland, 25 U.S. (12 Wheat.) 419 (1827) (tariff act bars state taxation of seller of imported goods) (both discussed *supra* in chapter 6) *with* Passenger Cases, 48 U.S. (7 How.) 282 (1849) (tariff act bars taxation of incoming passengers) *and* Pennsylvania v. Wheeling & Belmont Bridge Co., 54 U.S. (13 How.) 518 (1852) (steamboat license and compact for free navigation preclude state bridge) (both discussed *supra* in chapter 7).

[48]*See Prigg*, 41 U.S. (16 Pet.) at 626 (opinion of Taney, C.J.), 633 (opinion of Thompson, J.), 650 (opinion of Daniel, J.).

[49]*Id.* at 628.

[50]*Id.* at 653-54 (citing Sturges v. Crowninshield, 17 U.S.(4 Wheat.) 122 (1819)). *See generally supra* chapter 5. Daniel also invoked Thompson's argument in New York v. Miln, 36 U.S. (11 Pet.) 102 (1837), *supra* chapter 7, that the commerce power was not exclusive.

[51]*See* Wayman v. Southard, 23 U.S. (10 Wheat.) 1, 26 (1825) (dictum) (*supra* chapter 4) (denying state power to regulate federal court procedure); Chirac v. Lessee of Chirac, 15 U.S. (2 Wheat.) 259, 269 (1817) (*supra* chapter 5) (suggesting that only Congress could regulate naturalization). McLean, agreeing with

uniformity was so important in the fugitive slave field that it overcame the natural inference that when the Framers meant to forbid state action they said so.[52]

It seems perplexing that the anti-slavery Story went so far out of his way to strike down a law protecting free persons from being taken into slavery. His explanation that personal preferences must yield to the Constitution[53] seems weak, because in this case the Constitution did not seem to contradict Story's own convictions. Part of the answer may be that, as Daniel perceived, the exclusivity of federal power was a sword with two edges: in striking down a law protecting free blacks, Story established that the states could not help enforce the fugitive slave clause.[54] This does not explain Story's additional argument that the kidnapping law unconstitutionally discharged a fugitive slave, but the legal realist might surmise that it was the price of majority support for his exclusivity conclusion.[55]

C.   Other Fugitives

Article IV also contains a clause dealing with another kind of fugitive: any "person charged in any State with Treason, Felony, or other Crime" found in another state must "be delivered up" to the state in which he is so charged "on Demand."[56] In the same 1793 statute that specified the procedure for return of runaway slaves, Con-

---

Story, said the fugitive slave power was as exclusive as that over commerce, *Prigg*, 41 U.S. (16 Pet.) at 662. Because the Court had yet to hold that the commerce clause had any negative effect on state authority, this analogy fell somewhat short.

[52]That the Framers could not have intended to allow the states to frustrate the Constitution's purposes was a principle familiar since McCulloch v. Maryland, 17 U.S. (4 Wheat.) 316 (1819). Nevertheless as in *McCulloch* itself, *see supra* chapter 6, no implied limitation on state authority was necessary in *Prigg* in order to secure the national goal. Just as Congress could have immunized the national bank from state taxation, it could have outlawed state legislation that interfered with the recovery of runaways. Indeed, an alternative basis for *Prigg* itself was that Congress had already done so. See *Prigg*, 41 U.S. (16 Pet.) at 617-18.

[53]*See* G. DUNNE, JUSTICE JOSEPH STORY AND THE RISE OF THE SUPREME COURT 401 (1970).

[54]*Prigg*, 41 U.S. (16 Pet.) at 656-57. Daniel's fellow southerner Wayne held a different view, arguing that state "assistance" was likely to sabotage the constitutional goal, as in the case before him. *Id.* at 643-44. Daniel's prognosis, however, seems to have been correct. *See* C. SWISHER, ROGER B. TANEY 424 (1936) ("The major significance of the decision lies in the fact that many of the northern states took advantage of the advice that they might forbid their officers to aid in the enforcement of the federal Fugitive Slave Law, thereby rendering it ineffective."); *see also* 2 C. WARREN, THE SUPREME COURT IN UNITED STATES HISTORY 87 n.1 (rev. ed. 1928), adding that Story's son said the Justice had referred to the decision as "'a triumph of freedom.'" As noted by Fehrenbacher, this "triumph" was overturned when Congress passed a new and more effective fugitive slave provision in 1850. D. FEHRENBACHER, *supra* note 37, at 43.

[55]In Moore v. Illinois, 55 U.S. (14 How.) 13 (1852), the Court, in an opinion by Grier, upheld an Illinois conviction for secreting a fugitive slave, distinguishing *Prigg* on the basis of Story's peculiar concession in *Prigg* that exclusivity did not preclude the state from exercising its police power to rid itself of undesirable persons and emphasizing rather debatably that the Illinois law neither hindered nor assisted the master in recovering his slave. *Prigg*, 41 U.S. (16 Pet.) at 625. Grier also implied, however, that what Story had tried to settle in *Prigg* actually remained unsettled: "we would not wish it to be inferred, by any implication from what we have said, that any legislation of a State to aid and assist the claimant, and which does not directly nor indirectly delay, impede, or frustrate the reclamation of a fugitive, . . . is necessarily void." *Moore*, 55 U.S. (14 How.) at 19.

[56]U.S. CONST. art. IV, § 2, cl. 2.

gress also implemented this extradition clause, making it "the duty of the executive
authority" of the state to which the accused had fled to arrest and return him.[57] In
1861, however, when Kentucky sued to require Ohio's governor to deliver up a
fugitive from justice in *Kentucky v. Dennison*,[58] the Court held the Governor's duty
unenforceable.

Chief Justice Taney wrote for a unanimous Court, and he left no doubt that Ohio
was in the wrong. Ohio's position that helping a slave to escape was not a "Crime"
within article IV because not all states made that act criminal, Taney sensibly
observed, would engender just the sort of "controversy" the extradition clause was
meant to prevent and render it "useless for any practical purpose";[59] the broad term
"other Crime," contrasted with the restrictive "high misdemeanor" in the Articles of
Confederation,[60] extended the obligation to "every offence made punishable by the
law of the State in which it was committed."[61] Although the clause did not say so, that
obligation clearly lay on the Governor of the state where the fugitive was found
because similar words had been used in the Articles before there were any federal
authorities who could have taken action.[62] Finally, as with the fugitive slave clause in
Prigg, Congress had implied power to adopt regulations to implement this
prescription.[63]

Having said all this, Taney executed a sudden *volte-face*:

> [L]ooking to the subject-matter of this law, and the relations which the
> United States and the several States bear to each other, the court is of
> opinion, the words "it shall be the duty" [in the 1793 Act] were not used
> as mandatory and compulsory, but as declaratory of the moral duty which
> [article IV created]. . . . [T]he Federal Government, under the Con-
> stitution, has no power to impose on a State officer, as such, any duty
> whatever, and compel him to perform it; for if it possessed this power, it
> might overload the officer with duties which would fill up all his time, and
> disable him from performing his obligations to the State . . . .[64]

This was the first time the Court had based a decision on the implicit immunity of
states from federal legislation,[65] and it seemed to contradict Marshall's comment in

[57]Act of Feb. 12, 1793, ch. 7, § 1, 1 Stat. 302, 302.

[58]65 U.S. (24 How.) 66 (1860). *See generally* 5 C. SWISHER, *supra* note 2, at 685-90.

[59]*Dennison*, 65 U.S. (24 How.) at 102.

[60]ARTICLES OF CONFEDERATION art. 4, § 2.

[61]*Dennison*, 65 U.S. (24 How.) at 103. The words "Treason" and "Felony," he added, had been
included to show that political offenses were extraditable. *Id.* at 99-100. In support of Taney's construction, see Notes of James Madison (Aug. 28, 1787), *reprinted in* 2 THE RECORDS OF THE FEDERAL
CONVENTION OF 1787 437, 443 (M. Farrand ed. 1966) [hereinafter cited as 2 CONVENTION RECORDS] (the
present language was substituted for the phrasing taken from the Articles "in order to comprehend all
proper cases; it being doubtful whether 'high misdemeanor' had not a technical meaning too limited"). *See
also* C. PINCKNEY, *supra* note 12, *reprinted in* 3 CONVENTION RECORDS, *supra* note 12, at 112.

[62]*Dennison*, 65 U.S. (24 How.) at 102-03.

[63]*Id.* at 104; *cf. supra* text accompanying notes 29-44 (discussing *Prigg*).

[64]*Dennison*, 65 U.S. (24 How.) at 107-08.

[65]Suggestive but distinguishable dicta had appeared in *Prigg*, 41 U.S. (16 Pet.) at 616 ("it might well be
deemed an unconstitutional exercise of the power of interpretation to insist that the States are bound to
provide means to carry into effect the duties of the national government, nowhere delegated or intrusted

upholding a converse federal immunity in *McCulloch v. Maryland*[66] that the states needed no immunity since they had a political check through their representation in Congress. Taney could have pointed out that by conferring only limited federal powers the Framers had shown they considered the political check inadequate and that, unlike Congress, the states could not protect themselves by legislation. He might then have turned *McCulloch*'s actual holding to his advantage by arguing that the Court had already recognized implicit immunities needed to keep one government from destroying another.[67]

In *Dennison* itself, however, the inability of Congress to impose duties on state officials seems irrelevant,[68] for Taney had earlier confirmed that the *Constitution* required them to deliver fugitives to other states.[69] Reducing this plain limitation to a "moral duty" out of concern for state autonomy would essentially allow the Governor to decide which offenses were extraditable, and, as Taney had said earlier in his opinion, that would read the extradition clause right out of the Constitution.[70]

Some twenty years before, in *Holmes v. Jennison*,[71] the Taney Court had faced the related question whether a state could constitutionally deliver up a fugitive from a foreign country and had been unable to decide it. A man charged with murder in Quebec had been arrested in Vermont for purposes of extradition, and the Supreme Court was asked to release him.[72] Taney's well-crafted opinion made a strong case for the initially surprising conclusion that extradition constituted an "Agreement or Compact with . . . a foreign Power," which, under article I, section 10, a state could not make without congressional consent.[73] As Taney read it, the consent requirement was intended to prevent the states from meddling with foreign affairs to the possible detriment of national policy, and the states could not evade it simply by

---

to them by the Constitution"). McLean disputed this observation at the time, using the extradition clause as a counterexample. *See id.* at 664-65. Taney, however, cited neither *Prigg* nor anything else in this part of his *Dennison* opinion, and McLean silently went along with Taney.

[66]17 U.S. (4 Wheat.) 316, 398 (1819); *see* chapter 6 *supra*.

[67]One recent application of this general principle, despite the novelty of its particular result, appears in National League of Cities v. Usery, 426 U.S. 833 (1976), *overruled*, Garcia v. San Antonio Metro. Transit Auth., 105 S. Ct. 1005 (1985). The argument for state autonomy seems especially potent when Congress seeks not to limit state activities but to require state enforcement of federal law. *See* D. CURRIE, AIR POLLUTION—FEDERAL LAW AND ANALYSIS § 4.29 (1981).

[68]Taney distinguished the practice of state courts in entertaining federal claims as entirely voluntary. *Dennison*, 65 U.S. (24 How.) at 108-09. Later cases that hold Congress may require state courts to do so, *e.g.*, Testa v. Katt, 330 U.S. 386 (1947), seem questionable but may be distinguishable on the ground that the Constitution itself (in the supremacy clause) requires state judges to apply federal law. This distinction could support *Dennison*'s extradition statute as well; it, too, implements a constitutional duty. *See Prigg*, 41 U.S. (16 Pet.) at 664-66 (opinion of McLean, J.).

[69]*Dennison*, 65 U.S. (24 How.) at 103-04.

[70]*See* 3 J. STORY, *supra* note 12, at 676 (the extradition clause gave "strength to a great moral duty . . . by elevating the policy of the mutual suppression of crimes into a legal obligation"); *see also* C. SWISHER, *supra* note 2, at 690 (comparing *Dennison* to *Marbury v. Madison, supra* chapter 3) (Taney delivered a lecture to refractory northern governors "but refrained from applying . . . a coercive power which the federal government did not possess"). Another interpretation might be that the Court was lying low after the debacle of its activism in Scott v. Sandford, 60 U.S. (19 How.) 393 (1857), *infra* text accompanying notes 198-274.

[71]39 U.S. (14 Pet.) 540 (1840).

[72]*Id.* at 563-64.

[73]U.S. CONST. art. I, § 10, cl. 3.

neglecting to reduce an agreement to writing.[74] He unnecessarily went on to say that Vermont's action intruded on the implicitly exclusive power given the federal government with respect to foreign affairs.[75]

This latter conclusion contrasts strikingly with Taney's firm position that the states could regulate commerce[76] and with his argument in *Prigg* that they could enforce the fugitive slave clause.[77] Distinguishing Barbour's counterexample of the bankruptcy clause[78] by finding an overriding need for uniformity, Taney argued that the Constitution was designed "to make us, so far as regarded our foreign relations, one people, and one nation; and to cut off all communications between foreign governments, and the state authorities," and that conflicting state policies about extradition could cause problems for the whole country.[79] Finally, Taney noted that the treaty power could never be "dormant" in the same sense as ordinary legislative powers.[80] Rather, by declining to enter into extradition treaties for a number of years the United States had expressed a policy against extradition. A state could no more defy that policy than it could appoint an ambassador to a nation the President had declined to recognize.[81]

That the treaty power allows the President to make binding policy by inaction may seem questionable, but Taney put the arguments for exclusive federal power strongly, showing once again that he was no doctrinaire states'-righter.[82] He was joined, however, only by Story, McLean, and Wayne,[83] the most federal-minded of his brethren. McKinley missed this Term altogether,[84] and the other four Justices, for various reasons, thought there was no jurisdiction.[85] There was no decision on the

[74]*Holmes*, 39 U.S. (14 Pet.) at 572-74. For the contrary argument, see the concurring opinion of Redfield, J., on remand. *Ex parte* Holmes, 12 Vt. 631, 646 (1840) ("A plain unsophisticated mind would find it difficult to construe that a '*compact or agreement*,' which was confessedly mere *comity*, and of course might be done or omitted at pleasure.") (emphasis added). In the course of this discussion Taney made some useful comments on the difficult and important question of distinguishing compacts from treaties, which the states may not make even with congressional permission. *See Holmes*, 39 U.S. (14 Pet.) at 571-72; *see also* U.S. CONST. art. I, § 10. No meaningful comments on the compact clause appear in the Convention debates or in The Federalist.

[75]*Holmes*, 39 U.S. (14 Pet.) at 576-79.

[76]*See supra* chapter 7 (discussing the *License Cases*).

[77]*See supra* text accompanying notes 48-49.

[78]*Holmes*, 39 U.S. (14 Pet.) at 591-92 (opinion of Barbour, J.); *cf. supra* chapter 5 (discussing *Sturges v. Crowninshield*).

[79]*Holmes*, 39 U.S. (14 Pet.) at 575-76.

[80]*Id.* at 576-78.

[81]*Id.* at 574, 577.

[82]As in *Prigg*, however, Congress could perhaps have protected the federal interest without exclusivity by passing a law forbidding state extradition, though it is not immediately obvious to which express federal authority such a law would have been "necessary and proper."

[83]*See Holmes*, 39 U.S. (14 Pet.) at 561.

[84]*See* 39 U.S. (14 Pet.) at vii.

[85]*See Holmes*, 39 U.S. (14 Pet.) at 579-86 (Thompson, J., combining arguments that no constitutional provision was actually offended with the contention that none was properly invoked below); *id.* at 586-94 (Barbour, J., finding no jurisdiction because there was no agreement and federal power was not exclusive); *id.* at 594-98 (Catron, J., finding no jurisdiction because no agreement had been proved). Once again, the third edition of the reports brought with them another windy opinion by Baldwin. *See* 39 U.S. (14 Pet.) at 586-86x (3d ed. 1884) (finding no jurisdiction because a state habeas corpus judgment was neither civil nor final as allegedly required for Supreme Court review—a position that seemed to contradict Cohens v. Virginia, 19 U.S. (6 Wheat.) 264 (1821) (*supra* chapter 4)).

merits; Catron, however, made it clear he would have joined Taney if there had been proof that Vermont had arrested Holmes in response to a request from Quebec.[86] Thus a majority of the Democratic Court took a broad view in *Holmes* of both explicit and implicit limits on state power,[87] as it would do again two years later in *Prigg v. Pennsylvania.*[88]

D. Federal Immunities

In *Kentucky v. Dennison*[89] the Taney Court employed an implicit constitutional immunity to minimize federal interference with the states. The Court was equally sensitive, though, to the protection of federal activities from state action. In two widely separated decisions, for example, it unanimously held the Constitution forbade state taxation either of a federal officer in proportion to the value of his office[90] or of federal securities owned by a banking corporation.[91] These decisions extended federal immunity beyond the Marshall precedents they relied on: the taxes in both *McCulloch v. Maryland*[92] and *Weston v. City Council*[93] had been more or less discriminatory.[94] In the federal securities case, however, Justice Nelson pointed out that neither *McCulloch* nor *Weston* had relied on the discriminatory nature of the tax, and he repeated *McCulloch*'s unconvincing argument that a court could not be expected to administer a ban that was less than absolute.[95]

The famous 1859 decision in *Ableman v. Booth*,[96] however, provided the most

[86]*Holmes*, 39 U.S. (14 Pet.) at 595-96. The Vermont court, with a more complete record, took this to mean Holmes had to be released. *See Ex parte* Holmes, 12 Vt. 631, 633 (1840) (noting that Quebec had asked for extradition and that the Governor had apprised Quebec "that the surrender would be made agreeably to the order").

[87]*See* 2 C. WARREN, *supra* note 54, at 64-66 (declaring that Taney's "superbly able opinion" had "sustained the supremacy of the powers of the Federal Government, with a breadth and completeness . . . excelled by no one of Marshall's opinions" and reporting James Buchanan's accusation that portions of the opinion were " 'latitudinous and centralizing beyond anything I have ever read in any other judicial opinion' ").

[88]*See supra* notes 29-44 and accompanying text.

[89]65 U.S. (24 How.) 66 (1861).

[90]Dobbins v. Commissioners of Erie County, 41 U.S. (16 Pet.) 435 (1842).

[91]New York *ex rel.* Bank of Commerce v. Commissioners of Taxes, 67 U.S. (2 Black) 620 (1863).

[92]17 U.S. (4 Wheat.) 316 (1819).

[93]27 U.S. (2 Pet.) 449 (1829).

[94]*See* T. POWELL, VAGARIES AND VARIETIES IN CONSTITUTIONAL INTERPRETATION 92-93 (1956); *supra* chapter 6. Moreover, in both the federal officeholder and the federal securities cases the Court was resolving an unnecessary constitutional issue. In the former it admitted that the tax also effectively contradicted the statute fixing the federal officer's compensation, Dobbins v. Commissioners of Erie County, 41 U.S. (16 Pet.) 435, 449-50, and in the latter it simply ignored an Act of Congress expressly exempting " 'all stocks, bonds, and other securities of the United States' " from state taxation, New York *ex rel.* Bank of Commerce v. Commissioners of Taxes, 67 U.S. (2 Black) 620, 625.

[95]New York *ex rel.* Bank of Commerce v. Commissioners of Taxes, 67 U.S. (2 Black) 620, 629-34. The Court has since overruled *Dobbins*, holding that taxation of the income of federal employees had too speculative and uncertain an impact on the Government to sustain the conclusion that it was implicitly prohibited. Graves v. New York *ex rel.* O'Keefe, 306 U.S. 466 (1939) (incorporating arguments made in the converse case of Helvering v. Gerhardt, 304 U.S. 405 (1938)).

[96]62 U.S. (21 How.) 506 (1859). *See generally* C. SWISHER, *supra* note 2, at 653-75; 2 C. WARREN, *supra* note 54, at 258-66, 332-44; Beitzinger, *Federal Law Enforcement and the Booth Cases*, 41 MARQ. L. REV. 7 (1957).

striking instance of the protection afforded federal activities by the Supreme Court during Taney's tenure. A federal commissioner jailed Booth on charges of aiding the escape of a fugitive slave. The Wisconsin courts freed him on habeas corpus, holding unconstitutional the new Fugitive Slave Act that formed part of the Compromise of 1850, and ordered him released again on the same ground after he had been convicted in federal court.[97] The Supreme Court unanimously reversed, holding the state courts could not investigate the validity of a federal order of commitment.[98]

Because the state supreme court had refused to respond to the writ of error, Taney devoted much of his opinion to a restatement, in best Marshall fashion, of the necessity and propriety of Supreme Court review of state court decisions[99]—citing, however, neither *Martin v. Hunter's Lessee*[100] nor *Cohens v. Virginia*,[101] which were squarely in point.[102] He also cited nothing in support of his more interesting conclusion that the state could not discharge a federal prisoner. The opinion rests largely upon bold fiat:

> [N]o State can authorize one of its judges or courts to exercise judicial power . . . within the jurisdiction of another and independent Government. . . . Wisconsin had no more power to authorize these proceedings . . . than it would have had if the prisoner had been confined in Michigan, or in any other State of the Union, for an offence against the laws of the State in which he was imprisoned.[103]

Taney accompanied this conclusion with an *in terrorem* observation:

> If the judicial power exercised in this instance has been reserved to the States, no offence against the laws of the United States can be punished by their own courts, without the permission and according to the judgment of the courts of the State in which the party happens to be imprisoned . . . .[104]

Elsewhere in the opinion Taney quoted the supremacy clause, apparently to establish that the United States could "execute its own laws by its own tribunals, without interruption from a State,"[105] and in summing up the Wisconsin proceedings he said the state court had "supervise[d] and annul[led] the proceedings of a commissioner of the United States," as well as a federal judgment.[106]

This sketchy reasoning hints at several possible arguments. The supremacy clause

---

[97]*Ableman*, 62 U.S. (21 How.) at 507-08.

[98]*See* Warren, *Federal and State Court Interference*, 43 Harv. L. Rev. 345, 353 (1930) (noting that although state habeas for federal prisoners was "entirely incompatible with the constitutional relations of the Federal and State Governments," it had been practiced "for a period of eighty years"). Taney did not allude to this practice.

[99]*Ableman*, 62 U.S. (21 How.) at 517-23.

[100]14 U.S. (1 Wheat.) 304 (1816).

[101]19 U.S. (6 Wheat.) 264 (1821).

[102]*See supra* chapter 4.

[103]*Ableman*, 62 U.S. (21 How.) at 515-16.

[104]*Id.* at 514.

[105]*Id.* at 517.

[106]*Id.* at 513-14.

alone[107] lends little support; it binds state courts to follow the Constitution, not to respect unconstitutional exercises of federal authority.[108] The analogy to a Michigan prisoner was also not very helpful. If anything in the Constitution at the time forbade Wisconsin to meddle with other states' prisoners it was the full faith and credit clause,[109] which says nothing about the federal government.

Two passages in *Ableman* hinted at more promising arguments, but neither was adequately developed. First, the suggestion that state courts were required to respect federal judgments could have been supported by an argument that in giving federal courts criminal jurisdiction Congress must have intended to empower them to dispose effectively of the case. Even this was not conclusive, because the jurisdiction of a court was traditionally subject to collateral investigation,[110] and because the Supreme Court was soon to hold that the constitutionality of the statute defining an offense was "jurisdictional" in this sense.[111] Moreover, it was less clear that the finality argument applied to the commissioner's pretrial order, which may not have been a judicial judgment but which apparently was held equally immune from state examination.[112] Most important, Taney neglected to develop fully the statutory basis for this argument.

Second, the *in terrorem* passage seems to borrow a page from *McCulloch v. Maryland*,[113] where Marshall argued, in holding that states could not tax the national bank, that the Framers were too sensible to have allowed the states to frustrate the exercise of federal authority. As in *McCulloch*, Congress's power under the necessary and proper clause seemed fully adequate to protect federal interests without resort to an implied immunity;[114] but since this point had not troubled the Court in *McCulloch*, that case was a good starting point for analysis of *Ableman*. Nevertheless it did not necessarily follow that because a state could not tax federal operations it could not decide whether a federal imprisonment was legal. To tax federal activities necessarily burdens them; in *Ableman* the burden arose only from the risk that the state court might make a mistake in interpreting federal law, and the Supreme Court had jurisdiction to correct such a mistake on writ of error.[115] In any event, *McCulloch* was not even cited.[116]

[107]U.S. CONST. art. VI, cl. 2.

[108]*See* Arnold, *The Power of State Courts to Enjoin Federal Officers*, 73 YALE L.J. 1385, 1402 (1964).

[109]*But cf.* Nevada v. Hall. 440 U.S. 410 (1979) (full faith and credit clause does not require one state to respect another's sovereign immunity from suit). The due process clause of the fourteenth amendment now limits the geographical reach of state court jurisdiction. *See* World-Wide Volkswagen Corp. v. Woodson, 444 U.S. 286 (1980). The fourteenth amendment was adopted after *Ableman*, however, and there was no doubt that Booth was within the geographical reach of Wisconsin process.

[110]*See, e.g., Ex parte* Watkins, 28 U.S. (3 Pet.) 193 (1830); *In re* Booth, 3 Wis. 157, 178-212 (1855).

[111]*See Ex parte* Siebold, 100 U.S. 371 (1880).

[112]*See also* Tarble's Case, 80 U.S. (13 Wall.) 397 (1872) (reaffirming *Ableman* in the absence of any federal judgment).

[113]17 U.S. (4 Wheat.) 316, 362 (1819); *supra* chapter 6.

[114]For example, Congress could have given the federal courts exclusive jurisdiction to determine the validity of a federal commitment, made federal judgments binding on state courts, or provided for removal (as it has since done, 28 U.S.C. § 1442 (1976)) of state court suits against federal officers. *See* Tennessee v. Davis, 100 U.S. 257 (1880); The Moses Taylor, 71 U.S. (4 Wall.) 411 (1867) (upholding analogous removal and exclusivity provisions); *see also supra* chapter 6.

[115]*Ableman*, 62 U.S. (21 How.) at 525-26.

[116]The Court did not seem to find an implicit exclusivity in the statute giving federal courts habeas

Thus, unlike some commentators,[117] I find *Ableman* one of Taney's least effective performances.[118] Though he had at his disposal powerful arguments to support his Marshall-like conclusions in favor of federal supremacy, in the worst Marshall tradition he disdained to make them.[119]

II. FEDERAL JURISDICTION

A. *Luther v. Borden*

Sued in a federal diversity case for breaking into Luther's house, Borden defended on the ground that he had been carrying out orders of the Rhode Island government to suppress rebellion. Luther responded that the government for which Borden acted no longer was the legitimate government of Rhode Island. The circuit court,

---

jurisdiction. The Court had already established that implicit exclusivity was exceptional. *See* Houston v. Moore, 18 U.S. (15 Wheat.) 1 (1820), *discussed supra* in chapter 4. For example, the Court allowed state court replevin and trover actions against federal officers in Slocum v. Mayberry, 15 U.S. (2 Wheat.) 1, 12 (1817), and in Teal v. Felton, 53 U.S. (12 How.) 284 (1852). Taney might nevertheless have built on the unreasoned holding that state courts could not issue mandamus to federal officers, McClung v. Silliman, 19 U.S. (6 Wheat.) 598 (1821), but he did not do so.

[117]*See* C. SWISHER, *supra* note 2, at 662 (*Ableman* "marked the Chief Justice at his best"); 2 C. WARREN, *supra* note 54, at 336 (calling *Ableman* "the most powerful of all his notable opinions").

[118]As if that were not enough, after holding that the court below had no power to determine the issue, Taney added that it had erred on the merits: the challenged fugitive slave provisions were (for undisclosed reasons) constitutional. *Ableman*, 62 U.S. (21 How.) at 526. Apart from the contention that Congress had no power to implement the fugitive slave clause, the arguments of the judges below seemed not so frivolous as to warrant such cavalier dismissal. They had argued, for example, that the Act gave judicial duties to commissioners lacking the protections of article III, that there was a right to jury trial on the question whether the person captured was an escaped slave, and that due process required notice and opportunity to respond. *See In re* Booth, 3 Wis. 1, 36, 40-43, 64-70 (1854). For counterarguments based on the ability of Congress to leave matters to state courts and on the preliminary nature of the deprivation (an argument rejected in analogous circumstances in *Prigg*), see *Booth*, 3 Wis. at 82-84 (Crawford, J., dissenting).

[119]The Court also decided several cases giving a rather restrained interpretation to article IV's command that one state give full faith and credit "to the public Acts, Records, and judicial Proceedings" of another. U.S. CONST. art. IV, § 1. In Marshall's days the Court had held a sister-state judgment had to be enforced without reexamining its merits. Mills v. Duryee, 11 U.S. (7 Cranch) 481 (1813). Under Taney the Court allowed the enforcing state to apply to such a judgment a statute of limitations it would not have applied to a suit on its own judgments, McElmoyle v. Cohen, 38 U.S. (13 Pet.) 312 (1839), to limit to sixty days the time in which to sue on such a judgment, Bacon v. Howard, 61 U.S. (20 How.) 22 (1857), and to allow the limitation period to run while the debtor was outside the state, Bank of Alabama v. Dalton, 50 U.S. (9 How.) 522 (1850). Finally, in D'Arcy v. Ketchum, 52 U.S. (11 How.) 165 (1851), the Court held that one state did not have to enforce another's judgment entered without service of process on the defendant, even though the judgment would have been enforceable in the state where it was rendered.

Now that the due process clause of the fourteenth amendment renders a judgment entered without personal jurisdiction void even in the state where rendered, the *D'Arcy* rule seems obvious. In Taney's time, however, nothing in the Constitution seemed to invalidate such a judgment, and the statute implementing article IV appropriately provided that sister-state judgments be given "such faith and credit . . . as they have by law or usage in the courts of the state from whence [they] . . . are . . . taken." Act of May 26, 1790, ch. 11, 1 Stat. 122. To read traditional bases for declining to respect a foreign judgment into a provision designed to make that respect mandatory seems highly questionable.

rejecting this contention, held that no trespass had been committed, and the Supreme Court, in 1849, affirmed.[120]

Familiar to hordes of law students as the central fount of the political question doctrine, *Luther v. Borden* deserves closer attention lest it be taken to establish more than it actually held.[121]

Taney began his opinion for the Court by pointing to the chaotic result of holding an entire state government illegitimate:

> [T]he laws passed by its legislature during that time were nullities; its taxes wrongfully collected; its salaries and compensation to its officers illegally paid; its public accounts improperly settled; and the judgments and sentences of its courts in civil and criminal cases null and void, and the officers who carried their decisions into operation answerable as trespassers, if not in some cases as criminals.[122]

Later in the opinion he mentioned other practical difficulties: evidentiary problems would confound the inquiry whether the new state constitution under which Luther claimed had received the support of a majority of eligible voters;[123] also, because the issue would depend in part on witness credibility, juries might reach conflicting results in similar cases.[124]

Such considerations have become a part of today's political question discussion,[125] but it would be stretching things to call them the basis of *Luther*. The passage warning of chaotic results was not a holding of nonjusticiability but a prelude to a note of caution: "When the decision of this court might lead to such results, it becomes its duty to examine very carefully its own powers before it undertakes to exercise jurisdiction."[126] Taney did present the problems of proof and conflicting verdicts as additional reasons for declining to inquire whether the original state government had been superseded, but he did so only after he had plainly announced a more traditional and indisputable basis for his conclusion. Which faction consti-

---

[120]Luther v. Borden, 48 U.S. (7 How.) 1 (1849). Catron, Daniel, and, once again, McKinley "were absent on account of ill health when this case was argued." *Id. See generally* C. Swisher, *supra* note 2, at 522-27; W. Wiecek, The Guarantee Clause of the U.S. Constitution 111-29 (1972).

[121]At least two other decisions of the Taney period had political question overtones. Williams v. Suffolk Ins. Co., 38 U.S. (13 Pet.) 415, 421 (1839), an early salvo in a dispute that has continued to capture headlines in our own time, deferred to the President's decision that the "Buenos Ayrean" government had no authority over the Falkland Islands. Fellows v. Blacksmith, 60 U.S. (19 How.) 366, 372 (1856), refused to inquire whether those signing an Indian treaty had tribal authority to do so. The first case appears to conclude unsurprisingly that the President had acted within his authority on the merits. *Williams*, 38 U.S. (13 Pet.) at 420. *See generally* Henkin, *Is There a "Political Question" Doctrine?*, 85 Yale L. J. 597, 611-12 (1976). The second, saying only that "the courts can no more go behind [the treaty] for the purpose of annulling its effect and operation, than they can behind an act of Congress," *Fellows*, 60 U.S. (19 How.) at 372, seems harder to square with *Marbury's* obligation to say what the law is. Although courts typically decide questions of an agent's authority, *see generally* F. Mechem, Outlines of the Law of Agency (2d ed. 1903) *passim*, the congressional analogy is still troubling. *See also infra* notes 148, 291-92 and accompanying text, discussing *Rhode Island v. Massachusetts* and the *Prize Cases*.

[122]*Luther*, 48 U.S. (7 How.) at 38-39.

[123]*Id.* at 41-42.

[124]*Id.*

[125]*See, e.g.*, Baker v. Carr, 369 U.S. 186, 269 (1962) (Frankfurter, J., dissenting).

[126]*Luther*, 48 U.S. (7 How.) at 39.

tuted the legitimate government, Taney noted, was a question of state law.[127] The state supreme court, in holding that this inquiry "belonged to the political power and not to the judicial," had already held "that the charter government was the lawful and established government," and the circuit court was bound to "adopt and follow the decisions of the State courts in questions which concern merely the constitution and laws of the State."[128] The practical considerations Taney later raised were just icing on the cake; it is not at all clear they would have been taken to forbid federal resolution of the dispute had that not been contrary to state law.

The most interesting part of the *Luther* opinion, and the only part that seemed to invoke constitutional considerations, was also an afterthought following the state law decision:

> Moreover, the Constitution of the United States, as far as it has provided for an emergency of this kind, and authorized the general government to interfere in the domestic concerns of a State, has treated the subject as political in its nature, and placed the power in the hands of that department. . . .
>
> . . . For as the United States [in article IV] guarantee to each State a republican government, Congress must necessarily decide what government is established in the State before it can determine whether it is republican or not. And when the senators and representatives of a State are admitted into the councils of the Union, the authority of the government under which they are appointed, as well as its republican character, is recognized by the proper constitutional authority. And its decision is binding on every other department of the government . . . .[129]

Every link in this chain of bare conclusions is subject to serious counterattack. Article IV does not say Congress shall guarantee the states a republican government; it says the "United States" shall.[130] Article I nowhere declares that the House and Senate have authority to pass upon the legitimacy of a state government in seating their members.[131] Finally, the fact that Congress or one of its Houses may have power to determine a question does not mean its decision binds the courts or that no other branch has power to determine the same question. Having sworn to uphold the Constitution,[132] Congress passes regularly on the extent of its legislative authority, but that does not preclude the courts from holding a statute unconstitutional.[133]

None of this proves Taney's conclusion wrong. As Gerald Gunther has argued, "there is nothing in [*Marbury v. Madison*[134]] that precludes a constitutional inter-

---

[127]*Id.* at 40.

[128]*Id.* at 39-40.

[129]*Id.* at 42.

[130]U.S. CONST. art. IV, § 4; *see* W. WIECEK, *supra* note 120, at 77; Bonfield, *The Guarantee Clause of Article IV, Section 4: A Study in Constitutional Desuetude*, 46 MINN. L. REV. 513, 523 (1962).

[131]Powell v. McCormack, 395 U.S. 486, 550 (1969) (interpreting article I, § 5), would later hold that the "qualifications" to be judged by each house include only age, citizenship, and residence.

[132]U.S. CONST. art. VI, cl. 3.

[133]*See* A. BICKEL, THE LEAST DANGEROUS BRANCH 191 (1962) ("there is no textual reason [why judging member qualifications] . . . should be deemed proof against judicial intervention, any more than the language of the Commerce Clause").

[134]5 U.S. (1 Cranch) 137 (1803), *supra* chapter 3.

pretation which gives final authority to another branch" to make a particular determination.[135] First, the Court may find that the President or Congress has broad substantive discretion, as in receiving ambassadors or declaring war;[136] *Marbury* itself seemed to speak of "political" questions in this way.[137] Second, other provisions may deprive the courts of jurisdiction to remedy even errors of constitutional dimension; the familiar example of whether an impeached officer has committed "high Crimes and Misdemeanors"[138] is supported not only by the textual argument that the grant of a judicial function to the Senate[139] implies an exception to article III,[140] but also by history suggesting a deliberate exclusion of the courts.[141] The weakness of Taney's opinion lay not in recognizing that such provisions might exist, but in failing to demonstrate that the guarantee clause was one of them.[142]

Superficially more persuasive was his contention that the President had recognized the charter government by passing on its request for aid in putting down the rebellion, and that the Court had already held Congress had given him unreviewable discretion in determining whether there was a sufficient danger to justify action under the clause of article IV providing for the suppression of invasions and domestic violence.[143] This precedent, however, did not compel a finding of comparable discretion to resolve the distinct question whether the government requesting aid was a legitimate one. Indeed, President Tyler had explicitly disclaimed *any* discretion in this regard when recognizing the Rhode Island authorities, considering himself bound by Congress's actions in admitting the state to the Union and in continuing to seat its senators and representatives.[144] Finally, Taney's contention that judicial second-guessing in the face of domestic violence would make the constitutional provision "a guarantee of anarchy, and not of order"[145] rested on a debatable view of

---

[135]Gunther, *Judicial Hegemony and Legislative Autonomy: The* Nixon *Case and the Impeachment Process*, 22 U.C.L.A. L. Rev. 30, 34 (1974).

[136]U.S. Const. art. II, § 3; U.S. Const. art. I, § 8; *see* Henkin, *supra* note 121, at 608 (arguing that many "political question" decisions, including *Luther*, actually upheld the challenged action on the merits).

[137]*Marbury*, 5 U.S. (1 Cranch) at 165-66; *see supra* chapter 3.

[138]U.S. Const. art. II, § 4; *see, e.g.*, Wechsler, *Toward Neutral Principles of Constitutional Law*, 73 Harv. L. Rev. 1, 7-8 (1959).

[139]U.S. Const. art. I, § 3, cl. 6 ("The Senate shall have the sole Power to try all Impeachments.").

[140]*See* Scharpf, *Judicial Review and the Political Question: A Functional Analysis*, 75 Yale L.J. 517, 539-40 (1966). Textually, of course, a distinction is possible between trials and appeals.

[141]The Federalist No. 65 (A. Hamilton) (arguing that the Justices of the Supreme Court had insufficient numbers, prestige, and strength to shoulder such a sensitive function). It seems less clear, however, that the courts would or should accept Senate sanctions on a convicted officer that go beyond the prescribed maximum.

[142]Taney might have taken some comfort from the language of the clause, which, instead of being phrased as an enforceable limitation on the states themselves, directs affirmative federal action to "guarantee" an appropriate form of government. *See* Henkin, *supra* note 121, at 610. The clause not only contrasts with such obviously self-executing provisions as the ex post facto and contract clauses, but also contains a guarantee against invasion that judges could not really carry out; this, however, is scarcely conclusive. Neither the Convention debates, The Federalist, nor Story's treatise casts any light on the question.

[143]*Luther*, 48 U.S. (7 How.) at 42-45 (citing U.S. Const. art. IV, § 4 and Martin v. Mott, 25 U.S. (12 Wheat.) 19 (1827)).

[144]*See* W. Wiecek, *supra* note 120, at 105.

[145]*Luther*, 48 U.S. (7 How.) at 43. See the generalization of this argument in Baker v. Carr, 369 U.S. 186, 217 (1962), noting that political questions are often characterized by "an unusual need for unques-

the merits. Whether the requesting government met the guarantee clause's conditions was arguably irrelevant to the President's decision to use troops; the domestic
violence provision was designed to restore order, leaving Congress thereafter to
determine whether the existing government was "republican."[146]

In any event, the Court seemed at most to say only that the guarantee and violence
clauses committed the decision of the legitimacy of a state government to the final
determination of other branches;[147] the Court did not establish a general inability of
the courts to decide "political" questions.[148] What is most puzzling about *Luther*,
however, is why the Court thought the guarantee clause bore on the case at all.
Counsel did not seem to claim that the state government offended article IV;[149] thus,
rather than holding the guarantee clause unenforceable, as he is generally understood to have done, Taney must have concluded that it deprived the Court of

---

tioning adherence to a political decision already made." Taney added that the President's power to
recognize state governments was analogous to his power to recognize foreign ones. *Luther*, 48 U.S. (7
How.) at 44. The latter authority, however, derives from his powers (which apply only to foreign
countries) to receive and appoint ambassadors. *See* United States v. Belmont, 301 U.S. 324 (1937); U.S.
Const. art. II §§ 2, 3.

[146]*See* W. Wiecek, *supra* note 120, at 104 (giving Tyler's initial argument that "the executive could not
look into real or supposed defects of the existing government" but must recognize it until set aside "by
legal and peaceable proceedings"). Once again the Convention debates and The Federalist provide no
help. *Cf.* Conron, *Law, Politics, and Chief Justice Taney: A Reconsideration of the Luther v. Borden
Decision*, 11 Am. J. Legal Hist. 377, 383-84 (1967) (by concluding that the President and Congress had a
duty to determine the legitimacy of the state government, Taney was construing the clause on the merits in
the same breath with which he disclaimed the power to do so). See also *Luther*, 48 U.S. (7 How.) at 45, in
which Taney, upholding the declaration of martial law, added unnecessarily that "[u]nquestionably" a
permanent military government would not be republican, "and it would be the duty of Congress to
overthrow it." Justice Woodbury, dissenting alone and interminably from the conclusion upholding
martial law, did not appear to rely on the guarantee clause. *Id.* at 48.

[147]*See* W. Wiecek, *supra* note 120, at 123-24 (despite Taney's broad language, *Luther* established only
that the case itself was political, not that all guarantee clause cases were); Bonfield, *supra* note 130, at 535
(the broad statements about the guarantee clause were "dictum"; the Court held only "that Congress or
the President had the sole power to determine which of two contending state governments is legitimate");
Henkin, *supra* note 121, at 608 (*Luther* held "that the actions of Congress and the President in this case
were within their constitutional authority").

[148]At the end of the opinion Taney noted that "[m]uch of the argument . . . turned upon political
rights and political questions," on which the Court declined to express an opinion. *Luther*, 48 U.S. (7
How.) at 46-47. This seems not to mean as much as it might; counsel's argument had been filled with
rhetoric about the inherent right of people to change their own government, *see id.* at 28-29 (Mr.
Whipple), *id.* at 30-31 (Mr. Webster), and Taney seems to have been correctly observing that this was not
a legal argument at all.

Taney could also generalize about "political" matters, however, as Rhode Island v. Massachusetts, 37
U.S. (12 Pet.) 657 (1838), suggests. There he dissented alone from the assertion of jurisdiction to
determine an interstate boundary dispute on the unexplained ground that the rights in question were
"political" rather than "judicial." *Id.* at 752-53. He relied on a similar but inconclusive hint by Marshall in
Cherokee Nation v. Georgia, 30 U.S. (5 Pet.) 1, 20 (1831), *supra* chapter 4. Baldwin's response that the
Court's jurisdiction replaced the states' forgone rights to negotiate treaties and to declare war, and his
references to a boundary dispute provision in the Articles of Confederation, seem more convincing. *See*
Rhode Island v. Massachusetts, 37 U.S. (12 Pet.) at 721-31.

[149]*See* W. Wiecek, *supra* note 120, at 90, 112, 121 (noting only extrajudicial contentions that the Rhode
Island government was less than "republican" and observing that the Court held the clause "took the
matter out of the hands of all federal courts"); Henkin, *supra* note 121, at 608 n.33 (flatly denying that any
such claim was made).

authority to determine the legitimacy of the government under state law. Thus the clause appears to have played no necessary part in the decision; it was a gratuitous alternative ground of constitutional dimension and portentous significance that might better have been left out altogether.

B. Admiralty Jurisdiction

In 1825, in *The Steam-Boat Thomas Jefferson*,[150] that determined nationalist Story had held for a unanimous Marshall Court that a suit for wages earned on a Missouri River voyage lay beyond federal admiralty jurisdiction because that jurisdiction was historically confined to "waters within the ebb and flow of the tide."[151] In 1852, in *The Propeller Genesee Chief v. Fitzhugh*,[152] a nearly unanimous Court, in an opinion written by the supposedly less nationalistic Taney, held that admiralty jurisdiction embraced a suit arising out of a collision on Lake Ontario, where the tide was imperceptible.[153]

Picking up an obiter cue dropped by Story in the earlier case,[154] Congress had passed a statute purporting to extend the jurisdiction of the district courts to certain cases involving vessels on the Great Lakes and their connecting waters.[155] Loyal to uncited precedent and the spirit of article III, however, Taney rejected Story's suggestion that the commerce clause allowed Congress to give the courts cognizance of cases outside the judicial power defined by article III,[156] for

> it would be inconsistent with the plain and ordinary meaning of words, to call a law defining the jurisdiction of certain courts of the United States a regulation of commerce. . . .
> . . . The extent of the judicial power is carefully defined and limited, and Congress cannot enlarge it to suit even the wants of commerce . . . .[157]

[150]23 U.S. (10 Wheat.) 428 (1825).

[151]*Id.* at 429; *see supra* chapter 4. After Taney's appointment the Court unanimously confirmed this limitation in The Steam-Boat Orleans v. Phoebus, 36 U.S. (11 Pet.) 175 (1837) (Story, J.).

[152]53 U.S. (12 How.) 443 (1852).

[153]Only Daniel, *id.* at 463-65, who had dissented on historical grounds even from the assertion of jurisdiction over tidewaters within the states, *see* Waring v. Clarke, 46 U.S. (5 How.) 441, 503 (1847), disagreed. Woodbury and Grier had also dissented in *Waring*, but the former died before *The Genesee Chief*, and the latter had apparently been converted. *See generally* C. SWISHER, *supra* note 2, at 442-47.

[154]*The Thomas Jefferson*, 23 U.S. (10 Wheat.) at 430.

[155]Act of Feb. 26, 1845, ch. 20, 5 Stat. 726.

[156]*See also* THE FEDERALIST No. 80, at 539, No. 81, at 552 (A. Hamilton) (J. Cooke ed. 1961) (quoting the enumeration in article III as "the entire mass of the judicial authority of the union" and saying that federal judicial power had "been carefully restricted to those causes which are manifestly proper for the cognizance of the national judicature"); *cf.* Mossman v. Higginson, 4 U.S. (4 Dall.) 12, 14 (1800), *supra* chapter 1 (dismissing a suit by an alien because the opposing party was not alleged to be a citizen of any state: the statute "must receive a construction, consistent with the constitution," and "the legislative power of conferring jurisdiction on the federal Courts, is, in this respect, confined to suits *between citizens and foreigners*") (emphasis in original).

[157]*The Genesee Chief*, 53 U.S. (12 How.) at 452; *see also* Gibbons v. Ogden, 22 U.S. (9 Wheat.) 1, 196 (1826) (Marshall, C.J.), *supra* chapter 6 ("to regulate . . . is, to prescribe the rule by which commerce is to be governed").

Given this holding, the Court could sustain the Great Lakes Act only if the case was maritime, and *The Thomas Jefferson* seemed to say it was not.

Disdaining to argue that the earlier case had interpreted the original statutory admiralty provision more narrowly than the constitutional provision it mirrored,[158] Taney held Story's decision squarely against him on the constitutional issue and candidly overruled it. If the Court laid down "any rule by which the right of property should be determined," he conceded, the principle of stare decisis "should always be adhered to"; for "it is in the power of the legislature to amend [the rule] . . . without impairing rights acquired under it."[159] No such consideration required adherence to an erroneous jurisdictional decision, however, because the "rights of property and of parties will be the same by whatever court the law is administered"[160]—especially because, as his earlier statement implied, no other remedy existed short of constitutional amendment. This was, at the time, the Court's most comprehensive treatment of stare decisis in constitutional cases. It seems also to have been only the second time the Court had overruled a constitutional decision.[161]

Taney's reasons for rejecting Story's tidal limitation were clear and convincing. The lakes "are in truth inland seas. Different States border on them on one side, and a foreign nation on the other."[162] They were used for interstate and foreign commerce and had been the scene of naval battles and prize captures. "[T]here is certainly nothing in the ebb and flow of the tide that makes the waters peculiarly suitable for admiralty jurisdiction."[163] Whether or not Taney was right that the reason the English jurisdiction extended only to tidewaters was that "there was no navigable stream in the country beyond the ebb and flow of the tide," he was on solid ground in arguing that "there can be no reason for admiralty power over a public tide-water, which does not apply with equal force to any other public water used for commercial purposes and foreign trade."[164] There was no reason to think the flexible terms "admiralty" and "maritime" in the Constitution meant to petrify precedents unsuited to American conditions.[165]

[158]For an example of such a disparity between statutory and constitutional provisions, see *supra* chapter 3 (discussing Hepburn v. Ellzey, 6 U.S. (2 Cranch) 445 (1805)).

[159]*The Genesee Chief*, 53 U.S. (12 How.) at 458.

[160]*Id.* at 459. In this he overstated his case, because it had long been settled that federal maritime law governed admiralty cases. *See* Currie, *Federalism and the Admiralty: "The Devil's Own Mess"*, 1960 Sup. Ct. Rev. 158. The diversity of state laws had been given as a reason for extending admiralty jurisdiction in 1845. *See* C. Swisher, *supra* note 2, at 434.

[161]The first instance is discussed *infra* at text accompanying notes 170-82. For earlier discussions of stare decisis, see generally *supra* chapter 3.

[162]*The Genesee Chief*, 53 U.S. (12 How.) at 453.

[163]*Id.* at 454.

[164]*Id.* at 454, 457.

[165]The Court had already rejected the argument that British precedents were determinative in Waring v. Clarke, 46 U.S. (5 How.) 441, 457-59 (1847) (Wayne, J.), and in New Jersey Steam Nav. Co. v. Merchants' Bank, 47 U.S. (6 How.) 344, 386-92 (1848) (Nelson, J.); in both cases the Court cited earlier decisions for more than they had said. *See supra* chapter 1, discussing *La Vengeance* and *The Charming Betsey*. This conclusion was not without its problems. Extension of admiralty jurisdiction beyond English precedents not only enlarged federal judicial authority and the scope of federal maritime law; it also threatened a restriction of jury trial, because admiralty cases were typically tried by the judge alone. The Court had said in Marshall's day that the term "suits at common law" in the seventh amendment jury trial provision excluded equity and admiralty cases. *See* Parsons v. Bedford, 28 U.S. (3 Pet.) 433, 447 (1830) (dictum), *discussed supra* in chapter 4. Despite a general practice of referring to eighteenth-century

This was Taney at his best, reasoning powerfully from the purposes of article III as Marshall had done in upholding diversity jurisdiction in *Bank of United States v. Deveaux*,[166] and as Story had done with respect to federal question jurisdiction in *Martin v. Hunter's Lessee*.[167] Ideally he might have stated those purposes explicitly;[168] but the implications were clear enough. Thus *The Genesee Chief* seems one of the most satisfying of all early constitutional opinions, and it certainly does not reveal either Taney or his brethren as particularly grudging in their interpretation of federal power.[169]

C.   Diversity Cases

In diversity cases, as in admiralty, the Taney Court defined federal jurisdiction more broadly than had its nationalist forebears. In *Deveaux*, while upholding jurisdiction of an action by a corporation whose members were all alleged to be diverse to the defendant, Marshall had stated without explanation (and held in a companion case) that the corporation was not itself a "citizen" for diversity purposes.[170] Combined with Marshall's equally unexplained holding in *Strawbridge v. Curtiss*[171] that diversity jurisdiction lay only if all plaintiffs with joint interests were diverse to all defendants,[172] this rule excluded corporate litigation from the federal courts if any "member" of the corporation was a co-citizen of the opposite party. Just as the

---

English precedents to determine the scope of the seventh amendment, *see, e.g.*, Baltimore & C. Line v. Redman, 295 U.S. 654, 659 n.5 (1935), the Court allowed the definition of "common law" cases for jury trial purposes to ebb and flow with the tide of admiralty jurisdiction under article III. *See, e.g.*, Waring v. Clarke, 46 U.S. (5 How.) at 470 (Woodbury, J., dissenting).

Because the Great Lakes Act did provide for jury trial, *The Genesee Chief* presented the converse question whether Congress could authorize jury trial in a case *not* "at common law"; Taney rightly held it could. *See The Genesee Chief*, 53 U.S. (12 How.) at 459-602; U.S. CONST. amend. VII. The seventh amendment gives the right to a jury in certain cases, but it does not guarantee the right to a nonjury trial in others.

[166]9 U.S. (5 Cranch) 61 (1809); *see supra* chapter 3.

[167]14 U.S. (1 Wheat.) 304 (1816); *see supra* chapter 4.

[168]*Cf.* THE FEDERALIST No. 80, at 538 (A. Hamilton) (J. Cooke ed. 1961) (maritime cases so depend on the "laws of nations," and so commonly affect the "rights of foreigners," that they relate to the "public peace"); Southern Pac. Co. v. Jensen, 244 U.S. 205, 215 (1917) (Constitution aimed for "uniformity" in maritime law).

[169]In the same term, on the authority of *The Genesee Chief*, the Court upheld admiralty jurisdiction of a case arising above tidewater on the Mississippi River. *See* Fretz v. Bull, 53 U.S. (12 How.) 466, 468 (1852) (Wayne, J.). Six years later, in a full-dress opinion, it applied the holding to the Alabama River, which was concededly outside the scope of the Great Lakes Act and entirely within a single state. *See* Jackson v. The Steamboat Magnolia, 61 U.S. (20 How.) 296 (1858) (Grier, J.). Daniel dissented in both cases, and in the latter was joined by Campbell and Catron. *Fretz*, 53 U.S. (12 How.) at 472; *Jackson*, 61 U.S. (21 How.) at 303, 307, 322; *see also* People's Ferry Co. v. Beers, 61 U.S. (20 How.) 393, 402 (1857) (Catron, J.) (unanimously holding a shipbuilding contract nonmaritime: "it was a contract made on land, to be performed on land"; the "wages of the shipwrights had no reference to a voyage"); New Jersey Steam Nav. Co. v. Merchants' Bank, 47 U.S. (6 How.) 344, 392 (1848) (Nelson, J.) (holding five to two that a contract made on land for carriage of goods by sea was maritime, despite British precedents, because the service was "a maritime service, to be performed upon" waters within the admiralty jurisdiction).

[170]Bank of the United States v. Deveaux, 9 U.S. (5 Cranch) 61, 86 (1809), *supra* chapter 3.

[171]7 U.S. (3 Cranch) 267 (1806) *supra* chapter 3.

[172]*Strawbridge*, 7 U.S. (3 Cranch) at 267.

growth of internal commerce made the tidewater limitation on admiralty jurisdiction archaic, the rise of the corporation did the same for the restrictive part of *Deveaux*.[173] In the 1844 case of *Louisville, Cincinnati, and Charleston R.R. v. Letson*,[174] decided even before *The Genesee Chief*, the Court (without recorded dissent)[175] cut itself loose from *Deveaux* and ostensibly from *Strawbridge* as well, proclaiming that "[w]e do not think either of them maintainable upon the true principles of interpretation of the Constitution and the laws of the United States."[176]

"A corporation created by a state," wrote Justice Wayne, "seems to us to be a person, though an artificial one, inhabiting and belonging to that state, and therefore entitled, for the purpose of suing and being sued, to be deemed a citizen of that state."[177] This conclusion was essentially as unsupported as Marshall's contrary assertion thirty-five years before.[178] Wayne did cite Coke for the proposition that corporations were sometimes to be treated as "inhabitants."[179] He also cited *Deveaux* itself to show that this treatment was appropriate "'when the general spirit and purposes of the law requires it,'" and Wayne added that "the spirit and purposes of the law require[s] it" in the case before him.[180] Alas, he omitted to say why; though noting that a corporation shared with flesh-and-blood citizens the ability to contract, to sue, and to be sued,[181] he did not relate these facts to the "spirit and purposes" of the diversity clause.[182]

Justice Grier did somewhat better when more or less reaffirming *Letson* in the 1854 case of *Marshall v. Baltimore & Ohio Railroad*,[183] quoting from an earlier Catron opinion that argued that in the absence of federal authority outsiders would "'be compelled to submit their rights'" to local judges and juries "'and to contend with powerful corporations, where the chances of impartial justice would be greatly against them.'"[184] Unfortunately, Catron had dissociated himself from the implica-

---

[173]*See* J. FRANK, JUSTICE DANIEL DISSENTING 225 (1964).

[174]43 U.S. (2 How.) 497 (1844).

[175]On the background of *Letson* and related cases, see C. SWISHER, *supra* note 2, at 463 (noting also that on the apparent date of decision of *Letson* "only Justices Story, McLean, Baldwin, Wayne and Catron were present"); C. SWISHER, *supra* note 54, at 390. *See also* G. HENDERSON, *supra* note 1, at 60.

[176]*Letson*, 43 U.S. (2 How.) at 555. The Court correctly added that the earlier decisions seemed difficult to reconcile with Bank of United States v. Planters' Bank, 22 U.S. (9 Wheat.) 904, 910 (1826), which had held that a suit against a corporation in which a state was a shareholder was not a suit against the state.

[177]*Letson*, 43 U.S. (2 How.) at 555.

[178]*Deveaux*, 9 U.S. (5 Cranch) at 86; *see also supra* chapter 3.

[179]*Letson*, 43 U.S. (2 How.) at 558-59.

[180]*Id.* at 559.

[181]*Id.* at 558.

[182]He did say citizens should not be able to "exempt themselves" from federal jurisdiction by incorporating, *id.* at 552, but that problem had already been settled by *Deveaux*. *See supra* chapter 3. The problem in *Letson* was that the complete diversity rule would have deprived the court of jurisdiction if the railroad had *not* been incorporated. Indeed, one might have invoked the reasoning that sustained jurisdiction in *Deveaux* to support a *denial* of jurisdiction in *Letson*: citizens also ought not to lose their *exemption* from federal jurisdiction by virtue of incorporation.

[183]57 U.S. (16 How.) 314 (1853).

[184]*Id.* at 327 (quoting Rundle v. Delaware & Raritan Canal Co., 55 U.S. (14 How.) 80, 95 (1853) (concurring opinion)); *see also Marshall*, 57 U.S. (16 How.) at 329 (arguing that corporations themselves needed the protection of "an impartial tribunal" in other states, where local prejudices or jealousy might injuriously affect them). Grier also quoted Hamilton's explanation that diversity jurisdiction was a means

tions Grier later tried to draw from this passage,[185] observing that he had only been making *Deveaux*'s point that state incorporation laws could not "repeal the Constitution" by precluding jurisdiction when all relevant members of the corporation were diverse to the opposing party.[186] Grier's point would have seemed stronger had he explicitly noted that the existence of undisclosed owners or directors from outside the state seemed unlikely to diminish the probability that local tribunals may unduly favor local corporations[187]—the point seems far less obvious than what Taney left unsaid in *The Genesee Chief.*

Ironically, Grier began his *Marshall* opinion with a solemn declaration that "[t]here are no cases, where an adherence to the maxim of '*stare decisis*' is so absolutely necessary to the peace of society, as those which affect retroactively the jurisdiction of courts."[188] This was precisely the opposite of what the Court had said two terms earlier in *The Genesee Chief,*[189] to which Grier naturally made no reference. Grier's point also seemed especially inappropriate because *Letson*, the very decision he now pronounced immutable, had itself unceremoniously discarded another jurisdictional precedent.[190] Worse still, Grier went on to modify the very decision to which he protested he had to adhere: instead of deeming the corporation itself an article III citizen, as *Letson* had reasonably enough done, the Court indulged in a patently fallacious irrebuttable "presum[ption]" that the "persons who act under these [corporate] faculties, and use this corporate name," were "resident in the State which is the necessary *habitat* of the corporation."[191]

---

of enforcing the privileges and immunities protected by article IV. *Id.* at 326 (citing THE FEDERALIST No. 80 (A. Hamilton)).

[185]*See Marshall*, 57 U.S. (16 How.) at 338 (Catron, J.).

[186]*See Rundle*, 55 U.S. (14 How.) at 95. In both opinions Catron made it clear he considered the relevant members to include only "the president and directors," and not the shareholders. *Marshall*, 57 U.S. (16 How.) at 338; *Rundle*, 55 U.S. (14 How.) at 95. The majority in *Marshall* seemed to agree: stockholders were to be ignored because they were "not really parties," and their "representatives" were similarly irrelevant because the law conclusively "presumed" them to live in the state of incorporation. *See Marshall*, 57 U.S. (16 How.) at 328-29; Comment, *Limited Partnerships and Federal Diversity Jurisdiction*, 45 U. CHI. L. REV. 384, 405-06 (1978). Earlier decisions were less clear on this point. *Deveaux* had spoken vaguely of "members," 9 U.S. (5 Cranch) at 86, 91-92, which Professors Hart and Wechsler without explanation took to mean stockholders. *See* H. HART & H. WECHSLER, *supra* note 45, at 1085. Similarly, *Letson* spoke interchangeably of "members" and of "corporators," *see, e.g., Letson*, 43 U.S. (2 How.) at 508-10, and a decision between *Deveaux* and *Letson* had refused jurisdiction because of the citizenship of two individuals fuzzily denominated as "stockholders *and* corporators." Commercial & R.R. Bank v. Slocomb, 39 U.S. (14 Pet.) 60, 63 (1840) (emphasis added).

[187]*See* Comment, *supra* note 186, at 409 (limiting the observation to those "only beneficially interested").

[188]*Marshall*, 57 U.S. (16 How.) at 325.

[189]*See supra* text accompanying notes 159-61.

[190]Grier could have argued—but did not—that it was more serious to overrule a decision upholding jurisdiction than to overrule one denying it; nineteenth-century doctrine seems to have freely allowed collateral attack on judgments for want of jurisdiction. *See* Thompson v. Whitman, 85 U.S. (8 Wall.) 457 (1874). As an additional irony, one of the cases Grier managed to insist could not be abandoned was *Bank of United States v. Deveaux*, whose restrictive reasoning, as embodied in a companion decision, *Letson* had already overruled. *Letson*, 43 U.S. (2 How.) at 554-56.

[191]*Marshall*, 57 U.S. (16 How.) at 328. Catron, Daniel, and Campbell dissented. For a more recent and vigorous attack on the presumption, see McGovney, *A Supreme Court Fiction: Corporations in the Diverse Citizenship Jurisdiction of the Federal Courts*, 56 HARV. L. REV. 853 (1943). See also G. HENDERSON, *supra* note 1, at 62-63, explaining the presumption as a means of quieting the fear that

By means of foul or fair, therefore, the Court under Taney frankly departed from constitutional precedent in extending both admiralty and diversity jurisdiction beyond the limits set by Story and Marshall. The famous 1842 decision in *Swift v. Tyson*,[192] moreover, holding (in the apparent teeth of a federal statute) that federal courts in diversity cases could ignore state decisional law on "general commercial" matters, seems another startling leap beyond Marshall precedents, which appeared to deny the existence of any federal common law.[193] Story's opinion in *Swift* did not discuss the Constitution, but from a modern perspective he seems to have assumed that the grant of judicial power empowered the federal diversity court to make law.[194] The Court would hold as much in later admiralty cases,[195] but Story's successors were to reject this assumption a century later when *Swift* was finally overruled.[196]

With respect to other issues regarding the federal courts, the Taney period was relatively quiet.[197] One unforgettable diversity decision, however, remains for discus-

---

Letson might result in privileges and immunities for foreign corporations under article IV despite the holding of Bank of Augusta v. Earle, 38 U.S. (13 Pet.) 519 (1839), discussed *supra* notes 1-17 and accompanying text. *Cf. Marshall*, 57 U.S. (16 How.) at 352-53 (Campbell, J., dissenting) (discussing *Letson* and questioning "when the mischief will end"). Grier emphasized that the presumption could have no such consequence by reaffirming *Bank of Augusta*'s statement that a corporation had no existence outside its charter state. *Marshall*, 57 U.S. (16 How.) at 328. Because *Bank of Augusta* had explicitly held that diversity precedents did not govern privileges and immunities cases, the fear that *Letson* would be imported into article IV seems exaggerated. It certainly highlighted the distinction between the two clauses, however, and in neither *Letson* nor *Marshall* did the Court find it necessary to explain the consistency of its conclusion with *Bank of Augusta*.

[192]41 U.S. (16 Pet.) 1 (1842).

[193]See United States v. Coolidge, 14 U.S. (1 Wheat.) 415 (1816); United States v. Hudson, 12 U.S. (7 Cranch) 32 (1812); *see also supra* chapter 4. *Cf.* Kitch, *Regulation and the American Common Market*, in A. TARLOCK, REGULATION, FEDERALISM, AND INTERSTATE COMMERCE 9, 25 (1981) (by making recognition of foreign corporations optional, and concurrently opening to them federal courts taking an independent view of commercial law, the Court in *Swift*, *Letson*, and *Bank of Augusta* created "a judicial program of voluntary commercial integration": "while the federal courts recognized the paramount power of the states, they tendered to the states a system of uniform national commercial law, which the states were free to reject").

[194]*But see* the interesting arguments in R. BRIDWELL & R. WHITTEN, THE CONSTITUTION AND THE COMMON LAW 66-67 (1977), that the process of determining commercial customs was not viewed as lawmaking at the time of *Swift*, and in Conant, *The Commerce Clause, the Supremacy Clause, and the Law Merchant: Swift v. Tyson and the Unity of Commercial Law*, 15 J. MARITIME LAW & COMM. 153 (1984), that *Swift* was right because the law merchant was not "common law" within the Rules of Decision Act, Act of Sept. 24, 1789, ch. 20, § 34, 1 Stat. 73, 92.

[195]*See, e.g.*, Southern Pacific Co. v. Jensen, 244 U.S. 205, 215 (1917); *see also* Currie, *supra* note 160, at 158-64.

[196]*See* Erie R.R. v. Tompkins, 304 U.S. 64 (1938). The generally accepted purpose of the diversity jurisdiction of affording an unbiased forum, *see, e.g., Deveaux*, 9 U.S. (5 Cranch) at 87, does not support Story's assumption; like the transfer provision of 28 U.S.C. § 1404(a)(1976), see Van Dusen v. Barrack, 376 U.S. 612, 616-18 (1964), diversity seems designed to provide another court, not another body of law. *Cf.* Allstate Ins. Co. v. Hague, 449 U.S. 302, 309 (1981) (citing with apparent approval Home Ins. Co. v. Dick, 281 U.S. 397 (1930), which held a state court could not consistently with due process apply its own law to a controversy with wholly foreign contacts); D. CURRIE, FEDERAL COURTS: CASES AND MATERIALS 395 (3d ed. 1982) (*Erie* may be "an application of the principle that a disinterested forum may not frustrate the policies of an interested State").

[197]The Court reaffirmed Congress's power to exclude diversity cases created by assignment, *see* Sheldon v. Sill, 49 U.S. (8 How.) 441 (1850), and the impropriety (on statutory grounds) of deciding claims subject to executive review, *see* United States v. Ferreira, 54 U.S. (13 How.) 40 (1852). The Court also respected Jay's dictum that the United States could not be sued without its consent, *see* United States

sion, and because it also resolved an important issue of substantive congressional power, it is treated in the following section.

III. CONGRESSIONAL AND PRESIDENTIAL POWERS

A. *Scott v. Sandford*

Dred Scott, a Missouri slave, accompanied his master first to Illinois, where slavery did not exist, and then to Fort Snelling in what is now Minnesota, where slavery had been forbidden by the Missouri Compromise.[198] Allegedly sold to a New Yorker after returning to Missouri, Scott brought a diversity action in federal court claiming his freedom. The Supreme Court dismissed for lack of jurisdiction, and a majority of the Justices found Congress had no power to outlaw slavery in territories acquired by the Louisiana Purchase.[199]

---

v. McLemore, 45 U.S. (4 How.) 286 (1846), and narrowly construed mandamus to avoid undermining this immunity. *See* Reeside v. Walker, 52 U.S. (11 How.) 272 (1850); Brashear v. Mason, 47 U.S. (6 How.) 92 (1848). For the first time the Court rejected a case as collusive in Lord v. Veazie, 49 U.S. (8 How.) 251 (1850), by holding a feigned dispute not a "controversy" within article III. In a split decision it also upheld the standing of a state as owner of roads and canals to challenge a bridge that reduced its toll revenues. Pennsylvania v. Wheeling & Belmont Bridge Co., 54 U.S. (13 How.) 518 (1852). The only surprise not already mentioned came when the Court, in reaffirming *Marbury*'s limits on the original jurisdiction, refused to review a military conviction on the ground that the military commission that had entered it was not a judicial body. *See Ex parte* Vallandigham, 68 U.S. (1 Wall.) 243 (1864). *See also* Murray's Lessee v. Hoboken Land & Improvement Co., 59 U.S. (18 How.) 272, 284 (1856), upholding an extrajudicial distraint procedure for satisfying debts of a customs collector over the argument that only a court created under article III could determine the collector's liability: there were some "matters, involving public rights," that Congress "may or may not bring within the cognizance of the courts of the United States, as it may deem proper." Much later the Court was to take this passage as authority for allowing Congress to leave such matters to a court that did not meet the requirements of article III, *Ex parte* Bakelite Corp., 279 U.S. 438, 451 (1929). *Cf. supra* chapter 4, discussing *American Ins. Co. v. Canter*. As I have noted elsewhere, the Court's later reliance was misplaced. "*Murray*'s *Lessee* held only that the Government could collect debts . . . without suing at all, not that it could sue for the debt before judges lacking the protections of article III . . . . Article III may not require that courts be used at all, but it leaves no doubt as to how courts are to be constituted if they are created." Currie, *Bankruptcy Judges and the Independent Judiciary*, 16 CREIGHTON L. REV. 441, 450-51 (1983). Indeed, until the executive has determined that it believes the money owing, there is no controversy ripe for judicial decision.

[198] Act of March 6, 1820, ch. 22, § 8, 3 Stat. 545, 548:

> [I]n all that territory ceded by France to the United States, under the name of Louisiana, which lies north of thirty-six degrees and thirty minutes north latitude, not included within the limits of [Missouri], . . . slavery and involuntary servitude, otherwise than in the punishment of crimes, . . . is hereby, forever prohibited; *Provided always*, That any person escaping into the same, from whom labour or service is lawfully claimed, in any state or territory of the United States, such fugitive may be lawfully reclaimed and conveyed to the person claiming his or her labour or service as aforesaid.

[199] 60 U.S. (19 How.) 393 (1857). Among the anomalies associated with the case are that Curtis participated despite the fact that his brother argued for Scott, *see id.* at 399; C. SWISHER, *supra* note 2, at 613-14; that the Missouri Compromise had been repealed in 1854, at least in the Kansas and Nebraska territories where it was most important, Act of May 30, 1854, ch. 59, 10 Stat. 277; that two Justices communicated with President-elect Buchanan about the case while it was pending; and that Nelson had initially been assigned to dispose of the case without reaching any constitutional questions, *see* D. POTTER, THE IMPENDING CRISIS 1848-1861, 272-74 (1976); C. SWISHER, *supra* note 2, at 605, 616-19; 2 C. WARREN,

The best known decision of the Taney period, *Scott* has been widely lamented as
bad policy and bad judicial politics. What may not be so well recollected is that it was
also bad law.[200]

Scott based jurisdiction on the allegation that he was a citizen of Missouri suing a
citizen of New York. In a nation where individual states do not formally confer
citizenship, the statutory and constitutional references to "citizens" of different
states are hardly self-defining.[201] To the extent that diversity jurisdiction is based
upon a fear of state court bias,[202] one might expect the test to be whether the party
lives in another state.[203] To the extent that the clause was meant to avoid the risk that
one state might take umbrage at the maltreatment of its people in another,[204] one
might expect the test to be, as in respect to citizens of "foreign States" under the
same article, whether the party is deemed a citizen by the state.[205] Without considering either of these alternatives, however, Taney began his "opinion of the court"
with the surprising conclusion that the question was whether Scott was a citizen *of the
United States.*[206]

Decisions involving aliens before and after *Scott* have held that nationality rather
than domicile governs *foreign* citizenship for diversity purposes,[207] and that an alien is
not a "citizen" of an American state in which he lives.[208] Perhaps recognizing that
aliens are covered by a separate provision inapplicable to cases like *Scott*, Taney did
not invoke this line of authority. Instead, his argument that federal citizenship was

---

supra note 54, at 293-94. Much of the copious literature is listed, and some of the better pieces reprinted, in
THE DRED SCOTT DECISION: LAW OR POLITICS? (S. Kutler ed. 1967). The factual background is given in
intricate detail in W. EHRLICH, THEY HAVE NO RIGHTS—DRED SCOTT'S STRUGGLE FOR FREEDOM 9-134
(1979), and in V. HOPKINS, DRED SCOTT'S CASE 1-23 (1951). For a thorough and thoughtful discussion of
all aspects of the controversy, see D. FEHRENBACHER, *supra* note 37.

[200]For perceptive contemporaneous legal criticism, see *The Case of Dred Scott*, 20 MONTHLY LAW REP.
61 (1858); 85 N. AM. REV. 392 (1857). The most comprehensive modern treatment of the legal issues
appears in D. FEHRENBACHER, *supra* note 37.

[201]*See, e.g.*, U.S. CONST. art. III, § 2, cl. 1.

[202]*See, e.g.*, Bank of the United States v. Deveaux, 9 U.S. (5 Cranch) 61, 87 (1809), *supra* chapter 3.

[203]The Court has consistently used this test in situations not involving race. *See, e.g.*, Williamson v.
Osenton, 232 U.S. 619, 624-26 (1914). It was also the basic position of McLean's dissent: "Being a
freeman, and having his domicile in a State different from that of the defendant, he is a citizen within the
Act of Congress, and the courts of the Union are open to him." *Scott*, 60 U.S. (19 How.) at 531.

[204]*See, e.g.*, 3 ELLIOT'S DEBATES, *supra* chapter 3, note 42, at 557 (Mr. Marshall); 4 *id.* at 158-59
(Mr. Davie).

[205]*See, e.g.*, Murarka v. Bachrack Bros., 215 F. 2d 547, 553 (2d Cir. 1954). *But cf.* Sadat v. Mertes, 615
F.2d 1176, 1183 (7th Cir. 1980) (Egyptian nationality of dual national was not dominant where dual
national renounced allegiance to any foreign state). This was close to the position taken by Justice Curtis
in dissent: "every free person born on the soil of a State, who is a citizen of that State by force of its
Constitution or laws" is a citizen for diversity purposes. *Scott*, 60 U.S. (19 How.) at 576; *see also id.* at 582.
Curtis's limitation to persons born in the state seems artificial in light of this purpose.

[206]*Scott*, 60 U.S. (19 How.) at 404-05. Curtis, dissenting, agreed that this was the question. *Id.* at 571.
But see D. FEHRENBACHER, *supra* note 37, at 341-46; D. POTTER, *supra* note 199, at 275 ("If state citizenship
for Negroes existed, it would apparently qualify them to sue in a federal court under the diversity of
citizenship clause, regardless of whether they held federal citizenship or not . . . .").

[207]*See, e.g.*, Van der Schelling v. U.S. News & World Report, Inc., 213 F. Supp. 756 (E.D. Pa. 1963)
(American domiciled abroad not foreign "citizen" or "subject"), *aff'd*, 324 F.2d 956 (3d Cir. 1963), *cert.
denied*, 377 U.S. 906 (1964).

[208]*See, e.g.*, Breedlove v. Nicolet, 32 U.S. (7 Pet.) 413, 428, 431-32 (1833) (foreign nationals may sue
citizens of state where former are domiciled); Psinakis v. Psinakis, 221 F.2d 418, 420, 422 (3d Cir. 1955).

decisive was bound up with one of his reasons for holding that Scott was not a citizen. The naturalization power, Taney argued, had been given to Congress in order to prevent one state from foisting undesirables upon other states as "citizens" entitled to "privileges and immunities" under article IV. This purpose could be achieved only by holding that no one but a citizen of the United States could be a "citizen" of a state under articles III and IV, and that only Congress could confer national citizenship.[209]

This argument was clever, but vulnerable at several points. Although Taney's justification for the naturalization power conformed with that given in the Federalist,[210] as early as 1792 two Justices on circuit, disagreeing with that reading, had held the naturalization power was not exclusive.[211] As Taney noted, the Supreme Court had later said that it was.[212] It had done so however, without discussion, in a context suggesting its opinion turned on a preemptive federal statute, and in a passage unnecessary to the result;[213] years later it had held that the similarly phrased bankruptcy power in the same clause was not exclusive.[214] Moreover, Taney expressly declared elsewhere in Scott that Congress could not confer citizenship on American blacks;[215] Curtis observed in dissent that it was somewhat unusual to hold exclusive a federal power that did not exist at all.[216]

Nor was it at all clear that holding blacks "citizens" within article IV would entitle them, as Taney argued, "to enter every other State whenever they pleased, . . . go where they pleased at every hour of the day or night without molestation, . . . hold public meetings upon political affairs, and . . . keep and carry arms wherever they went."[217] The Court had already confirmed in Conner v. Elliott,[218] which nobody cited, that article IV outlawed only classifications based on citizenship itself; Taney did not parry Curtis's challenging riposte that mere citizenship would not entitle anyone to privileges for which he lacked other requisite qualifications such as age, sex, or race.[219] Finally, even if Taney's arguments demonstrated that the states could not create new citizens for purposes of article IV, it did not necessarily follow that they could not do so for purposes of article III. Taney himself had explicitly refused

[209]Scott, 60 U.S. (19 How.) at 405-06, 416-18, 422-23.

[210]THE FEDERALIST No. 42 (J. Madison) (not cited by Taney).

[211]Collet v. Collet, 2 U.S. (2 Dall.) 294, 296 (C.C.D. Pa. 1792).

[212]Scott, 60 U.S. (19 How.) at 405; see Chirac v. Lessee of Chirac, 15 U.S. (2 Wheat.) 259, 269 (1817) (Marshall, C.J.) (not cited by Taney). Accord, 3 J. STORY, supra note 12, at 1, 3.

[213]See supra chapter 5 (noting Chirac in discussion of Sturges v. Crowninshield, 17 U.S. (4 Wheat.) 122 (1819).

[214]Sturges v. Crowninshield, 17 U.S. (4 Wheat.) 122 (1819), supra chapter 5.

[215]Scott, 60 U.S. (19 How.) at 417-18 (citing no authority). This conclusion forced Taney to distinguish Indians, who had on occasion been made citizens, on the ground that they were "foreign." Id. at 403-04. The distinction flatly contradicted what Marshall had held in refusing a tribe the right to sue as a "foreign State." See Cherokee Nation v. Georgia, 30 U.S. (5 Pet.) 1 (1831), supra chapter 4.

[216]Scott, 60 U.S. (19 How.) at 578-79. Phrased differently, this objection becomes less compelling: it is not unthinkable that the Framers would simultaneously limit federal power and exclude states from the field entirely.

[217]Id. at 417.

[218]See supra notes 18-25 and accompanying text.

[219]Scott, 60 U.S. (19 How.) at 582-84. Curtis's argument suggests that a black citizen of one state could be enslaved in another, which seems hard to square with the apparent purposes of article IV. Reconciling the rejection of this conclusion with the neutrality principle correctly established in Conner, however, was a difficult problem which Taney made no effort to resolve.

in *Bank of Augusta v. Earle*[220] to follow a diversity precedent in determining an identical question of privileges and immunities,[221] and his successors would build on this refusal by holding a corporation not a citizen under article IV, though it effectively was one under article III.[222]

Because no one argued that Scott had been a "citizen" while he was a slave, all the Court needed to say was that no state could make him a citizen thereafter. Taney at least had a plausible, though tenuous argument to that effect, but, perhaps because of the way the jurisdictional plea was phrased,[223] he insisted on arguing that *no* person descended from an American slave had ever been a citizen for article III purposes. Other than people naturalized by the federal government, said Taney, United States citizens included only descendants of citizens of the states at the Constitution's adoption, and, Taney continued, blacks had been citizens of none of the states at that time.[224] Disputing the premise as well as the conclusion,[225] Curtis cited, among other authorities, an early North Carolina case explicitly declaring liberated slaves "citizens of North Carolina."[226] Curtis also demolished Taney's counterexamples: laws discriminating against blacks no more disproved citizenship than did those disadvantaging married women, and an Act of Congress limiting militia service to "white male citizen[s]"[227] implied, if anything, that there might be black citizens as well.[228]

Taney's arguments against the citizenship of free blacks thus left a good deal to be desired.[229] He has also been widely pilloried for going on to hold the Missouri Compromise unconstitutional: a court without jurisdiction, as many have said in criticism of *Marbury v. Madison* as well,[230] cannot properly decide the merits.[231] The

---

[220]38 U.S. (13 Pet.) 519 (1839).

[221]*See supra* text accompanying notes 1-17.

[222]*See* D. FEHRENBACHER, *supra* note 37, at 355-56; *compare* Paul v. Virginia, 75 U.S. (8 Wall.) 168 (1869), *with* Marshall v. Baltimore & O.R.R., 57 U.S. (16 How.) 314 (1853).

[223]The plea in abatement urged that Scott was not a citizen "because he is a negro of African descent; his ancestors were of pure African blood, and were brought into this country and sold as negro slaves." *Scott*, 60 U.S. (19 How.) at 396-97.

[224]*Id.* at 406-16, 419-22.

[225]*See supra* note 205.

[226]*Scott*, 60 U.S. (19 How.) at 573 (citing, inter alia, State v. Manuel, 20 N.C. (3 & 4 Dev. & Bat.) 114 (1838)). The issue in *Manuel* was whether certain guarantees in the state constitution were inapplicable to free blacks because they were not citizens. The North Carolina court said the provisions applied to people who were not citizens but added that free blacks had been citizens of North Carolina since the revolution. *Manuel*, 20 N.C. (3 & 4 Dev. & Bat.) at 120. Professor Swisher termed Curtis's evidence on this point "devastating." C. SWISHER, *supra* note 2, at 628; *see also* J. KETTNER, THE DEVELOPMENT OF AMERICAN CITIZENSHIP, 1608-1870, at 328 (1978).

[227]Act of May 8, 1792, ch. 33, § 1, 1 Stat. 271, *cited* (with a minor inaccuracy) *in Scott*, 60 U.S. (19 How.) at 587.

[228]*Scott*, 60 U.S. (19 How.) at 583, 586-87 (also effectively refuting other examples). Similarly, constitutional and statutory provisions recognizing that *some* blacks were slaves, for example, the importation clause of article 1, § 9, and the fugitive slave clause of article IV, cited by Taney in 60 U.S. (19 How.) at 411, said nothing about the status of others who were not. *See also* D. FEHRENBACHER, *supra* note 37, at 351-52, 361.

[229]Nor were they new arguments. For their antecedents, including an 1832 opinion by Taney as Attorney General, see D. FEHRENBACHER, *supra* note 37, at 64-73, 5 C. SWISHER, *supra* note 2, at 506-07.

[230]*See generally supra* chapter 3.

[231]*See, e.g.,* D. POTTER, *supra* note 199, at 281-82, and authorities cited therein. Curtis made the same accusation in his dissent. *See Scott*, 60 U.S. (19 How.) at 589.

validity of the Compromise, however, was also relevant to jurisdiction. As Taney said, if Congress could not abolish slavery in the territories, Scott remained a slave, and "no one supposes that a slave is a citizen of the State or of the United States."[232] Strong arguments remain that Taney should have been content with a single ground for finding a lack of jurisdiction. With two Justices dissenting and four others declining to decide whether the descendants of slaves could be citizens, however, Taney seems to have spoken for only three Justices on that issue.[233] Without the conclusions of Grier and Campbell that Scott remained a slave,[234] apparently no majority would have existed for a decision against jurisdiction.[235]

On the question whether Scott was still a slave the Justices produced an appalling cacophony of reasons. The most obvious basis for finding Scott not free was, as Taney at one point suggested, that a Missouri court had already so held;[236] but Daniel responded devastatingly that res judicata, an affirmative defense, had not been pleaded.[237] Nelson based his opinion solely on the ground that Missouri law governed the status of an alleged slave resident in Missouri, and that under that law Scott remained a slave.[238] On this narrow point Nelson had the support of three other justices[239] and a Supreme Court precedent that was not easy to distinguish;[240] it was

---

[232]*Scott*, 60 U.S. (19 How.) at 427.

[233]Wayne joined Taney's opinion in toto, *id.* at 454, and Daniel agreed that a descendant of slaves was not a citizen. *Id.* at 475-82. Nelson and Campbell expressly left the issue open, *id.* at 458, 493, and Grier said he agreed with Taney that Scott was still a slave, *id.* at 469. Catron argued that the defendant had waived the broader issue by pleading over on the merits. *Id.* at 518-19. Taney and Daniel, disagreeing, properly pointed to precedents holding that subject matter jurisdiction could be investigated at any time. *Id.* at 400-03, 472-75. Professor Fehrenbacher argues that because Taney's opinion purported to be that of the Court, concurring Justices should be taken to have agreed with everything in the opinion which they did not disclaim. D. FEHRENBACHER, *supra* note 37, at 326-30. I read four of them, however, as having disclaimed Taney's views on black citizenship in general. More troublesome is the fact that neither Grier nor Campbell announced his views from the bench. *See id.* at 315. They certainly left the impression at the time that they accepted everything Taney said, and withdrawing that support after the decision had been announced was questionable.

[234]Both Grier and Campbell agreed with Taney and Wayne that because Scott remained a slave there was no jurisdiction. *Id.* at 469 (Grier, J.), 517-18 (Campbell, J.).

[235]Nelson and Catron purported to decide only the merits. *Scott*, 60 U.S. (19 How.) at 458 (Nelson, J.), 519 (Catron, J.). Daniel's discussion of the slavery issue appeared to go only to the merits. *Id.* at 482-92. For criticism of the argument that the slavery issue should not have been decided, see D. POTTER, *supra* note 199, at 276-84 (observing that the dictum label enabled critics to reconcile defiance of the decision with their general respect for law by depriving the pronouncement of "ordinary judicial force"); Corwin, *The Dred Scott Decision, in the Light of Contemporary Legal Doctrines*, 17 AM. HIST. REV. 52, 55-59 (1911); Hagan, *The Dred Scott Decision*, 15 GEO. L.J. 95, 107-09 (1927).

[236]*Scott*, 60 U.S. (19 How.) at 453-54; *see* Scott v. Emerson, 15 Mo. 576, 585 (1852) (lower Missouri court opinion).

[237]*Scott*, 60 U.S. (19 How.) at 492-93. The judgment also may not have been sufficiently final because the state proceeding had been remanded to the trial court and was awaiting the federal decision. *See id.* at 453 (Taney, C.J.).

[238]*Id.* at 459-68.

[239]*See id.* at 455 (Wayne, J.), 469 (Grier, J.) 483-88 (Daniel, J.). Taney, *id.* at 452-54, Campbell, *id.* at 493-500, and Catron, *id.* at 519, used the same argument to dismiss the relevance of Scott's stay in Illinois, but all three seemed to base their decision with respect to the territorial stay solely on the invalidity of the Compromise.

[240]*See* Strader v. Graham, 51 U.S. (10 How.) 82, 94 (1851) (Taney, J.)(refusing to review a Kentucky decision holding that a trip to Ohio had not freed Kentucky slaves: "It was exclusively in the power of

indeed gratuitous that those three went on to join Taney, Campbell, and Catron in declaring the Compromise unconstitutional.

Once more, Taney's "opinion of the Court" label is misleading, for there seems to have been no consensus as to *why* Congress had no power to outlaw slavery in the area to which Scott had been taken. Apparently joined only by Wayne and Grier,[241] Taney began by arguing that the article IV authority to "make all needful Rules and Regulations respecting the Territory or other Property belonging to the United States"[242] extended only to those territories already within the country in 1789.[243] Because the language of the clause was general and the need for "Rules and

---

Kentucky to determine for itself whether their employment in another State should or should not make them free on their return.").

Technically, which state's law was determinative was irrelevant to the Supreme Court's jurisdiction in *Strader*. Moreover, unlike *Strader*, *Scott* arose in a federal court, which the dissenters argued was free to make its own decision, *Scott*, 60 U.S. (19 How.) at 593, 603-04; it has also been argued that the federal law involved in *Scott* was applicable without regard to state choice-of-law principles by virtue of the Supremacy Clause, Hagan, *supra* note 235, at 110. *Strader*, however, had also rejected an argument based on the Northwest Ordinance, not only because the Ordinance had ceased to be law when Ohio became a state, but also because it had never had extraterritorial effect. *Strader*, 51 U.S. (10 How.) at 94-97. This meant that *Strader*'s choice-of-law principle was not dictum but an alternative holding, that it applied to federal laws, and that it governed a lower federal court.

There remained the argument that the rule should be different in Scott's case because his master had been domiciled in free territory, but the Missouri court had already rejected that argument in Scott's earlier suit. *See* Scott v. Emerson, 15 Mo. 576 (1852). On the question whether a federal court would be free to ignore the Missouri decision, see *Scott*, 60 U.S. (19 How.) at 603 (Curtis, J.), shakily arguing, after conceding that the question was one of Missouri law, *id.* at 594, that federal courts were entitled to ignore state decisions involving "principles of universal jurisprudence" outside the commercial field. *See also id.* at 563 (McLean, J.), 604 (Curtis, J.) (invoking the questionable decision in Pease v. Peck, 59 U.S. (18 How.) 589, 599 (1855), that when (as evidently in *Scott*) "the decisions of the state court are not consistent, we do not feel bound to follow the last"); *Scott*, 60 U.S. (19 How.) at 466-67 (Nelson, J.) (finding the state decisions basically consistent and arguing, without mentioning *Pease*, that a state court was free to change its mind). *See generally supra* chapter 7 (discussing Gelpcke v. Dubuque, 68 U.S. (1 Wall.) 175 (1864); *supra* notes 120-49 and accompanying text (discussing Luther v. Borden, 48 U.S. (7 How.) 1 (1849)). Curtis finally argued that by consenting to Scott's territorial marriage his master had freed him, and that Missouri thus would impair the marriage contract in violation of article I, § 10 by declaring him a slave. *Scott*, 60 U.S. (19 How.) at 599-603; but because freedom was a consequence of the contract and not part of its obligation, and because the contract clause appeared inapplicable to judicial decisions, *see supra* chapter 7 (discussing *Gelpcke v. Dubuque*), this contention seems rather strained. The otherwise highly critical comment in the *Monthly Law Report* supported Nelson's opinion. *See The Case of Dred Scott*, 20 MONTHLY L. REP. 61, 110 (1858). For an informative discussion of the complex choice-of-law issues and a criticism of Nelson that seems to underplay both the Northwest Ordinance part of *Strader* and the obligation of federal courts to follow state court decisions, see D. FEHRENBACHER, *supra* note 37, at 50-61, 260-62, 385-86, 390-94.

[241]*See Scott*, 60 U.S. (19 How.) at 454 (Wayne, J.), 469 (Grier, J.). Catron expressly relied on the territorial clause for power to govern areas outside the 1789 boundary. *See id.* at 523. Campbell, who devoted his opinion to a narrow interpretation of that clause, said it "comprehends all the public domain, wherever it may be." *Id.* at 509. Daniel's apparent belief that the territorial clause provided the only argument for congressional authority suggests he did not take Taney's alternative thesis seriously. *See id.* at 488-89. Nelson presented his nonconstitutional thesis with the apparently exclusive observation that this thesis represented "the grounds upon which" he had "arrived at" his conclusion. *Id.* at 457.

[242]U.S. CONST. art. IV, § 3, cl. 2.

[243]*Scott*, 60 U.S. (19 How.) at 432-46. Taney correctly noted that the Court had left this question open in American Ins. Co. v. Canter, 26 U.S. (1 Pet.) 511, 542 (1828), *supra* chapter 4, where Marshall equivocated concerning the source of authority to set up courts for Florida. *Scott*, 60 U.S. (19 How.) at 442-43. It was embarrassing for Taney that Wayne had said for a unanimous Court in Cross v. Harrison, 57

Regulations" was just as great in the newly acquired territory, Taney's construction seems singularly unpersuasive;[244] he might as convincingly have argued that the ex post facto clause applied only to the thirteen original states. Not only did Taney inconsistently acknowledge that new states could be admitted from the area purchased from France,[245] but, as Curtis noted,[246] Taney destroyed the force of his own argument by conceding that Congress could govern that territory as an incident of its power to admit it to statehood.[247] Daniel and Campbell argued that the power to make rules and regulations was not a general power to govern;[248] Curtis observed that similar language in the commerce clause had already received its naturally broad interpretation,[249] and Catron dryly added that he had been ordering people hanged on the strength of article IV regulations on circuit for many years.[250]

U.S. (16 How.) 164, 192-93 (1853), invoked by Catron, *Scott*, 60 U.S. (19 How.) at 523, that article IV gave Congress power to govern California. That case implicated no act of Congress, however, so the statement was dictum. *Cf.* 1 J. KENT, COMMENTARIES ON AMERICAN LAW 384 (4th ed. New York 1840) (1st ed. New York 1826) (giving article IV as the source of the territorial power in a discussion of new as well as original territories).

[244]*See Scott*, 60 U.S. (19 How.) at 611-14 (Curtis, J., dissenting); *cf.* D. FEHRENBACHER, *supra* note 37, at 367-68 (construction "bizarre" and "eccentric"); D. POTTER, *supra* note 199, at 277 (Taney's construction of article IV "tortured").

[245]*Scott*, 60 U.S. (19 How.) at 477.

[246]*Id.* at 623-24.

[247]*Id.* at 446-49. Taney apparently hoped in this way to circumvent the precedent of the Northwest Ordinance, which had prohibited slavery in an area owned before the Constitution was adopted, but he gave no satisfactory reason for thinking the authority he found implicit in the statehood clause narrower than the power in the territorial provision. Daniel was on a sounder ground in arguing that the Ordinance itself was unconstitutional, *see id.* at 490-92, because the Articles of Confederation, under which the Ordinance was enacted, contained no provision remotely resembling article IV's authority to adopt regulations for territories. *See id.* at 608 (Curtis, J., dissenting) (this consideration entitled "to great weight"). As Curtis pointed out, however, Congress had effectively reenacted the Ordinance in 1789 under the new Constitution. *See id.* at 616-17. Catron distinguished the Ordinance, *see id.* at 522-23, on the basis of Tucker's argument that it had been approved not under article IV, but under article VI's provision that "All . . . Engagements entered into, before the Adoption of the Constitution, shall be as valid against the United States under this Constitution, as under the Confederation." U.S. CONST. art. VI, cl. 1; *see* St. G. Tucker, 1 *Appendix to Volume First. Part First of Blackstone's Commentaries* 280, in 1 BLACKSTONE'S COMMENTARIES: WITH NOTES OF REFERENCE TO THE CONSTITUTION AND LAWS, OF THE FEDERAL GOVERNMENT OF THE UNITED STATES; AND OF THE COMMONWEALTH OF VIRGINIA (St. G. Tucker ed. Philadelphia 1803 & photo. reprint 1965).

[248]*See Scott*, 60 U.S. (19 How.) at 489-90 (Daniel, J.) (no power "to impair the civil and political rights of the citizens of the United States" or to "exclude" slaveowners); *id.* at 501,514 (Campbell, J.):

> The recognition of a plenary power in Congress to dispose of the public domain, or to organize a Government over it, does not imply a corresponding authority to determine the internal polity, or to adjust the domestic relations, or the persons who may lawfully inhabit the territory . . . . [T]he power . . . is restricted to such administrative and conservatory acts as are needful for the preservation of the public domain, and its preparation for sale or disposition.

See Taney's similar suggestion, *id.* at 436-37, which was unnecessary in light of his conclusion that the power in question applied only to the original territories; see also his comparison, *id.* at 440, with the article I, § 8 power of Congress "to exercise exclusive Legislation in all Cases whatsoever" over the District of Columbia. For cogent criticism of these arguments, see D. FEHRENBACHER, *supra* note 37, at 368-70.

[249]*Scott*, 60 U.S. (19 How.) at 622-23; *see also id.* at 625-26 (where Curtis pointed out that if slavery lay outside congressional power, there seemed to be no one to define its numerous incidents in the territories).

[250]*Scott*, 60 U.S. (19 How.) at 522-23. The territorial clause was little discussed at the Convention. The

Catron had two far-fetched theses of his own, which nobody else joined. He relied first on the Louisiana treaty, which assured France that "the inhabitants of the ceded territory . . . shall be maintained and protected in the free enjoyment of their liberty, property, and . . . religion" until "incorporated in the Union of the United States, and admitted . . . to the enjoyment of all the rights, advantages, and immunities, of citizens of the United States."[251] Curtis responded with a number of debatable points about the meaning of the treaty,[252] and with the more telling objection that the supremacy clause gave treaties no precedence over later federal statutes.[253]

Catron's second point was no better:

> The Constitution having provided that "The citizens of each State shall be entitled to all privileges and immunities of citizens of the several States," the right to enjoy the territory as equals was reserved to the states, and to the citizens of the States . . . .
> . . . If the slaveholder is prohibited from going to the Territory with his slaves, . . . owners of slave property . . . might be almost as effectually excluded from removing into the Territory . . . as if the law declared that owners of slaves, as a class, should be excluded . . . .[254]

In other words, the privileges and immunities clause ensured slaveowners the same right as anyone else to inhabit the territories. The statute, however, *did* give slaveholders the same right as anyone else, for *no one* was allowed to hold slaves in the territory. Catron might as well have argued that equality entitled burglars to practice their calling in the territories.[255] Worse yet, he could make the clause relevant at all only by misquoting it. Article IV guarantees the citizen the privileges and immunities of citizens "in the several States," not "of the several States."[256] The text shows it to be a protection of outsiders from state discrimination, not a guarantee of equal treatment by Congress.

---

replacement of Madison's initial proposal of separate clauses authorizing Congress both to "dispose of the unappropriated lands" and to "institute temporary Governments for New States arising therein" by a single clause authorizing "all needful rules and regulations respecting the territory or 'other property'" seems to suggest the propriety of a broad construction. *See* Notes of James Madison (Aug. 18, 1787 and Aug. 30, 1787), *reprinted in* 2 CONVENTION RECORDS, *supra* note 61, at 324, 459.

[251]*Scott*, 60 U.S. (19 How.) at 524-26. On this point Catron had the support of William Rawle's treatise, *see* W. RAWLE, A VIEW OF THE CONSTITUTION OF THE UNITED STATES OF AMERICA 67-68 (2d ed. Philadelphia 1829)(1st ed. Philadelphia 1825); see also Story's ambiguous comment quoted *infra* note 265.

[252]*See Scott*, 60 U.S. (19 How.) at 630-32, arguing that the quoted passage applied only to those inhabiting the territory at the date of the treaty, that it did not say the inhabitants could "go upon the public domain ceded by the treaty, either with or without their slaves," and that it was a temporary provision that expired when Louisiana became a state. McLean added, without explanation, that a provision such as that found by Catron would have been outside the treaty power. *Id.* at 557.

[253]*Id.* at 629-30. Congress had repealed treaties by legislation as early as 1798, *see id.*, and its power to do so has been confirmed by more recent decisions. *See* The Chinese Exclusion Case, 130 U.S. 581 (1889); Whitney v. Robertson, 124 U.S. 190 (1888).

[254]*Scott*, 60 U.S. (19 How.) at 527.

[255]Compare the discussion of this clause in connection with Bank of Augusta v. Earle, 38 U.S. (13 Pet.) 519 (1839), and Conner v. Elliott, 59 U.S. (18 How.) 591 (1856) (both cases discussed *supra* notes 1-25 and accompanying text).

[256]U.S. CONST. art. IV, § 2, cl. 1.

It remains to explain the ground on which Chief Justice Taney, explicitly joined only by Wayne and Grier,[257] ultimately based his opinion. Having asserted that the Constitution limited Congress's power over the territories, Taney proceeded to give examples. Surely, he argued, Congress could not pass a law abridging the freedom of speech or religion in the territories, or denying the right to bear arms or to trial by jury there, or compelling people there to incriminate themselves.[258] Similarly, "the rights of private property have been guarded with equal care . . . by the fifth amendment . . . , which provides that no person shall be deprived of life, liberty, and property, without due process of law," and

> an act of Congress which deprives a citizen of the United States of his liberty or property, merely because he came himself or brought his property into a particular Territory of the United States, and who had committed no offence against the laws, could hardly be dignified with the name of due process of law.[259]

Nothing in the Constitution, he added, "gives Congress a greater power over slave property, or . . . entitles property of that kind to less protection than property of any other description. The only power conferred" was to protect the slaveowner's rights; a prohibition on slavery was "not warranted by the Constitution."[260]

Scholars have argued over the meaning of this passage,[261] but it was at least very possibly the first application of substantive due process in the Supreme Court, the original precedent for *Lochner v. New York*[262] and *Roe v. Wade*.[263] Despite Taney's blithe announcement, however, even the threshold question whether the amendments applied to the territories was disputable: fifty years later the Court would hold that some of them did not apply to certain other possessions,[264] and it had already

[257]*See supra* note 232.

[258]*Scott*, 60 U.S. (19 How.) at 450.

[259]*Id.*

[260]*Id.* at 452.

[261]Professor Swisher argued that Taney's due process point was a "suggestion, rather than . . . a necessary link in his argument," and that, much like Campbell, Taney had held Congress had power over a Territory "only to the extent of nurturing it into statehood." C. SWISHER, *supra* note 54, at 508; *see also* D. FEHRENBACHER, *supra* note 37, at 377-84. Taney did begin his discussion by defining Congress's authority as "the power to preserve and apply to the purposes for which it was acquired"; by denying that Congress had "a mere discretionary power" over "the person or property of a citizen," as it had in determining the form of territorial government; and by introducing the section in which he discussed due process by stating that "reference to a few provisions of the Constitution will illustrate" the proposition that Congress could "exercise no power . . . beyond what [the Constitution] . . . confers, nor lawfully deny any right which it has reserved." *Scott*, 60 U.S. (19 How.) at 448-50. If due process was only an illustration, however, Taney failed to explain why his implicit power to govern territories did not include the right to legislate on the subject of slavery. He never denied that such laws were related to preserving the territories for eventual statehood, and thus the several paragraphs devoted to the constitutional protection of slave property, *id.* at 450-52, seem to justify the conclusion of such careful observers as Professors Corwin and Potter that the due process clause was the basis of Taney's position. *See* D. POTTER, *supra* note 199, at 276; Corwin, *supra* note 235, at 61-63.

[262]198 U.S. 45 (1905).

[263]410 U.S. 113 (1973).

[264]*See, e.g.,* Dorr v. United States, 195 U.S. 138, 146-49 (1904) (defendant not entitled to jury in criminal trial held in the Philippines). The ambiguous and unexplained extension of the civil jury to the

held article III inapplicable to territorial courts in *American Insurance Co. v. Canter*.[265] More important, the idea that the due process clause limited the substantive powers of Congress also needed a bit of explaining. On its face the term "due process" seemed to speak of procedural regularity, as the Court had employed it the year before *Scott* in *Murray's Lessee v. Hoboken Land & Improvement Co.*[266] Still more fundamentally, although *Murray's Lessee*—not cited by Taney—had stated the contrary,[267] considerable historical evidence supports the position that "due process of law" was a separation-of-powers concept designed as a safeguard against unlicensed executive action, forbidding only deprivations not authorized by legislation or common law.[268] Finally, Taney did not respond to Curtis's crippling observation that no one had ever thought due process provisions offended by either federal or state bans on the international or interstate slave trade.[269]

From a lawyer's viewpoint *Scott* was a disreputable performance. The variety of feeble, poorly developed, and unnecessary constitutional arguments suggests, if nothing else, a determination to reach a predetermined conclusion at any price.[270]

Iowa Territory in Webster v. Reid, 52 U.S. (11 How.) 437, 460 (1850), may as likely have rested on the statute setting up the territory, which "extended the laws of the United States" to that area, as on the Constitution itself.

[265] 26 U.S. (1 Pet.) 511 (1828), *supra* chapter 4. Thomas Hart Benton's contemporaneous criticism of *Scott* was based on the argument that Congress's power over territories lay wholly outside the Constitution and thus was subject to no limitations whatever. *See* T. BENTON, HISTORICAL AND LEGAL EXAMINATION OF THAT PART OF THE DECISION OF THE SUPREME COURT OF THE UNITED STATES IN THE DRED SCOTT CASE, WHICH DECLARES THE UNCONSTITUTIONALITY OF THE MISSOURI COMPROMISE ACT, AND THE SELF-EXTENSION OF THE CONSTITUTION TO TERRITORIES, CARRYING SLAVERY ALONG WITH IT (New York 1857) (citing numerous congressional actions respecting territories that allegedly would have offended the Constitution had it applied). Thus Benton agreed with Campbell's view that article IV applied only to the regulation of federal property, but he and Campbell drew from the same premise opposite conclusions. *See also* 3 J. STORY, *supra* note 12, §§ 1311-1322 (equivocating as to the source of territorial power but finding it unlimited "unless so far as it is affected by stipulations in the cessions," *id.* § 1322, at 198).

[266] 59 U.S. (18 How.) 272 (1856); *see* D. POTTER, *supra* note 199, at 276 ("Up to that time, due process had been generally regarded as a matter of procedure . . . ."); 3 J. STORY, *supra* note 12, § 1783, at 661 (equating due process with common law procedure); Jurow, *Untimely Thoughts: A Reconsideration of the Origins of Due Process*, 19 AM. J. LEGAL HIST. 265, 272 (1975) (equating "process" with "writs").

[267] *Murray's Lessee*, 59 U.S. (18 How.) at 276.

[268] *See* Corwin, *The Doctrine of Due Process of Law Before the Civil War*, 24 HARV. L. REV. 366 (1911); *see also* Youngstown Sheet & Tube Co. v. Sawyer, 343 U.S. 579, 646 (1952) (Jackson, J., concurring) (juxtaposing article II's command that the President "take care that the Laws be faithfully executed" with the due process clause: "One gives a governmental authority that reaches so far as there is law, the other gives a private right that authority shall go no farther."). The congressional debates on the Bill of Rights reveal no discussion of the due process provision. *See generally* 1 ANNALS OF CONG. (J. Gales ed. 1789); Easterbrook, *Substance and Due Process*, 1982 SUP. CT. REV. 85, 95-100.

[269] *Scott*, 60 U.S. (19 How.) at 627. For additional criticism of Taney's due process argument, see D. FEHRENBACHER, *supra* note 37, at 328-84; Corwin, *supra* note 235, at 64-67.

[270] Notably, no serious constitutional objections were made to the Missouri Compromise line at the time of its enactment, or for many years thereafter. *See* T. BENTON, *supra* note 265, at 91-97. The long House debate in 1820 concerned the much more doubtful proposal to require Missouri to prohibit slavery *after statehood*; the Compromise itself was accepted essentially without debate by overwhelming majorities, including many Southerners. *See* 35 ANNALS OF CONG. 467-69 (1820)(Senate discussion of Compromise); 36 ANNALS OF CONG. 1576-88 (1820)(House discussion of Compromise, including speech of Mr. Kinsey of New Jersey, treating the Compromise line as a Southern proposal). A few Congressmen did incidentally suggest in the debate over the provision respecting slavery after statehood that, as Campbell later argued, article IV applied only to the use of federal property. *See, e.g.*, 35 ANNALS OF CONG. 1003

Curtis's dissent, however, is one of the great masterpieces of constitutional opinion-writing,[271] in which, calmly and painstakingly, he dismantled virtually every argument of his variegated adversaries. Along the way, in arguing that no exception should be carved out of Congress's powers "upon reasons purely political,"[272] he also delivered a classic statement on constitutional interpretation:

> [W]hen a strict interpretation of the Constitution, according to the fixed rules which govern the interpretation of laws, is abandoned, and the theoretical opinions of individuals are allowed to control its meaning, we have no longer a Constitution; we are under the government of individual men, who for the time being have power to declare what the Constitution is, according to their own views of what it ought to mean.[273]

It was a tragedy but not a surprise that within a year after this decision Curtis went back to Boston to practice law.[274]

B. *The Prize Cases*

In 1861, following the purported secession of a number of Southern states, President Lincoln proclaimed a blockade of Southern ports.[275] In 1863, by a five to four vote, the Supreme Court upheld the constitutionality of the proclamations.[276]

Justice Grier's unimpressive majority opinion treated the problem largely as one of "international law,"[277] paying scant attention to what today would appear to be the

---

(1820) (Mr. Smyth of Virginia); *id.* at 1160 (Mr. McLane of Delaware). Several Congressmen explicitly added, however, that Congress nevertheless had power to ban slavery in the territories. *See id.* at 940-41 (Mr. Smith of Maryland); *id.* at 1160 (Mr. McLane); *see also id.* at 1031-32 (Mr. Reid of Georgia) (anticipating Catron's treaty argument); 36 *id.* at 1379 (Mr. Darlington of Pennsylvania)(asserting that the power was "generally conceded").

The first serious assault on the principle underlying the Compromise was probably the series of resolutions offered by John C. Calhoun in 1847, CONG. GLOBE, 29th Cong., 2d Sess. 455 (1847), arguing that the states owned the territories in common and that Congress, as their agent, could not discriminate among the states. *See also id.* at App. 244 (Mr. Rhett of South Carolina); *id.* at 876 (Mr. Calhoun, opposing extension of the Compromise line to the Pacific). Daniel's argument in *Scott* echoed this trusteeship idea, but unlike Calhoun and Rhett he based Congress's territorial power on article IV. *See supra* notes 248-49 and accompanying text. The historical antecedents of the *Scott* arguments are splendidly treated in D. FEHRENBACHER, *supra* note 37, at 74-235.

[271]I have repeatedly referred to it, rather than McLean's pedestrian counterpart, for this reason. McLean's biographer conceded that "Curtis'[s] opinion was much the abler." F. WEISENBURGER, THE LIFE OF JOHN McLEAN 203 (1937); *see also* D. POTTER, *supra* note 199, at 278.

[272]*Scott*, 60 U.S. (19 How.) at 620.

[273]*Id.* at 621.

[274]*See* Curtis, *Memoir of Benjamin Robbins Curtis, L.L.D.*, in 1 A MEMOIR OF BENJAMIN ROBBINS CURTIS 243-44 (B.R. Curtis, Jr. ed. 1879)(saying the "controlling reason" for Curtis's resignation was financial but adding that Curtis "no longer felt that confidence in the Supreme Court which was essential to his useful co-operation with its members"); *see also* C. SWISHER, *supra* note 2, at 636-38.

[275]Proclamation No. 4, 12 Stat. 1258 (1861); Proclamation No. 5, 12 Stat. 1259 (1861).

[276]Prize Cases, 67 U.S. (2 Black) 635 (1863). *See generally* C. SWISHER, *supra* note 2, at 879-900; C. SWISHER, *supra* note 54, at 563-65.

[277]*Prize Cases*, 67 U.S. (2 Black) at 665-68.

real question—the consistency of the President's act with the Constitution and laws of the United States.[278] Justice Nelson accurately framed the issue in a literate dissent joined by Taney, Catron, and Clifford: only Congress had the power to declare war.[279]

Grier responded in part with the bald conclusion that Congress "cannot declare war against a State, or any number of States."[280] Even if true, this did not prove that the President could,[281] and Grier admitted the President had no power to "initiate or declare a war either against a foreign nation or a domestic State."[282] The President was, however, "Commander in Chief of the Army and Navy" under article II; Congress had authorized him to call out the armed forces to suppress insurrections; and that, said Grier, was what he had done.[283]

Though buried in a mass of irrelevancies, this seems to be a good argument. Nelson's protest that Congress could not delegate its power to declare war[284] missed the mark; article I shows that *defensive* responsibility can be delegated, as self-preservation demands, by specifically authorizing Congress to "provide for calling forth the Militia to execute the Laws of the Union, suppress Insurrections and repel Invasions."[285] Grier neglected to cite the Convention history that would have placed his conclusion beyond dispute: the original draft empowering Congress to "make" war was altered to the present form on Madison's and Gerry's motion, "leaving to the Executive the power to repel sudden attacks."[286]

Nelson left his most interesting objection for last: putting down an insurrection meant only fighting the insurgents themselves; to make enemies of innocent inhabitants of the territory under rebel control required a declaration of war.[287] Some limit to the presidential power of response does seem necessary to keep it from infringing the constitutional purpose that Congress shall make the basic decisions of war and peace;[288] subsequent events have illustrated the difficulty of drawing the line.[289] In the

---

[278]*See supra* chapter 2; *cf.* Ware v. Hylton, 3 U.S. (3 Dall.) 199, 230 (1796) (Chase, J.) (the obligations international law might impose toward other countries were irrelevant to Virginia's power to confiscate alien property as a domestic matter).

[279]*Prize Cases*, 67 U.S. (2 Black) at 688-90 (Nelson, J., dissenting).

[280]*Id.* at 668. This conclusion finds no support in the constitutional language and little in its apparent policy; it is hard to see why the Framers would not have wanted Congress to have a say in domestic as well as in international fighting.

[281]In view of the argument *supra* note 280, this more probably would mean the United States could never be formally at war with its own constituent parts.

[282]*Prize Cases*, 67 U.S. (2 Black) at 668.

[283]*Id.* This passage calls into question the suggestion in L. TRIBE, *supra* note 12, § 4-6, at 174, that the *Prize Cases* "recognized an inherent executive power . . . to repel an invasion or rebellion."

[284]*Prize Cases*, 67 U.S. (2 Black) at 693 (Nelson, J., dissenting).

[285]U.S. CONST. art. I. § 8, cl. 15. Nelson made nothing of the fact that the Navy instead of the militia enforced the blockade. Because no reason appears why the government should have less authority to use federal rather than state troops in an emergency, the militia seems to have been mentioned to avoid any argument that state officers were outside federal control.

[286]Notes of James Madison (Aug. 17, 1787), *reprinted in* 2 CONVENTION RECORDS, *supra* note 61, at 318-19.

[287]*Prize Cases*, 67 U.S. (2 Black) at 693-95.

[288]An attack on a foreign nation helping the rebels, for instance, would appear to cross the line between defensive and offensive action. Compare this argument with the controversy over the bombing of neutral Cambodia during the conflict in Vietnam.

[289]*See* G. GUNTHER, CASES AND MATERIALS ON CONSTITUTIONAL LAW 410-24 (10th ed. 1980)(collecting

context of a massive rebellion within the United States itself, however, the choice of a blockade seems to have been well within the discretion confided the President in choosing the necessary means of defense.[290]

Unfortunately, Grier did not put it quite that way. Whether the crisis required belligerent actions, he said, was for the President alone to decide: "[t]he proclamation of blockade is itself official and conclusive evidence to the Court that a state of war existed which demanded and authorized a recourse to such a measure."[291] If this meant to immunize from judicial scrutiny anything a President might do in the name of pursuing lawful hostilities, it went far indeed; but later Presidents would discover that despite Grier's extreme statement they did not have nearly so much latitude.[292]

Compared with *Scott* and the *Prize Cases*, the remaining efforts of the Taney Court with respect to federal legislative and executive power were anticlimactic. As mentioned in the previous chapter, the commerce power was construed rather broadly.[293] Similarly, in areas outside the commerce clause the Taney decisions tended to apply Marshall's generous interpretation of the necessary and proper clause, upholding statutes punishing the passing of counterfeit coins,[294] authorizing bankruptcy trustees to pass title free of mortgages,[295] and allowing distraint of the property of a delinquent customs collector.[296] In *Prigg*[297] and *Dennison*[298] the Taney Court even went beyond the necessary and proper clause to sustain the implicit

---

examples including the capture of American vessels abroad, the effort to rescue American hostages in Iran, the evacuation of Americans and others from Saigon, and of course the Vietnam conflict itself).

[290]Grier's alternative holding that Congress had retroactively validated the blockade by subsequent legislation was less convincing. His argument that the ex post facto clause (invoked by Nelson, *Prize Cases*, 67 U.S. (2 Black) at 697-98) had no application "in a tribunal administering public and international law," *id.* at 671, sounds almost like an assertion that the Constitution was off during the emergency—a conclusion the Court would emphatically deny a few years later in *Ex parte* Milligan, 71 U.S. (4 Wall.) 2, 118-21 (1866) (*infra* chapter 9). More charitably, Grier may have meant the clause applied only to criminal matters, as the Court (in cases he ignored) had long held. *See supra* chapter 2 (discussing Calder v. Bull, 3 U.S. (3 Dall.) 386 (1798)). The proclamation made it unlawful to take ships in and out of Southern ports, however, and that was what the claimants had done. That their punishment was forfeiture of goods does not seem to take the case out of the punitive category. *Cf. Ex parte* Garland, 71 U.S. (4 Wall.) 333 (1867); Cummings v. Missouri, 71 U.S. (4 Wall.) 277 (1867) (*infra* chapter 9) (both striking down laws retroactively disqualifying Confederate sympathizers from certain occupations).

[291]*Prize Cases*, 67 U.S. (2 Black) at 670. For a later refusal for want of information, expertise, and manageable standards to determine whether a President had gone too far in combating an enemy, see DaCosta v. Laird, 471 F.2d 1146 (2d Cir. 1973) (mining and bombing of North Vietnam).

[292]*See, e.g.*, Youngstown Sheet & Tube Co. v. Sawyer, 343 U.S. 579 (1952) (invalidating seizure of steel mills during Korean War): *Ex parte* Milligan, 71 U.S. (4 Wall.) 2 (1866) (*infra* chapter 9) (invalidating military trial of civilian during Civil War).

[293]*See, e.g.*, Foster v. Davenport, 63 U.S. (22 How.) 244 (1859); Pennsylvania v. Wheeling & Belmont Bridge Co., 59 U.S. (18 How.) 421 (1856); United States v. Marigold, 50 U.S. (9 How.) 560 (1850); United States v. Coombs, 37 U.S. (12 Pet.) 72 (1838) (all noted *supra* in chapter 7).

[294]United States v. Marigold, 50 U.S. (9 How.) 560 (1850).

[295]Houston v. City Bank, 47 U.S. (6 How.) 486 (1848).

[296]Murray's Lessee v. Hoboken Land & Improvement Co., 59 U.S. (18 How.) 272 (1856).

[297]Prigg v. Pennsylvania, 41 U.S. (16 Pet.) 539 (1842)(discussed *supra* notes 29-55 and accompanying text).

[298]Kentucky v. Dennison, 65 U.S. (24 How.) 66 (1861) (discussed *supra* notes 58-70 and accompanying text). *See also* Searight v Stokes, 44 U.S. (3 How.) 151 (1845) (dictum) (resolving in favor of federal power the long-disputed question whether the authority to "establish" post roads included the power to build them); 3 J. STORY, *supra* note 12, at 26-46 (anticipating the *Searight* dictum).

power of Congress to pass legislation implementing the constitutional provisions requiring states to surrender fugitive slaves and fugitives from justice. It found the military had "inherent" authority to determine the pay of its members[299] and could impose tariffs[300] and establish courts[301] in conquered territories; and it held the President had power to make a pardon conditional.[302] Distorted as it was by the corrosive slavery question, *Scott v. Sandford*[303] was the least representative decision of an era otherwise characterized by vigorous judicial support for federal power.[304]

[299]United States v. Eliason, 41 U.S. (16 Pet.) 291 (1842).
[300]Cross v. Harrison, 57 U.S. (16 How.) 164 (1854).
[301]Leitensdorfer v. Webb, 61 U.S. (20 How.) 176 (1858).
[302]*Ex parte* Wells, 59 U.S. (18 How.) 307 (1856).
[303]60 U.S. (19 How.) 393 (1857).

[304]As in earlier periods, the Bill of Rights figured hardly at all in the decisions of the Taney period. Cases concerning the scope of the admiralty jurisdiction indirectly involved the seventh amendment, but the amendment did not stand in the way of reinterpreting the maritime clause to suit American conditions. *See supra* text accompanying notes 150-69. The Court's conclusion in Barron v. Mayor of Baltimore, 32 U.S. (7 Pet.) 243, 247 (1833) (*supra* chapter 6), that the taking clause did not apply to the states, was reaffirmed and applied to other amendments in Withers v. Buckley, 61 U.S. (20 How.) 84 (1858)(taking), Permoli v. New Orleans, 44 U.S. (3 How.) 589 (1845)(religion), Fox v. Ohio, 46 U.S. (5 How.) 410 (1847) (double jeopardy) (alternative holding), and Smith v. Maryland, 59 U.S. (18 How.) 71 (1855) (search and seizure). Moore v. Illinois, 55 U.S. (14 How.) 13, 19-20 (1852), set a lasting precedent in stating that a single act could constitute separate offenses against state and federal authority despite the double jeopardy clause. Gilman v. Sheboygan, 67 U.S. (2 Black) 510, 513 (1863), a diversity case holding that a tax did not offend the taking provision of a state constitution, laid down an explanation that, though based on state precedent, had important implications for the similar fifth amendment provision: "That clause . . . refers solely to the exercise, by the State, of the right of eminent domain."

The most interesting Bill of Rights decision apart from *Scott* was Murray's Lessee v. Hoboken Land & Improvement Co., 59 U.S. (18 How.) 272 (1856), sustaining the summary distraint of a customs collector's property for approximately a million dollars he had failed to deliver after extracting it from importers. Equating due process with the "law of the land" clause in Magna Charta, as he said Coke had done, Curtis announced that the due process clause was "a restraint on the legislative as well as on the executive and judicial powers of the government." *Id.* at 276. The content of due process, he said, was determined by "those settled usages and modes of proceeding existing in the common and statute law of England, before the emigration of our ancestors, and which are shown not have been unsuited to their civil and political condition by having been acted on by them after the settlement of this country." *Id.* at 277. Plausible decisions construing state law-of-the-land clauses, *see* Corwin, *supra* note 268, contradicted the first of these propositions, and later decisions holding English practice neither a necessary nor a sufficient indicium of due process abandoned the second. *See, e.g.,* Powell v. Alabama, 287 U.S. 45 (1932) (requiring assigned defense counsel despite the absence of English precedent); Hurtado v. California, 110 U.S. 516 (1884) (*infra* chapter 11) (allowing prosecution by information where English practice required indictment); *see also* G. GUNTHER, *supra* note 289, at 477-78. Finding distraint historically supported, the Court in *Murray's Lessee* rejected a fourth amendment argument on the ground that the requirements applicable to warrants had "no reference to civil proceedings for the recovery of debts" any more than to ordinary executions. *Murray's Lessee* 59 U.S. (18 How.) at 285-86. A little history might have helped support this essentially bare conclusion.

Conclusion to Part Three

Though none of Marshall's successors could rival his unique opportunity to flesh out the skeletal Constitution, Taney's years as Chief Justice also furnished a good number of significant occasions. No era containing such great controversies as *Charles River Bridge*,[1] *Bank of Augusta v. Earle*,[2] *Prigg v. Pennsylvania*,[3] *Luther v. Borden*,[4] *Cooley v. Board of Wardens*,[5] *Ableman v. Booth*,[6] and the *Prize Cases*[7] can be described as uneventful, even apart from *Scott*. A summary of the achievements of the Court over which Taney presided would include a rather generous interpretation of congressional and presidential power (with the glaring exception of *Scott*); a striking expansion of federal judicial authority beyond the boundaries set by the Marshall Court; vigorous enforcement of the contract clause and other express and implied limitations upon the states; and a compromise that settled the festering negative commerce clause debate in a manner destined to protect vital federal interests against state infringement for much of the next hundred years.

All of this was accomplished, to be sure, with far more perceptible friction than the Marshall Court had generally allowed itself to exhibit. Unlike Marshall, Taney had no success in silencing colleagues with views of their own, and a comparison of those views with the few separate opinions that did see the light of day under Marshall strongly suggests that the differences of opinion ran much deeper after Marshall's departure. For the Taney Court was a fractious one. Story, McLean, and Wayne, all of whom sat with Marshall, tended to take relatively nationalist positions, as did the later-appointed Curtis; Barbour, Catron, Daniel, Campbell, and Wood-

---

[1]Charles River Bridge v. Warren Bridge, 36 U.S. (11 Pet.) 420 (1837); *supra* chapter 7.
[2]38 U.S. (13 Pet.) 519 (1839).
[3]41 U.S. (16 Pet.) 539 (1842).
[4]48 U.S. (7 How.) 1 (1849).
[5]53 U.S. (12 How.) 299 (1852); *supra* chapter 7.
[6]62 U.S. (21 How.) 506 (1859).
[7]67 U.S. (2 Black) 635 (1863).

bury tended to come out in favor of the states in doubtful cases.[8] Sectional alignments partially clouded this picture: for example, though Wayne managed to find it to the South's advantage to keep the states out of the fugitive slave business, he could not bring himself to find that Congress could forbid slavery in the territories.[9]

On occasions this lack of cohesiveness paralyzed the Taney Court. For ten years the Court sowed hopeless confusion in the commerce clause pasture; its contract clause cases hardly formed a consistent pattern; and *Scott* presented the spectacle of seven judges with nearly as many rationales for their common conclusion. Under Taney the Court became a gaggle of squabbling prima donnas; whether the fault was his or theirs, Taney never did exhibit Marshall's astounding powers of leadership.

Taney's inability to prevent institutional incoherence contrasts sharply with the exemplary quality of many of his own opinions. Even when he was apparently in error, as in *Charles River Bridge*, his writing was often characterized by an unusual lucidity and economy of style that left little doubt where he stood and why. At his best, as in *The Genesee Chief*[10] and the *License Cases*,[11] Taney was not only clear but also extremely persuasive. Like most of his brethren, he made far greater use of precedent than had Marshall, perhaps because not until his day was there a significant body of precedent to cite. He did on occasion exhibit Marshall's tendency to reach out for unnecessary constitutional issues, as in *Luther* and *Scott*. His *Scott* opinion was a disaster, and thereafter he seemed to lose much of his power; neither his unexplained contradictions in *Dennison*[12] nor his unfocused and unsupported ramblings in *Ableman* earned him additional garlands. On the whole, however, he was an able and convincing Justice. As his biographer remarked, he would have been remembered as such had not Dr. Sandford allegedly purchased a slave who had once been to Fort Snelling.[13]

Nor was it merely an exceptional longevity that made Taney by far the dominant figure on the Court in his time. Though he assigned the burden of speaking for the majority to others much more frequently than had Marshall, Taney still delivered substantially more Court opinions in constitutional cases than any of his colleagues, including a disproportionate number of the important ones: *Charles River Bridge*, *Bank of Augusta*, *Luther*, *The Genesee Chief*, *Ableman*, and *Dennison*—not to mention *Scott*, in which he invited the blame for what was labeled the Court's opinion. More to the point, the Chief Justice did not lose many battles. In nearly thirty years of constitutional litigation he apparently dissented in only five cases, and in only two of importance.[14] After the squabbling had subsided, the outcome almost always matched what Taney wanted.

---

[8]Apart from slavery, the Justices' major disagreements involved public contracts, state powers affecting commerce, and the expansion of admiralty and diversity jurisdiction.

[9]A converse instance is the narrow construction of the commerce power rendered by the nationalistic McLean in *Groves v. Slaughter*, 40 U.S. (15 Pet.) 449 (1841)(separate opinion), *supra* chapter 7, in order to uphold a state law limiting slavery.

[10]The Propeller Genesee Chief v. Fitzhugh, 53 U.S. (12 How.) 443 (1851).

[11]46 U.S. (5 How.) 504 (1847), *supra* chapter 7.

[12]Kentucky v. Dennison, 65 U.S. (24 How.) 66 (1861).

[13]*See* C. SWISHER, *supra* chapter 8, note 54, at 586.

[14]Prize Cases, 67 U.S. (2 Black) 635, 699 (1862); Passenger Cases, 48 U.S. (7 How.) 283, 464 (1849); *see supra* chapter 7.

The other two important figures in constitutional cases during Taney's tenure were Story and Curtis. More federalist than Marshall, Story was somewhat out of place among his later colleagues, and he expressed his discomfiture by dissenting vehemently from their first three constitutional decisions—although he and Taney soon discovered that they had many views in common.[15] Most of Story's work was substantial and well-crafted. In both *Prigg*[16] and the *Miln*[17] dissent he seemed unconvincing and strained, but his opinions in *Charles River Bridge*[18] and *Briscoe*[19] were among the best in the whole period.[20]

It is an enormous pity that Curtis spent only six years on the Court, for in that short time he distinguished himself as perhaps the most powerful occupant of the bench. This assessment rests in large part on two of his nine constitutional opinions, *Cooley* and the *Scott* dissent. Although both *Cooley* and his important opinions in *Conner v. Elliott*[21] and *Murray's Lessee v. Hoboken Land & Improvement Co.*[22] show that Curtis shared Marshall's unfortunate inclination to lay down conclusory pronouncements as if he were a lawgiver, he also shared Marshall's rare gift of magisterial style that made this, in its way, convincing. What was more remarkable about *Cooley*, however, were Curtis's ability to bring irreconcilable factions together and his prescient statesmanship: as Marshall had done so often before him, Curtis wrote a constitutional provision that was to last. Most impressive of all of Curtis's efforts, however, was his *Scott* opinion, one of the best examples of legal craftsmanship to be found anywhere in the United States Reports.

These three pretty well exhaust the roster of stars who sat between 1836 and 1864. Perhaps the best of the others was Thompson, like Story a holdover from an earlier era in which he had done much of his best work.[23] Never one to write much for the Court, he displayed strong reasoning powers in his short *Briscoe* concurrence and an admirable sense of restraint for the majority in *Groves*. No extreme nationalist, he was the only Justice to join Story's *Charles River Bridge* dissent in defense of vested rights.

Important for his longevity and the vehemence of his opinions, McLean exhibited more bluster than sound reasoning. He distorted commerce clause precedents to further his nationalist position, let his abolitionist views lead him into inconsistent and unnecessary support for state power in *Groves*, and added very little in his long *Scott* dissent. At times a fierce protector of contracts who found tax exemptions that were invisible to the majority of his brethren,[24] he strangely dissented from the

[15]*See* G. DUNNE, *supra* chapter 8, note 53, at 391-92; J. McCLELLAN, JOSEPH STORY AND THE AMERICAN CONSTITUTION 293-94 (1971).

[16]41 U.S. (16 Pet.) at 626.

[17]New York v. Miln, 36 U.S. (11 Pet.) 102, 153 (1837), *supra* chapter 7.

[18]*Charles River Bridge*, 36 U.S. (11 Pet.) at 583, *supra* chapter 7.

[19]Briscoe v. Bank of Kentucky, 36 U.S. (11 Pet.) 257, 328 (1837), *supra* chapter 7.

[20]*See* J. McCLELLAN, *supra* note 14, at 294 (quoting Taney's lament on Story's death that his loss was "utterly irreparable in this generation; for there is nobody equal to him").

[21]59 U.S. (18 How.) 591 (1856).

[22]59 U.S. (18 How.) 272 (1856).

[23]*See, e.g.*, Ogden v. Saunders, 25 U.S. (12 Wheat.) 213, 292 (1827)(Thompson, J., separate opinion); Brown v. Maryland, 25 U.S. (12 Wheat.) 419, 449 (1827)(Thompson, J., dissenting). *See generally supra* chapter 6.

[24]*See, e.g.*, Ohio Life Ins. & Trust Co. v. Debolt, 57 U.S. (16 How.) 416 (1853), *supra* chapter 7.

enforcement of mortgage rights in *Bronson*. His best opinion came in *Prigg*, where he alone argued persuasively that the kidnapping law conflicted with neither the federal statute nor the constitutional right of discharge. Even in *Prigg*, however, McLean neglected to make clear whether he was concurring or dissenting.[25]

Baldwin managed to write almost nothing of interest for the Court in a constitutional case, largely confining himself to a series of mostly tardy concurrences I have already described as long and boring.[26] Wayne, appointed before Taney and still on the Court when Taney died, had remarkably little to show for his tenure.[27] A nationalist except in *Scott*, Wayne deserves notice as a Southerner who cast the decisive vote to uphold Lincoln's blockade in the *Prize Cases*. Barbour, who wrote competently for state authority in *Miln*, was a minor figure who vanished after a handful of years.[28] Catron, whose service substantially coincided with Taney's, wrote barely enough to reveal himself as somewhat more state-minded than the Court and to discredit himself badly in *Scott*. McKinley was a cipher, serving fifteen years and leaving virtually no trace.[29] Daniel, who seemed to care little for legal reasoning, was a knee-jerk antifederalist who dissented regularly in cases involving admiralty, diversity, or contracts and who denied federal power over internal improvements.[30] Nelson was an unimpressive plodder in the mainstream who wrote little over a long period; his chief claim to fame was his unique refusal to reach the constitutional issue in *Scott*.[31] Woodbury stayed only briefly and had little impact; he was unusually long-winded and relatively state-oriented in admiralty and contract cases.[32] Another

[25]C. SWISHER, *supra* chapter 8, note 2, at 46, confirms the general understanding that McLean, who repeatedly angled for a Presidential nomination while on the Bench, "was one of the most politically minded of all the Justices." For detailed discussion of McLean's perennial ambitions, his willingness to make extrajudicial statements, his inability to resist dicta, and his penchant for hard work, see F. WEISENBURGER, *supra* chapter 8, note 271.

[26]C. SWISHER, *supra* chapter 8, note 2, at 50-52 & n.53, notes Baldwin's uncertain emotional health and financial difficulties and Taney's fear that the "evil" "temper of Judge Baldwin's opinions . . . will grow" to the point where "[i]t will . . . be necessary . . . to take some step to guard the tribunal from misconstruction."

[27]*See generally* A. LAWRENCE, JAMES MOORE WAYNE, SOUTHERN UNIONIST 113-14 (1943)(Wayne lacked the gifts of Story, Taney, Curtis, and Campbell, and his opinions "lack judicial craftsmanship," but he was "a diligent, useful and conscientous Justice").

[28]For Story's rather approving view of Barbour, see G. DUNNE, *supra* chapter 8, note 53, at 382-83.

[29]McKinley officially missed four entire terms (1840, 1843, 1847, and 1850), two on account of "indisposition," one because of an "important session" on circuit, and one for undisclosed reasons. *See* 39 U.S. (14 Pet.) at vii; 42 U.S. (1 How.) at lxxi; 47 U.S. (6 How.) following title page; 49 U.S. (8 How.) at iii. At his death Taney said McKinley had been "faithful and assiduous in the discharge of his duties while his health was sufficient to undergo the labor." 55 U.S. (14 How.) at v; *see also* C. SWISHER, *supra* chapter 8, note 2, at 66-67, 463 (noting in addition his time spent in the business of manufacturing rope). McKinley, says Professor Swisher, "made no significant contribution to legal thinking in any form." *Id.* at 67. *See generally* Currie, *The Most Insignificant Justice: A Preliminary Inquiry*, 50 U. CHI. L. REV. 466, 471-73 (1983).

[30]*See* J. FRANK, *supra* chapter 8, note 173, at 236, 243, 274 (after 1848 Daniel became a "[s]outhern sectionalist of the most extreme sort"; he dissented alone more than twice as often as any of his contemporaries; though a weak stylist and not so gifted as Curtis, Campbell, and Taney, he was "at least as good as all the rest"); C. SWISHER, *supra* chapter 8, note 2, at 69-70 (describing Daniel as "not untypical of an extreme element in the South in his time"); *see also* G. DUNNE, *supra* chapter 8, note 53, at 383 (Story viewed Daniel as "a man of 'prodigiously small calibre'").

[31]C. SWISHER, *supra* chapter 8, note 2, at 221, terms Nelson "stable, sound, and unspectacular."

[32]*See* J. FRANK, *supra* chapter 7, note 173, at 274 (noting with considerable justification that, while Daniel was no stylist, "at his worst he was not as bad as Woodbury").

mainstream Justice of long service, Grier was notably uninspired. Of his two significant majority opinions, *Marshall*[33] was incomplete on diversity policy and embarrassing on precedent, and the *Prize Cases* seemed largely off the point. Campbell was a more erudite and less extreme version of Daniel who spoke infrequently for the Court before secession, which he had opposed, drew him back to Alabama.[34]

The others—Clifford, Miller, Swayne, Davis, and Field—were appointed late and belong to the following period. Clifford commenced his career with a leap into the natural-law position that the United States could not repeal its own grants,[35] a position he was later to denounce in a related context with some eloquence.[36] Miller began to attract attention with two clever opinions avoiding protection for what others thought were vested rights.[37] Before Taney's death Swayne wrote only two constitutional opinions, one strongly pro-state,[38] the other strongly anti-state,[39] and both essentially lawless. Davis and Field were not heard from at all.

It was a stormy time but one of essential continuity; a time of several great controversies and many small ones; a time of three or four Justices who were of substantial parts and of a number of others who were not.

[33]Marshall v. Baltimore & O.R.R., 57 U.S. (16 How.) 314 (1853).

[34]C. SWISHER, *supra* chapter 8, note 2, at 450, describes Campbell in the context of his learned historical dissents in the admiralty cases as, with the exception of Story, "probably the outstanding scholar on the Court during the Taney period." *See also* H. CONNOR, JOHN ARCHIBALD CAMPBELL 261 (1920) (describing Campbell's mind as "massive rather than analytical" and calling him "clear in his conceptions, but without imagination"); J. FRANK, *supra* chapter 8, note 173, at 173 ("Campbell did with genius what Daniel did in a work-a-day way, and the two were basically like-minded"). For Campbell's views on secession, see H. CONNOR, *supra*, at 118-19.

[35]Rice v. Railroad Co., 66 U.S. (1 Black) 358, 373 (1862) (dictum).

[36]Loan Ass'n v. Topeka, 87 U.S. (20 Wall.) 655, 667 (1875)(dissenting opinion). *See infra* chapter 10.

[37]Bridge Proprietors v. Hoboken Land & Improvement Co., 68 U.S. (1 Wall.) 116 (1864); Gelpcke v. Dubuque, 68 U.S. (1 Wall.) 175, 207 (1864)(dissenting opinion)(discussed *supra* in chapter 7).

[38]Conway v. Taylor's Executor, 66 U.S. (1 Black) 603 (1862), *supra* chapter 7.

[39]Gelpcke v. Dubuque, 68 U.S. (1 Wall.) 175 (1864), *supra* chapter 7.

Part Four

Chief Justice Chase
1865–1873

Introduction to Part Four

The appointment of Salmon P. Chase as Chief Justice in December 1864, like that of his predecessor in 1836, marked the beginning of a new epoch in the Court's history. Not only had the Civil War altered the legal landscape dramatically; Chase was to preside over an essentially new complement of Justices. Of those who had sat more than a few years with Chief Justice Taney, only Samuel Nelson and Robert Grier were to remain for a significant time. With them were six newcomers appointed between 1858 and 1864, five of them by Abraham Lincoln and four of them Republicans: Nathan Clifford, Noah H. Swayne, Samuel F. Miller, David Davis, Stephen J. Fields, and Chase himself. These eight Justices were to sit together through most of the period until Chase's death in 1873. Taney's longtime colleagues James M. Wayne and John Catron were gone by 1867, while William Strong, Joseph P. Bradley, and Ward Hunt, appointed near the end of Chase's tenure, played relatively minor roles. The work of the Chase period was largely done by eight men.[1]

[1] JUSTICES OF THE SUPREME COURT DURING THE TIME OF CHIEF JUSTICE CHASE

		1864	66	68	70	72
James M. Wayne	(1835–1867)					
John Catron	(1837–1865)					
Samuel Nelson	(1845–1872)					
Robert C. Grier	(1846–1870)					
Nathan Clifford	(1858–1881)					
Noah H. Swayne	(1862–1881)					
Samuel F. Miller	(1862–1890)					
David Davis	(1862–1877)					
Stephen J. Field	(1863–1897)					
Salmon P. Chase	(1864–1873)					
William Strong	(1870–1880)					
Joseph P. Bradley	(1870–1892)					
Ward Hunt	(1872–1882)					

SOURCE: G. GUNTHER, CASES AND MATERIALS ON CONSTITUTIONAL LAW (10th ed. 1980), app. A.

285

Chase was Chief Justice for less than nine years, but his tenure was a time of important constitutional decisions. Most of the significant cases fall into three categories. The best known involved a variety of questions arising out of the Civil War itself. Less dramatic but of comparable impact on future litigation and of comparable jurisprudential interest were a number of decisions determining the inhibitory effect of the commerce clause on state legislation. Finally, at the very end of the Chase period, the Court for the first time turned to the task of interpreting the amendments adopted as a result of the war, a labor that would absorb a major part of the energies of Justices down to the present day.[2]

One conspicuous feature of the Chase period should be noted at the outset: the enormous increase in the Justices' workload. In the first seventy-five years of its existence, the Court had produced sixty-eight volumes of decisions; in Chase's nine terms it produced fifteen. The increase in constitutional litigation was more striking still: in less than nine years under Chase, the Court resolved as many constitutional cases as it had in the preceding twenty-eight years.[3]

[2]The leading general histories of the Court during the Chase period are Charles Fairman's excellent HISTORY OF THE SUPREME COURT OF THE UNITED STATES, vol. 6 (1971) [hereinafter cited as FAIRMAN, HISTORY], and Charles Warren's THE SUPREME COURT IN UNITED STATES HISTORY (2d ed. 1926), vol. 2. The best biographies of the Justices are C. FAIRMAN, MR. JUSTICE MILLER AND THE SUPREME COURT 1862–1890 (1939) [hereinafter cited as FAIRMAN, MILLER]; and C. SWISHER, STEPHEN J. FIELD, CRAFTSMAN OF THE LAW (1930). Others include W. KING, LINCOLN'S MANAGER: DAVID DAVIS (1960); P. CLIFFORD, NATHAN CLIFFORD, DEMOCRAT (1922); A. HART, SALMON PORTLAND CHASE (1899); A. LAWRENCE, JAMES MOORE WAYNE, SOUTHERN UNIONIST (1943); and J. SCHUCKERS, THE LIFE AND PUBLIC SERVICES OF SALMON PORTLAND CHASE (1874), which oddly makes virtually no reference to Supreme Court decisions.

[3]For discussion of the increasing docket problems *see, e.g.*, FAIRMAN, MILLER, *supra* note 2, at 401-08; F. FRANKFURTER & J. LANDIS, THE BUSINESS OF THE SUPREME COURT, ch. 6 (1928).

9

Civil War and Reconstruction

An event as catalysmic as the Civil War was bound to place considerable strain on the Constitution, and the brunt of the judicial burden of putting it back in shape was borne in the decade following the war itself—the period considered in this part.

A series of landmark opinions characterizes this aspect of the Court's work. *Ex parte Milligan*[1] invalidated military trials of civilians. *Cummings v. Missouri*[2] and *Ex parte Garland*[3] struck down state and federal test oaths enacted after the war. *Mississippi v. Johnson*,[4] *Georgia v. Stanton*,[5] *Ex parte McCardle*,[6] and *United States v. Klein*[7] laid down important principles of federal jurisdiction in the course of generally unavailing attempts to obtain a judicial test of Reconstruction measures. *Texas v. White*[8] finally established both the illegality of secession and the validity of the basic Reconstruction principle. Wartime financial measures produced several important opinions culminating in the invalidation of paper tender under questionable circumstances in *Hepburn v. Griswold*[9] and in the prompt overruling of that case after two new Justices were appointed.[10]

The thirteenth and fourteenth amendments were among the principal legacies of the rebellion; yet because their interpretation first confronted the Court during the last days of Chase's tenure, the decisions addressing them are considered in the chapter that follows.

[1]71 U.S. (4 Wall.) 2 (1866).
[2]71 U.S. (4 Wall.) 277 (1867).
[3]71 U.S. (4 Wall.) 333 (1867).
[4]71 U.S. (4 Wall.) 475 (1867).
[5]73 U.S. (6 Wall.) 50 (1868).
[6]74 U.S. (7 Wall.) 506 (1869).
[7]80 U.S. (13 Wall.) 128 (1872).
[8]74 U.S. (7 Wall.) 700 (1869).
[9]75 U.S. (8 Wall.) 603 (1870).
[10]Legal Tender Cases, 79 U.S. (12 Wall.) 457 (1872).

I. MILITARY TRIALS AND TEST OATHS

A. *Ex parte Milligan*

Sentenced to death by a military commission in Indiana during the war for giving aid
to the rebellion, Milligan sought habeas corpus from a federal circuit court. On
certified questions the Supreme Court held, in a celebrated 1866 opinion by Lincoln's old friend David Davis, that the military trial of a civilian under such circumstances was unconstitutional.[11]

Davis's discussion of the constitutional question begins with one of the Court's
most stirring affirmations of the rule of law:

> The Constitution of the United States is a law for rulers and people,
> equally in war and peace, and covers with the shield of its protection all
> classes of men, at all times, and under all circumstances. No doctrine,
> involving more pernicious consequences, was ever invented by the wit of
> man than that any of its provisions can be suspended during any of the
> great exigencies of government.[12]

The merits, wrote Davis, were plain from the words of the Constitution. "Every
trial involves the exercise of judicial power," and article III vests that power in " 'one
supreme court and such inferior courts as the Congress may from time to time ordain
and establish.' " "One of the plainest constitutional provisions was, therefore,
infringed when Milligan was tried by a court not ordained and established by
Congress, and not composed of judges appointed during good behavior."[13] Moreover, the sixth amendment had been offended as well, for it guaranteed that " 'in all

[11]71 U.S. (4 Wall.) 2 (1866). The question had been avoided during the war itself in *Ex parte
Vallandigham*, 68 U.S. (1 Wall.) 243 (1864), where the Court held it had no jurisdiction to review directly
the judgment of a military commission. *See supra* chapter 8. Of the various jurisdictional objections
brushed aside in *Milligan*, the only one of interest was that the case was moot because it should be
presumed that the petitioner had been hanged as directed. "[E]ven the suggestion [that the military had
executed Milligan while his case was pending]," said Davis, "is injurious to the Executive, and we dismiss
it from further consideration." 71 U.S. (4 Wall.) at 118. In fact, Milligan had been reprieved and was later
released in accordance with the Supreme Court's decision. *See* 2 C. WARREN, *supra* introduction to part
four, note 2, at 427 n.1. For the guess that the Court would not have reached the same bold decision on the
merits while the war was still going, see, for example, C. SWISHER, *supra* introduction to part 4, note 2, at
138; L. TRIBE, AMERICAN CONSTITUTIONAL LAW 181 (1978). For a comprehensive description of the case
and its historical context, see FAIRMAN, HISTORY, *supra* introduction to part four, note 2, at 185-237.

[12]71 U.S. (4 Wall.) at 120-21; *see also id.* at 123-24:

> When peace prevails, and the authority of the government is undisputed, there is no
> difficulty of preserving the safeguards of liberty; . . . but if society is disturbed by civil
> commotion—if the passions of men are aroused and the restraints of law weakened, if not
> disregarded—these safeguards need, and should receive, the watchful care of those in-
> trusted with the guardianship of the Constitution and laws.

But cf. 1 G. LEFEBVRE, THE FRENCH REVOLUTION 125 (1962) (" [T]hat one could not govern in time of war
and revolution as in time of peace— . . . that . . . rights . . . depended upon circumstances . . . [—] was to
become the doctrine of the [French] revolutionary government.").

[13]71 U.S. (4 Wall.) at 121-22 (quoting U.S. CONST. art III, § 1).

criminal prosecutions the accused shall enjoy the right to a . . . trial by an impartial jury.'"[14]

Having said this, Davis began in dicta to take much of it back. First, he conceded, soldiers were not entitled to jury trials for military offenses, for the fifth amendment excepts from its grand-jury requirement "'cases arising in the land or naval forces, or in the militia, when in actual service, in time of war or public danger,'" and "the framers, . . . doubtless, meant to limit the right of trial by jury, in the sixth amendment, to those persons who were subject to indictment or presentment in the fifth."[15] Though unnecessary to the decision, this concession was necessitated by long-standing practice and was in accord with an earlier dictum.[16] Moreover, though one may feel queasy over the Court's conclusion that the fifth amendment's military exception applies to the sixth as well, it helps to reconcile the conviction that the Framers had not meant to abolish traditional courts-martial with the apparently uncompromising text of the Constitution.[17]

More troubling is what follows:

> If, in foreign invasion or civil war, the courts are actually closed, and it is impossible to administer criminal justice according to law, *then*, on the theatre of active military operations, where war really prevails, there is a necessity to furnish a substitute for the civil authority, thus overthrown, to preserve the safety of the army and society; and as no power is left but the military, it is allowed to govern by martial rule until the laws can have their free course. As necessity creates the rule, so it limits its duration; for, if this government is continued *after* the courts are reinstated, it is a gross usurpation of power. . . . Because, during the late Rebellion [martial rule] could have been enforced in Virginia, where the national authority was overturned and the courts driven out, it does not follow that it should obtain in Indiana, where that authority was never disputed, and justice was always administered.[18]

There was no occasion to say any of this, for, as the Court emphasized in Indiana "the courts were open," and there were no hostile armies.[19] More disturbing yet is the implication of this obiter pronouncement, for it undermines the very basis of the Court's decision. If military courts may try civilians whenever military necessity demands it, then neither article III nor the jury provision is plain on its face after all. Moreover, while in the purely formal sense the Court may still be right that the

[14]*Id.* at 122-23 (quoting U.S. Const. amend. VI).

[15]*Id.* at 123 (quoting U.S. Const. amend V).

[16]*See* Dynes v. Hoover, 61 U.S. (20 How.) 65, 79 (1858).

[17]A still earlier precedent involving territorial courts, American Ins. Co. v. Canter, 26 U.S. (1 Pet.) 511 (1828), provides further evidence that article III was not quite so ironclad as Davis would have us believe, but the special status of the Territories and the Court's explicit statement that its permissive holding did not apply within the states, *id.* at 546, make Davis's failure to distinguish the case a matter more of style than of substance. *See supra* chapter 4. For a more general discussion of the problem of judicial power outside article III, see Currie, *Bankruptcy Judges and the Independent Judiciary*, 16 Creighton L. Rev. 441 (1983).

[18]71 U.S. (4 Wall.) at 127.

[19]*Id.* at 126-27.

Constitution is not "suspended" in an emergency, it might as well be, for apparently its provisions implicitly include exceptions for emergency conditions.

Davis's dicta thus deprive his earlier ringing statements of much of their force. Unfortunately, however, it is difficult to escape the conclusion that he was right about military tribunals in places where war had interrupted the civil courts. Just as it is hard to believe the Framers meant by ostensibly unqualified language to overturn the tradition of sovereign immunity,[20] it is hard to believe they meant to do away with the tradition that occupying armies may temporarily govern.[21] *Milligan* was not the occasion for saying so; Davis could have satisfied the demands of candor without appearing to destroy the basis of his own holding. Rather than overemphasizing the constitutional text and then taking it back, Davis might better have begun by observing that it was unnecessary to decide whether the Framers meant to do away with traditional military powers to govern either military personnel or conquered territories; it was enough that neither of those traditions came close to justifying an implied exception for the case at hand, and that a strong showing would be required to demonstrate that the Framers had not meant what they said.[22]

[20]*See supra* chapter 1 (discussing Chisholm v. Georgia, 2 U.S. (2 Dall.) 419 (1793)).

[21]*See ex parte* Quirin, 317 U.S. 1, 39 (1942) (allowing military trials of enemies for violating the laws of war):

> The object of [§ 2 of article III] was to preserve unimpaired trial by jury in all those cases in which it had been recognized by the common law and in all cases of a like nature as they might arise in the future, . . . but not to bring within the sweep of the guaranty those cases in which it was then well understood that a jury trial could not be demanded as of right (citation omitted).

Article III's tenure requirement was not discussed. *Cf. infra* text accompanying notes 173-206 and note 191 (discussing Texas v. White, 74 U.S. (7 Wall.) 700 (1869), and The Grapeshot, 76 U.S. (9 Wall.) 129 (1870)). In Miller v. United States, 78 U.S. (11 Wall.) 268 (1871) (Strong, J.), the Court, upholding over two dissents (Field and Clifford) the power of Congress to confiscate rebel property without a jury on the acceptable ground that this was not punishment for crime at all, went to the shocking extreme of declaring that exercises of the war powers were *never* "affected by the restrictions imposed by the fifth and sixth amendments." *Id.* at 305-06. Counsel for the United States had so argued in *Milligan*, 71 U.S. (4 Wall.) at 20-21, 102-05 (argument of Messrs. Speed and Butler), quoting a speech by John Quincy Adams, *id.* at 104 (quoting Cong. Globe, 24th Cong., 1st Sess. 433 (statement of Rep. Adams)). *Cf.* Fairman, History, *supra* introduction to part four, note 2, at 201. ("A competent Attorney General would never have permitted such an outlandish argument to be made . . . ."). The decision in *Milligan*, which rejected this position, was naturally ignored in *Miller*.

[22]For the position that Davis's distinction was in accord with that drawn in English common law, see Fairman, Miller, *supra* introduction to part four, note 2, at 96, and the argument of counsel for the petitioner, 71 U.S. (4 Wall.) at 47 (argument of Mr. Garfield) (quoting M. Hale, The History of the Common Law of England 42-43 (Runnington ed., London 1820) (1st ed. London 1713)). *Cf.* 1 W. Blackstone, Commentaries *400:

> [T]he necessity of order and discipline in an army is the only thing which can give [martial law] countenance; and therefore it ought not to be permitted in time of peace, when the king's courts are open for all persons to receive justice according to the laws of the land.

Not altogether easy to distinguish, of course, is the later *Ex parte* Quirin, 317 U.S. 1 (1942). *See supra* note 21. It might be argued that Milligan too was an enemy spy offending the laws of war. So to hold, however, would come close to saying that every case of treason is outside the jury and judge protections of article III—a hard position to maintain since it is the same article that narrowly defines the substantive offense itself.

Davis's opinion was joined by Nelson, Grier, Clifford, and Field—the Court's four Northern Democrats. Chase, with his fellow Republicans Swayne and Miller and the old Georgian Wayne, concurred on narrower grounds.[23] There was no need, they said, to hold that Congress had no power to authorize military trials of civilians in cases like Milligan's, for Congress had never purported to do so. Indeed, they argued, it had forbidden them. The statute that gave the circuit court jurisdiction of Milligan's habeas corpus petition required the release of all military prisoners once a civil grand jury had met and failed to indict them, and Milligan fell squarely within the statutory terms.[24]

Convincing enough on this point,[25] Chase opened himself to his own criticism by adding that he thought Congress could have authorized a military trial.[26] The bulk of his argument was devoted to a demonstration of the relatively easy conclusion that military tribunals may be necessary and proper to the raising and governance of armies and to the conduct of war.[27] On the harder question whether those powers were not limited by the explicit guarantees invoked by the majority, Chase said only that the fifth amendment exception for "'[c]ases arising in the land or naval forces'" should be construed to include "protection and defence as well as . . . internal administration."[28] Language proposed by the state conventions ratifying the original Constitution was plausibly if unconvincingly invoked to support this broad interpretation,[29] but the language actually chosen by Congress is not conducive to

[23]71 U.S. (4 Wall.) at 132-42. This was not the first time the sturdy Southerner had been more supportive of Yankee war powers than several of his Northern brethren. *See supra* chapter 8 (discussing the Prize Cases, 67 U.S. (2 Black) 635 (1863), where Wayne cast the decisive vote to uphold Lincoln's blockade of Southern ports).

[24]71 U.S. (4 Wall.) at 133-36 (invoking the Act of Mar. 3, 1863, ch. 81, §§ 2, 3, 12 Stat. 755, 755-56 (expired by its own terms at end of war)). Davis relied on this statute to support the circuit court's jurisdiction over Milligan's petition, *see id.* at 115-16; he did not discuss whether it also required his release, and this argument was not much pressed by counsel.

[25]Fairman terms this "an exceedingly generous construction of the statute that authorized the suspension of the privilege of the writ of habeas corpus—imputing to Congress an intention at the same time to prohibit the military trial of civilians . . . ." FAIRMAN, HISTORY, *supra* introduction to part four, note 2, at 210. In light of the Court's familiar principle of construing statutes if possible to avoid having to find government action unconstitutional, however, Chase's position seems entirely reasonable.

[26]71 U.S. (4 Wall.) at 136-42. Fairman agrees that Chase's constitutional discussion was as unnecessary as Davis's but adds fairly enough that "it seems that the minority would have been content to confine themselves to the facts of the particular case if the majority had done so." FAIRMAN, MILLER, *supra* introduction to part four, note 2, at 97 n.60. For contemporaneous criticism of the majority for deciding too much, see 1 AM. L. REV. 572 (1867), *quoted in* 2 C. WARREN, *supra* introduction to part four, note 2, at 441-42.

[27]Even on this issue one must be wary, as Marshall warned, not to extend the logic of the relation between means and ends to its extreme without regard to the "spirit" of the Constitution. This spirit includes the notion that the people as well as the states retain some unspecified interests not subject to federal incursion. *See* chapter 6, *supra* (discussing McCulloch v. Maryland, 17 U.S. (4 Wheat.) 316 (1819)); *see also* Reid v. Covert, 354 U.S. 1, 19-41 (1957) (holding, without relying on the limitations invoked in *Milligan*, that the necessary and proper clause did not authorize court-martial of civilians connected with the armed services); *cf.* U.S. CONST. amend IX ("The enumeration in the Constitution, of certain rights, shall not be construed to deny or disparage others retained by the people").

[28]71 U.S. (4 Wall.) at 137-39 (quoting U.S. CONST. amend V).

[29]*Id.* at 138 ("'except in such cases as may arise in the *government and regulation* of the land forces'" (emphasis added)).

Chase's conclusion, and even the rejected terminology did not compel the Court to equate Indiana with Virginia.

Despite Davis's brave words, then, the difference between him and Chase seems one of degree rather than of principle. The whole Court conceded unnecessarily that civil courts and juries would yield in the face of military necessity; Chase differed from Davis only in thinking the situation in Indiana serious enough to justify a military tribunal.[30] Nonetheless, many of our most important rights turn on subjective questions of degree; and *Milligan*'s willingness to reject a plea of military necessity, though falling short of the romantic vision with which the opinion began, stands nonetheless as an important landmark in the judicial protection of civil liberties.[31]

B.   The Test Oath Cases

At the end of the war both Congress and the people of Missouri adopted provisions requiring that persons seeking to carry on specified professional occupations subscribe to an oath that they had never given aid to the rebellion.[32] Missouri convicted a priest for practicing his calling without taking the state oath, and a former Confederate Congressman asked the Supreme Court for permission to practice before it without taking the federal one. In the famous decisions in *Cummings v. Missouri*[33]

---

[30]*See id.* at 140 (stressing that Indiana "was the theatre of military operations, had been actually invaded, and was constantly threatened with invasion" and that it was apparently the home of "a powerful secret association . . . plotting insurrection").

[31]Along the way Chase offered an interesting insight into a constitutional question distinct from that resolved by the majority: since Congress was the lawmaker and the President the Commander-in-Chief under article II, Chase wrote, "Congress cannot direct the conduct of campaigns, nor can the President, . . . *without the sanction of Congress*, institute tribunals for the trial and punishment of offences, either of soldiers or civilians, unless in cases of a controlling necessity . . . ." *Id.* at 139-40 (emphasis added). Both halves of this statement seem reasonable enough, but Chase had no occasion for making it since he had already concluded that Congress had *forbidden* the President to set up such tribunals without discussing whether it had power to impose such a restriction. *Cf.* Youngstown Sheet & Tube Co. v. Sawyer, 343 U.S. 579 (1952) (Justice Black's opinion for the Court seeming to announce that the President could not seize the steel mills to assure war production without statutory authorization, though a majority of Justices concluded that Congress had *forbidden* the seizure); *supra* chapter 4 (discussing the Flying Fish, 6 U.S. (2 Cranch) 170 (1804)).

[32]The federal statute was the Act of July 2, 1862, ch. 128, 12 Stat. 502, which read in part:

> [E]very person elected or appointed to any office of honor or profit under the government of the United States . . . shall, before entering upon the duties of such office, . . . take and subscribe the following oath or affirmation: "I, A.B., do solemnly swear (or affirm) that I have never voluntarily borne arms against the United States . . . ; that I have voluntarily given no aid . . . to persons engaged in armed hostility thereto."

Missouri's provision was part of its newly adopted Constitution:

> The oath to be taken as aforesaid shall be known as the Oath of Loyalty, and shall be in the following terms:
> "I, A.B., do solemnly swear . . . that I have always been truly and loyally on the side of the United States against all enemies thereof, foreign and domestic . . . ."
> Within sixty days after the constitution takes effect, every person in this State holding any office of honor, trust, or profit . . . shall take and subscribe the said oath.

Mo. CONST. of 1865, art. II, §§ 6, 7.

[33]71 U.S. (4 Wall.) 277 (1867).

and *Ex parte Garland*,[34] a closely divided Court held both requirements unconstitutional.[35]

Both decisions were written by Justice Field, a California Democrat appointed by Lincoln. Disqualification from an occupation, he argued with impressive support from history and from the impeachment provisions of the Constitution, was a traditional punishment for crime.[36] Thus the oath laws both made criminal certain acts that had not been forbidden when committed and inflicted additional punishments for those that had been; they therefore were ex post facto laws prohibited to both Congress and the states by sections 9 and 10 of article I.[37] It was no excuse, said Field, that the laws disqualified not rebel sympathizers as such but only those refusing to take the oath, for the result was the same: "To make the enjoyment of a right dependent upon an impossible condition is equivalent to an absolute denial of the right . . . . [I]f that which cannot be accomplished by means looking directly to the end, can be accomplished by indirect means, the inhibition may be evaded at pleasure."[38] Indeed, the oath requirement was worse than a direct disqualification of those who had aided the rebellion; a direct disqualification would have occurred only after a finding of guilt, while, as Alexander Hamilton had said, oath provisions "'oblige the citizen to establish his own innocence to avoid the penalty.'"[39]

Moreover, Field announced, the oath requirements were bills of attainder proscribed by the same two sections. This term, he stated without citation, was meant to embrace what the English had called bills of pains and penalties as well as technical attainders imposing death, and thus included any "legislative act which inflicts punishment without a judicial trial."[40] Historical examples were given of bills that

[34]71 U.S. (4 Wall.) 333 (1867).

[35]For a discussion of the test oath cases and reaction to them, see FAIRMAN, HISTORY, *supra* introduction to part four, note 2, at 240-48. A similar oath requirement for access to the courts was struck down in Pierce v. Carskadon, 83 U.S. (16 Wall.) 234 (1873), over the dissent of Justice Bradley.

[36]*Cummings*, 71 U.S. (4 Wall.) at 320-22.

[37]*Id.* at 327-28; *Garland*, 71 U.S. (4 Wall.) at 377-78.

[38]*Cummings*, 71 U.S. (4 Wall.) at 327, 329.

[39]*Id.* at 331.

[40]*Id.* at 323. Field cited nothing for this important departure from the conceded common-law meaning of the term, though Story, whom Field quoted a paragraph later for the proposition that " '([b]ills of this sort' " had commonly been enacted in the heat of " 'violent political excitements,' " had made the same unexplained equation, citing a conclusory dictum of Marshall. J. STORY, COMMENTARIES ON THE CONSTITUTION OF THE UNITED STATES § 1338 (Boston 1833) (citing Fletcher v. Peck, 10 U.S. (6 Cranch.) 87, 138 (1810) ("A bill of attainder may affect the life of an individual, or may confiscate his property, or may do both.")). Professor Berger has castigated the Court for extending the term beyond its established meaning, arguing plausibly enough that the presumption should be that the Framers used common-law terms in their understood sense, particularly where, as with the bills of attainder clause, a provision was adopted without debate. Berger, *Bills of Attainder, A Study of Amendment by the Court*, 63 CORN. L. REV. 355, 367, 380 (1978); *see also Garland*, 71 U.S. (4 Wall.) at 387 (Miller, J., dissenting) (complaining that the traditional bill of attainder had provided for "corruption of the blood": "[t]he party attainted lost all inheritable quality, and could neither receive nor transmit any property . . . by inheritance."); *cf. supra* chapter 2 (discussing Calder v. Bull, 3 U.S. (3 Dall.) 385 (1798)). But Berger offers no reason to explain why the Framers would have wanted to distinguish sharply between death and other penalties inflicted by legislation without trial; they expressed no antipathy to the death penalty as such, nor even to judicially imposed corruption of blood, except in the specific case of treason against the United States. *See* U.S. CONST. art. III, § 3; *see also* 3 J. ELLIOT, THE DEBATES IN THE SEVERAL STATE CONVENTIONS ON THE ADOPTION OF THE FEDERAL CONSTITUTION 236 (2d ed. Wash., D.C. 1836) (1st ed. Wash. D.C.) (statement

had named classes of offenders rather than individuals, and of bills that had imposed conditional punishments.[41] In effect, Field concluded, the oath provisions deprived persons who had aided the rebellion of their professions without judicial trial; and, once again, "[i]f the inhibition can be evaded by the form of the enactment, its insertion in the fundamental law was a vain and futile proceeding."[42] Finally, one of the petitioners had received a presidential pardon that freed him from punishment for his Confederate activities; to remit him to the choice between perjury and disqualification, the Court concluded, was to impair the effect of the pardon.[43]

As in *Milligan*, there were only five votes against the constitutionality of the challenged measures, and this time the division was on strict party lines. Justice Wayne, who had disagreed with the majority in *Milligan*, joined his Democratic brethren in the oath cases;[44] Davis, who had differed from his fellow Republicans in the earlier case, joined them in arguing that the oath provisions ought to have been upheld.[45] Justice Miller's well-written dissent, covering both cases, made a variety of arguments, based upon the form of the oath requirements, that seem, as Field said, to permit the constitutional safeguards to be evaded at pleasure.[46] Miller's essential contention, however, was more thought-provoking. The disqualification of rebel sympathizers, he argued, was not punishment at all, but only a prophylactic measure to protect the public in the future.[47] Both Congress and the state had the right to make certain that practitioners possessed "the proper qualifications for the discharge of their duties," and "fidelity to the government under which he lives" was "among

---

of Mr. Nicholas) (stressing that condemnation without trial was the vice which the clause was meant to prevent).

[41]*Cummings*, 71 U.S. (4 Wall.) at 323-24.

[42]*Id.* at 325.

[43]*Garland*, 71 U.S. (4 Wall.) at 380-81. The Court also added, in a passage significant for a much later controversy, *see* P. KURLAND, WATERGATE AND THE CONSTITUTION 136-48 (1978), that the President could pardon offenses "before legal proceedings are taken" as well as after. *Garland,* 71 U.S. (4 Wall.) at 380; *see* 2 THE RECORDS OF THE FEDERAL CONVENTION OF 1787, at 426 (rev. ed. M. Farrand 1937) [hereinafter cited as CONVENTION RECORDS]:

> Mr. L. Martin moved to insert the words "after conviction" after the words "reprieves and pardons".
> Mr. Wilson objected that pardon before conviction might be necessary in order to obtain the testimony of accomplices . . . Mr. L. Martin withdrew his motion.

[44]Wayne himself had been declared an "alien enemy" and his property confiscated by his own state of Georgia during the war. *See* A. LAWRENCE, *supra* introduction to part four, note 2 at 189.

[45]*Garland*, 71 U.S. (4 Wall.) at 382-99; *Cummings*, 71 U.S. (4 Wall.) at 332.

[46]Unlike a bill of attainder, said Miller, the laws in question did not identify any individuals who were to be punished; furthermore, the oath requirement was neither retrospective nor criminal. *Garland*, 71 U.S. (4 Wall.) at 389-92 (dissenting opinion). Miller further argued that attorneys could have been disqualified before the statute was imposed on the ground that disloyalty showed bad character. *Id.* at 393. That can hardly be a complete apology for the statute, which made disqualification mandatory and contained a very broad list of disqualifying acts. *See id* at 374-77. For contemporaneous criticism, see J. POMEROY, AN INTRODUCTION TO THE CONSTITUTIONAL LAW OF THE UNITED STATES 329 (1870), arguing that what distinguished the oath requirements from bills of attainder was "the entire absence of the judicial element. There is no adjudication; no usurpation of the functions of courts; no persons or class of persons, either by name or by description, are, by the mere force and operation of the enactment, convicted of any crime existing or alleged."

[47]*Garland*, 71 U.S. (4 Wall.) at 393-96.

the most essential qualifications which should be required in a lawyer."[48] Since the laws under examination did not inflict punishment, Miller concluded, they were neither ex post facto laws nor bills of attainder, and they did not contradict the pardon.[49]

Miller's position cannot be lightly dismissed. Incompetent medical treatment cannot retroactively be made a crime; but it does not follow that it cannot be taken into account in determining whether to allow a doctor to continue plying his trade, and one may legitimately doubt the Framers meant to forbid its consideration.[50] If one agrees with Miller on this point, one is led to ask whether the disqualification in question was intended as punishment or as protection; Marshall had cautioned about the difficulties of investigating legislative motives as early as 1810.[51] Miller accepted the challenge frankly if less than convincingly:

> The history of the time when this statute was passed—the darkest hour of our great struggle—the necessity for its existence, the humane character of the President who signed the bill, and the face of the law itself, all show that it was purely a qualification, exacted in self-defence, of all who took part in administering the government in any of its departments, and that it was not passed for the purpose of inflicting punishment, however merited, for past offences.[52]

Justice Field did not deny that past behavior might sometimes be considered in determining qualifications, and he seemed to agree that the legislative motive was determinative. The Missouri oath, he said in *Cummings*, "was exacted, not from any notion that the several acts designated indicated unfitness for the callings, but because it was thought that the several acts deserved punishment . . . ."[53] Unlike Miller, he based his conclusion as to motive on objective considerations:

> It is evident from the nature of the pursuits and professions of the parties, placed under disabilities by the constitution of Missouri, that many of the acts, from the taint of which they must purge themselves, have no possible relation to their fitness for those pursuits and professions. There can be no connection between the fact that Mr. Cummings entered or left the State of Missouri to avoid enrolment or draft in the military service of the United States and his fitness to teach the doctrines or administer the sacraments of his church; nor can a fact of this kind or the expression of words of sympathy with some of the persons drawn into the Rebellion constitute any evidence of the unfitness of the attorney or counsellor to practice his profession, or of the professor to teach the ordinary branches

---

[48]*Id.* at 385.

[49]*Id.* at 396-97. That retroactive punishment was the hallmark of an ex post facto law had been established in Calder v. Bull, 3 U.S. (3 Dall.) 385 (1798), *discussed supra in* chapter 2.

[50]*Cf.* Hawker v. New York, 170 U.S. 189, 196 (1898) (upholding a ban on medical practice by convicted felons: "The State is not seeking to further punish a criminal, but only to protect its citizens from physicians of bad character.").

[51]Fletcher v. Peck, 10 U.S. (6 Cranch) 87, 130 (1810); *see supra* chapter 5.

[52]*Garland*, 71 U.S. (4 Wall.) at 396.

[53]*Cummings*, 71 U.S. (4 Wall.) at 320.

of education, or of the want of business knowledge or business capacity in the manager of a corporation, or in any director or trustee.[54]

At least with respect to the priest in *Cummings*, Field seems to have had the better of this argument, and Miller made no attempt to show that past acts of disloyalty were relevant to the qualifications of the clergy. Even Field was careful to point out that neither case involved qualifications for public office,[55] where Miller's position becomes much more compelling: could the Framers really have meant to require admission into the councils of government of people who had demonstrated their desire to sabotage it?[56] Miller placed his reliance on the intimate role of attorneys in the governmental process: "They are, by the nature of their duties, the moulders of public sentiment on questions of government, and are every day engaged in aiding in the construction and enforcement of the laws."[57] I think I side with Field on this one, but it seems to me both sides argued ably for supportable positions[58] in a case to which the Constitution gave no clear answer.[59]

II. RECONSTRUCTION

The Court made few friends among the dominant radical faction by striking down military trials and test oaths; there were those who labeled *Milligan* and the oath cases "Dred Scott II and III."[60] A series of cases immediately following appeared to confront the Court with a still more explosive issue: the constitutionality of the statutes providing for the fate of the former Confederate States. This set of cases produced several important rulings respecting the powers of the federal courts, but some of the central substantive issues remained unsettled. The Court tended to treat the latter as hot potatoes, and the other branches of government were only too willing to help see to it that they were never completely resolved.[61]

The substantive issues were both fundamental and difficult. Among other things,

[54]*Id*. at 319-20.

[55]*Garland*, 71 U.S. (4 Wall.) at 378.

[56]*See* Garner v. Board of Public Works, 341 U.S. 716, 720 (1951) (allowing inquiry into past affiliations of applicants for municipal employment: "Past conduct may well relate to present fitness; past loyalty may have a reasonable relationship to present and future trust."). After Wayne's death, the Court divided 4-4 over the validity of an oath of past loyalty as a qualification for voting. *See* FAIRMAN, HISTORY, *supra* introduction to part four, note 2, at 613-16; C. SWISHER, *supra* introduction to part four, note 2, at 154 n.21.

[57]*Garland*, 71 U.S. (4 Wall.) at 386.

[58]The similar question of citizenship requirements for Bar admission was to divide a much later Court. *See In re* Griffiths, 413 U.S. 717 (1973) (holding that Connecticut's exclusion of aliens from the practice of law violated the equal protection clause of the fourteenth amendment).

[59]For an excellent discussion of later bill-of-attainder cases, see Note, *The Bounds of Legislative Specification: A Suggested Approach to the Bill of Attainder Clause*, 72 YALE L.J. 330 (1962).

[60]*See* FAIRMAN, HISTORY, *supra* introduction to part four, note 2, 216, 218, 219, 232, 236, 245; C. SWISHER, *supra* introduction to part four, note 2, at 152; 2 C. WARREN, *supra* introduction to part four, note 2, 430-32.

[61]For general discussions of the Reconstruction cases see FAIRMAN, HISTORY, *supra* introduction to part four, note 2, chs. 8-10, 12; S. KUTLER, JUDICIAL POWER AND RECONSTRUCTION POLITICS, chs. 5-6 (1968); 2 C. WARREN, *supra* introduction to part four, note 2, ch. 30.

Congress had subordinated the elected governments of ten Southern states to military authority[62] and made both black suffrage and ratification of the fourteenth amendment conditions of admitting their representatives to Congress.[63] Not only was it less than obvious what constitutional provisions might support such legislation; on its face the statute seemed a gross breach of Congress's constitutional obligation to guarantee each state a republican form of government,[64] a denial of the constitutional right of representation in Congress,[65] and a perversion of the ratification provisions of article V.[66] It also raised the article III and jury-trial problems already identified in *Ex parte Milligan.*[67]

The Radical argument that the Southern states were no longer parts of the Union and thus could be treated as conquered territories[68] was contrary to the premise on

[62]Act of Mar. 2, 1867, ch. 153, §§ 1-3, 6, 14 Stat. 428, 428-29 (expired upon readmission of rebel states to representation in Congress). The Act directed the military to keep the peace and punish offenders and declared that "any civil governments" in those states were "provisional only, and in all respects subject to the paramount authority of the United States." *Id.* § 6, 14 Stat. at 429. Tennessee, which was safely in Republican hands and had ratified the fourteenth amendment, *see* FAIRMAN, HISTORY, *supra* introduction to part four, note 2, at 99, 132, 264 n.41, was not included. Act of Mar. 2, 1867, ch. 153, § 6, 14 Stat. 428, 429.

[63]Act of Mar. 2, 1867, ch. 153, § 5, 14 Stat. 428, 429. A supplementary act, in response to the difficulties experienced by loyalists attempting to vote, provided that military authorities conduct elections for the state constitutional conventions contemplated by the basic reconstruction law. Act of Mar. 23, 1867, ch. 6, 15 Stat. 2; *see* FAIRMAN, HISTORY, *supra* introduction to part four, note 2, at 317-27 (criticizing Chief Justice Chase for stepping outside the judicial role to draft the supplementary bill).

[64]U.S. CONST. art. IV, § 4 ("The United States shall guarantee to every State in this Union a Republican Form of Government . . . ."). President Johnson invoked this clause and the clauses cited *infra* text accompanying notes 65-67, among others, in the message accompanying his veto of the basic reconstruction bill, Act of Mar. 2, 1867, ch. 153, 14 Stat. 428 (enacted over presidential veto). CONG. GLOBE, 39th Cong., 2d Sess. 1729, 1731-32 (House), 1969, 1971-72 (Senate) (1867) [hereinafter cited as Johnson Veto Message], *reprinted in* 6 J. RICHARDSON, A COMPILATION OF THE MESSAGES AND PAPERS OF THE PRESIDENTS 498, 506-10 (1900).

[65]U.S. CONST. art. I, §§ 2, 3 ("The House of Representatives shall be composed of Members chosen every second Year by the People of the several States . . . . The Senate . . . shall be composed of two Senators from each State . . . ."); *see also* U.S. CONST. art. V ("[N]o State, without its Consent, shall be deprived of its equal Suffrage in the Senate."). Moreover, to the extent that the question pertained to the "Qualifications" of Senators and Representatives, *but see* Powell v. McCormack, 395 U.S. 486 (1969) (holding "Qualifications" limited to the constitutional requirements of age, citizenship, and residence), it was by no means clear that either House could surrender by statute its constitutional authority as "Judge of the . . . Qualifications of its own Members," U.S. CONST. art I, § 5. *See* A. McLAUGHLIN, A CONSTITUTIONAL HISTORY OF THE UNITED STATES 677-78 (1935) (discussing President Johnson's veto, on similar grounds, of a bill to "readmit" Arkansas to congressional representation).

[66]U.S. CONST. art V (providing that amendments become law "when ratified by the Legislatures [or Conventions] of three fourths of the several States"); *see* Johnson Veto Message, *supra* note 64, at 1729, 1969, *reprinted in* 6 J. RICHARDSON, *supra* note 64, at 500 (arguing that the sole purpose of military rule was "as a means of coercing the people into the adoption of principles and measures to which it is known that they are opposed, and upon which they have an undeniable right to exercise their own judgment").

[67]*See supra* notes 11-31 and accompanying text.

[68]*See, e.g.*, CONG. GLOBE, 39th Cong., 1st Sess. 73 (1865) (statement of Rep. Stevens) (arguing that the war "broke all the ties" with the seceding states and that they had to apply for admission as new states under article IV); *id.* at 24 (statement of Sen. Howard) (describing the rebel states as "simply conquered communities, subjugated by the arms of the United States—communities in which the right of self-government does not now exist"); *id.* at 31 (statement of Rep. Stevens) (objecting to the presentation of credentials on behalf of Representatives from Tennessee: "The State of Tennessee is not known to this

which the North had fought the war.[69] The argument that military rule was a means to
the establishment of truly republican government[70] involved, among other things, a
substantial redefinition of what "Republican" meant, if not an actual play on the
word.[71] The most effective argument in favor of military rule was that put forward by
Davis in his dictum in *Milligan*:[72] the relevant constitutional provisions were subject
to implicit exceptions for military necessity. Unlike Indiana, the seceding states had
taken arms against the nation, and a measure of military occupation could be

---

House nor to Congress."). Compare the more subtle variant of this argument employed by Representatives Shellabarger and Bingham, *id*. at 142-45, 156-59, and later espoused for the Court by Chase, *see infra*
text accompanying notes 175-91: though secession was unlawful, the states had forfeited their rights. *See*
FAIRMAN, HISTORY *supra* introduction to part four, note 2, at 119, 123, 268, 268, 288-89 (describing views of
Rep. Stevens and Shellabarger). The Act itself began by reciting in its own justification that "no legal state
governments . . . now exist[ ]" in the rebel states. Act of Mar. 2, 1867, ch. 153, § 1, 14 Stat. 428, 428. As
Fairman says, this was also a swipe at Andrew Johnson's efforts at *presidential* reconstruction. FAIRMAN,
HISTORY, *supra* introduction to part four, note 2, at 298.

[69]*See* CONST. GLOBE, 39th Cong., 1st Sess. 292 (1866) (statement of Sen. Nesmith):

> Why should we involve ourselves in the paradoxical absurdity of denying the right of
> secession, of fighting them for four years to enforce that denial, and when they admit their
> failure by the last arbitrament, turn round and admit that they have accomplished their
> purpose, and are to-day outside the Union?

See also Johnson Veto Message, *supra* note 64, at 1730, 1970 *reprinted in* 6 J. RICHARDSON, *supra* note 64,
at 503-04. In his first inaugural address President Lincoln had argued that secession was unconstitutional
and had expressed his determination to enforce federal law throughout the nation. Lincoln's First
Inaugural Address, in 6 J. RICHARDSON, *supra* note 64, at 5, 7; in calling up troops he noted the need for
measures "for the protection of the National Constitution and the preservation of the National Union by
the suppression of the insurrectionary combinations now existing in several States for opposing the laws of
the Union," Proclamation of May 3, 1861, in 6 J. RICHARDSON, *supra* note 64, at 15; in addressing a special
war session of Congress on July 4, 1861 he described his efforts "to prevent, if possible, the consummation
of such attempt to destroy the Federal Union," Special Session Message (July 4, 1861), in 6 J.
RICHARDSON, *supra* note 64, at 20; in his first Annual Message that December he emphasized that he had
"thought it proper to keep the integrity of the Union prominent as the primary object of the contest on our
part," Message of December 3, 1861, in 6 J. RICHARDSON, *supra* note 64, at 54; and in the Emancipation
Proclamation he declared that "hereafter, as heretofore, the war will be prosecuted for the object of
practically restoring the constitutional relation between the United States and each of the States and the
people thereof in which States that relation is or may be suspended or disturbed," Proclamation of
September 22, 1862, in 6 J. RICHARDSON, *supra* note 64, at 96.

[70]*See, e.g.*, CONG. GLOBE, 39th Cong., 1st Sess. 143, 145 (1866) (statement of Rep. Shellabarger)
(suggesting that President Johnson had invoked the clause guaranteeing a republican form of government
as authority for his own earlier efforts at reconstruction in the teeth of state constitutions). To create
governments under the clause in the face of anarchy, however, as Johnson did, is not the same as to set
aside governments already established.

[71]Racial qualifications for voting had not been thought to subject Northern governments to congressional tinkering in the past. Only five states permitted blacks to vote at the time of the war. *See* FAIRMAN,
HISTORY, *supra* introduction to part four, note 2, at 96. Several states rejected proposals for black suffrage
between 1865 and 1867, *see id*. at 128 n.121, and Tennessee had been readmitted to Congress without
black voting, *see id*. at 264 n.41. Shellabarger's argument was that a "[r]epublican" government meant one
that was "loyal." CONG. GLOBE, 39th Cong., 1st Sess. 145 (1866); *see also* A. MCLAUGHLIN, *supra* note 65,
at 643 ("A state government, that is seized by 'rebels' and made to do their will, can scarcely be considered
a free constitutional government. Technically, a state not in the possession of its loyal citizens is not,
constitutionally speaking, republican." (footnote omitted)). In the Constitutional Convention the term
"republican" had been contrasted with monarchy. *See* 1 CONVENTION RECORDS, *supra* note 43, at 206.

[72]*See supra* notes 15-22 and accompanying text.

defended as inherent in putting down the insurrection.[73] Davis had also insisted, however, that military rule could not be "continued *after* the courts are reinstated,"[74] and the provisions of the new law were to be applied whether or not the civil tribunals were open.[75]

A. *Mississippi v. Johnson*

These troubling questions were first pressed upon the Court in 1867, when Mississippi filed an original action in the Supreme Court to enjoin the President from enforcing the Reconstruction Acts, on the ground that they were unconstitutional. In a brief opinion by Chief Justice Chase, the Court unanimously held it had "no jurisdiction of a bill to enjoin the President in the performance of his official duties."[76]

The legal basis of this conclusion was left in obscurity. Since Andrew Johnson was apparently a citizen of Tennessee,[77] the case seemed to fall within article III's provisions for federal judicial authority over "Controversies . . . between a State and Citizens of another State"[78] and for original Supreme Court jurisdiction over "Cases . . . in which a State shall be a Party."[79] As an original matter, one might have argued with considerable force that the general expressions of article III were not intended to override the tradition of sovereign immunity,[80] and that a suit to enjoin an officer

[73]This much was conceded by Senator Doolittle, one of the most articulate opponents of reconstruction. *See* Cong. Globe, 39th Cong., 1st Sess. 271-72 (1866).

[74]*Milligan*, 71 U.S. (4 Wall.) at 127.

[75]Many thought *Milligan* spelled the doom of the provisions for military rule. Davis himself did not, emphasizing that he had expressly recognized the power to authorize military trials "in insurrectionary States." *See* S. Kutler, *supra* note 61, at 67, 95. For an able defense of military jurisdiction on the ground that it was "for Congress . . . to determine when the war has so far ended that this work [of restoring peaceful relations] can be safely and successfully completed," see 13 Op. Att'y Gen. 59, 65 (1869). Professor Fairman, who has given us a superb account of the intricate legislative history of the Reconstruction Acts, Fairman, History, *supra* introduction to part four, note 2, chs. 3, 6, refrains from expressing a categorical judgment on their constitutionality, but does seem to view the legislation on the whole as necessary and desirable in light of Southern intransigence. *See id.* at 333-55, 591-98.

[76]Mississippi v. Johnson, 71 U.S. (4 Wall.) 475, 501 (1867).

[77]*See id.* at 475 (reciting the allegations of the complaint); *id.* at 501 (assuming the allegation of citizenship to be true). In the case that follows, Georgia v. Stanton, 73 U.S. (6 Wall.) 50 (1868), it was argued that federal officers "have no State citizenship," but have their "official residence" in the District of Columbia, *id.* at 53-54; *see infra* notes 99-122 and accompanying text; the Court did not pick up the suggestion. Johnson's Tennessee citizenship was used as an argument against the Radical theory of Reconstruction: if Tennessee was no longer a state, he was not qualified to be President. *See* Cong. Globe, 39th Cong. 1st Sess. 118 (1865) (statement of Rep. Finck) (quoting U.S. Const. art II, § 1, which requires that the President be a citizen of the United States).

[78]U.S. Const. art III, § 2, para. 1.

[79]U.S. Const. art III, § 2, para. 2; *see* Marbury v. Madison, 5 U.S. (1 Cranch) 137, 173-75 (1803). The case would also appear to fall within the statutory grant of original Supreme Court jurisdiction. Judiciary Act of 1789, ch. 20, § 13, 1 Stat. 73, 78 ("[T]he Supreme Court shall have . . . jurisdiction of all controversies of a civil nature . . . between a state and citizens of other states, or aliens, in which . . . case it shall have original but not exclusive jurisdiction.") By modern standards Mississippi's case also arose under federal law, but there was no statute at the time giving the trial courts jurisdiction on that basis.

[80]*See supra* chapter 1 (discussing Chisholm v. Georgia, 2 U.S. (2 Dall.) 419 (1793)).

from acting in his official capacity was in effect one against the government;[81] but the Court had already rejected the latter proposition in the analogous state-officer case of *Osborn v. Bank of the United States*.[82] Chase disclaimed reliance on sovereign immunity—expressly reserving the question whether in appropriate cases a state might sue the United States itself.[83]

Much of the *Johnson* opinion was devoted to showing that *Marbury v. Madison*[84] was not precedent for the injunction requested. Marshall had made clear in the earlier case that even a cabinet officer could be subjected to a court order in some cases, emphasizing that it was "not by the office of the person to whom the writ is directed, but the nature of the thing to be done, that the propriety . . . of issuing a *mandamus* is to be determined."[85] But *Marbury*, as Chase insisted, had expressly been limited to compelling the performance of "ministerial" acts;[86] Marshall had specifically disavowed any authority "to inquire how the executive, or executive officers, perform duties in which they have a discretion."[87] The enforcement of the Reconstruction Acts, Chase continued, involved the exercise of executive discretion: the President was required to appoint military commanders, to provide the necessary troops, and to supervise the commanders in carrying out their duties.[88] Judicial enforcement of such nonministerial duties, said Chase, would in Marshall's words be "'an absurd and excessive extravagance'"; the fact that the present suit sought not "to enforce action by the Executive . . . but to restrain such action under legislation alleged to be unconstitutional" did not take it "out of the general principles which forbid judicial interference with the exercise of Executive discretion."[89]

This passage, whose essence would seem equally applicable to suits against other government officers,[90] wholly fails to persuade. The distinction the Court brushed aside is crucial; the President may have broad discretion in executing a valid law, but he has no discretion to enforce an invalid one since he has no discretion to violate the Constitution.

Less frivolous was the suggestion later in the opinion that the President enjoyed a special immunity from suit by virtue of his unique position: "The Congress is the legislative department of the government; the President is the executive department. Neither can be restrained in its action by the judicial department; though the acts of both, when performed, are, in proper cases, subject to its cognizance."[91] The consequences of such an injunction, Chase continued, were so grave as to make plain its "impropriety":

[81]*See supra* chapter 4 (discussing Osborn v. Bank of the United States, 22 U.S. (9 Wheat.) 738 (1824)).
[82]22 U.S. (9 Wheat.) 738 (1824).
[83]*Johnson*, 71 U.S. (4 Wall.) at 501.
[84]5 U.S. (1 Cranch) 137 (1803).
[85]*Id.* at 170; *see supra* chapter 3.
[86]*See Johnson*, 71 U.S. (4 Wall.) at 498-99.
[87]*Marbury*, 5 U.S. (1 Cranch) at 170.
[88]*Johnson*, 71 U.S. (4 Wall.) at 499.
[89]*Id.* (quoting and paraphrasing *Marbury*, 5 U.S. (1 Cranch) at 170)). For an approving view of Chase's argument respecting discretion, see FAIRMAN, HISTORY, *supra* introduction to part four, note 2, at 381 n.57.
[90]Indeed, though the opinion notably failed to discuss the fact, the military commander of the district including Mississippi had been named as an additional defendant. *See Johnson*, 71 U.S. (4 Wall.) at 475, 497.
[91]*Id.* at 500.

If the President refuse obedience, it is needless to observe that the court is without power to enforce its process. If, on the other hand, the President complies with the order of the court and refuses to execute the acts of Congress, is it not clear that a collision may occur between the executive and legislative departments of the government?[92]

Surely, Chase argued, Congress could not be enjoined from enacting an unconstitutional law; and how could an injunction against Presidential enforcement of such a law be distinguished?[93]

Distinguishing the two cases is child's play: the Constitution expressly immunizes members of Congress from being questioned about their legislative actions "in any other Place";[94] it makes no comparable provision for the President. Moreover, the argument that the Framers must have meant to avoid the risk of a direct confrontation between the branches had already been blunted in *Marbury*; conflict is likely when a Secretary of State is ordered about as well. Now the negative inference from the congressional immunity is not airtight, for that provision may have been inserted out of an abundance of caution with no intention of foreclosing an implicit presidential immunity;[95] and, as counsel argued, the indispensability of the President makes his immunity argument far stronger than that of his subordinates.[96] Thus, a respectable argument might have been made in favor of holding as a constitutional matter that the President himself could not be enjoined,[97] but neither of Chase's arguments seems to fill the bill.[98]

[92]*Id.* at 500-01.

[93]*Id.* at 500.

[94]U.S. CONST. art I, § 6.

[95]*See* Nixon v. Fitzgerald, 457 U.S. 731, 784 n.27, 786 n.31 (1982) (finding a presidential immunity from damage actions, apparently in the Constitution itself, and rejecting any negative inference from the explicit congressional immunity); *cf.* Hans v. Louisiana, 134 U.S. 1 (1890) (finding an implication of state immunity from suit by its own citizens although the eleventh amendment immunized it in express terms only from suits by citizens of other states and by aliens).

[96]*Johnson*, 71 U.S. (4 Wall.) at 487-90 (argument by Attorney General Stanbery) (With the President in jail for contempt, "there is not a law of the United States that can be executed, not an officer that can be appointed or . . . removed."); *see also* P. KURLAND, *supra* note 43, at 131-36 (arguing on this basis for an implicit presidential immunity against criminal process); *cf.* 3 J. STORY, *supra* note 40, at 419 (President immune from arrest); Memorandum for the United States Concerning the Vice President's Claim for Constitutional Immunity at 15-20, *In re* Proceedings of the Grand Jury Impaneled Dec. 5, 1972, No. Civ. 73-965 (D. Md. 1973) (President Nixon's Justice Department's response to Vice President Agnew's defense of immunity from criminal prosecution; arguing that only the President is indispensable, and only in his case would conviction be inconsistent with the constitutional powers of prosecution and pardon), *cited in* D. CURRIE, FEDERAL COURTS—CASES & MATERIALS 611 (3d ed. 1982).

[97]The Court specifically reserved the question whether the President could be required "to perform a purely ministerial act, . . . or may be held amenable, in any case, otherwise than by impeachment for crime." *Johnson*, 71 U.S. (4 Wall.) at 498; *see also* United States v. Nixon, 418 U.S. 683 (1974) (upholding an order to produce tapes without even adverting to any argument of immunity from process); Nixon v. Sirica, 487 F.2d 700, 708-12 & n.53 (D.C. Cir. 1973) (ordering production of Watergate tapes, distinguishing *Johnson* on its own flimsy "discretionary" ground).

[98]*See* FAIRMAN, HISTORY, *supra* introduction to part four, note 2, at 382-83 (arguing that a contrary decision would have "subverted" "something very fundamental to the constitutional system" and praising the President for protecting his office at the cost of defending a law he bitterly opposed); S. KUTLER, *supra* note 61, at 96-97 (arguing that *Johnson* was correctly decided and pointing out that none of the Justices supposedly hostile to Reconstruction dissented).

B. *Georgia v. Stanton*

Educated by Mississippi's misadventure, Georgia sought to enjoin not the President but his subordinates, the Secretary of War and two of his generals, from enforcing the Reconstruction Act. Once again the Supreme Court's original jurisdiction was invoked, and once again without success.[99] The judgment was again unanimous; the Chief Justice, who disagreed with the Court's reasons, declined to give any of his own.[100]

It is noteworthy that Justice Nelson, writing for the majority, did not rely on *Mississippi v. Johnson*; apparently, despite some of the language in that opinion and the fact that a subordinate officer had been named as an additional defendant,[101] the Court had not meant in the earlier case to hold that no officer could be enjoined from enforcing an unconstitutional law. Rather, the case was largely governed, in the eyes of the majority, by *Cherokee Nation v. Georgia*,[102] in which the Court had refused to entertain a suit by the tribe to enjoin Georgia from exercising jurisdiction over its reservation. As in *Cherokee Nation*, the complaint in *Stanton* called "for the judgment of the court upon political questions, and, upon rights, not of persons or property, but of a political character," and thus did not "belong to the jurisdiction of a court, either in law or equity."[103]

Nelson properly acknowledged that the language on which he relied had been unnecessary to the result in *Cherokee Nation*, since the Court had held the tribe not a "foreign State" entitled to sue in the Supreme Court.[104] Nevertheless, the language had in fact been used,[105] and on the "political" issue the cases were analogous: both concerned the protection of an established government against an arguably usurping rival. So, the reader will recall, had the famous decision in *Luther v. Borden*[106] where, in refusing to determine which of two contending factions was the legitimate government of Rhode Island, Taney had suggested, among other things, that the question was "political."[107] Predictably, counsel opposing the suit in *Stanton* argued that *Luther* had placed the constitutionality of Reconstruction beyond judicial ken by classifying it as a "political question."[108]

Although no earlier decision had established as a general principle that questions of political import were nonjusticiable—indeed, such recent decisions as *Milligan*, *Cummings*, and *Garland* had demonstrated the contrary—a substantial argument could have been made on the basis of precedent for a refusal ever to consider the validity of Reconstruction. In the first place, the guarantee of a republican form of

[99]73 U.S. (6 Wall.) 50 (1868).

[100]*Id.* at 77-78. For speculation as to Chase's position, see FAIRMAN, HISTORY, *supra* introduction to part four, note 2, at 393.

[101]*See supra* text accompanying notes 76-98 and note 91.

[102]30 U.S. (5 Pet.) 1 (1831). *See supra* chapter 4.

[103]73 U.S. (6 Wall.) at 77, 76.

[104]*Id.* at 74 (quoting *Cherokee Nation*, 30 U.S. (5 Pet.) at 29-30).

[105]"The bill requires us to control the legislature of Georgia, and to restrain the exertion of its physical force. The propriety of such an interposition by the court may be well questioned. It savours too much of the exercise of political power to be within the proper province of the judicial department." *Cherokee Nation*, 30 U.S. (5 Pet.) at 20.

[106]48 U.S. (7 How.) 1 (1849). *See supra* chapter 8.

[107]*Id.* at 42, 46.

[108]73 U.S. (6 Wall.) at 61 (argument by Mr. Stanbery).

government was a principal basis both for justifying the statute and for attacking it,[109] and one of the things clearly, if unnecessarily and unconvincingly, said in *Luther* was that the administration of this clause was entrusted exclusively to the other branches of government.[110] Moreover, the *Prize Cases*[111] might well have been called into service in support of such a decision; for in upholding the President's blockade of Southern ports during the war, the Court had flatly, if unnecessarily, suggested that judges could never second-guess the responsible political authority as to the degree of force necessary to put down the rebellion.[112]

It is striking that neither the *Prize Cases* nor even *Luther* was mentioned in the *Stanton* opinion. In fact, passages in the opinion strongly suggest that the Court did not consider the case analogous to *Luther* and did not mean to classify the issue of Reconstruction as "political" in the sense in which that term is understood today. First, in distinguishing the interstate boundary dispute the Court had resolved in *Rhode Island v. Massachusetts*,[113] Nelson described the question in the earlier case as "not a political question, but one of property" having only an incidental effect on sovereignty, because the state "as the original and ultimate proprietor" had the right of escheat over all lands within its borders.[114] While this may trivialize the *Rhode Island* holding,[115] the implication seems to be that it was the fact that Georgia sued in its sovereign capacity in *Stanton*, and not the nature of the underlying issue, that made the case too "political" for judicial cognizance.[116]

This impression is strengthened by the penultimate paragraph of the *Stanton* opinion, in which Nelson dismissed the importance of an allegation that enforcement of the Reconstruction laws would deprive the state of the use of its public buildings. The loss of property, he wrote, had been alleged "only by way of showing one of the grievances resulting from the threatened destruction of the State, . . . not as a specific ground of relief"; protecting the state's property would not justify the broad injunctive relief the state had requested and "would have called for a very different bill" from the one before the Court.[117] This may represent an unjustifiably hostile reading of the complaint,[118] but it also suggests the trouble was indeed not with the issue but

---

[109]*See supra* text accompanying notes 61-71.

[110]*See* 48 U.S. (7 How.) at 42-43; *supra* chapter 8.

[111]67 U.S. (2 Black) 635 (1863).

[112] Whether the President . . . has met with such armed hostile resistance . . . as will compel him to accord to them the character of belligerents, is a question to be decided *by him*, and this court must be governed by the decisions and acts of the political department . . . to which this power was entrusted.

Id. at 670; *see supra* chapter 8. Professor Fairman seems to view *Stanton* as a political-question case and to think it rightly decided. FAIRMAN, HISTORY, *supra* introduction to part four, note 2, at 393-96.

[113]37 U.S. (12 Pet.) 657 (1838); *see supra* chapter 8.

[114]*Stanton*, 73 U.S. (6 Wall.) at 73.

[115]The Court in *Rhode Island* never referred to the state's property interest; it relied on the express provision in the Articles of Confederation for settlement of boundary disputes and on the fact that the states had surrendered authority to settle them by either war or treaty. 37 U.S. (12 Pet.) at 723-31. The second argument applied equally to *Stanton*.

[116]*See also Stanton*, 73 U.S. (6 Wall.) at 76 (stressing that "the *rights* in danger . . . must be *rights* of persons or property, not merely political *rights*" (emphasis added)).

[117]*Id.* at 77.

[118]*See id.* at 53 (declaring that the state had averred that it was the "owner of certain real estate and buildings . . . (the State capitol, . . . and Executive mansion), and of other real and personal property, exceeding in value $5,000,000; and that putting the acts of Congress into execution . . . would deprive it of

with the party. The history of the Cherokee litigation invoked by the Court is equally instructive: after throwing out the tribe's suit with intimations that the case was "political," the Court held the laws the tribe had challenged unconstitutional in an action by a missionary whose personal rights were at stake.[119] Thus, despite its misleading terminology, *Stanton* seems to have held not that Reconstruction was a political issue but, in accord with the distinction earlier drawn in the *Wheeling Bridge* case,[120] that the state had no standing to assert merely political interests;[121] the door seemed to have been left open for an attack by someone in the position of that missionary in the land of the Cherokees.[122]

C. *Ex parte McCardle*

Such a plaintiff was not long in presenting himself: an editor imprisoned by the military authorities in Mississippi on charges of having published "incendiary and libellous" articles[123] sought habeas corpus on the ground that the Reconstruction Acts were unconstitutional. When the circuit court denied relief, he appealed to the Supreme Court as provided in an 1867 statute.[124] As if to demonstrate that *Stanton*

---

the possession and enjoyment of its property."). For the more persuasive argument of counsel that the threat to state property was too conjectural to constitute a ripe controversy, see *id.* at 57-60 (argument by Mr. Stanbery).

In the absence of Justice Grier, the court later divided equally along party lines and refused Georgia permission to file an amended complaint more clearly alleging a property right. *See* 2 C. WARREN, *supra* introduction to part four, note 2, at 463-64. Kutler views Nelson's reference to property rights in *Stanton* as inviting an amended pleading and Grier's absence as crucial to avoiding a test of Reconstruction. S. KUTLER, *supra* note 61, at 99, 113.

[119]Worcester v. Georgia, 31 U.S. (6 Pet.) 515 (1832); *see supra* chapter 6.

[120]Pennsylvania v. Wheeling & Belmont Bridge Co. (I), 54 U.S. (13 How.) 518, 559-62 (1852); *see supra* chapter 7.

[121]For conflicting contemporaneous interpretations of the *Stanton* decision, see 2 C. WARREN, *supra* introduction to part four, note 2, at 472-73. The confusion between political questions and standing was later perpetuated in the famous opinion in Massachusetts v. Mellon, 262 U.S. 447 (1923), which, in denying a state standing to assert its sovereign interest in keeping Congress within its powers, invoked *Stanton* and declared that the "question, *as it is thus presented*, is political and not judicial in character." *Id.* at 483 (emphasis added).

[122]For a real political-question case decided during the Chase period, see United States v. Holliday, 70 U.S. (3 Wall.) 407 (1866) (Miller, J.). There the Court deferred to the Executive as to whether the Chippewas were still to be treated as an Indian nation for purposes of a statute forbidding liquor sale to certain Indians: "In reference to all matters of this kind, it is the rule of this court to follow the action of the executive and other political departments of the government, whose more special duty it is to determine such affairs." *Id.* at 419. The statute in question seemed expressly to make the executive's position decisive, for it applied to "any *Indian* under the charge of any Indian superintendent or Indian agent appointed by the United States." *Id.* at 408. Miller's language went further, as it had to in order to sustain the constitutionality of the act under the Indian commerce clause of article I, § 8, U.S. CONST. art. I, § 8; *see infra* chapter 10; since there was no doubt that the Chippewas were in fact "Indians," the loose terminology of the opinion need not be taken as carte blanche for Congress to extend its powers by declaring all inhabitants of Kentucky, for example, to be "Indians." *Cf.* Williams v. Suffolk Ins. Co., 38 U.S. (13 Pet.) 415 (1839), noted *supra* in chapter 8, (deferring to the executive on the question of sovereignty over the Falkland Islands).

[123]*Ex parte* McCardle, 74 U.S. (7 Wall.) 506, 508 (1869).

[124]Act of Feb. 5, 1867, ch. 28, § 1, 14 Stat. 385, 386 (repealed 1868).

had not really been a political-question case, the Court upheld its jurisdiction.[125] While the case was pending, however, Congress repealed the provision under which the appeal had been taken.[126] Thereupon the Court dismissed without dissent in an 1869 opinion by Chief Justice Chase.[127]

The opinion made it seem quite simple. Article III gave the Supreme Court appellate jurisdiction of specified cases "with such Exceptions . . . as the Congress shall make,"[128] and Congress had made an exception by repealing the jurisdictional provision.[129] The text of the Constitution makes this conclusion appear obvious; but a moment's reflection should reveal that, if taken literally, the exceptions clause provides Congress with a ready means of frustrating Supreme Court review of its acts. If, as some passages in *Marbury v. Madison* suggest, judicial review is merely an unavoidable incident of the duty of judges to decide cases properly before them,[130] this conclusion is no cause for reexamining the statement in *McCardle*. Yet other passages in *Marbury*, made persuasive by explicit statements of Convention delegates and in the *Federalist*,[131] indicate that the Court thought the Framers had created judicial review as a means of enforcing the constitutional limits on congressional power.[132] On this view, to take the exceptions clause literally would give Congress a means of avoiding a critical check on its powers; even stronger than *Marbury*'s presumption that the Framers did not mean to leave Congress as sole judge of its own powers is the presumption that they did not both create a judicial check and render it avoidable at the whim of Congress.[133] Thus, as most modern commentators have concluded,[134] the issue was by no means so simple as Chase made it appear in *McCardle*.[135]

[125]73 U.S. (6 Wall.) 318 (1868) (Chase, C.J.). The political-question issue, however, was not discussed; the argument concerned the interpretation of the provision for appeals.

[126]Act of March 27, 1868, ch. 34, § 2, 15 Stat. 44 (enacted over presidential veto) (amending Judiciary Act of 1789, 1 Stat. 73, and repealing Act of Feb. 5, 1867, ch. 28, § 1, 14 Stat. 385, 386). For the history of this provision, courageously vetoed by President Johnson during proceedings for his own impeachment, see FAIRMAN, HISTORY, *supra* introduction to part four, note 2, at 459-69; 2 C. WARREN, *supra* introduction to part four, note 2, at 473-80.

[127]For a thorough discussion of the legal issues, see Van Alstyne, *A Critical Guide to Ex parte McCardle*, 15 ARIZ. L. REV. 229 (1973).

[128]U.S. CONST. art III, § 2.

[129]74 U.S. (7 Wall.) at 514 ("The power to make exceptions to the appellate jurisdiction of this court is given by express words.").

[130]*E.g.*, 5 U.S. (1 Cranch) at 177-78 ("It is, emphatically, the province and duty of the judicial department, to say what the law is . . . . So, if a law be in opposition to the constitution; . . . the court must determine which of these conflicting rules governs the case . . . .").

[131]For citations of supporting statements by Convention delegates and in the *Federalist*, see *supra* chapter 3.

[132]5 U.S. (1 Cranch) at 176, 178 (arguing that the reason for a written constitution was to limit legislative power and that to deny judicial review would give Congress "a practical and real omnipotence, with the same breath which professes to restrict their powers within narrow limits"). For a discussion of the ambivalence of *Marbury* on this point, see *supra* chapter 3.

[133]President Johnson's message vetoing the repeal of the Court's jurisdiction argued among other things that the deprivation of jurisdiction was "not in harmony with the spirit and intention of the Constitution" because "it establishes a precedent which, if followed, may eventually sweep away every check on arbitrary and unconstitutional legislation." CONG. GLOBE 40th Cong., 2d Sess. 2094, 2094 (Senate), 2165, 2165 (House) (1868), *reprinted in* 6 J. RICHARDSON, *supra* note 64, at 646, 647.

[134]*See, e.g.*, authorities cited *supra* in chapter 1 (discussing Wiscart v. D'Auchy, 3 U.S. (3 Dall.) 321

On the other hand, the last paragraph of the opinion removes the suspicion that the Court meant to establish that Congress's power to make exceptions to its appellate jurisdiction was absolute:

> Counsel seem to have supposed, if effect be given to the repealing act in question, that the whole appellate power of the court, in cases of *habeas corpus*, is denied. But this is an error. The act of 1868 does not except from that jurisdiction any cases but appeals from Circuit Courts under the act of 1867. It does not affect the jurisdiction which was previously exercised.[136]

What this cryptic message meant was demonstrated soon enough when another military prisoner sought Supreme Court review of a similar denial of habeas corpus, not by appeal but by petitions for habeas corpus and certiorari under the Judiciary Act of 1789.[137] In *Ex parte Yerger*,[138] also in 1869, the Court in another apparently unanimous Chase opinion upheld its jurisdiction. It was true that the appellate power was "subject to exception and regulation by Congress,"[139] but because a complete denial of Supreme Court review "must greatly weaken the efficacy of the writ . . . and seriously hinder the establishment of . . . uniformity in deciding upon questions of personal rights,"[140] no such construction of the statute would be adopted

---

(1796)); authorities cited *supra* in chapter 2 (discussing Martin v. Hunter's Lessee, 14 U.S. (1 Wheat.) 304 (1816)). *Contra,* H. WECHSLER, THE COURTS AND THE CONSTITUTION 7 (1965):

> Federal courts . . . do not pass on constitutional questions because there is a special function vested in them to enforce the Constitution or police the other agencies of government. They do so rather for the reason that they must decide a litigated issue that is otherwise within their jurisdiction and in doing so must give effect to the supreme law of the land.

[135]The argument that the repealing act could not be applied to a pending case was rejected summarily; precedent had established "that no judgment could be rendered in a suit after the repeal of the act under which it was brought"; cases cited to the contrary were distinguished as involving "the exercise of judicial power by the legislature, or of legislative interference with courts in the exercising of continuing jurisdiction." 74 U.S. (7 Wall.) at 514; *see also* Van Alstyne, *supra* note 127, at 245 (characterizing this "perfunctory discussion" as "quite correct, given the fact that the case had not come to decision by the date the Act became effective").

[136]74 U.S. (7 Wall.) at 515.

[137]*Ex parte* Yerger, 75 U.S. (8 Wall.) 85 (1869) (holding that jurisdiction existed under the Judiciary Act of 1789, ch. 20, § 14, 1 Stat. 73, 81-82 (current version at 28 U.S.C. § 1651 (1976)). For earlier decisions respecting review of judicial imprisonments under this provision, see *supra* chapter 3 (discussing *Ex parte* Bollman, 8 U.S. (4 Cranch) 75 (1807)). In *Yerger*, Chase reaffirmed that this jurisdiction was appellate and thus constitutional. 75 U.S. (8 Wall.) at 97-102. In this connection he cast belated aspersions on Marshall's conclusion in *Marbury*, 5 U.S. (1 Cranch) at 174, that Congress could not enlarge the Supreme Court's original jurisdiction:

> If the question were a new one, it would, perhaps, deserve inquiry whether Congress might not, under the power to make exceptions from this appellate jurisdiction, extend the original jurisdiction to other cases than those expressly enumerated in the Constitution; and especially, in view of the constitutional guaranty of the writ of *habeas corpus*, to cases arising upon petition for that writ.

75 U.S. (8 Wall.) at 97.

[138]75 U.S. (8 Wall.) 85 (1869). Professor Fairman says Miller dissented without opinion, FAIRMAN, HISTORY, *supra* introduction to part four, note 2, at 583, but the official report does not say so.

[139]75 U.S. (8 Wall.) at 102.

[140]*Id.* at 103.

without a clearer statement by Congress; as *McCardle* had said, the repealing statute took away only the jurisdiction conferred in 1867, not that which had been confirmed in 1789.[141]

At this point it appeared that a judicial test of Reconstruction was imminent, but the military came to the rescue: Yerger was turned over to the civilian authorities, and the case became moot.[142] Thus, despite an intervening decision yet to be discussed,[143] the Reconstruction cases failed to produce a decision on the validity of the provisions for military trials.

That all three branches were happy to avoid the confrontation was plain enough. Not only had Congress deprived the Court of jurisdiction over a pending case in a deliberate effort to prevent a decision; it had been the scene of a number of far more drastic proposals to insulate congressional actions from judicial scrutiny.[144] The Executive had done its part by releasing Yerger when all else had failed. The Court's attitude is suggested by its transparently weak *Johnson* opinion, by its failure to assert continued jurisdiction in *McCardle* under the 1789 act on which it relied in *Yerger*,[145] and by its explicit decision, over the protest of Grier and Field, to postpone action in *McCardle* pending passage of the bill to take away its jurisdiction.[146] At the same time, however, the Court studiously avoided giving a definitive opinion on Congress's power to limit its jurisdiction, and in both respects it seems to have been wise not to be bold. For the Court was fighting for its future, and, like Marshall in *Marbury*,[147] it did so tenaciously. With the *Dred Scott* debacle in the wings, and with a little help from the other branches, the Court managed to tread the narrow path between rendering a judgment that might have been ignored[148] and holding that Congress had the right to prevent judicial review.

[141]*Id.* at 103-05; *cf.* Van Alstyne, *supra* note 127, at 249 ("*McCardle*, in short, upheld only an inessential exception to the Supreme Court's jurisdiction, and did not curtail any of its important authority."). Indeed, as Van Alstyne further argues, the repealing act made no "Exception" at all: it merely regulated the manner in which jurisdiction should be exercised. *Id.* at 250-54.

[142]*See* FAIRMAN, HISTORY, *supra* introduction to part four, note 2, at 584-91; 2 C. WARREN, *supra* introduction to part four, note 2, at 496-97 & n.1.

[143]*See infra* text accompanying notes 174-206 (discussing Texas v. White, 74 U.S. (7 Wall.) 700 (1869)).

[144]See S. KUTLER, *supra* note 61, at 64-88 (noting that various court-curbing measures failed so long as there was no immediate danger to the Reconstruction Acts, but that the Republican party was determined "to protect its reconstruction legislation" from the Court); 2 C. WARREN, *supra* introduction to part four, note 2, at 466-72, 491-96 (discussing bills to require a two-thirds vote to invalidate federal statutes, to deprive the Supreme Court of jurisdiction over Reconstruction Act cases, and to abolish judicial review entirely).

[145]For discussion of the possibility of so relying, see Van Alstyne, *supra* note 127, at 245-48.

[146]*See* 2 C. WARREN, *supra* introduction to part four, note 2, at 480-84. Warren reprints Grier's eloquent statement: "By the postponement of this case, we shall subject ourselves, whether justly or unjustly, to the imputation that we have evaded the performance of duty imposed on us by the Constitution, and waited for legislative interposition to supersede our action, and relieve us from responsibility." *Id.* at 482 (quoting National Intelligencer, Mar. 31, Apr. 6, 1868; Chicago Republican, Apr. 3, 1868; Indianapolis Journal, Apr. 2, 3, 1868). *But see* FAIRMAN, HISTORY, *supra* introduction to part four, note 2, at 479-80 (denying that the Court acted improperly). Fairman notes that both the democratic Senator Reverdy Johnson and a leading member of the Bar who had been an intimate of Chief Justice Taney had defended the Court from the charge of undue delay. *id.* at 468.

[147]*See supra* chapter 3.

[148]Chase wrote to another judge that the Court would "doubtless" have held the provision for military trials unconstitutional had it taken jurisdiction in *McCardle*. *See* FAIRMAN, HISTORY, *supra* introduction to part four, note 2, at 494 (quoting Letter from Chief Justice Salmon P. Chase to District Judge Robert A.

D. *United States v. Klein*

Indeed, before three years were out, the Court found a somewhat less explosive context in which to say that Congress's power over the appellate jurisdiction was not absolute after all. Congress had authorized the owner of property that had fallen into government hands during the war to recover the property's proceeds if he could demonstrate that he had not given aid or comfort to the rebellion,[149] and the Supreme Court had held in an earlier case that a presidential pardon, by purging the owner of his offense, satisfied this burden of proof.[150] Armed with a pardon, Klein obtained a judgment from the Court of Claims for the value of cotton taken by the government. While an appeal was pending, Congress enacted a law providing that a pardon should be taken instead as proof that the owner had aided the rebellion, and that upon such proof the suit should be dismissed for want of jurisdiction.[151] Without dissent on the central issue, the Court in an important 1872 Chase opinion held the new provisions unconstitutional.[152]

"Undoubtedly," said Chase, "the legislature has complete control over the organization and existence of [the Court of Claims] and may confer or withhold the right of appeal from its decisions"; if the statute "simply denied the right of appeal in a particular class of cases, there could be no doubt that it must be regarded as an exercise of the power of Congress to make 'such exceptions from the appellate jurisdiction' as should seem to it expedient."[153] "But," he continued, "the language of the proviso shows plainly that it does not intend to withhold appellate jurisdiction except as a means to an end. Its great and controlling purpose is to deny to pardons granted by the President the effect which this court had adjudged them to have."[154] To "dismiss the appeal" when a pardon showed "that the judgment must be affirmed" would allow "one party to the controversy to decide it in its own favor," and permit Congress to "prescribe rules of decision to the Judicial Department . . . in cases pending before it."[155] Moreover, the statute was "liable to just exception as impairing the effect of a pardon, and thus infringing the constitutional power of the Executive."[156]

Hill (May 1, 1869)); *see also* Hughes, *Salmon P. Chase: Chief Justice*, 18 VAND. L. REV. 569, 595 (1965) (asserting that "the Court performed like an expert, if aged, escape artist").

[149]Act of Mar. 12, 1863, ch. 120, § 3, 12 Stat. 820, 820, *quoted in* United States v. Klein, 80 U.S. (13 Wall.) 128, 131 (1872).

[150]United States v. Padelford, 76 U.S. (9 Wall.) 531, 542-43 (1870) (Chase, C.J.).

[151]Act of July 12, 1870, ch. 251, 16 Stat. 230, 235, *quoted in* United States v. Klein, 80 U.S. (13 Wall.) 128, 133-34 (1872).

[152]United States v. Klein, 80 U.S. (13 Wall.) 128, 147-48 (1872). Miller and Bradley, while arguing that the prior case was distinguishable because there the claimant had been pardoned *before* his property was seized, agreed that Congress had no power "to prescribe to the judiciary the effect to be given to an act of pardon or amnesty by the President." *Id.* at 148. For a brief background of the case, see FAIRMAN, HISTORY, *supra* introduction to part four, note 2, at 840-46. The most comprehensive legal analysis is Young, *Congressional Regulation of Federal Courts' Jurisdiction and Processes: United States v. Klein Revisited*, 1981 WIS. L. REV. 1189.

[153]80 U.S. (13 Wall.) at 145.

[154]*Id.*

[155]*Id.* at 146.

[156]*Id.* at 147.

Several distinct arguments appear in this jumble of reasoning, not all of them convincing. It had been equally obvious in *McCardle* that the denial of jurisdiction had been "a means to" the "end" of frustrating whatever substantive rights the applicant might have had, and that by depriving the Court of jurisdiction the United States had "decide[d]" the controversy "in its own favor." Yet the Court in *McCardle* had blandly deferred to the congressional command with no suggestion that either legislative motive or the effect on substantive rights was relevant.[157] As for "prescrib[ing] rules of decision to the Judicial Department," that is what legislation is all about, and *McCardle* itself had involved a "pending" case.[158]

Nevertheless, there were important differences between *Klein* and McCardle. First, in *Klein* Congress had foreclosed all judicial relief, while in *McCardle* it had left open not only the trial courts but an alternate route to the Supreme Court itself; only in *Klein* could it be argued that by closing all the courts Congress had effectively denied a substantive constitutional right.[159] Moreover, the law in *McCardle* had impartially excluded appeals by all habeas corpus applicants; the law in *Klein* discriminated against those claimants who had been pardoned. Since the Court had earlier suggested that the purpose of the pardon was to place its beneficiary on a par with those who had never aided the rebellion,[160] the Court could well view this discrimination as "impairing the effect" of the pardon—just as the Court might view a denial of jurisdiction over actions brought by Roman Catholics as an abridgement of their free exercise of religion even if Congress is under no general duty to provide a forum for the vindication of constitutional rights.[161] Thus it appears that the most *Klein* may even arguably have established is that Congress may not selectively close all the courts to claims of a class of litigants constitutionally entitled to equal treatment on the merits.

There is, however, a third basis for distinguishing *McCardle*, emphasized by the Court itself,[162] that makes it questionable whether *Klein* really established so much as the proposition just stated. As Henry Hart saw it, Congress had not deprived the Court of power to decide the case; it had attempted "to tell the court *how* to decide it" and indeed to do so "in accordance with a rule of law independently unconstitutional."[163] To Hart, *Klein* was like the later case of *Yakus v. United States*,[164] where Justice Rutledge, with the apparent agreement of the Court, had drawn the following distinction:

[157]*See supra* notes 123-36 and accompanying text.

[158]*See supra* notes 126-27 and accompanying text.

[159]The right in question was the right conferred by the pardon as previously interpreted. *Klein*, 80 U.S. (13 Wall.) at 147.

[160]United States v. Padelford, 76 U.S. (9 Wall.) 531, 542-43 (1870).

[161]*See* Van Alstyne, *supra* note 127, at 263; *cf.* Elrod v. Burns, 427 U.S. 347 (1976) (forbidding political discrimination in government employment although the Constitution gave no right to a government job). Similarly, *Klein* conceded that there need be no Court of Claims at all, and no appeal from its decisions. 80 U.S. (13 Wall.) at 145; *see* Young, *supra* note 152, at 1230-33 (arguing that the discriminatory nature of the proviso was the reason sovereign immunity did not bar the action).

[162]*See supra* note 155 and accompanying text.

[163]P. BATOR, P. MISHKIN, D. SHAPIRO & H. WECHSLER, HART & WECHSLER'S THE FEDERAL COURTS AND THE FEDERAL SYSTEM 316, 337 (2d ed. 1973) [hereinafter cited as HART & WECHSLER] (Hart's well-known discussion of congressional control of the distribution of judicial power); *accord*, Young, *supra* note 152, at 1215-24 (giving a much fuller explanation).

[164]321 U.S. 414 (1944).

It is one thing for Congress to withhold jurisdiction. It is entirely another to confer it and direct that it be exercised in a manner inconsistent with constitutional requirements or, what in some instances may be the same thing, without regard to them . . . . [W]henever the judicial power is called into play, it is responsible directly to the fundamental law and no other authority can intervene to force or authorize the judicial body to disregard it.[165]

I have argued above that whether Congress may withdraw jurisdiction of entire constitutional cases depends upon whether one emphasizes those passages in *Marbury v. Madison* insisting that judicial review is a fundamental check on other branches or those describing it merely as a consequence of the judge's own obligation not to violate the Constitution.[166] Rutledge's position, however, seems to follow even from the latter view. If the judge merely refuses to hear a case he keeps his hands clean; if he inflicts punishment on a defendant without listening to his constitutional objections, as Rutledge argued was the case in *Yakus*, he arguably violates the Constitution.

The harder question was whether *Klein* really was a case in which the Court was ordered to decide a case according to an unconstitutional rule. If, as the Chief Justice at one point suggested, the statute merely directed the Supreme Court "to dismiss the *appeal*,"[167] the *Yakus* argument appears misplaced; the Court then was simply forbidden to act.[168] As Chase elsewhere recognized, however, what the statute actually required was that the Court "dismiss the *cause*"[169]—that is, as the government requested, that it "remand" the case to the Court of Claims "with a mandate that the same be dismissed for want of jurisdiction."[170] The Court was thus told not to decline jurisdiction but to exercise it: to deprive the claimant of an existing judgment in his favor if it found, in the Court's words, "that the judgment must be affirmed"[171] because of the pardon. For Congress to have required the denial, on this basis, of relief on the *merits* would have unconstitutionally impaired the pardon. Although a contrary argument can be made,[172] there is therefore a strong case for finding that

[165]*Id.* at 468 (dissenting opinion). The majority held there had been an adequate prior opportunity for judicial review, which the defendant had forfeited.

[166]*See supra* notes 130-33 and accompanying text.

[167]80 U.S. (13 Wall.) at 146 (emphasis added).

[168]A grant of jurisdiction to decide against but not in favor of a pardoned claimant might have been vulnerable to the argument that the exercise of article III's "judicial Power" required the authority to decide either way if at all; but the statute in *Klein* avoided this objection, for it required dismissal on proof of a pardon without a decision on the merits one way or the other.

[169]80 U.S. (13 Wall.) at 146 (emphasis added).

[170]*Id.* at 130. For a convincing demonstration that the government's position correctly reflected the intentions of Congress, see Young, *supra* note 152, at 1203-09. *See also* CONG. GLOBE, 41st Cong., 2d Sess. 3824 (1870) (statement of Senator Edmunds) ("[W]e say they shall dismiss the case out of court for want of jurisdiction; not dismiss the appeal, but dismiss the case—everything."), *quoted in* Young, *supra* note 152, at 1208.

[171]80 U.S. (13 Wall.) at 146.

[172]Viewing this situation from the point before Klein brought his suit in the Court of Claims, the ultimate result was the same as if the courts had never been given jurisdiction over claims by persons whose rebel activities had been pardoned; the Supreme Court was directed merely to keep the lower court from giving Klein a judicial remedy. At the time Congress restricted jurisdiction, however, Klein had already had a favorable judgment, and the Court was ordered to take it away because of the pardon.

Klein fell on the wrong side of Justice Rutledge's principle that a court may not be ordered to violate the Constitution.[173]

In short, *Klein* does establish the welcome if unsurprising proposition that Congress's power to limit federal court jurisdiction, like all its other powers, is subject to limitations found elsewhere in the Constitution. *McCardle* was distinguishable, though the Court was not entirely clear in saying why. Chase deserves some credit for smelling a rat, even if he could not quite identify it; the unsatisfying quality of his opinion may to a large extent be forgiven in view of the difficulty, after a hundred years of second-guessing, of coming up with a wholly satisfactory explanation.

E. *Texas v. White*

At the outbreak of the war Texas owned federal bonds, which, according to state law, it could transfer only over the signature of the Governor. After secession the rebel legislature repealed the signature requirement, and the bonds were sold. When the war was over, the partly reconstructed state brought an action in the Supreme Court to recover the bonds, and in an 1869 Chase opinion it prevailed.[174]

There was a threshold problem: the Supreme Court had jurisdiction only if the suit was between "a State and Citizens of another State,"[175] and Texas had purported to secede from the Union.[176] Thus the Chief Justice found it necessary to hold that secession was unconstitutional. He did so in a single paragraph: the Articles of Confederation had declared the Union "perpetual"; the preamble to the 1789 Constitution had declared that the new Union was to be even "more perfect"; and "[w]hat can be indissoluble if a perpetual Union, made more perfect, is not?"[177]

---

[173]A final possible basis for distinguishing *Klein* from *McCardle* was that Klein had won in the lower court and McCardle had lost. In this light Chase's statement that the United States was attempting to decide its own controversy, *see supra* note 155 and accompanying text, takes on added significance. On several prior occasions the Justices had said that neither the Executive nor Congress could revise judicial decisions, *see* Gordon v. United States, 69 U.S. (2 Wall.) 561 (1865); United States v. Ferreira, 54 U.S. (13 How.) 40 (1852); Hayburn's Case, 2 U.S. (2 Dall.) 409 (C.C.D.N.Y., C.C.D. Pa., C.C.D.N.C. 1792), *discussed supra in* chapter 1, and one of the reasons given had been that to do so was to exercise judicial power, *see Hayburn's Case*, 2 U.S. (2 Dall.) at 410. While the statute in *McCardle* had left the lower court's denial of relief standing, that in *Klein* directed the Supreme Court to set aside a decision already rendered; the rule that Congress itself could not reverse the decision would be meaningless if Congress could order the Supreme Court to do so. Pennsylvania v. Wheeling & Belmont Bridge Co. (II), 59 U.S. (18 How.) 421 (1856), which Chase distinguished on the obscure basis that the statute in question had created "new circumstances," 80 U.S. (13 Wall.) at 146-47, does not detract from this argument; Congress's decision to authorize a bridge over the Ohio River did not contradict the Court's holding that earlier statutes had forbidden it. On the other hand, Congress had not directed the Court to reverse Klein's case alone; it had enacted a general change in the law, and a long line of cases had already established that such a law could be applied to cases on appeal when it was enacted. *E.g.*, The Schooner Peggy, 5 U.S. (1 Cranch) 103, 110 (1801) (Marshall, C.J.); *see* HART & WECHSLER, *supra* note 163, at 316 n.4; *see also* Young, *supra* note 152, at 1238-40.

[174]Texas v. White, 74 U.S. (7 Wall.) 700 (1869). The case and its intricate aftermath are extensively described in FAIRMAN, HISTORY, *supra* introduction to part four, note 2, at 619-76.

[175]U.S. CONST. art III, § 2, para. 1. Since Texas had brought an original action in the Supreme Court, the Court had jurisdiction only if the suit was one "in which a State [was] a Party." U.S. CONST. art III, § 2, para. 1; *see* Marbury v. Madison, 5 U.S. (1 Cranch) 137, 173-75 (1803); *see also supra* notes 78-79.

[176]*See* 74 U.S. (7 Wall.) at 722-24.

[177]*Id.* at 724-25; *see also* White v. Hart, 80 U.S. (13 Wall.) 646, 649-52 (1872) (Swayne, J.) (reaffirming

This hardly seems an adequate treatment of an issue on which reasonable people had differed to the point of civil war.[178] It was an act of considerable audacity to treat the mere statement of purpose in the preamble as if, contrary to its natural reading, it imposed legally binding limitations on the states.[179] As for the Articles, they had been superseded by the new Constitution. Indeed this very supersession, as well as the arguments that accompanied it, furnished an embarrassing argument in favor of secession. The Convention had deliberately chosen to ignore the procedure prescribed in the Articles for their own amendment,[180] invoking a variety of justifications ranging from popular sovereignty and the right of revolution[181] to the position that a breach of the Articles by one state dissolved the obligations of the others.[182] At least the first two arguments were still available in 1861,[183] but Chase did not stop to rebut any of them.

---

that Georgia had never left the Union and holding therefore that she was forbidden to impair contractual obligations notwithstanding her attempted secession). The *White v. Hart* opinion added nothing to the reasoning of *Texas v. White*, nor did it cite the *Texas* decision.

[178]For an argument in favor of the right of secession by a highly respected northern observer, see W. RAWLE, A VIEW OF THE CONSTITUTION OF THE UNITED STATES OF AMERICA 295-310 (2d ed. Philadelphia 1829) (1st ed. Philadelphia 1825). We pass quickly over the objection that, so far as the mere text was concerned, the reason the earlier union was less "perfect" might have been precisely that it *was* perpetual, for that could (and should) have been refuted by a little history: it was the weakness of the central govenment under the Articles of Confederation, not its permanence, that gave rise to the call for revision. *See, e.g.*, 1 CONVENTION RECORDS, *supra* note 43, at 18-27 (argument of Edmund Randolph in laying his plan before the Convention, spelling out the weakness of the Articles, finding them "totally inadequate to the peace, safety and security of the confederation," and declaring "the absolute necessity of a more energetic government"); *see also* 2 J. ELLIOT, *supra* note 40, at 185-90 (statement of Mr. Ellsworth), 208-15 (statement of Mr. Livingston), 430-31 (statement of Mr. Wilson); 3 *id.* at 26-27 (statement of Gov. Randolph), 226 (statement of Mr. Marshall); 4 *id.* at 253 (statement of Mr. Pinckney); 1 J. STORY, *supra* note 40, at 226-51.

[179]One might as persuasively argue that the preamble's recitation of the purpose to "promote the general Welfare" empowered by Congress, in the teeth of the enumeration of limited powers emphasized by the tenth amendment and confirmed in McCulloch v. Maryland, 17 U.S. (4 Wheat.) 316 (1819), to take any steps appropriate to achieving that goal. *See* 1 J. STORY, *supra* note 40, at 445 ("The preamble never can be resorted to, to enlarge the powers confided to the general government . . . . Its true office is to expound the nature, and extent, and application of the powers actually conferred by the constitution, and not substantively to create them.")

[180]   And the articles of this confederation shall be inviolably observed by every State, and the Union shall be perpetual; nor shall any alteration at any time hereafter be made in any of them, unless such alteration be agreed to in a Congress of the United States, and be afterwards confirmed by the Legislatures of every State.

ARTICLES OF CONFEDERATION, art. 13. Contrast U.S. CONST. art VII ("The Ratification of the Conventions of nine States, shall be sufficient for the Establishment of this Constitution between the States so ratifying . . . .").

[181]*See, e.g.*, 1 CONVENTION RECORDS, *supra* note 43, at 262 (statement of Gov. Randolph) ("There are great seasons when persons with limited powers are justified in exceeding them . . . ."); 2 *id.* at 469 (statement of Mr. Wilson) ("We must go to the original powers of Society, The House on fire must be extinguished, without a scrupulous regard to ordinary rights."). Compare the insistence in the Declaration of Independence on the "Right of the People to alter or to abolish" a bad government. The Declaration of Independence para. 2 (U.S. 1776).

[182]*E.g.*, 1 CONVENTION RECORDS, *supra* note 43, at 314 (statement of Mr. Madison).

[183]Madison, who used the breach argument himself in 1787, *see supra* note 182, argued that ratification by conventions rather than by state legislatures would make that argument inapplicable to the new Constitution. 1 CONVENTION RECORDS, *supra* note 43, at 122-23; *see also infra* notes 186-89 and accompanying text.

The Confederacy itself, as the Court was later to hold,[184] was easy to strike down if the states had not legally seceded; article I, section 10 expressly forbids the states to enter into any "Alliance, or Confederation."[185] If secession was lawful, however, even the Confederacy was not an alliance among states, and the secession question was harder. The best argument was based upon an important change of language from the Articles to the Constitution: while the former were a "firm league of friendship" among "sovereign[ ]" states,[186] the latter was "the supreme Law of the Land."[187] The Articles may have been a treaty voidable upon breach, but the "more perfect" Constitution was not; and Texas had unilaterally declared inoperative within its borders what the Constitution said was supreme law, "any Thing in the Constitution or Laws of any State to the Contrary notwithstanding."[188] Even this argument was not conclusive, since the whole question was whether Texas was still part of the "Land"; while it is scarcely the most natural inference, it would not have been wholly inconsistent for the Framers to require that states respect federal law only so long as they chose to remain in the Union. The interesting fact is that the supremacy clause argument was not made.[189]

Surprisingly, Chase went on to hold that the illegality of secession did not answer the jurisdictional objection. Though Texas had not left the Union, it had forfeited its right to sue:

> All admit that, during this condition of civil war, the rights of the State as a member, and of her people as citizens of the Union, were suspended. The government and the citizens of the State, refusing to recognize their constitutional obligations, assumed the character of enemies, and incurred the consequences of rebellion.[190]

Thus Chase, and the majority of the Court with him, accepted without supporting argument the standard Radical view of a one-sided secession: the Southern states had annihilated their rights but not their obligations.[191] This was a pretty shaky thesis; if Texas was still a state, article III seemed to give it the right to sue.

The Court's findings of forfeiture meant that Texas's right to sue depended upon the legitimacy of the provisional governments set up with federal approval after the defeat of the rebellion. "[S]o long as the war continued," wrote Chase, the President had power "as commander-in-chief" to "institute temporary governments within insurgent districts" or to "take measures . . . for the restoration of State government

---

[184]Williams v. Bruffy, 96 U.S. 176, 182 (1878) (Field, J.).

[185]U.S. Const. art I, § 10.

[186]Articles of Confederation, arts. 2, 3.

[187]U.S. Const. art VI, para. 2.

[188]*Id.*

[189]It had, however, been made by Justice Story in his *Commentaries*. J. Story, *supra* note 40, at 308-09, 318-22. Professor Fairman finds the issue simple: "The Constitution . . . allowed for amendment but not for dissolution; it did not speak to the situation where secession in arms had been attempted." Fairman, History, *supra* introduction to part four, note 2, at 641 (footnote omitted). This appears to turn the Constitution on its head: the tenth amendment reserves to the states all powers not prohibited by the Constitution. Madison's argument that ratification by conventions would make the Union permanent, on the other hand, *see supra* note 183, strongly supports the Court's conclusion; it was not cited.

[190]74 U.S. (7 Wall.) at 727.

[191]*See supra* note 190 and accompanying text.

faithful to the Union"—"employing, however, . . . only such means and agents as were authorized by constitutional laws."[192] Whether presidential Reconstruction "was, in all respects, warranted by the Constitution," it was unnecessary to decide;[193] it was "primarily" up to Congress to restore constitutional government through article IV's guarantee of "a republican government";[194] and Congress had recognized Texas's civil government as a "provisional" one in the Reconstruction Acts themselves.[195]

For this proposition Chase relied on precedent: his predecessor's famous statement in *Luther v. Borden*[196] that "'it rests with Congress to decide what government is the established one in a State.'"[197] The quoted statement was not only of questionable persuasiveness, as I have elsewhere argued;[198] it was also unnecessary to the result in *Luther*. The plaintiff had not relied on the guarantee clause, and the Court ultimately held that the federal court must defer to state courts in determining the question because it was a matter of state law.[199] Even the dicta of *Luther*, moreover, did not clearly point to Chase's conclusion. At one point Taney had seemed to say that the guarantee clause issue was for each House of Congress to decide in determining whether to seat elected senators and representatives;[200] and, as three dissenters argued in *Texas v. White*, those Houses had suggested that Texas was not a state by denying it representation.[201] Furthermore, even the passage invoked by Chase seemed to cut against his decision to determine the legality of secession and forfeiture of the right to sue: if Congress alone had power to decide whether Texas had a legitimate state government, the Court had no business reaching either question. Finally, Chase's ultimate holding that Congress had given Texas authority to sue made it unnecessary to discuss whether the state had earlier lost that right; Chase seemed eager to take the occasion to affirm as much of standard Radical doctrine as he could.[202]

[192]74 U.S. (7 Wall.) at 730; *see also* Stewart v. Kahn, 78 U.S. (11 Wall.) 493, 506-07 (1871) (Swayne, J.) (upholding Congress's authority under its powers "to declare war . . . and . . . suppress insurrections" to suspend civil statutes of limitations in state courts during the time the war precluded suit: "[The power] carries with it inherently the power to guard against the immediate renewal of the conflict, and to remedy the evils which have arisen from its rise and progress."); The Grapeshot, 76 U.S. (9 Wall.) 129, 131-33 (1870) (Chase, C.J.) (upholding the President's military authority to establish a civil tribunal in reoccupied Louisiana during the war).

[193]74 U.S. (7 Wall.) at 729.

[194]*Id.* at 730 (quoting Luther v. Borden, 48 U.S. (7 How.) 1, 42 (1849) (Taney, C.J.)).

[195]*Id.* at 730-31.

[196]48 U.S. (7 How.) 1 (1849) (Taney, C.J.).

[197]*Texas*, 74 U.S. (7 Wall.) at 730 (quoting *Luther*, 48 U.S. (7 How.) at 42 (Taney, C.J.)).

[198]*See supra* chapter 8.

[199]*Luther*, 48 U.S. (7 How.) at 40.

[200]*Id.* at 42.

[201]74 U.S. (7 Wall.) at 738 (Grier, Swayne, and Miller, J.J.).

[202]Grier's dissent, *id.* at 737-39, substantially joined on the jurisdictional issue by Swayne and Miller, *id.* at 741, was no more satisfying. Professing to find the question of statehood one of "fact" rather than law, Grier noted that Texas was not represented in Congress, and invoked Marshall's holding that the District of Columbia was not a "State" for article III purposes because it did not elect Congressmen. *Id.* at 737, 738 (quoting Hepburn v. Ellzey, 6 U.S. (2 Cranch.) 445, 452 (1805), *supra* chapter 3). But the District of Columbia was not *entitled* to representation under the plain terms of the Constitution. If Texas had no right to secede, it seemed still to have the right to elect Congressmen; Grier seemed to be saying that Congress could deny a state the right to sue by unconstitutionally excluding it from its own halls.

Having upheld jurisdiction, the Court held Texas could get its bonds back; the rebel act authorizing sale without the Governor's signature was invalid because it had been passed "in furtherance or support of rebellion . . . ."[203] Grier alone protested: if Texas had not left the Union, it had the power to repeal its own legislation.[204] This plausible position was made more convincing by the singular failure of the majority to identify what provision of the Constitution the repealing act offended; unlike secession, the sale of state property did not on its face contradict federal law. Chase seems to have viewed the raising of funds for rebellious purposes as inseparable from secession itself;[205] but this conclusion, like so much else in his opinion, would have benefited from further explication.[206]

In *Texas v. White* the Court went out of its way to embrace the Radical position that secession and all acts that served it were illegal, that the seceding states had nevertheless forfeited their rights, and that Congress could determine under the

----

[203]*Id.* at 732-34.

[204]*Id.* at 739-40.

[205]*See id.* at 726 ("[T]he ordinance of secession . . . and all the acts of her legislature intended to give effect to that ordinance, were absolutely null."). Easier than *Texas v. White* were cases holding void acts of the central government of the Confederate States, since the Confederacy itself was unconstitutional. *See, e.g.,* Hickman v. Jones, 76 U.S. (9 Wall.) 197, 200-01 (1870) (Swayne, J.) (allowing damages against those responsible for trying the plaintiff under Confederate authority for "treason" against the Confederacy); United States v. Keehler, 76 U.S. (9 Wall.) 83, 86-87 (1870) (Miller, J.) (holding it no defense to an action against a postmaster who had unlawfully paid out government funds that he had done so in conformity with an act of the Confederate Congress); *supra* note 177 and accompanying text.

On the other hand, the Court managed to avoid massive disruptions by acknowledging acts of the Confederacy not directly in furtherance of the rebellion on the basis that the Confederacy was a "de facto" government. Thus in Thorington v. Smith, 75 U.S. (8 Wall.) 1 (1869) (Chase, C.J.), the Court enforced a contractual obligation to pay for land in Confederate money, and in Delmas v. Insurance Co., 81 U.S. (14 Wall.) 661 (1872) (Miller, J.), it held such a contract had been unconstitutionally impaired. *See also* Mauran v. Insurance Co., 73 U.S. (6 Wall.) 1 (1868) (Nelson, J.) (holding a seizure by the rebels to be a "capture" within an exception to a marine insurance policy). What is interesting are the dicta in *Texas v. White* suggesting that it was the same de facto doctrine that would justify the Court in upholding acts of the rebel *state* governments that were "necessary to peace and good order" and not "in furtherance or support of the rebellion." 74 U.S. (7 Wall.) at 733 (citing "acts sanctioning and protecting marriage and the domestic relations, governing the course of descents, regulating the conveyance and transfer of property, . . . and providing remedies for injuries to person and estate"). For reasons never adequately stated but probably related to its holding that Texas had forfeited its right to sue, the Court seemed to think that by unlawfully attempting to secede the state government had lost all its powers. But in Horn v. Lockhart, 84 U.S. (17 Wall.) 570, 580 (1873) (Field, J.), where the issue was the validity of a wartime Alabama probate decree, the Court said:

> [T]he acts of the several States in their individual capacities, . . . so far as they did not impair . . . the supremacy of the National authority, . . . are . . . to be treated as valid and binding. The existence of a state of insurrection and war did not loosen the bonds of society, or do away with civil government, or the regular administration of the laws.

[206]That actions supporting the rebellion were punishable as treason, U.S. CONST. art. III, § 3, and suppressable as insurrection, U.S. CONST. art. I, § 8, does not prove them unconstitutional, and the provision forbidding states to "engage in War," U.S. CONST. art. I, § 10, had an exception for cases of actual or threatened invasion. A strong argument could have been made that the exception did not apply to an "invasion" by federal troops seeking to enforce federal law, but Chase did not make it. For extensive criticism of the nonconstitutional aspects of the decision, some of which were promptly repudiated in other cases, see FAIRMAN, HISTORY, *supra* introduction to part four, note 2, at 643-62, accusing Chase of "want of rigor in analysis," *id.* at 648.

guarantee clause how they were to be governed. It did so essentially by fiat, without serious consideration of the opposing arguments.

III. Financial Measures

As it had in the area of federal and state relations, the Civil War produced a revolution in the area of finance. As usual, the Supreme Court was asked to hold everything that was new unconstitutional; after one important setback, the Court confirmed the new order.

A. Federal Taxes

The first confrontation came in the field of federal taxation. Before the war, tariffs on imported goods had provided the principal source of federal revenue. To meet the extraordinary expenses of the emergency, Congress not only raised tariffs but imposed a variety of internal taxes, including one on the income of insurance companies and on the amounts they had insured.[207] In the 1869 case of *Pacific Insurance Co. v. Soule*,[208] the Court rejected the argument that this tax was a direct one required by article I to be apportioned among the states according to population.[209] Justice Swayne's unsatisfying opinion carefully selected for quotation or unattributed paraphrase those relatively unconvincing passages from the carriage tax case of *Hylton v. United States*[210] that favored his conclusion (the dicta that perhaps only land and poll taxes were direct[211] and the wishful argument that direct taxes meant those that could be fairly apportioned[212]) and ignored the more persuasive argument of Justice Paterson that the carriage tax had been an indirect effort to reach what an income tax reached directly—the income itself.[213]

[207]Act of June 30, 1864, ch. 173, §§ 105, 120, 13 Stat. 223, 276, 283-84, *amended by* Act of July 13, 1866, ch. 184, 14 Stat. 98; *see* J. Schuckers, *supra* introduction to part four, note 2, at 222-23; Dam, *The Legal Tender Cases*, 1981 Sup. Ct. Rev. 367, 371.

[208]74 U.S. (7 Wall.) 433 (1869).

[209]U.S. Const. art. I, § 2 ("Representatives and direct Taxes shall be apportioned among the several States . . . according to their respective numbers . . . ."); U.S. Const. art I, § 9 ("No Capitation, or other direct, Tax, shall be laid, unless in Proportion to the Census or Enumeration herein before directed to be taken.").

[210]3 U.S. (3 Dall.) 171 (1796).

[211]*Id.* at 175 (Chase, J.), 177 (Paterson, J.), 183 (Iredell, J.); the first two were quoted by Swayne, *Soule*, 74 U.S. (7 Wall.) at 444-45, with references to the approving views of several prominent commentators.

[212]*Hylton*, 3 U.S. (3 Dall.) at 174 (Chase, J.), 179-80 (Paterson, J.), 181-83 (Iredell, J.), *restated in Soule*, 74 U.S. (7 Wall.) at 446 (Swayne, J.).

[213]*Hylton*, 3 U.S. (3 Dall.) at 180-81. Paterson had quoted Adam Smith's explanation: "[T]he state, not knowing how to tax directly and proportionally the revenue of its subjects, endeavors to tax it indirectly, by taxing their expense . . . ." *Id.* at 180 (quoting A. Smith, An Inquiry into the Nature and Causes of the Wealth of Nations 692 (J. McCulloch ed. London 1838) (1st ed. London 1776)). Counsel for the taxpayer in *Soule* not only invoked Smith; he stated an alternative interpretation that would also make sense of the term "direct" while arguably outlawing the income tax. "The ordinary test of the difference between *direct* and *indirect* taxes, is whether the tax falls ultimately on the tax-payer, or whether, through the tax-payer, it falls ultimately on the consumer." 74 U.S. (7 Wall.) at 437-38, 440 (argument of Mr.

More novel and more complicated was *Veazie Bank v. Fenno*,[214] an 1869 Chase decision upholding a prohibitive federal tax on state bank notes[215] against a variety of constitutional objections. The first issue was easy after *Soule:* on the basis of the tests employed in that case, this tax was not direct.[216] More troublesome was the argument, advanced by Nelson and Davis in dissent,[217] that the tax in effect was one on the states that had created the banks, and that it was thus forbidden by an implicit immunity analogous to the immunity of federal banks to state taxes recognized in *McCulloch v. Maryland*.[218] It was true that *McCulloch* had described this immunity in dictum as a one-way street: the supremacy clause operated only in favor of federal immunity, and the states were protected by their representation in Congress.[219] Yet the case for state immunity was arguably stronger than that for federal immunity in *McCulloch*: precisely because the supremacy clause worked only one way, the states could not protect themselves by legislation as Congress could protect its instrumentalities.[220]

Wills). For criticism of the *Hylton* opinions and a discussion of the meaning of "direct" taxes, see *supra* chapter 2.

For a discussion of *Farrington v. Saunders*, an unreported 1871 case in which the Court divided 4-4 over the validity of the cotton tax imposed by the Act of July 13, 1866, ch. 184 § 1, 14 Stat. 98, 98, see FAIRMAN, HISTORY, *supra* introduction to part four, note 2, at 883-95. Field, Nelson, and Clifford thought the cotton tax direct, probably on the basis of Paterson's suggestion in *Hylton*, 3 U.S. (3 Dall.) at 177, that a tax on "the immediate product of land" might be considered one on the land itself. FAIRMAN, HISTORY, *supra* introduction to part four, note 2, at 890. Davis, Nelson, and Clifford thought it a tax on exports forbidden by section 10 of article I of the Constitution, apparently because (as argued by counsel) so much cotton was exported. FAIRMAN, HISTORY, *supra* introduction to part four, note 2, at 884. Chase was absent. Counsel had also made the interesting argument that if the tax was not direct it violated the requirement that indirect taxes be "uniform throughout the United States," U.S. CONST. art I, § 8, because all cotton was grown in the South. FAIRMAN, HISTORY, *supra* note 4, at 885 (argument of former Justice Curtis). Compare a similar argument made by Justice Nelson in the commerce clause context. *See infra* chapter 10.

[214]75 U.S. (8 Wall.) 533 (1869); *see* FAIRMAN, HISTORY, *supra* introduction to part four, note 2, at 711-12; Dam, *supra* note 207, at 374-76.

[215]Act of July 13, 1866, ch. 184, § 9, cl. 2, 14 Stat. 98, 146 (repealed 1870). Similar notes had earlier been unsuccessfully attacked on the ground that they were bills of credit, which the states were forbidden by section 10 of article I to issue. Briscoe v. Bank of Kentucky, 36 U.S. (11 Pet.) 257 (1837); *see supra* chapter 7. The tax on them was part of Chase's pet project as Treasury Secretary to replace them with a federal currency based in large part on national-bank notes. *See* J. SCHUCKERS, *supra* introduction to part four, note 2, at 240-41, 296-97; Dam, *supra* note 207, at 375.

[216]75 U.S. (8 Wall.) at 540-47 (citing *Soule* and the passages it had quoted from *Hylton*). After pointing out that Congress had never imposed direct taxes on anything but land and slaves, the Court concluded:

> [i]t may further be taken as established upon the testimony of Paterson, that the words direct taxes, as used in the Constitution, comprehended only capitation taxes, and taxes on land, and perhaps taxes on personal property by general valuation and assessment of the various descriptions possessed within the several States.

Id. at 546.

[217]*Id.* at 554-56.

[218]17 U.S. (4 Wheat.) 316, 431-32 (1819) (Marshall, C.J.) ("[T]he power to tax involves the power to destroy"; to allow states to tax federal activities would make the federal Government "dependent on the States.").

[219]*Id.* at 428, 435.

[220]*See supra* chapter 6. The power of Congress to exempt federal securities from state taxation had in fact just been confirmed in another Chase opinion. *See* Bank v. Supervisors, 74 U.S. (7 Wall.) 26, 30-31 (1869); *infra* note 247.

The Court had already recognized this argument by holding in *Kentucky v. Dennison*[221] that Congress could not impose duties on state officers under the extradition clause; there seemed no reason not to apply the same reasoning to federal taxes, and the Court was soon to do so.[222] Indeed, the Court in *Veazie Bank* conceded the principle,[223] but insisted that the tax was on the banks' contracts and not on the process of governing.[224] This distinction would equally have sustained the state tax in *McCulloch*. A better basis of decision might have been that (in apparent contrast to the national bank in *McCulloch*) "[t]here was nothing in the case showing that [Veazie Bank] sustained any relation to the State as a financial agent, or that its authority to issue notes was conferred or exercised with any special reference to other than private interests."[225]

The final and most interesting argument in *Veazie Bank* was that the measure was a tax in form only; in substance it was an ill-disguised attempt to forbid the state banks to issue notes at all. Though there seems little doubt that this characterization was correct,[226] the Court piously said that the oppressiveness of a tax was no ground for holding it unconstitutional.[227] This was hardly an answer. Notwithstanding the reluctance Marshall had expressed to investigate legislative motive in *Fletcher v. Peck*,[228] he had cautioned in *McCulloch* that Congress could not invoke its powers as a "pretext" for interfering with matters reserved to the states.[229] As later Justices not known for judicial activism were to insist, a total refusal to investigate the motive or effect of a tax would make a mockery of the careful enumeration of limited federal

[221]65 U.S. (24 How.) 66, 107-10 (1861); *see supra* chapter 8.

[222]*See infra*, conclusion to part four (discussing Collector v. Day, 78 U.S. (11 Wall.) 113 (1871)).

[223]   It may be admitted that the reserved rights of the States, such as the right to pass laws, to give effect to laws through executive action, to administer justice through the courts, and to employ all necessary agencies for legitimate purposes of State government, are not proper subjects of the taxing power of Congress.

75 U.S. (8 Wall.) at 547.

[224]*Id.* at 547-48.

[225]This passage appears in the reporter's statement of the case, *id.* at 535, but not in the opinion itself. The argument that even the national bank had essentially served private interests had been made in *McCulloch* and ignored. *See supra* chapter 6, and authorities cited therein. The decision in Briscoe v. Bank of Kentucky, 36 U.S. (11 Pet.) 257 (1837); *see supra* note 215, that state bank notes were not those of the state for purposes of the bills of credit clause also lent some support to the decision that the tax in *Veazie Bank* was not one on the state. *See* 75 U.S. (8 Wall.) at 552 (Nelson, J., dissenting).

[226]*See* 75 U.S. (8 Wall.) at 556 (Nelson, J., dissenting):

[T]he purpose is scarcely concealed, in the opinion of the court, namely, to encourage the National banks. It is sufficient to add, that the burden of the tax, while it has encouraged these banks, has proved fatal to those of the States, and if we are at liberty to judge of the purpose of an act, from the consequences that have followed, it is not, perhaps, going too far to say, that these consequences were intended.

See also Dam, *supra* note 207, at 375 ("The power to tax was used with unprecedented effectiveness to destroy."). The rise of checking accounts not subject to the tax, however, substantially frustrated the congressional goal; in the long run the chief effect of the tax was to accelerate the movement from notes to checks as the principal medium of exchange. See J. WHITE, BANKING LAW 23 (1976).

[227]75 U.S. (8 Wall.) at 548.

[228]10 U.S. (6 Cranch) 87, 130 (1810); *see supra* chapter 5.

[229]17 U.S. (4 Wheat.) at 423. Also ignored in *Veazie Bank* was the apparent conclusion of the whole Court shortly before that the question in the test-oath cases was whether or not the legislature's intention had been to punish. *See supra* notes 33-43 and accompanying text.

powers recognized in *McCulloch:* Congress could effectively regulate anything it pleased simply by calling the price of action a tax instead of a penalty.[230] Yet Madison had noted in the Convention that taxes were often properly laid for ulterior reasons,[231] and Justice Robert Jackson later said with much force that it was impossible to formulate a tax law without making decisions about social or economic priorities.[232] Moreover, the First Congress, whose views have often and for good reason been given special deference,[233] had imposed discriminatory taxes to encourage American shipping.[234] Thus the question of motive in taxation scarcely seems to admit of such a simple answer as Chase offered in *Veazie Bank.*

In any event, Chase unnecessarily went on to announce an alternative ground that made it easier for later Justices to explain away his apparent conclusion that motive could not be investigated:[235] it was irrelevant, he said, whether Congress had attempted to outlaw state bank notes under the guise of taxing them, because Congress could have outlawed them directly.[236] Congress, wrote Chase, had undoubted authority "to provide a circulation of coin," and it was "settled by . . . uniform practice . . . and by repeated decisions, that Congress may constitutionally authorize the emission of bills of credit."[237] Having this power to "provide a currency, . . . Congress may . . . secure the benefit of it to the people by appropriate legislation."[238] Just as it had denied the status of legal tender to foreign coins and outlawed counterfeiting, Congress might therefore "restrain . . . the circulation as money of any notes not issued under its own authority. Without this power, indeed, its attempts to secure a sound and uniform currency for the country must be futile."[239]

All of this seems more than a little glib and was certainly generous in its interpretation of congressional power. The only explicit authority referred to was the power to coin money,[240] and, as the next important financial controversy was to show, there was considerable doubt whether that power even authorized the issuance of paper money,[241] much less empowered Congress to forbid state bank notes. Neither the constitutional source of the alleged power to issue bills of credit nor the alleged

---

[230]*See, e.g.,* United States v. Kahriger, 345 U.S. 22, 38 (1953) (Frankfurter, J., dissenting from the upholding of a tax on the business of accepting wagers); Child Labor Tax Case, 259 U.S. 20, 36-38 (1922) (Taft, C.J., joined by Holmes, J.) (striking down a prohibitive tax on goods manufactured by child labor); *cf.* 1 J. KENT, COMMENTARIES ON AMERICAN LAW 393-94 n.c. (4th ed. New York 1840) (1st ed. New York 1826) (arguing that taxes could be laid only for the purposes specified in article I, § 8: "to pay the Debts and provide for the common Defence and general Welfare of the United States").

[231]2 CONVENTION RECORDS, *supra* note 43, at 276 (discussing the clause forbidding the Senate to intitate revenue measures); *see also* J. STORY, *supra* note 40, at 430-440 (defending the validity of taxes laid for purposes other than collection of revenue).

[232]United States v. Kahriger, 345 U.S. 22, 35 (1953) (concurring opinion).

[233]*See, e.g., supra* chapter 4 (discussing Martin v. Hunter's Lessee, 14 U.S. (1 Wheat.) 304 (1816); *supra* chapter 6 (discussing *McCulloch*).

[234]Act of July 20, 1789, ch. 3, 1 Stat. 27 (repealed 1970).

[235]*See, e.g.,* Child Labor Tax Case, 259 U.S. 20, 41-42 (1922).

[236]75 U.S. (8 Wall.) at 548-49.

[237]*Id.* at 548.

[238]*Id.* at 549.

[239]*Id.* The dissenters did not discuss this issue.

[240]*Id.* at 548-49 (citing U.S. CONST. art I, § 8).

[241]*See infra* text accompanying notes 249-314 (discussing the legal-tender litigation).

decisions upholding it were cited.[242] The legislative precedent of the ban on counter-feit coins was of little use, since that had been authorized explicitly by article I,[243] and the necessity of outlawing state notes in order to "secure a sound and uniform currency," which was the heart of the argument, was stated as a bald conclusion. No allusion was made to the several Supreme Court precedents that would have been helpful: neither to *McCulloch*, with its broad test for necessity and propriety and its finding that the national bank was constitutional,[244] nor to the broad conclusions reached by the Taney court under the commerce clause,[245] nor to *United States v. Marigold*,[246] which upheld the power to outlaw the mere *passing* of counterfeit coins, nor to Chase's own decision in the preceding Term that Congress had power to immunize paper money from state taxation.[247] As in *Texas v. White*,[248] the Chief Justice seems to have been at pains to run roughshod over all possible objections and little concerned to give persuasive reasons for his debatable conclusions.

B.   Legal Tender

An even greater controversy over wartime financial policy reached the Court the same Term in *Hepburn v. Griswold*.[249] In a notorious split decision,[250] the Court, speaking through Chase, held that Congress had no power to make its paper money

[242]The Supreme Court decision closest to being on point was Bank v. Supervisors, 74 U.S. (7 Wall.) 26 (1869), upholding Congress's power to immunize paper money from state taxation, where Chase had said it was "not seriously questioned" in argument that the notes had been issued "as a means to ends entirely within the constitutional power of the government." *Id.* at 29.

[243]U.S. CONST. art. I, § 8 ("The Congress shall have Power . . . [t]o provide for the Punishment of counterfeiting the Securities and current Coin of the United States. . . .").

[244]17 U.S. (4 Wheat.) 316 (1819); *see supra* chapter 6.

[245]*See, e.g.*, Foster v. Davenport, 63 U.S. (22 How.) 244 (1859) (upholding licensing of lighters confined to Mobile harbor on the ground that they were servicing vessels engaged in interstate and foreign commerce); United States v. Coombs, 37 U.S. (12 Pet.) 72 (1838) (upholding power to punish theft of shipwrecked goods); *supra* chapters 7, 8.

[246]50 U.S. (9 How.) 560 (1850); *see supra* chapter 8.

[247]   [W]e think it clearly within the discretion of Congress to determine whether, in view of all the circumstances attending the issue of the notes, their usefulness, as a means of carrying on the government, would be enhanced by exemption from taxation; and within the constitutional power of Congress, having resolved the question of usefulness affirmatively, to provide by laws for such exemption.

Bank v. Supervisors, 74 U.S. (7 Wall.) 26, 30-31 (1869). Nothing had been cited in support of this conclusion either.

[248]*See supra* notes 174-206 and accompanying text.

[249]75 U.S. (8 Wall.) 603 (1870).

[250]Miller, Swayne, and Davis dissented; Nelson, Clifford, and Field joined Chase's opinion. For discussion of the lamentable circumstances surrounding the vacillating vote of the aged Grier, who was said to agree with the majority that the Act was invalid as applied to debts incurred before its passage, *id.* at 626, and of his resignation under pressure from his brethren before the decision was actually announced from the bench, see FAIRMAN, HISTORY, *supra* introduction to part four, note 2, at 716-19 (doubting that Grier really believed the law unconstitutional and chastising Chase for proceeding to decision with such a questionable majority). *See also id.* at 739 (quoting from a memorandum by Justice Miller: "'We do not say he did not agree to the opinion. We only ask, of what value was his concurrence, and of what value is the judgment under such circumstances?'"); FAIRMAN, MILLER, *supra* introduction to part four, note 2, at 164-66 (describing how Grier came to change his vote).

legal tender. The contrast with the latitudinarian approach of *Veazie Bank* was striking, and *Veazie Bank* was not even cited.[251]

In 1860, when only gold and silver coins were legal tender for debts, Hepburn gave Griswold a note promising to pay 11,250 "dollars." Two years later Congress authorized the issuance of paper money and declared it "a legal tender in payment of all debts, public and private."[252] Hepburn tendered payment in this paper money, which had depreciated in value;[253] the Supreme Court held Griswold did not have to accept it. The statute making paper money legal tender, wrote Chase—who as Lincoln's Secretary of Treasury had supported the measure[254]—was "not a means appropriate . . . to carry into effect any express power vested in Congress"; it was "inconsistent with the spirit of the Constitution"; and it was "prohibited by the Constitution" as well.[255]

The opinion begins by reaffirming the power of judicial review, repeating Marshall's arguments, in best Marshall style, without attribution.[256] It also intones, again without citation—and, the result suggests, without conviction—the familiar canon that "acts of Congress must be regarded as constitutional, unless clearly shown to be otherwise."[257] Moreover, said Chase in echo of *McCulloch v. Maryland*,[258] the

[251]Professor Fairman's *History* devotes a hundred pages to discussion of this controversy, clearly disapproving of much about Chase's conduct but commenting only obliquely on the constitutional merits. FAIRMAN, HISTORY, *supra* introduction to part four, note 2, at 677-775. An excellent early analysis of the legal issues is Thayer, *Legal Tender*, 1 HARV. L. REV. 73 (1887), *reprinted in* J. THAYER, LEGAL ESSAYS 60-90 (1908). For an enlightening explanation of the financial issues underlying the legislation, see Dam, *supra* note 207.

[252]Act of Feb. 25, 1862, ch. 33, § 1, 12 Stat. 345, 345. In earlier cases the Court had construed the Act narrowly so as to avoid the constitutional question. *See* Bronson v. Rodes, 74 U.S. (7 Wall.) 229, 249-50 (1869) (Chase, C.J.) (holding over Miller's dissent that a contractual obligation in "'dollars payable in gold and silver coin'" was not a "debt" within the tender provision but "an agreement to deliver a certain weight of standard gold"); Lane County v. Oregon, 74 U.S. (7 Wall.) 71, 77 (1869) (Chase, J.) (holding, in part because of a separate statutory reference to federal "taxes," that the "debts" for which the notes were made tender did not include state taxes, and adding that "it is not easy to see upon what principle the national legislature *can* interfere with the exercise" of state power to tax (emphasis added)). The tender issue had also been expressly reserved in Bank v. Supervisors, 74 U.S. (7 Wall.) 26, 29-30 (1869), where the notes were held immune from state taxation. In *Hepburn* itself, Chase found the statutory terms too clear to permit holding them applicable only to future contracts, despite the principle that laws "are not to receive an interpretation which conflicts with acknowledged principles of justice and equity, if another sense, consonant with those principles, can be given to them." 75 U.S. (8 Wall.) at 606-10. Grier alone disagreed. *See id.* at 626.

[253]75 U.S. (8 Wall.) at 608.

[254]*See* FAIRMAN, HISTORY, *supra* introduction to part four, note 2, at 684-87. In *Hepburn*, Chase adverted obliquely to his change of heart, contrasting "patriotic" acquiescence by "many" "amid the tumult of the late civil war" with "considerate reflection" "under the influence of the calmer time." 75 U.S. (8 Wall.) at 625-26. Later, when his earlier advocacy was used against him by a new majority, he acknowledged it expressly (though in the third person) and said bravely enough that "[e]xamination and reflection under more propitious circumstances have satisfied him that this opinion was erroneous . . . ." Legal Tender Cases, 79 U.S. (12 Wall.) 457, 576 (1871) (dissenting opinion).

[255]75 U.S. (8 Wall.) at 625. Though the only question before the Court was retroactive application of the law, the first of Chase's arguments seemed strongly to imply that the Act could not be applied prospectively either; he so argued in the later Legal Tender Cases, 79 U.S. (12 Wall.) 457, 582-86 (1871) (dissenting opinion).

[256]75 U.S. (8 Wall.) at 610-12; *see* Marbury v. Madison, 5 U.S. (1 Cranch) 137 (1803).

[257]75 U.S. (8 Wall.) at 610.

[258]17 U.S. (4 Wheat.) 316, 407-12 (1819).

necessary and proper clause confirmed that Congress had "extensive" powers "in-cidental" to "the exercise of the powers expressly granted," and "a very large part, if not the largest part," of federal functions "have been performed in the exercise of powers thus implied."[259] Neither the necessary and proper clause nor the tenth amendment, he persuasively emphasized, "is to be taken as restricting any exercise of power fairly warranted by legitimate derivation from one of the enumerated or express powers."[260] The test of whether a law went beyond congressional authority, he concluded, was that laid down in *McCulloch:* "'Let the end be legitimate, let it be within the scope of the Constitution, and all means which are appropriate, which are plainly adapted to that end, which are not prohibited, but consistent with the letter and spirit of the Constitution, are constitutional.'"[261]

Applying this test, Chase first concluded that paper tender was not an "appropri-ate" means of carrying out any of Congress's enumerated powers. The power to "coin money," he said, quite without elaboration, applied only to "the precious metals."[262] This brusque treatment may strike the modern reader as surprisingly literal; the Court has not taken the copyright clause's reference to "Writing,"[263] for example, as limited to the written word.[264] Throughout the legal tender litigation, however, proponents of the paper money placed little emphasis on the coinage clause; while we may have wished for a better explanation, it seems that the obvious differences between coins and promises illustrated elsewhere in the opinion[265] were understood at the time to have made the choice of the term "coin" a deliberately narrow one.[266] But if this was so, a respectable argument could have been made that the coinage clause by negative implication *forbade* Congress to issue paper money.[267] Though later opinions did invoke this contention against the law,[268] they did not give

---

[259]75 U.S. (8 Wall.) at 613.

[260]*Id.* at 613-14. Both clauses, wrote Chase, were "admonitory," leaving no room to doubt either that Congress had incidental powers or that those powers were limited. *Id.* at 614. Marshall had said as much in *McCulloch* as well. *See* 17 U.S. (4 Wheat.) at 406, 420-21. Contrast the later statement in Hammer v. Dagenhart, 247 U.S. 251 (1918), properly repudiated in United States v. Darby, 312 U.S. 10, 115-17 (1941), that an act forbidding interstate traffic in goods made by child labor "in a two-fold sense is repugnant to the Constitution. It not only transcends the authority delegated to Congress over commerce but also exerts a power as to a purely local matter to which the federal authority does not extend." 247 U.S. at 276.

[261]75 U.S. (8 Wall.) at 614 (quoting 17 U.S. (4 Wheat.) at 421). For a discussion of this test, see *supra* chapter 6.

[262]75 U.S. (8 Wall.) at 615-16.

[263]U.S. Const. art. I, § 8.

[264]*See, e.g.,* Burrow-Giles Lithograph Co. v. Sarony, 111 U.S. 53 (1884) (Miller, J.), *infra* chapter 13 (holding photographs protected).

[265]*See* 75 U.S. (8 Wall.) at 608 (observing that the value of tender notes "sank in July, 1864, to the rate of two dollars and eighty-five cents for a dollar in gold").

[266]Miller conceded in dissent that the coinage provision did not itself support making paper tender. *Id.* at 627.

[267]See the argument of O. W. Holmes, Jr., in a note to 1 J. Kent, Commentaries on American Law 272 n.1 (12th ed. 1873) (1st ed. New York 1826): "[I]f the Constitution says expressly that Congress shall have power to make metallic legal tender, how can it be taken to say by implication that Congress shall have power to make paper money legal tender?" Holmes had first made this argument in 4 Am. L. Rev. 768 (1870). *See* Fairman, History, *supra* introduction to part four, note 2, at 715.

[268]*E.g.,* Legal Tender Cases, 79 U.S. (12 Wall.) 457, 624 (1871) (Field, J., dissenting); *see infra* note 313.

it especial prominence,[269] and Chase, who made a variety of arguments, did not mention it at all.[270]

The argument that Chase did take seriously was that paper tender was necessary and proper to the exercise of the war powers, of the commerce power, and of the power to borrow money.[271] No one doubted, he conceded, that Congress could issue ordinary bills of credit as paper money to facilitate the exercise of these powers, though unfortunately he did not bother to spell out why.[272] But the fact that at the

[269]In *McCulloch* Marshall had rejected the parallel argument that by authorizing Congress to make certain acts criminal the Framers had implicitly forbidden it to criminalize others, 17 U.S. (4 Wheat.) at 416-17, and the Court had confirmed Marshall's conclusion in United States v. Marigold, 50 U.S. (9 How.) 560 (1850) (upholding a ban on the passing of counterfeit coins). The analogy is not decisive since the Framers may have had different reasons for including the coinage and counterfeiting clauses; but the Court nonetheless made effective use of it when *Hepburn* was overruled. Legal Tender Cases, 79 U.S. (12 Wall.) 457, 536-37, 544-47 (1871). For further arguments against the negative implication, see Thayer, *supra* note 251, at 83-88, *reprinted in* J. THAYER, *supra* note 251, at 73-79, observing that the coinage clause was thought neither to preclude ordinary bills of credit nor make coins legal tender.

[270]Nor did Chase, like his dissenting brethren Field and Clifford in the case overruling *Hepburn*, Legal Tender Cases, 79 U.S. (12 Wall.) 457, 587, 635 (1871); *see infra* note 313, rely on the Convention's rejection of a proposal (taken from article 9 of the Articles of Confederation) to authorize Congress explicitly to "emit bills on the credit of the United States," 2 CONVENTION RECORDS *supra* note 43, at 182. Professor Dam argues that, by omitting express authority, the Framers meant to prohibit bills of credit as contrasted with promissory notes, just as they had in the case of the states in article I, § 10. *See* Dam, *supra* note 207, at 382-90; Craig v. Missouri, 29 U.S. (4 Pet.) 410, 431-32 (1830). In support of this argument, Dam relies largely on a private note by Madison explaining to posterity (but not to his colleagues) his own vote ("[S]triking out the words," wrote Madison, "would not disable the Govt [*sic*] from the use of *public notes* as far as they could be safe & proper & would only cut off the pretext for a paper *currency* and particularly for making the bills a tender," *id.* at 310 note (emphasis added)). Madison, however, spoke only for himself. As Professor Thayer long ago pointed out, Thayer, *supra* note 251, at 74-78, *reprinted in* J. THAYER, *supra* note 251, at 61-67, though Mason and apparently others agreed with Madison that Congress "would not have the power unless it were expressed," Gorham of Massachusetts ("Ghorum" in Madison's notes) argued "for striking out, without inserting any prohibition," so as not to encourage Congress to act lightly; Gorham believed that "[t]he power as far as it will be necessary or safe, is involved in that of borrowing." 2 CONVENTION RECORDS, *supra* note 43, at 309. Thus, despite Professor Dam's persuasive reading of Madison's own position, Justice Bradley seems right that the language was "struck out with diverse views of members," Legal Tender Cases, 79 U.S. (12 Wall.) 457, 559 (1871) (concurring opinion), and that, like the Framers' rejection of an explicit power of incorporation, *id.*, the omission does not demonstrate that the Convention as a whole thought it was prohibiting what it declined to authorize expressly—even if such an intention would be the equivalent of an express prohibition. *See* FAIRMAN, MILLER, *supra* introduction to part four, note 2 at 159 ("[T]his was not a vote to forbid the issue of notes, since it was concurred in by several members who had made it clear that they were opposed to an absolute prohibition."). Moreover, as both Thayer and Dam pointed out, the argument from the omitted proposal proves too much: what was stricken was authority to issue bills of credit at all, not merely to make them legal tender. *See* Dam, *supra* note 207, at 389-90; Thayer, *supra* note 251, at 78-80, *reprinted in* J. THAYER, *supra* note 251, at 67-69. Congress had been issuing bills with general acquiescence since the War of 1812, and neither Chase nor any other Justice questioned their constitutionality. *See Hepburn*, 75 U.S. at 616; *supra* notes 237-38 and accompanying text (discussing Veazie Bank v. Fenno, 75 U.S. (8 Wall.) 533 (1869)).

[271]75 U.S. (8 Wall.) at 616-17.

[272]*Id.* at 616, 619 (adding without citation that the Court had recently so held). The reference was apparently to Bank v. Supervisors, 74 U.S. (7 Wall.) 26 (1869), and to Veazie Bank v. Fenno, 75 U.S. (8 Wall.) 533 (1869); *see supra* text accompanying notes 241-42, where the question had not been argued. *See also* Legal Tender Cases, 79 U.S. (12 Wall.) 457, 574-75 (1871) (Chase, C.J., dissenting) (explaining that *Veazie Bank* had based the authority to issue bills on the borrowing power, with additional currency powers derived from the commerce clause).

same time other notes that were not legal tender "circulated freely and without discount" was strong "evidence that all the useful purposes of the notes would have been fully answered without making them a legal tender for pre-existing debts."[273] In any event, it was by no means clear "that any appreciable advantage is gained by compelling creditors to receive them in satisfaction of *pre-existing* debts,"[274] as in *Hepburn;* and furthermore,

> whatever benefit is possible is far more than outweighed by the losses of property, the derangement of business, the fluctuations of currency and values, and the increase of prices to the people and the government, and the long train of evils which flow from the use of irredeemable paper money.[275]

This was a clever argument, and not wholly unconvincing; if the tender provision did not facilitate government operations, it could hardly be "necessary" even in the loose sense employed by Marshall.[276] On closer scrutiny, however, Chase's argument begins to fall apart. In the first place, he was judging the legal-tender law in hindsight; he seemed to be saying that every law that failed to accomplish its purpose also fell outside the necessary and proper clause. One would have thought the question was whether the measure appeared necessary at the time of its adoption,[277] and on that basis one might think that Congress was within its rights in expecting that people would be likely to accept paper money at a smaller discount if their creditors would have to accept it too.[278] Besides, Chase admitted that his evidence of the inutility of tender was somewhat flawed; since the nontender notes that had retained a value comparable to that of tender notes had been exchangeable for them, one may be skeptical of his easy conclusion that they derived their desirability essentially from the government's promise to receive them in satisfaction of public dues.[279] More

[273]75 U.S. (8 Wall.) at 620.

[274]*Id.* at 621 (emphasis added).

[275]*Id.* For discussion of the adverse effects of the tender legislation, see FAIRMAN, HISTORY, *supra* introduction to part four, note 2, at 690-91.

[276]Indeed, Chase came close to saying that tender did not even meet the still more lenient test that Marshall had employed in the earlier case of United States v. Fisher, 6 U.S. (2 Cranch) 358, 396 (1805) ("Congress must possess the choice of means, and must be empowered to use any means which are in fact conducive to the exercise of a power granted by the constitution."), since a measure that is wholly useless is not even "conducive" to the exercise of a granted power.

[277]*See* FAIRMAN, MILLER, *supra* introduction to part four, note 2, at 162 ("[I]t is not good constitutional law to say that a measure is invalid because we see it worked out badly."). For a contemporaneous criticism on the same ground, see 4 AM. L. REV. 586, 606-09 (1870).

[278]*See* 75 U.S. (8 Wall.) at 634 (Miller, J., dissenting); *see also* Legal Tender Cases, 79 U.S. (12 Wall.) 457, 543 (1871) (Strong, J.). This argument, moreover, seems as applicable to old debts as to new ones: the more creditors are required to accept paper money, the more likely it is that its owner can realize its full value. *See* Thayer, *supra* note 251, at 94, *reprinted in* J. THAYER, *supra* note 251, at 87 ("To make the currency do the usual office of money more effectually and fully, is legitimate regulation of the currency."). Professor Dam, however, is dubious: "[N]ot every new use increases value . . . . [I]t is, of course, an empirical question." Dam, *supra* note 207, at 393.

[279]75 U.S. (8 Wall.) at 620. Professor Dam, who finds Chase's conclusion (as later repeated by Field, Legal Tender Cases, 79 U.S. (12 Wall.) 457, 647 (1871) (dissenting opinion)) "compelling," does not advert to this fact. Dam *supra* note 207, at 393-94, 409. Professor Dam persuasively argues, however, that the real necessity for making the notes tender was to protect the banks from having to pay out gold or keep

fundamentally, the Chief Justice's assumption that the test was whether the same goal could have been accomplished without paper tender[280] seemed to contradict Marshall's insistence that a measure could be "necessary" without being indispensable;[281] as Miller noted in dissent,[282] there was nothing in *McCulloch* to suggest that Congress must choose the least intrusive means.[283] Finally, in balancing the utility of the tender provision against its adverse effects on property and financial stability, Chase, without authority or explanation, added a brand new and debatable dimension to the Marshall calculus he purported to be applying: he seems to have read the requirement that a law be "proper" to demand that its benefits outweigh its costs—in the eyes, of course, of the judges.[284]

Having amply if unconvincingly disposed of the case on the ground that paper tender for existing debts was not an "appropriate" means of effectuating any express congressional power, Chase imitated Marshall once again by going on to find two additional grounds for his conclusions. The first, once more purporting to apply the passage from *McCulloch* already quoted,[285] was that the tender law offended the "spirit" of the Constitution. One of the "cardinal principles" of that document, Chase wrote without citing the preamble in which the phrase appeared, was "the establishment of justice."[286] What was "just," in turn, was indicated in part by the clause forbidding the states to impair the obligation of contracts.[287] Although that clause did not itself limit the authority of Congress, its spirit was meant to "pervade the entire body of legislation"; "a law not made in pursuance of an express power, which necessarily and in its direct operation impairs the obligation of contracts, is inconsistent with the spirit of the Constitution."[288] The same was true of the fifth amendment ban on the taking of property for public use without just compensation,

---

gold in reserve—and thus was to prevent the collapse of the banks. *Id.* at 405-08; *see also id.* at 410 ("Collapse of the big city banks, which were in early 1862 the Treasury's indispensable link with the financial markets, might well have led to the collapse of the Union. Or at least a Court sitting in 1862 might reasonably have so feared.").

[280]*See, e.g., supra* text accompanying note 273.

[281]McCulloch v. Maryland, 17 U.S. (4 Wheat.) 316, 414 (1819) (contrasting the provision in article I § 10 forbidding all state import duties not "absolutely necessary" for the execution of inspection laws); *id.* at 424 (rejecting the relevance of Congress's option of relying on state banks); *cf.* Dam, *supra* note 207, at 411 ("[E]ven if the bonds could have been sold directly to the public for specie, Congress was not required to use this constitutionally less offensive method . . . .").

[282]75 U.S. (8 Wall.) at 628-31.

[283]It is also striking that Chase nowhere attempted to compare the necessity of the tender law with that of other measures that had been upheld in the past; as Miller argued, it is not obvious that tender was appreciably less necessary to the powers invoked than was either the national bank or the tax on state notes that Chase himself had voted to uphold the same term in Veazie Bank v. Fenno, 75 U.S. (8 Wall.) 533 (1869).

[284]*See supra* notes 274-75 and accompanying text. Without citing it, Chase properly rejected Marshall's position that it was for Congress alone to determine "the degree of . . . necessity" of any measure "really calculated to effect any of the objects entrusted to the government," *McCulloch*, 17 U.S. (4 Wheat.) at 423, which threatened to eliminate judicial review af any measure adopted under the necessary and proper clause. *Hepburn*, 75 U.S. (8 Wall.) at 617-18.

[285]*See supra* text accompanying note 261.

[286]75 U.S. (8 Wall.) at 622.

[287]*Id.* at 623 (quoting U.S. Const. art. I, § 10).

[288]*Id.*

which did apply to Congress: "If such property cannot be taken for the benefit of all, . . . it is difficult to understand how it can be so taken for the benefit of a part without violating the spirit of the prohibition."[289]

One is tempted to protest with Miller[290] that the contract clause, like the legal-tender clause of the same section, applied only to the states, that it was not even clear that property had been "taken" in the constitutional sense, and that "justice" was an open-ended notion that would allow judges to pass upon the wisdom of every law. One is tempted to add that the preamble is at best a guide to interpreting clauses with teeth in them, and that the supremacy clause requires acceptance of statutes that comply with the provisions of the Constitution without regard to its "spirit."[291] Yet Chase's position does not seem to have been that the Court may disregard all unjust laws.[292] He explicitly purported to apply Marshall's test for measures adopted under the necessary and proper clause, and in explaining why a federal bankruptcy law would not offend his principles he expressly distinguished laws passed under Congress's express powers.[293] In effect, as he had earlier construed the word "proper" to require that laws incidental to express powers be utilitarian,[294] so he now construed it to require that they also be just. Moreover, he qualified even that relatively modest conclusion by professing to find the content of "justice" not in general notions of propriety but in analogous constitutional provisions. Finally, Chase appeared superficially to have impressive support for his restrictive reading of the term "proper," for Marshall had said in the famous *McCulloch* passage quoted above that a law was not necessary and proper unless it satisfied the "spirit" as well as the terms of the Constitution.[295]

Nevertheless, there are grave objections to Chase's reasoning. First, by failing to tie his arguments to the words "necessary and proper," Chase left the door open for a later argument that his decision had established the general power of the courts to invalidate unjust legislation, and he nowhere said "justice" was to be found *solely* in analogous provisions.[296] More fundamentally, he never explained why he thought "proper" should for the first time be construed, as it need not have been, to mean

---

[289]*Id.* at 623-24.

[290]*Id.* at 627, 637-38 (dissenting opinion).

[291]*See supra* chapter 2 (discussing Calder v. Bull, 3 U.S. (3 Dall.) 386 (1798)); *supra* chapter 5 (discussing Fletcher v. Peck, 10 U.S. (6 Cranch) 87 (1810)). Moreover, if one were free to look at the "spirit" rather than the text of the governing provisions, one might as convincingly argue that the purpose of the enumerated powers in article I was to authorize Congress, as Randolph had proposed, 1 CONVENTION RECORDS, *supra* note 43, at 21, to deal with all subjects of national concern, which surely included deciding what would be legal tender. Yet the choice of specific provisions over general ones seems to have been deliberate. *See also* Thayer, *supra* note 251, at 89-91, *reprinted in* J. THAYER, *supra* note 251, at 80-83.

[292]Speaking in dissent in the Legal Tender Cases, 79 U.S. (12 Wall.) 457 (1871), when *Hepburn* was overruled, see *infra* note 313, Field did invoke the natural-law utterances of his predecessors, apparently as a limitation on any exercise of congressional power. Chase invoked them too in a separate dissent in the later case, but apparently for a more limited purpose. *See infra* note 296.

[293]75 U.S. (8 Wall.) at 623.

[294]*See supra* note 284 and accompanying text.

[295]*See supra* text accompanying note 261.

[296]The next Term, in dissent, he defined "justice" by reference to the natural-law musings of Marshall and of the earlier Justice Chase. *See* Legal Tender Cases, 79 U.S. (12 Wall.) 457, 581-82 (1871) (Chase, C.J., dissenting).

"just." Though Marshall had encouraged such an interpretation by his reference to the "spirit" of the Constitution, he had expressly (if not very convincingly) argued that "proper" was not a second and more stringent requirement but served instead to ameliorate the degree of necessity that might otherwise have been required.[297] The context suggests that what Marshall meant by his "spirit" reference was that the necessary and proper clause was part of an enumeration designed to give Congress only limited authority and thus should not be read so expansively as to defeat the purpose of the enumeration itself.[298] It was a substantial step beyond that position for Chase to equate "proper" with conformity to the purposes underlying distinct provisions that the Framers had expressly made inapplicable to the case before him.

Beyond the foregoing argument, Chase found yet a third ground on which to declare the tender law unconstitutional: it deprived creditors of their property without due process of law, in violation of the fifth amendment.[299] This was the second time this thesis had surfaced in the Supreme Court. The first was in the *Dred Scott* case, on which Chase understandably neglected to rely; there Chief Justice Taney, apparently speaking for less than a majority of the Justices,[300] had said quite without explanation that for Congress to provide that a man lost his property in slaves by bringing them across a territorial line "could hardly be dignified with the name of due process of law."[301] Chase did no better in *Hepburn*: contracts were property, the loss of value was "direct and inevitable," and, "whatever may be the operation of" the tender act, "due process of law makes no part of it."[302] What due process meant he made no effort to say,[303] and it was no clearer then than it had been at the time of *Scott*—except for the uncited precedent itself—that the clause was meant to outlaw substantively arbitrary legislation.[304] Furthermore, as with the question of the taking clause, it was not certain that there had been a "deprivation": the next Term a new majority was to say, again without adequate demonstration, that both clauses applied "only to a direct appropriation, and not to consequential injuries resulting from the exercise of lawful power."[305] Finally, the equation of

---

[297]*McCulloch*, 17 U.S. (4 Wheat.) at 418-19. Yet another possibility is that "proper" meant "not contrary to limitations found in other provisions of this Constitution," such as the ex post facto clause. "Proper" is a peculiarly vague and uninformative word with which to express that idea, and to modern eyes this interpretation makes the word redundant. Moreover, if the Framers thought this point needed explicit statement, one would expect them to have added "proper" to other grants of congressional power (*e.g.*, the commerce clause) as well.

[298]*See supra* chapter 6. As Miller pointed out in dissent, legal tender could scarcely be considered "an invasion of the rights reserved to the States," since it was "among the subjects of legislation forbidden to the States" by article I, § 10. 75 U.S. (8 Wall.) at 627.

[299]75 U.S. (8 Wall.) at 624-25.

[300]*See supra* chapter 8.

[301]Scott v. Sandford, 60 U.S. (19 How.) 393, 450 (1857); *see supra* chapter 8.

[302]75 U.S. (8 Wall.) at 624.

[303]In contrast to later cases, there was no suggestion that a strong state interest might justify the alleged deprivation. *Cf.* Lochner v. New York, 198 U.S. 45 (1905) (finding "no reasonable foundation for holding" a limitation on work hours "to be necessary or appropriate as a health law"); Munn v. Illinois, 94 U.S. 113 (1877) (upholding regulation of rates of grain elevators "'affected with a public interest'" "when such regulation becomes necessary for the public good").

[304]*See supra* chapter 8 (discussing Scott v. Sandford, 60 U.S. (19 How.) 393 (1857)).

[305]Legal Tender Cases, 79 U.S. (12 Wall.) 457, 551 (1871). Miller had argued in his *Hepburn* dissent that Chase's reasoning would preclude a declaration of war or abolition of a tariff, since the former would

contract with property was at least as slippery and dangerous as the converse feat Marshall had performed in holding a taking of property impaired the contract by which it had been granted; and Marshall had at least come up with plausible reasons for his conclusion.[306] All Chase told us was that "[a] very large proportion of the property of civilized men exists in the form of contracts,"[307] which is only to say that they represent much of what is of value; in every law school contract and property are the subjects of separate courses, and there was room for a historical argument that the phrase, "life, liberty, and property" referred to the losses traditionally inflicted as punishment for crime.[308]

Justice Miller's concise and readable dissent, joined by Swayne and Davis, said most of the right things.[309] The very next Term, following the retirement of the decrepit Grier[310] and the appointment of the Republicans Strong and Bradley,[311] Justice Strong said them well again,[312] this time for a 5-to-4 majority, in the *Legal Tender Cases*;[313] *Hepburn v. Griswold* was formally overruled.[314]

"lessen[ ]" "the value of every ship" and the latter "sink the capital employed in the manufacture" of articles previously subject to duties. 75 U.S. (8 Wall.) at 637 (dissenting opinion). Chase conceded the principle but disputed its application: while the issuance of a manufacturing charter causes only a "contingent and incidental" injury to competitors, the loss to creditors in the tender cases was "direct and inevitable." *Id.* at 624. The ease with which the distinction between "direct" and "incidental" effects could be employed to support either result suggests it was little more than a label for the judges' independent conclusions.

[306]Fletcher v. Peck, 10 U.S. (6 Cranch) 87, 136-37 (1810); *see supra* chapter 5.

[307]75 U.S. (8 Wall.) at 624.

[308]*See* Shattuck, *The True Meaning of the Term "Liberty" in Those Clauses in the Federal and State Constitutions Which Protect "Life, Liberty, and Property,"* 4 HARV. L. REV. 365 (1890).

[309]75 U.S. (8 Wall.) at 626-39.

[310]*See supra* note 250.

[311]For rejection of the contention that President Grant packed the Court in order to assure the overruling of *Hepburn*, see 2 C. WARREN, *supra* introduction to part four, note 2, at 516-19.

[312]As a state judge in Pennsylvania, Strong had already written an opinion upholding the legislation. Shollenberger v. Brinton, 52 Pa. 9, 56 (1866). There is a decided flavor in his Supreme Court opinion of Marshall's emphasis on the intolerable consequences of an adverse decision. He began by saying that if there were no authority to issue paper tender the government would be "without those means of self-preservation which, all must admit, may, in certain contingencies, become indispensable." 79 U.S. (12 Wall.) at 529. Once this was said, it was pretty clear what the result would be, for the Framers could hardly have meant to create a government whose powers were not adequate to deal with foreseeable emergencies. This sort of argument makes interpretation of the actual provisions supererogatory; as Chase came close to saying all bad laws were unconstitutional, so Strong seemed to hint that all good laws were valid. *See supra* chapters 3,4 (discussing Marbury v. Madison, 5 U.S. (1 Cranch) 137 (1803), and Cohens v. Virginia, 19 U.S. (6 Wheat.) 264 (1821)).

Strong may also be faulted for declining to specify to which of the enumerated powers the tender laws were necessary and proper, though he dilated at length upon the degree of their necessity for the good of the country. In this discussion he did stress the war effort and the need to raise money for government expenditures, so that we may say he implicitly related tender to the war powers and to the borrowing of money. At another point, however, he expressly said it was not necessary that the measure be ancillary to any one of the specified powers; it was "allowable to group together any number of them and infer from them all that the power claimed has been conferred." 79 U.S. (12 Wall.) at 534. Technically, this conclusion may be unobjectionable, but it seems to suggest a leniency in reviewing congressional actions that borders on no review at all.

Finally, as Field pointed out in dissent, 79 U.S. (12 Wall.) at 664-66, Strong was on dangerous ground in arguing, *id.* at 534-35, that the existence of the Bill of Rights implied that Congress had broad powers not expressly listed in the Constitution; it was to preclude the inference that a particular power was

One of the principal lessons of this episode is how little general statements of governing principles contribute to the outcome of particular cases. The opinions on both sides of the legal tender controversy faithfully echoed Marshall's tests for determining the validity of laws passed under the necessary and proper clause, and in so doing they reached diametrically opposite results. It seems reasonably clear that it was the second legal tender decision that more accurately captured the spirit of Marshall's formulation; *Hepburn v. Griswold*, like *Scott v. Sandford*, was an aberration in a history of generally sympathetic interpretation of the affirmative grants of congressional power. *Hepburn*'s due process holding, on the other hand, while flatly repudiated in the *Legal Tender Cases* and later ignored, was the harbinger of an idea whose time was to come again.

In dealing with the great issues arising out of the Civil War and its aftermath, the Court revealed deep divisions, sometimes along party lines. Congress and the President did not always get their way: the majority rejected both military trials and test oaths and originally rejected legal tender as well, and despite its efforts to avoid an ultimate confrontation over Reconstruction the Court managed in *United States v. Klein* to set significant though poorly defined limits to Congress's power to destroy the Court's own essential functions. All the wartime financial measures, however, eventually passed muster; and in *Texas v. White*, Chase finally succeeded in writing most of the Radical philosophy of Reconstruction into the Constitution.

---

authorized because others were prohibited that the ninth amendment provided that "[t]he enumeration in the Constitution, of certain rights, shall not be construed to deny or disparage others retained by the people." U.S. CONST. amend. IX; 1 ANNALS OF CONG. 456 (J. Gales ed. 1789) (statement of Mr. Madison); *supra* chapter 2.

Justice Bradley, whose concurring opinion, 79 U.S. (12 Wall.) at 554-70, showed off his historical knowledge without adding much of substance, did discuss the Convention history and even more brazenly spoke out for Congress's essentially unlimited powers: the federal government was "invested with all those inherent and implied powers which, at the time of adopting the Constitution, were generally considered to belong to every government as such, and as being essential to the exercise of its functions." *Id.* at 556.

[313]79 U.S. (12 Wall.) 457 (1871). Chase's dissent, *id.* at 570-87, joined by Clifford, Field, and Nelson, restated most of his arguments from *Hepburn*, adding references to the Convention and to United States v. Dewitt, 76 U.S. (9 Wall.) 41 (1870), where the Court had struck down a law regulating the inflammability of oil not passing in interstate or foreign commerce on the ground that any impact of the law on taxes was too remote to make the measure necessary and proper to the taxing power. Clifford wrote nearly fifty pages, 79 U.S. (12 Wall.) at 587-634, and remarkably managed to add essentially nothing beyond another discussion of the Convention history. *See* Currie, *The Most Insignificant Justice*, 50 U. CHI. L. REV. 466, 474-77 (1983). Field's equally lengthy offering, 79 U.S. (12 Wall.) at 634-81, detailed the Convention history, drew a negative inference from the coinage power, and invoked the natural law passages of Fletcher v. Peck, 10 U.S. (6 Cranch) 87 (1810), and of Calder v. Bull, 3 U.S. (3 Dall.) 386 (1798). Significantly, in light of Field's later opinions, *e.g.*, Munn v. Illinois, 94 U.S. 113, 136 (1877) (dissenting opinion), he did not mention due process. Nelson, as usual, was mercifully silent. *Cf. supra*, chapter 7 (discussing the License Cases, 46 U.S. (5 How.) 504 (1847), and the Passenger Cases, 48 U.S. (7 How.) 283 (1849)).

[314]79 U.S. (12 Wall.) at 553. For criticism of Chase's efforts to preclude reconsideration of the issue by invoking an apparently fictitious agreement that the outcome of other cases would be governed by *Hepburn* and an inapplicable principle limiting the reopening of judgments in cases already decided, see FAIRMAN, HISTORY, *supra* introduction to part four, note 2, at 738-52.

10

Limitations on State Power

The Civil War and Reconstruction cases considered in the preceding chapter were the most prominent feature of the constitutional work of the Supreme Court during the time of Chief Justice Chase. There remain for discussion not only the celebrated *Slaughter-House Cases*, in which a sharply divided Court wrestled for the first time with the construction of the amendments adopted in response to the war, but a plethora of other decisions, most of which also dealt with limitations on the powers of the states.

I. The Commerce Clause

In 1851, after years of haggling,[1] a majority of the Justices had agreed, in the famous case of *Cooley v. Board of Wardens*, that the commerce clause of article I, though phrased simply as a grant of authority to Congress, implicitly precluded the states from enacting laws on commercial "subjects" that were "in their nature national, or admit only one uniform system, or plan of regulation."[2] In *Cooley* itself, however, the challenged state law had been upheld. In the remaining fourteen years of Chief Justice Taney's tenure, moreover, despite frequent opportunities, the *Cooley* doctrine had never again been mentioned, and no state law had been struck down explicitly on the basis of the commerce clause.[3] It was during Chase's tenure that the Court resuscitated *Cooley* and first made the negative effect of the clause a reality.[4]

---

[1] *See supra* chapters 6, 7.

[2] 53 U.S. (12 How.) 298, 319 (1852) (upholding state regulation of pilotage).

[3] *See supra* chapter 7.

[4] *See* Pomeroy, *The Power of Congress to Regulate Inter-State Commerce,* 4 S.L. Rev. (n.s.) 357, 358 (1878) ("The entire subject was, for a long time, tacitly surrendered to the domain of the individual states . . . . The last fifteen years, however, have witnessed a complete revolution both in opinion and in practice.").

The road the Court traveled in so doing was by no means smooth; the confused body of decisions handed down in this field by Chase and his brethren suggests the depth of the can of worms that *Cooley* had opened up and that we have never since succeeded in closing.

A. *Gilman v. Philadelphia*

The Court's first significant encounter with the commerce clause after Chase's appointment came in 1866 in *Gilman v. Philadelphia*,[5] in which a wharf owner attacked a Pennsylvania statute authorizing the construction of a bridge over the Schuylkill River that would prevent vessels from reaching his dock.[6] In upholding the law,[7] Justice Swayne relied principally upon Marshall's cryptic opinion in *Willson v. Black Bird Creek Marsh Co.*,[8] which had similarly permitted a state, in the absence of congressional action, to obstruct a navigable stream. As the three dissenters in *Gilman* observed, it was not at all clear that Congress had not acted.[9] More important for present purposes, *Gilman* represented a significant extension of the *Willson* case and a sharp turn away from the attitude apparently expressed in *Cooley*.

In the first place, as Clifford noted in dissent,[10] Marshall had spoken of the creek in

[5]70 U.S. (3 Wall.) 713 (1866).

[6]The year before, the Court had divided 4-4, without opinions, over the legality of a bridge over the Hudson. The Albany Bridge Case, 69 U.S. (2 Wall.) 403 (1865), *noted in* 6 C. FAIRMAN, HISTORY OF THE SUPREME COURT OF THE UNITED STATES 51 (1971). *Cooley* itself had been reaffirmed in Steamship Co. v. Joliffe, 69 U.S. (2 Wall.) 450 (1865) (Field, J.), despite the passage of a federal statute purporting to license pilots and to replace the existing system of pilotage; over the dissents of Miller, Wayne, and Clifford, *id.* at 463, four Justices concluded that the statute referred only "to pilots having charge of steamers on the voyage, and not to port pilots," *id.* at 461. *Cooley* was reaffirmed once more in an unduly wordy Swayne opinion in 1872. *Ex parte* McNiel, 80 U.S. (13 Wall.) 236 (1872). The Kansas Indians, 72 U.S. (5 Wall.) 737 (1867) (Davis, J.), and The New York Indians, 72 U.S. (5 Wall.) 761 (1867) (Nelson, J.), striking down state taxes on Indian lands shortly after *Gilman*, seem, like Worcester v. Georgia, 31 U.S. (6 Pet.) 515 (1832), to have been based essentially upon treaties and not upon the Indian commerce clause. For a discussion of *Worcester*, see *supra* chapter 6.

[7]70 U.S. (3 Wall.) at 732.

[8]27 U.S. (2 Pet.) 245 (1829); *see supra* chapter 6.

[9]70 U.S. (3 Wall.) at 732-44 (Clifford, J., dissenting, joined by Wayne, J., and Davis, J.). The Court had held in Gibbons v. Ogden, 22 U.S. (9 Wheat.) 1 (1824), that a federal coasting license preempted a state law giving others exclusive rights to navigate the Hudson River. Though a similar license had been ignored in *Willson*, another had been one of the grounds for the later holding that Congress had forbidden obstruction of the Ohio River. Pennsylvania v. Wheeling & Belmont Bridge Co. (I), 54 U.S. (13 How.) 518 (1852); *see supra* chapters 6, 7; *see also* Pomeroy, *supra* note 4, at 378 (finding it "difficult to reconcile" *Gilman* with *Wheeling Bridge I*); Wintersteen, *The Commerce Clause and the State*, 28 AM. L. REG. (n.s.) 733, 744 (1889) (describing *Gilman* as "receding" from *Wheeling Bridge* and praising it as "practical" because a contrary result would have deprived the states of power to "establish[ ] new avenues of land . . . communication").

The license argument highlighted the standing problem that the Court resolved in favor of the plaintiff on the authority of *Wheeling Bridge I*, 70 U.S. (3 Wall.) at 722-24; although, as argued, the wharf owners were "'not the owners of licensed coasting vessels'" nor themselves engaged in navigation, it was enough that they suffered "specific injury" from the obstruction of the stream. *Id.* at 722.

[10]70 U.S. (3 Wall.) at 743 (paraphrasing 27 U.S. (2 Pet.) at 251-52). In fact it was Mr. Wirt, representing the defendants, and not Marshall who had used the word "sluggish" in describing the creek. 27 U.S. (2 Pet.) at 249.

Willson "as a low, sluggish water, of little or no importance, and treated the erection described in the bill of complaint as one adapted to reclaim the adjacent marshes and as essential to the public health"; *Gilman* upheld a purely commercial measure[11] obstructing what Swayne conceded to be significant navigation.[12] Further, although Swayne, with his penchant for reciting hornbook rules rather than giving reasons,[13] paraphrased Justice Curtis's *Cooley* test at one point in his opinion,[14] he made no effort to apply it to the case. If he had, he might have had difficulty explaining why the construction of bridges over navigable waters was not a subject requiring uniformity; one might have thought there was no more serious threat to commerce than obstructions that might prohibit the passage of vessels entirely. Yet Swayne concluded quite implausibly and without explanation that "[b]ridges are of the same nature with ferries" and thus fell within the powers that Marshall had said were " 'not surrendered to the General Government.' "[15] This would mean, if taken seriously, that the states could obstruct any river they liked unless Congress had told them not to; and that would seem to mean there was precious little left of the *Cooley* doctrine. Indeed, at the end of his opinion Swayne appeared to revert to Taney's extreme position that the commerce clause did not limit the states at all: "Until the dormant power of the Constitution is awakened and made effective, by appropriate legislation, the reserved power of the States is plenary. . . ."[16]

In appearing to embrace the three inconsistent positions of Marshall, Curtis, and Taney in a single case, Swayne made clear only that if the Court was to make sense out of the commerce clause it would have to start assigning the opinions to someone else; but in upholding the bridge in *Gilman* the Court seemed to take a very dim view of the negative effect of the commerce clause.

B. The *Portwardens Case* and *Crandall v. Nevada*

Within two years after *Gilman*, however, the Court seemed to repudiate most of what that case stood for, without even citing it, and to take an even more nationalistic view than that taken in *Cooley*—without the dissent of Swayne or of anyone else.

The occasion was *Steamship Co. v. Portwardens*,[17] and the year was 1867. The opinion was delivered by Chase: Louisiana lacked power to impose a five-dollar tax on vessels entering the port of New Orleans. One ground was that the law offended the ban on "Dut[ies] of Tonnage" found in article I, section 10;[18] intended to prevent

---

[11]The only justification offered for the bridge in the statement of the case was that it would "connect parts of one street . . . having one part on the east and one part on the west of the stream" and thus improve transportation by land. 70 U.S. (3 Wall.) at 719.

[12]The Schuylkill was "navigable . . . for vessels drawing from eighteen to twenty feet of water," and "[c]ommerce has been carried on in all kinds of vessels for many years to and from the complainants' property." *Id.* at 721.

[13]*Cf.* Conway v. Taylor's Executor, 66 U.S. (1 Black) 603 (1862), *discussed supra in* chapter 6.

[14]70 U.S. (3 Wall.) at 726-27.

[15]*Id.* at 726 (quoting Gibbons v. Ogden, 22 U.S. (9 Wheat.) 1, 203 (1824)). Ferries, unlike bridges, do not prevent the passage of other vessels.

[16]70 U.S. (3 Wall.) at 732; *see supra* chapter 7 (discussing the License Cases, 46 U.S. (5 How.) 504 (1847), and the Passenger Cases, 48 U.S. (7 How.) 283 (1849)).

[17]73 U.S. (6 Wall.) 31 (1867).

[18]U.S. Const. art. I, § 10.

evasion of the ban on import taxes, this provision had to be construed despite its narrow wording to embrace "not only a *pro rata* tax . . . . but any duty on the ship" in order to accomplish its purpose.[19] Before reaching this reasonable conclusion, however, Chase had already determined that the law also offended the commerce clause.

The tax in question, Chase wrote, was "a regulation of commerce."[20] This conclusion itself seemed to contradict the distinction drawn by Marshall in *Gibbons v. Ogden*[21] and to imply, surprisingly, that the commerce clause gave Congress power to impose taxes. Chase explained with some persuasiveness, however, that the purpose of the clause was "to place . . . commerce beyond interruption or embarrassment arising from the conflicting or hostile State regulations" and that the tax, which imposed a "serious burden," therefore "work[ed] the very mischief against which the Constitution intended to protect commerce among the States."[22] This of course could have been said with much greater force in *Gilman*, where the state law had been upheld: one would have thought a physical obstruction of navigation a far more serious "embarrassment" of commerce than a paltry five-dollar tax.[23] The Court might have attempted to reconcile the two cases by arguing that the whole port of New Orleans was more essential to commerce than a few miles of the Schuylkill,[24] but it did not do so; and thus the two decisions seemed to stand the *Cooley* test on its head.[25]

Even more interesting than the result, however, was the approach taken by Chase to the general question of the effect of the commerce clause on state law. Swayne had just finished saying the states retained power until Congress acted;[26] the Chief Justice

---

[19]73 U.S. (6 Wall.) at 34-35. See also the State Tonnage Tax Cases, 79 U.S. (12 Wall.) 204 (1871), where, in a typically uninformative Clifford opinion, the Court unanimously held that, although a state could impose a property tax on vessels, it could not measure the tax by tonnage as a surrogate for value. Later cases were to take a more functional view. *See, e.g.*, Packet Co. v. Keokuk, 95 U.S. 80 (1877) (Strong, J.) (wharfage fee may be proportioned to tonnage); Cannon v. New Orleans, 87 U.S. (20 Wall.) 577, 581 (1874) (Miller, J.) (tonnage tax "a contribution claimed for the privilege of arriving or departing from a port").

[20]73 U.S. (6 Wall.) at 33.

[21]22 U.S. (9 Wheat.) 1 (1824). The bans on state import and tonnage taxes in U.S. CONST. art. I, § 10, Marshall argued, did not imply that otherwise the states were free to regulate interstate commerce; for the Constitution treated the tax and commerce powers as "distinct from each other," and the prohibitions "presuppose the existence of that which they restrain, not of that which they do not purport to restrain." 22 U.S. (9 Wheat.) at 201-03; *see also supra* chapter 7 (discussing the Passenger Cases, 48 U.S. (7 How.) 283 (1849)).

[22]73 U.S. (6 Wall.) at 33. For discussion of the purposes of the clause, see *supra* chapter 6.

[23]Money has depreciated since 1867, but the ship tax struck down in the State Tonnage Tax Cases, 79 U.S. (12 Wall.) 204, 211 (1871), was one dollar *per ton* and thus upwards of three hundred dollars for some vessels; those in the Passenger Cases, 48 U.S. (7 How.) 283 (1849), had been one to two dollars *per passenger, id.* at 284-85.

[24]*See* T. COOLEY, CONSTITUTIONAL LIMITATIONS 593 (1868) ("[T]he same structure might constitute a material obstruction in the Ohio or the Mississippi, where vessels are constantly passing, which would be unobjectionable on a stream which a boat only enters at intervals of weeks or months.").

[25]Marshall's familiar but questionable principle that the power to tax was the power to destroy, McCulloch v. Maryland, 17 U.S. (4 Wheat.) 316, 431 (1819), would have supported the *Portwardens* decision, but it would equally have outlawed the pilotage charges upheld in *Cooley*. *Cooley's* insistence on investigating the degree of necessity for uniformity seems hard to reconcile with a rigid rule that all taxes on commerce are forbidden. For a discussion of *McCulloch*, see *supra* chapter 6.

[26]*See supra* text accompanying note 16.

said "the regulation of commerce among the States is in Congress" alone[27] with certain exceptions. The first class of exceptions included "quarantine and other health laws, laws concerning the domestic police, and laws regulating the internal trade of a State," which "have always been held not to be within the grant to Congress."[28] The second, exemplified by *Cooley*, consisted of "cases in which, either by express provision or by omission to exercise its own powers, Congress has left to the regulation of States matters clearly within its commercial powers."[29] Finally, the charge assessed in *Cooley* was based "not only on State laws but upon contract," for "[p]ilotage is compensation for services performed; half pilotage is compensation for services which the pilot has put himself in readiness to perform by labor, risk, and cost . . . ."[30]

Apart from the obvious difficulty of explaining the duty of an unwilling shipowner to pay for a pilot as one based on contract,[31] this statement of the law was revolutionary. Ignoring the *Cooley* test altogether, Chase seemed to be returning to Marshall's notion of reserved powers,[32] with a strong and startling suggestion that such matters as the quarantine of foreign vessels were not within congressional cognizance at all. More important, Chase seemed to be saying that states could regulate matters that did fall within the commerce power only with congressional permission. This seemed to take back *Cooley*'s conclusion that the states were free to regulate commerce in the absence of congressional action unless the subject demanded uniformity,[33] and it squarely contradicted *Cooley*'s express determination that Congress could not authorize states to regulate commerce.[34] Finally, Chase was the first spokesman for the Court to espouse the recurring fallacy that in some undefined cases congressional inaction was to be treated as if it were permissive or prohibitory legislation[35]—though the Constitution makes clear that Congress can act only by affirmative vote of both Houses.[36] Thus in two short years, without dissent and without significant changes in membership, the Court had gone from saying the states could impede commerce unless Congress had said otherwise to essentially the opposite position that they could not do so unless authorized by Congress.

Adding to the confusion was the virtually contemporaneous decision in *Crandall*

[27]73 U.S. (6 Wall.) at 34.

[28]*Id.* at 33. These are powers "properly within State jurisdiction," which are "not affected by the grant of power [to Congress] to regulate commerce," in spite of the fact that they are powers "which may . . . affect commerce." *Id.*

[29]*Id.*

[30]*Id.* at 34.

[31]Field, concluding in Steamship Co. v. Joliffe, 69 U.S. (2 Wall.) 450, 456-57 (1865), that repeal of a statute giving a rejected pilot half his fee did not affect rights previously vested, had unnecessarily attempted to explain the right as quasi-contractual. Miller's answer was devastating: "Here is no element of contract; no consent of minds; no services rendered . . . . It is purely a case of a violation of the law in refusing to perform what it enjoins . . . ." *Id.* at 468 (Miller, J., dissenting).

[32]*See supra* text accompanying notes 8-16.

[33]*See supra* text accompanying note 2.

[34]53 U.S. (12 How.) at 317 ("If the states were divested of the power to legislate on this subject by the grant of the commercial power to Congress, it is plain this act could not confer upon them power thus to legislate."); *see supra* chapter 7.

[35]*See, e.g.,* Dowling, *Interstate Commerce and State Power*, 27 VA. L. REV. 1, 5-6 (1940).

[36]U.S. CONST. art. I, §§ 1, 7; *see* T. POWELL, VAGARIES AND VARIETIES IN CONSTITUTIONAL INTERPRETATION 162 (1956) (describing the congressional-inaction theory as "sheer make-believe").

v. Nevada,[37] in which, while invalidating a tax on passengers leaving the state on grounds quite difficult to discover in the Constitution,[38] all the Justices but Clifford and Chase[39] doubted there was a commerce clause violation because the subject seemed neither "uniform" nor "national" within the *Cooley* test.[40] Justice Miller, who wrote the opinion, did not bother saying why that was so or how uniformity could be the test after what Chase had said in *Portwardens*,[41] and he made no effort to distinguish that case. There was no apparent reason to think ships required more uniformity than trains, or commerce entering the state more than that departing, or freight more than passengers; the Court did not revive the rejected contention that passenger traffic was not commerce.[42] Indeed, by modern standards the tax in *Crandall* was more offensive in commerce clause terms than that in *Portwardens*, for only the former applied *solely* to interstate travelers; if the purpose of the clause was, as Chase had said, to protect interstate commerce against "interruption or embarrassment," one might have thought its most obvious effect was to protect it from outright discrimination.[43] Fortunately for consistency, neither Miller's dicta about commerce in *Crandall* nor the commerce basis of *Portwardens* was necessary to the result; but they did raise a serious question whether the Court had any idea of what it was doing.[44]

C.   *Woodruff v. Parham*

The year after *Crandall* was decided, Justice Miller had another opportunity to write a narrow interpretation of the negative effect of the commerce clause in an opinion

---

[37]73 U.S. (6 Wall.) 35 (1868).

[38]*See infra* conclusion to part four, text accompanying notes 32-34.

[39]73 U.S. (6 Wall.) at 49 (Clifford, J., dissenting, joined by Chase, C.J.). Clifford's brief opinion was nothing but a conclusion: "the State legislature cannot impose any such burden upon commerce among the several States." *Id.*

[40]*Id.* at 43.

[41]The one thing the two preceding decisions had had in common was Marshall's idea of reserved state powers, which Miller did not mention.

[42]*See supra* chapter 6 (discussing Gibbons v. Ogden, 22 U.S. (9 Wheat.) 1 (1824)).

[43]*See, e.g.*, Philadelphia v. New Jersey, 437 U.S. 617 (1978) (striking down a law forbidding the importation of most solid or liquid waste); South Carolina State Highway Dep't. v. Barnwell Bros. Inc., 303 U.S. 177, 185 n.2 (1938) (Stone, J.) ("[W]hen the regulation is of such a character that its burden falls principally upon those without the state, legislative action is not likely to be subjected to those political restraints which are normally exerted on legislation . . . ."); THE FEDERALIST No. 22 (A. Hamilton) (describing the purpose of the clause as being to suppress "'the interfering and unneighborly regulations of some States'"); L. TRIBE, AMERICAN CONSTITUTIONAL LAW 326 (1978) ("any state action which imposes special or distinct burdens on out-of-state interests unrepresented in the state's political process" viewed with suspicion); *cf. supra* chapter 6 (discussing McCulloch v. Maryland, 17 U.S. (4 Wheat.) 316 (1819)). Moreover, a tax of one dollar per passenger seems, in *Portwarden's* own terms, a more "serious burden" than one of five dollars on an entire ship. Several Justices had pronounced a similar tax on incoming passengers from abroad invalid on commerce clause grounds as early as 1849. *See supra* chapter 7 (discussing the Passenger Cases, 48 U.S. (7 How.) 283 (1849)).

[44]Much later Miller himself was to treat *Crandall* as if it had struck the tax down on commerce clause grounds. *See* C. FAIRMAN, *supra note* 6, at 1307 n.14; *see also* Pomeroy, *supra note* 4, at 364 (writing in 1878: "I think it very clear from later decisions that the views of the [] dissenting judges [on the commerce issue] would now be adopted by the court as correct.").

for the Court. Alabama had levied a tax on the sale of goods at auction, and the Court upheld it as applied to goods brought in from other states and sold in their original package.[45] Most of the opinion was devoted to a well-written though disputable refutation of Marshall's dictum that the import-export clause forbade state taxation of imports from other states.[46] In the last few paragraphs Miller also rejected an attack based on the commerce clause.

The key to the case, in Miller's opinion, was that "[t]here is no attempt to discriminate injuriously against the products of other States": the tax was "imposed alike upon all sales made in Mobile, . . . whether the goods sold are the produce of [Alabama] or some other [state]."[47] A tax applicable only to out-of-state goods, he stated flatly, would be contrary to the commerce clause.[48] But, he noted in connection with his import clause argument, if a state could not subject such goods to a nondiscriminatory tax, it could not require a merchant who bought his wares elsewhere to "contribute a dollar to support its government, improve its thoroughfares or educate its children."[49] Miller seemed to be suggesting, as counsel had argued, that "it would be strange" if the Constitution required the state "to work a discrimination against its own manufacturers."[50] All of this must strike a responsive chord in the modern reader, for much of what Miller said about the commerce clause

[45]Woodruff v. Parham, 75 U.S. (8 Wall.) 123 (1869).

[46]75 U.S. (8 Wall.) at 130-40 (disavowing Brown v. Maryland, 25 U.S. (12 Wheat.) 419, 449 (1827)). Miller stressed the absence of any reference by the Framers to taxes on "imports" from other states, and correctly dismissed Marshall's statement as unexplained dictum. He reclassified Almy v. California, 65 U.S. (24 How.) 169 (1861), which had held that a state tax on gold shipped from California to New York offended the import-export clause, as based on the commerce clause and on "the rule laid down in Crandall v. Nevada," 75 U.S. (8 Wall.) at 138, since, as he rightly observed, the fact that the shipment was interstate and not foreign "seems to have escaped the attention of counsel . . . and of the Chief Justice who delivered the opinion," id. at 137. See supra chapter 7. As Nelson said in dissent, 75 U.S. (8 Wall.) at 142-44, the words of the prohibition did not distinguish between interstate and foreign trade, and the commerce clause expressly equated them; and there was something to his argument that at least some of the policies underlying the imports clause applied equally to interstate traffic, id. at 144. See supra chapter 6; see also T. POWELL, supra note 36, at 182 ("When the Framers spoke in 1787, the states were substantially sovereign, and their exercises of sovereign powers in adversely affecting trade from sister states was one of the factors leading to the Annapolis conference . . . ."). In a companion case reaching the same result as Woodruff, the Court seems to have overlooked an allegation that some of the goods had come from foreign countries. Hinson v. Lott, 75 U.S. (8 Wall.) 148, 149 (1869). See also Low v. Austin, 80 U.S. (13 Wall.) 29 (1872) (Field, J.), which uncritically and unanimously followed the implications of Marshall's ill-conceived Brown opinion in holding the same clause forbade a nondiscriminatory property tax on imported goods while they remained in their original package, though some of the purposes of the clause suggested it outlawed only taxes on imports as such. See supra chapter 6; Michelin Tire Corp. v. Wages, 423 U.S. 276 (1976) (overruling Low). The arguably erroneous view that the imports clause barred even nondiscriminatory taxes weighed heavily in Miller's refusal to hold that it applied to imports from other states. See 75 U.S. (8 Wall.) at 137; see also 4 J. ELLIOT, THE DEBATES IN THE SEVERAL STATE CONVENTIONS ON THE ADOPTION OF THE FEDERAL CONSTITUTION 80 (2d ed. Wash., D.C. 1836) (1st ed. Wash., D.C. 1827-1830) (comments by Gov. Johnston indicating that at the time of the North Carolina Ratifying Convention, some states were in fact taxing goods imported from other states).

[47]75 U.S. (8 Wall.) at 140.

[48]Id.

[49]Id. at 137.

[50]Id. at 128 (Mr. Phillips). Marshall's reasoning in McCulloch, though not the absolute rule Marshall laid down in that case, also supports Miller's distinction: when a legislature can harm disfavored interests only by inflicting similar burdens on its own favorites, the political process provides its own check on arbitrary action. 17 U.S. (4 Wheat.) 316, 428, 435 (1819).

in *Woodruff* has survived: discrimination is almost always contrary to the clause,[51] but interstate commerce may be required to pay its way.[52]

Shaken from his usual lethargy, Justice Nelson dissented alone, making the intelligent objection that a ban on discrimination was not enough to protect producers in other states: a New York tax on "all sales of cotton, tobacco, or rice . . . would be a tax without any discrimination; and yet it would be in fact, in its operation and effect, exclusively upon these Southern products."[53] There is a sense, of course, in which such a tax could be found discriminatory; as Nelson's example portended, the Court has not found discrimination a self-defining concept in later cases.[54]

What is most interesting about *Woodruff* is once again the Court's treatment of prior law. Miller's discrimination principle would appear to mean that the Court was wrong to rely on the commerce clause in *Portwardens*, where the tax evidently applied to ships entering the port from other places in the same state;[55] yet *Portwardens* was nowhere cited, nor were any of the other recent commerce clause cases. Miller elected to write as if the case before him were the first in which the Court had had occasion to develop a theory of the effect of the clause on state law. Most jarringly, the test he enunciated was a brand-new one that seemed to depart from all of the inconsistent theses that had been espoused in the past five years without even adverting to them. In a companion case[56] he attempted to show that he was really applying the *Cooley* test, which he had embraced in *Crandall*;[57] but by saying that discrimination and nothing else brought state legislation within the requirement of national uniformity he really appeared to be using the familiar formula as a cover for an entirely new approach. The pretense seemed certain to produce confusion in future cases as to whether the need for uniformity or discrimination or both was the constitutional test.

D. Railroad Taxes

Justice Miller's conclusion in *Woodruff* that discrimination was the key to the validity of state laws affecting commerce proved as fleeting as it was novel. Within four years the Court was to strike down one nondiscriminatory tax on commerce clause grounds,[58] and Miller was to complain because it refused to strike down another.[59]

[51]*See, e.g.*, Philadelphia v. New Jersey, 437 U.S. 617 (1978).

[52]*See, e.g.*, Western Live Stock v. Bureau of Revenue, 303 U.S. 250, 254 (1938).

[53]75 U.S. (8 Wall.) at 145-46.

[54]*See, e.g.*, Exxon Corp. v. Governor of Maryland, 437 U.S. 117 (1978) (upholding a law forbidding refiners to operate retail service stations though no gasoline was refined in Maryland); Hunt v. Washington State Apple Advertising Comm'n, 432 U.S. 333 (1977) (holding discriminatory a law requiring that all apples sold bear their federal grade or none at all, because the enacting state had no grading system of its own); Dean Milk Co. v. Madison, 340 U.S. 349 (1951) (invalidating as discriminatory a requirement that milk be processed within five miles of the place of sale, though the rule excluded milk from elsewhere in the same state as well).

[55]*See supra* text accompanying notes 17-36.

[56]Hinson v. Lott, 75 U.S. (8 Wall.) 148, 152 (1869).

[57]*See supra* text accompanying notes 37-40.

[58]Case of the State Freight Tax, 82 U.S. (15 Wall.) 232 (1873).

[59]State Tax on Railway Gross Receipts, 82 U.S. (15 Wall.) 284 (1873).

Pennsylvania had imposed two taxes on railroads doing business within its borders: a flat charge of two to five cents per ton of freight carried anywhere in Pennsylvania,[60] and a levy of 0.75% of the gross receipts of railroads incorporated there.[61] To Justices Swayne and Davis, both taxes were constitutional as applied to interstate shipments and their proceeds: as they said of the freight tax, neither discriminated against interstate commerce,[62] and that should have sufficed under *Woodruff*—which they did not cite.

The majority, however, held the first charge unconstitutional in the *Case of the State Freight Tax*[63] in 1873—apparently the first time that any state law had been struck down solely on commerce clause grounds.[64] Since interstate freight carriage was interstate commerce, Justice Strong wrote, the freight tax regulated interstate commerce;[65] if a state could impose a two-cent tax it could impose a prohibitive one;[66] and interstate transportation was a subject—unlike the construction of bridges over local streams in *Gilman*[67]—requiring uniform regulation.[68] In support of these conclusions Strong relied on *Crandall* and another decision striking down a state tax without invoking the commerce clause[69] and ignored the one precedent in his favor: the opinion against the ship tax in *Portwardens*.[70]

Cooley,[71] the source of the uniformity test professedly applied, was also not cited—perhaps because it would have been difficult to reconcile with the decision that the freight tax was invalid. Not only could it have been argued with as much force that the power to charge pilot fees was also the power to destroy;[72] interstate

---

[60]Case of the State Freight Tax, 82 U.S. (15 Wall.) at 232-33.

[61]State Tax on Railway Gross Receipts, 82 U.S. (15 Wall.) 284, 284-85 (1873).

[62]*Id.* at 282.

[63]82 U.S. (15 Wall.) 232 (1873).

[64]*See* Pomeroy, *supra* note 4, at 365 ("Few more important decisions have been made concerning the regulation of commerce since the leading case of Gibbons v. Ogden.").

[65]82 U.S. (15 Wall.) at 275-76.

[66]*Id.* at 276. In contrast to the opinion in *Portwardens*, Strong did not bother describing the burden actually imposed as a "serious" one. *See supra* text accompanying note 22.

[67]*See supra* text accompanying notes 16-17.

[68]82 U.S. (15 Wall.) at 279-80. Strong noted once again that the stream in *Gilman* had been "wholly within a [single] State . . ." and, like Marshall in Gibbons v. Ogden, 22 U.S. (9 Wheat.) 1 (1824), speculated that perhaps the states had no power to regulate interstate commerce as such at all: "Cases that have sustained State laws, alleged to be regulations of commerce among the States, have been such as related to bridges or dams across streams wholly within a State, police or health laws, or subjects of a kindred nature, not strictly commercial regulations." 82 U.S. (15 Wall.) at 279.

[69]82 U.S. (15 Wall.) at 280-81. That the privilege of traveling to the seat of government recognized in *Crandall, infra*, conclusion to part four, text accompanying notes 9-11, applied to the shipment of freight everywhere in the country seems questionable, and the *Crandall* opinion seemed to suggest that even a discriminatory tax would not offend the commerce clause. *See supra* text accompanying notes 37-43. The other case cited was Almy v. California, 65 U.S. (24 How.) 169 (1861), which had been based on the import-export clause, and reexplained on commerce clause grounds in Woodruff v. Parham, 75 U.S. (8 Wall.) at 137-38. *See supra* note 46.

[70]Strong argued that the tax was indistinguishable from a tariff on the entry and exit of goods from the state, 82 U.S. (15 Wall.) at 276; but a tariff applies only to incoming commerce, while the freight tax was even-handed.

[71]*See supra* text accompanying notes 2-4.

[72]*See* Greeley, *What is the Test of a Regulation of Foreign or Interstate Commerce?* 1 HARV. L. REV. 159, 181 (1887) (pointing out that Strong's argument was enough to outlaw any state measure affecting interstate or foreign commerce).

transportation had been the "subject" of state law in *Cooley* in exactly the same sense as it was in the *Freight Tax Case*. If nothing else, it had become evident that under the *Cooley* test everything depended on how the relevant "subject" was defined, and that the Court was prepared to define it inconsistently and without explanation. No effort was made to distinguish *Woodruff* either. Without attribution, the majority pooh-poohed its discrimination principle by begging the question: "if an act to tax interstate or foreign commerce is unconstitutional, it is not cured by including in its provisions subjects within the domain of the State."[73]

In a second opinion by Strong, immediately following, the Court *upheld* the second Pennsylvania tax in the case of the *State Tax on Railway Gross Receipts*.[74] Unlike the freight tax, this one was said to fall upon railroad property—its money— rather than on the transportation of freight, and thus, although its effect on interstate commerce might be the same as that of the freight tax, it was not a regulation of commerce at all.[75] A more sterile distinction can scarcely be imagined: if the Framers meant to protect commerce from interference, as Strong had said in the *Freight-Tax Case*,[76] one would think the effect rather than the form of the exaction decisive.[77]

Miller made this objection in his dissent in the *Gross Receipts* case, and Field and

[73]82 U.S. (15 Wall.) at 277. The intervening decision in Paul v. Virginia, 75 U.S. (8 Wall.) 168 (1869) (Field, J.) (alternative holding); *see also infra*, conclusion to part four, text accompanying notes 5, 20, which allowed a state to discriminate against foreign insurance corporations, suggests a possible distinction: if a foreign insurer's agreement is not an interstate transaction because both parties signed it in the same state, perhaps the sale of goods after their importation is not either. But to hold that the tax in *Woodruff* was not a regulation of interstate commerce would seem to suggest that a *discriminatory* tax on the sale of out-of-state goods would also pass muster; and that would seem squarely contrary to the purpose of the clause.

In light of future developments it is noteworthy that the Court in the *Freight Tax Case* treated as part of interstate commerce a rail journey that began and ended within a single state—where the freight was then taken out of the state by ship. 82 U.S. (15 Wall.) at 234. The point passed without discussion. Marshall had said in Gibbons v. Ogden, 22 U.S. (9 Wheat.) 1, 195 (1824), that Congress's power extended to those parts of an interstate trip within a single state, but the *Freight Tax* case was an extension of his conclusion; for in *Gibbons* the entire journey had taken place in the same vessel.

[74]82 U.S. (15 Wall.) 284 (1873).

[75]*Id.* at 294-95. For a thorough exploration of the later history of the formalistic distinctions made by Strong in these cases, see Powell, *Indirect Encroachment on Federal Authority by the Taxing Powers of the States* (pt. 2), 31 HARV. L. REV. 572 (1918). For criticism, see part 5 of the same article, 32 HARV. L. REV. 234, 2144 (1919) (noting that in these and other early cases the Justices "were prone to indulge in nominalism and conceptualism in finding what was the subject taxed" and "seemed to be feeling their way in the dark").

[76]82 U.S. (15 Wall.) at 275.

[77]*See* Kitch, *Regulation and the American Common Market*, in REGULATION, FEDERALISM, AND INTERSTATE COMMERCE (A. Tarlock, ed. 1981) (terming the distinction "bizarre"). Kitch argues that in terms of effects the freight tax was indeed the *less* harmful to interstate commerce: "the flat tax on freight per pound weighed more heavily on the short haul, largely intrastate, traffic while the gross receipts tax directly taxed that portion of the revenue derived from the out-of-state haul." *Id.* at 28. The Court's formal distinction was made to appear still more inexplicable by Strong's insistence that, although the freight tax was nominally levied upon the railroads, in "practical operation" its "burden" could be passed on to the shipper. 82 U.S. (15 Wall.) at 272-75; *cf. id.* at 294 (defending the gross receipts tax: "A tax upon the occupation of a physician . . . measured by . . . income . . . will hardly be claimed to be a tax on his patients . . . , though the burden ultimately falls upon them."). On Strong's behalf it should be said, as he noted, that a similarly formalistic distinction had been drawn in determining whether states could impose taxes based upon the value of federal government securities. See 82 U.S. (15 Wall.) at 272 ("[T]he decisions turned upon the question, what was the subject of the tax . . . .").

Hunt joined him.[78] What was interesting about Miller's position was the facile way in which he abandoned all he had said about the commerce clause in *Woodruff v. Parham*. There he had said a tax on out-of-state goods was permissible because not discriminatory;[79] here he said interstate commerce was "exempted . . . from [state] . . . control" entirely.[80] In *Woodruff* he had said interstate commerce must pay its fair share of the cost of government;[81] in the *Gross Receipts* case he said (in italics) that *"by no device or evasion . . . can a State compel citizens of other States to pay to it a tax, contribution, or toll, for the privilege of having their goods transported through that State."*[82] Miller's principle was, as usual, clear and simple; the only trouble was that he kept enunciating different principles every time a new case came along.

There is one passage in the *Freight Tax* case that suggests why the Court properly concluded that nondiscrimination alone would not be enough to assure interstate traffic an equal opportunity. Although the argument was not carried through, it points toward a possible basis for legitimately distinguishing between the two railroad taxes:

> It is of national importance that . . . there should be but one regulating power, for if one State can . . . tax persons or property passing through it, . . . every other may, and thus commercial intercourse between States remote from each other may be destroyed. . . .[F]or though it might bear the imposition of a single tax it would be crushed under the load of many.[83]

In other words, since the freight tax was not apportioned to the length of travel, cumulative burdens imposed by several states on the same shipment—even though not discriminatory—could have placed interstate traffic at a competitive disadvantage by subjecting it alone to multiple exactions.[84] Unlike the freight tax, however, the gross-receipts provision applied only to Pennsylvania corporations; if each state taxed only its own companies, there was no risk of multiple taxation. Thus the result

---

[78]82 U.S. (15 Wall.) at 298.

[79]*See supra* text accompanying notes 47-48, 51-52.

[80]82 U.S. (15 Wall.) at 299.

[81]75 U.S. (8 Wall.) at 136-37.

[82]82 U.S. (15 Wall.) at 299. The Court conceded in the *Freight Tax* case that a state could charge a fee for the actual use of its own facilities, such as a toll road or canal, but properly concluded that no such facilities were involved in the case of a privately owned railroad. 82 U.S. (15 Wall.) at 277-79. Miller also acknowledged in the *Gross Receipts* case that the state could impose a property tax on the instrumentalities of interstate commerce, 82 U.S. (15 Wall.) at 299; he did not explain how this concession was to be squared with his theory. For support of Miller's views on the ground that Pennsylvania was exploiting its geographical position in both cases by imposing taxes falling largely on unrepresented outsiders, see Brown, *The Open Economy: Mr. Justice Frankfurter and the Position of the Judiciary*, 67 YALE L. J. 219, 229-30 (1957).

[83]82 U.S. (15 Wall.) at 280.

[84]*See* Western Live Stock v. Bureau of Revenue, 303 U.S. 250, 255-56 (1938); L. TRIBE, *supra* note 43, at 360-69; Note, *The Multiple Burden Theory in Interstate Commerce Taxation*, 40 COLUM. L. REV. 653 (1940). Professor Powell remarks:

> If we discard all the doctrinal disquisitions of the opinions and look only to the results of the decisions, we find that the controlling motive of the Supreme Court has been the desire to prevent the states from imposing on interstate commerce any peculiar or unusual

of the two railroad decisions can be reconciled if one assumes, as the Court would actually later hold, that no other state could tax the same gross receipts;[85] but Strong nowhere suggested that this was the basis of his distinction.[86]

The circle was closed by Chase's 1873 opinion for a unanimous Court in *Osborne v. Mobile*,[87] upholding a tax that not only posed a patent risk of multiple taxation but actually discriminated against interstate commerce as well.[88] Miller held his peace; apparently discrimination, which in *Woodruff* he had said was determinative, was no longer either necessary or sufficient to show invalidity.[89]

Chase's death spares us from pursuing the saga further in this article; his successor was left with precedents reflecting just about every conceivable view of the commerce clause problem. The overall tendency of commerce clause decisions during

---

burden . . . . What the court is insistent upon is that there must be adequate safeguards against subjecting interstate commerce to heavier taxation than local commerce.

Powell, *Indirect Encroachment on Federal Authority by the Taxing Powers of the States* (pt. 7), 32 HARV. L. REV. 902, 917-18 (1919). The tax in *Portwardens, see supra* text accompanying notes 17-44, which the Court also struck down, posed the same risk of multiple burdens. Of course the Court might have insisted upon a showing that other states actually did tax the same transaction. *See* L. TRIBE, *supra* note 43, at 360 (citing General Motors Corp. v. Washington, 377 U.S. 436 (1964)). A freight tax proportioned to miles traveled would have avoided this possibility, *see* L. TRIBE, *supra* note 43, at 367-69, and cases cited; yet Strong's blunderbuss opinion seemed to mean that such a tax would be unconstitutional too—though he did note that the tax in question was not so proportioned, 82 U.S. (15 Wall.) at 273, 278.

[85] Fargo v. Michigan, 121 U.S. 230 (1887) (Miller, J.), *infra* chapter 12 (invalidating a gross-receipts tax on out-of-state corporations, even though apportioned to their local earnings). Even before the first *Gross Receipts* decision the Court had similarly held, without explicitly invoking the commerce clause, that ships could be subjected to property taxes only in their home port, Hays v. Pacific Mail S.S. Co., 58 U.S. (7 How.) 596 (1855), *cited supra* in chapter 7; and it soon wrote this distinction into the commerce clause itself, Morgan v. Parham, 83 U.S. (16 Wall.) 471, 479 (1873) (Hunt, J.). As later cases have suggested, there may be more equitable formulas for apportioning the power to tax interstate operations among the states affected. *See, e.g.,* Moorman Mfg. Co. v. Blair, 437 U.S. 267 (1978); L. TRIBE, *supra* note 43, at 367-69.

[86] Strong did indicate his awareness that the tax reached only domestic corporations; an alternative basis for upholding the tax was that it was laid on the franchise granted by Pennsylvania. 82 U.S. (15 Wall.) at 296 ("It is not to be questioned that the States may tax the franchises of companies created by them . . . ."). Ironically, the *Gross Receipts* decision was overruled shortly after the Court had demonstrated, by precluding taxation by other states, *supra* note 85, that there was ample justification for the distinction Justice Strong had originally drawn. Philadelphia & So. S.S. Co. v. Pennsylvania, 122 U.S. 326 (1887) *infra* chapter 12, (per Bradley, J., who had been with the majority in the original *Gross Receipts* case).

[87] 83 U.S. (16 Wall.) 479 (1873).

[88] The city imposed a license tax of $50 on express companies operating only within the city, of $100 on those operating only within the state, and of $500 on those "having a business extending beyond the limits of the State." *Id.* at 480. Like the gross-receipts tax, wrote Chase, this exaction fell upon "a business carried on" in the state; it was immaterial that the business in question included "the making of contracts . . . for . . . transportation beyond it" or that it might "'increase the cost of transportation . . . .'" *Id.* at 482-83. The Court added that there was no discrimination against citizens of other states—proving there was no violation of the privileges and immunities clause but ignoring *Woodruff's* distinct principle forbidding discrimination against interstate commerce itself. *Id.* at 481-82.

[89] *See also* Ward v. Maryland, 79 U.S. (12 Wall.) 418, 432 (1871) (Bradley, J., concurring) (arguing that a state tax on sales by sample would violate the commerce clause even if it applied equally to local sellers, since it would "effectually" require foreign manufacturers to "establish[] commercial houses" within the state). This rather extreme view was to become an alternative holding in Robbins v. Shelby County, 120 U.S. 489 (1887), written by Bradley himself. In *Ward* the Court found a discrimination against outsiders in violation of article IV. *See infra,* conclusion to part four, text accompanying note 23.

Chase's time seemed lenient. The only measures struck down were the taxes on arriving ships and on interstate freight; the states were apparently free to obstruct navigable rivers and even to discriminate against interstate operations, so long as they did not make the mistake of labeling a tax as one on interstate commerce itself.[90] In doctrinal terms the Court's efforts in this field can be described only as a disaster.[91]

II. The Slaughter-House Cases

The thirteenth amendment,[92] abolishing slavery, was proclaimed law in 1865; the fourteenth,[93] extending citizenship to blacks and protecting them against official discrimination, in 1868; the fifteenth,[94] giving them the vote, in 1870. Beginning in 1866, Congress, on the strength of these provisions, enacted a series of statutes designed to make the vision of equality concrete.[95] These statutes were to engage the Court's most serious attention shortly after Chase's death. But in the meantime, in two historic cases in 1873, the Court was asked for the first time to interpret the amendments themselves.

The critical decision came in a case remote from the amendments' central purpose of racial justice.[96] Louisiana had given a partial monopoly of the slaughtering business to one company;[97] its competitors argued that this created an "involuntary servitude," abridged their "privileges or immunities," denied them "equal protection of the laws," and "deprived" them of "liberty, or property, without due process of law," in violation of the thirteenth and fourteenth amendments. By a bare majority,[98] the Court rejected all four objections in an opinion by Justice Miller.

The thirteenth amendment contention was nothing but a play on words: the whole tenor of the congressional debate confirms that, as Miller said, "servitude" was included to prevent evasion of the ban on slavery, not to forbid limitations on the right to use one's property.[99] In light of later developments, it is noteworthy that the equal protection and due process arguments were given equally short shrift.

[90]See 2 C. Warren, The Supreme Court in United States History 626 (rev. ed. 1926) (until the *Freight Tax Case,* in this period "only a few interstate commerce cases had been considered, but in each the Court had taken a pronounced stand in favor of State regulation . . . .").

[91]In his classic study of early commerce clause decisions, Professor Frankfurter passed over the entire Chase period, observing that Chase's contribution "consists in the main of fugitive and confused themes in the Supreme Court's symphonic evolution of the commerce clause." F. Frankfurter, The Commerce Clause Under Marshall, Taney, and Waite 74 (1937).

[92]U.S. Const. amend. XIII.

[93]U.S. Const. amend. XIV.

[94]U.S. Const. amend. XV.

[95]See Act of Mar. 1, 1875, ch. 114, 18 Stat. 335; Act of Apr. 20, 1871, ch. 22, *repealed by* Act of Feb. 8, 1894, ch. 25, 28 Stat. 36; Act of Feb. 28, 1871, ch. 99, 16 Stat. 433, *repealed by* Act of Feb. 8, 1894, ch. 25, 28 Stat. 36; Act of May 31, 1870, ch. 114, 16 Stat. 140, *repealed by* Act of Feb. 8, 1894, ch. 25, 28 Stat. 36, 37; Act of Apr. 9, 1866, ch. 31, 14 Stat. 27. *See infra* chapter 11.

[96]Slaughter-House Cases, 83 U.S. (16 Wall.) 36 (1873). The background of the litigation is described in detail in C. Fairman, *supra* note 6, at 1301-88.

[97]As the Court emphasized, the statute did not forbid others to do their own slaughtering; it required them to do it on the company's premises and to pay a fee for the privilege. 83 U.S. (16 Wall.) at 42, 61.

[98]Field's dissent, 83 U.S. at 83, was joined by Chase, Bradley, and Swayne; the last two added dissenting opinions of their own. *Id.* at 83, 111, 124.

[99]*Id.* at 68-69; *see* Clyatt v. United States, 197 U.S. 207 (1905) (upholding, on the basis of the thirteenth

First, since the purpose of the former clause was to set aside laws discriminating against blacks, the Court "doubt[ed] very much whether any action . . . not directed by way of discrimination against the negroes as a class, or on account of their race, would ever be held to come within the purview of this provision."[100] This might have been a plausible enough holding if documented, as I shall discuss below;[101] but it was not the holding. Miller expressly reserved the question of nonracial discrimination until "some case of State oppression, by denial of equal justice in its courts," was presented[102]—leaving the reader with the bare conclusion that *Slaughter-House* was not such a case and with no immediate clue as to why he thought the clause applied only to injustices committed in the courts.[103]

The due process discussion was even more perfunctory: the fourteenth amendment provision subjected the states to the same limitations to which the fifth subjected the federal government; and

> under no construction of that provision that we have ever seen, or any that we deem admissible, can the restraint imposed by the State of Louisiana upon the exercise of their trade by the butchers of New Orleans be held to be a deprivation of property within the meaning of that provision.[104]

Miller did not even say whether he meant that there had been no deprivation or that the rights involved were not property, let alone explain what he thought either "deprivation" or "property" meant. There is language in the context of an earlier and apparently gratuitous discussion of the scope of Louisiana's police power[105] that suggests he thought there had been no deprivation;[106] but, unlike later Justices,[107] he nowhere attempted to tie his police power discussion to the due process clause, and he did not even cite the Court's recent declaration in the *Legal Tender Cases*[108] that the clause applied "only to a direct appropriation, and not to consequential injuries

---

amendment, a federal statute outlawing peonage); CONG. GLOBE, 38th Cong. *passim* (1864-65). Field gave the thirteenth amendment argument a glance by suggesting that a person excluded from an occupation was not truly free, but he fell short of resting his dissent on that provision. 83 U.S. (16 Wall.) at 89-93.

[100]83 U.S. (16 Wall.) at 81.

[101]*See infra* text accompanying notes 114-118.

[102]83 U.S. (16 Wall.) at 81. During oral argument in a later railroad case, Miller emphatically denied that he had meant in *Slaughter-House* to limit the clause to the protection of blacks. *See* C. FAIRMAN, MR. JUSTICE MILLER AND THE SUPREME COURT, 1862-1890, at 187 (1939).

[103]Bradley concluded, without giving reasons, that the law denied equal protection, 83 U.S. (16 Wall.) at 122; the other dissenters relied on other provisions.

[104]*Id.* at 81.

[105]After giving examples of British monopolies, explaining that limiting the place and manner of slaughtering was a standard means of combating nuisances, and invoking *McCulloch v. Maryland*'s test for the necessity and propriety of federal laws, *see supra* chapter 6, Miller concluded that Louisiana's "authority . . . to pass the present statute is ample," unless there was something to the contrary in either the state or the federal constitution. 83 U.S. (16 Wall.) at 66. Why he thought the Supreme Court had power to determine anything beyond the federal question when reviewing a state-court judgment he did not say.

[106]*See* 83 U.S. (16 Wall.) at 61-62 (denying that the complaining butchers had been "deprived of the right to labor" or that the law "seriously interfere[d]" with their business).

[107]*See infra* chapter 11.

[108]*See supra* chapter 9.

resulting from the exercise of lawful power."[109] Finally, the statement that the Court had "[n]ever seen" a construction of the clause that would invalidate the monopoly was not easy to take at face value, since both Taney in *Dred Scott*[110] and Chase in the repudiated *Hepburn v. Griswold*[111] had employed due process to strike down federal statutes in what arguably were analogous circumstances; some explanation of what the clause did mean seems to have been in order.[112]

The bulk of both the majority and dissenting opinions, however, was devoted to the question whether the monopoly offended the provision that "no State shall . . . abridge the privileges or immunities of citizens of the United States."[113] Miller's negative answer was simply stated: the introductory clause of the amendment spoke separately of state and of national citizenship; therefore the privileges and immunities of "citizens of the United States" were those "belonging to a citizen of the United States as such," not those enjoyed by virtue of state citizenship.[114] From this critical conclusion the result followed easily: unlike rights secured by federal treaties or by the thirteenth amendment, the right to slaughter animals did not "owe [its] existence to the Federal government, its National character, its Constitution, or its laws," and thus was not a privilege of *national* citizenship.[115]

The difficulty, of course, was with Miller's apparent conclusion that the sole office of the clause was to protect rights already given by some other federal law. Apart from the amendment's less than conclusive reference to dual citizenship,[116] his sole justification was that a broader holding would "radically change [] the whole theory

[109]79 U.S. (12 Wall.) 457, 551 (1872).

[110]Scott v. Sandford, 60 U.S. (19 How.) 393 (1857); *see supra* chapter 8.

[111]75 U.S. (8 Wall.) 603 (1870); *see supra* chapter 9.

[112]Both Bradley and Swayne invoked due process. The former announced that the "right of choice" of profession was "liberty" and the "occupation" itself "property," 83 U.S. (16 Wall.) at 122, the latter that "liberty" meant "freedom from all restraints but such as are justly imposed by law" and that "property" embraced anything with "exchangeable value," including labor, *id.* at 127. Neither gave reasons. Both neglected to reveal why there was a "deprivation," and Bradley made no effort to explain why "due process of law" was wanting. Swayne seemed to contradict his own conclusions by proclaiming, once more without argument, that the phrase meant "the application of the law as it exists in the fair and regular course of administrative procedure." *Id.* Interestingly in light of his later opinions, *e.g.*, Munn v. Illinois, 94 U.S. 113, 136 (1876) (dissenting opinion), *infra* chapter 11, Field's dissent did not invoke due process.

Swayne added that "[n]o searching analysis [was] necessary to eliminate [sic] the meaning" of the first section of the fourteenth amendment; there was "no room for construction" because its language was "intelligible and direct." 83 U.S. (16 Wall.) at 126. Said Fairman: "This throws more light upon Justice Swayne than upon the Amendment." C. FAIRMAN, *supra* note 6, at 1363.

[113]U.S. CONST. amend. XIV, § 1.

[114]83 U.S. (16 Wall.) at 73-75. For an approving view based solely on the text of the amendment, see A. MCLAUGHLIN, A CONSTITUTIONAL HISTORY OF THE UNITED STATES 729 (1935).

[115]83 U.S. (16 Wall.) at 79-80. Other examples of privileges of national citizenship given by Miller were habeas corpus, the right to travel on federal government business recognized in Crandall v. Nevada, 73 U.S. (6 Wall.) 35 (1868); *see infra*, conclusion to part four, text accompanying notes 32-34, and "[t]he right to peaceably assemble and petition for redress of grievances." *Id.* at 79.

[116]"All persons born or naturalized in the United States, and subject to the jurisdiction thereof, are citizens of the United States and of the State wherein they reside." U.S. CONST. amend. XIV, § 1; *see* 83 U.S. (16 Wall.) at 73-74. The most obvious explanation of this language was that it was meant to overturn Chief Justice Taney's conclusion in *Dred Scott* that even free blacks were not state citizens entitled to invoke the diversity jurisdiction, *see supra* chapter 8, not to limit the scope of the privileges or immunities clause. Indeed the citizenship clause was added long after the inclusion of the protection of privileges and immunities. *See* CONG. GLOBE, 39th Cong., 1st Sess. 2286, 2869, 2890 (1866).

of the relations of the State and Federal governments to each other and of both these governments to the people"[117]—which quite arguably was precisely what the authors of the amendment had in mind.[118] The dissenters did not hesitate to argue that Miller's interpretation wrote the privileges or immunities clause entirely out of the Constitution.[119] Though Miller disdained to cite it, there was nevertheless some legislative history to support the view that the clause created no new rights. Moreover, the dissenters overstated their objection, since the fifth section of the amendment gave Congress explicit authority to pass legislation to enforce the rights it protected, and it was not clear that Congress had previously had such power with regard to some of the federal rights identified in the debate as intended to be protected.[120]

There was also, however, legislative history to support no fewer than three other interpretations of the privileges or immunities clause, all of which were put forward by the dissenting Justices. In presenting the proposal to the Senate, Senator Howard had said among other things that it was designed, as Justice Black later argued,[121] to make the Bill of Rights applicable to the states.[122] Still other passages in the debates

[117]83 U.S. (16 Wall.) at 78.

[118]See J. tenBroek, The Antislavery Origins of the Fourteenth Amendment 185, 204 (1951).

[119]   If this inhibition . . . only refers . . . to such privileges and immunities as were before its adoption specially designated in the Constitution or necessarily implied as belonging to citizens of the United States, it was a vain and idle enactment . . . . With privileges and immunities thus designated or implied no State could ever have interfered by its laws, and no new constitutional provision was required to inhibit such interference. The supremacy of the Constitution and the laws of the United States always controlled any State legislation of that character.

83 U.S. (16 Wall.) at 96 (Field, J., dissenting, joined by Chase, C.J., and Swayne & Bradley, JJ.); see also J. Ely, Democracy and Distrust 22 (1980); C. Fairman, supra note 6, at 1354; L. Tribe, supra note 43, 423-24.

[120]See, e.g., Cong. Globe, 39th Cong., 1st. Sess. 2542-43 (remarks of Rep. Bingham) (arguing that the amendment "takes from no State any right that ever pertained to it" but merely authorized Congress for the first time to protect federal rights against state abridgement), 2961 (remarks of Sen. Poland) (arguing that it merely gave Congress power to enforce the privileges and immunities clause of article IV: "State legislation was allowed to override it, and as no express power was by the Constitution granted to Congress to enforce it, it became really a dead letter."). Contrast the express authority of Congress to enforce the full faith and credit clause of the same article. U.S. Const. art. IV, § 1. That Congress had been held to have implicit power to enforce the adjacent fugitive slave provision, see supra chapter 8 (discussing Prigg v. Pennsylvania, 41 U.S. (16 Pet.) 539 (1842)), does not detract from the clearly expressed desires of Bingham and Poland to avoid any doubt of congressional enforcement authority.

[121]E.g., Adamson v. California, 332 U.S. 46, 71-72 (1947) (Black, J., dissenting).

[122]Cong. Globe, 39th Cong., 1st Sess. 2766 (1866) (summarizing the Bill of Rights, noting its inapplicability to the states, and declaring it "[t]he great object of the first section of this amendment . . . to restrain the power of the States and compel them at all times to respect these great fundamental guarantees."); see also Adamson v. California, 332 U.S. 46, 71-72, 93-123 (1947) (Black, J., dissenting); O'Neil v. Vermont, 144 U.S. 323, 360-64 (1892) (Field, J., dissenting); Slaughter-House Cases, 83 U.S. (16 Wall.) 36, 118 (1873) (Bradley, J., dissenting); Crosskey, Charles Fairman, "Legislative History," and the Constitutional Limitations on State Authority, 22 U. Chi. L. Rev. 1, 6 (1954); Curtis, The Fourteenth Amendment and the Bill of Rights, 14 Conn. L. Rev. 237 (1982). It is not entirely clear that Justice Miller rejected the incorporation theory in Slaughter-House; indeed, Professor Ely takes Miller's inclusion of the right to assemble and petition the Government among the privileges of national citizenship, see supra note 115, as indicating that the Court actually embraced incorporation. J. Ely, supra note 119, at 196-97. Miller's reference is ambiguous; he may have meant only that the states were forbidden to interfere with citizens assembling to petition the federal government, and he conspicuously neglected to refer to the Bill of Rights as a whole.

seemed to suggest that Congress meant to give federal protection to all privileges or immunities that were "fundamental" in the sense described by Justice Washington in his famous circuit court interpretation, in *Corfield v. Coryell*,[123] of the privileges and immunities clause of article IV.[124] Finally, numerous legislators suggested that the principal aim of the amendment was to provide a firm constitutional basis for the Civil Rights Act of 1866,[125] which had outlawed racially discriminatory state action.[126] As Field said in dissent, what article IV

> did for the protection of the citizens of one State against hostile and discriminating legislation of other States, the fourteenth amendment does for the protection of every citizen of the United States against hostile and discriminating legislation against him in favor of others, whether they reside in the same or in different States.[127]

The textual difficulty with the incorporation theory pointed out by the second Justice Harlan[128] seems less compelling than Professor Fairman's demonstration that nobody thought the amendment invalidated the numerous provisions permitting trials for infamous crimes without indictment that were adopted by states and approved by Congress shortly after its adoption, and that Senator Howard's interpretation was apparently shared by virtually none of the many others who spoke to the clause in the debates.[129] The fundamental-rights notion reflects once again the

[123]6 Fed. Cas. 546 (C.C.E.D. Pa. 1823) (No. 3,230).

[124]*E.g.*, CONG. GLOBE, 39th Cong., 1st Sess. 2765 (1866) (remarks of Sen. Howard) (quoting from *Corfield v. Coryell*, 6 Fed. Cas. at 551-52); *see* 83 U.S. (16 Wall.) at 114-19 (Bradley, J., dissenting); United States v. Hall, 26 Fed. Cas. 79, 81 (C.C.S.D. Ala. 1871) (No. 15,282) (Woods, J.); *cf.* Kurland, *The Privileges or Immunities Clause: "Its Hour Come Round at Last"?*, 1972 WASH. U.L.Q. 405, 419 (arguing for a modified version of the fundamental rights view). Ely finds

> the most plausible interpretation of the Privileges or Immunities Clause to be, as it must be, the one suggested by its language—that it was a delegation to future constitutional decision-makers to protect certain rights that the document neither lists, at least not exhaustively, nor even in any specific way gives directions for finding.

J. ELY, *supra* note 119, at 28-30.

[125]Act of April 9, 1866, ch. 31, § 1, 14 Stat. 27, 27.

[126]*E.g.*, CONG. GLOBE, 39th Cong., 1st Sess. 2459 (1866) (remarks of Rep. Stevens), 2465 (remarks of Rep. Thayer), 2498 (remarks of Rep. Broomall), 2502 (remarks of Rep. Raymond), 2511 (remarks of Rep. Eliot), 2538 (remarks of Rep. Rogers), 2896 (remarks of Sens. Doolittle, Fessenden, and Howard); *see also* 83 U.S. (16 Wall.) at 97 (Field, J., dissenting).

[127]83 U.S. (16 Wall.) at 100-01.

[128]Duncan v. Louisiana, 391 U.S. 145, 179 n.9 (1968) (dissenting opinion) ("The great words of the four clauses of the first section of the Fourteenth Amendment would have been an exceedingly peculiar way to say that 'The rights heretofore guaranteed against federal intrusion by the first eight Amendments are henceforth guaranteed against state intrusion as well.' "). If one wishes to be technical, it is hard to see how a state could "abridge" the privileges in the Bill of Rights, since the only rights there confirmed were of freedom from federal action. *See* A. McLAUGHLIN, *supra* note 114, at 730-31 & n.18. But see Crosskey's observation that the first amendment demonstrated it was not unusual "to forbid the 'abridging' . . . of a 'right' not previously existing against the agency forbidden, and not *formally* created against it in the prohibition itself": for the "*'right of the people* peaceably to assemble, and to petition the Government,'" which Congress was forbidden to abridge, "did not exist previously against Congress . . . ." 2 W. CROSSKEY, POLITICS AND THE CONSTITUTION IN THE HISTORY OF THE UNITED STATES 1094 (1953).

[129]Fairman, *Does the Fourteenth Amendment Incorporate the Bill of Rights?* 2 STAN. L. REV. 5 (1949). The existence of the due process clause in the amendment provides another argument against incorpo-

incessant quest for the judicial holy grail; perhaps at long last we have discovered a clause that lets us strike down any law we do not like.[130] There is no textual reason why the clause could not have created a new and undefined class of federal privileges, and if that is what the Framers meant to do it is no objection that they may have misunderstood what Justice Washington was talking about on circuit, or that he may have misunderstood article IV.[131]

The basic objection to the fundamental-rights argument, as well as to Miller's interpretation and to the incorporation thesis, is that none of them may reflect what most of the Framers actually had in mind. The dominant theme in the debates, as Fairman has shown,[132] was to provide a constitutional basis for the Civil Rights Act of 1866, which provided that all persons

> born in the United States and not subject to any foreign power, excluding Indians not taxed, are hereby declared to be citizens of the United States; and such citizens, of every race and color, without regard to any previous condition of slavery or involuntary servitude, . . . shall have the same right, in every State and Territory in the United States, to make and enforce contracts, to sue, be parties, and give evidence, to inherit, purchase, lease, sell, hold, and convey real and personal property, and to full and equal benefit of all laws and proceedings for the security of persons and property, as is enjoyed by white citizens, and shall be subject to like punishment, pains, and penalties, and to none other, any law, statute, ordinance, regulation, or custom, to the contrary not-withstanding.[133]

There is no doubt what this statute was: a simple prohibition of official racial discrimination. It created no substantive federal rights, however fundamental; it did not make the Bill of Rights apply to the states. But it did more than enforce rights already existing; it provided that the rights that states chose to give white people were the measure of the rights of nonwhites too.

Speaker after speaker proclaimed that it was this statute for which the fourteenth amendment would provide an unassailable constitutional base.[134] If the language

---

ration; it suggests that when the drafters of the amendment meant to make bill of rights provisions apply to the states, they said so. The later argument that the *due process* clause incorporates the Bill of Rights is even more questionable, for it makes all the other provisions of the original bill redundant. Moreover, the incorporation thesis would probably have been of no use to those challenging the monopoly in *Slaughter-House* itself, for it is hard to find anything in the first eight amendments that forbids monopolies—unless it be the due process clause itself, which the fourteenth amendment expressly made applicable to the states without the need of incorporation.

[130]*Cf. supra* chapters 2, 5, 10 (discussing *Calder v. Bull*, *Fletcher v. Peck*, and *Hepburn v. Griswold*).

[131]The Court had made clear before the fourteenth amendment debates that the original privileges and immunities clause was merely a protection of outsiders from discrimination in respect to privileges created by state law; Washington held, despite some loose language, that it gave no protection even where there was discrimination unless the right was fundamental. *See* Fairman, *supra* note 129, at 9-15; *supra* chapter 8 (discussing Conner v. Elliott, 59 U.S. (18 How.) 591 (1856)).

[132]*See* Fairman, *supra* note 129, *passim*.

[133]Act of Apr. 9, 1866, ch. 31, § 1, 14 Stat. 27, 27.

[134]*See* R. Berger, Government by Judiciary, ch. 2 (1977); 5 C. Swisher, History of the Supreme Court of the United States 415 (1974); *supra* note 126; *see also* Fairman, *supra* note 129, *passim*. Fairman concludes, nevertheless, that "Justice Cardozo's gloss on the due process clause—what is

actually adopted did not permit such an interpretation, such statements could not alter its meaning. But a comparison of the amendment with the statute shows that the text is admirably designed to accomplish just what the speakers said it would do.

The statute did three things. First, it extended citizenship without regard to race; this provision was essentially copied into the first clause of the amendment. Second, the statute forbade racial discrimination with respect to certain enumerated rights: to contract, to sue, to deal with property; and at the end it forbade racial discrimination in the infliction of punishment. The second clause of the fourteenth amendment seems to generalize these provisions: all legal privileges and immunities are protected—not only the privileges of contracting and suing, and not only the immmunity from punishment.[135] That the provision is merely a guarantee of equal treatment is strongly suggested by the choice of the language of article IV, which the Court had already so construed: as Field said,[136] the original Constitution forbade discrimination against citizens of other states;[137] the new provision, like the statute it was meant to sustain, extended the same protection to a state's own citizens—without regard to race.[138]

It may be objected that Field's interpretation cannot be accepted because it makes the equal protection clause redundant;[139] every student knows that the latter clause

---

'implicit in the concept of ordered liberty'—comes as close as one can to catching the vague aspirations that were hung upon the privileges and immunities clause." Fairman, *supra* note 129, at 139 (citing Palko v. Connecticut, 302 U.S. 319, 325 (1937)); *see* also Royall, *The Fourteenth Amendment,* 4 S.L. Rev. 558, 571 (1878) (arguing that the fourteenth amendment incorporated, and did not merely make constitutional, statutes such as the Civil Rights Bill).

[135]Berger denies that there was any generalization: the privileges and immunities protected were only those listed in the Civil Rights Act. R. Berger, *supra* note 134, ch. 2. There seems no reason to doubt, however, that the Framers meant to employ the term as broadly as it had been construed in article IV. *See* Corfield v. Coryell, 6 Fed. Cas. 456 (C.C.E.D. Pa. 1823) (No. 3,230) (declaring that the term included all rights that were "fundamental").

[136]*See* supra text accompanying note 127.

[137]*See* Paul v. Virginia, 75 U.S. (8 Wall.) 168, 180 (1869) (dictum); Conner v. Elliott, 59 U.S. (18 How.) 591, 594 (1856), *discussed in supra* chapter 8;, *see also* Ward v. Maryland, 79 U.S. (12 Wall.) 418, 430-32 (1871) (Clifford, J.) (striking down a tax that discriminated against citizens of other states). It is worth noting Miller's own explanation of the article IV provision in *Slaughter-House* itself:

> Its sole purpose was to declare to the several States, that whatever those rights, as you grant or establish them to your own citizens, or as you limit or qualify, or impose restrictions on their exercise, the same, neither more nor less, shall be the measure of the rights of citizens of other States within your jurisdiction.

83 U.S. (16 Wall.) at 77; *accord* 2 J. Kent, Commentaries on American Law 71 (1st ed. New York 1826); 3 J. Story, Commentaries on the Constitution of the United States § 1800 (Boston 1833).

[138]*See* Crosskey, *supra* note 122, at 7-9 (agreeing that this was the purpose of the amendment but arguing that it was accomplished by the equal protection clause, not by the clause repeating the terms of article IV that the Framers meant to amend); for further elaboration, *see* 2 W. Crosskey *supra* note 128, at 1083-1158. Ely concurs: "[T]he slightest attention to language will indicate that it is the Equal Protection Clause that follows the command of equality strategy, while the Privileges or Immunities Clause proceeds by purporting to extend to everyone a set of entitlements." J. Ely, *supra* note 119, at 24. Ely adds, fairly enough, that statements indicating a desire for equality or an intention to justify the 1866 act are not necessarily inconsistent with a desire to confer additional rights as well. *Id.* at 23, 199. As indicated in the text, I think the language of the amendment, in light of its origins, also cuts in favor of Field's interpretation.

[139]*See* J. Ely, *supra* note 119, at 24.

does precisely what Field said was done by privileges or immunities.[140] The text of the statute the amendment was designed to justify once again suggests an answer. The third feature of the 1866 act was to give to nonwhites "the full and equal benefit of all laws and proceedings for the security of persons and property, as is enjoyed by white citizens."[141] As Miller recognized in the introductory part of his *Slaughter-House* opinion, there were two distinct problems with which the mere abolition of slavery did not deal: the southern states had adopted Black Codes denying blacks a variety of privileges and immunities, and "[i]t was said that their lives were at the mercy of bad men, either because of the laws for their protection were insufficient or were not enforced."[142] Against this background equal protection seems to mean that the states must protect blacks to the same extent that they protect whites: by punishing those who do them injury.[143] "Protection of the laws" is, after all, a peculiar way to express a general freedom from discrimination; it may well have been the privileges or immunities clause instead that was meant to protect blacks' rights to contract, to sue, and to hold property.

The next objection to Field's position is that the privileges or immunities clause cannot possibly have been an anti-discrimination provision because it is too broad; since it is not confined to racial discrimination, it would mean that the state could not bar two-year-olds from driving trucks or halfwits from teaching school. This objection, it will be noted, is just as applicable to the equal protection clause, which the Court has used for the same purpose; the Court has dealt with it, as Field did,[144] essentially by saying the intention was not to outlaw reasonable classifications.[145] An

[140]*E.g.,* Missouri *ex rel.* Gaines v. Canada, 305 U.S. 337 (1938) (equal access to public education).

[141]Act of Apr. 9, 1866, ch. 31, § 1, 14, Stat. 27, 27.

[142]83 U.S. (16 Wall.) at 70.

[143]Compare the remarks of Senator Cowan, discussing the definition of citizenship: Even the foreigner, while not a citizen, "is entitled, to a certain extent, to the protection of the laws. You cannot murder him with impunity . . . . You cannot commit an assault and battery upon him . . . . He has a right to the protection of the laws." CONG. GLOBE, 39th Cong., 1st Sess. 2890 (1866). Blackstone speaks of protection of the laws in a similar fashion: "For in vain would rights be declared, in vain directed to be observed, if there were no method of recovering and asserting those rights, when wrongly withheld or invaded. This is what we mean properly, when we speak of the protection of the law." 1 W. BLACKSTONE, COMMENTARIES *55-56; *see also* J. TENBROEK, *supra* note 101, at 26-29, 96-98, 163-79, 192-221 (arguing that "equal protection" had been used in this sense ever since the earliest days of abolitionism and not in the sense of improper classifications); *cf.* Willing, *Protection by Law Enforcement: The Emerging Constitutional Right*, 35 RUTGERS L. REV. 1, 60 (1982) (even in the traditional terms of *Slaughter-House,* preservation of effective law enforcement when a state fails to provide it is a "right" guaranteed by the federal government). Senator Howard, however, spoke of the equal-protection and due process clauses in a broader sense as intended to "abolish[] all class legislation and do[] away with the injustice of subjecting one caste of persons to a code not applicable to another. . . . It protects the black man in his fundamental rights as a citizen with the same shield which it throws over the white man." CONG. GLOBE, 39th Cong., 1st Sess. 2766 (1866).

[144]   The State may prescribe such regulations for every pursuit and calling of life as will promote the public health, secure the good order and advance the general prosperity of society, but when once prescribed, the pursuit or calling must be free to be followed by every citizen who is within the conditions designated, and will conform to the regulations.

83 U.S. (16 Wall.) at 110.

[145]See, for example, the Court's analysis in Massachusetts Board of Retirement v. Murgia, 427 U.S. 307 (1976);

Through mandatory retirement at age 50, the legislature seeks to protect the public by assuring physical preparedness of its uniformed police. . . . [M]andatory retirement at 50

alternative construction that takes no great liberties with the text seems to correspond much better with its expressed purpose: despite the broad drafting, privileges or immunities are secured only against racial discrimination, for that was the only thing forbidden by the statute whose constitutionality the amendment was meant to assure.[146]

Thus Miller may have been on the right track to suggest that equal protection was a safeguard only against racial discrimination[147]—though the use of the broader term "person" in contrast to "citizen" in that clause and the fact that it would not be unreasonable to guarantee literally everyone equal *protection* in the narrow sense suggest that his argument is more persuasive as applied to privileges or immunities. Miller may also have been suggesting a plausibly narrow interpretation of equal protection when he hinted that the clause might apply only if justice was denied in the courts[148]—he seems to have had some perception that the clause referred only to procedures for the redress of wrongs. What he failed to do, however, was to read the privileges or immunities clause broadly enough to accomplish what he acknowledged to be the purpose of the amendment;[149] thereafter it seemed inevitable that the Court would have to read the equal protection clause, despite its arguably distinct purpose, in such a way as to fill the gap.[150] Just how the Court should have construed the privileges or immunities clause it is not easy to say, but Miller seems to have selected an interpretation particularly difficult to reconcile with the history of the amendment,[151] and without adequate attention to the problem.

Just as Miller's opinion diverted discrimination analysis from privileges or immunities to equal protection, it diverted fundamental-rights analysis to the due process clause. While his interment of the privileges or immunities approach has so far been permanent, the due process argument was to rise again despite the blows it had received in the *Legal Tender Cases*[152] and in *Slaughter-House* itself. All of this, however, is material for later study,[153] for only one more fourteenth amendment case

---

serves to remove from police service those whose fitness for uniformed work presumptively has diminished with age. This clearly is rationally related to the State's objective.

Id. at 314-15.

[146]Some members of Congress had also referred to the need to enable Congress to enforce the privileges of Northerners in the South already protected by article IV. *See supra* note 103. But power to punish violations of an existing duty is a far cry from a general prohibition of classifications the Court finds unreasonable.

[147]*See supra* text accompanying note 100. Given this passage and others indicating that "the pervading purpose" of all three civil-war amendments (13th–15th) was "the freedom of the slave race, the security and firm establishment of that freedom, and the protection of the newly-made freeman and citizen from the oppressions of those who had formerly exercised unlimited dominion over him," 83 U.S. (16 Wall.) at 71, it seems more than a little odd to suggest, as Kutler does, that Miller's opinion "laid the foundation for the legal subversion of Negro hopes for full equality." *See* S. KUTLER, JUDICIAL POWER AND RECONSTRUCTION POLITICS 165 (1968).

[148]*See supra* text accompanying notes 102-03.

[149]*See* 83 U.S. (16 Wall.) at 70; L. TRIBE, *supra note* 43, at 419 n.26.

[150]One result of this, as I shall argue in the next chapter, was that the original purpose of the equal protection clause was largely forgotten and the powers of Congress to enforce it accordingly may have been too narrowly construed.

[151]For a nearly contemporaneous criticism of the Court for ignoring the legislative history, see Royall, *supra* note 134, at 563.

[152]79 U.S. (12 Wall.) 457 (1871); *see supra* chapter 9.

[153]*See infra* chapter 11.

was decided before Chase's death: *Bradwell v. State*,[154] which immediately follows *Slaughter-House* in the official reports.

If Field's theory of privileges or immunities had prevailed, *Bradwell* would have been an interesting case testing whether the amendment forbade only racial discrimination: it concerned an Illinois decision that only males could practice law. Justice Bradley, who disagreed with *Slaughter-House*, had to face that issue in a concurring opinion. In so doing, rather than limiting the clause to race, he uttered some benighted observations about the woman's place in the home, some of which he had the temerity to attribute to "the Creator;"[155] his basic point was that the discrimination was acceptable on the merits. After *Slaughter-House*, however, the privileges or immunities claim was easy: as Miller said for the Court, the clause did not forbid discrimination of any kind, and there was no federal right to practice law.[156] Most revealing with respect to later developments is the total absence of any argument that sex discrimination in bar admission offended the equal protection clause; apparently it had not yet occurred to anybody that "protection of the laws" included the right to be a lawyer.

Chief Justice Chase dissented alone in *Bradwell*.[157] He did not have the courtesy to tell us why.

[154] 83 U.S. (16 Wall.) 130 (1873).

[155] *Id.* at 141-42. Swayne and Field, who had also dissented in *Slaughter-House*, joined Bradley's opinion.

[156] *Id.* at 139. An argument had also been made on the basis of article IV's guarantee of equal privileges for citizens of other states. Miller's conclusive response was that, although Ms. Bradwell had been born in Vermont, she had become an Illinois citizen by residing there, in accordance with the first clause of the fourteenth amendment. *Id.* at 138; *see also* Corker, Bradwell v. State: *Some Reflections Prompted by Myra Bradwell's Hard Case that Made "Bad Law"*, 53 WASH. L. REV. 215 (1978) (suggesting that the issue may have been moot by the time the court decided it, since Illinois had passed legislation prohibiting most sex-based restrictions on employment, Act of March 22, 1872, 1871-72 Ill. Laws 578).

[157] 83 U.S. (16 Wall.) at 142.

Conclusion to Part Four

The principal constitutional task of the court under Chase was to deal with the many important and varied issues arising directly or indirectly out of the Civil War. Apart from the war issues, questions of the extent of congressional power were scarce and of relatively minor interest. The commerce clause was read, not surprisingly, to authorize federal regulation of liquor sales to Indians,[1] registration of ship mortgages,[2] permission to build railroad bridges,[3] and inspection of vessels carrying goods and passengers on an intrastate portion of an interstate journey,[4] though the famous and peculiar decision in *Paul v. Virginia* that states could regulate insurance because it was not commerce[5] seemed to mean that Congress could not regulate it at all. Thus although the Court generally construed congressional powers amply,[6] it was not prepared to ignore the fact that Congress had only the powers the Constitution enumerated; and it made this point by appropriately holding, in *United States v. Dewitt*, that the only oil whose flammability Congress could limit was that moving in

---

[1]United States v. Holliday, 70 U.S. (3 Wall.) 407 (1866) (Miller, J.).

[2]White's Bank v. Smith, 74 U.S. (7 Wall.) 646 (1869) (Nelson, J.).

[3]The Clinton Bridge, 77 U.S. (10 Wall.) 454 (1870) (Nelson, J.)

[4]The Daniel Ball, 77 U.S. (10 Wall.) 557 (1851) (Field, J.).

[5]75 U.S. (8 Wall.) 168, 183 (1869) (Field, J.) (alternative holding) ("The policies are simple contracts of indemnity against loss by fire, . . . not articles of commerce . . . . They are not subjects of trade and barter offered in the market as something having an existence and value independent of the parties to them . . . ."); *accord*, Ducat v. Chicago, 77 U.S. (10 Wall.) 410 (1871) (Nelson, J.); *see* United States v. South-Eastern Underwriters Association, 322 U.S. 533, 539, 546–47 (1944) (overruling this holding); *supra* chapter 10, note 73 (discussing the alternative ground that the transactions in question were not interstate); *infra* text accompanying notes 20-22 (discussing whether the state law in *Paul* offended the privileges and immunities clause).

[6]*Cf.* License Tax Cases, 72 U.S. (5 Wall.) 462 (Chase, C.J.) (upholding a privilege tax on activities assumed to be beyond Congress's regulatory powers because, in contrast to the steamboat license in Gibbons v. Ogden, 22 U.S. (9 Wheat.) 1 (1824) (*see supra* chapter 6), the statute did not purport to give a right to engage in the licensed activities without regard to state law).

interstate or foreign commerce.[7] Apart from the oath and military-trial cases and the ups and downs of due process in the two controversies over legal tender,[8] little attention was given to provisions limiting the enumerated congressional powers; of most significance for the future was the plausible holding in *Pumpelly v. Green Bay Co.* that the flooding of land by a dam was a taking of property within the meaning of the Wisconsin constitution.[9]

Similarly, the reconstruction cases account for most of the important decisions of the Chase years respecting the powers of the federal courts. In other expectable decisions the Justices reaffirmed that Congress could not subject the Court's decisions to revision by other branches,[10] held that a county was to be treated as a "citizen" for diversity purposes,[11] and allowed removal from a state court on the basis of a federal defense.[12] Auguring most for the future was the appearance of two dissents from the decision in *Davis v. Gray*,[13] which seemed only to follow Marshall's holding in *Osborn v. Bank of the United States* that the eleventh amendment did not preclude suits to enjoin state officers from acting unconstitutionally;[14] in the next few

[7] 76 U.S. (9 Wall.) 41 (1870) (Chase, C.J.).

[8] *See also* Osborn v. Nicholson, 80 U.S. (13 Wall.) 654 (1872) (Swayne, J.) (suggesting without explanation that the due process clause forbade congressional impairment of contracts); Stewart v. Kahn, 78 U.S. (11 Wall.) 493 (1871) (Swayne, J.) (holding due process not offended by revival of causes of action barred by the statute of limitations during the war).

[9] 80 U.S. (13 Wall.) 166 (1872) (Miller, J.); *see also* Yates v. Milwaukee, 77 U.S. (10 Wall.) 497 (1871) (Miller, J.) (holding in a case coming from federal circuit court, without stating what provision was at stake, that a city could not order the removal, without compensation, of a wharf that posed no threat to navigation).

[10] Gordon v. United States, 69 U.S. (2 Wall.) 561 (1865) (without opinion). Taney's draft opinion, belatedly printed at 117 U.S. 697 (1885) (Appendix), was not the opinion of the Court. For antecedents, see *supra* chapter 1 (discussing Hayburn's Case, 2 U.S. (2 Dall.) 409 (1799)), and *supra* chapter 8 (discussing United States v. Ferreira, 54 U.S. (13 How.) 40 (1852)).

[11] Cowles v. Mercer County, 74 U.S. (7 Wall.) 118 (1869) (Chase, C.J.);*cf.* Marshall v. Baltimore & O.R.R., 57 U.S. (16 How.) 314 (1854) (fictitiously deeming all persons representing a private corporation to be citizens of its state of incorporation), *discussed supra in* chapter 8. In the case of a county this presumption makes more sense, *see* P. BATOR, P. MISHKIN, D. SHAPIRO & H. WECHSLER, HART AND WECHSLER'S THE FEDERAL COURTS AND THE FEDERAL SYSTEM 1089 (2d ed. 1973), and the risk of bias seems quite real, since otherwise the outsider would have to sue the county in its own courts.

[12] The Mayor v. Cooper, 73 U.S. (6 Wall.) 247 (1868) (Swayne, J.). Marshall had presaged this result in Cohens v. Virginia, 19 U.S. (6 Wheat.) 264, 379 (1821), *discussed supra in* chapter 4, saying that a case arose under federal law whenever the claim of either party relied on federal law, and many times (as in *Cohens* itself) the Court had reviewed state-court decisions where a defendant's federal right had been denied. *See also* Justices v. Murray, 76 U.S. (9 Wall.) 274 (1870) (Nelson, J.) (properly holding the seventh amendment forbade retrial after removal of fact questions already determined by a state-court jury); The Alicia, 74 U.S. (7 Wall.) 571 (1869) (Chase, C.J.) (holding Congress without power to order transfer of appeals in prize cases to the Supreme Court on the highly technical ground that the trial court's decree had been vacated by the filing of an appeal); *cf. supra* chapter 3 (discussing *Ex parte* Bollman, 8 U.S. (4 Cranch) 75 (1807)).

[13] 83 U.S. (16 Wall.) 203 (1873) (Swayne, J.). The suit was to enjoin a state official from conveying to others lands claimed by the plaintiffs. Chase joined Davis's dissent. *Id.* at 233.

[14] 22 U.S. (9 Wheat.) 738 (1824), *discussed supra in* chapter 4. The dissenters (Davis and Chase) made no attempt to distinguish *Osborn*, saying in one brief paragraph only that the effect of the decision was "to deprive the State of the power to dispose, in its own way, of its public lands." 83 U.S. (16 Wall.) at 233. Later cases were to make it important whether title had already passed to the plaintiffs, but the Court gave this question no attention, and it did not distinguish Governor of Georgia v. Madrazo, 26 U.S. (1 Pet.) 110 (1828), which had placed an ill-defined limitation on *Osborn*.

years the Court was to develop highly sophisticated distinctions in this area.[15]

By far the greatest number of cases, as in the Taney period, dealt with constitutional limits on the powers of the states. The *Slaughter-House Cases* and *Bradwell* seemed to portend a narrow application of the new fourteenth amendment. The Court finally invalidated two state taxes for obstructing interstate commerce, but on the whole it was not particularly aggressive in applying the limiting effect of the commerce clause. Contract clause litigation, as usual, dominated the docket in terms of sheer numbers, but no interesting new questions were decided.[16] In obedience to Marshall's ill-conceived reasoning in *Brown v. Maryland*,[17] the imports-exports clause was held to bar nondiscriminatory taxes on goods in the hands of their importer[18] but to allow taxes after he had sold them, without even discussing whether they were discriminatory.[19] *Paul v. Virginia*[20] confirmed the debatable implication of *Bank of Augusta v. Earle*[21] that corporations were not "Citizen[s]" for purposes of article IV's privileges and immunities clause despite what the Court had done for them under the similar language of article III;[22] *Ward v. Maryland* properly repeated that the clause forbade discriminatory taxes on out-of-state traders;[23] and *Bradwell v. State* appropriately concluded that it ceased to protect individuals who had become citizens of the state of whose action they complained.[24]

[15]*See infra* chapter 12. On the related question of the implicit immunity of the *federal* government from suit, see The Davis, 77 U.S. (10 Wall.) 15 (1870) (Miller, J.) (allowing a salvage claim against government property because it was not in government possession); The Siren, 74 U.S. (7 Wall.) 152 (1869) (Field, J.) (holding that the United States had consented to claims against a fund by filing a claim of its own).

[16]The Court reaffirmed that states could reserve the right to alter corporate charters, e.g., Pennsylvania College Cases, 80 U.S. (13 Wall.) 190 (1872) (Clifford, J.); it appeared both to embrace and to reject the unexplained suggestion of Gelpcke v. Dubuque, 68 U.S. (1 Wall.) 175, 206 (1864) (*see supra* chapter 7) that the clause forbade judicial as well as legislative impairment. *Compare* Havemeyer v. Iowa County, 70 U.S. (3 Wall.) 294, 303 (1866) (Swayne, J.) ("if the contract, when made, was valid . . . no subsequent action by . . . the judiciary can impair its obligation"), *and* Thomson v. Lee County, 70 U.S. (3 Wall.) 327, 331 (1866) (Davis, J.) ("change in judicial decision cannot be allowed to render [contracts] invalid"), *and* Butz v. Muscatine, 75 U.S. (8 Wall.) 575, 583-84 (1869) (Swayne, J.) (Court has as much duty "to protect the contract from [judicial action] as from [legislation]"), *with* Railroad Co. v. Rock, 71 U.S. (4 Wall.) 177, 181 (1867) (Miller, J.) (invalidation by state court not unconstitutional unless in support of state statute), *and* Railroad Co. v. McClure, 77 U.S. (10 Wall.) 511, 515 (1871) (Swayne, J.) (state court invalidation of bonds outside Court jurisdiction), *and* Bank of West Tennessee v. Citizens' Bank, 81 U.S. (14 Wall.) 9, 10 (1872) (Swayne, J.) (state court refusal to enforce bank obligation outside Court jurisdiction). *See generally* C. FAIRMAN, *supra* chapter 10, note 6, at 918–1116 (discussing *Gelpcke* and other municipal bond cases). Most interesting was the addition of Miller, Chase, and Field to the list of dissenters denying that states had power to give contractual tax exemptions. Washington Univ. v. Rouse, 75 U.S. (8 Wall.) 439, 443–44 (1869) (Miller, J., dissenting); *see supra* chapter 7. Though he lost this battle, Miller's ideas would soon persuade the Court in an analogous field of state regulation. *See* Stone v. Mississippi, 101 U.S. 814 (1880) (state had no power to promise not to revoke lottery charter). The remaining twenty-odd contract clause decisions merely applied settled law.

[17]25 U.S. (12 Wheat.) 419 (1827); *see supra* chapter 6.

[18]Low v. Austin, 80 U.S. (13 Wall.) 29 (1872) (Field, J.); *see supra* chapter 10, note 46.

[19]Waring v. Mayor, 75 U.S. (8 Wall.) 110 (1869) (Clifford, J.).

[20]75 U.S. (8 Wall.) 168, 177-82 (1869) (Field, J.); *see also supra* text accompanying note 5 (discussing *Paul's* holding that insurance was not commerce).

[21]38 U.S. (13 Pet.) 519 (1839); *see supra* chapter 8.

[22]*See supra* note 11.

[23]79 U.S. (12 Wall.) 418, 432 (1871); *see supra* chapter 10, note 89. *Cf. supra* chapter 8 (discussing Conner v. Elliott).

[24]83 U.S. (16 Wall.) 130, 139 (1873); *see supra* chapter 10, notes 154-56 and accompanying text. The full

More interesting are a handful of decisions dealing with implicit governmental immunities. On the one side, *Collector v. Day*[25] finally recognized, contrary to dicta in *McCulloch v. Maryland*[26] and to the thrust of the *Veazie Bank* case,[27] that the constitutional argument that Congress could not tax the states was at least as strong as its converse.[28] On the other, the Court was faithful to the purposes of federal immunity in holding, despite the implications of *Cooley v. Board of Wardens*,[29] that Congress could waive the implicit federal immunity,[30] and *Tarble's Case* reaffirmed the inability of state courts to free federal prisoners on the apparent basis of *McCulloch*'s argument that the states may not impede federal functions.[31] Most important and most questionable, however, was the famous decision in *Crandall v. Nevada*,[32] in which the Court, after disdaining the aid of a commerce clause argument that had prevailed against an indistinguishable state law in the immediately preceding case,[33] elected to rely on *McCulloch* for the proposition that Nevada's tax on passengers leaving the state interfered with government operations (and with an unpedigreed correlative right of the citizen) by obstructing travel to government offices—*without saying that the passengers in question were on their way to visit the government.* This opinion was by Miller, who would soon afterward hold, without invoking any constitutional provision, that a city could not issue bonds to promote private industry.[34] The natural-law overtones of the *Crandall* opinion were reflected

---

faith and credit clause was held in Christmas v. Russell, 72 U.S. (5 Wall.) 290 (1866) (Clifford, J.), not to permit one state to look behind another's judgment for fraud or on the ground that the original claim had been barred by time; Cheever v. Wilson, 76 U.S. (9 Wall.) 108 (1870) (Swayne, J.), required respect for a divorce rendered at a wife's separate domicile. See also the two confusing and minor full faith and credit decisions in Green v. Van Buskirk, 72 U.S. (5 Wall.) 290 (1867) (Clifford, J.), and 74 U.S. (7 Wall.) 139 (1869) (Davis, J.) (writ of attachment granted by Illinois court in suit between New York citizens binding on New York courts). The Court also reaffirmed the inapplicability of the Bill of Rights to the states in the pre-fourteenth-amendment cases of Pervear v. Commissioners, 72 U.S. (5 Wall.) 475 (1867) (Chase, C.J.) (cruel and unusual punishment), and Twitchell v. Commonwealth, 74 U.S. (7 Wall.) 321 (1869) (Chase, C.J.) (right to be informed of charge).

[25]78 U.S. (11 Wall.) 113 (1871) (Nelson, J.).

[26]17 U.S. (4 Wheat.) 316 (1819). *See supra* chapter 6.

[27]75 U.S. (8 Wall.) 533 (1870); *see supra* chapter 9.

[28]*Cf. supra* chapter 9 (discussing Lane County v. Oregon, 74 U.S. (7 Wall.) 71 (1869)); chapter 8, *supra* 10 (discussing Kentucky v. Dennison, 65 U.S. (24 How.) 66 (1860)). *See also* United States v. Railroad Co., 84 U.S. (17 Wall.) 332 (1873) (Hunt, J.), decided after Chase's death but before the appointment of his successor, barring a federal tax on interest paid to a city, which was treated as a state for this purpose—over dissents arguing the principle was inapplicable because the activity in question was essentially proprietary. *Cf. supra* chapter 6 (discussing Bank of United States v. Planters' Bank, 22 U.S. (9 Wheat.) 904 (1824)).

[29]53 U.S. (15 How.) 299 (1852); *see supra* chapter 10, text accompanying notes 1-4.

[30]Van Allen v. Assessors, 70 U.S. (3 Wall.) 573 (1866) (Nelson, J.). *See also* the peculiar decisions in Thomson v. Pacific R.R., 76 U.S. (9 Wall.) 579 (1870) (Chase, C.J.), that a state may tax a federal corporation if it also gives it a charter, which hardly seems to reduce the risk of disrupting federal interests, and in Society for Savings v. Coite, 73 U.S. (6 Wall.) 594 (1868) (Clifford, J.), allowing the state to tax the franchise of a corporation though its funds were partly invested in federal securities that, as reaffirmed in Banks v. Mayor, 74 U.S. (7 Wall.) 16 (1869) (Chase, C.J.), could not themselves be taxed.

[31]80 U.S. (13 Wall.) 397 (1872) (Field, J.); *see supra* chapter 8 (discussing Ableman v. Booth, 62 U.S. (21 How.) 506 (1859)).

[32]73 U.S. (6 Wall.) 35 (1868) (Miller, J.).

[33]*See supra* chapter 10 text accompanying notes 37-43.

[34]Loan Ass'n v. Topeka, 87 U.S. (20 Wall.) 655 (1875). *See infra* chapter 11.

not only in *Hepburn v. Griswold*, from which Miller loudly dissented,[35] but also in three contemporaneous decisions rejecting state claims of what the Court viewed as extraterritorial powers.[36] In another case, nevertheless, the Court emphatically denied that it had authority to invalidate laws simply because they offended "fundamental principles."[37]

Moving from the decisions to the Justices, one finds as usual that the business of writing significant opinions was largely confined to a handful of the Court's members. Catron never sat after Chase was appointed, Wayne disappeared without writing a word after delivering a decisive vote against test oaths, and Hunt barely put in an appearance at the end. Nelson was as inconspicuous as he had been during twenty years with Taney,[38] Grier noteworthy only because of the unfortunate effects of his senility in the legal-tender controversy. Clifford and Swayne, for perfectly adequate reasons, were never assigned anything of importance; they were two of the poorest opinion-writers ever to sit on the Court.[39] Davis wrote essentially nothing but that stirring and ultimately disappointing opinion against military trials in *Milligan*; it is surprising only that it took him so long to discover that he would really be better off in the Senate. Even the famous Bradley, who served only three years with Chase, barely got his feet wet during this period, contributing little beyond a scattergun dissent in *Slaughter-House*, a few embarrassing remarks about women in *Bradwell*, and a disturbing suggestion in the *Legal Tender Cases* that Congress could do anything that governments were ordinarily empowered to do.

We have reduced the field to four Justices: Miller, Field, Chase, and Strong. The last of these is in a way the most remarkable, for in a time as brief as that of Bradley, Strong far outshone his more celebrated colleague, writing opinions for the Court not only in the towering *Legal Tender Cases* but also in the climactic railroad-tax cases that represented the mature commerce clause judgment of the Chase period. Chief Justices aside, only the notable Curtis[40] had been given such responsibility so soon. Moreover, though Strong's two commerce clause decisions appear poorly explained to modern eyes, his *Legal Tender* opinion was both powerful and reminiscent of Marshall in its confidence that the men in Philadelphia had granted us a perfect constitution.

---

[35]75 U.S. (8 Wall.) 603, 626 (1870); *see supra* chapter 9.

[36]State Tax on Foreign Held Bonds, 82 U.S. (15 Wall.) 300 (1873) (Field, J.); Railroad Co. v. Jackson, 74 U.S. (7 Wall.) 262 (1869) (Nelson, J.); Gilman v. Lockwood, 71 U.S. (4 Wall.) 409 (1867) (Clifford, J.); *cf.* Wilkinson v. Leland, 27 U.S. (2 Pet.) 627, 655 (1829) (Story, J.) (limiting reach of state authority to state territorial boundaries), *noted supra in* chapter 5. See also the unexplained holding denying city authority to order removal of a wharf in Yates v. Milwaukee, 77 U.S. (10 Wall.) 497 (1871) (*see supra* note 9), which can probably be attributed to a state taking provision; and the suggestions of natural law limits on retroactive legislation in Gordon v. United States, 74 U.S. (7 Wall.) 188 (1868) (Grier, J.), Locke v. New Orleans, 71 U.S. (4 Wall.) 172 (1867) (Field, J.), and Freeborn v. Smith, 69 U.S. (2 Wall.) 160 (1865) (Grier, J.).

[37]Gunn v. Barry, 82 U.S. (15 Wall.) 610, 623 (1873) (Swayne, J.).

[38]*See supra* chapters 7, 8.

[39]*See* C. FAIRMAN, *supra* chapter 10, note 6, at 77 ("In his day Clifford was at once the most prolix and most pedestrian member of the Court."); *see also* Currie, *The Most Insignificant Justice: A Preliminary Inquiry*, 50 U. CHI. L. REV. 466, 473-77 (1983) (discussing Clifford's high ranking on scale of Inanities Per Page).

[40]*See supra* chapters 7, 8.

Chase himself, appreciating like his two immediate predecessors the prerogatives of his office, dominated the civil-war and reconstruction cases, and in so doing he seems to have been more politician than legal craftsman.[41] In *Johnson* and *McCardle* he saved the Reconstruction Acts from the risk of invalidation and the Court from that of reprisal; in *Klein* he asserted the Court's ultimate independence from Congress; in *Texas v. White* he gave Radical theory the imprimatur of the judges. Not one of these four opinions is satisfying from the standpoint of legal analysis. Chase's opinions in the legal-tender controversies represent the triumph of policy preferences over legal reasoning. That on the taxation of state banknotes in *Veazie,* with which his legal-tender opinions clash, is little more than a bare conclusion; and so is his concurrence in *Milligan* unnecessarily affirming the power of Congress to authorize military trials. It is interesting that despite his propensity to assign important cases to himself he was one of a minority who had nothing to say about the fourteenth amendment in the *Slaughter-House Cases.*

Apart from Chase, clearly the most influential member of this Court was Miller,[42] and it was no fluke that it was he who spoke for the *Slaughter-House* majority. His name crops up everywhere, and everywhere it is associated with a strong and controversial position. Several times he expressed forceful and general theories of the commerce clause; often alone he continued to fulminate against the effort to extend the contract clause to judicial action; it was he who revived the cry that states could not contract away their tax powers and elevated Taney's offhand remark about the right to travel[43] to a constitutional principle in *Crandall.* He wrote always with exemplary clarity and brevity, and often with great effect; his dissents in the oath cases and in the first legal-tender decision are among the best reasoned opinions of the period. Sometimes, as in *Hepburn* and in the municipal bond cases, he was the reasonable voice of obedience to written law. Other opinions, however, confirmed a tendency to reach the desired result without much attention to the relevant sources. Further criticism may be directed at his cavalier dismissals of the equal protection and due process claims in *Slaughter-House* and his persistent contempt for precedent in commerce clause cases, which made his inherently reasonable but ever-changing general theories of the clause appear cynical afterthoughts designed to shore up a preconceived determination. Most troubling, however, is his free and easy fabrication of a right to travel in *Crandall,* where even his own audacious thesis did not appear to support the result he reached. The picture that emerges is of a strong judge with unusually great abilities and little respect for the law.

I come at last to Field, who was destined to sit for nearly thirty years with Miller and whose fundamental disagreements with him were to form the central theme of Court history for nearly twenty years after Chase had disappeared. This polarization had manifested itself strongly before 1873. Field wrote to invalidate the test oaths

---

[41]*See* C. FAIRMAN *supra* chapter 10, note 6, at 1474-77.

[42]*See* C. FAIRMAN, *supra* chapter 10, note 100 at 3 (quoting Chase's view that Miller was clearly the "'dominant personality'" on the Court in his early years), 63 (speaking of constitutional law as a field where Miller's "preeminence was undisputed"), 248 (concluding that Miller's "strength lay in the wisdom of his judgments rather than in the artistry of their doctrinal elaboration"), 426 ("When Justice Miller died it was generally remarked that the Court had lost the ablest of its members and the greatest figure in constitutional law since Marshall.").

[43]Passenger Cases, 48 U.S. (7 How.) 283, 492 (1849) (dissenting opinion); *see supra* chapter 7.

and Miller to uphold them; Miller wrote the majority opinion for the slaughtering monopoly and Field the most notable opinion against it; they wrote on opposite sides of the legal-tender controversy. Field was less likely to support Radical measures than Miller, and later cases confirm *Slaughter-House*'s implication that he was more likely to find ways of protecting economic freedom.[44] In style Field was notably more prolix and pompous than Miller, but his best opinions—in *Slaughter-House* and the oath cases—show that Miller had a worthy adversary in terms of intellectual power.

With two strong and youthful Justices ranged on apparently opposite sides of the major issues that were about to confront the Court, the stage was set for the appointment of a new Chief Justice in 1874.

[44]*E.g.*, Munn v. Illinois, 94 U.S. 113 (1877). *See infra* chapter 11.

Part Five

Chief Justice Waite
1874–1888

Introduction to Part Five

Chief Justice Chase died in May, 1873. It was not until January of the next year, following several unfortunate attempts, that President Grant succeeded in filling his position. When he did, there was widespread skepticism at the wisdom of the choice; though his predecessors had been former Senators, Attorneys General, Secretaries of State, and members of the Constitutional Convention, Morrison R. Waite was a provincial lawyer from Toledo, Ohio.[1] Waite was to preside for fourteen years over a Court that contained such giants as Samuel Miller, Stephen Field, and Joseph Bradley, and he was to do a highly creditable job.

Waite's tenure divides naturally into two periods.[2] His initial colleagues, besides

---

[1] *See* C. MAGRATH, MORRISON R. WAITE: THE TRIUMPH OF CHARACTER (1963), ch. 1; 2 C. WARREN, THE SUPREME COURT IN UNITED STATES HISTORY 552-61; Graham, *The Waite Court and the Fourteenth Amendment*, 17 VAND. L. REV. 525 (1964), noting that alone among Chief Justices Waite had garnered the title "His Accidency."

[2] JUSTICES OF THE SUPREME COURT DURING THE TIME OF CHIEF JUSTICE WAITE

		1874	76	78	80	82	84	86	88
Nathan Clifford	1858–1881								
Noah H. Swayne	1862–1881								
Samuel F. Miller	1862–1890								
David Davis	1862–1877								
Stephen J. Field	1863–1897								
William Strong	1870–1880								
Joseph P. Bradley	1870–1892								
Ward Hunt	1872–1882								
Morrison R. Waite	1874–1888								
John M. Harlan	1877–1911								
William B. Woods	1880–1887								
Stanley Matthews	1881–1889								
Horace Gray	1881–1902								
Samuel Blatchford	1882–1893								
Lucius Q. C. Lamar	1888–1893								

Miller, Field, and Bradley, included Nathan Clifford, Noah H. Swayne, David
Davis, William Strong, and Ward Hunt. Davis was replaced by John M. Harlan in
1877; the other eight sat together until 1880. Then, in a two-year period, there was a
sudden turnover: Strong and the decrepit trio of Clifford, Swayne, and Hunt[3] were
replaced by William B. Woods, Stanley Matthews, Horace Gray, and Samuel
Blatchford. These four, together with Waite, Miller, Field, Bradley, and Harlan,
were to sit together essentially until Waite's death in 1888, and most of them to
dissappear soon after. However, the importance of the new appointments around
1880 should not be exaggerated, for they largely involved minor players.[4] The heart
of the Court—and it was an extraordinary one—consisted of Waite, Miller, Field,
Bradley, and Harlan, who sat together for all but three of the entire fourteen years.[5]
    The principal constitutional business of the Court during Waite's Chief Jus-
ticeship was to put meat on the essentially bare bones of the fourteenth amendment.
In doing so the Court came down with such familiar decisions as *Munn v. Illinois,
Mugler v. Kansas, Yick Wo v. Hopkins, Hurtado v. California*, and the *Civil Rights
Cases*; and in general it allowed a fairly wide scope for state authority. On the other
hand, the Court under Waite went far beyond its predecessors in using the commerce
clause to limit state power, as illustrated by such famous cases as *Henderson v. New
York, Hall v. DeCuir*, and the *Wabash* case. It was also during this period that the
Court, in decisions including *Louisiana v. Jumel, In re Ayers*, and the *Virginia
Coupon Cases*, developed many of the distinctions that still dominate the law
surrounding suits against state officers. Finally, the Court addressed for the first time
the meaning of several important provisions of the Bill of Rights, including freedom
of religion in the polygamy case of *Reynolds v. United States* and both search and
seizure and self-incrimination in *Boyd v. United States*.
    Dominating the entire period, as in the time of Chief Justice Chase, were Miller
and Field—the former an Iowa Republican basically supporting broad legislative
discretion, the latter a California Democrat inclined to the protection of property. So
long as he was there, Miller's views prevailed on the whole. Later Justices would to a
large extent implement Field's views; but we are getting ahead of the story.

SOURCE: G. GUNTHER, CASES AND MATERIALS ON CONSTITUTIONAL LAW (10th ed. 1980), App. A. Biog-
raphies of the period include MAGRATH, *supra* note 1; C. FAIRMAN, MR. JUSTICE MILLER AND THE SUPREME
COURT (1939); C. SWISHER, STEPHEN J. FIELD, CRAFTSMAN OF THE LAW (1930); F. LATHAM, THE GREAT
DISSENTER: JOHN MARSHALL HARLAN (1970); W. CATE, LUCIUS Q. C. LAMAR (1935); W. KING, LINCOLN'S
MANAGER, DAVID DAVIS (1960); P. CLIFFORD, NATHAN CLIFFORD, DEMOCRAT (1922). *See also* Fairman, *Mr.
Justice Bradley*, in MR. JUSTICE 69-95 (A. Dunham and P. Kurland eds. 1964); Fairman, *What Makes a
Great Justice? Mr. Justice Bradley and the Supreme Court, 1870–1892*, 30 B.U.L. REV. 49 (1950); Westin,
John Marshall Harlan and the Constitutional Rights of Negroes: The Transformation of a Southerner, 66
YALE L. J. 637 (1957).
    [3]*See* FAIRMAN, MILLER, *supra* note 2, ch. xvi.
    [4]For discussion of the changes in membership *see* 2 WARREN, *supra* note 1, at 563, 622-25, arguing that
they ushered in a more nationalistic period.
    [5]The background of the Justices is also instructive. In 1857, when the *Dred Scott* case was decided, a
majority of the Justices were Southerners and all but two of them Democrats; from Justice Wayne's death
in 1867 until the appointment of Harlan in 1877 there was no Southerner on the Court at all, and not a
single Democrat was appointed after 1863 until Lucius Quintus Cincinnatus Lamar in the very year of
Waite's death—twenty-five years later.

11

The Civil War Amendments

In the *Slaughter-House Cases*, shortly before Chase's death, the Court in a famous Miller opinion had held that neither the thirteenth nor the fourteenth amendment outlawed a state-created monopoly of the slaughtering business. In so doing, the Court arguably reduced the privileges or immunities clause to nothing more than authority for congressional enforcement of rights found elsewhere in federal law, hinted that equal protection might apply only to racial classifications, and dismissed a due-process argument with little more than a bare conclusion.[1]

The Court under Waite was presented with the task of filling in some of the remaining blanks. After *Slaughter-House*, the privileges-or-immunities cases were treated as easy, and perhaps they were: since neither the right to sell liquor,[2] the right to vote,[3] the right to a civil jury,[4] nor the right to bear arms[5] was independently

---

[1]83 U.S. (16 Wall.) 36 (1873). *See supra* chapter 10.

[2]Bartmeyer v. Iowa, 85 U.S. (18 Wall.) 129, 133 (1874) (Miller, J.). Miller unnecessarily and questionably added without explanation that in any event the privileges or immunities clause had no effect on laws passed before its adoption: "the most liberal advocate[s] . . . have contended for nothing more than that the rights of the citizen previously existing, and dependent wholly on state laws for their recognition, are now placed under the protection of the Federal government . . . ." *Id.* at 133. *Cf. supra* chapter 2, discussing *Cooper v. Telfair*. Field, who had dissented in *Slaughter-House*, argued that although the clause protected "the fundamental rights belonging to citizens of all free governments" against state action, it did not "interfere [ ] in any respect with the police power of the state." *Id.* at 138-40 (concurring opinion). *See also* Butchers' Union Co. v. Crescent City Co., 111 U.S. 746, 754-66 (1884), where both Field and Bradley relied on their dissenting arguments in *Slaughter-House* to explain their concurrence in a decision allowing Louisiana to repeal the monopoly upheld in the earlier case. Harlan and Woods, moreover, joined Bradley's opinion. If nothing else, Field was tenacious. *Cf. infra* chapter 13, discussing the legal-tender question.

[3]Minor v. Happersett, 88 U.S. (21 Wall.) 162, 171 (1875) (Waite, C.J.): "The amendment did not add to the privileges and immunities of a citizen. It simply furnished an additional guaranty for the protection of such as he already had." *Slaughter-House*, the source of this interpretation, was not cited. The equal protection clause, significantly, was not mentioned at all; but Waite's negative inferences drawn from § 2 of the fourteenth amendment (which reduced the representation of any state denying the vote to black

protected against state action, none of them was a privilege of national citizenship protected by the fourteenth amendment.[6] The central issues to which the Court devoted its attention in this period were three: the meaning of the due process clause, the meaning of equal protection, and the scope of Congress's authority to enforce the prohibitions of the amendments.

I. DUE PROCESS

Due process, the Court had said in upholding a federal distraint procedure against fifth-amendment objections in *Murray's Lessee v. Hoboken Land & Improvement Co.* in 1856, meant the same thing as the "law of the land" provision of Magna Charta, with one important difference: it was "a restraint on the legislative as well as on the executive and judicial powers of the government."[7] The test for determining whether a challenged "process" met the constitutional standard, the Court added without explanation, was essentially historical: "we must look to those settled usages and modes of proceeding existing in the common and statute law of England, before the emigration of our ancestors, and which are shown not to have been unsuited to their civil and political condition by having been acted on by them after the settlement of this country."[8]

----

males) and from the adoption of the fifteenth (guaranteeing black suffrage) (88 U.S. (2 Wall.) at 174-75) would have been equally effective against an equal-protection argument. *See infra* text accompanying notes 115-18. Waite also declared, without suggesting that the question was committed to other branches (*cf. supra* chapter 8, discussing *Luther v. Borden*), that the meaning of a "Republican Form of Government" guaranteed by article IV was settled by state practices in 1789, when no state permitted women to vote. *See* 88 U.S. (21 Wall.) at 175-76 (also rejecting arguments based on the due process and bill of attainder clauses). *Cf. supra* chapter 9, discussing the Reconstruction Acts.

[4]Walker v. Sauvinet, 92 U.S. 90, 92 (1876) (Waite, C.J.): Because the seventh amendment "relates only to trials in the courts of the United States" (Edwards v. Elliott, 88 U.S. (21 Wall.) 532 (1874) (Clifford, J.)), "[a] trial by jury in suits at common law pending in the State courts is not . . . a privilege or immunity of national citizenship . . . ." Nor did due process require a jury: "Due process of law is process due according to the law of the land," which in this case meant "the law of the State." *Id.* at 93. For further discussion of due process *see infra* text accompanying notes 7-83. Field and Clifford dissented without opinion. Yet Clifford had written *Edwards v. Elliott, supra,* in which the seventh amendment claim had been summarily rejected with a citation to *Barron v. Baltimore* (*see supra* chapter 6) and in which claims based on privileges or immunities, due process, and equal protection had not even been deemed worthy of reply, 88 U.S. (21 Wall.) at 544, 557. He seemed to owe an explanation.

[5]Presser v. Illinois, 116 U.S. 252, 264-65, 267, 268 (1866) (Woods, J.): "We have not been referred to any statute of the United States which confers upon the plaintiff in error the privilege which he asserts"; the second amendment's "right . . . to keep and bear arms" neither limited the states nor implied the right "to drill or parade with arms in cities and towns"; the first amendment protected "the right peaceably to assemble" only if "the purpose of the assembly was to petition the government for a redress of grievances." Due process, attainder, and ex post facto objections were brushed aside as "so clearly untenable as to require no discussion." The long lapse of time between *Presser* and the last previous privileges-or-immunities case suggests that most lawyers had got the message and had shifted their reliance to other clauses.

[6]In the jury case, *supra* note 4, the Court for the first time clearly rejected the thesis that the rights protected by the first eight amendments against federal interference were "national" privileges in the relevant sense, and it did so without discussion. For the bearing of *Slaughter-House* on this question, *see supra* chapter 10.

[7]59 U.S. (18 How.) 272, 276 (1856) (Curtis, J.). *See supra* chapter 8. No reason was given to support this critical conclusion.

[8]59 U.S. (18 How.) at 277.

In the *Dred Scott* case[9] and in *Hepburn v. Griswold*[10] the same clause had been relied on before Waite's day to strike down federal statutes on the ground that they were substantively objectionable.[11] In neither case had the Justices paused to explain how a clause phrased in terms of "process" could demand anything more than an adequate procedure. *Hepburn*, however, was overruled almost before the country had had time to read it,[12] and *Scott* was scarcely a popular decision after the Civil War. In *Slaughter-House*, Miller had shrugged off a due-process attack on the butchers' monopoly as though the counsel for the plaintiffs had had a screw loose;[13] one might have thought at the time that the clause had been limited to the procedural context that its words suggested.

A. Procedural Cases

In terms of the results it reached, the Court under Waite was faithful to Miller's promise of a sparing interpretation of the due process clause; even in the traditional area of procedure it never struck down any measure on due-process grounds. In

[9]Scott v. Sandford, 60 U.S. (19 How.) 393, 450 (1857) (Taney, C.J.):

> An act of Congress which deprives a citizen of the United States of his liberty or property, merely because he came himself or brought his property into a particular territory of the United States, and who had committed no offence against the laws, could hardly be dignified with the name of due process of law.

Whether Taney actually spoke for a majority on this issue, and whether he really meant to base his holding on the due process clause, have both been disputed. *See supra* chapter 8. For abolitionist views that the due process clause had the opposite effect of outlawing slavery, *see* J. tenBroek, The Antislavery Origins of the Fourteenth Amendment 98-100 (1951).

[10]75 U.S. (8 Wall.) 603, 524 (1870) (Chase, C.J.) (alternate holding): contracts were property; requiring their owners to accept paper money in place of coin deprived them of property: and "whatever may be the operation of such an act, due process of law makes no part of it." *See supra* chapter 9.

[11]The idea had been further propagated by Judge Cooley's influential treatise in 1868 without reference to *Scott*: under due process or the related state provisions preventing deprivations not in accordance with "the law of the land," the validity of government action was to be tested "by those principles of civil liberty and constitutional defence which have become established in our system of law, and not by any rules that pertain to forms of procedure only." This conclusion appeared to be based essentially on Justice Johnson's equally unexplained dictum in *Bank of Columbia v. Okely*, *supra* chapter 4, that "law of the land" in the Maryland constitution was "meant to secure the individual from the arbitrary exercise of the powers of government, unrestrained by the established principles of private rights and distributive justice." Cited by Cooley without explication was the leading state case treating such a provision as a limit on substantive arbitrariness (Wynehamer v. People, 13 N.Y. 378 (1856)); contrary decisions collected by Professor Corwin in the leading article cited in chapter 8 *supra* were ignored. T. Cooley, Constitutional Limitations 355-56 (1868).

[12]Legal Tender Cases, 79 U.S. (12 Wall.) 457, 553 (1871). Justice Strong, writing for the Court, argued that the taking and due-process provisions had "always been understood as referring only to a direct appropriation, and not to consequential injuries resulting from the exercise of lawful power." *Id.* at 551. *See supra* chapter 9.

[13]83 U.S. (16 Wall.) 36, 80-81 (1873):

> [I]t is sufficient to say that under no construction of that provision that we have ever seen, or any that we deem admissible, can the restraint imposed by the State of Louisiana upon the exercise of their trade by the butchers of New Orleans be held to be a deprivation of property within the meaning of that provision.

See supra chapter 10.

Pennoyer v. Neff, to be sure, the Court did announce that an in personam judgment entered without personal service within the state would offend due process.[14] What due process had to do with this question was suggested by Justice Field's statement that due process meant "a course of legal proceedings according to those rules and principles which have been established in our systems of jurisprudence"[15] and by his elaborate demonstration that tradition limited the power of a state to persons and property within its borders.[16] Not only was this pronouncement entirely obiter;[17] its reasoning was wholly in line with *Murray's Lessee*'s principle that history was the test of due process. *Pennoyer* was the first Supreme Court case, however, to suggest that due process had something to do with the extraterritorial authority of the states; it was therefore an important step toward the later position that due process limited the extraterritorial reach of state substantive laws as well.[18]

More interesting and novel was Justice Matthews's scholarly 1884 opinion in *Hurtado v. California*,[19] concluding—despite suggestive passages in Coke's Institutes and flat statements by Kent and Story[20]—that indictment by a grand jury had not been considered an element of due process in England[21] and—without mentioning

---

[14]95 U.S. 714, 733 (1878) (Field, J.).

[15]*Id.*

[16]*Id.* at 722-32. Since the original basis for this tradition was the practical limitation of power to affect absent parties, article IV's requirement that one state respect the judgments of another might have led the Court to question whether it was appropriate to American conditions. *See* R. Cramton, D. Currie, and H. Kay, Conflict of Laws—Cases, Comments, Questions 525-27 (3d ed. 1981); International Shoe Co. v. Washington, 326 U.S. 310, 316 (1945) (Stone, C.J.):

> [N]ow that the *capias ad respondendum* has given way to personal service of summons or other form of notice, due process requires only that in order to subject a defendant to a judgment *in personam*, if he be not present within the territory of the forum, he have certain minimum contacts with it such that the maintenance of the suit does not offend "traditional notions of fair play and substantial justice."

Justice Hunt's dissenting objection in *Pennoyer* that it was hypertechnical to insist on attachment of local land before rather than after judgment (95 U.S. at 736-48) was amply refuted by Field's concern for advance notice going beyond mere publication (*id.* at 726-27); but this did not explain Field's dictum (*id.*) that actual notice by mail would not have sufficed. Later cases have properly separated the notice and the territorial aspects of due process. *See, e.g.*, Mullane v. Central Hanover Bank, 339 U.S. 306 (1950) (Jackson, J.). For the argument that due process historically had nothing to do with territoriality, *see* Whitten, *The Constitutional Limitations on State-Court Jurisdiction (Part 2)*, 14 Creighton L. Rev. 735 (1981).

[17]The fourteenth amendment had not been in force at the time the questioned judgment was entered; the holding was only that, as had been established in D'Arcy v. Ketchum, 52 U.S. (11 How.) 165, 176 (1851) (Catron, J.), *supra* chapter 8, and later cases cited by Field, a statutory requirement of full faith and credit did not require a federal court to respect a decision rendered without personal jurisdiction. Field did note that it was "beginning to be considered, as it always ought to have been," that such judgments were void even where rendered because "contrary to the first principles of justice," 95 U.S. at 732, but he neither based his holding on this ground nor said whether the Supreme Court had power to make such a ruling in reviewing a state-court proceeding.

[18]*E.g.*, Home Ins. Co. v. Dick, 281 U.S. 397 (1930) (Brandeis, J.), striking down the application of Texas law to a contract said to have no connection with Texas at the time it was made. *See generally* B. Currie, Selected Essays on the Conflict of Laws, ch. 5 (1963); R. Cramton, D. Currie, and H. Kay, *supra* note 16, chapter 3.

[19]110 U.S. 516 (1884).

[20]2 W. Kent, Commentaries 13 (2d ed. 1832); 3 J. Story, Commentaries on the Constitution of the United States § 1783 (1833), both invoking Coke.

[21]110 U.S. at 522-28. Blackstone, cited by Harlan in an equally learned dissent (*id.* at 544), had flatly

Pennoyer, which had stated the contrary—that the *Murray* test was a one-way street. That a procedure was traditional was, as in *Murray* itself, an adequate ground for upholding it; that it was not traditional was an insufficient reason for striking it down. To hold otherwise, said Matthews, would "deny every quality of the law but its age, and . . . render it incapable of progress or improvement"; "flexibility and capacity for growth and adaptation is the peculiar boast and excellence of the common law"; and (in light of *Murray*) in this country a purely historical test would preclude even legislative correction.[22] Thus due process "must be held to guarantee not particular forms of procedure, but the very substance of individual rights to life, liberty, and property"—to assure that state law remained "within the limits of those fundamental principles of liberty and justice which lie at the base of all our civil and political institutions . . . ."[23] Judged by this standard, the commencement of a murder prosecution by information easily passed muster: "[i]t is merely a preliminary proceeding, and can result in no final judgment, except as the consequence of a regular judicial trial, conducted precisely as in cases of indictments."[24]

This was not the first time the Court had squarely held, without considering some highly relevant legislative history,[25] that the fourteenth amendment did not incorporate all of the protections guaranteed against federal action by the Bill of Rights;[26] and, though this conclusion may well have been correct,[27] Matthews's argument that the decision to make only due process and not other enumerated rights apply to the states must have been deliberate[28] was not wholly convincing in light of Harlan's dissenting observation that it appeared to exclude even notice of the accusation,[29]

---

said the common law required an indictment for public prosecution of anything more serious than a misdemeanor; but that was not necessarily the same as saying the requirement was an element of due process. *See also* Easterbrook, *Substance and Due Process*, 1982 SUP. CT. REV. 85, 102-03, arguing that *Hurtado* departed from Coke's view of due process but that Coke had misunderstood Magna Charta; 2 W. CROSSKEY, POLITICS AND THE CONSTITUTION IN THE HISTORY OF THE UNITED STATES 1136-41 (1953), terming the decision flatly wrong.

[22]110 U.S. at 528-32.

[23]*Id.* at 532, 535.

[24]*Id.* at 538. Harlan put the contrary case strongly in dissent, giving evidence of the high value the Framers had placed on the grand jury as a protection against prosecutorial oppression and of the universality of the requirement at the time both the fifth and the fourteenth amendments had been adopted. *Id.* at 550-58.

[25]*See supra* chapter 10.

[26]*See* Walker v. Sauvinet, 92 U.S. 90 (1876), *supra* note 4 (civil jury); Davidson v. New Orleans, 96 U.S. 97 (1878) (dictum) (taking without compensation). For later examples during the Waite period, *see* Presser v. Illinois, *supra* note 5 (right to bear arms); In re Sawyer, 124 U.S. 200, 219 (1888) (Gray, J.) (dictum) (criminal jury and compulsory process). Professor Crosskey (*supra* note 21, vol. 2, at 1102-10) made the less sweeping argument that due process incorporated all the *procedural* guarantees of the Bill of Rights, invoking Justice Curtis's declaration that the first step in determining compliance with the similar provision of the fifth amendment was to determine whether the procedure in question conflicted with any other constitutional provision (Murray's Lessee v. Hoboken Land and Improv. Co. 59 U.S. (18 How.) 272, 277 (1856)). But since the procedural provisions in the Bill of Rights applied only to the federal government, it was much easier to say they determined the process "due" from the United States than that "due" from a state; and that the fourteenth amendment did not incorporate the grand-jury requirement seems a particularly compelling conclusion in light of the materials on contemporary understanding reported by Professor Fairman (*see supra* chapter 10).

[27]*See supra* chapter 10.

[28]110 U.S. at 534-35.

[29]*Id.* at 547-50, invoking the sixth amendment and concluding that this and other components of due

which certainly seemed "fundamental" enough to meet the Court's own test of due process.[30] Given *Murray*'s holding that due process operated as a limit on legislative power, however, *Hurtado*'s rejection of a purely historical test was entirely reasonable; it does not seem likely that the Framers of the amendment meant to prevent all changes in the law of procedure, and the words surely do not suggest that they did. But the net result of the Court's conclusions was that the due process clause made the judges censors over what was "fundamental" in judicial procedure; and there is no evidence that the Framers had that in mind either.[31] That the trouble lay with *Murray*'s blithe conclusion that due process limited the legislature seemed not to occur to anyone,[32] and perhaps it was too late to change it anyway.

Thus in the procedural domain the Court managed both to construe due process in a manner highly deferential to state legislative judgments and at the same time to establish itself as the protector and definer of "fundamental" procedural rights.[33] Despite the discouraging tone of the *Slaughter-House* opinion, however, it was in the substantive area that the Waite Court rendered its most interesting due-process decisions; and it is to those decisions that we now turn.

---

process had been specifically mentioned because they were "so essential to the safety of the people that it was deemed wise to avoid the possibility that Congress, in regulating the processes of law, would impair or destroy them."

[30]*See also* Kennard v. Louisiana ex rel. Morgan, 92 U.S. 480, 483 (1876)(Waite, C.J.), quoted by the majority in *Hurtado*, 110 U.S. at 533, stressing even in a civil case that due process was satisfied because the law provided, among other things, for "notifying [the defendant] of the case he is required to meet . . . ."

[31]For judicial development of the converse proposition that traditional procedures might *offend* due process if they denied fundamental rights, *see* Easterbrook, *supra* note 21, 1982 Sup. Ct. Rev. at 105–09. *See also id.* at 94, arguing that, in light of its placement amid a number of specifically enumerated procedural provisions, it was "inconceivable" that due process "could have been designed as a general authorization to courts to find and enforce whatever procedures judges thought important. . . ."

[32]Indeed, Matthews took the occasion to reaffirm that, although the same words in English law had meant only that the King could act against his subjects only in accordance with law, their mere incorporation into a written Constitution "necessarily" transformed them into a safeguard of "fundamental" rights against legislative encroachment. *Id.* at 531–32.

[33]Other procedural due-process decisions of the Waite period include McMillan v. Anderson, 95 U.S. 37 (1877) (Miller, J.), invoking history without citing *Murray's Lessee* in upholding a procedure for collection of state taxes by seizure of assets after notice but without prior hearing; Springer v. United States, 102 U.S. 586, 593-94 (1881) (Swayne, J.), upholding a distraint procedure for collection of federal taxes; Davidson v. New Orleans, 96 U.S. 97, 105 (1878) (Miller, J.), upholding a procedure for the assessment of swamp-clearing costs because it provided for notice and a fair judicial hearing; Hagan v. Reclamation Dist., 111 U.S. 701, 711-12 (1884) (Field, J.), upholding another assessment procedure although the hearing followed the assessment itself; United States v. Union Pac. R. R., 98 U.S. 569, 591-93, 604 (1879) (Miller, J.), holding on the same territorial basis employed to limit state-court process in *Pennoyer v. Neff* (text accompanying notes 14-18 supra) that due process did not forbid Congress to authorize nationwide service in federal courts; Ker v. Illinois, 119 U.S. 436, 439-40 (1886) (Miller, J.), holding that, whether or not a kidnapping of the defendant by federal officials comported with due process, it did not cause his later state conviction to offend that requirement; Spencer v. Merchant, 125 U.S. 345, 356-58 (1888) (Gray, J.), holding over two dissents and without giving reasons that, although notice and hearing might be required for administrative allocation of an assessment among benefited owners, the legislature could make the allocation with no hearing at all. For later efforts to explain the distinction, *see* Bi-Metallic Inv. Co. v. State Bd. of Equalization, 239 U.S. 441 (1915) (Holmes, J.) (impracticability and political checks).

B. *Bartemeyer v. Iowa*

Even before Waite's appointment, in the first important due-process case decided after the death of Chase, the Court unanimously upheld state authority to prohibit the sale of liquor.[34] After *Slaughter-House*, the privileges-or-immunities claim was frivolous; yet Miller devoted much of his brief opinion to it[35] and never bothered to deal adequately with the somewhat more open question whether the law offended due process.

Without a definitive rejection by the majority, dissenters in *Slaughter-House* had proclaimed that the right to pursue a calling was "property" or "liberty" protected by the due process clause,[36] and in contrast to *Slaughter-House* there seemed no doubt that the seller in *Bartemeyer* had been "deprived" of that right. Given the coolness of Miller's reaction to the due-process claim in the earlier case, one might have concluded from his silence in *Bartemeyer* that, despite *Scott* and *Hepburn*, due process had no substantive dimension—had he not, quite without explanation, conceded that if the liquor in question had belonged to the defendant before its sale was forbidden there would have been a "grave" due-process question.[37] It seemed incumbent on Miller to explain why there was no similar difficulty in applying the law to liquor acquired after the law was passed; but he elected not to do so.

Concurring separately, both Bradley and Field were perspicacious enough to offer a reason: unlike the monopoly that both had voted to condemn in *Slaughter-House*, the liquor law was, as the former put it, a regulation "intended for the preservation of the public health and the public order."[38] Neither Justice paused to explain how this police-power test related to the unpromising text or origins of the fourteenth amendment. Perhaps they meant that police-power measures by definition constituted "due process of law," so as to justify any resultant deprivation of liberty or property; perhaps—as later opinions would suggest—they meant the police power qualified the definitions of "liberty" and "property" themselves, so that its exercise deprived no one of any protected interest at all.[39] Language in both

[34]85 U.S. (18 Wall.) 129 (1874).

[35]*Id.* at 132-33.

[36]*See supra* chapter 10.

[37]85 U.S. (18 Wall.) at 133. The remainder of the opinion was devoted to showing that the defendant had not established that he owned the liquor early enough to raise the question. *Id.* at 134-35. *See* T. COOLEY, *supra* note 11, at 583-84, noting that state courts tended to uphold prohibition laws even though they destroyed property rights in existing liquor.

[38]*Id.* at 137 (Bradley, J., concurring). *See also id.* at 138 (Field, J., concurring): "No one has ever pretended . . . that the fourteenth amendment interferes in any respect with the police power of the state." *See* Scott, *Justice Bradley's Evolving Concept of the Fourteenth Amendment from the Slaughter-House Cases to the Civil Rights Cases*, 25 RUTGERS L. REV. 552, 560-61 (1971), finding Bradley inconsistent because the law he voted to strike down in *Slaughter-House* had also been defended as a police-power measure seriously designed to protect health. Bradley had there declared that the monopoly features of the law had "not the faintest semblance" of a police regulation and that the police-power justification was a mere "pretence." 83 U.S. (16 Wall.) at 111, 120.

[39]*See infra* text accompanying notes 48-55, 67-74. This seems to have been the view taken by Judge Cooley, who had given wide currency to the notion that the due-process limitation was defined in terms of the police power. The validity of government action under the due-process clause, Cooley argued, was determined by "those principles of civil liberty and constitutional defence which have become established

opinions casting doubt upon the application of the law to liquor previously owned,[40] moreover, left the relationship between due process and the police power somewhat ambiguous; while the history of the police power concept in defining state power to affect interstate or foreign commerce[41] suggested that the power itself was scarcely self-defining. Though the concurring Justices' treatment of the problem could hardly be termed exemplary,[42] however, they had managed to enunciate the first clear theory of substantive due process, and Miller had missed yet another opportunity to say something useful in support of a narrow reading of the clause.[43]

C.   The Granger Cases

The Court itself first seriously addressed the substantive reach of due process in 1877, when in a series of decisions it rejected a quiverful of constitutional challenges to state laws limiting the rates chargeable by railroads and other businesses.

The Chief Justice, in *Munn v. Illinois*,[44] larded the lead opinion with quotable if unsupported expressions of deference to the legislative judgment: "Every statute is presumed to be constitutional"; "[i]f there is doubt, the expressed will of the

---

in our system of law"; the "chief restriction" was "that vested rights must not be disturbed"; but all property was held subject to the police power. T. COOLEY, *supra* note 11, at 356-58, 572-73. The last proposition was supported by a long quotation from Chief Justice Parker of Massachusetts; its connection with due process was essentially a bare conclusion.

[40]*See* 85 U.S. (18 Wall.) at 136 (Bradley, J., concurring), stressing that because there was no adequate allegation that the liquor in question had been owned before its sale was forbidden "the question of depriving a person of property without due process of law does not arise" and adding that "[n]o one has ever doubted that a legislature may prohibit the vending of articles deemed injurious to the safety of society, provided it does not interfere with vested rights of property"; *id.* at 137-38 (Field, J., concurring).

[41]*See supra* chapter 7, and *cf. infra* chapter 12.

[42]Field, moreover, had discovered the due process clause only after losing the fight to establish a broad scope for privileges or immunities; unlike Swayne and Bradley, he had not invoked due process in the *Slaughter-House Cases. See supra* chapter 10. Swayne had nothing to say in *Bartemeyer*.

[43]Chief Justice Waite added another important datum in 1875, when without dissent he wrote to uphold a statute denying women the right to vote:

> The right of suffrage, when granted, will be protected. He who has it can only be deprived of it by due process of law, but in order to claim protection he must first show that he has the right.

Minor v. Happersett, 88 U.S. (21 Wall.) 162, 176 (1875). This passage seemed, quite without explanation, both to portend a rather broad interpretation of liberty and property and to limit the clause to the protection of rights previously given by state law. Superficially, this formulation conformed with *Bartemeyer*'s suggested distinction between old and new liquor; but it left unexplained why the Court had not been bothered by Iowa'a destruction in that case of the preexisting freedom to engage in the liquor business.

[44]94 U.S. 113 (1877). Companion cases involving both local and interstate railroads, Chicago, B. & Q. R.R. v. Iowa, 94 U.S. 155 (1877), and Peik v. Chicago & Nw. Ry., 94 U.S. 164 (1877), also written by Waite, added nothing significant on the due-process question. For the background of the Granger Cases, *see* Fairman, *The So-Called Granger Cases, Lord Hale, and Justice Bradley*, 5 STAN. L. REV. 587 (1953); 2 C. WARREN, *supra* introduction to part five, note 1, chapter 33, and C. SWISHER, *supra*, introduction to part five, note 2, ch. xiv; for Bradley's substantial role in drafting the opinion see C. FAIRMAN, *supra*, and C. MAGRATH, *supra*, introduction to part five, note 1, ch. 10. An impressive and detailed investigation of the facts is found in Kitch and Bowler, *The Facts of Munn v. Illinois*, 1978 SUP. CT. REV. 313.

legislature should be sustained"; "we must assume that, if a state of facts could exist that would justify such legislation, it actually did exist when the statute now under consideration was passed"; "[f]or protection against abuses by legislatures the people must resort to the polls, not to the courts."[45] None of this was very helpful in determining whether or not rate regulation was within the state's power, but it certainly seemed to stack the deck in the state's favor.

The most straightforward part of the *Munn* opinion was historical: rate regulation had been common in England before the Revolution, and it had long been practiced by Congress in the District of Columbia with no suggestion of a due-process problem under the fifth amendment.[46] Field and Strong contested this view of history in dissent;[47] but given Waite's interpretation it would have sufficed to point out that, whatever the applicability of the clause to substantive rate regulation, this history satisfied the test of "settled usage[ ]" laid down in *Murray's Lessee*.

Murray's Lessee, however, was not cited, nor were any of the other precedents applying the due process clauses. Unwilling to rely on the established equation of "due process" with historical precedent, Waite insisted on explaining that the businessmen in *Munn* had not been "deprive[d]" of property at all. At common law,

> when private property is "affected with a public interest, it ceases to be *juris privati* only." . . . When, therefore, one devotes his property to a use in which the public has an interest, he, in effect, grants to the public an interest in that use, and must submit to be controlled by the public for the common good, to the extent of the interest he has thus created.[48]

Because the handful of Chicago grain elevators regulated in *Munn* had "a 'virtual' monopoly" position over the transportation of grain from west to east, they were "affected with a public interest"[49]—and the regulation did not deprive the owners of property.

[45]94 U.S. at 123, 132, 134.

[46]*Id.* at 125-30, 133-34.

[47]*Id.* at 139-40, 146-54. Field distinguished most of Waite's examples as based upon conditions imposed and accepted in the grant of special privileges: "the State, in exercising its power of prescribing the compensation, only determines the conditions upon which its concession shall be enjoyed." The District of Columbia instances he dismissed on the ground they had never been tested in the Court; usury laws he explained away on the ground that they were a relaxation of an earlier total ban on the lending of money—proving only that the common law had once permitted even greater restrictions on the use of property than a mere limitation of the rental for its use.

[48]*Id.* at 126. That this discussion related to determining whether Munn had been "deprive[d]" of property is indicated *id.* at 123.

[49]*Id.* at 130-32. In a companion case *Munn* was extended to a railroad, without mention of any virtual monopoly, simply because railroads were "carriers for hire, . . . given extraordinary powers, in order that they may the better serve the public in that capacity." Chicago, B. & Q. R.R. v. Iowa, 94 U.S. 155, 161 (Waite, C.J.). Field and Strong dissented without opinion, though the fact that the railroad had been incorporated seemed to bring the case within their admission that rate regulation could be made a condition of the grant of a franchise. *See supra* note 47. *See* Kitch and Bowler, *supra* note 44, 1978 SUP. CT. REV. at 341-43, arguing that "[t]he central analytic flaw" in *Munn* was "the failure to connect the copiously cited precedents, most of them relating to common carriers, to the elevator business" and doubting that Waite meant to imply that every business with substantial economic power was "affected with a public interest" or to "lay the constitutional foundation for pervasive economic regulation . . . ." *But see infra* note 58.

Thus for the first time the Court in *Munn* explicitly focused upon the definition of "property" in the fourteenth amendment, holding essentially by fiat that property rights in certain businesses were qualified by the public interest.[50] It followed, said Waite, that it was immaterial that the owners had built their elevators before the rate law was adopted: "What they did was from the beginning subject to the power of the body politic to require them to conform to such regulations as might be established by the proper authorities for the common good."[51]

Field, pointing to the fictitious nature of the "grant" concocted by the Court,[52] argued with some force that "[a]ll that is beneficial in property arises from its use, and the fruits of that use," and that deprivation of the right to use property was therefore a loss of property itself.[53] Adding an impressively broad definition of "liberty,"[54] he explained his acceptance of the police power in *Bartemeyer*: "The doctrine that each one must so use his own as not to injure his neighbor—*sic utere tuo ut alienum non laedas*—is the rule by which every member of society must possess and enjoy his property . . . ."[55] In effect, Field too was willing to say that the ownership of property did not carry with it a right to harm others, but without much explanation he denied that the charging of unreasonable rates fell within that principle.[56] What Field again conspicuously neglected to do, however, was to say why he believed that deprivation of property rights by rate regulation was "without due

[50]No consideration was given to the question whether state or federal law determined the extent of property rights presumably conferred by the state. *Cf.* chapter 5 *supra*, discussing *Ogden v. Saunders* and the related question under the contract clause.

[51]94 U.S. at 133. This seemed pretty well to dispose of the "grave question" of old liquor, which the Court had so assiduously avoided in *Bartemeyer*; as Field and Strong showed in dissent, any property right could be defined away if five judges were prepared to reach the undisprovable conclusion that its use was "affected with a public interest." *Id.* at 140-41.

[52]*Id.* at 140, 149.

[53]*Id.* at 141. He did not stop to distinguish the *Legal Tender Cases*, which had suggested an arguably narrower interpretation of the term "deprived." *See supra* note 12.

[54]   By the term "liberty," as used in the provision, something more is meant than mere freedom from physical restraint or the bounds of a prison. It means freedom to go where one may choose, and to act in such manner, not inconsistent with the equal rights of others, as his judgment may dictate for the promotion of his happiness; that is, to pursue such callings and avocations as may be most suitable to develop his capacities, and give to them their highest enjoyment.

94 U.S. at 142. No support was given for this conclusion.

[55]*Id.* at 145.

[56]His statement that the police power embraced "[w]hatever affects the peace, good order, morals, and health of the community" (*id.* at 145) could easily have covered rate regulation; his conclusion that it did not (*id.* at 146) was based almost entirely on his view of history, *see supra* note 47. His statement that the grain elevators in question were "not nuisances" and that their use "in no respect prevents others from using and enjoying their property" (*id.* at 148) suggests a possible basis of distinction: the neighbors cannot protect themselves against nuisances, but they need not contract for the storage of grain. Why this difference should have been of constitutional dimension Field did not say. *See also* T. COOLEY, *supra* note 11, at 572:

The police of a State . . . embraces its system of internal regulation, by which it is sought not only to preserve the public order and to prevent offences against the State, but also to establish for the intercourse of citizen with citizen those rules of good manners and good neighborhood which are calculated to prevent a conflict of rights, and to insure to each the uninterrupted enjoyment of his own, so far as is reasonably consistent with a like enjoyment of rights by others.

process of law," or to cite either of the two discredited decisions that lent support to his premise.

More significantly, the majority nowhere took issue with Field's crucial assumption. By stressing the public interest in grain elevators, the Court seemed to imply that they were extraordinary, and that similar regulation of other businesses might not pass muster.[57] By employing the rhetoric of substantive due process without ever having justified its acceptance, moreover, Waite made it easy for his successors to argue that the principle had already been established—and thus to invalidate laws on the basis of the purely factual and always arguable judgment that the subject was not "affected by a public interest."[58] Once again Waite and his deferential brethren had resisted the effort to transform due process into a tool for general judicial censorship; once again they had failed to put the questionable idea to rest.[59]

D. *Davidson v. New Orleans*

The following year Miller seemed to try very hard to do just that when a disgruntled landowner raised due-process objections to the assessment of his land to raise funds for swamp drainage. The swollen due-process docket, he announced for the Court, attested to a widespread and "strange misconception of the scope of this provision":

> [I]t would seem . . . that the clause . . . is looked upon as a means of bringing to the test of the decision of this court the abstract opinions of every unsuccessful litigant in a State court of the justice of the decision against him, and of the merits of the legislation on which such a decision may be founded.[60]

Even if property had been taken without compensation, "it must be remembered that, when the fourteenth amendment was adopted, the provision on that subject, in immediate juxtaposition in the fifth amendment with the one we are construing, was

[57]*See, e.g.*, T. COOLEY, *supra* note 11, at 734-38 (6th ed. 1890), reading *Munn* as limiting price regulation to cases involving exclusive or special privileges or the use of public property and adding that "[t]he mere fact that the public have an interest in the existence of the business, and are accommodated by it, cannot be sufficient . . . ."

[58]*See* C. MAGRATH, *supra* introduction to part five, note 1, at 187-88; F. FRANKFURTER, THE COMMERCE CLAUSE UNDER MARSHALL, TANEY, AND WAITE 84-88 (1937), arguing that by this language Waite "surely meant no more than that the Court must be able to attribute to the legislature the fulfillment of a public interest, and thereby relieve it of the imputation of sheer arbitrariness." *Accord*, Fairman, *supra* note 44, 5 STAN. L. REV. at 656-58, showing that this interpretation was far more clearly stated in a Bradley memorandum from which Waite drew heavily in writing his opinion and adding that "[a]n illustration, invoked to make new legislation congenial to the mind, was twisted [by later decisions] into a device for preventing further innovation."

[59]R. McCLOSKEY, THE AMERICAN SUPREME COURT 127-35 (1960), goes further, viewing Waite's opinion not as a careless slip in asserting a broad policy of self-restraint but as a cautious and deliberate step toward Field's still too revolutionary thesis that protection for vested rights could respectably be anchored in the historically inapposite due process clauses. The results of the Waite Court's later encounters with this issue, however, seem to cast doubt on this explanation. *See* especially text accompanying notes 75-83 *infra*, discussing *Powell v. Pennsylvania*.

[60]Davidson v. New Orleans, 96 U.S. 97, 104 (1878).

left out, and this was taken."[61] The measure in question, moreover, was a tax for public purposes; the law provided for notice and opportunity to contest the charge; and

> it is not possible to hold that a party has, without due process of law, been deprived of his property, when, as regards the issues affecting it, he has, by the laws of the State, a fair trial in a court of justice, according to the modes of proceeding applicable to such a case.[62]

All of this came within a hair's breadth of saying that due process meant nothing more than a fair trial; and Bradley alone, giving no reasons, protested in concurrence the unequivocal conclusion that due process did not forbid uncompensated takings.[63]

In a single gratuitous sentence, however, Miller managed to undermine his own apparent conclusion:

> It seems to us that a statute which declares in terms, and without more, that the full and exclusive title of a described piece of land, which is now in A., shall be and is hereby vested in B., would, if effectual, deprive A. of his property without due process of law, within the meaning of the constitutional provision.[64]

[61]*Id.* at 105.

[62]*Id.* at 104-05.

[63]*Id.* at 107. Miller emphatically conceded that due process limited state legislative authority: although the barons who had extracted Magna Charta's original law-of-the-land provision had had no intention "to protect themselves against the enactment of laws by the Parliament of England," the derivative clause in the fourteenth amendment would be "of no avail" if a state could "make any thing due process of law which, by its own legislation, it chooses to declare such." *Accord*, T. COOLEY, *supra* note 11, at 354. As an original matter this was unconvincing: there would have been nothing futile about extending to the states a separation-of-powers provision designed to assure the approval of the popularly elected legislature before a person could be deprived of his property. *See* Youngstown Sheet & Tube Co. v. Sawyer, 343 U.S. 579, 655 (1952) (Jackson, J., concurring): "[with] all its defects, delays and inconveniences, men have discovered no technique for long preserving free government except that the Executive be under the law, and that the law be made by parliamentary deliberations." Miller's conclusion, nevertheless, was compelled by *Murray's Lessee*, *supra* text accompanying note 7; indeed the argument was stronger in *Davidson* than in *Murray*, for only the fourteenth amendment and not the fifth could be argued to have been concerned solely with federal-state relations. *See also* Arrowsmith v. Harmoning, 118 U.S. 194, 196 (1886) (Waite, C.J.), where in rejecting for understandable practical reasons the notion that every error in the application of state law was a failure of due process the Court seemed to express indifference to the original English purpose of assuring that no one be deprived of property except in accordance with law. In any event, Miller's concession that due process limited legislation was not inconsistent with holding that it required only fair procedure.

[64]96 U.S. at 102. *See also* Campbell v. Holt, 115 U.S. 620, 623 (1885) (dictum), where in allowing a state to reinstate a contract action barred by the statute of limitations ("[w]e are unable to see how a man can be said to have *property* in the bar of the statute as a defence to his promise to pay," *id.* at 629) Miller added that the result would be otherwise "in an action to recover real or personal property": "by the law in existence before the repealing act [in such a case], the property had become the defendant's, . . . and to give the act the effect of transferring this title to plaintiff, would be to deprive him of his property without due process of law."

In the Sinking-Fund Cases, 99 U.S. 700, 718-19 (1879), Chief Justice Waite relied in part on the due process clause for the statement (which in one sense would have followed from the simple enumeration of federal powers) that "[t]he United States cannot any more than a State interfere with private rights, except

In light of this passage, it was not surprising that litigants continued even after *Davidson* to bombard the Court with arguments based upon the "strange misconception" that it was free under the due process clause to reexamine the "merits of . . . legislation."[65] Without giving the faintest semblance of an explanation and in the same opinion in which he appeared to say due process went only to procedure, Miller had seemed to announce that due process required the legislature to have an acceptable substantive reason for depriving a person of property.[66]

E. *Mugler v. Kansas*

After *Davidson*, though the Court under Waite never found a state law to offend due process, it made no more efforts to establish that the clause had nothing to do with "the merits of . . . legislation." On the contrary, the Court's own opinions began to speak in Justice Field's police-power terms without even explaining what they had to do with the fourteenth amendment.[67] The climax of this development came in 1887,

---

for legitimate governmental purposes." In this case the Court managed over dissents by Strong, Bradley, and Field to uphold a requirement that funds be set aside to pay debts not yet due on the debatable ground that a general power of amendment reserved in contracts with the debtors allowed any later provision that could have been prescribed at the time credit was extended.

[65]Eight years later, in upholding as a reasonable means of deterrence a provision for double damages in tort actions against railroads for failure to fence their tracks, Field echoed Miller's surprise at the continuing "misconception" while encouraging it by saying that, so long as adequate rules for enforcement were followed, due process did not affect laws "enacted within the legitimate sphere of legislative power." Missouri Pac. Ry. v. Humes, 115 U.S. 512, 519-20 (1885).

[66]To conclude on the basis of the first passages quoted in the text that Miller would have permitted giving A's land to B without any reason after a "fair trial" of the relevant "issues" would be to accuse him of insisting on a pointless formality, for in such a case there would be no issues to be tried.

[67]In upholding in the same year an ordinance forbidding the operation of locomotives in a city street, for example, the Chief Justice relied heavily on the police power and on Field's maxim *sic utere tuo*, adding that "[a]ll property . . . is subject to the *legitimate* control of the government" and that "*[a]ppropriate* regulation of the use of property is not 'taking' property, within the meaning of the constitutional prohibition" (emphasis added). Though he also said the state court's judgment was "final as to the reasonableness of the action," Waite seemed to be suggesting not only that a court might investigate whether a regulation was in some sense "appropriate" or "legitimate" but also, ignoring Miller's contrary declaration in *Davidson*, that the due process clause did forbid uncompensated takings. Railroad Co. v. Richmond, 96 U.S. 521, 528-29 (1878). Strong dissented without opinion.

Still clearer was Field's own statement for the Court in upholding a prohibition on the nighttime operation of laundries:

> [I]t is of the utmost consequence in a city subject, as San Francisco is, . . . to high winds, and composed principally within the limits designated of wooden buildings, that regulations of a strict character should be adopted to prevent the possibility of fires. That occupations in which continuous fires are necessary should cease at certain hours of the night would seem to be, under such circumstances, a reasonable regulation as a measure of precaution. At any rate, of its necessity for the purpose designated the municipal authorities are the appropriate judges.

Soon Hing v. Crowley, 113 U.S. 703, 708 (1885). *See also* Head v. Amoskeag Mfg. Co., 113 U.S. 9, 26 (1885) (Gray, J.), upholding a statute authorizing a riparian proprietor to flood the land of others upon payment of damages, partly on the ground that it was "a just and reasonable exercise of the power of the legislature" to adjust the mutually dependent rights of all landowners abutting the stream and noting that "without some such regulation" the water power "could not be beneficially used."

when Justice Harlan held that a state could prohibit the manufacture of beer even for one's own use:

> [I]t is difficult to perceive any ground for the judiciary to declare that the prohibition . . . is not fairly adapted to the end of protecting the community against the evils which confessedly result from the excessive use of ardent spirits . . . . [W]e cannot shut out of view the facts, within the knowledge of all, that the public health, the public morals, and the public safety, may be endangered by the general use of intoxicating drinks. . . . [I]f, in the judgment of the legislature, the manufacture of intoxicating liquors for the maker's own use, as a beverage, would tend to cripple, if it did not defeat, the effort to guard the community against the evils attending the excessive use of such liquors, it is not for the courts, upon their views as to what is best and safest for the community, to disregard the legislative determination of that question.[68]

It was irrelevant, Harlan added, that the breweries in question had been in existence before the prohibition law was passed; "the State did not . . . give any assurance . . . that its legislation . . . would remain unchanged," and "[i]t cannot be supposed that the States intended, by adopting th[e] Amendment, to impose restraints upon the exercise of their powers for the protection of the safety, health, or morals of the community."[69]

There is a decided attitude of deference to legislative judgment in this opinion, but the stress on the police-power basis of the law strongly implies that no regulation would be upheld unless it fell within the Court's conception of that power, and another passage made the implication explicit.[70] Indeed, there are pronounced echoes in the quoted passage of Marshall's test for the necessity and propriety of a measure enacted by Congress to carry out the powers expressly given it by the Constitution:[71] public health is a legitimate end, and the prohibition seems "fairly adapted" to that goal. It is easy enough to see why this test is relevant in deciding whether a federal law is necessary and proper to effectuate the limited functions entrusted to Congress;[72] it is harder to relate it to the provision that states may not deprive persons of property without due process of law. Without explanation, the

---

[68]123 U.S. 623, 661-62 (1887).

[69]Id. at 664, 669.

[70] The courts are not bound by mere forms, nor are they to be misled by mere pretences . . . . If, therefore, a statute purporting to have been enacted to protect the public health, the public morals, or the public safety, has no real or substantial relation to those objects, . . . it is the duty of the courts to so adjudge, and thereby to give effect to the Constitution.

Id. at 661.

[71] Let the end be legitimate, let it be within the scope of the constitution, and all means which are appropriate, which are plainly adapted to that end, which are not prohibited, but consist with the letter and spirit of the constitution, are constitutional.

McCulloch v. Maryland, 17 U.S. (4 Wheat.) 316, 421 (1819).

[72]U.S. Const., art. I, § 8: "The Congress shall have Power . . . To make all Laws which shall be necessary and proper for carrying into Execution the foregoing Powers, and all other Powers vested by this Constitution in the Government of the United States, or in any Department or Officer thereof." The legitimacy of the end is made relevant by the requirement that the law carry other granted powers into execution, the appropriateness of the means by the requirement that it be "necessary and proper" to that goal. See supra chapter 6.

Court had begun to treat the states as though they too had only enumerated powers—to enact measures "fairly adapted" to the protection of public safety, health, morals, and order.

On this assumption, *Mugler* was an easy case; even Field objected only to the provision requiring destruction of liquor already manufactured and of brewing utensils, both of which he argued might have legitimate uses.[73] Miller said nothing, presumably because he found the result congenial; but the Court had traveled a long way from the narrow view of due process that Miller had tried to express in *Davidson*.[74]

F. *Powell v. Pennsylvania*

Though Field had every reason to be satisfied that the Court had swallowed his police-power thesis in *Mugler*, in its final encounter with due process in this period the Court showed that it still differed sharply with Field in determining the crucial question of the scope of that power. With Harlan writing again, the Court just after Waite's death in 1888 and before appointment of his successor upheld a statute flatly forbidding the sale of oleomargarine, going so far as to reject the offer of evidence that the defendant's product was both wholesome and nutritious.[75] Although "the privilege of pursuing an ordinary calling" was indeed protected by the fourteenth amendment,[76] *Mugler* had settled that the amendment "was not designed to interfere with the exercise of" the police power.[77] The healthfulness of the particular defendant's product would not prove that *no* oleomargarine was injurious;[78] it therefore must be "assumed" that other margarine was harmful; and whether the danger was such as to require "the entire suppression of the business, rather than its regulation in such manner as to permit the manufacture and sale of articles of that class that do not contain noxious ingredients, are questions of fact and of public policy which belong to the legislative department to determine."[79]

[73]123 U.S. at 677-78.

[74]Indeed, at one point, ignoring *Davidson*'s flat statement that a taking without compensation was not within the due-process clause, Harlan announced a general test for distinguishing between regulation and taking that has been influential in many later cases: "A prohibition simply upon the use of property for purposes that are declared, by valid legislation, to be injurious to the health, morals, or safety of the community, cannot, in any just sense, be deemed a taking or an appropriation of property for the public benefit. Such legislation does not disturb the owner in control or use of his property for lawful purposes, nor restrict his right to dispose of it, but is only a declaration by the State that its use by any one, for certain forbidden purposes, is prejudicial to the public interests." *Id.* at 668-69. He seemed to be saying, reasonably enough, that a property right did not include the right "to inflict injury upon the community," *id.* at 669, 665; but he also seemed to be implying that the fourteenth amendment might forbid uncompensated takings after all.

[75]Powell v. Pennsylvania, 127 U.S. 678, 681-82, 684 (1888).

[76]*Id.* at 684.

[77]*Id.* at 683.

[78]*Id.* at 684.

[79]*Id.* at 684-85. Despite the "grave" question perceived fifteen years earlier in *Bartemeyer*, the Court did not even bother replying to the allegation (*id.* at 682) that the margarine in question had been manufactured before the law was enacted. Justice Field, in his lone dissent, relied in part on this allegation, distinguishing articles that "could not be used without injury to the health of the community . . . ." *Id.* at 698-99.

Field's reply was not only predictable; given the Court's notion that due process forbade regulation not fairly designed to protect health or public order, it seemed overwhelming:

> [O]ne would suppose that it would be a matter for congratulation on the part of the State, that in the progress of science a means had been discovered by which a new article of food could be produced, equally healthy and nutritious with, and less expensive than, one already existing . . . . If that which is forbidden is not injurious to the health or morals of the people, . . . it derives no validity by calling it a police or health law.[80]

Amen, Brother Field; if there was ever a case for substantive due process, this was it. In essence the margarine ban seemed simply a transfer of wealth to the dairy industry, and even Miller in *Davidson* had conceded that a legislature could not give one man's property to another.[81] General formulas never decide concrete controversies, Brother Field; the important part of *Mugler* for the majority was its deference to the legislative judgment. But be patient, Brother Field, for general formulas can be manipulated in one direction as well as in another. If, as *Powell* suggests, the Justices did not really believe in substantive due process,[82] they might better have said so directly; as it was, all a Court full of Field's disciples would have to do was to differ over the assessment of the facts, and Field would have his day.[83] Alas, O Miller! Those who fail to take the tide at its flood commonly end up missing the boat.

G.   Related Issues

During Waite's tenure the Court thus expended considerable energy both in staving off and in encouraging the development of due process into a shield for protecting

[80]*Id*. at 689, 695.

[81]The statute had replaced one forbidding the palming off of margarine as butter, the title of the act itself retained a reference to "fraud," and the Court said in passing that the legislature had determined that the law would "prevent frauds." *Id*. at 679-686. But the Court nowhere discussed the fraud problem, explaining only that the statute was a reasonable health measure; and Field dismissed the title as a holdover from a more limited draft, concluding that the statute itself was "not designed . . . to protect against deception," *id*. at 688. No one argued that protection of the butter industry from competition was itself a legitimate police-power goal. *Cf*. Sunstein, *Public Values, Private Interests, and the Equal Protection Clause*, 1982 SUP. CT. REV. 127, 131-38, arguing that in equal-protection cases the Court has insisted that some justification for legislation be offered beyond a "naked preference [ ]" for one person or class over another and adding that in many cases the Court has "stretched far to find a justification" that satisfies this standard. *Powell* is a classic example of the same approach to due process. *See also* E. FREUND, THE POLICE POWER § 134 (1904) (arguing that *Powell* "reached the extreme limit of tolerance"); E. CORWIN, LIBERTY AGAINST GOVERNMENT 149 (1948): "In the Mugler case the Court marched uphill; in the Powell case it marched down again."

[82]But *see* C. MAGRATH, *supra*, introduction to part five, note 1, ch. 10.

[83]*See, e.g.*, Lochner v. New York, 198 U.S. 45 (1905) (Peckham, J.) (limitation on hours of employment offends due process); C. FAIRMAN, MILLER, *supra* introduction to part five, note 2 at 206. *See also* McCurdy, *Justice Field and the Jurisprudence of Government-Business Relations; Some Parameters of Laissez Faire Constitutionalism, 1863-1897*, in AMERICAN LAW AND THE CONSTITUTIONAL ORDER 246, 249-51 (Friedman & Scheiber eds. 1978), denying that Field himself would have joined *Lochner*, noting that his *Slaughter-House* dissent had been in opposition to monopoly, and arguing that later Justices had "wrenched Field's principles out of their original context." The fact remains that Field was an avid advocate of substantive due process.

substantive interests against legislative interference. In a more limited field, the contract clause of article I, § 10 had served this same office from the beginning; and although in a multitude of routine cases Waite and his brethren continued to enforce this clause according to the guidelines laid down by their forebears,[84] it was fully in keeping with their general deference to legislative judgment that in one critical respect they created a new and broadly defined loophole in the protection afforded to the beneficiaries of public promises.

The opening wedge had been inserted by no lesser a friend of the contract clause than John Marshall himself, who in holding the clause applied to government contracts had warned in passing that there were limits to the authority of a state legislature to "abridge the powers" of its successors.[85] He did not define the source of those limits; and no concrete use of his concession was made in the Supreme Court until Justice Catron's dissenting objection in 1854 that Ohio had no power to grant contractual tax exemptions.[86] That the idea was still alive, however, had been manifested shortly before Waite's accession by a Miller dissent associating his name and those of Chase and Field with Catron's long-repudiated position respecting taxes;[87] and in the Waite years Miller was to find an outlet for his views outside the tax field that would command the agreement of a unanimous bench.

The development began inconspicuously. Convicted of running a lottery, a defendant argued that he had been authorized to do so by a contract with the state. Affirming a decision that the law on which he relied had been passed in violation of a procedural provision of the state constitution,[88] Field added unnecessarily and without explanation the following portentous language:

> We are not prepared to admit that it is competent for one legislature, by any contract with an individual, to restrain the power of a subsequent legislature to legislate for the public welfare, and to that end to suppress any and all practices tending to corrupt the public morals.[89]

The next term, in the hands of Justice Bradley, the refusal to admit became an unequivocal but equally conclusory denial, for which only the previous statement

[84]*See* B. WRIGHT, THE CONTRACT CLAUSE OF THE CONSTITUTION 94, 95 (1938), citing the cases: "Between 1873 and 1888 there were twenty-nine cases in which state legislation was held unconstitutional because of an impairment of the obligation of contracts. . . . [T]he clause reached its peak at about the end of the Waite period." *But see* Kainen, *Nineteenth Century Interpretations of the Federal Contract Clause: The Transformation from Vested to Substantive Rights Against the State*, 31 BUFF. L. REV. 381, 385 (1982), finding "strict construction with a vengeance" in a case holding that a charter authorizing a railroad to set its own rates was not impaired by a later legislative decision to limit the rates it could charge (Railroad Commission Cases, 116 U.S. 307 (1886)).

[85]Fletcher v. Peck, 10 U.S. (6 Cranch.) 87, 135 (1810). *See supra* chapter 5.

[86]Piqua Branch of State Bank v. Knoop, 57 U.S. (16 How.) 369, 404-05 (Dec. Term 1853) (dissenting opinion). *See supra* chapter 7.

[87]Washington Univ. v. Rouse, 75 U.S. (8 Wall.) 439, 443-44 (1870) (dissenting opinion), noted *supra* in the conclusion to part four: "To hold, then, that any one of the annual legislatures can, by contract, deprive the state forever of the power of taxation, is to hold that they can destroy the government which they are appointed to serve . . . ." On the question of stare decisis, Miller said "there may be questions touching the powers of legislative bodies, which can never be finally closed by the decisions of a court." He did not say why.

[88]Boyd v. Alabama, 94 U.S. 645, 650 (1877). The opinion also doubted whether the contract had actually authorized a lottery. *Id*. at 649-50.

[89]*Id*. at 650.

was cited. After concluding fairly enough both that the legislature had reserved the right to repeal a beer company's charter and that the contract gave no "greater or more sacred right than any citizen had to manufacture malt liquor,"[90] the Court felt unable to resist adding that the legislature "had no power" to give a perpetual right to make intoxicating beverages: neither the police power itself nor the legislature's discretion as to the means of exercising it could be "bargained away" by contract.[91]

This alternative holding became the sole basis for decision in 1880, when in *Stone v. Mississippi* the Court confronted a contract that unmistakably purported to grant the right to run a lottery for twenty-five years.[92] The police power, said Waite, "extends to all matters affecting the public health or the public morals," including the prevention of lotteries; "[a]ll agree," as shown by two earlier opinions, "that the legislature cannot bargain away the police power."[93] Taxation was different; it was merely "incident to" the functions of government, while it was for the preservation of public health and morals that government itself was organized.[94] No reference was made to the Mississippi constitution to support these conclusions; indeed, Waite went so far as to say, as a matter of mere fiat, that the people themselves had no power to renounce their police power.[95]

In light of the tenth amendment,[96] one might have thought that, apart from such limits as the federal Constitution might impose, the Supreme Court had no business telling either the people or the legislature of Mississippi what their powers were. In fact, after uttering all these natural-law platitudes, Waite polished off his opinion by giving a distinct reason for his conclusion based clearly on federal law: "[t]he contracts which the Constitution protects are those that relate to property rights, not

[90]Beer Co. v. Massachusetts, 97 U.S. 25, 31-32 (1878). *See also* Fertilizing Co. v. Hyde Park, 97 U.S. 659 (1878) (Swayne, J.), holding that a charter authorizing the operation of a fertilizer plant for fifty years did not promise not to require its relocation when it became a nuisance.

[91]97 U.S. at 33.

[92]101 U.S. 814, 815, 817 (1880).

[93]*Id.* at 817-19. For another discussion of the development of this doctrine with reference to earlier state decisions, *see* B. WRIGHT, *supra* note 84, at 196-203. Cooley (*supra* note 11, at 574-77) had maintained that contracts were subject to the police power, but it was not clear to what extent he relied on implied reservations in the contracts themselves and to what extent on legislative inability to contract.

[94]101 U.S. at 819-20.

[95]*Id.* at 819. *See also* Butchers' Union Co. v. Crescent City Co., 111 U.S. 746, 751 (1884) (Miller, J.), extending the *Stone* principle to hold that Louisiana could repeal the slaughtering monopoly upheld over fourteenth amendment objections in the *Slaughter-House Cases* because "a wise policy forbids the legislative body to divest itself of the power to enact laws for the preservation of health and the repression of crime." The abatement of existing slaughterhouses as nuisances would have fit easily into this formulation, but Miller did not explain how the authorization of *additional* facilities could be considered a health measure. *See id.* at 760-61 (Bradley, Harlan, and Woods, JJ., concurring), denying that the repeal was a police measure and (like Field in a separate opinion) basing concurrence on the grounds rejected in *Slaughter-House*. Miller did not advert to earlier decisions protecting exclusive bridge franchises against impairment, e.g., The Binghamton Bridge, 70 U.S. (3 Wall.) 51 (Dec. Term 1865), nor did he object when the Court shortly afterwards held the state could not repeal monopolies of gas and water service, distinguishing *Crescent City* on the flimsy and conclusory ground that the latter were not "ordinary business[es]" but "franchise[s]" involving the laying of pipes in city streets. New Orleans Gas Co. v. Louisiana Light Co., 115 U.S. 650, 669 (1885); New Orleans Water-Works v. Rivers, 115 U.S. 674 (1885) (both by Harlan J.).

[96]"The powers not delegated to the United States by the Constitution, nor prohibited by it to the States, are reserved to the States respectively, or to the people."

governmental."[97] No reason was offered for his debatable interpretation other than the foregoing discussion; but at least it had the virtue of not usurping the state's authority to define its own powers.[98]

It may appear surprising that it was Field, the most avid exponent of protection for substantive rights under the inauspicious due process clause, who took the lead in watering down the explicit protection of the contract clause. His due-process and contract views, however, had one important attribute in common: when Field was done the test of state power to affect not only contracts but a broad range of other rights not yet fully defined was the uncertain scope of the "police power."[99]

Natural-law notions had appeared in Supreme Court opinions before, usually in defense of vested rights;[100] the rise of due process as a substantive limitation was to provide a nominally more acceptable outlet for this propensity. The beer and lottery cases presented the converse spectacle of natural law being employed to *defeat* rights that otherwise appeared to be vested, in accord with the deferential attitude of the times; and Justice Miller's famous opinion for the Court in *Loan Association v. Topeka*[101] was in the same mold. There, five years before *Stone v. Mississippi*, the Court permitted a city to weasel out of its bond obligations because they had

[97]101 U.S. at 820. *Cf.* Butler v. Pennsylvania, 51 U.S. (10 How.) 402, 451 (1850) (Daniel, J.), *supra* chapter 7, employing a similar explanation in holding the jobs of government officers unprotected by the clause. *Butler* was not cited in *Stone*. It was, however, relied on in Newton v. Commissioners, 100 U.S. 548, 559 (1880) (Swayne, J.) (alternative holding), which seemed to talk both of the meaning of "Contract" in article I and of inherent limits on state power in concluding that "there can be no contract" agreeing not to move a county seat because the subject was "'governmental'" and the ability to meet changing needs "vital to the public welfare." *Cf.* Maynard v, Hill, 125 U.S. 190, 210-14 (1888) (Field, J.), holding despite Story's contrary statement in the *Dartmouth College* case (see *supra* chapter 5) that marriage was not a "contract" within the meaning of the clause. *But see* Hall v. Wisconsin, 103 U.S. 5 (1880) (Swayne, J.) (discussed in B. WRIGHT, *supra* note 84, at 221-23), where the same Justice who had written *Newton* significantly omitted to cite *Butler* in holding that the state's employment of "commission-ers" to conduct an agricultural survey had created a protected contract rather than a "public office."

[98]In another important limiting decision the Court finally settled on Justice Miller's position that the contract clause limited only legislative action, New Orleans Waterworks Co. v. Louisiana Sugar Ref. Co., 125 U.S. 18, 30 (1888) (Gray, J.), after having suggested the contrary as recently as Douglass v. County of Pike, 101 U.S. 677, 687 (1880) (Waite, C.J.). For the background of this controversy, *see supra* chapter 7. *See also* several decisions permitting states to erect retroactive procedural roadblocks to the enforcement of their own bond obligations: Antoni v. Greenhow, 107 U.S. 769 (1883) (Waite, C.J.) (state that promised to accept interest coupons in payment of taxes may require bondholder to pay first and then sue to establish his right); Moore v. Greenhow, 114 U.S. 338 (1885) (Matthews, J.) (same); In re Ayers, 123 U.S. 443, 494-96 (1887) (Matthews, J.) (alternative holding) (suit against taxpayer who has tendered coupons as payment no impairment of agreement to accept coupons since taxpayer has defense on merits). *Cf.* the related use of sovereign immunity as a shield against enforcement of state bonds by narrow construction of precedents allowing suits against state officers, *infra* chapter 12; and *cf.* Railroad Co. v. Tennessee, 101 U.S. 337 (1880) (Waite, C.J.), allowing repeal of a provision permitting the state to be sued on its contracts because even under prior law there had been no way to enforce the judgment. The dissents of Field and Harlan in the *Antoni* case are overpowering.

[99]For an impressive presentation of the view that the gradual replacement of contract-clause by due-process limitations reflected the decline of the underlying conviction that rights "vested" under prior law were either a necessary or a sufficient measure of the interests deserving substantive protection, *see* Kainen, *supra* note 84; for the argument that Field's contract-clause views showed him no doctrinaire apologist for property rights, see McCurdy, *supra* note 83.

[100]*See, e.g., supra*, chapters 2 and 5, discussing *Calder v. Bull* and *Fletcher v. Peck*.

[101]87 U.S. (20 Wall.) 655 (1875).

committed tax revenues to assist a private manufacturer, and because "there can be no lawful tax which is not laid for a *public purpose*."[102] As Clifford alone protested in an unwontedly cogent and concise dissent,[103] Miller nowhere tied this conclusion to either the federal or the state constitution, relying instead on cases drawn indiscriminately from a variety of states and echoing without attribution the natural-law utterances of earlier Justices:

> There are limitations on [state and federal] power which grow out of the essential nature of all free governments. Implied reservations of individual rights, without which the social compact could not exist, and which are respected by all governments entitled to the name . . . . To lay with one hand the power of the government on the property of the citizen, and with the other to bestow it upon favored individuals to aid private enterprises and build up private fortunes, is none the less a robbery because it is done under the forms of law and is called taxation.[104]

This was the same Miller who, as *Davidson* illustrates, was the Court's foremost opponent of the effort to find in the due process clause authority for the judges to invalidate laws on the basis of their own notions of sound policy.[105] A charitable reader might argue that Miller was actually giving a traditionally narrow interpretation to the terms "taxation" and "legislation" in the state constitution; even he explicitly declined to apply the *Topeka* rule in cases coming from state courts, where the sole question open was federal.[106] In any event, it is perhaps no more surprising to find the otherwise deferential Miller inventing extraconstitutional public-purpose limitations than to find the economic-liberty enthusiast Field diluting the contract clause. Both examples seem only to illustrate the tendency of judges to discover that they have maximum flexibility to do whatever they think is just; and it may be this as much as the possible reluctance of his colleagues that restrained Miller from ever putting the last nail in the coffin of substantive due process.

[102]*Id.* at 664-65 (emphasis in original).

[103]*Id.* at 667-70.

[104]*Id.* at 663-64.

[105]*See also* C. FAIRMAN, *supra*, introduction to part five, note 2, at 67-68, describing Miller as an advocate of "judicial restraint" who "thought that the Court ought not to invent constitutional limitations . . . ."

[106]*See* Davidson v. New Orleans, 96 U.S. 97, 105 (1878), describing *Topeka* as based upon "principles of general constitutional law." In Cole v. La Grange, 113 U.S. 1 (1885), Justice Gray cited *Topeka* in reaching the same result explicitly on the basis of the state constitution. This opinion also had important implications for the taking clause of the fifth amendment, for one of Gray's conclusions was that, although a similar clause in the state constitution "regards the right of eminent domain, and not the power to tax," its requirement of compensation of takings for *public* use implied there could be no taking for private use at all: "Otherwise, as it makes no provision for compensation except when the use is public, it would permit private property to be taken or appropriated for private use without any compensation whatever." A tax, he added interestingly, "requires no other compensation than the taxpayer receives in being protected by the government to the support of which he contributes." *Id.* at 7-8. *See* Epstein, *Not Deference, but Doctrine: The Eminent Domain Clause*, 1982 SUP. CT. REV. 351, 372-73.

II. EQUAL PROTECTION

A. *Strauder v. West Virginia*

Slaughter-House had emphasized that racial equality was the central concern of the fourteenth amendment, but it was not until 1880 that the Supreme Court first had the opportunity to apply the amendment in the context of alleged racial discrimination. Three decisions in that year, all written by Justice Strong, dealt with the exclusion of blacks from criminal juries.

The most important of these cases for present purposes was *Strauder v. West Virginia*,[107] in which state legislation explicitly limited jury service to whites.[108] Eloquently echoing the relevant passages from *Slaughter-House*, Strong reaffirmed that the amendment "was designed to assure to the colored race the enjoyment of all the civil rights that under the law are enjoyed by white persons . . . ." "What is this," he asked after paraphrasing the text, "but declaring that the law in the States shall be the same for the black as for the white; that all persons, whether colored or white, shall stand equal before the laws of the States, and, in regard to the colored race, for whose protection the amendment was primarily designed, that no discrimination shall be made against them by law because of their color?"[109] "[P]rejudices often exist against particular classes in the community, which sway the judgment of jurors"; "protection of life and liberty against race or color prejudice" was "a legal right" under the amendment; and "[i]t is not easy to comprehend how it can be said that while every white man is entitled to a trial by a jury selected . . . without discrimination against his color, and a negro is not, the latter is equally protected by the law with the former." The state remained free to "confine the selection to males, to freeholders, to citizens, to persons within certain ages, or to persons having educational qualifications," because history showed the purpose of the amendment was to prevent "discrimination because of race or color." But if a law "exclud[ed] all white men from jury service, thus denying them the privilege of participating equally with the blacks in the administration of justice, we apprehend no one would be heard to claim that it would not be a denial to white men of the equal protection of the laws."[110]

The result seems obvious today. There was no doubt that West Virginia discriminated against blacks or that black equality was the central thrust of the amendment. One may quibble over whether as an original matter the clause applicable to *Strauder* was that guaranteeing equal protection or that securing privileges and immunities against state abridgement;[111] but after the narrow construction given the latter clause in *Slaughter-House*, equal protection was the only remaining avenue for accomplishing the Framers' purpose. Neither the opinion's strong suggestion that history limited the all-encompassing language of that clause to racial discrimination nor the

[107]100 U.S. 303 (1880).
[108]*Id.* at 305.
[109]*Id.* at 306-08.
[110]*Id.* at 308-10.
[111]*See supra* chapter 10.

clear statement that it forbade discrimination against whites[112] was new or implausible.[113] But there are nevertheless difficulties with the opinion.

The first problem is in identifying just whose right was being protected. It was obvious that potential black jurors had been the victims of discrimination, and the Court said so, noting that "colored people"—like whites in the converse hypothetical already quoted—"are singled out and expressly denied by a statute all right to participate in the administration of the law, as jurors . . . ."[114] No potential juror was complaining, however, and earlier cases had suggested that a litigant might not be allowed to assert the rights of others.[115] Moreover, as Field and Clifford protested in dissent[116] and as legislative history confirms,[117] there was good reason to believe the fourteenth amendment protected only "civil" and not "political" rights.[118] For both reasons it would have been difficult for Strong to base his decision on an infringement of the rights of potential black jurors.

In fact he did not do so. After pointing out the denial of equality to potential jurors, Strong attempted to show that the rights of the criminal defendant had also been infringed: "compelling a colored man to submit to a trial for his life by a jury . . . from which the State has expressly excluded every man of his race, because of color

[112]Strong added "Celtic Irishmen," 100 U.S. at 308, arguably extending the clause beyond the strictly racial. There were nevertheless hints that the discrimination forbidden was that "implying inferiority," and the statement about exclusion of whites from juries was explicitly made in the context of "those states where the colored people constitute a majority . . . ." *Id.* Thus the dicta of *Strauder* did not wholly exclude the notion of "benign" racial classifications.

[113]*See supra* chapter 10.

[114]100 U.S. at 308.

[115]*E.g., Owings v. Norwood, supra* chapter 3. Moreover, a finding that the defendant's own rights were at stake was necessary to the Court's further holding (100 U.S. at 310-12) that he was entitled to remove the case to federal court under a statute limited to prosecutions "against any person who is denied, or cannot enforce, in the judicial tribunals of the State, . . . any right secured *to him*" under certain federal laws (emphasis added).

[116]100 U.S. at 349, 366-68, taking comfort from the fact that no one had thought the privileges and immunities clause of article IV had given outsiders the right to sit as jurors and arguing that the passage of the fifteenth amendment showed no one had thought political rights were included in the fourteenth either. Field might have added that § 2 of the fourteenth amendment itself provided for a reduction in representation if a state excluded blacks from voting (*see* Reynolds v. Sims, 377 U.S. 533, 593-94 (1964) (Harlan, J., dissenting)). None of these arguments is conclusive. Equal protection arguably covers rights that the different language of article IV did not; on its face the fifteenth amendment might have been adopted out of an abundance of caution rather than a conviction that the fourteenth did not do the job (*cf.* text accompanying notes 208-16 *infra*, discussing the relationship between the thirteenth and fourteenth amendments); and § 2 might merely have prescribed a remedy for what § 1 had forbidden.

[117]*See, e.g.,* CONG. GLOBE, 39th Cong. 1st Sess. (1866), pp. 2459 (Mr. Stevens), 2462-63 (Mr. Garfield), 2469 (Mr. Kelley), 2530 (Mr. Randall), 2539 (Mr. Farnsworth), 2542 (Mr. Bingham), 2765 (Mr. Howard), 3035 (Mr. Henderson), all denying that the fourteenth amendment would give blacks the right to vote.

[118]*See* United States v. Reese, 92 U.S. 214, 217-18 (1976) (dictum), saying that until the fifteenth amendment there was no bar to racial discrimination in voting; Reynolds v. Sims, 377 U.S. 533 (1964), ignoring Justice Harlan's overwhelming exposition of legislative history in holding that the equal protection clause applied to state legislative apportionments; R. BERGER, GOVERNMENT BY JUDICIARY, ch. 4 (1977); Van Alsytne, *The Fourteenth Amendment, The "Right" to Vote, and the Understanding of the Thirty-Ninth Congress,* 1965 SUP. CT. REV. 33, 72, dismissing the significance of § 2 of the amendment, conceding "an original understanding that § 1 . . . would not itself immediately invalidate state suffrage laws severely restricting the right to vote," and adding that there was no "clear, uniform understanding that the open-ended phrases of § 1 . . . would foreclose a different application in the future." *Cf.* Professor Bickel's related discussion of segregation and miscegenation, note 143 *infra*.

alone, . . . is . . . a denial *to him* of equal legal protection."[119] But this was not so obvious. What lay behind it was the express fear that whites might not try a black fairly;[120] yet Strong stoutly insisted in a companion case that equal protection did not guarantee that any black actually sit on the jury or even be eligible for jury service, so long as there was no showing of discrimination against black jurors.[121] The Court thus appears at first glance to have confounded the rights of the defendant with those of the potential juror: it seems no more likely that an all-white jury will try a black fairly just because the absence of blacks is not deliberate.[122] Moreover, in focusing on the defendant's rights, the opinion implied an unexamined and not inevitable definition of equality itself. In a sense all defendants were treated equally; all were tried by a jury for which only whites were eligible.[123] The law operated unequally on the races in much the same way a uniform tax operates unequally on rich and poor; the text of the amendment does not tell us in such a case whether it is the amount extracted or its impact upon the taxpayer that must be equal.

Despite these difficulties, however, *Strauder* seems on balance to have been rightly decided. In one sense, as Strong emphasized, there was indeed inequality: only blacks were tried by juries from which members of their race had been excluded. The risk of prejudice from all-white juries suggested why this arrangement might place blacks at a disadvantage, and the amendment's purpose of protecting blacks against discrimination suggests that this disadvantage made the law unequal in the constitutional sense. Moreover, the logic of Strong's position did not in fact demand that blacks actually be represented on the jury; the problem was not prejudice itself but that the statute exposed blacks more than whites to the risk of a prejudiced jury.

B.   Judicial and Executive Discrimination

In *Strauder*, blacks had been excluded from juries by statute, but the Court made clear in two companion cases that the equal protection clause forbade judicial or executive officers to exclude them as well:

> Whoever, by virtue of public position under a State government, deprives another of property, life, or liberty, without due process of law, or denies or takes away the equal protection of the laws, violates the constitutional inhibition; and as he acts in the name and for the State, and is clothed with the State's power, his act is that of the State.[124]

---

[119]100 U.S. at 309 (emphasis added). Strong similarly stressed the rights of unspecified black defendants in upholding a federal statute punishing a judge who had excluded blacks from juries in the companion case of Ex parte Virginia, 100 U.S. 339, 345 (1880).

[120]*See supra* text accompanying notes 109-110.

[121]Virginia v. Rives, 100 U.S. 322-23 (1880): "A mixed jury in any particular case is not essential to the equal protection of the laws . . . ."

[122]Justice Field thought the logic of the defendant's argument would require that *all* jurors and the judge as well be black. 100 U.S. at 368-69 (dissenting opinion).

[123]*See Developments in the Law—Equal Protection*, 82 HARV. L. REV. 1065, 1164 (1969): "if *A* likes scotch and *B* only bourbon, to give each a bottle of scotch treats them alike with respect to what they are given, but not respect to what they would have preferred."

[124]Ex parte Virginia, 100 U.S. 339, 347 (1880), (Strong, J.), upholding federal prosecution of a state

Field's objection that "[i]f an executive or judicial officer exercises power with which he is not invested by law, and does unauthorized acts, the State is not responsible for them"[125] was to surface again in occasional fourteenth amendment cases[126] and to become a part of the Court's explanation for allowing injunctive suits to be brought against state officers despite the eleventh amendment.[127] The contrast between the broad language of the amendment and other provisions expressly applicable only to the passage of "laws,"[128] however, cut against Field's position; and there seemed no reason to think the amendment's purpose of protecting blacks from official discrimination any less applicable to judicial or executive than to legislative action.

To say that judicial officers were forbidden to discriminate against blacks, however, was not to settle the question how discrimination was to be proved; and a passage in one of the 1880 cases seemed to suggest that the complaining party had to shoulder a substantial burden. Allegations that blacks "had never been allowed to serve as jurors in the county . . . in any case in which a colored man was interested," wrote Justice Strong, "fall short of showing . . . that there had been any discrimination against the defendants because of their color or race," for "the jury which indicted them, and the panel summoned to try them, may have been impartially selected."[129] The following Term, however, in *Neal v. Delaware*, the Court held that proof of a similar pattern of all-white juries "presented a *prima facie* case" of deliberate exclusion:

> It was, we think . . . a violent presumption which the State court indulged, that such uniform exclusion of that race from juries, during a period of many years, was solely because, in the judgment of those officers, fairly exercised, the black race in Delaware were utterly disqualified, by want of intelligence, experience, or moral integrity, to sit on juries.[130]

Justice Harlan did not mention the 1880 case, on which the dissenters relied;[131] but the conflict may be more apparent than real. Not only had the language quoted from that decision been entirely unnecessary to the result; there seems to have been no allegation in the first case that the exclusion of blacks had been deliberate. Thus the two cases together seem to establish what we know as the law today: that the equal

---

judge for excluding blacks from juries. *See also* Virginia v. Rives, 100 U.S. 313, 318 (1880) (Strong, J.) (dictum), holding the statute did not allow removal of a criminal case to federal court on the basis of a prediction that a state judge would violate state law making blacks eligible for jury duty: "It is doubtless true that a State may act through different agencies,—either by its legislative, its executive, or its judicial authorities; and the prohibitions of the amendment extend to all action of the State denying equal protection of the laws, whether it be action by one of these agencies or by another."

[125]*Id.* at 334. In the next two sentences he inconsistently acknowledged that the Supreme Court could reverse the judge's "erroneous ruling" in such a case, though the ruling offended federal law only if the judge's action was that of the state.

[126]*See, e.g.*, Barney v. City of New York, 193 U.S. 430, 437 (1904); Snowden v. Hughes, 321 U.S. 1, 17 (1944) (Frankfurter, J., concurring). But *see* Home Tel. & Tel. Co. v. City of Los Angeles, 227 U.S. 278, 287-89 (1913); United States v. Raines, 362 U.S. 17, 25-26 (1960).

[127]*See infra* chapter 12.

[128]*See supra* chapters 2 and 7, discussing the ex post facto and contract clauses of article I, § 10.

[129]Virginia v. Rives, 100 U.S. 313, 322 (1880).

[130]103 U.S. 370, 397 (1881).

[131]*Id.* at 398 (Waite, C.J.) and 401-02 (Field, J.).

protection clause forbids only deliberate discrimination and that circumstantial evidence may be strong enough to prove it.[132] That is all that was necessarily involved in the more famous and unanimous later decision in *Yick Wo v. Hopkins*, where the Court set aside convictions for operating laundries without official permission because the governing ordinance, though neutral on its face, had been applied in a discriminatory manner:

> It appears that both petitioners have complied with every requisite, deemed by the law or by the public officers charged with its administration, necessary for the protection of neighboring property from fire, or as a precaution against injury to the public health . . . . And while th[e] consent of the supervisors is withheld from them and from two hundred others who have also petitioned, all of whom happen to be Chinese subjects, eighty others, not Chinese subjects, are permitted to carry on the same business under similar conditions. The fact of this discrimination is admitted. No reason for it is shown, and the conclusion cannot be resisted, that no reason for it exists except hostility to the race and nationality to which the petitioners belong . . . .[133]

In all of this the Court seems to have captured the spirit of the amendment perfectly. If its efforts failed to stamp out official actions treating one race less favorably overall in objective terms than another, it was not essentially for want of judicial will.[134]

C. *Pace v. Alabama*

More questionable from today's perspective, however, was the unanimous 1883 decision in *Pace v. Alabama*[135] upholding a statute imposing more severe penalties

---

[132]*See* Washington v. Davis, 426 U.S. 229, 239, 241 (1976).

[133]118 U.S. 356, 374 (1886) (Matthews, J.). This decision shows that it made a difference that the Court chose to view this sort of discrimination as falling within the equal protection rather than the privileges or immunities clause; for the latter speaks only of "Citizen[s]" and the former of all "Person[s]," and the parties in *Yick Wo* were not American citizens. *See id.* at 369. The choice of the equal protection clause also made it easier for the Court to conclude (without giving any reasons) that a corporation was protected against official discrimination (Santa Clara County v. Southern Pacific R.R., 118 U.S. 394, 396 (1886) (Waite, C.J.)), although corporations had been held not "Citizen[s]" within other constitutional provisions. *See supra* chapters 3 and 10, discussing *Bank of United States v. Deveaux* (dictum) (diversity jurisdiction of article III), and *Paul v. Virginia* (privileges and immunities clause of article IV).

[134]For a less favorable view, *see* C. MAGRATH, *supra*, introduction to part five, note 1, ch. 8; for a comprehensive discussion of the jury cases, *see* Schmidt, *Juries, Jurisdiction, and Race Discrimination: The Lost Promise of Strauder v. West Virginia*, 61 TEX. L. REV. 1401 (1983). For the view that Field was insufficiently sensitive to actual discrimination in Chinese laundry cases prior to *Yick Wo, see* SWISHER, *supra*, introduction to part five, note 2, ch. 9, contrasting a still earlier position Field had taken on circuit. *See also* text accompanying notes 167-218 *infra*, discussing the Court's response to statutes purporting to enforce the Civil War amendments. Other passages in *Yick Wo* suggested a quite distinct theory that was not so easy to fit within the equal protection clause: that the state had given its administrative officers so much discretion that they *might* treat Chinese unequally. 118 U.S. at 366-73. What the amendment seems to preclude is actual discrimination; one might as well argue that the state constitution denied equal protection because it left the legislature room to pass discriminatory legislation. But the Court, after making the argument of unbridled discretion, acknowledged that it was not necessary to rely on it because the law had in fact been discriminatorily applied. *Id.* at 373. The discretion argument has a substantial later history in first amendment cases, *e.g.*, Staub v. City of Baxley, 355 U.S. 313 (1958).

[135]106 U.S. 583 (1883).

for living "in adultery or fornication" when the parties were of different races. As in *Strauder*, the critical question was what the fourteenth amendment meant by the term "equal," and again the Court answered the question without acknowledging that it existed.

Field conceded in his two-page opinion that blacks could not be subjected to greater punishment than whites "for the same offence."[136] But Alabama, he concluded, had treated all persons guilty of the same offense equally. The law imposed one punishment "when the persons . . . are both white and when they are both black" and another "where the two sexes are of different races"; under each provision blacks and whites were subjected to identical sanctions.[137]

Field's characterization was not necessarily inaccurate; the crucial question was whether it was enough to satisfy the constitutional standard. It was true that blacks and whites were equally disabled from living with members of other races. But it was also true that both blacks and whites were penalized more heavily for living with certain individuals than they would have been if they had been of another race; and a later Court was to find that the significant inequality.[138] The question was whether separation of the races was "equal" in the fourteenth amendment sense because it impartially denied both blacks and whites certain privileges on racial grounds; and Justice Harlan, who later would protest in a famous dissent that it was not,[139] went along with the majority's contrary conclusions in *Pace*.[140]

The language of the amendment does not answer the question,[141] and the debates on the amendment itself contain little that is relevant. Most nearly in point are some rather telling statements by important Republicans that the equal-rights provisions of statutory measures being considered at the same time would not legalize miscegenation or forbid segregated schools, in part because, as *Pace* concluded, "your law forbidding marriages between whites and blacks operates alike on both races."[142]

[136]*Id.* at 584.

[137]*Id.* at 585.

[138]Loving v. Virginia, 388 U.S. 1 (1967) (invalidating miscegenation law).

[139]Plessy v. Ferguson, 163 U.S. 537, 557, 559 (1896) (dissenting opinion). Even in *Plessy*, Harlan's inspiring declaration that "[o]ur Constitution is color-blind" was qualified by his perception that what was physically equal might be psychologically unequal: everyone knew that the law segregating trains "had its origin in the purpose, not so much to exclude white persons from railroad cars occupied by blacks, as to exclude colored people from coaches occupied by or assigned to white persons. . . . [T]he law . . . , practically, puts the brand of servitude and degradation upon a large class of our fellow citizens . . . ."

[140]Contrast Railroad Co. v. Brown, 84 U.S. (17 Wall.) 445, 452-53 (1874) (Davis, J.), construing a charter provision requiring "that no person shall be excluded from the cars on account of color" to outlaw separate-but-equal accommodations: although "the words taken literally might bear" the opposite interpretation, ". . . evidently Congress did not use them in any such limited sense" since "self-interest" would preclude railroads from refusing to transport blacks at all. *Brown* was not cited in *Pace*.

[141]Nor does the correct insistence in Shelley v. Kraemer, 334 U.S. 1, 22 (1948), that equal protection is guaranteed to "the individual" rather than to blacks as a class; the question remains whether the clause requires that one individual be treated the same as or only as well as another.

[142]CONG. GLOBE, 39th Cong., 1st Sess. 322 (1866) (Sen. Trumbull), discussing the bill to expand the powers of the Freedmen's Bureau; *id.* at 420 (same); *id.* at 505-06 (Sen. Fessenden), discussing the 1866 Civil Rights Act: A black man "has the same right to make a contract of marriage with a white woman that a white man has with a black woman." *See also id.* at 632-33 (Rep. Moulton), arguing that marriage was not a "civil" right that would be protected by the Civil Rights Act but a "social right." *Cf. supra* text accompanying notes 117-18, discussing "political" rights such as suffrage; *id.* at 1117 (Sen. Wilson on segregated schools).

This falls short of a conclusive demonstration that Congress and the ratifying state legislatures affirmatively embraced the same view of the equal protection clause.[143] It does make it seem more likely than not that they would have done so if they had resolved the issue explicitly; but their failure to address the question in the debates on the amendment itself is also consistent with a desire to leave it to future Congresses and courts to give content to their general command of racial equality.[144] If this was what the Framers meant, Field can no more be faulted for following the understanding of his time than his successors can be for taking today's more attractive view that equality is not satisfied by balancing one racially defined disability against another.[145]

Field can be criticized, however, for not perceiving the complexity of the problem. Moreover, he ignored entirely the possibility, later accepted by the Court in the school-segregation cases, that laws objectively imposing equal disabilities on both races might nevertheless place blacks at a relative disadvantage because they were known to be motivated by the sense that blacks were inferior.[146] This approach would create an interesting and different problem of interpreting the legislative history. It would suggest that laws like the one in *Pace* did not in fact meet the logical test of equality that their Republican defenders said they met, and the question would be whether to hold them to their general criterion or to their specific belief that miscegenation laws were not unequal. That miscegenation laws had just such a stigmatizing purpose had been not only acknowledged but heavily relied upon in the *Dred Scott* case in support of the argument that blacks were not citizens;[147] yet Field

[143]Professor Bickel, relying on the statements noted above, concluded that the fourteenth amendment, "as originally understood, was meant to apply neither to . . . antimiscegenation statutes, nor segregation." Bickel, *The Original Understanding and the Segregation Decision*, 69 HARV. L. REV. 1, 58 (1955). *See also* R. BERGER, *supra* note 118, ch. 7; Avins, *Anti-Miscegenation Laws and the Fourteenth Amendment: The Original Intent*, 52 VA. L. REV. 1224 (1966), and Pittman, *The Fourteenth Amendment: Its Intended Effect on Anti-Miscegenation Laws*, 43 N.C.L. REV. 92 (1964), all agreeing with Bickel's view of the original understanding but arguing that it was binding; Kelly, *The Fourteenth Amendment Reconsidered*, 54 MICH. L. REV. 1049, 1081-84 (1956), contrasting repeated assurances that the amendment merely constitutionalized the 1866 statute with Senator Howard's statement that it would "abolish[ ] all class legislation" (CONG. GLOBE, 39th Cong., 1st Sess. 2766 (1866)).

[144]*See* Bickel, *supra* note 143, at 59-65, arguing that Congress had built into the amendment a capacity for expansion beyond its own specific views of equality.

[145]In some contexts, equality clearly permits one disadvantage to be canceled by another: paying two people with the same dollar bill is impossible. *See also infra* note 159, discussing *Missouri v. Lewis*, which upheld separate courts for different geographical areas in part because there was no showing that one court was inferior to the other. Consider also whether most of us would so readily jump to the opposite conclusion in a marriage case if the participants were not of different sexes. Perhaps what these examples suggest is that one's conception of equality may be influenced by the significance of the discrepancy in treatment and by the degree of necessity for it as well as by logical exercises. For a perceptive argument that equality is not only far from self-defining but "empty," *see* Westen, *The Meaning of Equality in Law, Science, Math, and Morals: A Reply* , 81 MICH. L. REV. 604, 611-13 (1983), pointing out that because no two things are equal in every respect equality "means that they are identical in *all significant* . . . respects" and thus "derives its entire meaning from normative standards that logically precede it . . . ." *See also id.* at 624-25 n. 36, discussing *Pace*.

[146]Brown v. Board of Education, 347 U.S. 483, 494 (1954): "To separate [black children] from others of similar age and qualification solely because of their race generates a feeling of inferiority . . . ." See also Justice Harlan's dissent in *Plessy v. Ferguson, supra* note 139; Black, *The Lawfulness of the Segregation Decisions*, 69 YALE L. J. 421 (1960).

[147]Scott v. Sandford, 60 U.S. (19 How.) 393, 413, 416 (1857) (Taney, C. J.), chapter 8 *supra. See* Karst,

did not even address the question whether a law could be said to treat blacks and whites equally when as Taney said it imposed a "mark of degradation" on the former alone.[148]

D.   Nonracial Cases

Both in *Slaughter-House* and in *Strauder* the Court came close to saying that in light of its history the equal protection clause applied only to racial classifications. At least ten cases presented the Waite Court with the question whether the clause outlawed classifications not based on race. Although in none of them did the Court find a violation of the clause, in none did it repeat its suggestion that the clause applied only to race; and in none did it give a satisfactory reason for its conclusion.

The first such case was *Munn v. Illinois*,[149] decided before *Strauder*, in which, after rejecting a due-process challenge to the regulation of grain-elevator rates in Chicago,[150] Chief Justice Waite summarily dismissed an equal-protection objection:

> Certainly it cannot be claimed that this [clause] prevents the State from regulating the fares of hackmen or the charges of draymen in Chicago, unless it does the same thing in every place within its jurisdiction. But, as has been seen, the power to regulate the business of warehouses depends upon the same principle as the power to regulate hackmen and draymen, and what cannot be done in the one case in this particular cannot be done in the other.[151]

Apparently, the clause did not forbid geographical discrimination, but the reader was not told why; and Waite did not say why it was permissible to regulate grain elevators without also regulating other businesses similarly "affected with a public interest."

Later opinions generally did no better. In *Missouri v. Lewis*, for example, the Court upheld a law providing separate appellate courts for metropolitan Saint Louis and for the rest of the state essentially because it treated all people in the Saint Louis area equally.[152] In *Missouri Pacific Ry. v. Humes* it upheld a law imposing double

Foreword: Equal Citizenship Under the Fourteenth Amendment, 91 Harv. L. Rev. 1, 13, 48 (1977): "What matters most about *Dred Scott* today is that the Court's assumptions about racial inferiority and restricted citizenship were just what the drafters of the Civil War amendments . . . sought to overturn. . . . The chief target of the equal citizenship principle is the stigma of caste."

[148]*Cf.* the statement in *Strauder v. West Virginia*, text accompanying notes 107–23 *supra*, that exclusion of blacks from juries was "practically a brand upon them, . . . an assertion of their inferiority . . . ." 100 U.S. at 308. In *Strauder*, of course, there was inequality in a more objective sense as well. Indeed, the conclusion that the law in *Pace* imposed no greater objective burden on blacks than on whites is true only on the assumption that in the relevant geographical area there were not significantly fewer blacks than whites. Miscegenation laws have a more severe effect on small minority groups than on others because they place off limits to them a larger part of the total population.

[149]94 U.S. 113 (1877).
[150]*See supra* text accompanying notes 44-59.
[151]94 U.S. at 134-35.
[152]101 U.S. 22, 31 (1880) (Bradley, J.).

damages on railroads that failed to fence their property because it treated all railroads alike.[153] In *Powell v. Pennsylvania* it upheld a law outlawing oleomargarine because it applied equally to everyone in the margarine business.[154] No suggestion was made in any of these opinions to explain why it was appropriate to single out Saint Louis residents, or railroads, or margarine for special treatment,[155] and those were the classifications that had been challenged.[156]

One answer might have been that in a sense there was no inequality in any of these cases at all, since none of the characteristics used as the basis for classification was (like race) immutable. Everyone, for example, was forbidden to sell oleomargarine, and no one could run a railroad without risking double-damage liability.[157] Both these laws were arguably no more unequal than a law forbidding everybody to steal. Yet even the law of theft is unequal in another sense, for it singles out those who steal for unfavorable treatment.[158] The Framers of the clause could hardly have intended to legalize theft, but the Court nowhere suggested that the effect of the provision was limited to classifications based on immutable characteristics.[159]

Occasional hints dropped by the Waite Court suggest an alternative interpretation that would explain the validity of theft laws without denying that they resulted in disparity of treatment. In upholding an ordinance barring locomotives from a single street, for example, the Chief Justice observed that "other streets may not be situated like Broad Street, neither may there be the same reasons why steam transportation should be excluded from them";[160] and in upholding an ordinance forbidding the night operation of laundries against a charge of underinclusiveness, Justice Field noted that "[t]here may be no risks attending the business of others, certainly not as great as where fires are constantly required to carry them on."[161]

---

[153]115 U.S. 512, 523 (1885) (Field, J.). *See also* the Railroad Commission Cases, 116 U.S. 307, 336 (1886) (Waite, C. J.) (rate regulation upheld because "it applies equally to all persons or corporations owning or operating railroads in the State").

[154]127 U.S. 678, 687 (1888) (Harlan, J.).

[155]The closest thing to an explanation was in *Missouri v. Lewis*, where in an earlier passage the Court had said "[c]onvenience, if not necessity, often requires" the division of a state into administrative or judicial districts. 101 U.S. at 30-31. The analogy to different treatment by two different states, *id.* at 31-32, is unconvincing; the amendment speaks to individual states.

[156]*See* Tussman & tenBroek, *The Equal Protection of the Laws*, 37 CAL. L. REV. 341, 345 (1949), criticizing the margarine opinion's "easy dismissal of the equal protection issue on the grounds that the law applies equally to all to whom it applies . . . . By the same token a law applying to red-haired makers of margarine would satisfy the requirements of equality."

[157]*See* 2 W. CROSSKEY, *supra* note 21, at 1099: "to say that a law discriminates between farmers and others is really to say that it discriminates between agriculture and other employments. Such a law would, therefore, involve no inequality *as between 'persons'*; [but] . . . only an inequality *as between types of behavior* . . ." and thus should not be held to deny equal protection (emphasis added).

[158]*See* Westen, *supra* note 145, 81 MICH. L. REV. at 615-16.

[159]*Missouri v. Lewis* also presented the *Pace* problem of determining whether equality required identical or only equally favorable treatment. The Court took the latter view without saying why: "It is not for us, nor for any other tribunal, to say that these courts do not afford equal security for the due administration of the laws . . . ." 101 U.S. at 33. *Cf.* text accompanying notes 135–48 *supra*.

[160]Railroad Co. v. Richmond, 96 U.S. 521, 529 (1878).

[161]Soon Hing v. Crowley, 113 U.S. 703, 708 (1885). *Cf.* Missouri Pac. Ry. v. Mackey, 127 U.S. 205, 210 (1888) (Field, J.), upholding a law abrogating the fellow-servant rule for railroads only:

[T]he hazardous character of the business of operating a railway would seem to call for

These passages seemed to imply without explanation that the clause forbade only those inequalities that were unjustified.[162] The absolute language of the amendment surely does not encourage this conclusion. Field made it linguistically plausible by implying in another case that equality meant like treatment of those "similarly situated,"[163] but it is not clear that is what the framers of the amendment had in mind either. Once it was assumed that the clause was not limited to racial classifications, some such limit had to be inferred to avoid the absurd conclusion that there could be no classifications at all. But the breadth of the authority implied by such an interpretation might have induced the Court to explain why it thought that in adopting a provision whose motivating cause was the elimination of racial discrimination the framers of the amendment had meant to make the judges censors of the reasonableness of all state laws.

At the same time, however, that the Court seemed to say the equal protection clause required an acceptable reason for any classification, it demonstrated indifference to whether such a reason actually existed. After saying in the locomotive case that other streets "may" not present the same problem, for example, the Court specifically added that it was "the special duty of the city authorities to make the necessary discriminations in this particular."[164] As in the case of substantive due process,[165] the Court seemed simultaneously to have found a questionable and unexplained limiting principle in the Constitution and to have indicated that it would make no effort to enforce it.[166]

---

special legislation. . . . The business of other corporations is not subject to similar dangers . . . .

Less convincing was the additional conclusion that "it is simply a question of legislative discretion whether the same liabilities shall be applied . . . to persons using steam in manufactories," which would seem to present comparable dangers. *Id.*

[162]*See also* Wurts v. Hoagland, 114 U.S. 606, 615 (1885) (Gray, J.) (upholding assessment for drainage of wetlands because "the statute is applicable to all lands of the same kind"); Kentucky Railroad Tax Cases, 115 U.S. 321, 337, (1885) (Matthews, J.) ("[t]he different nature and uses of their property justify" differential tax treatment of railroad and other property); Hayes v. Missouri, 120 U.S. 68, 71, 72 (1887) (Field, J.) (allowing state to authorize more peremptory challenges in large cities than elsewhere because of the "difficulty of securing . . . an impartial jury in cities of that size" resulting from their "mixed population," large numbers of criminals, and the "unfortunate disposition on the part of business men [there] to escape from jury duty"); Dow v. Beidelman, 125 U.S. 680, 691 (1888) (Gray, J.) (allowing differential rail charges according to length of line as indicator of "amount of . . . business" because "a uniform rate . . . might operate unjustly . . .").

[163]Barbier v. Connolly, 113 U.S. 27, 32 (1885) (also upholding a ban on night laundries). How the Court was to determine who was "similarly situated" Field did not say. *See* Tussman & tenBroek, *supra* note 156, 37 CAL. L. REV. at 346: "A reasonable classification is one which includes all persons who are similarly situated *with respect to the purpose of the law*" (emphasis added). For discussion of possible administrative, political, or emergency justification for an imperfect fit between the classification and the law's purpose, *see id.* at 346-53.

[164]Railroad Co. v. Richmond, *supra* note 160, 96 U.S. at 529.

[165]*See supra* text accompanying notes 75-83, discussing *Powell v. Pennsylvania.*

[166]*See* Tussman & tenBroek, *supra* note 156, 37 CAL. L. REV. at 368-72, adding later examples. Also of interest are two opinions that seemed to allow evasion of the purposes of the clause by concluding that foreign corporations were not "within the jurisdiction" of a state within the meaning of that provision until they had qualified to do business and thus could be subjected to discriminatory privilege taxes. Philadelphia Fire Ass'n v. New York, 119 U.S. 110, 119-120 (1886) (Blatchford, J.); Pembina Consolidated Silver Mining Co. v. Pennsylvania, 125 U.S. 181, 189 (1888) (Field, J.). Harlan dissented in the first case; a

III. Enforcement and Related Questions

A. *United States v. Reese*

Unlike most of the provisions of the original Constitution limiting state authority,[167] all three of the Civil War amendments explicitly provided that "[the] Congress shall have power to enforce this article by appropriate legislation."[168] In an interesting series of cases involving statutes passed under these provisions, the Court under Waite resolved significant questions both of the scope of the enforcement power and of the meaning of the provisions that Congress was attempting to enforce.

The first was *United States v. Reese* in 1876, in which municipal officers were on trial for denying a black man the right to vote on the ground of race.[169] Ignoring both the canon of strict construction of penal statutes and that demanding that statutes be construed if possible to preserve their validity, Chief Justice Waite unnecessarily read the provision in question to forbid the denial of the right to vote on *any* ground[170] and thus had an easy time in finding that it went beyond Congress's power.[171] The only right given by the fifteenth amendment was "exemption from discrimination in the exercise of the elective franchise on account of race, color, or previous condition of servitude"; it was this right that Congress was given power to enforce; and thus "[i]t is only when the wrongful refusal . . . is because of race, color, or previous condition of servitude, that Congress can interfere, and provide for its punishment."[172] With some qualification to prevent evasion,[173] this conclusion seems

---

modern variant of the Court's theory was more recently rejected when a state was held forbidden to exclude illegal aliens from public schools. Plyler v. Doe, 457 U.S. 202, 214 (1982): "th[e] debate clearly confirms the understanding that the phrase 'within its jurisdiction' was intended in a broad sense to offer the guarantee of equal protection to all within a state's boundaries, and to all upon whom the State would impose the obligation of its laws."

[167]*See* U.S. Const. art. I, § 10; art. IV, § 2. Contrast the full faith and credit clause of art. IV, § 1: "And the Congress may by general Laws prescribe the Manner in which such Acts, Records and Proceedings shall be proved, and the Effect thereof."

[168] U.S. Const. amend. XIII, § 2; amend. XV, § 2. The wording of amend. XIV, § 5 is slightly different: "The Congress shall have power to enforce, by appropriate legislation, the provisions of this article."

[169]92 U.S. 214, 215-16 (1876). For a discussion of *Reese* and of the other cases in this section in historical context, *see* 2 Warren, *supra*, introduction to part five, note 1, ch. 34.

[170]As Justice Hunt observed in a cogent dissent, the first section of the statute recognized a right to be free of racial discrimination in voting, and the sections under which the defendant was prosecuted made it an offense to deny the right to vote "as aforesaid." 92 U.S. at 241-45, also relying on uncited legislative history. The statute appears *id.* at 239-40, Act of May 31, 1870, ch. 114, § § 1-4, 16 Stat. 140, repealed by 28 Stat. 36, 37 (1894).

[171]Since the election was municipal, there was no room for an argument that the statute could be justified by Congress's power to regulate the "Times, Places, and Manner" of electing Senators or Representatives, U.S. Const. art. I, § 4. *See* 92 U.S. at 215, 218. *Cf. infra* note 174, discussing *Ex parte Yarbrough*.

[172]92 U.S. at 218. On the question what remedies Congress can provide when there *has* been a violation of the Civil War amendments, *see* Strauder v. West Virginia, 100 U.S. 303, 310-12 (1880) (Strong, J.), holding that Congress could provide for removal of cases to federal court when the state courts were disabled from providing equal protection, and Ex parte Virginia, 100 U.S. 339, 345-48 (1880) (Strong, J.), holding that Congress could make it a crime for a state-court judge to exclude blacks from juries:

> Whatever legislation is appropriate, that is, adapted to carry out the objects the amend-
> ments have in view, whatever tends to enforce submission to the prohibitions they contain,

obvious from the language and evident purpose of the enforcement provision.[174] The trouble was that the prosecution before the Court was for the denial of the vote on racial grounds and thus clearly within the enforcement power. The Court got around

---

and to secure to all persons the enjoyment of perfect equality of civil rights and the equal protection of the laws against State denial or invasion, if not prohibited, is brought within the domain of congressional power.

Cf. McCulloch v. Maryland, supra chapter 6 (necessary and proper clause).

Justice Field dissented in both cases. Removal, he argued, was inconsistent with the limitations article III placed on the judicial power, because the offense did not arise under federal law (100 U.S. at 336-37). Justice Strong responded that the Court had just held that removal was permissible "when a right under the Federal Constitution or laws is involved" (*id.* at 312, citing Tennessee v. Davis, 100 U.S. 257 (1880) (Strong, J.)). But *Davis* was an easy case in which a federal officer had removed on the basis of a substantive federal defense of immunity from state law (see *supra* chapter 4, discussing *Cohens v. Virginia*); in *Strauder* the only federal question was whether trial by a state-court jury from which blacks had been excluded denied equal protection, and that was relevant only in determining the question of jurisdiction itself. An argument might have been made for federal-question jurisdiction even in this bootstrap posture: the Supreme Court could have reviewed a state-court decision on the ground that blacks had been excluded; *Osborn v. Bank of United States* (*supra* chapter 4) had held that the original jurisdiction was as broad as the appellate, and that when there was jurisdiction over one issue the court could decide the whole case. But Strong chose instead to overlook the distinction between *Strauder* and *Davis*.

Field also argued that state judges were implicitly immune from federal sanctions under such decisions as *Kentucky v. Dennison* and *Collector v. Day*, discussed in chapter 8 and in the conclusion to part four *supra* (100 U.S. at 358-62). Strong replied that the fourteenth amendment, unlike the extradition clause in *Dennison*, "expressly gives authority for congressional interference" (100 U.S. at 347-48); but *Collector v. Day* had found a state judge's salary implicitly immune from the explicit federal tax power. Strong could have strengthened his case by observing that the all-purpose *Osborn* decision had also held an action against a state officer permissible despite the explicit eleventh amendment ban on suits against the state itself. Moreover, unlike the tax power, the authority to enforce the fourteenth amendment, which speaks solely to state action, would be reduced to almost nothing if Congress could not provide remedies against state officers; mere review of state-court proceedings could have been provided without the enforcement clause by virtue of article III. *Cf.* Fitzpatrick v. Bitzer, 427 U.S. 445 (1976), holding Congress could make the state itself suable under the fourteenth amendment. Strong made no such argument; indeed, he went out of his way to make the debatable point that the selection of jurors was not a "judicial act," thus implicitly detracting from his own brave conclusion that "[w]e cannot perceive how holding an office under a State . . . can relieve the holder from obligation to obey the Constitution of the United States, or take away the power of Congress to punish his disobedience." 100 U.S. at 348-49.

The *Strauder* and *Virginia* cases seem to refute Professor tenBroek's argument (*supra* note 9, at 204-05) that the enforcement clause of the fourteenth amendment was nugatory unless construed to permit Congress to outlaw purely private action.

[173]*See* Katzenbach v. Morgan, 384 U.S. 641 (1966), holding that Congress could outlaw English literacy tests for voters literate in Spanish in part because of the risk that the state law might be a disguised method of racial discrimination; Oregon v. Mitchell, 400 U.S. 112, 216 (1970) (Harlan J., concurring in the decision that Congress could outlaw literacy tests altogether: "Th[e] danger of violation of § 1 of the Fifteenth Amendment was sufficient to authorize the exercise of congressional power under § 2"). *Cf. United States v. Coombs*, discussed *supra* in chapters 7 and 8, holding that the necessary and proper clause empowered Congress to regulate the acts of persons not themselves engaged in interstate or foreign commerce if their action "interferes with, obstructs or prevents such commerce."

[174]Contrast Ex parte Siebold, 100 U.S. 371, 382-94 (1880) (Bradley, J.) (stuffing ballot box), and Ex parte Yarbrough, 110 U.S. 651, 660-62 (1884) (Miller, J.) (private interference with black voter), upholding broader measures respecting the integrity of *congressional* elections in view of Congress's explicit authority to regulate the "Times, Places, and Manner" of such elections (U.S. Const. art. I, § 4). Justice Miller, however, did not clearly rely on that provision in *Yarbrough*. Beginning his discussion with the Marshall-like assertion (*cf. supra* chapter 4, discussing *Cohens v. Virginia)* that without power to

this difficulty by proclaiming, in sharp contrast to modern conceptions of standing or of severability,[175] that it had no power to rewrite an overbroad statute.[176]

B.   *Cruikshank* and *Harris*

Later the same Term, in *United States v. Cruikshank*,[177] the Court in another Waite opinion dealing with a statute punishing conspiracies to deny any constitutional right[178] continued to construe the amendments according to their limited terms. The indictment charged violation of a variety of constitutional provisions, but the Court found most of them inapplicable to private action and held that no offense had been stated.[179] The right to assemble for lawful purposes and the right to bear arms were protected by the first and second amendments against encroachment by Congress alone;[180] the due process and equal protection clauses of the fourteenth amendment, limiting only the states, added nothing to the rights of one citizen against another;[181] and there was no allegation that the defendants had acted under state authority.[182]

---

outlaw voter intimidation the federal government would be helpless (110 U.S. at 657-58), Miller listed measures Congress had undertaken under its power over congressional elections as well as under other powers and concluded by terming it "a waste of time to seek for specific sources of the power to pass these laws" (*id.* at 666). His view seems to have been that Congress had whatever powers it ought to have, notwithstanding the enumeration of its authority and the tenth amendment. *Cf. infra* chapter 13, discussing *United States v. Kagama. See also* United States v. Waddell, 112 U.S. 76 (power to protect federally granted homestead land from private invasion under the property clause of article IV); United States v. Hall, 98 U.S. 343 (1879) (Clifford, J.) (power to forbid embezzlement of veteran's federal pension).

[175]*See, e.g.,* United States v. Raines, 362 U.S. 17 (1960), refusing in a case involving official action to determine whether the statute unconstitutionally reached private action as well and disapproving *Reese* except to the extent it was based upon the conclusion that the statute as narrowed "no longer gave an intelligible warning of the conduct it prohibited." *Id.* at 22. For language in *Reese* suggesting this conclusion, *see* 92 U.S. at 219-20; for consideration of the question whether *Raines* was based on severability or standing or both, *see* H. HART & H. WECHSLER, THE FEDERAL COURTS AND THE FEDERAL SYSTEM 184-99 (2d ed. 1973); Monagahan, *Overbreadth*, 1981 SUP. CT. REV. 1, 3-14, arguing that severability relates only to a court's willingness to construe a statute to exclude unconstitutional applications but acknowledging today's "presumption of severability." As an original matter of statutory interpretation, it would seem odd to conclude that a Congress legislating to protect voting rights would rather have no statute at all than a statute limited to offenses based on race. *See* Stern, *Separability and Separability Clauses in the Supreme Court*, 51 HARV. L. REV. 76, 99 (1937), adding (at 79-82) that severability had been the norm before *Reese* and citing, inter alia, T. COOLEY, *supra* note 11, at 180-81.

[176]92 U.S. at 220-21. For a fuller discussion of the severability problem distinguishing cases in which separate "parts" of a provision were invalid from those involving invalid applications of a single "part" *see* Baldwin v. Franks, 120 U.S. 678, 685-86 (1887) (Waite, C. J.), refusing to allow prosecution for violation of a federal treaty right because the statute also forbade violation of rights given by state law. *See also* the *Trade-Mark Cases, infra* chapter 13.

[177]92 U.S. 542 (1876).

[178]Act of May 31, 1870, ch. x, § 6, 16 Stat. 141 (current version 18 U.S.C. § 241), quoted 92 U.S. at 548.

[179]General counts alleging in terms of the statute itself simply a conspiracy to deny unspecified constitutional rights were held too vague. *Id.* at 557-59. Clifford's "dissent," 92 U.S. at 559-59, was really a concurrence on the ground that the entire indictment was too vague.

[180]*Id.* at 552-53.

[181]*Id.* at 554-55.

[182]The same reasoning would have disposed of an additional count alleging interference with the right to vote; the Court elected to rely instead on the fact that there was no allegation that the denial was based

This decision seems perfectly obvious too,[183] and Waite reaffirmed in the context of equal protection the appropriately restrictive view of the enforcement power he had embraced in *Reese*: "The only obligation resting upon the United States is to see that the States do not deny the right . . . . The power of the national government is limited to the enforcement of this guaranty."[184] The implication seemed to be that Congress could not outlaw private action under the enforcement clause, but that was not what the case held; Congress had forbidden only violations of the Constitution, and the holding was that the equal protection and due process clauses themselves did not forbid private action.

Reese's view of the enforcement power and *Cruikshank*'s view of the substantive provisions of the fourteenth amendment were brought together in *United States v. Harris*[185] in 1883, a prosecution for lynching under a federal statute making it a crime for any two persons to conspire to deprive another of "the equal protection of the laws."[186] As in *Cruikshank*, said Justice Woods, the equal protection clause prohibited only state action;[187] as in *Cruikshank*, there was no allegation that the defendants had been acting for the state or that the state had failed in its duty;[188] and thus (as in

---

on race as required by the fifteenth amendment, citing *Reese*. *Id*. at 555-56. The argument that by choosing this ground in both *Cruikshank* and *Reese* the Court embraced Bradley's peculiar position that the fifteenth amendment authorized Congress to forbid private interference with voting on racial grounds (see Benedict, *Preserving Federalism: Reconstruction and the Waite Court*, 1978 SUP. CT. REV. 39, 71-74, citing United States v. Cruikshank, 25 Fed. Cas. 707, 712 (No. 14,897) (C.C.D. La. 1874)), seems to confuse deciding with refusing to decide; and Bradley's position seemed irreconcilable with what the whole Court said with regard to the similarly worded fourteenth amendment in reviewing his *Cruikshank* decision. But Bradley had drawn the same distinction himself, explaining that by forbidding states to interfere with what it described as the "right" to vote on racial grounds the fifteenth amendment implicitly established a right against private as well as official interference. 25 Fed. Cas. at 712.

[183]Later cases have shown that it is not always so easy to determine whether it is the state that is responsible for doing what states are forbidden to do, e.g., Shelley v. Kraemer, 334 U.S. 1 (1948) (judicial enforcement of discriminatory private covenant); Burton v. Wilmington Parking Auth., 365 U.S. 715 (1961) (discrimination by lessee of state property), but they have adhered to Waite's conclusion. Even United States v. Guest, 383 U.S. 745 (1966), and Griffin v. Breckenridge, 403 U.S. 88 (1971), to the extent they upheld Congress's power to reach purely private actions, did so on the basis not of the fourteenth amendment but of the thirteenth and of the implicit right to travel recognized in *Crandall v. Nevada*, discussed *supra* in the conclusion to part four, neither of which in the Court's view was limited to state action.

[184]92 U.S. at 555. This formulation is properly broad enough to allow Congress to see to it that private persons do not induce or assist the state in denying fourteenth amendment rights, see United States v. Price, 383 U.S. 787 (1966) (punishment of private parties "jointly engaged" with state officers in killing civil-rights workers without due process of law). Cf. *supra* note 173, discussing the power to forbid practices that may lead to racial discrimination in voting.

[185]106 U.S. 629 (1883).

[186]R.S. § 5519, quoted 106 U.S. at 632.

[187]*Id*. at 638-39.

[188]*Id*. at 639-40. There were allegations that the defendants had conspired to prevent the state from affording the victims equal protection of the laws, *id*. at 631, and outlawing private conduct that interferes with the state's duties may sometimes be within the enforcement clause, *see supra* note 184. But the specific facts alleged in the complaint showed that the interference complained of consisted of private mistreatment of the lynching victims themselves, which was indistinguishable from private mistreatment of anyone else; and to hold Congress could outlaw that without more would effectively expunge the state-action limitation.

Reese, which was not cited at this point), Congress could not make the proscribed activity a crime.[189]

A strong argument can be made, on the basis of the origins of the equal protection clause, that private lynching was among the evils that Congress was meant to have power to forbid. Although none of the prohibitory clauses of the amendment speaks directly to private action, the equal protection clause seems to impose upon the states a unique duty to take affirmative action to protect black persons from private attack. That, as I have argued above, was the clear sense of a parallel provision in the 1866 Civil Rights Act for which the clause was evidently intended to assure a constitutional base; and, as Justice Miller acknowledged in *Slaughter-House*, the failure of states to protect blacks was one of the problems that prompted the adoption of the fourteenth amendment.[190] Thus a state that systematically failed to prosecute those who committed offenses against blacks would itself violate the equal protection clause. In light of the broad reading given a similar grant in the necessary-and-proper clause,[191] a strong argument could be made that in such circumstances a federal prohibition of the private activity itself would be an appropriate means of remedying the state's failure to afford equal protection.[192]

Harris does not foreclose this interpretation.[193] In the first place, Justice Woods emphasized that there was no finding or allegation that the state had been derelict in its own constitutional duty;[194] that Congress cannot act when the Constitution has not been violated does not prove it cannot act when there is a violation.[195] Besides, Congress had attempted not to remedy a state's denial of equal protection but to

---

[189]*Id.* at 640. *Reese* was cited later in support of the proposition that the statute could not be limited to such applications as might be justified by the thirteenth amendment, *id.* at 641-42.

[190]*See supra* chapter 10. *See also* Frantz, *Congressional Power to Enforce the Fourteenth Amendment Against Private Acts,* 73 YALE L.J. 1353, 1354-57 (1964), relying largely upon the report of the joint committee that drafted the amendment for the conclusion that the *central* problem with which the amendment was meant to deal was the failure of states to protect blacks from "private aggression;" TENBROEK, *supra* note 9, at 163-79, 186-87.

[191]*See supra* chapter 6, discussing *McCulloch v. Maryland; supra* note 173, quoting from *United States v. Coombs.*

[192]*See* Frantz, *supra* note 190, 73 YALE L.J. at 1358-59, quoting the argument of Rep. Garfield in the debate on the 1871 Klu Klux Klan Act (CONG. GLOBE, 42d Cong., 1st Sess. 153 (App.) (1871); Frank and Munro, *The Original Understanding of "Equal Protection of the Laws,"* 50 COLUM. L. REV. 131, 164-65 (1950), also quoting from the 1871 debates; TENBROEK, *supra* note 9, at 96-98, 206.

[193]*See* Frantz, *supra* note 190, 73 YALE L. J. at 1377-79; Benedict, *supra* note 182, at 66-67.

[194]*See* 106 U.S. at 639-40.

[195]That Woods so understood his explicit reservation is strongly suggested by his own earlier opinion on circuit in United States v. Hall, 26 Fed. Cas. 79, 81-82 (No. 15,282) (C.C.S.D. Ala. 1871): "denying the equal protection of the laws includes the omission to protect," and if the state fails to protect citizens "the only appropriate legislation" under § 5 "is that which will operate directly on offenders and offenses and protect the rights which the amendment secures." The holding in that case that this principle allowed Congress to punish private infringements of speech and assembly (*id.* at 81) was based on a broad view of privileges and immunities rejected in the *Slaughter-House Cases.* Justice Bradley, on circuit in *Cruikshank,* had taken the position that Congress could act against private conduct under the fifteenth amendment as well if the states did not protect the right of blacks to vote, 25 Fed. Cas. 707, (No. 14,897) (C.C.D. La. 1874). *See also* TENBROEK, *supra* note 9, at 206-07, making a similar plea for the due process clause. An affirmative duty to protect the citizen, however, is harder to derive from a requirement that no state deprive persons of liberty or property without due process or deny the right to vote than from one phrased in terms of "protection of the laws."

punish private citizens for violating the clause; the Court was quite right that the clause itself did not forbid private action.[196]

C. *The Civil Rights Cases*

The famous *Civil Rights Cases*[197] of 1883 followed easily from *Harris*. Congress had attempted to outlaw racial discrimination by private owners of inns, theaters, and railroads;[198] the fourteenth amendment limited only "State action"; and the only power of Congress, said Bradley, was "[t]o adopt appropriate legislation for correcting the effects of such prohibited State laws and State acts, and thus to render them effectually null, void, and innocuous."[199]

Justice Harlan, who had not participated in deciding any of the earlier cases on the merits,[200] dissented alone in the *Civil Rights Cases*, giving three interesting answers to the majority. First, anticipating the arguments in much later cases, he contended that if state action was required the requirement was satisfied:

> In every material sense applicable to the practical enforcement of the Fourteenth Amendment, railroad corporations, keepers of inns, and managers of places of public amusement are agents or instrumentalities of the State, because they are charged with duties to the public, and are amenable, in respect of their duties and functions to governmental regulation.[201]

That everyone the state may regulate is himself the state seems something of a contradiction in terms, and today it would mean the explicit reference to state action was no limitation at all.[202] Moreover, the *Dartmouth College* case, in a related context, had drawn a clear line between the state itself and those whose activities

---

[196]*See* H. FRIENDLY, THE DARTMOUTH COLLEGE CASE AND THE PUBLIC-PRIVATE PENUMBRA 17 (1968), conceding that in some instances a state may violate the amendment by failing to act but emphasizing that "it is the *state's* conduct, whether action or inaction, not the *private* conduct, that gives rise to constitutional attack; it still cannot be doubted that the Fourteenth Amendment was designed to protect the citizen against government and not against other citizens."

[197]109 U.S. 3 (1883).

[198]Act of March 1, 1875, ch. 114, § 1, 18 Stat. 335, quoted 109 U.S. at 9.

[199]109 U.S. at 11. This formulation again does not rule out the possibility that a federal lynch law might be an appropriate means of correcting a state's failure to afford equal protection to blacks. *See* Frantz, *supra* note 190, 73 YALE L. J. at 1365-70, 1380-81, stressing Bradley's emphasis (109 U.S. at 14) on the fact that the law was not limited to states that refused to protect the rights of blacks and his earlier broad circuit-court opinion in *Cruikshank, supra* note 195. Whether racial discrimination was meant to fall within equal protection rather than privileges and immunities is another question. *See supra* chapter 10. For a less sympathetic view of the Civil Rights Cases, *see* Scott, *supra* note 38, 25 RUTGERS L. REV. at 562-69, accusing Bradley of changing his position in order to preserve the 1877 compromise that put an end to Reconstruction.

[200]Appointed after *Reese* and *Cruikshank*, Harlan had thought the Supreme Court had no jurisdiction in *Harris*. *See* 106 U.S. at 644.

[201]109 U.S. at 58-59.

[202]Modern decisions rejecting Harlan's argument include Moose Lodge v. Irvis, 407 U.S. 163 (1972) (private club with liquor license); Jackson v. Metropolitan Edison Co., 419 U.S. 345 (1974) (regulated public utility).

merely served the public interest;[203] against this background it seems that Harlan was stretching things considerably.

Harlan based a second argument on the fact that section 5 authorized Congress to enforce not only the prohibitions of the amendment but all of its "provisions." The opening clause conferring citizenship on all persons born in the country said nothing about states; and citizenship itself, he argued, "necessarily imports at least equality of civil rights among citizens of every race in the same State"—apparently as against both state and private action.[204] Of course citizenship had never meant this before the amendment was adopted, as Justice Curtis had shown in his dissent in the *Dred Scott* case.[205] Moreover, Harlan's entirely unsubstantiated conclusion rendered the prohibitory clauses of the amendment redundant, and his suggestion that citizenship alone conferred as a federal matter all rights that were "fundamental in citizenship in a free republican government"[206] was an indirect challenge to the authority of the *Slaughter-House Cases*, where the Court had taken great pains to show that nothing in the prohibitory clauses of the same amendment conferred any such rights.[207]

---

[203]*See supra* chapter 5. In *Dartmouth College*, the Court rejected the argument that because a state was free to break agreements with its own agencies it was equally free with respect to a privately owned college. For discussion of the relation between *Dartmouth College* and later state-action decisions under the fourteenth amendment, *see* H. FRIENDLY, *supra* note 196, passim.

[204]109 U.S. at 46-48. Harlan added that citizenship entailed freedom from discrimination "by the State, or its officers, or by individuals or corporations exercising public functions or authority," but his zeal to avoid reliance in this section of the opinion on prohibitions limited to state action suggests that he did not mean in this passage to argue that such persons were in effect the state. For the suggestion that abolitionists had seen citizenship in the same light as Harlan, *see* tenBroek, *supra* note 9, at 87-91; for approval of Harlan's view, *see* C. BLACK, STRUCTURE AND RELATIONSHIP IN CONSTITUTIONAL LAW 65 (1969).

[205]*See supra* chapter 8.

[206]109 U.S. at 47.

[207]*See supra* chapter 10. It seemed more likely that the citizenship provision was meant simply to overrule *Scott's* exclusion of blacks from whatever rights, like those of the diversity jurisdiction and of the two privileges and immunities clauses, were defined in terms of citizenship.

A more serious question of the meaning of the citizenship clause was presented in the interesting case of Elk v. Wilkins, 112 U.S. 94 (1884). Alleging he had been denied the right to vote because he was an Indian, Elk invoked the fifteenth amendment. But that amendment protects only "citizens of the United States," and the fourteenth amendment extended citizenship only to those "born or naturalized in the United States and subject to the jurisdiction thereof." There was little doubt that Elk had been "born . . . in the United States," since Marshall had long ago established that Indian reservations were within the states where they were located. *Fletcher v. Peck, supra* chapter 5; *see also Cherokee Nation v. Georgia, supra* chapter 4 (holding Indian nation not "foreign" for purposes of article III jurisdiction). There was also no doubt that Elk was "subject to the jurisdiction" of the United States at the time he attempted to vote, for he alleged that he lived in Omaha and had severed all connection with his tribe. 112 U.S. at 95. However, all the Justices seemed to agree that he had not been "subject to the jurisdiction" while still a member of the tribe, despite the fact that Congress had some authority over tribal Indians (see the Indian commerce clause of art. I, § 8, and *United States v. Kagama, infra* chapter 13); and the legislative history was abundantly clear on this point. *See, e.g.,* CONG. GLOBE, 39th Cong., 1st Sess. 2890 (Senator Howard, sponsor of the citizenship provision (*see id.* at 2869), declaring an exception for "Indians not taxed" (*cf.* art. I., § 2 (basis of representation)) unnecessary because Indians were not "subject to the jurisdiction" while they "maintain their tribal relations"); *id.* at 2892 (Senator Trumbull, saying reservation Indians not included). The difficult question not resolved by the text was whether the requirements that a person be "born . . . in the United States" and "subject to the jurisdiction thereof" both had to be met *at the same time*.

Justice Gray concluded for the majority that the amendment had provided citizenship only by birth or

Harlan's final suggestion was that the prohibition of private discrimination in theaters and the like was authorized by the thirteenth amendment, which nobody contended was limited to state action: "Neither slavery nor involuntary servitude . . . shall exist within the United States . . . ."[208] The difficulty was in establishing that exlcusion from a theater was a form of slavery. Harlan's central argument that slaves were victims of discrimination[209] does not do the trick; that all men are mammals does not prove that all mammals are men. Previous constitutional history, moreover, refutes the notion that the absence of slavery meant freedom from either official or private discrimination; the books are full of laws in both Northern and Southern states discriminating against free blacks before the Civil War.[210] Legislative history detracts further from Harlan's conclusion. Senator Henderson, for example, who had introduced the proposed amendment, had expressly denied that it would result in "negro equality."[211] Supporters of the amendment who later contended that it

---

by naturalization and appeared to think it improbable that the Framers of the amendment intended to give Indians a right of unilateral naturalization denied to foreigners. 112 at U.S. at 102-03 (invoking "the principle that no one can become a citizen of a nation without its consent" and mentioning children born to foreign diplomats in this country).

The "consent" terminology begged the question, since the country may have consented in adopting the fourteenth amendment; but Gray's argument is intuitively appealing. His only supporting authority, however, was a series of statutes granting citizenship to Indians, which he argued would have been "superfluous" (id. at 104) if Indians could become citizens by their own action. Harlan's dissenting reply (joined by Woods) was devastating: "those statutes had reference to tribes, the members of which could not, while they continued in tribal relations, acquire the citizenship granted by the Amendment." id. at 116. Harlan responded, moreover, with an improbability argument of his own: it was inconceivable that those who wrote the amendment meant to exclude Indians who had already become assimilated while granting citizenship to blacks born in slavery (id. at 120-21), especially in light of congressional references in the debates both on the amendment itself and on an earlier statutory provision employing the words "Indians not taxed" that seemed to confirm his conclusion (id. at 114, 117-18, citing Senator Trumbull's remarks in the statutory context respecting "the Indian when he shall have cast off his wild habits, and submitted to the laws of organized society and become a citizen" (CONG. GLOBE, 39th Cong., 1st Sess. 528), and two remarks in the constitutional debate speaking of citizenship for Indians who "come" within our "limits" or "jurisdiction" and "are civilized," id. at 2890-94). None of this seems conclusive, but Harlan certainly won more points than Gray for the strength of his opinion.

[208]Early decisions agreeing with Harlan's thirteenth amendment views in upholding antidiscrimination provisions of the 1866 Civil Rights Act include United States v. Rhodes, 27 Fed. Cas. 785, 794 (No. 16,151) (D. Ky. 1866) (Swayne, J.), and People v. Washington, 36 Cal. 658 (1869). Contra, Bowlin v. Commonwealth, 65 Ky. 5 (1867); People v. Brady, 40 Cal. 198, 215-17 (1870).

[209]109 U.S. at 35-36, terming discrimination a "necessary incident []" or "badge[]" of slavery.

[210]Both majority and dissenting opinions in the Dred Scott case had recited numerous examples. See supra chapter 8. The language of the amendment was taken consciously from that of article VI of the Northwest Ordinance (1 Stat. 51, 53 n. (a)) (see CONG. GLOBE, 39th Cong., 1st Sess. 1488-89 (1864) (Sen. Howard)), and virulently discriminatory laws against blacks existed in both Illinois and Indiana, which had incorporated the Ordinance into their own constitutions. See Hamilton, The Legislative and Judicial History of the Thirteenth Amendment, 9 NAT. BAR J. 26, 48-53 (1951): "It was universally understood that Article VI did not confer any political or civil rights on Negroes."

[211]See CONG. GLOBE, 38th Cong., 1st Sess. 1465 (1864):

> I will not be intimidated by fears of negro equality. . . . [I]n passing this amendment we do not confer upon the negro the right to vote. We give him no right except his freedom, and leave the rest to the states.

For an effort to make a contrary case out of the fears of opponents and a few vague allusions lifted from their antislavery context, see TENBROEK, supra note 9, at 138-51, concluding that the fourteenth amend-

The Civil War Amendments 401

gave Congress authority to ban mere racial discrimination made no such claim when there was still time to vote it down; those who had spoken of "slavery" and "auction blocks" in the debates on the amendment itself[212] revealed that it outlawed "[a]ny statute which is not equal to all" only after it was safely on the books.[213] Noting the historic gap between freedom and equality, Justice Bradley concluded that ordinary discrimination had "nothing to do with slavery."[214] Despite the fact that a majority of Justices much later embraced it,[215] Harlan's position seems to represent a triumph of the Trojan Horse theory of constitutional adjudication.[216]

---

ment had really been implicit in the thirteenth all along. The general flavor of the debates is suggested by the quotations in note 212 *infra*.

[212]*E.g.*, CONG. GLOBE, 38th Cong., 1st Sess. 1314 (1864) (Sen. Trumbull):

> [I]n my judgment, the only effectual way of ridding the country of slavery, and so that it cannot be resuscitated, is by an amendment of the Constitution forever forbidding it within the jurisdiction of the United States. That accomplished, we are forever freed of this troublesome question. . . . We take this question entirely away from the politics of the country. We relieve Congress of sectional strifes, and we . . . restore to a whole race that freedom which is theirs by the gift of God. . . .

See also id. at 1320-24 (Sen. Wilson): ("when this amendment shall be consummated . . . the slave mart, pen and auction blocks will disappear").

[213]CONG. GLOBE, 39th Cong., 1st Sess. 474-75 (Sen. Trumbull):

> I regard the bill . . . as the most important measure that has been under consideration since the adoption of the Constitutional Amendment abolishing slavery. That amendment declared that all persons in the United States should be free. This measure is intended to give effect to that declaration and secure to all persons . . . practical freedom. There is very little importance in the general declaration of abstract truths and principles unless they can be carried into effect. . . . The purpose of the bill under consideration is to destroy [the State's] discriminations, and to carry into effect the constitutional amendment. . . . [A]ny statute which is not equal to all, and which deprives any citizen of civil rights which are secured to other citizens, is an unjust encroachment upon his liberty; and is . . . a badge of servitude which by the Constitution is prohibited. . . . Then, under the constitutional amendment which we have now adopted, and which declares slavery shall no longer exist, and which authorizes Congress by appropriate legislation to carry this provision into effect, I hold that we have the right to pass any law which, in our judgment, is deemed appropriate and which will accomplish the end in view, to secure freedom to all people in the United States.

See also id. at 603 (Sen. Wilson): ("[f]or the better security of these new-born civil rights . . ."). For detailed consideration of the debates both on the amendment itself and on the Civil Rights Act, see C. FAIRMAN, HISTORY, *supra* introduction to part four, note 2, ch. XIX.

[214]109 U.S. at 24-25. Invoking Bradley's reference to congressional power to abolish all "badges and incidents of slavery" and his earlier broad reading of the thirteenth amendment on circuit in *Cruikshank*, 25 Fed. Cas. at 711 ("disability to be a citizen and enjoy equal rights was deemed one form or badge of servitude"), Professor Benedict (*supra* note 182, 1978 SUP. CT. REV. at 70-71, 75-77) argues that the Court in the *Civil Rights Cases* "acquiesced" in an expansive view of Congress's enforcement power. But the proof of the pudding seems to lie in its application; for Bradley concluded that discrimination was not a badge or incident of slavery.

[215]Jones v. Alfred H. Mayer Co., 392 U.S. 409 (1968).

[216]For a spirited defense of Harlan's position, see Kinoy, *The Constitutional Right of Negro Freedom*, 21 RUTGERS L. REV. 387 (1967). *See also* F. LATHAM, *supra*, introduction to part five, note 2, at 41, noting that Harlan had originally opposed adoption of the thirteenth amendment. Harlan's best argument was that one of the cases before the Court involved an interstate rail journey that Congress clearly had power to regulate under the commerce clause. See 109 U.S. at 60-61, properly invoking *Hall v. DeCuir, infra* chapter 12, where the Court had held a comparable state law fell because it infringed Congress's exclusive authority. Rather than feebly responding that "the sections in question are not conceived in any such view" (*id.* at 19) (to which Harlan replied (*id.* at 60) that Congress need not "accurately recite . . . the

It has become fashionable to criticize the Waite Court for undermining Congress's powers under the Civil War amendments and thus for abandoning blacks to the mercies of Southern hostility.[217] Others have argued that the Court actually went pretty far to sustain the essence of congressional authority while striking down particular excesses.[218] I think the truth lies in between: the Court's restrictive inter-pretations of the Constitution were unavoidable, but by manipulating the statutory issues of coverage and severability the Court went out of its way to incapacitate the enforcement authorities after it was too late politically to expect Congress to fill the gap by enacting narrower statutes.

---

particular provision authorizing its enactment"), the Court might better have relied on its conclusion in *Reese* (text accompanying note 176 *supra*) that it lacked authority to cut an overbroad statute down to constitutional size. The extreme view of the commerce clause that more recently enabled the Court to uphold a modern version of the law struck down in the *Civil Rights Cases* was unheard of in 1883. *Compare* Katzenbach v. McClung, 379 U.S. 294 (1964) (discrimination reduces restaurant attendance and thus interstate food shipments), *with* the *Trademark Cases*, *infra* chapter 13 (no power to regulate trademarks outside interstate and foreign commerce).

[217]*See, e.g.*, C. MAGRATH, *supra* introduction to part five, note 1, ch. 8; Graham, *supra* introduction to part five, note 1, 17 VAND L. REV.; and authorities cited in Benedict, *supra* note 182 at 40 n. 2.

[218]*See* Benedict, *supra* note 182.

12

Commerce and Sovereign Immunity

As the Chase period was dominated by civil-war and reconstruction issues, the Waite era was chiefly characterized by controversies over the postwar amendments. The ordinary business of constitutional litigation, however, did not await the completion of these herculean tasks.

In a flock of cases Waite and his brethren continued to struggle with the scope of state authority to affect interstate and foreign commerce. A long series of decisions enabled the Court to work its way to a comprehensible and clean test for determining when state and federal officers could be sued despite the sovereign-immunity principle illustrated by the eleventh amendment. And yet another group of cases dealt with a variety of questions respecting other powers of Congress.

The present chapter considers the commerce and immunity cases, the next chapter those relating to congressional authority.

I. The Commerce Clause and the States

In the famous *Cooley* case in 1851 a majority of the Court had finally declared that the grant of power to Congress to regulate interstate and foreign commerce implicitly limited state power as well.[1] In 1873 the Court for the first time had relied solely on the commerce clause as the sole basis for striking down an exercise of state power.[2] During the Waite period the Court was to decide over fifty cases in which it was alleged that state action offended the commerce clause. In contrast to its hands-off attitude toward state regulation under the fourteenth amendment during the same period,[3] the Waite Court wielded the commerce clause with unprecedented vigor to

[1] *See supra* chapter 7.
[2] *See supra* chapter 10, discussing the *Case of the State Freight Tax.*
[3] *See supra* chapter 11.

403

clear away state measures that it thought interfered with the free flow of commerce.[4] In the process, however, it left the law an intellectual shambles.

A. Discrimination and Uniformity

The period began auspiciously enough in *Welton v. Missouri*[5] in 1876, where the Court without dissent reaffirmed the dictum of *Woodruff v. Parham*[6] that a tax discriminating against sellers of out-of-state goods offended the commerce clause.[7] To reach this result, Field had to ignore a contrary intervening decision,[8] and he

---

[4]*See* F. FRANKFURTER, THE COMMERCE CLAUSE UNDER MARSHALL, TANEY AND WAITE 74-75 (1937): the Waite period "brought to fruition Marshall's theory of the restrictions upon state authority immanent in the commerce clause"; 2 C. WARREN, THE SUPREME COURT IN UNITED STATES HISTORY 626 (rev. ed. 1926): "From the beginning of Chief Justice Waite's term of office, . . . the Court reversed its policy and upheld the National authority over commerce [by striking down state laws] in practically every case of importance coming before it." *See also* The Lottawanna, 88 U.S. (21 Wall.) 558, 575 (1875) (Bradley, J.) (dictum), foreshadowing a whole body of decisions enforcing a distinct and equally questionable implicit limitation on state laws derived from the extension of federal judicial power over maritime cases in article III:

> [T]o place the rules and limits of maritime law under the disposal and regulation of the several States . . . would have defeated the uniformity and consistency at which the Constitution aimed on all subjects of a commercial character affecting the intercourse of the States with each other or with foreign states.

For the development of this doctrine, *see* Currie, *Federalism and the Admiralty—The Devil's Own Mess*, 1960 SUP. CT. REV. 158.

[5]91 U.S. 275 (1876). In two earlier cases the Court had upheld taxes imposed by a state on its own railroad corporations. Delaware Railroad Tax, 85 U.S. (18 Wall.) 206, 232 (1874) (Field, J.) (tax on corporate stock and income proportional to track within state); Railroad Co. v. Maryland, 88 U.S. (21 Wall.) 456, 471-72 (1875) (Bradley, J.) (charter requirement reserving twenty percent of income to state). The first was based on *State Tax on Railway Gross Receipts*, *supra* chapter 10, and added nothing to its reasoning. The second might well have invoked the same authority but did not, enunciating instead the apparently broader principle that the power to create a corporation included the power to impose conditions on the grant. *See* note 74 *infra*, discussing the *Wabash* case. Miller dissented alone without mentioning the commerce clause. 88 U.S. (21 Wall.) at 475.

[6]*See supra* chapter 10. *Woodruff* was quoted at 91 U.S. 282-83.

[7]The tax was laid on the privilege of selling goods "which are not the growth, produce, or manufacture of this State, by going from place to place . . . ." 91 U.S. at 275. Though the sale itself took place after interstate transportation had ceased, Field said, as the purpose of the clause seems to require, that "the commercial power continues until the commodity has ceased to be the subject of discriminating legislation by reason of its foreign character." *Id.* at 282. Contrast McCready v. Virginia, 94 U.S. 391, 396-97 (1877) (Waite, C.J.), upholding a state's power to limit the planting and harvesting of oysters to its own residents in part because "[c]ommerce has nothing to do with land while producing, but only with the product after it has become the subject of trade." Strictly speaking, the discrimination in *McCready* was against nonresidents and not against interstate commerce; and the Court also argued, as it had emphasized in rejecting the more pertinent privileges-and-immunities objection under article IV, that the state was the owner of submerged lands and could thus do as it pleased with them. For repudiation of this ownership theory in a commerce-clause case having to do with minnows, *see* Hughes v. Oklahoma, 441 U.S. 322 (1979). The only other significant case of the Waite period involving interstate privileges and immunities was Chemung Canal Bank v. Lowery, 93 U.S. 72, 77-78 (1876) (Bradley, J.), upholding a provision tolling the statute of limitations only when the plaintiff was a resident of the forum state on the questionable ground that there was "a valid reason for the discrimination." *See supra* chapter 8, discussing *Conner v. Elliott.*

[8]*See* the discussion of *Osborne v. Mobile* in chapter 10 *supra*.

unnecessarily both reaffirmed the much broader argument that interstate "transportation and exchange of commodities . . . requires uniformity of regulation"[9] and embraced the questionable thesis that congressional "inaction on this subject, when considered with reference to its legislation with respect to foreign commerce, is equivalent to a declaration that inter-State commerce shall be free and untrammelled."[10] But protectionism was at the heart of what the clause was meant to avoid,[11] and *Welton*'s nondiscrimination principle has become a pillar of modern commerce-clause analysis.[12]

Both this principle and *Welton*'s generalization that transportation required uniform regulation might have been pressed into service in support of Justice Miller's opinion for the Court the same year in *Henderson v. Mayor of New York*,[13] striking down a provision requiring a shipowner to post a bond to indemnify the state in the event that an immigrant passenger became a public charge, or alternatively to pay a fee for each passenger.[14] Yet although the law applied solely to the transportation of persons from abroad, neither of *Welton*'s principles was invoked at all.

Part of a scheme to protect the state against the expenses of supporting penurious immigrants, the New York provisions had a long history of their own in the Supreme Court. A related provision requiring the filing of information on incoming passengers had been upheld in *New York v. Miln*[15] in 1837 as an exercise of the state's police power, which Marshall had said in *Gibbons v. Ogden*[16] was unaffected by the grant of power to Congress over interstate and foreign commerce. Twelve years later, in the *Passenger Cases*,[17] a provision imposing a tax for each incoming passenger had been struck down by a sharply divided Court despite the argument that it too served to protect the state from the burden of supporting needy newcomers. There was, however, no opinion for the Court and no unanimity as to the reasons for decision.[18]

The bond requirement in *Henderson*, Miller persuasively argued, was nothing but a means of coercing payment of a tax like the one held invalid in the *Passenger Cases*: nobody would post a $300 bond when he could pay a $1.50 tax instead.[19] But Miller forthrightly declined to rely on the unsatisfying precedent of the *Passenger Cases*,[20]

[9]91 U.S. at 280. *Cf. supra* chapter 10, discussing the *Case of the State Freight Tax*.

[10]91 U.S. at 282. Cf. Steamship Co. v. Portwardens, *supra* chapter 10, where Chase had espoused but not applied the equally questionable and essentially contradictory thesis that in some cases Congress's silence meant the states were free to regulate commerce.

[11]See the discussion of *Crandall v. Nevada* in chapter 10 *supra*.

[12]*See, e.g.*, Philadelphia v. New Jersey, 437 U.S. 617 (1978) (state cannot discriminatorily exclude waste generated in other states). Other applications of this principle during the Waite period include Cook v. Pennsylvania, 97 U.S. 566 (1878) (discriminatory tax on sale of foreign goods at auction); Guy v. Baltimore, 100 U.S. 434, 442 (1880) (Harlan, J.) (discriminatory charges for use of publicly owned wharf); and Walling v. Michigan, 116 U.S. 446 (1886) (Bradley, J.) (discriminatory tax on sale of foreign liquor).

[13]92 U.S. 259 (1876).

[14]*See id.* at 260-61.

[15]*See supra* chapter 7.

[16]*See supra* chapter 6.

[17]*See supra* chapter 7.

[18]Although several Justices invoked the commerce clause, the one basis for decision that appeared to be embraced by a majority was that the tax offended both the statutory scheme omitting to impose federal taxes on passengers and a treaty guaranteeing British subjects "free" entry.

[19]92 U.S. at 268-69.

[20]*Id.* at 269-70.

and he did not bother with the unconvincing statutory and treaty arguments that had apparently been the basis of that decision. He relied directly on the commerce clause as expounded by *Cooley*, and in so doing expressly confirmed *Cooley*'s implication that it was irrelevant whether the law had been enacted under the police power.[21]

Cooley had settled, wrote Miller, that Congress's power to regulate commerce was exclusive with respect to " 'whatever subjects of this power are in their nature national or admit of one uniform system or plan of regulation.' "[22] The New York law "prescribes terms or conditions on which alone the vessel can discharge its passengers" and thus "is a regulation of commerce."[23] Any "regulation which imposes onerous, perhaps impossible, conditions on those engaged in active commerce with foreign nations . . . concern[s] the exterior relation of this whole nation with other nations and governments" and "must of necessity be national in its character"; and it was "equally clear that the matter of these statutes may be, and ought to be, the subject of a uniform system or plan."[24] The police-power justification for the law was in Miller's view somewhat contrived, because its burden fell on wealthy and industrious immigrants as well as on the needy.[25] In any event, though it was unnecessary to say whether states could "protect themselves against *actual* paupers, vagrants, criminals, and diseased persons,"[26] Miller cast considerable doubt on their ability to do so by announcing that "[n]othing is gained" by saying that the state acted under its police power: "whenever the statute of a State invades the domain of legislation which belongs exclusively to the Congress of the United States, it is void, no matter under what class of powers it may fall . . . ."[27]

As an original matter, Miller's argument that the crucial question under a provision designed to assure that commerce is not interrupted should be the effect of a challenged measure rather than the source of power under which it is enacted seems unanswerable.[28] He nowhere acknowledged, however, that the police-power theory he was for the first time explicitly abandoning had been the basis on which *Miln* had been decided and on which Marshall had relied to explain the validity of quarantine laws. He made no effort to distinguish either *Miln* or *Cooley* itself, in both of which state laws equally prescribing conditions for interstate or foreign commerce had been upheld.[29] He ignored recent precedents invalidating state taxes on incoming ships

[21]*See supra* chapter 7.

[22]92 U.S. at 272-73.

[23]*Id.* at 271.

[24]*Id.* at 273.

[25]*Id.* at 269. This argument seems weak; taxation of those who can afford it is a common means of taking care of those who cannot.

[26]*Id.* at 275 (emphasis in original).

[27]*Id.* at 271-72.

[28]*See supra* chapter 6, discussing *Gibbons v. Ogden*.

[29]*Miln* and *Cooley* as well as the quarantine laws could perhaps have been distinguished as imposing less severe burdens on commerce; but all would fall under the theory of *Welton* and of the *Freight Tax* case that interstate and foreign transportation required uniform regulation or none at all. *See* Morgan v. Louisiana, 118 U.S. 455, 464, 465 (1886) (Miller, J.), consistently casting doubt on the police-power theory while relying on *Cooley* to uphold a quarantine law on the ground of varying local needs and adding, without noting the contrary holding in *Cooley*, that Congress had effectively approved state quarantine measures subsequently adopted.

and on interstate freight shipments although both their results and their reasons would have given him strong support.[30] Finally, he was no better in explaining why the subject in question required a uniform national law than Curtis had been in *Cooley* in showing that pilotage did not;[31] and that made it hard to predict how the Court would apply the *Cooley* test in future cases.

In the companion case of *Chy Lung v. Freeman*,[32] Miller applied similar reasoning to strike down a California statute that appeared to be more narrowly tailored to the problem of actually undesirable immigrants that the Court had reserved in *Henderson*. California required a bond not for all immigrants but only for those believed by an inspector to present special risks, including "lewd and debauched women."[33] Stressing that the law gave full discretion to the inspector to determine the facts and to compromise the bond requirement by the payment of whatever sum he thought proper—twenty percent of which went into his own pocket[34]—the Court once again doubted the legitimacy of the asserted protective purpose and reserved the question of the power to exclude actual undesirables.[35] The manifest purpose of the law, Miller concluded, was "money"; the statute gave the inspector "the power to prevent entirely vessels engaged in a foreign trade . . . from carrying passengers, or to compel them to submit to systematic extortion of the grossest kind."[36] Giving a reason why the power to regulate such matters should be exclusive, Miller came close to saying, despite *Miln*, that the states could never regulate foreign commerce at all:

> The passage of laws which concern the admission of citizens and subjects of foreign nations to our shores belongs to Congress, and not to the States. It has the power to regulate commerce with foreign nations: the responsibility for the character of those regulations, and for the manner of their execution, belongs solely to the national government. If it be otherwise, a single State can, at her pleasure, embroil us in disastrous quarrels with other nations.[37]

---

[30]*Steamship Co. v. Portwardens* had said a five-dollar tax on an entire ship imposed a "serious burden" impermissible in the absence of congressional authorization; the *Case of the State Freight Tax* had said the power to tax commerce was the power to destroy it, that interstate transportation was a subject requiring uniform regulation, and that state taxation of commerce with ports outside the state posed a risk of multiple taxation. *See supra* chapter 10.

[31]*See supra* chapter 7.

[32]92 U.S. 275 (1876).

[33]*Id.* at 277-78.

[34]*Id.* at 278.

[35]*Id.* at 280.

[36]*Id.* at 280, 278.

[37]*Id.* at 280. To Professor Warren (*supra*, introduction to part five, note 1, v.2, at 628), *Henderson* and *Chy Lung* meant the whole subject of "immigration" was beyond state power. See also People v. Compagnie Generale Transatlantique, 107 U.S. 59, 61 (1883) (Miller, J.), rejecting the argument that a charge for incoming passengers could be defended as a fee for determining whether they were criminals, paupers, or otherwise excludable: because the "Imports" and "Exports" which article I, § 10 protected from state taxation did not include "free human beings," the "inspection Laws" excepted from that prohibition (and thus implicitly from the negative effect of the commerce clause) applied only to the inspection of "personal property." Contrast Turner v. Maryland, 107 U.S. 38 (1883) (Blatchford, J.), upholding as inspection laws provisions regulating packaging and requiring examination of goods intended for foreign export and extracting a fee for the services provided—although local transactions were exempted.

Again the decision was unanimous. Whatever may be said of Miller's disdain for authority and his disinclination to explain how in *Henderson* he applied the law to the facts, he seemed at least, like Curtis before him,[38] to have freed the Court from a confusing accumulation of precedents.

B. Additional Theories

In the very same year, however, the certainty became unglued again. In upholding the application of a state wrongful-death law to an accident occurring in interstate commerce in *Sherlock v. Alling*,[39] Justice Field referred neither to *Henderson* nor to the uniformity test it had employed, saying only that the law in question affected commerce only "indirectly."[40] Why that was so, and why it mattered, Field did not bother to say; one might have thought the seriousness of the burden rather than its directness was relevant to the Framers' assumed purpose of preventing obstructions to commerce.

The next year, in *Peik v. Chicago & Northwestern Ry.*,[41] the court adopted still a third formulation in upholding state authority to limit the rates charged for interstate rail journeys. There was no denying that, like the law in *Henderson*, the rate law set forth "conditions" for engaging in commerce. *Welton* had said that the interstate shipment of goods required uniform regulation. The power to limit rates seems to pose the same risk of disrupting commerce as the power to tax, and its exercise seems no less "direct."[42] Yet Waite disposed of the commerce-clause objection in a single paragraph without citing any authority or attempting to distinguish any of the precedents.[43] The commerce in question "directly affects the people of Wisconsin"; its rates therefore were "of domestic concern"; and "until Congress undertakes to legislate for those who are without the State, Wisconsin may provide for those within, even though it may indirectly affect those without."[44] In this cryptic passage,

---

[38]*See supra* chapter 7, discussing *Cooley.*

[39]93 U.S. 99 (1876).

[40]*Id.* at 102-04. Field added that the law was not discriminatory and that Congress had not legislated on the subject; but nondiscriminatory burdens had been struck down before (*see* the *Freight Tax* case, chapter 10 supra), and Field himself had said in *Welton* (note 10 *supra*) that congressional silence should be taken as a declaration that commerce should not be burdened.

[41]94 U.S. 164 (1877).

[42]*See* Pomeroy, *The Power of Congress to Regulate Inter-State Commerce*, 4 So. L. REV. (N.S.) 357, 372 (1878): "These statutes . . . act *directly* upon a commerce which is inter-state; they do not, like laws imposing a tax upon gross receipts from traffic, affect such commerce *indirectly*; they assume to regulate and control it *as commerce*, and have no other object and design."

[43]*Henderson* could have been distinguished on the ground that the tax there in question applied only to foreign commerce and thus was discriminatory, while the rate regulation was evenhanded; and Field had noted that the wrongful-death law in *Sherlock* was a "general" and evenhanded one. Neither *Henderson* nor *Peik*, however, mentioned discrimination.

[44]94 U.S. at 177-78. In the companion cases of Munn v. Illinois, 94 U.S. 113, 135 (1877), and Chicago, B. & Q. R.R. v. Iowa, 94 U.S. 155, 163 (1877), Waite applied the same reasoning to the regulation of grain elevators and of a railroad located entirely in one state. Waite did not fall for the seductive conclusion that these cases did not involve interstate commerce at all, conceding that both the railroad and the elevators handled goods being sent interstate. *Cf.* Stafford v. Wallace, 258 U.S. 495, 516 (1922), upholding federal regulation of stockyards as "a throat through which the current [of interstate commerce] flows . . . ."

Waite without explanation shifted the focus from the effect of a law on commerce to its extraterritorial effect.[45]

Later the same Term, in *Foster v. Master and Wardens*,[46] the Court struck down on commerce-clause grounds a Louisiana law giving port officials a monopoly of the business of inspecting for damage to the hatches and cargo of arriving ships. Without referring to any of the three divergent tests laid down in the three preceding cases, Justice Swayne for a still unanimous Court relied on an earlier decision striking down a tax on incoming ships, observing simply that the provisions in question were "a clog and a blow to all [foreign and interstate] commerce in the port to which they relate."[47] So, it might as easily have been concluded, were the wrongful-death and rate provisions upheld in *Sherlock* and *Peik*. Moreover, the monopoly provision satisfied the tests of validity laid down in both those cases. Like the rate law, it operated directly only on persons within the state; more clearly than the death law, its effect on commerce itself was indirect, since its prohibition was directed to local inspectors and not to shipowners. No effort was made to explain why uniformity was more necessary than in regard to rates or tort remedies, and there was no suggestion that the law applied only to interstate and foreign commerce. From the rationale of this opinion one might almost have concluded that Swayne thought every state law void that imposed any burden on commerce, had it not been for a precedent of his own allowing a state to block commerce entirely by building a bridge over a navigable stream.[48] At the end of the opinion, however, Swayne went out of his way to take back what Miller had tried to establish in *Henderson* by referring to the recognized power of the states "to establish inspection, quarantine, health, and other regulations, within the sphere of their acknowledged authority."[49] In less than two years, four Justices had enunciated four inconsistent views of the commerce clause, and every one of them had spoken for a unanimous Court.

---

[45]See Pomeroy, *supra* n.42, 4 So. L. Rev. (N.S.) 393 (1878): "While I am firmly of the opinion that each state ought to be entitled to regulate the rates of fare and freight of railways . . . operating within its territory, . . . yet it seems to me very difficult to reconcile the reasoning of the court in these three cases with the principles which have been settled by the prior course of decision." The relevance of extraterritorial application became clear in Western Union Tel. Co. v. Pendleton, 122 U.S. 347, 358-59 (1887) (Field, J.), when the Court held invalid an Indiana law prescribing rules to govern the manner of delivering telegrams sent from Indiana to other states: the state of delivery might prescribe conflicting rules, and the net effect might be to prevent interstate messages entirely. *Cf.* text accompanying notes 57-64 *infra*, discussing *Hall v. DeCuir*. Thus the commerce clause was invoked before either due process or full faith and credit as a limitation on state choice of law.

[46]94 U.S. 246 (1877).

[47]*Id.* at 247, citing *Steamship Co. v. Portwardens*, *supra* chapter 10.

[48]*Gilman v. Philadelphia*, *supra* chapter 10. Cases of the Waite period reaffirming *Gilman* include Pound v. Turck, 95 U.S. 459 (1878) (Miller, J.) (involving a dam), Escanaba Co. v. Chicago, 107 U.S. 678 (1883) (Field, J.), and Willamette Iron Bridge Co. v. Hatch, 125 U.S. 1 (1888) (Bradley, J.), which concerned a bridge limiting access to the port of Portland, Oregon, from the Pacific Ocean. Soon after this decision, Congress decided it was time to require federal permission to obstruct navigable waters. Act of Sept. 19, 1890, ch. 907, § 7, 26 Stat. 426, 454 (current version at 33 U.S.C. § 401). *Cf.* County of Mobile v. Kendall, 102 U.S. 691, 699 (1881) (Field, J.), decided partly in reliance on the bridge and dam cases but much easier to justify in terms of the purposes of the commerce clause: a state's dredging of harbors promoted rather than interfered with navigation.

[49]94 U.S. at 248.

The implications of Swayne's opinion were explicitly confirmed by Justice Strong for another unanimous bench the following Term in *Railroad Co. v. Husen*, [50] holding unconstitutional a statute that basically excluded Texas, Mexican, or Indian cattle from entering Missouri during eight months of the year. Congress's power over both interstate and foreign commerce was "necessarily exclusive,"[51] but the states had not surrendered their "police power."[52] Thus a state could exclude convicts, paupers, or "animals having contagious or infectious diseases,"[53] but Missouri had gone too far; as New York in *Henderson* had taxed self-sufficient as well as indigent immigrants, and as California in *Chy Lung* had excluded people who were not lewd or debauched, Missouri had excluded healthy as well as diseased cattle.[54]

Police power had become the test again by rewriting *Henderson*, without any protest by its author; but in contrast to the due-process cases, where police power was also emerging as the test,[55] the Court in *Husen* made clear it would scrutinize state laws very closely to make sure that the state had not interfered any more with interstate or foreign transportation than was "absolutely necessary for its self-protection."[56]

C.   Segregation and rates

Surveying the wreckage in 1878, Waite observed with some justice that "it would be a useless task" to formulate a general test for determining the limits of state power to affect interstate commerce; it would be "far better to leave a matter of such delicacy to be settled in each case upon a view of the particular rights involved."[57] Like his brethren, however, he could not resist the urge to lay down a general test after all, and it was the one Field had espoused in *Sherlock v. Alling*: "State legislation which seeks to impose a direct burden upon inter-state commerce, or to interfere directly with its freedom, does encroach upon the exclusive power of Congress."[58]

[50]95 U.S. 465 (1878).

[51]*Id.* at 469.

[52]*Id.* at 470.

[53]*Id.* at 471.

[54]*Id.* at 472-73. One might respond that it is the essence of a quarantine law to exclude all persons coming from disease-infected areas because of the difficulty of determining at the time of entry whether a particular individual is afflicted; but the Court may have been right that it was unnecessary to provide more than a delay to allow assurance against latent disease.

[55]*See supra* chapter 11.

[56]95 U.S. at 472. *See* Pomeroy, *supra* note 42, 4 So. L. Rev. (N.S.) at 402, explaining *Husen* in Field's terms of direct and indirect burdens: "whatever be the nature and extent of the police power, its exercise can only affect inter-state or foreign commerce *indirectly*; as soon as it operates upon such commerce *directly*, and becomes a 'regulation' thereof, it is either absolutely void or is voidable by congressional legislation"; Greeley, *What Is the Test of a Regulation of Foreign or Interstate Commerce?*, 1 HARV. L. REV. 159, 177-79 (1887), attempting to rationalize *Husen* on the ground that "the Court thought that the law was passed for the purpose of discriminating against the cattle of other States."

[57]Hall v. DeCuir, 95 U.S. 485, 488 (1878).

[58]*Id.* Waite also repeated Field's conclusion (note 10 *supra*) that the failure of Congress to act on the subject was the equivalent of a declaration that commerce should be free of restrictions. *Id.* at 490. It was evidently this offhand remark that led Professor Pomeroy, *supra* note 42, 4 So. L. Rev. (N.S.) at 370, to the basically misleading suggestion that *Hall*, like *Gibbons v. Ogden*, was based upon conflict with federal statutes.

It was ostensibly on this basis that Waite concluded for a still ostensibly unanimous Court[59] in *Hall v. DeCuir* that a law forbidding racial segregation in public conveyances could not constitutionally be applied to a ship traveling to and from another state. Yet Waite made no effort to show why the impact of this law upon commerce was any more "direct" than that of the wrongful-death law upheld in *Sherlock* or of the rate law he himself had written to uphold in *Peik*.[60] Nor did he advert to the police power, which the two immediately preceding decisions had said would justify far more burdensome regulations that seemed equally direct, such as the complete exclusion of paupers and diseased cattle.[61] In fact, his explanation of why the antisegregation law was impermissible suggested that he really was concerned not with the directness of the burden on commerce but with the degree of interference and thus, as in *Cooley* and *Henderson*, with the need of uniformity:

> No carrier of passengers can conduct his business with satisfaction to himself, or comfort to those employing him, if on one side of a State line his passengers, both white and colored, must be permitted to occupy the same cabin, and on the other be kept separate.[62]

No effort was made to show that in fact there were conflicting rules, or why the danger was any less acute in the area of wrongful death or rate regulation, let alone the total exclusion of paupers. In fact, the inconvenience even of actually conflicting regulations in *Hall* seems trifling in comparison with the prospect of rate restrictions that could render interstate traffic entirely unprofitable: all the owner would have to do would be to shift passengers from one cabin to another at the state line.[63] Waite's analysis did have the virtue of focusing on the fact that the subject was one, like the taxes on interstate freight shipments, on which varying state laws might subject interstate commerce to burdens not shared by local competitors. Nevertheless, like *Cooley* itself, whose general test the Court seemed to be actually applying, the freight-tax case that had given the most direct support to Waite's analysis was not cited.[64]

[59]*See* C. MAGRATH, *supra* introduction to part five, note 1, at 140, reporting that Miller, Strong, and Hunt had disagreed in conference but refrained from dissenting publicly.

[60]In fact, though Waite cited *Peik*'s companion cases dealing with regulation of businesses wholly within one state, *id.* at 487-88, he conspicuously neglected to cite *Peik* itself.

[61]There was no suggestion that the law in *Hall* discriminated against interstate commerce, for it applied impartially to all carriers in the state. *Id.* at 485-86.

[62]*Id.* at 489. Implicit in this passage was the unarticulated premise that a state law requiring segregated transportation would not offend the equal protection clause. *Cf. supra* chapter 11, discussing *Pace v. Alabama*. The crucial nature of this assumption may explain why Justice Clifford devoted a substantial portion of his long and boring concurrence to the otherwise irrelevant argument that the states were free to operate racially segregated schools (95 U.S. at 504-06)—though Clifford himself apparently did not see the connection.

[63]Clifford, who also (*id.* at 495-97) invoked the federal coasting license that the Court had pulled out of its pocket before whenever it wanted to invalidate state laws (*see supra* chapters 6 and 7), contended unconvincingly that a carrier could not operate at all if one state required and the next forbade separate cabins for the races. 95 U.S. at 497-98.

[64]*See Case of the State Freight Tax, supra* chapter 10. Waite himself relied primarily upon the *Freight Tax* case in 1882 in holding that Texas could not tax interstate telegraph messages, which as he said seemed precisely analogous. Telegraph Co. v. Texas, 105 U.S. 460, 465-66 (1882). Again he did not bother distinguishing rate regulation. See also *Western Union Tel. Co. v. Pendleton, supra* note 45.

Eight years later, in *Wabash, St. L. & Pac. Ry. v. Illinois*,[65] Justice Miller relied heavily on *Hall v. DeCuir* and on the *Freight Tax Case* in holding for a divided Court, despite the recent *Peik* decision,[66] that a state lacked power to outlaw discriminatory rates for the portion of an interstate rail journey within its borders.[67] It was "impossible," he said, "to see any distinction in its effect upon commerce . . . , between a statute which regulates the charges for transportation, and a statute which levies a tax for the benefit of the state upon the same transportation";[68] and if each state were free to set its own rules governing rates on a single trip, the "embarrassments upon interstate transportation . . . might" as in *Hall* "be too oppressive to be submitted to."[69] The governing principle, as in *Henderson*, was the need for uniformity: "this species of regulation is one which must be, if established at all, of a general and national character . . . ."[70]

What had made both *Freight Tax* and *Hall* especially strong cases in modern terms for freedom from state regulation was the risk that applying the laws of two or more states to a single shipment might subject interstate transportation to burdens not shared by local traffic and thus put it at a competitive disadvantage. Miller made no attempt to show anything comparable either to multiple taxation or to the necessity for moving passengers to new seats at every border; his exposition of the burden of the rate law demonstrated only that it limited the parties' freedom of contract just as it would have if the transporation had been wholly within one state.[71] Indeed, the rate law did not appear to subject interstate traffic to the risk of special burdens. For Illinois had attempted to regulate only the fares charged within its own borders; if other states imposed different rules for their part of the same journey, the only adjustment needed would be the trivial cost of consulting several states' rules in determining the total fare.

That even a single state rate law might make interstate commerce so unrewarding as to discourage it would of course have been an argument for saying national regulation was needed;[72] but too many other laws with similar potential had been upheld to make that self-evident.[73] If that was his principle, Miller relied most heavily

---

[65]118 U.S. 557 (1886). Bradley, Waite, and Gray dissented.

[66]*See supra* text accompanying notes 41-45. Miller had gone along with *Peik*, but now he explained (112 U.S. at 568-70) that the commerce clause objection had been so minor in relation to the overriding due-process question at the time of the earlier case that it had not been given adequate consideration. Miller did not stop to refute Waite's argument in *Peik* that what mattered was the effect on outsiders rather than upon commerce itself.

[67]*See id.* at 564, reporting that the state had held the statute "inoperative upon that part of the contract which has reference to transportation outside of the State . . . ."

[68]*Id.* at 570. Professor Pomeroy, *supra note* 42, 4 So. L. Rev. (N.S.) at 372, had anticipated this equation.

[69]118 U.S. at 572.

[70]*Id.* at 577.

[71]*Id.* at 575-76.

[72]*See* F. Frankfurter, *supra note* 4, at 100, deeming the dissent in *Wabash* "a rather extreme instance of deference to local authority" without offering any reasons.

[73]*E.g., The License Cases, supra* chapter 7 (sale of imported liquor); *Cooley v. Board of Wardens, supra* chapter 7 (pilotage); *Sherlock v. Alling, supra* text accompanying notes 39-40 (wrongful death); *State Tax on Railway Gross Receipts, supra* chapter 10 (tax by incorporating state); and see the dicta as to exclusion of undesirables in *Husen, supra* text accompanying note 53.

on the wrong cases;[74] and apart from them he gave us essentially only his conclusion that uniformity was required.[75]

D.   Taxes and Police Powers

The implication of *Wabash* that the Court took very seriously its assumed responsibility to protect interstate commerce from state interference was confirmed the next year in *Robbins v. Shelby County,* [76] where in striking down a tax on the sale of goods by sample by anyone without a licensed place of business in the county the Court said it was irrelevant whether the tax was discriminatory:[77] since the power to tax was the power to destroy, "[i]nterstate commerce cannot be taxed at all . . . ."[78] It would seem

[74]Other cases relied on involved either similar risks of multiple taxes or actual discrimination. *E.g.*, *Telegraph Co. v. Texas*, *supra* note 64 (interstate messages); Pickard v. Pullman Southern Car Co., 117 U.S. 34 (1886) (Blatchford, J.) (tax on railroad cars); *Welton v. Missouri*, *supra* text accompanying notes 5-12 (tax on sellers of foreign goods). The dissenters, apart from citing *Peik* and decisions allowing dams and bridges over navigable streams (118 U.S. at 581-85, 592-93), argued basically that the state could regulate railroad rates because it had chartered the railroad: *"Omne majus continet in se minus"* (*id.* at 587)—which as every student knows is not always true (*cf.*, *e.g.*, Insurance Co. v. Morse, 87 U.S. (20 Wall.) 445 (1874) (Hunt, J.), and Barron v. Burnside, 121 U.S. 186 (1887) (Blatchford, J.), both holding a state could not condition the right to do local business on waiver of the right to invoke federal jurisdiction), and which the dissenters themselves rejected in conceding that the commerce clause forbade both taxes and discriminatory regulations respecting the goods carried on railroads chartered by or even owned by the state itself (118 U.S. at 589).

[75]It was shortly after this decision that Congress entered the field by creating the Interstate Commerce Commission to regulate interstate rail rates. Act of Feb. 4, 1887, ch. 104, 24 Stat. 379 (1887).

[76]120 U.S. 489 (1887) (Bradley, J.).

[77]Along the way Bradley had eclectically recited *Cooley*'s uniformity test, Marshall's police-power distinction, and Field's thesis that "incidental" burdens on commerce were permissible, *id.* at 492-94, and at the end he added that the tax did seem discriminatory (*id.* at 498), although, as Waite, Field, and Gray stressed in dissent, it also applied to instate businesses that had no place of business in Shelby County (*id.* at 502). The bare notion of nondiscrimination does not answer the question whether the clause demands that outsiders be treated as well as merchants in the city itself or only as well as those elsewhere in the same state. The principle of virtual representation that seems to underlie the commerce clause appears to suggest the latter, but the Court has apparently continued to take the contrary position espoused in *Robbins*. See Dean Milk Co. v. Madison, 340 U.S. 349 (1951).

[78]120 U.S. at 495, 497. Similar language was used in Leloup v. Port of Mobile, 127 U.S. 640, 645, 648 (1888) (Bradley, J.), striking down a nondiscriminatory license tax on the interstate telegraph business and overruling *Osborne v. Mobile*, *supra* chapter 10. That interstate commerce could not be taxed at all seemed counter to Miller's insistence, in allowing a state to tax the sale of goods imported from other states, that interstate commerce should pay its own way (see *Woodruff v. Parham*, *supra* chapter 10). The dissenters in *Robbins* argued forcefully that the commerce clause did not require the states to place their own manufacturers at a disadvantage, 120 U.S. at 501-02; yet Miller went along in *Robbins* without comment.

Perhaps there was in *Robbins* and in *Leloup* a risk of multiple taxation not present in the earlier case. When, for example, the sale itself is interstate, there is a danger that two states may tax it and thus subject it to cumulative burdens beyond those imposed on local businesses. *See*, T. POWELL, VAGARIES AND VARIETIES IN CONSTITUTIONAL INTERPRETATION 190 (1956), adding that in such cases "the earlier notion was that no tax was better than two." *Cf. supra* chapter 10, discussing the *Case of the State Freight Tax*. If that was what troubled the Justices in *Robbins*, they managed to suppress it while stating a much broader rule. *See* Lockhart, *The Sales Tax in Interstate Commerce*, 52 HARV. L. REV. 617, 621-28 (1939). Shortly after *Robbins*, indeed, the Court made clear that multiple taxation was not its sole concern by overruling a

to follow that the power to regulate commerce was also the power to destroy it; yet the year following *Robbins*, in *Smith v. Alabama*, the Court over only one dissent upheld the application to interstate transportation of a statute requiring state certification of the competence of railway engineers.[79] Since there was no federal common law, said Justice Matthews, the whole subject of "the rights and duties of common carriers" was necessarily regulated by state law until Congress acted.[80] *Sherlock* had held the states could provide redress if those engaged in interstate transportation negligently caused injury; it followed that they could "prescribe the precautions and safeguards foreseen to be necessary and proper to prevent by anticipation those wrongs . . . ."[81] The law was not a regulation of commerce at all but rather "an act . . . within the . . . admitted power reserved to the State to regulate the relative rights of persons . . . within its territorial jurisdiction . . . to secure . . . safety of persons and property"; it affected transactions in commerce "only indirectly, incidentally, and remotely, and not so as to burden or impede them . . . ."[82]

The obvious contrast between this conclusion and the holdings in *Wabash* and *Hall* that the states could regulate neither railroad rates nor the segregation of steamboat passengers cried out for justification. There had been no federal common law to govern the relationship between a carrier and its customers in the prior cases either; the effect of the engineer rule seemed no more indirect than that of the laws there struck down; Strong had said in the *Freight Tax* case that the entire subject of interstate transportation required uniform regulation.[83] The potential burden of the

---

precedent allowing a state to tax the gross receipts earned by its own railroads in interstate commerce (Philadelphia & So. S.S. Co. v. Pennsylvania, 122 U.S. 326 (1887) (Bradley, J.), overruling *State Tax on Railway Gross Receipts*, *supra* chapter 10), although it had just established that no other state could tax the same receipts (Fargo v. Michigan, 121 U.S. 230 (1887)). *See* Lockhart, *Gross Receipts Taxes on Interstate Transportation and Communication*, 57 HARV. L. REV. 40, 48 (1943), pointing out that the tax struck down in *Fargo* was properly apportioned to miles traveled within the taxing state. The Court really did seem almost to think the states could not tax interstate commerce at all. *See* POWELL, *supra*, at 180, citing *Robbins* as evidence of a longstanding principle that "[t]here is no *Cooley* rule governing state taxation."

For qualifications of this principle, *see* Packet Co. v. Keokuk, 95 U.S. 80 (1877) (Strong, J.), one of several decisions of this period sensibly holding that a fee for the use of a city wharf was neither a tax forbidden by the commerce clause nor a "Duty on Tonnage" prohibited by article I, § 10, although measured by the tonnage of the ship; Transportation Co. v. Wheeling, 99 U.S. 273 (1879) (Clifford, J.), an incompetent opinion upholding an ad valorem property tax on a ship in its home port; Wiggins Ferry Co. v. East St. Louis, 107 U.S. 365 (1883) (Woods, J.) (upholding a license tax on ship in its home port). The risk of multiple taxation in the last two cases was removed, without mention of the problem, by Gloucester Ferry Co. v. Pennsylvania, 114 U.S. 196 (1885), a wordy Field opinion holding that an interstate ferry company could not be taxed according to its capital stock outside its home state, and invoking authority that the ferries themselves were similarly protected. *See supra* chapter 7, discussing *Hays v. Pacific Mail S.S. Co. See also* the twin Bradley opinions in Brown v. Houston, 114 U.S. 622 (1885), and Coe v. Errol, 116 U.S. 517, 525 (1886), respectively holding that interstate transportation for purposes of immunity from nondiscriminatory state property taxes ended when a ship reached its berth and did not begin until the goods "are committed to the common carrier for transportation out of the state to the state of their destination, or have started on their ultimate passage to that state." *Welton*, of course, had stated a different rule for discriminatory taxation, *see supra* note 7.

[79]124 U.S. 465 (1888).

[80]*Id.* at 476-78.

[81]*Id.* at 476-77.

[82]*Id.* at 482.

[83]*See supra* chapter 10.

law in *Smith*, moreover, seems indistinguishable from that of the antisegregation law, since differing state competency requirements might make it necessary to change engineers at every state line. Yet neither *Hall* nor *Wabash* was so much as cited, presumably because of the Court's conclusion that the engineer rule was not a regulation of commerce at all; and this conclusion itself contradicted *Henderson*'s sensible principle that every law prescribing the conditions upon which commerce could be conducted was a regulation of commerce. Evidently, the distinguishing factor was that the law in *Smith* was a safety measure within what Matthews never quite referred to as the police power; but why the police power did not also include the protection of citizens from discriminatory rates or racial segregation[84] he did not say.[85]

If the implication to be drawn from *Smith* was that ordinary commerce-clause limitations did not apply to legitimate measures for the protection of health and safety, it was soon to be dispelled. Forty years earlier, in the *License Cases*, the Court had unanimously held that the states were free to forbid the sale of liquor imported from other states, and three Justices had expressly invoked the police power.[86] In 1888, however, casting doubt on the correctness of the earlier decision while distinguishing it,[87] the Court over a trenchant Harlan dissent joined by Waite and Gray[88] held in *Bowman v. Chicago & Northwestern Ry.* that a state could not forbid that importation itself as part of a general prohibition law.[89]

In a long and poorly constructed opinion, Matthews reaffirmed the concession in *Husen* that a state could forbid the importation of diseased animals or decayed food, which "may be rightly outlawed as intrinsically and directly the immediate sources and causes of destruction to human health and life."[90] The same would appear to be true of liquor, on whose unhealthful propensities the Court had waxed eloquent only a few months before in *Mugler v. Kansas*, in holding that a law prohibiting the manufacture and sale of liquor fell within the police power.[91] Yet liquor, Matthews argued, was different from diseased animals or decayed food: the latter were "not legitimate subjects of trade and commerce," and thus their prohibition was not a regulation of commerce at all.[92] This seemed to beg the question, for the same could

[84]Waite had described rate regulation in *Munn* as an exercise of the police power, 94 U.S. at 125. *See also* the broad definitions of this power in the other due-process cases discussed in chapter 11 *supra*.

[85]The sole dissenter (124 U.S. at 483) was Bradley, whose opinion in *Robbins* suggested he might view any regulation of commerce, like any tax upon it, as impermissible; yet Bradley's position was as inconsistent as the Court's, for he had also dissented from the conclusion in *Wabash* that the states were forbidden to regulate interstate rates. He wrote no opinion in *Smith* to explain why he thought states could regulate railroad rates but not the competence of railway engineers.

[86]*See supra* chapter 7.

[87]125 U.S. 465, 476-79, 498-500 (1888).

[88]*Id.* at 509-24.

[89]For the related provisions banning manufacture and sale within the state, see *id.* at 474-75; for the Court's express holding that it was irrelevant that the law did not discriminate against interstate commerce, see *id.* at 495-96, citing *Robbins v. Shelby County*, *supra* text accompanying notes 76-78.

[90]125 U.S. at 489, 491.

[91]*See supra* chapter 11.

[92]*Id.* at 489. It did not seem to trouble Matthews that this interpretation cast doubt on the ability of Congress to deal with the interstate shipment of diseased animals. The later suggestion that the liquor legislation was void because of its extraterritorial effect on shippers outside the state (*id.* at 498),

have been said of liquor. It also left the reader to wonder about the police-power justification that Matthews himself had used to uphold a safety law that did affect "legitimate" commerce in *Smith v. Alabama*, which in *Bowman* he chose not to cite. Once it was decided that the exclusion of liquor could not be justified on a police-power theory, the case was easy; for outside the police-power cases the Court had struck down less burdensome measures on the ground that the power to impose them was the power to exclude goods entirely,[93] and the law in *Bowman* was an absolute prohibition.

It is a relief that with the *Bowman* decision we have reached the end of the commerce clause decisions of the Waite period, for they do not make elevating reading.[94]

II. Sovereign Immunity

As originally drafted, article III seemed to give the federal courts power to enter judgments against nonconsenting governments despite a contrary English tradition that arguably was only a formality: the judicial power was extended both to "Controversies between a State . . . and citizens of another State" or foreign state and to "Controversies to which the United States shall be a Party." In *Chisholm v. Georgia*, the Court had confirmed this inference as to states, dropping hints that the same might not be true of the United States, essentially because of the practical difficulties of enforcing the judgment. But the country lost no time in demonstrating that it thought the Court was wrong in permitting states to be sued under the general language of article III; the eleventh amendment, adopted as a response to *Chisholm*, flatly provided that the judicial power should not be construed to extend to "any suit in law or equity, commenced or prosecuted against one of the United States by Citizens of another State, or by Citizens or Subjects of any Foreign State."[95]

Marshall had managed to deprive this provision of much of its apparent force in *Osborn v. Bank of the United States* by permitting suits to be filed against state officers for injunctive and restorative relief that had the same effect as if the state itself had been the defendant,[96] and in *Davis v. Gray* the Chase Court had reaffirmed if not extended Marshall's decision.[97] Already in *Davis*, however, there were inarticulate signs of a reaction; two Justices dissented without seriously attempting to distinguish *Osborn*. More important, Marshall himself in a later and opaquely worded decision had indicated there were occasions on which a suit against an officer would be barred on the ground that it was effectively against the state itself;[98] and a

---

furthermore, seemed equally applicable to the exclusion of diseased animals, which Matthews had said was within state power.

[93]*E.g.*, *Robbins v. Shelby County*, *supra* text accompanying notes 76-78.

[94]*Cf.* the contemporary assessment by Greeley, *supra* note 56, 1 Harv. L. Rev. at 159: "While these cases almost always commend themselves to our common sense as actual decisions upon the facts, the reasoning upon which the decisions are based is meager and unsatisfactory . . . ."

[95]*See supra* chapter 1.

[96]*See supra* chapter 4.

[97]*See* conclusion to part four, *supra*.

[98]*See supra* chapter 4, discussing *Governor of Georgia v. Madrazo*.

series of decisions during the Waite period were to wrestle, not always satisfactorily, with Marshall's distinction.[99]

A.   *United States v. Lee*

Osborn had been reaffirmed by the Waite Court without much ado in the 1876 Bradley opinion in *Board of Liquidation v. McComb*, allowing suit to enjoin a state officer from issuing additional bonds in such a way as to impair the contractual rights of bondholders.[100] Six years later the same principle was for the first time applied to suits against federal officers in an important but surprisingly controversial opinion by Justice Miller.[101] The action was brought to recover from federal agents a Virginia estate the government had illegally taken for nonpayment of taxes.[102] Miller's eloquent opinion began with serious doubts whether the United States itself should be held immune from suit, both because the original formalistic reasons for the English doctrine seemed anachronistic in a country where sovereignty lay with the people and because, as Justice Wilson had argued in *Chisholm*, the petition of right had made the doctrine meaningless even in England.[103] But the holding was only that the precedents, which Miller ably marshaled, permitted suits to obtain possession of assets unlawfully held by government officials even if the government itself could not be sued;[104] and he polished it off by inveighing rightly if irrelevantly against the injustice of denying a remedy in such a case.[105]

---

[99]For an enlightening study of the cases considered in this section, *see* C. JACOBS, THE ELEVENTH AMENDMENT AND SOVEREIGN IMMUNITY 110-31 (1972).

[100]92 U.S. 531 (1876). The original bondholders had accepted their bonds in exchange for earlier bonds of a higher face value, in the expectation that reduction of the total state debt would improve their chances of being repaid. The issuance of additional bonds to cover the full amount of an unrelated state obligation was held to defeat the contractual scheme and to create "an unjust discrimination between one class of creditors and another." *Id.* at 539-40. Citing *Osborn* and *Davis*, the Court in a single conclusory paragraph said "an unconstitutional law" would not prevent mandamus to require an officer to perform "a plain official duty" or, as in *McComb* itself, an injunction to prevent its violation. *Id.* at 541. Field did not participate (*id.*).

[101]United States v. Lee, 106 U.S. 196 (1882).

[102]The land had belonged to the family of General Robert E. Lee. The government, the Court found, had improperly refused to accept payment of taxes from anyone but an actual owner, and the estate had become the site of the Arlington National Cemetery and of a "military station." *Id.* at 198-204.

[103]*Id.* at 205-09. Miller's observation that the petition of right had disappeared with the King suggests the anomalous result that sovereign immunity is a more serious obstruction to suits against the government here than it was in England. *See* L. JAFFE, JUDICIAL CONTROL OF ADMINISTRATIVE ACTION 197 (1965). Gray had an interesting and different view in dissent (106 U.S. at 238): the petition of right had fallen into disuse because it "was so tedious and expensive," so that it provided essentially no remedy until long after our Constitution was adopted.

[104]106 U.S. at 209-18. Miller added that because the case involved a taking without compensation it was analogous to those permitting habeas corpus against government officers, *id.* at 218, 220, but the analogy is flawed. Not only does the supension clause of article I, § 9 explicitly contemplate a judicial remedy; the statutes authorizing habeas against federal officers constituted a waiver of immunity, and the Court had not yet faced the problem of habeas against state officers. *Cf.* chapter 3 *supra*, discussing mandamus in connection with *Marbury v. Madison*. For Justice Wilson's contract-clause variant of Miller's argument that the taking clause *implicitly* created a judicial remedy, *see supra* chapter 1, discussing *Chisholm v. Georgia*, and compare *Marbury*'s effective conclusion that judicial review was implicit in all constitutional limitations. *See also* the suggestion, 106 U.S. at 219-20, important for later cases, that the mere assertion

The only surprise was the lengthy and scholarly dissent by Justice Gray, joined by
Waite, Bradley, and Woods.[106] Gray defended the immunity of the United States
itself not only on the basis of repeated Supreme Court dicta but also on the policy
ground that even in a republic "it is essential to the common defence and general
welfare that the sovereign should not, without its consent, be dispossessed by judicial
process of forts, arsenals, military posts, and ships of war, necessary to guard the
national existence against insurrection and invasion . . . ."[107] To dispossess the
government's agents, he rightly observed, was to dispossess the government itself;[108]
and he argued persuasively that English courts would not have allowed sovereign
immunity to be circumvented in a suit like *Lee* by naming a subordinate official as a
defendant.[109] American precedent was Gray's most difficult obstacle, and he explained it as follows:

> In those cases in which judgments have . . . been rendered by this court
> against individuals concerning money or property in which a State had an
> interest, either the money was in the personal possession of the defen-
> dants and not in the possession of the State, or the suit was to restrain the
> defendants by injunction from doing acts in violation of the Constitution
> of the United States.[110]

Osborn itself was the hardest case to square with this explanation, for in addition
to allowing an injunction against the collection of unconstitutional state taxes, the
Court in that case had approved an order directing the return of taxes already
collected and held by the state treasurer in a chest in the state treasury. The Court
had said, without apparent relevance to the immunity question, that the money had
not been commingled with state funds;[111] but even if for some reason that mattered,[112]
it was hardly the same as saying that the chest was not in the state's possession at all.[113]

---

of official authority could not preclude suit when the executive had no power to authorize the officer's
action.

[105]*Id.* at 218-23.

[106]*Id.* at 223-51.

[107]*Id.* at 226-27.

[108]*Id.* at 226. Miller responded by disparaging fears of "imaginary evils" in light of "at least two wars"
successfully concluded despite the suability of government officers, argued that the government itself was
not bound by a decree against the officer, and concluded with much force that vital interests could be
protected by exercising the power of eminent domain. *Id.* at 217, 221-22. Fears of state-court interference
with legitimate federal interests that had led to the denial of state-court power to issue habeas corpus to
federal officers in *Abelman v. Booth* and in *Tarble's Case* (chapters 8, 10 *supra*) were brushed off in *Lee*, as
they should have been in the habeas cases, by reference to the possibility of removal. 106 U.S. at 222-23.

[109]106 U.S. at 227-34, properly distinguishing actions for damages (which the officer himself and not the
Crown would presumably pay) from ejectment actions, "'the effect of which may be to turn the crown out
of possession.'"

[110]*Id.* at 242.

[111]22 U.S. (9 Wheat.) 738, 833-36, 869 (1824).

[112]The relevance of this fact to the remedial question whether an officer could be ordered to return the
money was suggested by Marshall's further statement (*id.* at 868) that "detinue might have been
maintained . . . had it been in the power of the bank . . . to establish the identity of the property sued
for." There was no problem in identifying the land in *Lee*.

[113]If the officer does not hold the property on behalf of the government, the effect of the order is not to
put the government out of possession; in such a case one cannot say the suit is effectively against the state

Since the officers in *Osborn* had been acting for the state, and since the state can act only through agents, the order to return the tax money, like the order in *Lee*, had the same effect as an order against the government itself.[114] If this was not enough to make *Osborn* a suit against the state, it was hard to see why it made *Lee* a suit against the United States.

Gray's best American counterexample was *Governor of Georgia v. Madrazo*,[115] in which, despite *Osborn*, Marshall had disallowed a suit for the return of property acquired by the state after it had allegedly been taken unlawfully from the claimant by someone else. Gray thought this case "illustrate[d] the distinction between the possession of the State by its agents, and the possession of the agents in their own right."[116] But no more in *Madrazo* than in *Osborn* itself had Marshall pretended that the treasurer in the bank case had been off on a frolic of his own. What he said was that the Governor in *Madrazo* had been named in his official capacity and that "no case is made which justifies a decree against him personally": "He has acted in obedience to a law of the state, . . . and has done nothing in violation of any law of the United States."[117] Why the Governor could not be personally liable for holding the plaintiff's property even if he had acted under a valid state law, Marshall did not say;[118] but it seems clear that nothing of the sort could have been said in either *Osborn* or *Lee*, where the government officers had taken the property in violation of law.[119]

---

without first determining the question of the state's title, and even then the government's right to sue the prevailing plaintiff (*see supra* note 108) will protect it from disseisin as it could not against dispossession. *See* United States v. Peters, 9 U.S. (5 Cranch) 115, 139 (1803): "it can never be alleged that a mere suggestion of title in a state to property, in possession of an individual, must arrest the proceedings of the court, and prevent their looking into the suggestion, and examining the validity of the title."

[114]The same was true of the initial injunction in *Osborn*, which the Court seemed also to approve; and if Gray did not concede the correctness of this order by his reference to injunctions "concerning money or property in which the state had an interest" (a clear reference to *Davis v. Gray*, conclusion to part four *supra*), he failed to distinguish it at all. Gray may have meant that the degree of interference with government had been less in *Osborn* because the property had not yet been put to actual governmental use, but that hardly seems to make the action any less one against the government: whatever the burden of coughing up the money was, it was the state and not the treasurer who bore it.

[115]26 U.S. (1 Pet.) 110 (1828). *See supra* chapter 4.

[116]106 U.S. at 245, emphasizing Marshall's statement that Madrazo sought money that had been "'mixed up with . . . general [state] funds'" and "'slaves in possession of the government,'" 26 U.S. (1 Pet.) at 123. Curiously, Gray downplayed the significance of this decision (saying it "does not appear to us to have any important bearing, except" for the point quoted in the text), since the distinction for which he cited the case was crucial to his argument.

[117]26 U.S. (1 Pet.) at 123-24.

[118]The simplest explanation would be that it cannot be tortious for an official to act "in obedience to a law of the state." *See* W. PROSSER, TORTS 127 (4th ed. 1971). *Cf.* the more modern doctrine of official immunity, *see* Spalding v. Vilas, 161 U.S. 483 (1896), though to apply that doctrine to relief not affecting the officer's own pocketbook would seem hard to justify in terms of its purpose of not deterring exercise of official duties. *See* Supreme Court of Virginia v. Consumers Union, 446 U.S. 719 (1980) (holding judges immune from injunction in rulemaking capacity but not in acting as prosecutors in disciplinary proceedings). Marshall had spoken of such an immunity in his *Osborn* opinion, 22 U.S. (9 Wheat.) at 865-66. *Cf.* the much criticized conclusion in Larson v. Domestic & Foreign Commerce Corp., 337 U.S. 682, 702 (1947), an injunction case not speaking of official immunity, that an officer's action would be considered individual and not sovereign "only if it is not within the officer's statutory powers or . . . if the powers . . . are constitutionally void." An alternative explanation is that the Governor did not have actual custody of any property belonging to the plaintiff.

[119]An argument for official immunity from damages can be made even in such a situation, see Butz v.

Gray's heroic effort thus seems to have come too late; the horse had left the barn in *Osborn*, and because of the precedents Gray was not prepared to follow the logic of his argument to its otherwise convincing conclusion.[120]

B. *Louisiana v. Jumel*

The very same Term, however, *Lee* was distinguished without adequate explanation in an important Waite opinion[121] whose spirit seemed more in keeping with the dissent the Chief Justice had joined in *Lee*.[122] Louisiana had welshed on contractual obligations to its bondholders, and the Court conceded that it had offended the contract clause.[123] Despite *Osborn* and *Lee*, the Court over strong dissents by Field and Harlan held that state officers could not be compelled to take a variety of actions or to refrain from others in order to assure payment of the state's obligations.[124]

"The question," said Waite, "is whether the contract can be enforced . . . by coercing the agents and officers of the State, whose authority has been withdrawn in violation of the contract, without the State in its political capacity being a party to the proceedings."[125] The answer was no; the reasons were obscure. Waite complained that the extensive relief sought, which included the collection and disbursement of a tax to pay off the bonds, would require the officers "to act contrary to the positive orders of the . . . State" and the court to "assure control of the administration of the affairs of the State,"[126] but he neglected to say why what was undesirable was also

---

Economou, 438 U.S. 478, 517 (1978) (Rehnquist, J., dissenting) (distinguishing injunctive relief or mandamus); but Marshall in *Madrazo* clearly based his conclusion that the officer could not be held liable on the fact that he had offended neither federal nor state law.

[120]Gray also invoked The Exchange, 11 U.S. (7 Cranch) 116 (1812), which had relied on sovereign immunity to preclude an action in rem to recover a ship alleged to have been wrongfully taken on the order of a foreign sovereign (106 U.S. at 235). Without suggesting a distinction between suing an officer and suing the ship itself (see Ex parte New York, 256 U.S. 503 (1921) (holding an in rem action against a state vessel barred in a case in which title was not disputed), Miller answered (106 U.S. 209) that cases involving foreign relations were distinguishable because based upon deference to "the political branch" in matters that "might involve war or peace." Though *The Exchange* had said in passing that such considerations were "of great weight," 11 U.S. (7 Cranch) at 146, that was not the basis of its holding; but its actual argument that the United States had implicitly promised not to assert jurisdiction over ships operated by foreign sovereigns by inviting them to our ports was equally inapplicable to a case like *Lee*.

[121]Louisiana v. Jumel, 107 U.S. 711 (1883).

[122]*See* C. JACOBS, *supra note* 99, at 121, terming *Jumel* and New Hampshire v. Louisiana, 108 U.S. 76 (1883) (Waite, C.J.), which unanimously denied a state standing to evade the eleventh amendment by suing on behalf of its citizens, a "turning point in the application . . . of sovereign immunity."

[123]107 U.S. at 719-21.

[124]The plaintiffs had asked that the defendants be enjoined from recognizing the validity of the impairing legislation, from ignoring the original law under which the bonds had been issued, and from obstructing its enforcement; that they be ordered to restore any money diverted from the purpose of paying interest, to apply available funds to the satisfaction of bond obligations, and to collect taxes for the same purpose in accord with the original legislation. *Id.* at 717-18.

[125]*Id.* at 721.

[126]*Id.* at 721, 722. *See also id.* at 727, adding that it would "require the court to assume all the executive authority of the State, so far as it related to the enforcement of this law, and to supervise the conduct of all persons charged with any official duty in respect to the levy, collection, and disbursement of the tax . . . ." These conclusions were facilitated by the conspicuous failure of the plaintiffs, noted by the Court at

impermissible.[127] He added that the officers were not trustees, that their duty was to the state alone, and that they had "no contract relations with the bondholders,"[128] but he did not say why any of this mattered. He distinguished *Osborn* because the money had not "become mixed" with other funds in the treasury and *Lee* because in *Jumel* the state had title and not merely possession.[129] He did not say why either title or commingling was relevant, and he made no direct effort to distinguish the relief sought in *Jumel* from the injunction against tax collection that *Osborn* had also allowed.

Field and Harlan, in separate dissenting opinions, made the obvious arguments from precedent[130] and protested with considerable justice that the decision effectively emasculated the contract clause.[131] That objection might more properly have been addressed to the Framers of the eleventh amendment, which the dissenters' own position equally emasculated; but so far as had yet appeared they seemed to have precedent on their side in performing that operation. Miller, it should be noted, joined the majority without explaining why the great principles of justice he had said in *Lee* required officers to disgorge land the government had taken did not also require them to honor the state's contractual obligations.

Marshall's *Madrazo* opinion was not cited, but it suggests a possible basis for distinction. Relief had been denied in *Madrazo* in part because there was no basis for an order against the Governor "personally." In *Osborn* and in *Lee* the officers had committed torts by unlawfully seizing or detaining the plaintiffs' property; an agent is liable for his own torts even if they are committed on behalf of his employer.[132] But an agent is not ordinarily liable on contracts made for his principal;[133] and, as Waite noted in *Jumel*, the bonds were contracts of the state: "[t]he officers . . . have no contract relations with the bondholders."[134] The problem was thus not that the suit was against the state, but that the officers were the wrong parties; more clearly than the Governor in *Madrazo*, they were not liable for what the state had done.[135] This

---

721-22, to ask directly "for the payment of the bonds and coupons they hold." In the context of the remedial difficulties suggested by the statement quoted at the beginning of this note, the failure of the plaintiffs to ask to be paid outright seems to be the basis for Waite's further announcement that they "do not occupy the position of creditors of the State demanding payment from an executive officer charged with the ministerial duty of taking the money from the state treasury and handing it over to them," *id.* at 727. One suspects, however, that the failure to make the most obvious plea for relief reflects an unexplained conviction that, despite the quoted reference to "creditors," it had no chance of succeeding.

[127]The supremacy clause would appear to dispel any concern about conflicts between state law and an order based on the federal Constitution; and Waite maintained that the illegality of such judicial displacement of "the political power" as the plaintiffs sought "needs no argument" (*id.* at 727-28).

[128]*Id.* at 722-23, 726.

[129]*Id.* at 724-27.

[130]*Id.* at 735-37 (Field, J.), 756-60 (Harlan, J.).

[131]*Id.* at 733 (Field, J.), 760 (Harlan, J.).

[132]*See* 1 F. MECHEM, A TREATISE ON THE LAW OF AGENCY, §§ 1452, 1455, 1457 (2d ed. 1914) (citing trespass and conversion cases).

[133]*See id.*, §§ 1357, 1406.

[134]107 U.S. at 723. *See also id.* at 721: "the State has violated its contract . . . ."

[135]*See* F. MECHEM, *supra* note 132, § 1482: "An agent is not usually liable to third persons for the breach of his principal's contracts with . . . third persons even though the performance of those contracts was confided to those agents by the principal." Story had drawn the same distinction in connection with suits against federal officers in 1833. 3 J. STORY, COMMENTARIES ON THE CONSTITUTION OF THE UNITED STATES, §

may explain why it mattered to Waite that, in contrast to *Lee*, the state had title to the money; for that meant the plaintiff's claim was in contract rather than in tort.[136] Significantly, Waite never invoked the eleventh amendment and never argued that the suit was one against the state; he may simply have concluded that the officers were not liable on the merits for the breach of a contract to which they were not parties.

The dissenters argued with some force that the officers were indeed liable because the original state statutes had given them ministerial duties enforceable by mandamus,[137] but they said nothing to impair Marshall's sensible distinction: the mere fact that a suit is not barred by the eleventh amendment does not justify relief against a person who has committed no actionable wrong.[138] Whether this really was the basis of *Jumel*, however, is not clear. The passages deploring the intrusiveness of the extensive relief sought suggest the narrower conclusion that the case failed simply because of the unavailability of such a sweeping remedy; the way the issue was

---

1671 (1933). Mechem reserved the question whether there might be a tort action by the third party against an agent who had *disabled* his principal from performing; but it had been the legislature's decision in *Jumel* to renege on the bonds.

[136]This may also explain why it mattered that the money in *Osborn* had not yet been commingled with other funds in the treasury: commingling might have destroyed a detinue claim by making it impossible to identify the particular dollars the officers had taken. See the quotation from *Osborn* in note 112 *supra*. As Waite said, the officer would remain liable for damages, but not for the return of the specific coins taken. 107 U.S. at 725. *See also id.*, explaining the injunction in *Davis v. Gray* (conclusion to part four *supra*) on the ground that the plaintiff had equitable title to the lands in question, which might mean the officer had committed a tort and not merely helped the state to break its contract when he transferred them to someone else; *id.* at 726, explaining *McComb* on the ground that the same officers sued in *Jumel* had been "trustees" of the bonds themselves in the earlier case—trustees can be sued by their beneficiaries.

[137]107 U.S. at 734, 737-38, 742-44 (Field, J.) (citing, inter alia, *Marbury v. Madison, supra* chapter 3); 747-48, 758-59, 764-67 (Harlan, J.). Waite answered with the conclusion that the officer's duty was owed only to his principal (*id.* at 723), citing an English case that Harlan plausibly distinguished (id. at 753). Although Mechem (*supra* note 132, § 1447) generally confirmed Waite's conclusion in the context of private agents given money to pay third parties, the mandamus cases cited by the dissenters suggest a different rule in public-officer cases, and by 1914 Mechem could report even in the private context a conflict of authority whether the agent could be held liable to the creditor on the theory that he was a third-party beneficiary of the contract between principal and agent (*id.*, § 1449). Waite also said the state had dissolved any duty on the officer by enacting the legislation repudiating the bonds (107 U.S. at 721); the dissenters responded that *McComb* had flatly declared that an unconstitutional law would not prevent mandamus (*see supra* note 100). Waite argued that only the repudiation itself and not the removal of the officers' duty was unconstitutional. Federal jurisdiction to grant mandamus even in a removed case otherwise within federal jurisdiction was doubtful in light of the ill-considered decision in McClung v. Silliman, 19 U.S. (6 Wheat.) 598 (1821) (mandamus case not within diversity jurisdiction), which Harlan did not deal with fairly in arguing (107 U.S. at 761-64) for jurisdiction; but this was an issue apart from either sovereign immunity or the merits.

In discussing English authorities, Harlan obliquely suggested as well that the officers were trustees of the bond money and thus suable by the beneficiaries (*id.* at 755). Waite responded rather lamely that the state itself was the trustee, if there was one, and that the officers were under no duty to separate the earmarked tax receipts from other funds in the state treasury (*id.* at 722-23, 726). The legislation provided that the tax revenue was "'set apart and appropriated to that purpose [bond payment] and no other.'" 107 U.S. at 737 (Field, J., dissenting). *See* F. MECHEM, *supra* note 132, § 1450: "whether a mere revocable agency or an irrevocable trust has been created seems to depend on the intention of the principal . . . . Where a trust has been created, it may be enforced by the beneficiary as in other cases."

[138]*See* C. JACOBS, supra n. 99, at 103-05, taking the same view of *Madrazo*.

phrased hints at the broader conclusion that the Court thought a federal court lacked authority *ever* to "enforce[]" a state's contract "by coercing" its "agents and officers." That a court was not bound to grant the most extreme relief requested[139] and that the argument of practical effect on the government had been rejected in *Osborn* and *Lee* prove only that Marshall's liability argument was the most acceptable justification for *Jumel*, not that it was the actual basis of the Court's unusually uninformative opinion.

C. *The Virginia Coupon Cases*

Louisiana was not the only southern state to renege on bonds issued by her Reconstruction government; a series of 1885 cases involving similar efforts by Virginia[140] starkly confronted the Court with the question of just what it had meant in *Jumel*. Virginia had promised not simply to repay the funds invested in her bonds but to accept interest coupons in payment of taxes, yet in accord with later statutes her tax collectors had rejected the tender of coupons and begun to enforce the tax against bondholders by seizing their assets. Relying on *Osborn* and *Lee*, the Court in a turgid set of opinions by Justice Matthews managed to allow three distinct remedies against the offending officials: injunctions against the further seizure of assets,[141] damages for the harm done by past seizures,[142] and restoration of property unlawfully taken.[143]

The principle governing all three cases was stated in *Poindexter v. Greenhow*. The tax collector, like the officers in *Osborn* and *Lee*, had committed or threatened to commit a tort by taking the plaintiff's property; he had no defense because the state law purporting to authorize his action offended the contract clause;[144] and the action

---

[139]107 U.S. at 751 (Harlan, J., dissenting). An injunction against diversion of the funds to other uses, clearly embraced in the prayer for relief (*see supra* note 124), would have been closely analogous in remedial terms to the relief upheld in *McComb* and in *Davis*.

[140]Virginia Coupon Cases, 114 U.S. 269 (1885) (all written by Matthews, J.).

[141]Allen v. Baltimore & O. R.R., 114 U.S. 311 (1885).

[142]White v. Greenhow, 114 U.S. 307 (1885); Chaffin v. Taylor, 114 U.S. 309 (1885).

[143]Poindexter v. Greenhow, 114 U.S. 270 (1885).

[144]*Id.* at 282-83, 288-90. It was in this context that Matthews made the statement, made famous when repeated in Ex parte Young, 209 U.S. 123, 160 (1908), that because of the unconstitutionality of the state law the officer stood "stripped of his official character," 114 U.S. at 288. Notably problematic was Matthews's further effort, *id.* at 290-93, to justify the *Osborn* principle as an original matter on the ground that, because the state was forbidden to impair contracts, no impairment was the act of the state. This would mean there was no such thing as violation of the contract clause, or of the fourteenth amendment either, since both applied only to state action; and Bradley rightly protested in dissent that "to say that it is not the State that acts is to make a misuse of terms" when what was meant was that the state had acted unconstitutionally (*id.* at 335). There was no such difficulty with the original thesis of *Osborn*: since the agent's liability seems to have been based not on the state's infraction of the Constitution but on the agent's own common-law tort (*see* H. Hart & H. Wechsler, The Federal Courts and the Federal System 930-36 (2d ed. 1973)), *Osborn* does not present the contradictory spectacle of treating the officer as if he were the state for substantive purposes but not in determining jurisdiction. This point was emphasized by *Poindexter*'s companion case of Carter v. Greenhow, 114 U.S. 317, 322 (1885), where a trespass action like that upheld in White v. Greenhow, *supra* note 124, was held not to fall within the statute (now 28 U.S.C. § 1343 (3)) giving federal courts jurisdiction of actions to redress the deprivation, under color of state law, of "any rights, privileges or immunities secured by the Constitution . . . ." Though the Court's reasoning seems somewhat off the point, the decision shows that the sole function of the contract clause in

was "not an attempt to compel officers of the State to do the acts which constitute a performance of its contract . . . ."[145] The last statement would have provided a basis for distinguishing *Jumel* on the ground that officers were not liable for breach of contract, but it was not so used; *Jumel* was cavalierly distinguished on the ground that the present actions were "not for the purpose of controlling the discretion of executive officers, or administering funds actually in the public treasury."[146]

Two years earlier, Miller, who had written *Lee*, had said in dictum essentially what Matthews said in *Poindexter*.[147] Now, however, he joined Bradley, Waite, and Gray in arguing that all of the *Coupon Cases* were "virtually suits against the State of Virginia to compel a specific performance by the State of her agreement" and thus forbidden by the eleventh amendment.[148] The difficulty was that it had been equally true in both *Lee* and *Osborn* that the suit was "virtually" against the government, and the Court had nevertheless allowed relief because the officer himself had committed a wrong. To get around the precedents, Bradley argued that a citizen could sue an officer only "where the State or its officers moves against *him*," and not "to coerce the State into a fulfilment of its contracts."[149] But Bradley's categories were not mutually exclusive;[150] *Poindexter* and its companion cases involved efforts to coerce contract compliance by remedying or preventing official seizure of property. Significantly, Bradley made no reference to *Jumel*, which because of its vague

---

White was to invalidate a defense based on the unconstitutional statute, not to provide the plaintiff with a cause of action.

[145]114 U.S. at 293.

[146]*Id.*

[147]Cunningham v. Macon & Brunswick R.R., 109 U.S. 446, 452 (1883), explaining that in cases like *Lee* the officer "is not sued as, or because he is, the officer of the government, but as an individual, and the court is not ousted of jurisdiction because he *asserts* authority as such officer. To make out his defence he must show that his authority was sufficient in law to protect him." *See also id.* at 456. The discussion of authority as a defense reinforces the hypothesis in note 118 *supra* as to the reason the Governor could not be held personally liable in *Madrazo*. Miller's explanation of why the case before him was different from *Lee* seemed to suggest the nonliability theory discussed in connection with *Jumel*: describing the action as one to foreclose a mortgage on state property, he said the state was not only an indispensable party but "the only proper defendant," because "[n]o one sued has any personal interest in the matter or any official authority to grant the relief asked" (109 U.S. at 456-57). Harlan and Field, dissenting, argued that, as in *Osborn* and *Lee*, the plaintiff had also attacked the transaction by which the state had sought to acquire the property (*id.* at 458-64), and Miller's own statement of the case seems to support that interpretation (*id.* at 448). On this view the result but not the reasoning of *Cunningham* was a step away from Miller's own position in *Lee*.

[148]114 U.S. at 330-31, 332-33 (Bradley, J., dissenting). There were two technical difficulties with the application of the eleventh amendment to *Poindexter*, which had been brought in state court by a citizen of Virginia, *id.* at 273, for the amendment limits only "the Judicial power of the United States" and applies only to suits brought "by Citizens of *another* State . . . or Foreign State." Matthews did not exploit these difficulties but treated the case as if the amendment applied. Bradley, anticipating an argument soon to be adopted by the Court (Hans v. Louisiana, 134 U.S. 1 (1890)), argued that the reason the amendment had not limited suits against a state by its own citizens was that "the judicial power was not granted to the United States by the original Constitution in such cases" (114 U.S. at 337-38). He said nothing about the fact that the action had been brought in state court; but the eleventh amendment on its face seems to limit the Supreme Court's power to review a case within its terms regardless of the court in which it is originally brought.

[149]*Id.* at 336, also distinguishing between "cases of State aggression" and "of refusal to fulfill obligations."

[150]*See* C. JACOBS, *supra* note 99, at 125.

reasoning could have been argued to support a general inability to give relief having the effect of specific performance; instead he rather feebly argued that the tender of coupons had not extinguished the tax liability but only given the taxpayer a setoff against the state's claim, so that the seizure of his property was not tortious at all.[151] It was still not entirely clear whether *Jumel* was based on the nonliability of the defendants or on the impropriety of the requested remedy; but neither the majority nor the dissenters in the Virginia cases seemed to think it meant the courts could never take action against officers that would effectively hold the states to their contracts.

D.   *Hagood v. Southern* and *In re Ayers*

In the next case, in 1886, it was South Carolina that had refused to honor its bonds, and Matthews wrote for the Court once again.[152] This time, however, the result was different.

In *Hagood* the essential relief sought was not to prevent or to redress a tort committed by the officer in the name of tax collection but, as in *Jumel*, to compel the officer to take affirmative action by levying taxes to pay off its obligations.[153] Even in *Poindexter*, Matthews had distinguished cases involving "an attempt to compel officers to do the acts which constitute a performance of its contract," and *Hagood*, like *Jumel*, was such a case: the state was "the actual party to the alleged contract the performance of which is decreed, the one required to perform the decree, and the only party by whom it can be performed."[154] The governing distinction was restated:

> A broad line of demarcation separates from such cases as the present, in which the decrees require, by affirmative official action on the part of the defendants, the performance of an obligation which belongs to the State in its political capacity, those in which actions at law or suits in equity are maintained against defendants who, while claiming to act as officers of the State, violate and invade the personal and property rights of the plaintiffs, under color or authority, unconstitutional and void.[155]

[151]114 U.S. at 333-34.

[152]Hagood v. Southern, 117 U.S. 52 (1886).

[153]*See id.* at 58-59, 65-67. There were also prayers requesting injunctions against seizure of property in satisfaction of taxes after tender of "revenue bond scrip," as in the Virginia cases, but the Court held that none of the plaintiffs had standing to seek such relief: only one had tendered coupons in payment of taxes, and the bonds had been issued as security for that plaintiff's own debt; to give the principal debtor rights against his surety was "to reverse the order of the obligation" and "to convert [a] debtor into a creditor" (*id.* at 63-65).

[154]*Id.* at 67, adding that "these suits are accurately described as bills for the specific performance of a contract between the complainants and the State of South Carolina, who are the only parties to it" and that "the things required by the decrees to be done" "are the very things which, when done . . . , constitute a performance of the alleged contract by the State." On the following page Matthews declared that "[t]he case thus comes directly within the authority of *Louisiana vs. Jumel* . . . ." *See also id.* at 70, quoting *Jumel*'s statement that the officers "'have no contract relations with the bondholders.'"

[155]*Id.* at 70. Harlan and Field, adhering to their view that *Jumel* had been wrongly decided, agreed (*id.* at 71) that it was indistinguishable.

In light of *Poindexter* and *McComb*, which *Hagood* expressly reaffirmed,[156] Matthew's references to specific performance could not be read as adopting the argument that every order having the *effect* of enforcing a state contract was forbidden, and his new and influential term "affirmative official action"[157] did not include either mandamus[158] or restoration of property illegally held. The absence of any renewed argument that the relief sought would involve administering the state's executive branch[159] and the repeated emphasis on the fact that only the state was party to the contract strongly suggest that Matthews was explaining both *Hagood* and *Jumel* on the ground that there was no basis on which to hold the officer responsible for the breach, but he did not quite say so. In fact, he injected an interesting new twist borrowed from the dissenters in the Virginia cases[160] that shifted attention away from substantive liability and back to the *Osborn* question of state immunity: because the state was "the real party against which relief is sought, . . . the suit is . . . substantially within the prohibition of the XIth amendment. . . ."[161] This change in emphasis may seem minor, but it deprived the Court's theory of the power of reconciling the cases. To say that an officer could not be held responsible unless he had committed a wrong was almost self-evident; to say the suit was against the state because the officer was not liable contradicted *Osborn*'s principle that no one was a party who had not been sued.

That this was indeed the Court's theory was finally confirmed in yet another Matthews opinion in the climactic 1887 case of *In re Ayers*, holding despite *Poindexter* that a Virginia officer could not be enjoined from *suing* to collect taxes after tender of the coupons the state had agreed to accept as payment:[162]

> The action has been sustained only in those instances where the act complained of, considered apart from the official authority alleged as its justification, and as the personal act of the individual defendant, constituted a violation of right for which the plaintiff was entitled to a remedy at law or in equity against the wrongdoer in his individual character.
>
> The present case stands upon a footing altogether different. . . . The acts alleged in the bill as threatened by the defendants . . . are violations of the assumed contract between the State of Virginia and the complainants, only as they are considered to be the acts of the State of Virginia. *The defendants, as individuals, not being parties to that contract, are not capable in law of committing a breach of it. . . .*

[156]*Id.* at 69-71.

[157]*See* Larson v. Domestic & Foreign Commerce Corp., 337 U.S. 682, 691 n.11 (1949) (dictum): "a suit may fail, as one against the sovereign, even if it is claimed that the officer being sued has acted unconstitutionally or beyond his statutory powers, if the relief requested can not be granted by merely ordering the cessation of the conduct complained of but will require affirmative action by the sovereign or the disposition of unquestionably sovereign property."

[158]*See also* Cunningham v. Macon & Brunswick R.R., *supra* note 147, 109 U.S. at 452-53, 456 (dictum) (cited approvingly 117 U.S. at 69), declaring that mandamus would lie in a proper case because the law imposed on the official a duty to act affirmatively in favor of a third party.

[159]The relevant language from *Jumel* was quoted, 117 U.S. at 68, but in the context of the statement that *Jumel* was in point because the suit was one for specific performance.

[160]*See supra* note 148.

[161]117 U.S. at 67.

[162]123 U.S. 443, 450 (1887).

[F]or the reasons given, we adjudge the suit . . . in which the injunctions were granted against the present petitioners, to be in substance and in law a suit against the State of Virginia. It is, therefore, within the prohibition of the 11th Amendment . . . .[163]

Matthews conceded that this conclusion was contrary to what Marshall had said in *Osborn*, but he said Marshall had taken that back in *Madrazo*, where he had said that when "'there is no [other] party against whom a decree can be made,'" "'the State itself may be considered as a party on the record.'"[164] The quotation is accurate, but, unlike the alternative suggestion in the same opinion that the Governor was not liable on the merits for detaining the plaintiff's property, it makes Marshall himself appear inconsistent: the real-party-in-interest theory should have barred *Osborn* as well as *Madrazo*, since the effect of the action in either case was to dispossess the government. Logic as well as consistency supports the alternative explanation: if no defendant has committed an actionable wrong, the thing to do is to dismiss on the merits, not to pretend that the suit is against someone who has not been sued.[165]

Whether the proper theory was immunity or nonliability, however, the challenge to the Court in *Ayers* was to show why, if seizing the taxpayer's property was a tort, suing to acquire the same property was not. In part the answer was that the plaintiffs had no standing to object because they had not tendered coupons or been threatened with suit.[166] More fundamentally, however, the Court also concluded that the mere filing of suit violated no right of the coupon-holder himself because he retained the right to raise his tender as a defense; "it is not to be assumed in advance" that such a defense would be erroneously rejected.[167] Matthews seemed to invoke the familiar principle that to institute a losing lawsuit is not itself unlawful unless malicious;[168] and

---

[163]*Id*. at 502-03, 507 (emphasis added). Field, explaining his earlier dissent in *Jumel* on the ground that the state had there consented that its officers might be sued, concurred on grounds broad enough to overrule *Osborn* itself: "To enjoin the officers of the Commonwealth, charged with the supervision and management of legal proceedings in her behalf, from bringing suits in her name, is nothing less than to enjoin the Commonwealth, for only by her officers can such suits be instituted and prosecuted." *Id*. at 508-10. That a consenting state could be sued had been established in Clark v. Barnard, 108 U.S. 436, 447-48 (1883) (Matthews, J.), on the sensible basis that, despite the ostensibly absolute language of the amendment, the immunity it gave a state was "a personal privilege which it may waive at pleasure." *Cf*. chapter 4 *supra*, discussing *Bank of Columbia v. Okely* (jury trial); Neirbo Co. v. Bethlehem Shipbuilding Corp., 308 U.S. 165, 167-68 (1939) (venue limitation lost unless raised because it "relates to the convenience of litigants"). Immunity had been waivable in England, *see supra* text accompanying note 103.

[164]123 U.S. at 487-89, quoting from 26 U.S. (1 Pet.) at 123-24.

[165]There was a practical reason why it was necessary for Matthews to cast his distinction in jurisdictional rather than substantive terms in *Ayers*: the case was before him on petition for habeas corpus on behalf of an official imprisoned for disobeying the injunction, and habeas lay to attack a judgment only if the convicting court had lacked jurisdiction. *See* 123 U.S. at 485-87. It would nevertheless seem unfair to conclude this was why Matthews elected to adopt the eleventh-amendment approach; he had already done so in *Hagood v. Southern, supra* note 161, where the Court's authority to review the original order did not depend on a jurisdictional classification.

[166]123 U.S. at 496. *Cf. supra* note 153, noting a similar holding in *Hagood*.

[167]*Id*. at 494-95. *See also id*. at 509 (Field, J., concurring).

[168]*See* C. JACOBS, *supra* note 99, at 131: "If *Ayers* means anything, it is that mere institution of proceedings by a state officer in state courts is not tortious, despite the unconstitutionality of the legislation for which enforcement was sought."

although *Ayers* looks today like a textbook instance of malicious prosecution in light of *Poindexter*'s holding that the state had no right to reject the coupons, it seems that the extension of that tort to the filing of civil cases had not yet been accomplished at the time of that decision.[169] All Harlan could do in solitary dissent was to protest, as he had in *Jumel*, that the decision allowed the states to violate the Constitution with impunity;[170] but that hardly seemed a sufficient reason to enjoin an officer from committing an act that did not violate the plaintiff's rights.

Thus by the end of Waite's tenure the Court had slowly worked its way to a clear and comprehensible theory for determining when a state or federal officer could be sued in federal court and when he could not.[171] The problem was not easy, and the Court's test was not self-applying, as *Jumel* and *Poindexter* both show. Despite his crying need for a good editor, Justice Matthews, with much help from Miller, deserves considerable credit for having wrestled with the problem until he had developed a principle that came close not only to explaining the cases but also to providing an impeccable justification for the otherwise perplexing distinctions the Court had drawn. It is a shame, however, that the very same breath that finally fully articulated this principle also transformed it into one that seemed internally inconsistent and that bore no perceptible relation to the purpose of the amendment whose scope it was now said to define.[172]

---

[169]*See* W. Prosser, Torts 850-53 (4th ed. 1971).

[170]123 U.S. at 515-16.

[171]*But see* Orth, *The Interpretation of the Eleventh Amendment, 1798-1908: A Case Study of Judicial Power*, 1983 U. Ill. L.R. 423, 429, 449, arguing that *Madrazo* had not significantly qualified *Osborn*, that the decisions of the Waite period substantially departed from Marshall's view, and that their cause was the knowledge that decrees against Southern officials at that time could not have been enforced.

[172]Apart from the immunity cases and the federal-question issues mentioned *supra* in chapter 11 in connection with the power to enforce the fourteenth amendment, there were few significant decisions respecting the powers of federal courts during the Waite period. *See also* The Lottawanna, 88 U.S. (21 Wall.) 558, 574-75 (1875) (Bradley, J.), declaring that article III's provision extending the judicial power to admiralty cases contemplated uniform application of "[t]he general system of maritime law" rather than state law; Börs v. Preston, 111 U.S. 252 (1884) (Harlan, J.), holding the Constitution's grant of original Supreme Court jurisdiction not exclusive; Pacific R.R. Removal Cases, 115 U.S. 1 (1885) (Bradley, J.), reaffirming the principle of *Osborn v. Bank of the United States (supra* chapter 4) that any suit by or against a federal corporation arose under federal law; Wisconsin v. Pelican Ins. Co., 127 U.S. 265 (1888) (Gray, J.), holding that article III's provisions for Supreme Court jurisdiction of "Controversies" between a state and citizens of another state was limited to civil cases and thus did not include a suit to recover on a judgment entered in an action the Court deemed "penal"; and the unconstitutional-condition cases mentioned *supra* note 74. With *Börs* compare *Marbury v. Madison (supra* chapter 3); with *Pelican* compare *Cohens v. Virginia (supra* chapter 4).

13

The Powers of Congress

An important series of decisions during the Waite period, considered in connection with the civil-war amendments in chapter 11, passed upon the enforcement powers given by those amendments to Congress. Other enumerated congressional powers were the subject of a handful of interesting if less earthshaking decisions in this period, and in a few of those cases the Justices enunciated surprisingly broad views of inherent federal powers. In *Kilbourn v. Thompson*, however, the Court appeared to recede from a decision of the Marshall era in giving a narrow scope to congressional powers to investigate and to punish for contempt. Finally, at the very end of Waite's term—and of its first century—the Court at last began to give content to several central provisions of the Bill of Rights that limited congressional authority.

I. Enumerated and Implied Powers

A.   Interstate and Foreign Commerce

As usual, the commerce clause figured prominently in the decisions of the Waite period respecting congressional authority. The first two commerce clause decisions seemed to follow easily from *Gibbons v. Ogden*,[1] where the Marshall Court had unsurprisingly upheld federal power to license interstate steamboats and confirmed that the power was limited to commerce affecting more than one state. In *Pensacola Tel. Co. v. Western Union Tel. Co.* in 1878, Chief Justice Waite wrote a neat little opinion citing *Gibbons* and explaining why Congress had like power to authorize the operation of an interstate telegraph, pointing out—as had also been illustrated by *Gibbons*—that Congress's power was not limited to means of communication that

---

[1] *See supra* chapter 6.

had existed when the Constitution was adopted.[2] The only peculiar features of the case were Waite's failure to rely on *Gibbons* for his further conclusion that a state-granted monopoly was overridden by federal authorization[3] and Field's unaccountable dissenting insistence that *Bank of Augusta v. Earle*,[4] which had involved neither interstate commerce nor a statute granting federal permission, had held the states had complete authority to exclude foreign corporations.[5]

The second case presented the other side of the coin. In the *Trade-Mark Cases* in 1879, with Justice Miller writing, the Court predictably struck down an act of Congress purporting to regulate trademarks throughout the United States because it was not limited to those used in interstate or foreign commerce.[6] Again, the oddest aspect of the opinion was the neglect of pertinent authority: a few years earlier the Court had reached the same conclusion as to a statute regulating the composition of lighting oils.[7]

[2]96 U.S. 1, 9, 11 (1878), citing *Gibbons*: "commercial intercourse is an element of commerce . . . ." For an approving early view, *see* Wintersteen, *The Commerce Clause and the State*, 28 AM. L. REG. (N.S.) 733, 736 (1889), noting that the scope of the power had not expanded but only the occasions for its exercise. The Court also relied (96 U.S. at 9-10) on Congress's power "to establish Post Offices and post Roads," U.S. CONST. art. I, § 8, which it sensibly said were "established to facilitate the transmission of intelligence." *Cf.* chapter 8 *supra*, discussing *Searight v. Stokes*; California v. Central Pac. R.R., 127 U.S. 1, 39-40 (1888) (Bradley, J.), upholding congressional power to charter interstate railroads.

[3]96 U.S. at 11-12, construing the federal statute giving any telegraph company "the right to construct, maintain, and operate lines of telegraph" (*id.* at 3) as a declaration "that the erection of telegraph lines shall, so far as State interference is concerned, be free to all who will submit to the conditions imposed by Congress . . . ." *Cf.* Gibbons v. Ogden, 22 U.S. (9 Wheat.) 1, 213 (1824): "a license to do any particular thing, is a permission or authority . . . ." Field and Hunt, dissenting, argued with some degree of strain that the statute authorized telegraph operation only on the public domain although it expressly mentioned post roads (which included all railroads) as well, and although the telegraph in question was along a railroad right of way. *See* 96 U.S. at 3-5, 16-17, 24.

[4]*See supra* chapter 8.

[5]96 U.S. at 19-24, also invoking *Paul v. Virginia*, *supra* chapters 8, 10. Waite made the appropriate reply, 96 U.S. at 12-13. *See* F. FRANKFURTER, THE COMMERCE CLAUSE UNDER MARSHALL, TANEY AND WAITE 103-09 (1937), terming the decision obvious and Field's views "anachronistic." Professor Pomeroy, however, writing at the time of the *Pensacola* decision, was sympathetic to Field's position. *See* Pomeroy, *The Power of Congress to Regulate Interstate Commerce*, 4 So. L. REV. (N.S.) 357, 395-97 (1878).

[6]100 U.S. 82, 96-98 (1879). There were no dissents. As early as 1838 the Court had held Congress had authority under the necessary and proper clause to protect interstate or foreign commerce against theft by persons not themselves engaged in commerce (*United States v. Coombs, supra* chapters 7, 8), and the same theory should have supported protecting trademarks used in commerce against infringement by local competitors. But the statute forbade infringement of marks that were not used in interstate or foreign commerce at all. The argument that the statute should be upheld as applied to marks that *were* so used failed for the good reason that there were inadequate allegations in the present cases of interstate or foreign use (100 U.S. at 98; *see id.* at 82-83, revealing only that in two of the three cases the mark was owned by a foreign manufacturer) and for the inferior reason of the narrow view of severability adopted in *United States v. Reese, supra* chapter 11 (100 U.S. at 98-99).

[7]*United States v. Dewitt*, discussed in the conclusion to part four *supra*. *See* Wintersteen, *supra* note 2, 28 AM. L. REG. (N.S.) at 747. Miller expressly reserved the question whether a trademark law not limited to interstate or foreign commerce might be justified as necessary and proper to implement a treaty protecting the rights of foreign nationals (100 U.S. at 99; *cf.* Missouri v. Holland, 252 U.S. 416 (1920) (holding treaty power not limited to subjects within enumerated powers of Congress)); though counsel had made such an argument in passing (100 U.S. at 88), Miller professed that no such question was presented (*id.* at 93). A better response might have been that, as he had said in connection with the commerce clause argument (*see supra* note 6), the statute was broader than the treaty power could justify. For the fate of an argument based on the copyright clause, *see infra* text accompanying notes 32-36.

The next case was more doubtful. With Waite writing again, *Lord v. Steamship Co.* in 1881 unanimously upheld application of a federal law limiting shipowners' liability to a vessel traveling on the high seas between two points in the same state.[8] Although the case concerned the relationship between American cargo owners and an American ship that never touched at a foreign port,[9] the Court held the vessel was engaged in "commerce with foreign nations," essentially because of the risk in such a voyage of conflict with foreign interests: "If in her navigation she inflicted a wrong on another country, the United States, and not the State of California, must answer for what was done."[10] This rationale would clearly support federal imposition of safety measures, and of liability for their violation, on all ships in waters where foreign commerce was carried on; and there was uncited authority for congressional power to protect commerce from interference by persons not themselves engaged in interstate or foreign operations.[11] But *limiting* the liability of local ships would hardly seem conducive to the safety of foreign commerce even if liability for a collision with a foreign ship were in issue, which it was not; it is hard to see how the regulation in issue bore any relation to the dangers of foreign conflict on which the opinion relied. At one point the Court did note that the ship was outside the boundaries of any state,[12] perhaps implying that California law could not reach the case; but there seemed to be nothing in the federal Constitution to limit California's authority to apply her law to a transaction so intimately concerned with California interests,[13] and if there had been it still would have been hard to fit a case not involving a foreign nation into a grant of federal power expressly applicable only to commerce "with foreign Nations."[14]

In the *Head Money Cases* in 1884 Justice Miller wrote to hold that Congress could tax shipowners for alien passengers brought into this country.[15] As he said, the logic of *Henderson v. Mayor of New York*[16] seemed to compel this conclusion: the reason the states could not tax such passengers was that to do so was to regulate foreign commerce.[17] It was nevertheless startling to discover that the power to regulate

[8]102 U.S. 541 (1881).

[9]*Id.* at 542.

[10]*Id.* at 544.

[11]*United States v. Coombs, supra* chapters 7, 8 (theft of shipwrecked goods).

[12]102 U.S. at 544.

[13]*Cf.* Alaska Packers Ass'n v. Industrial Acc. Comm'n, 294 U.S. 532 (1935) (upholding application of California compensation law to Alaska accident involving employee hired in California). Earlier cases had reflected a more strictly territorial view, *see* R. CRAMTON, D. CURRIE, and H. KAY, CONFLICT OF LAWS—CASES, COMMENTS, QUESTIONS, ch. 3 (3d ed. 1981), but none of them had been decided by 1881, none involved facts occurring outside of any state or country, and the Court in *Lord* did not refer to the due process clause, on which the later decisions relied.

[14]Later cases developed the better theory that a limitation law was necessary and proper to the implementation of the admiralty jurisdiction of the federal courts (U.S. CONST., art. III, § 1), which administered a federal common law that the Framers could hardly have meant to be incapable of legislative improvement. *See, e.g.*, Detroit Trust Co. v. The Thomas Barlum, 293 U.S. 21, 42-45 (1934) (dictum) (upholding a ship-mortgage law on the same theory); Lehigh Valley R.R. v. Pennsylvania, 145 U.S. 192, 203 (1892), explaining *Lord* on this ground.

[15]112 U.S. 580.

[16]*See supra* chapter 12.

[17]112 U.S. at 590-93. *See* T. POWELL, VAGARIES AND VARIETIES IN CONSTITUTIONAL INTERPRETATION 64-65 (1956).

commerce included the power to tax it. Marshall had said in *McCulloch v. Maryland* that the tax power could not be incidental to another power,[18] and since the raising of revenue needed to finance any legitimate federal activity would be equally necessary and proper to the exercise of some substantive power, Miller's theory seemed to mean the tax power need not have been expressly conferred at all.[19] More interesting still was his further conclusion that because the fee had been imposed under the commerce power it did not, like a tax, have to promote the general welfare;[20] one might have thought the purpose of this limitation was to restrict the ends for which federal revenue could be collected and that it could not be evaded by labeling the exaction as an exercise of some other power.[21]

B. Indians

The final commerce-clause case of the period is the most interesting, but not because of what the Court said about the commerce clause itself. Congress had outlawed

---

[18]17 U.S. (4 Wheat.) 316, 411 (1819): "The power of creating a corporation . . . is not, like the power of making war, or levying taxes, or of regulating commerce, a great substantive and independent power, which cannot be implied as incidental to other powers, or used as a means of executing them."

[19]It might therefore have been better in *Henderson* to have avoided the conclusion that taxation was itself regulation; it would have sufficed to say the commerce clause precluded the states from passing any measure that interfered unduly with the Framers' goal of freedom of commerce.

[20]112 U.S. at 595-96. *See* U.S. CONST., art. I, § 8: "The Congress shall have Power to lay and collect Taxes, Duties, Imposts and Excises, to pay the Debts and provide for the common Defence and general Welfare of the United States; but all Duties, Imports, and Excises shall be uniform throughout the United States . . . ." Counsel had argued that because some of the funds collected were to be used to support indigent immigrants (*see* 112 U.S. at 590) the tax was "for the benefit of a few individuals, in a limited locality," and thus did not promote "the general Welfare" (112 U.S. at 582). Though he found it unnecessary to decide whether the general-welfare test was met, Miller suggested without elaboration that "it would not be difficult" to do so (*id.* at 595). Easiest to sustain on this basis would have been the portion of tax moneys going to defray expenses of inspecting immigrants (*id.* at 590), which were not only of general in the sense of national benefit but also incidental to the specifically granted power to regulate foreign commerce. Perhaps the care of needy immigrants could be defended on the same basis; if not the Court would have had to deal with Madison's plausible argument that "general welfare" was a shorthand reference to the enumerated objects of federal authority. *See* United States v. Butler, 297 U.S. 1, 65-66 (1936) (dictum), where the Madison view was finally rejected; Articles of Confederation, art. 8, where the same term was used simply in connection with a designation of the sources of funds to discharge otherwise legitimate debts and not to expand congressional spending power.

[21]*Cf.* Railway Labor Executives' Ass'n v. Gibbons, 455 U.S. 457, 468-69 (1982), holding the bankruptcy clause requirement of uniformity (U.S. CONST. art. I, § 8) could not be evaded by passing a disuniform law under the commerce clause: "if we were to hold that Congress had the power to enact nonuniform bankruptcy laws pursuant to the Commerce Clause, we would eradicate from the Constitution a limitation on the power of Congress to enact bankruptcy laws." Whether the uniformity clause was really offended by the law in *Gibbons* is a separate and more debatable question. *See* Baird, *Bankruptcy Procedure and State-Created Rights: The Lessons of Gibbons and Marathon*, 1982 SUP. CT. REV. 25, 30-36.

Miller did squarely hold, however, that the exaction in the *Head Money Cases* met the further requirement (*see supra* note 20) that an excise be "uniform throughout the United States," although it was to be collected only where immigrants were landed by ship: "The tax is uniform when it operates with the same force and effect in every place where the subject of it is found." 112 U.S. at 594. *Cf. Woodruff v. Parham, supra* chapter 10, where Miller had taken a similarly formal view of the question whether a state tax discriminated against interstate commerce, in the teeth of a dissent showing how a facially nondiscriminatory exaction could be used to disadvantage producers of goods produced only in other states.

murder of one Indian by another on Indian reservations within the states as well as the territories, and the Court upheld the statute in *United States v. Kagama* in 1886.[22] Rejecting the temptation to read the Indian commerce clause as general authority to regulate Indian affairs—which in light of the special status of the Indians might not have been implausible—[23] Miller stuck to a literal reading: murder between Indians on a reservation had nothing to do with commerce.[24] Nor did Miller argue directly that federal legislation was necessary either to implement implicit treaty obligations to protect the Indians[25] or to tidy up conditions resulting in or from Indian wars,[26] or that the United States had retained sufficient interest in lands reserved for the Indians that Congress could legislate for reservation government under the property clause of article IV.[27] Instead he insisted that Congress had a general power over Indian affairs that he made no real effort to locate in any clause of the Constitution:

> The power of the General Government over these remnants of a race once powerful, now weak and diminished in numbers, is necessary to

[22]118 U.S. 375 (1886).

[23]*Cf.* F. COHEN, HANDBOOK OF FEDERAL INDIAN LAW 92 (1941): "The commerce clause in the field of Indian affairs was for many decades broadly interpreted to include not only transactions by which Indians sought to dispose of land or other property in exchange for money, liquor, munitions, or other goods, but also aspects of intercourse which had little or no relation to commerce, such as travel, crimes by whites against Indians or Indians against whites, survey of land, trespass and settlement by whites in the Indian country, the fixing of boundaries, and the furnishing of articles, services and money by federal government." None of these examples, however, had to do with purely internal Indian affairs.

[24]118 U.S. at 378-79:

> [W]e think it would be a very strained construction of this clause, that a system of criminal laws for Indians living peaceably in their reservations, which left out the entire code of trade and intercourse laws justly enacted under that provision, and established punishments for the common-law crimes of murder, manslaughter, arson, burglary, larceny, and the like, without any reference to their relation to any kind of commerce, was authorized by the grant of power to regulate commerce with the Indian tribes.

[25]*See* Rice, *The Position of the American Indians in the Law of the United States*, 16 J. COMP. LEG. 78, 80-81 (3d series 1934): "by a broad reading of these treaties the national government obtained from the Indians themselves authority to legislate for them to carry out the purpose of the treaties." *Cf. Worcester v. Georgia, supra* chapter 6, taking the easier step of holding treaties implicitly forbade state interference with tribal autonomy. One cryptic sentence in *Kagama* could be taken to suggest this approach: "From [the Indians'] very weakness and helplessness, so largely due to the course of dealing of the Federal Government with them and the treaties in which it has been promised, there arises a duty of protection, and with it the power." 118 U.S. at 384. But the stress in this oblique reference to treaties was on the Indians' dependence, not on the treaties themselves, and the treaty theme was nowhere further developed.

[26]*See* F. COHEN, *supra* note 23, at 93-94; "In international law conquest brings legal power to govern." *Cf. supra* chapter 9, discussing the argument that federal administration of Southern states after the Civil War was justified by Congress's war powers.

[27]"The Congress shall have Power to dispose of and make all needful Rules and Regulations respecting the Territory or other Property belonging to the United States . . . ." Indeed, Miller went so far as to disparage the relevance of this clause even to support the validity of the statute as applied to reservations within the *territories*, saying, in terms reminiscent of the *Dred Scott* case (*supra* chapter 8) but without citing it, that the power to govern territories "arises not so much from" article IV "as from the ownership of the country in which the Territories are, and the rights of exclusive sovereignty which must exist in the National Government, and can be found nowhere else." 118 U.S. at 380. *See* Missouri, K. & T. Ry. v. Roberts, 152 U.S. 114, 116 (1894), upholding federal power to grant a right of way over a reservation: "Though the lands of the Indians were reserved by treaty for their occupation, the fee was always under the control of the government . . . ."

their protection, as well as to the safety of those among whom they dwell. It must exist in that government, because it never has existed anywhere else, because the theatre of its exercise is within the geographical limits of the United States, because it has never been denied, and because it alone can enforce its laws on all the tribes.[28]

All of this flatly contradicted Marshall's convincing assurance in *McCulloch* that Congress had only the powers enumerated in the Constitution,[29] as well as the explicit terms of the tenth amendment that confirmed Marshall's conclusion;[30] and the unexplained assumption that the states had no power over the matter seemed to have no support in the Constitution either.[31]

C.   The Copyright Clause

Apart from the commerce-clause cases, the most interesting questions of the scope of enumerated powers during the Waite period concerned the copyright clause. The *Trade-Mark Cases*, where as noted the Court held the commerce power did not authorize general federal regulation of trademarks,[32] also held the legislation could

---

[28]118 U.S. at 384-85. In support of his correct conclusion that reservations were within the United States, Miller properly invoked *Cherokee Nation v. Georgia, supra* chapter 4, where the Court had held a tribe was not a "foreign State" entitled to sue a state under article III (118 U.S. at 379). In doing so, Miller managed to misstate the reason for the *Cherokee* decision, for Marshall had held that the tribe was not "foreign," not that it was not a "State."

[29]*See supra* chapter 6; F. COHEN, *supra* note 23, at 90: "Reference to the so-called 'plenary' power of Congress over the Indians . . . becomes so frequent in recent cases that it may seem captious to point out that there is excellent authority for the view that Congress has no constitutional power over Indians except what is conferred by the Commerce Clause and other clauses of the Constitution," citing Marshall: "That instrument confers on Congress the powers of war and peace; of making treaties, and of regulating commerce . . . with the Indian tribes. These powers comprehend all that is required for the regulation of our intercourse with the Indians." Worcester v. Georgia, 31 U.S. (6 Pet.) 515, 558 (1832). A later and more impersonal version of Cohen's book, though obscure, seems more sympathetic to broadening the powers of the agency for which he wrote: "Properly viewed in its historical context, [the plenary power doctrine] was sensible. Otherwise, the dependent tribes would have had extraterritoriality." U.S. SOLICITOR FOR THE DEPT. OF INTERIOR, FEDERAL INDIAN LAW 33 (1958). *But see* W. WILLOUGHBY, THE CONSTITUTIONAL LAW OF THE UNITED STATES 386 (2d ed. 1929), finding in *Kagama* "a dangerous implication, namely, that a Federal power can be deduced from practical need for its exercise."

[30]"The powers not delegated to the United States by this Constitution, nor prohibited by it to the States, are reserved to the States respectively, or to the people." For a later example analogous to *Kagama, see* United States v. Curtiss-Wright Export Corp., 299 U.S. 304, 315-16 (1936) (dictum): "The broad statement that the federal government can exercise no powers except those specifically enumerated in the Constitution, and such implied powers as are necessary and proper to carry into effect the enumerated powers, is categorically true only in respect of our internal affairs." The tenth amendment, it should be noted, does not contain the word "internal." It is interesting that Miller's efforts to show that Indians were not regarded as foreign nations (118 U.S. at 379, 384-85) made it more difficult to make the plausible argument that, if Congress had a general and unstated authority over foreign affairs, Indian affairs fell within it.

[31]Given Miller's conclusion that murder was not commerce, a lack of state power could hardly have been based on the commerce clause; the decision in *Worcester v. Georgia* that the state lacked power over reservation affairs was based on treaties and federal statutes (*see supra* chapter 6), and the United States could hardly bootstrap itself into general authority over Indians by forbidding the states to act.

[32]*See supra* text accompanying notes 6-7.

not be sustained under the copyright and patent powers. The relevant clause of the Constitution, Miller observed, authorized Congress to protect the rights of "'authors and inventors . . . to their respective writings and discoveries'" and referred only to "the fruits of intellectual labor."[33] "The ordinary trade-mark," in contrast, did not "depend upon novelty, invention, discovery, or any work of the brain. . . . It is simply founded on priority of appropriation."[34] That a trademark may indeed be a creation of considerable ingenuity that could properly be copyrighted seems no answer to this argument; though Miller did not make this point, nothing in the reports suggests any such claim was made for the trademarks in question.[35] More broadly, Miller's conclusion seems equally supportable on the ground that the trademark law served to prevent confusion of goods[36] rather than, as the Constitution requires, to "promote the Progress of Science and useful Arts" by encouraging creative activity.

Miller wrote for the Court again in *Burrow-Giles Lithographic Co. v. Sarony* in 1884 to hold that photographs came within the definition of "Writings" in the copyright clause.[37] The literal objection that pictures were not words was ably refuted by reference to Congress's conclusion in passing copyright laws immediately after 1789 that charts, maps, and engravings were included,[38] and as in the telegraph case the Court persuasively concluded that the novelty of the means employed was no reason for construing the general terms of the Constitution more narrowly than their purpose required.[39] The final objection was that a photograph displayed no original-ity because it simply copied what already existed in nature; Miller convincingly found artistic contribution in the choice and arrangement of the subject.[40]

Overall, both the cases discussed in this section and those respecting authority to enforce the Civil War amendments[41] seem to show that during Waite's term as Chief Justice the Court took a reasonably balanced and straightforward view of the list of congressional powers, neither confining them artificially nor refusing to recognize that they were intended to have limits. *Kagama* was the most conspicuous departure from this pattern,[42] and it came in an area long recognized as one of special federal competence.[43]

[33]100 U.S. at 93, 94, quoting U.S. CONST., art. I, § 8.

[34]100 U.S. at 94.

[35]Even if it had been, Miller's overbreadth argument would have been as applicable to the copyright claim as to the commerce argument to which he himself applied it (*see supra* note 6).

[36]*See* H. NIMS, THE LAW OF UNFAIR COMPETITION AND TRADE-MARKS, §§ 185-88 (4th ed. 1947).

[37]111 U.S. 53 (1884).

[38]*Id.* at 56-57. Miller had already said engravings and prints were "writings" in the *Trade-Mark Cases*, 100 U.S. at 94 (dictum).

[39]111 U.S. at 57-58. *Cf. supra* text accompanying notes 1-5, discussing *Pensacola Tel. Co. v. Western Union Tel. Co.*.

[40]111 U.S. at 58-60.

[41]*See supra* chapter 11.

[42]*See also supra* chapter 11, discussing *Ex parte Yarbrough*.

[43]Less interesting additional decisions tend to confirm these observations. In Kohl v. United States, 91 U.S. 367 (1876), the Court for the first time upheld the power of Congress to provide for condemnation of property in order to carry out its granted powers. This holding had been anticipated by 3 J. STORY, COMMENTARIES ON THE CONSTITUTION OF THE UNITED STATES 46 (1833). Though Justice Strong accurately described the authority as incidental (91 U.S. at 372), he strangely neglected to mention the necessary and proper clause. He also repeated the tactic, questionable in light of the ninth amendment (*see supra* chapter 9, discussing the *Legal Tender Cases*), of inferring the existence of congressional power from a limitation

D.   Investigations and Immunities

In *Anderson v. Dunn*, in 1821, the Supreme Court had held that the House of Representatives had implicit authority to punish nonmembers for contempt, on the basis of necessity: "[t]he public functionaries must be left at liberty to exercise the powers which the people have intrusted to them."[44] Yet when the House imprisoned

---

in the Bill of Rights on its exercise, in this case the fifth amendment's ban on taking without compensation. 92 U.S. at 372-73. A few years later Justice Field, who had dissented in *Kohl* on the ground that Congress had not granted condemnation authority nor given the courts jurisdiction of condemnation cases, *id.* at 378-79, wrote for the entire Court to say that the power was inherent and "requires no constitutional recognition." United States v. Jones, 109 U.S. 513, 518 (1883). Cf. *United States v. Kagama, supra.*

Scholey v. Rew, 90 U.S. (23 Wall.) 331, 347-48 (1875), and Springer v. United States, 102 U.S. 586, 602 (1881), held that neither an inheritance tax nor an income tax was direct and thus that neither had to be apportioned among the states by population. Neither opinion added to the understanding of what constituted a direct tax (*cf. supra* chapters 2, 9). In the former Clifford said only that an inheritance tax was no different from an earlier income tax that had been upheld, without saying why; in the latter Swayne concluded flatly and without adequate support that only land and capitation taxes were direct, ignoring Justice Paterson's reliance in *Hylton v. United States, supra* chapter 1, on a quotation from Adam Smith suggesting that income taxes were the most direct of all.

United States v. Fox, 95 U.S. 670 (1878) (Field, J.), unsurprisingly held that the bankruptcy power did not authorize Congress to outlaw fraud by any person who later became bankrupt. Embry v. Palmer, 107 U.S. 3 (1883) (Matthews, J.), held Congress under article III and its power over the District of Columbia could require a state to respect a District judgment. United States v. Arjona, 120 U.S. 479, 484-88 (1887) (Waite, C.J.), upheld a law against counterfeiting foreign money as an exercise of Congress's power to punish crimes against the law of nations (art. I, § 8), which the Court convincingly argued required one nation to prevent harm to the interests of another. Juilliard v. Greenman, 110 U.S. 421 (1884), in a good opinion by Justice Gray repeating much of what Strong had said in the earlier *Legal Tender Cases* (*see supra* chapter 9), held that the power to borrow money included the power to make paper money legal tender even in peacetime. Field tenaciously continued to dissent, adding (*id.* at 458) that what had first been advocated as a wartime necessity was now argued to be a measure "that may be adopted at any time." Professor Dam, in *The Legal Tender Cases*, 1981 SUP. CT. REV. 367, 410-11, confirms that the case for legal tender was significantly weaker in *Juilliard* than it had been the time before; nevertheless Marshall's classic formulation in *McCulloch v. Maryland* had not required Congress to choose the least intrusive means of attaining a legitimate goal. Passages from *Juilliard* quoted by Dam (*id.* at 395-96) as evidence of a search for "inherent authority" seem so related to the demonstration that tender was incidental to borrowing as to appear quite innocuous in comparison with *Kagama.*

More questionable was the leading separation-of-powers decision in United States v. Perkins, 116 U.S. 483, 485 (1886) (Matthews, J.), where without discussion the Court effectively cleared the way for civil service by holding that the power to vest appointment of inferior officers in heads of departments (U.S. CONST. art. II, § 2) carried with it authority to limit the right to remove them. See 3 J. STORY, *supra* note 43, at 388, anticipating this result. In so holding, the Court seemed oblivious to the strong arguments for unified executive control that a later Court was to draw with respect to other officers from the provisions of article II, § § 1, 3, vesting the executive authority in a single President and directing him to take care that the laws were faithfully executed. *See* Myers v. United States, 272 U.S. 52 (1926). The particular limitation in *Perkins*, however—a requirement of court martial for removal of a naval officer—was arguably compatible with presidental control because it permitted a discharge for failure to carry out presidential orders. *See also* Ex parte Siebold, 100 U.S. 371, 397-98 (1880) (Bradley, J.), upholding Congress's power under article II, § 2 ("the Congress may by Law vest the Appointment of such inferior Officers, as they think proper, in the President alone, in the Courts of Law, or in the Heads of Departments") to empower judges to appoint election supervisors, rejecting the plausible dictum in Matter of Hennen, 38 U.S. (13 Pet.) 230, 257-58 (1839), that the power "was no doubt intended to be exercised by the department . . . to which the official to be appointed most appropriately belonged" but adding more narrowly that "[i]t cannot be affirmed that the appointment of the officers in question could, with any greater propriety, . . . have been assigned to any other depositary of official power . . . ."

[44]*See supra* chapter 6.

a witness for refusing to cooperate with an investigation into the operations of a "real-estate pool" in which a debtor of the Government was interested, the Court in *Kilbourn v. Thompson* in 1881 held the House had acted beyond its powers.[45]

Justice Miller began by casting aspersions on the arguments that supported the House's contempt power itself. The House of Commons, on whose authority much stress had been placed in argument, was distinguished on the probably irrelevant ground that, unlike our House of Representatives, it had historically exercised judicial as well as legislative powers.[46] The point of this lengthy and learned exercise, however, was blunted when the Court expressly refused to decide whether the contempt power might nevertheless be implicit, as *Anderson* had held, in aid of legitimate legislative functions.[47] For the ground of decision was that the House had had no power to conduct the investigation itself:

> we are sure that no person can be punished for contumacy as a witness before either House, unless his testimony is required in a matter into which that House has jurisdiction to inquire, and we feel equally sure that neither of these bodies possesses the general power of making inquiry into the private affairs of the citizen.[48]

Any determination of the rights of the government or of its debtor with respect to the pool, Miller added, could be made only by a court;[49] and the investigation "could result in no valid legislation on the subject to which the inquiry referred."[50]

Miller's persuasive insistence that congressional investigations be limited to legitimate legislative purposes became a popular bulwark against investigatory excesses in a much later period.[51] He nowhere denied, however, that the authority to enact legislation implied the right of the House to inform itself as to the need for legislation

---

[45]103 U.S. 168 (1881).

[46]*Id.* at 182-89, also suggesting that a legislative contempt citation might run afoul of the due process clause and suggesting a negative implication from the explicit authority of each House to "punish its Members for disorderly Behavior," U.S. Const. art. I, § 5: "These provisions are equally instructive in what they authorize and in what they do not authorize." For criticism of Miller's history, see Landis, *Constitutional Limitations on the Congressional Power of Investigation*, 40 Harv. L. Rev. 153, 159-64 (1926), giving evidence that Parliament's power was independent of any judicial function; T. Taylor, Grand Inquest 47 n. 16 (1955): "[I]t was specifically to protect and aid the exercise of *legislative* actions that the contempt and investigative powers grew up."

[47]103 U.S. at 189.

[48]*Id.* at 190.

[49]*Id.* at 192-94, calling the investigation a usurpation of judicial authority and terming article III's vesting of that authority in the courts as "equivalent to a declaration that no judicial power is vested in the Congress or either branch of it," except in impeachment and other enumerated instances. *Cf. supra* chapters 4 and 9, discussing *American Ins. Co. v. Canter* and *Ex parte Milligan.*

[50]103 U.S. at 195. *Anderson* was therefore distinguishable on the ground that no showing had been made in that case that the contempt citation was based on disobedience of an invalid order; but Miller chose to treat *Anderson* as having held the House's determination conclusive and to say it had been wrongly decided. *Id.* at 196-200.

[51]*See, e.g.*, Taylor, *supra* note 46, at 47; Watkins v. United States, 354 U.S. 178, 187, 194, 215 (1957), holding due process required that a witness be given adequate information to enable him to determine whether the questions posed were pertinent to a legitimate legislative purpose, citing *Kilbourn* as forbidding investigations into judicial matters, and adding that "there is no general authority to expose the private affairs of individuals without justification in terms of the functions of Congress."

or to employ coercive means to obtain the necessary information;[52] indeed, he conceded as much with respect to the impeachment power.[53] The problem in *Kilbourn* seems rather to have been that the House had made no effort to tie its investigation to any legitimate legislative purpose, leaving it open to Miller's conclusion that it was prying into matters that were none of its constitutional concern.[54]

The invalidity of the contempt citation did not end the case, for Kilbourn was seeking damages for his unlawful arrest, and article I, § 6 provided that "for any Speech or Debate in either House," neither Senators nor Representatives should be "questioned in any other Place." Making good use of English and state decisions intepreting similar provisions,[55] Miller sensibly read the words "Speech or Debate" generously in light of their purpose of avoiding interference with the legislative process:

> The reason of the rule is as forcible in its application to written reports presented in that body by its committees, to resolutions offered, which though in writing, must be reproduced in speech, and to the act of voting, whether it is done vocally or by passing between the tellers. In short, to things generally done in a session of the House by one of its members in relation to the business before it.[56]

Thus the members of Congress who had instigated Kilbourn's imprisonment for contempt were immune from damages for their illegal action. The unfortunate functionary who had merely carried out their orders, however, was not.[57] There was no discussion of his possible immunity; perhaps Miller thought it conclusive that the speech or debate clause spoke only of "Senators and Representatives," and the passage he quoted from an English case had flatly said, without reasons, that a subordinate was not protected.[58] As an accommodation between legislative freedom and the demands of law and order, Miller's compromise perhaps had something to recommend it in policy too; but a later Court, more impressed by the increasing inability of Congress to act without the aid of employees, has concluded that the purposes of the clause require that it be construed to include those acting for the members as well.[59]

---

[52]*See* Landis, *supra* note 46, at 161-209, giving exhaustive examples of such investigations by Houses of Parliament and of both state and national legislatures and finding them implicitly authorized because indispensable to exercise of legislative powers; McGrain v. Daugherty, 273 U.S. 135, 160-78 (1927), upholding the Senate's authority.

[53]103 U.S. at 190.

[54]*See* Landis, *supra* note 46, 40 HARV. L. REV. at 214-20, arguing that poor argument and lack of legislative experience led the Court to overlook the obvious connection of the inquiry to possible legislation; TAYLOR, *supra* note 46, at 312 n. 53, denying that the House had had any such legitimate purpose.

[55]103 U.S. at 201-04.

[56]*Id.* at 204. *See also id.* at 203, quoting from a similar Massachusetts decision: "'These privileges are thus secured, not with the intention of protecting the members against prosecution for their own benefit, but to support the rights of the people, by enabling their representatives to execute the functions of their office without fear of prosecutions, civil or criminal.'"

[57]*Id.* at 205.

[58]*Id.* at 202.

[59]United States v. Gravel, 408 U.S. 606, 616-22 (1972).

II. THE BILL OF RIGHTS

It is no doubt attributable as much to jurisdictional limitations and to the limited activity of the early Congress as to the law-abiding character of its members that, apart from an occasional due-process objection, very few federal actions were challenged in the Supreme Court as offending provisions of the first eight amendments during the first hundred years. It was not until the Waite period, for example, that the Court was called upon to determine the meaning of the first amendment's guarantees of freedom of religion, speech, and the press; and even then there was only one momentous first-amendment decision.

A. Freedom of Religion

That decision was *Reynolds v. United States*, where Chief Justice Waite for a unanimous Court in 1879 upheld the authority of Congress to outlaw polygamy in the territories among Mormons who argued that the practice was required by their religious beliefs.[60] To read the amendment as licensing wholesale religious exceptions from general laws, Waite showed, would have unacceptable consequences: the Framers could hardly have meant to permit human sacrifice even in the name of religion.[61] For evidence as to what the Framers *had* meant, he turned reasonably enough to Jefferson, who had been influential in the campaign that resulted in adoption of the first-amendment provision: "'it is time enough for the rightful purposes of civil government for its officers to interfere when principles break out into overt acts against peace and good order.'"[62] Waite's conclusion was a broad one: "Congress was deprived of all legislative power over mere opinion, but was left free to reach actions which were in violation of social duties or subversive of good order."[63]

At first glance the Court's reasoning seems to have gone too far: a rigid distinction between opinions and actions would allow Congress to forbid the holding of ordinary religious services. Not only would such a conclusion be as difficult to attribute to those intent on preserving religious liberty as the authorization of human sacrifice; it also seems to contradict the express language forbidding interference with "the free *Exercise*" of religion.[64] Waite's reference to actions "in violation of social duties or

[60] 98 U.S. 145, 161 (1879). As in the uncited *Scott v. Sandford* (*supra* chapter 8), the Court had no difficulty with the application of the Bill of Rights to the territories, notwithstanding the holding of *American Ins. Co. v. Canter* (*supra* chapter 4) that article III's limitations on the nature of federal courts did not apply there. As the language and purpose of the amendment suggest, Waite said simply that "[r]eligious freedom is guaranteed everywhere throughout the United States, so far as congressional interference is concerned." 98 U.S. at 162.

[61] *Id.* at 166.

[62] *Id.* at 163, quoting the preamble to a Virginia statute drafted by Jefferson to "'establish[] religious freedom.'" *See also id.* at 164, quoting similar expressions in a later Jefferson letter in the context of the first amendment itself.

[63] *Id.* at 164.

[64] *See* P. KURLAND, RELIGION AND THE LAW 22 (1962); L. TRIBE, AMERICAN CONSTITUTIONAL LAW 838 n. 13 (1978); Magrath, *Chief Justice Waite and the "Twin Relic": Reynolds v. United States*, 18 VAND. L. REV. 507, 531 (1964).

subversive of good order" suggests a limitation, as does his repeated insistence that the amendment did not create exceptions from generally applicable laws: if it did, "then those who do not make polygamy a part of their religious belief may be found guilty and punished, while those who do, must be acquitted and go free."[65] The implication seems to be that the effect of the clause is to prevent discrimination on account of religion, not to give the religious special exemptions from laws protecting secular interests.[66]

Waite's position is not the only plausible middle ground between two extreme interpretations that the Framers could not have intended. A recognition that the amendment does not permit human sacrifice is equally consistent with the later Court's view that even nondiscriminatory incursions on religious interests, like those on the interest in expression, may be justified only by an overbalancing governmental interest;[67] and reasonable judges might well differ as to the fate of the polygamy rule on such a subjective test.[68] We have also been warned by responsible scholars against attributing all the views of either Jefferson or the equally influential Madison to the Framers in general.[69]

In this instance, however, there is much evidence to suggest that Jefferson's position was widely shared. To begin with, the bulk of complaints about infringement of religious liberty during the preconstitutional period apparently concerned outright discrimination against dissenters from the dominant sect.[70] There were also pleas for exemption of conscientious objectors from military service;[71] but the heated congressional debate over the merits of an independent proposal to this effect when

---

[65]98 U.S. at 166. *See also id.* at 166-67:

> Can a man excuse his practices to the contrary because of his religious belief? To permit this would be to make the professed doctrines of religious belief superior to the law of the land, and in effect to permit every citizen to become a law unto himself. Government could exist only in name under such circumstances.

[66]*See* Magrath, *supra* note 64, 18 VAND. L. REV. at 531-32, also approving of this reasoning. This was basically the view taken in Judge Cooley's influential treatise: "the State is not to inquire into or take notice of religious belief, when the citizen performs his duty to the State and to his fellows." T. COOLEY, CONSTITUTIONAL LIMITATIONS 467-70 (1868).

[67]*See, e.g.,* Sherbert v. Verner, 374 U.S. 398 (1963) (Sabbatarians exempt from Saturday work as condition of unemployment benefits).

[68]*Cf.* the decision, which seems extreme even on a balancing test, that a compulsory education law could not be enforced against those with religious objections to learning. Wisconsin v. Yoder, 406 U.S. 205 (1972).

[69]*See, e.g.,* Corwin, *The Supreme Court as National School Board,* 14 LAW & CONTEMP. PROBS. 3, 10-13 (1949), noting that Jefferson was out of the country when the amendment was drafted; M. HOWE, THE GARDEN AND THE WILDERNESS 10 (1965). Both Corwin and Howe were questioning the significance of Jefferson's views in interpreting the separate prohibition of laws "respecting an Establishment" of religion.

[70]*E.g.,* Peter Stuyvesant's 1657 banning of Quakers, the conviction of Anne Hutchinson and persecution of John Clarke for propagating unorthodox views, Virginia and North Carolina laws barring nonconformists from performing marriages, holding offices, or attending schools, and a Virginia law outlawing certain disfavored opinions. See the enlightening collection of historical materials in A. STOKES & L. PFEFFER, CHURCH AND STATE IN THE UNITED STATES 8-10, 17, 67-71 (1964); Gianella, *Religious Liberty, Nonestablishment, and Doctrinal Development (Part I),* 80 HARV. L. REV. 1381, 1386 (1967).

[71]*See* Freeman, *A Remonstrance for Conscience,* 106 U. PA. L. REV. 806, 808-13 (1958).

the Bill of Rights was being considered[72] suggests that Congress did not think the free exercise clause itself conferred any such exemption. Moreover, whatever may be said of conscientious refusal to perform secular duties, Jefferson's view that religious liberty did not authorize *action* contrary to the public order was shared by the much-cited Roger Williams,[73] written into the Northwest Ordinance[74] and into treaties concluded under the Articles of Confederation,[75] and adopted by several original states besides Virginia.[76] In the absence of any suggestion that the Framers meant to depart from what appears to have been a widespread understanding about the proper limits of religious freedom,[77] Waite seems to have been on firm historical

[72]1 ANNALS OF CONG. 778-81 (1789). The brief debate on the free exercise clause itself (*id.* at 757-61) is unenlightening. The progress of the amendment through Congress is told in STOKES & PFEFFER, *supra* note 70, at 92-100.

[73]   There goes many a ship to sea, with many hundred souls in one ship, whose weal and woe is common, and is a true picture of a commonwealth, or a human combination or society. It hath fallen out sometimes, that both papists and protestants, Jews and Turks, may be embarked in one ship; upon which supposal I affirm, that all the liberty of conscience, that ever I pleaded for, turns upon these two hinges—that none of the papists, protestants, Jews, or Turks, be forced to come to the ship's prayers or worship, nor compelled from their own particular prayers or worship, if they practice any. I further add, that I never denied, that nothwithstanding this liberty, the commander of this ship ought to command the ship's course, yea, and also command that justice, peace and sobriety, be kept and practiced, both among the seamen and all the passengers. If any of the seamen refuse to perform their services, or passengers to pay their freight; if any refuse to help, in person or purse, towards the common charges or defence; if any refuse to obey the common laws and orders of the ship, concerning their common peace of preservation; if any shall mutiny and rise up against their commanders and officers; if any should preach or write that there ought to be no commanders or officers, because all are equal in Christ, therefore no masters nor officers, no laws nor orders, nor corrections nor punishments;—I say, I never denied, but in such cases, whatever is pretended, the commander or commanders may judge, resist, compel and punish such transgressors, according to their deserts and merits.

Quoted in STOKES & PFEFFER, *supra* note 70, at 15.

[74]"No person, demeaning himself in a peaceable and orderly manner, shall ever be molested on account of his mode of worship or religious sentiments, in the said territory." Ordinance for the Government of the Territory of the United States north-west of the river Ohio (July 13, 1787), art. I, 1 Stat. 51, 52 n. (a).

[75]*E.g.*, 1782 treaty with the Netherlands, quoted in STOKES & PFEFFER, *supra* note 70, at 85: "there shall be an entire and perfect liberty of conscience allowed to the subjects and inhabitants of each party, and their families; and no one shall be molested in regard to this worship, provided he submits, as to the public demonstration of it, to the laws of the country."

[76]*See* STOKES & PFEFFER, *supra* note 70, at 18, 75, 77, quoting the 1663 Rhode Island charter ("behaving themselves peaceably and quietly, and not using this libertie to lycentiousnesse and profanesse, nor to the injury or outward disturbance of others"), the 1818 Connecticut constitution ("the right hereby declared and established shall not be construed as to excuse acts of licentiousness or to justify practices inconsistent with the peace and safety of the State"), and the 1790 Massachusetts Constitution ("provided he doth not disturb the public peace, or obstruct others in their religious worship").

[77]Proponents of the position that the free exercise clause gives special exemptions from general laws tend to argue on the basis of policy rather than history. *E.g.*, Choper, *The Religion Clauses of the First Amendment: Reconciling the Conflict*, 41 U. PITT. L. REV. 673, 688-90 (1980) (enforcing gym-shorts rule against those with religious objections to showing legs would seriously impair religious freedom to serve trivial interest). *Cf.* Gianella, *supra* note 70, 80 HARV. L. REV. at 1388, discussing the similar case of sacramental wine in ostensibly historical terms (prohibition impossible to justify "[f]or those who take inviolability of conscience as seriously as did the founding fathers") without citing any historical analogies. Even if Gianella is right, one may wonder whether the Framers would have thought that polygamy would pose a similarly insignificant threat to the public order.

ground; and although he might have been more thorough in his use of historical sources, he deserves credit for a sound approach to the problem.[78]

B.   Freedom of Expression

Two cases with overtones of freedom of expression also engaged the Court during the Waite period. The first was *Ex parte Jackson*, where in 1878 Justice Field wrote to sustain a statute excluding circulars relating to lotteries from the mails.[79] The opinion began with the broad statement that the power "to establish Post Offices and Post Roads" included authority to determine what might be carried in the mail and that "[t]he right to designate what shall be carried necessarily involves the right to determine what shall be excluded."[80] But Field stopped short of concluding that because Congress need not have established a post office at all its power over the content of mail was without limit: no regulation could "be enforced . . . against the transportation of printed matter in the mail, . . . so as to interfere in any manner with the freedom of the press. Liberty of circulating," he emphasized, "is as essential to that freedom as liberty of publishing; indeed, without the circulation, the publication would be of little value." Thus, Field concluded, "[i]f . . . printed matter be excluded from the mails, its transportation in any other way cannot be forbidden by Congress."[81] Unless he meant to imply that the converse was also true, this conclusion was wholly gratuitous. But Field did not conclude that the law was valid simply because Congress had left open other channels of communication; the actual holding was his arguably narrower conclusion, after declaring the availability of other

---

[78]Waite's conclusion may be further strengthened by the fact that to construe the free exercise clause to confer special exemptions from general laws brings it into conflict with the modern view that the establishment clause of the same amendment *prohibits* government action whose primary effect is to aid religion, *see* Lemon v. Kurtzman, 403 U.S. 602 (1971). For historical criticism of the latter position, *see, e.g.*, Corwin, *supra* note 69, 14 LAW AND CONTEMP. PROBS. at 9-16, and M. HOWE, *supra* note 69, passim. For an effort to reconcile the two clauses, *see* P. KURLAND, *supra* note 64, at 17-18, 22, arguing that the two clauses

> must be read to mean that religion may not be used as a classification for purposes of governmental action, whether that action be the conferring of rights or privileges or the imposition of duties or obligations . . . . To permit individuals to be excused from compliance with the law solely on the basis of religious belief is to subject others to punishment for failure to subscribe to those same beliefs.

See also Ely, *Legislative and Administrative Motivation in Constitutional Law*, 79 YALE L. J. 1205, 1314 (1970); Kurland, *The Irrelevance of the Constitution: The Religion Clauses of the First Amendment and the Supreme Court*, 24 VILL. L. REV. 3, 15, 17-18, 24 (1978), noting the unpopularity of this interpretation with other scholars and with the modern Court.

[79]96 U.S. 727 (1878).

[80]*Id.* at 732, citing U.S. CONST. art. I, § 8.

[81]*Id.* at 733, adding that the fourth amendment limited the power to open mail. *See also id.* at 732: "The difficulty . . . arises, not from the want of power in Congress to prescribe regulations as to what shall constitute mail matter, but from the necessity of enforcing them consistently with rights reserved to the people . . . ." There was no suggestion that the commercial nature of the publication in question took it outside the unrestricted terms of the first amendment. *See* Valentine v. Chrestensen, 316 U.S. 52 (1942), denying protection to commercial advertising; Virginia Pharmacy Bd. v. Virginia Consumer Council, 425 U.S. 748 (1976) (contra).

channels, that Congress could "refuse its facilities for the distribution of matter deemed injurious to the public morals."[82]

The opinion is certainly unclear as to the exact reason for this conclusion; and even the narrowest interpretation of the decision would give pause today. Government censorship of the acceptability of written materials on the ground that their content is "injurious to the public morals" has rightly become suspect, and because the ban was not limited to circulars advertising *illegal* lotteries[83] it could not be sustained as a means of preventing incitement to criminal activity.[84] Today, moreover, it has become clear that the availability of other means of communication is not enough; when the government makes a facility available for the exchange of information, it is limited in its ability to discriminate according to content.[85] All of this, however, has developed through years of experience in first-amendment litigation and could scarcely have been expected to emerge full-blown in the Court's first encounter with the clause. Field's opinion is wholly conclusory, and in sharp contrast to *Reynolds* he made no effort to determine what the Framers of the first amendment had had in mind; but he deserves a little credit for recognizing that the government's proprietary position may not be a complete answer to all constitutional questions.

The second case was *Ex parte Curtis*, where in 1882 Waite wrote to uphold a statute forbidding one government employee to receive a political contribution from another.[86] Waite did not advert to a first-amendment problem at all, merely finding the statute necessary and proper "to promote efficiency and integrity in the discharge of official duties": "If persons in public employ may be called on by those in authority to contribute from their personal income to the expenses of political campaigns, . . . a refusal may lead to putting good men out of the service, [and] liberal payments may be made the ground for keeping poor ones in."[87]

Only Justice Bradley, dissenting, perceived the threat such a law posed to first-amendment values. In so doing, more clearly than Field in *Jackson*, Bradley stressed

---

[82]96 U.S. at 736, drawing an analogy to obscene materials and adding only the disturbingly broad observation that lotteries were "institutions which are supposed to have a demoralizing influence among the people." No one suggested, as four Justices would argue in connection with a later effort to exclude lottery tickets from interstate commerce, that the regulation was outside the purpose for which the power had been granted because designed to discourage an activity that Congress had no authority to forbid outright. *See* the Lottery Case, 188 U.S. 321 (1903) (Fuller, C.J., dissenting); *cf. supra* chapter 6, discussing *McCulloch v. Maryland*.

[83]96 U.S. at 728.

[84]*See* Pittsburgh Press Co. v. Human Relations Comm'n, 413 U.S. 376 (1973) (sustaining ban on advertisement of jobs available on illegally discriminatory basis).

[85]*See, e.g.*, Widmar v. Vincent, 454 U.S. 263, 277 (1981), holding a state university could not exclude a religious group from use of a generally available auditorium: "Having created a forum generally open to student groups, the University seeks to enforce a content-based exclusion of religious speech. Its exclusionary policy violates the fundamental principle that a state regulation of speech should be content-neutral . . . ."; Lamont v. Postmaster General, 381 U.S. 301, 302, 305 (1965), holding Congress could not require a request by the addressee for mail delivery of "communist political propaganda" and quoting from an earlier dissent of Justice Holmes: "'The United States may give up the Post Office when it sees fit, but while it carries it on the use of the mails is almost as much a part of free speech as the right to use our tongues . . . .'" *See generally* Stone, *Content Regulation and the First Amendment*, 25 WM. & MARY L. REV. 189 (1984).

[86]106 U.S. 371 (1882).

[87]*Id.* at 373, 375.

that the power of the government to run its own operations could not be used to impair other rights. Not only was the right to apply for public office (questionably) "a fundamental right of which the legislature cannot deprive the citizen"; Congress could not "clog its exercise with conditions that are repugnant to his other fundamental rights."[88] "To deny to a man the privilege of associating and making joint contributions with such other citizens as he may choose," Bradley continued, "is an unjust restraint of his right to propagate and promote his views on public affairs" and thus, even though imposed only as condition of public employment, contrary to the spirit of the first amendment.[89]

Like Field in *Jackson*, Bradley made no effort to demonstrate that his conclusions were consistent with the expectations of the Framers,[90] but it was inexcusable for the majority not to respond to his argument. As a matter of first principle, Bradley's opinion seems a far more realistic assessment of the deterrent effect of such conditions attached to public privileges than Holmes's famous and simplistic statement that there was no constitutional right to be a policeman;[91] and although later decisions have confirmed the Court's conclusion that limits on the political activities of government employees can be justified by the compelling interests indentified by Waite in the *Curtis* opinion,[92] they have accepted Bradley's perception that such limitations have to be analyzed in terms of their impact on first-amendment freedoms.[93]

C.   Search, Seizure, and Self-Incrimination

The last great Bill of Rights decision of the Waite period was the 1886 case of *Boyd v. United States*, in which the Court held unconstitutional an act of Congress providing for the compulsory production of documents relevant to proceedings to forfeit illegally imported goods.[94] The statute, said Justice Bradley, both authorized "unreasonable searches and seizures" in violation of the fourth amendment and "compelled" the owner of the goods "to be a witness against himself" in violation of the fifth. The two prohibitions, as Bradley saw them, were intimately related. "For the

---

[88]*Id.* at 376.

[89]*Id.* at 376-77.

[90]That giving money for political purposes was a form of "Speech," while certainly plausible in terms of the values of speech itself, *see* Buckley v. Valeo, 424 U.S. 1, 14-23 (1976), was surely not obvious; and there is substantial support for the view that at least the "freedom . . . of the press" as employed in the first amendment was understood to relate only to freedom from such "previous restraints" as licensing. *See, e.g.*, L. LEVY, LEGACY OF SUPPRESSION (1964). The congressional debates on the amendment (1 ANNALS OF CONG. 757-61 (1789)) contain nothing about either speech or press. Since neither opinion in *Jackson* explored these issues, this is fortunately not the place to do so.

[91]McAuliffe v. Mayor of New Bedford, 155 Mass. 216, 220, 29 N.E. 517 (1892).

[92]United Public Workers v. Mitchell, 330 U.S. 75 (1947); Civil Service Comm'n v. Letter Carriers, 413 U.S. 548 (1973), both upholding the Hatch Act provision forbidding federal employees to take "any active part in political management or in political campaigns."

[93]*See, e.g.*, Elrod v. Burns, 427 U.S. 347 (1976), limiting the use of political criteria for discharging government employees. *See generally* Van Alstyne, *The Demise of the Right-Privilege Distinction in Constitutional Law*, 81 HARV. L. REV. 1439 (1968). *Cf.* the Waite Court's own recognition, *supra* chapter 12, that the power of a state to exclude foreign corporations did not allow it to condition permission to do business on a surrender of the right to litigate in federal court.

[94]116 U.S. 616 (1886).

'unreasonable searches and seizures' condemned in the Fourth Amendment are almost always made for the purpose of compelling a man to give evidence against himself. . . ."[95] "Breaking into a house and opening boxes and drawers are circumstances of aggravation; but any forcible and compulsory extortion of a man's own testimony or of his private papers to be used as evidence to convict him of crime or to forfeit his goods" was within the principle of the fourth amendment.[96]

As Miller and Waite noted in a concurring opinion, not all "searches and seizures" are forbidden, but only those that are "unreasonable."[97] Even on the assumption that an order to produce evidence was a "search[]" or a "seizure[]," therefore, Bradley's conclusion was by no means self-evident. The interposition of a neutral magistrate between the policeman and the citizen, often stressed in holding warrantless searches or seizures unreasonable,[98] was assured by the statute's requirement of a court order to compel production. Indeed, such an order poses even less danger than an ex parte warrant because it affords the opportunity to argue against production by moving to quash.[99] Nor was there any trace in *Boyd* of the overbreadth problem that had characterized the general warrants and writs of assistance that Bradley acknowledged had been the immediate impetus for adoption of the fourth amendment,[100] for the order specified production of a single document described with particularity.[101] The key to Bradley's fourth-amendment conclusion lies in his view that even a specific warrant would not have justified seizure of property merely for use as evidence to support a criminal or quasi-criminal proceeding: seizure was permissible only when "the government is entitled to the possession of the property," as in the case of stolen goods.[102] There was language in the leading English case to support this conclusion;[103] and even when the Court finally repudiated the "mere evidence" rule it did not refute Bradley's history but, startlingly, appeared to argue that the amendment had shrunk because the Framers' respect for property had become outmoded.[104] Thus by reference to history Bradley sought to establish that the purpose of the amendment was to allow the suppression of evidence, not merely to outlaw unduly intrusive methods of obtaining it;[105] and this purpose would be thwarted if, in recognition of the obvious textual difficulties pointed out by Miller

[95]*Id.* at 633.

[96]*Id.* at 630.

[97]*Id.* at 641.

[98]*E.g.*, Johnson v. United States, 333 U.S. 10, 13-14 (1948).

[99]*See* Zurcher v. Stanford Daily, 436 U.S. 547, 570 (1978) (Stewart, J., dissenting from allowance of a search); 2 W. LaFave, Search and Seizure 209-10 (1978).

[100]116 U.S. at 625. For the colonial writs of assistance, *see* N. Lasson, The History and Development of the Fourth Amendment to the United States Constitution, ch. II (1937); for a summary of the inconclusive legislative history of the amendment, see *id.*, ch. III.

[101]116 U.S. at 619.

[102]*Id.* at 623.

[103]*See id.* at 626-29, quoting from Entick v. Carrington, 19 Howell's State Trials 1029 (1765).

[104]Warden v. Hayden, 387 U.S. 294, 300-10 (1967) (Brennan, J.). Bradley's view of the history and its application to "the milder discovery device employed in *Boyd*" are approved and *Hayden* criticized in White, *Forgotten Points in the Exclusionary Rule Debate*, 81 Mich. L. Rev. 1273, 1274-77 (1983). Bradley's view of the "mere evidence" rule is supported in T. Cooley, *supra* note 66, at 305-06.

[105]The question whether the amendment protects the interest in privacy of information is relevant also to the later issue of electronic surveillance not involving a traditional trespass. *See* Posner, *Rethinking the Fourth Amendment*, 1981 Sup. Ct. Rev. 49, 51 & n. 7, 8; Stone, *The Scope of the Fourth Amendment: Privacy and the Police Use of Spies, Secret Agents, and Informers*, 1976 Am. B.F. Res. J. 1193.

and Waite in a concurring opinion,[106] production orders were held not to be searches or seizures.[107] Bradley may not have been right about all this;[108] but he certainly made an impressive effort to tie his unobvious conclusions to the history and purposes of the provision.

Miller and Waite, concurring separately,[109] would have rested the decision on Bradley's more straightforward alternative basis that the owner of the seized goods had been compelled to produce evidence against himself,[110] but later cases have shown that even this argument is open to debate. All Bradley had to say on this

[106]116 U.S. at 638-41. The use of coercion, however, makes it easy to argue that there has been an effective seizure, and the prosecutor's plan was to search through the document after its production. *See id.* at 621-22 (Bradley, J.), 639 (Miller, J., concurring, conceding the presence of coercion in discussing the self-incrimination claim). Miller objected that there was no seizure because Boyd was not deprived of possession but required only to bring the document to court (*id.* at 640), but the statute provided that the owner should retain custody of his papers "except pending their examination in court," *id. See* White, *supra* note 104, 81 MICH. L. REV. at 1277 n. 20: "the respondent must yield at least temporary possession of the documents, and it is hard to see how that is not 'a seizure.'"

[107]Moreover, the risk of a general fishing expedition by subpoena conjures up the same overbreadth problems the Framers explicitly addressed by requiring that a warrant "particularly describ[e]" not only "the place to be searched" but also "the persons or things to be seized." The obvious counterargument, employed when the Court began moving away from *Boyd*'s fourth-amendment conclusion, was that the Framers could hardly have intended to place such an unreasonable obstruction in the way of law enforcement, especially in light of the sixth amendment's explicit guarantee to a criminal defendant of the right to "compulsory process for obtaining Witnesses in his favor." If every subpoena duces tecum is a search or seizure of property, then every subpoena ad testificandum is a search or seizure of the person; and if all searches or seizures to obtain mere evidence are unreasonable, there may be no subpoenas at all. *See* Hale v. Henkel, 201 U.S. 43, 73 (1906), declaring judicial subpoenas permissible because "it would be 'utterly impossible to carry on the administration of justice'" without them. Yet as Bradley said, 116 U.S. at 631, federal prosecutors had been forced to live with just such a limitation, based on chancery practice, until the time of the Civil War: "one cardinal rule of the court of chancery is never to decree a discovery which might tend to convict the party of a crime, or to forfeit his property." *Accord*, United States v. Saline Bank, 26 U.S. (1 Pet.) 100, 104 (1828) (Marshall, C.J.); J. STORY, EQUITY JURISPRUDENCE § § 1482-88, 1494 (4th ed. 1836): "it is against the genius of the common law to compel a party to accuse himself; and it is against the general principles of Equity, to aid in the enforcement of penalties or forfeitures." For the further demise of *Boyd*'s fourth-amendment holding, *see* Oklahoma Press Pub. Co. v. Walling, 327 U.S. 186, 195, 208 (1946) (Rutledge, J.): "these cases present no question of actual search and seizure, but raise only the question whether orders of court for the production of specified records have been validly made . . . . [T]he Fourth [Amendment], if applicable, at the most guards against abuse only by way of too much indefiniteness or breadth in the things required to be 'particularly described' . . ."; United States v. Dionisio, 410 U.S. 1, 9 (1973): "It is clear that a subpoena to appear before a grand jury is not a 'seizure' in the Fourth Amendment sense . . ."; In re Horowitz, 482 F.2d 72, 79 (2d Cir. 1973) (Friendly, J.): "Th[ose] decisions . . . suggest that the Court may be moving toward the position . . . that restriction on overbroad *subpoenas duces tecum* rests not on the Fourth Amendment but on the less rigid requirements of the due process clause."

[108]*Entick v. Carrington*, on which Bradley principally relied (*see supra* note 103), involved a warrantless general search. Lord Hale (2 PLEAS OF THE CROWN 113, 116, 149 (1736)) had said the law allowed search for stolen or "uncustomed" goods but said neither that nothing else could be searched for nor that the defendant's lack of a possessory interest was the reason seizure was allowed. For criticism of this branch of the *Boyd* opinion, *see* J. LANDYNSKI, SEARCH AND SEIZURE AND THE SUPREME COURT 58-60 (1966), discussing *Entick* and noting that in speaking equally of "persons, houses, papers and effects" "the amendment does not appear to endow papers with any special sanctity."

[109]116 U.S. at 638-41.

[110]116 U.S. at 639. *Cf.* the passage from Story's EQUITY JURISPRUDENCE quoted *supra* note 107. The Court had no difficulty with the fact that the fifth amendment speaks only to "criminal" proceedings and that the statute described the forfeiture as civil; forfeiture was imposed as punishment for the illegal act, and thus the proceeding was "in substance and effect a criminal one," *id.* at 634. *Cf. supra* chapter 9, discussing the test-oath cases; but *cf.* also *La Vengeance*, discussed *supra* in chapter 1.

subject, without exploring the possible purposes of the provision, was the unnecessarily sweeping and since-abandoned conclusion that "we have been unable to perceive that the seizure of a man's private books and papers to be used in evidence against him is substantially different from compelling him to be a witness against himself."[111] To the extent that the unreliability of coerced testimony is the basis of the self-incrimination provision, it seems inapplicable to what later Justices in upholding such measures as compulsory breath and blood tests have referred to as nontestimonial compulsion;[112] and what Boyd was directed to produce was a record already in existence. Unlike Bradley's hypothesized use of evidence physically taken from a defendant, however, an order to produce incriminating evidence subjects the accused to the same unpalatable "trilemma" that is commonly said to underlie the rule as applied to testimony in open court: the choice among contumacy, falsification, and self-accusation.[113] Bradley missed all this in his essentially conclusory treatment of the self-incrimination issue; but he cannot be said to have been insensitive to the protection of the citizen from undue government intrusion.[114]

[111]116 U.S. at 633. *But see* Andresen v. Maryland, 427 U.S. 463, 473 (1976), allowing use of documentary evidence obtained in a lawful search of the defendant's premises: "petitioner was not asked to say or to do anything . . . . 'A party is privileged from producing the evidence but not from its production.'"

[112]*E.g.*, Schmerber v. California, 384 U.S. 757, 761 (1966). *See* 3 H. WIGMORE, EVIDENCE, § 2263 (1904).

[113]*See, e.g.*, Murphy v. Waterfront Comm'n, 378 U.S. 52, 55 (1964); Meltzer, *Required Records, the McCarran Act, and the Privilege Against Self-Incrimination*, 18 U. CHI. L. REV. 687, 692-93, 700-01, 707 (1951), arguing on this ground that ownership of the materials is irrelevant: "A party directed to produce an incriminating document would be tempted to destroy, conceal, or withhold it . . . . If the privilege is designed to protect witnesses from unpleasant choices, its applicability should not depend on title because title is irrelevant to the attractiveness of the alternatives . . . ." The Court itself has tended to speak in terms of Wigmore's argument that in producing a document the accused implicitly vouches for its authenticity and thus incriminates himself testimonially. *See, e.g.*, Schmerber v. California, *supra* note 112, 384 U.S. at 761; 3 H. WIGMORE, *supra* note 112, § 2264. The fictitious nature of this authentication seems to cut against the argument, however, and later opinions have questioned it in saying an accused could be ordered to produce documents he had not personally prepared. *See* Fisher v. United States, 425 U.S. 391, 412-13 (1976): "production would express nothing more than the taxpayer's belief that the papers are those described in the subpoena."

[114]The congressional debates (1 ANNALS OF CONG. 782-83 (1789)) cast no light on either the fourth- or the fifth-amendment issues raised in *Boyd*. As Professor White points out, the result in *Boyd* was to reverse a judgment based upon the evidence unlawfully obtained, necessarily implying that the introduction of the evidence was itself improper and applying an unstated exclusionary rule for cases in which the owner had a continuing right to the return of his property. White, *supra* note 104, 81 MICH. L. REV. at 1277. But this was hardly surprising since the fifth amendment, which the Court expressly found to have been violated, explicitly speaks to the use of evidence; *Boyd* therefore need not be read to say anything about exclusion of evidence obtained only by unlawful search or seizure.

Other Bill of Rights decisions of the Waite period began to deal with other guarantees respecting the criminal process. *See* Ex parte Lange, 85 U.S. (18 Wall.) 163, 170, 175 (1874) (Miller, J.) (though unnecessary to decide whether double jeopardy clause of fifth amendment applies to punishments other than "life or limb," its "spirit" and common law forbid resentencing after service of sentence begun); Reynolds v. United States, 98 U.S. 145, 158-60 (1879) (Waite, C.J.) (sixth amendment does not require that defendant be confronted with witness whose unavailability he has caused); Wilkerson v. Utah, 99 U.S. 130, 134-35 (1879) (Clifford, J.) (shooting of murderer not cruel and unusual punishment); Ex parte Wilson, 114 U.S. 417, 426-29 (1885) (Gray, J.) (crime punishable by hard labor "infamous" and thus subject to grand-jury requirement of fifth amendment); Mackin v. United States, 117 U.S. 348, 352-54 (1886) (Gray, J.) (same for crime punishable by imprisonment in penitentiary); Spies v. Illinois, 123 U.S. 131, 170-80 (1887) (Waite, C. J.) (sixth-amendment requirement of "impartial" jury, even if applicable to states, satisfied by juror's assertion of ability to try case fairly despite opinion as to guilt of accused).

Conclusion to Part Five

The overall inclinations of the Court during the Waite period can be easily discerned. Resisting the invitation to employ the fourteenth amendment as a tool for censoring the desirability of state legislation, the Court in general gave broad scope to state power to legislate in matters of local concern, even beginning to water down the contract clause's protection for vested rights by holding the police power inalienable. At the same time, however, the Court enforced the implicit limitations of the commerce clause with increasing vigor to keep open the channels of interstate and foreign commerce, limiting the states in this field essentially to the building of bridges and the protection of health and safety and even there drawing the line at a state's attempt to shield itself from outside liquor. Moreover, the same opinions that repeatedly upheld laws against substantive due-process objections increasingly began to say that the police power was the test under that clause as well; the Court seemed to be moving toward a unified conception of state authority based largely upon a vague police-power notion found nowhere in the Constitution.[1]

Federal powers on the whole were construed neither too broadly nor too narrowly. The most interesting cases on federal authority concerned the eleventh amendment, and in those cases, though the Court ultimately found a persuasive rationale to support its distinctions, it often gave the impression of going out of its

[1]Professor McCloskey views the restrictive commerce clause cases as evidence of the Court's eagerness to read laissez-faire notions into the Constitution generally, noting that shortly after holding the states could not regulate such matters as interstate rates the Court disemboweled both the Interstate Commerce Act and the Sherman Act, Congress's two significant efforts at economic regulation (citing ICC v. Cincinnati, N.O., & T.P. Ry., 167 U.S. 479 (1897), and United States v. E.C. Knight Co., 156 U.S. 1 (1895)). R. McCLOSKEY, THE AMERICAN SUPREME COURT 124-27 (1960). This juxtaposition leaves out of account the significant changes in Court membership between 1888 and 1895 (including the replacement of Waite, Miller, Bradley, and Matthews, all of whom had been generally tolerant of economic regulation that did not interfere with the independent free-trade policy of the commerce clause); and it fails to explain why it was Miller, the greatest opponent of substantive due process, who took the lead in asserting the negative effect of the commerce clause.

way to limit previous decisions in order to protect the states from having to pay up on improvidently issued bonds. Perhaps in terms of their underlying philosophy these cases may be related to the Court's deference in the police-power cases to what it considered overriding public necessity; perhaps they reflected more generally the overall judicial restraint the Court manifested in most noncommerce-clause cases during this time.

Indeed, Felix Frankfurter with much force pointed to judicial restraint as the hallmark of Waite's own achievement.[2] His opinion in *Munn*, one of the most influential cases of the time, went to great extremes in declining to investigate the factual basis for a legislative judgment. In commerce-clause cases he was the Court's leading exponent of broad state power, going so far in the *Granger Cases* as to suggest that the states could regulate commerce as much as they liked so long as they did not "directly" affect persons outside their borders.

The list of Waite's opinions reads like a roster of the most significant cases of his time; like his predecessors, he appropriately kept many of the biggest cases for himself. As Frankfurter has pointed out, Waite lacked the grand style of Miller or Marshall, and few of his opinions make gripping reading.[3] Yet there was a brevity and straightforwardness about Waite that might well have been emulated by more of his colleagues and successors. When an issue was easy, like the state-action limitation in *Cruikshank* or the power of Congress to override a state monopoly of interstate communications in *Pensacola*, Waite did not waste time making the case look difficult. In the polygamy case of *Reynolds v. United States* he made effective use of historical materials and seems basically to have captured the spirit of the free exercise clause. His opinion in *Hall v. DeCuir*, though by modern standards exaggerating the impediment of an antisegregation law to commerce, was one of the few contemporary commerce-clause opinions to make an effort to explain the nature of the obstruction. On the other hand, he gave wholly inadequate attention to the commerce question in the *Granger Cases*; he bought trouble in *Munn* by enunciating an unsubstantiated public-interest test under the due process clause; he relied on nothing in the relevant state constitution in holding the state without power to promise not to forbid lotteries in *Stone v. Mississippi*; he strained unconvincingly in arguing in *Lord* that a journey between two California cities involved commerce with foreign nations. In *Louisiana v. Jumel* he was short on reasons for his conclusion and on bases for distinguishing precedents that had allowed suits to remedy acts of state officers; in *Ex parte Curtis* he seemed insensitive to the plausible first-amendment claims made by Bradley on behalf of government employees. In general, however, Waite comes through as a conscientious Justice with a modest view of his own function and a healthy distaste for long and tedious opinions.[4]

Waite's great ally in pursuing the principle of judicial restraint (except in commerce-clause cases) was Miller. Indeed, it might be more correct to put it the other

[2]F. FRANKFURTER, THE COMMERCE CLAUSE UNDER MARSHALL, TANEY AND WAITE 80-82 (1937). *See also* C. MAGRATH, MORRISON R. WAITE: THE TRIUMPH OF CHARACTER 209 (1963).

[3]*See* F. FRANKFURTER, *supra* note 2, at 79-80.

[4]Indeed, in striking contrast to some of its predecessors, the Waite Court in general (with certain notable exceptions) set a pattern of conciseness that might well be an example to its successors. For the view that Waite not only "restored respectability" to a Court in need of rehabilitation but also was the equal of Miller, Field, and Harlan in everything but style, *see* C. MAGRATH, *supra* note 2, at 274, 320-21.

way around, for Miller had distinguished himself as the Court's leading advocate of judicial restraint for many years before Waite was appointed.[5] Miller displayed rare power as a writer of opinions; there is scarcely a Miller opinion that is not a pleasure to read. In terms of brevity, lucidity, and style they are almost all models to be emulated by any judge; and he usually went right to the heart of the problem.

For all his power, Miller had an irritating habit of slighting the difficult question. He never explained in *Bartemeyer v. Iowa*, for instance, why a prospective liquor law did not offend due process, and his application of the uniformity test to the passenger-bond requirement in *Henderson* and to the rate regulation in *Wabash* was little more than a bare conclusion. He also exposed himself to charges of inconsistency. His vigorous efforts to keep state officers from being sued in bond cases seemed to depart from the spirit of his eloquent *Lee* opinion limiting the immunity of federal officers. There was a tension between his insistence that his brethren had no right to substitute views for the will of the legislature and his willingness to look beyond the Constitution for limits on state tax power in *Loan Association v. Topeka* and for congressional powers over Indians in *United States v. Kagama*. Nevertheless, the clarity of his opinions, his understanding of the nature of the problems before him, and his efforts to lay down comprehensible tests to carry out the purposes of various constitutional provisions mark him as one of the greatest constitutional judges we have ever had.[6]

Field, often in dissent, was the Court's unfailing advocate of judicial intervention; his opinions are most notably characterized by a dogged and consistent concern for the protection of economic, though not always of vested, rights. Field had a tendency to assume his most important conclusions—such as that the due process clause limited states to the exercise of their police powers, and that equal protection could be satisfied by imposing comparable discriminations on members of different races. In upholding a state wrongful-death law as applied to interstate commerce, he confused the law and ignored precedent by enunciating the unsubstantiated conclusion that only "direct" burdens were prohibited, and he failed to explain how his test applied to the case at hand. His positions that Congress could not license interstate telegraphs or punish state judges who denied federal rights seemed extreme. Given his assumptions, however, Field could argue forcefully in applying them, as shown by his demonstration of the unreasonableness of the margarine ban in *Powell v. Pennsylvania*. Moreover, Field came closer than any of his contemporaries to making sense of the equal protection clause by beginning to explain that classifications would be upheld if there was a reasonable basis for them.

Apart from his straightforward opinion for the Court in the *Civil Rights Cases*, Bradley wrote surprisingly few important majority opinions, principal among them the ambitious but unsettling equation of a subpoena with a search or seizure in *Boyd v. United States* and the poorly explained conclusion in *Robbins* that even a nondiscriminatory tax on drummers for out-of-state goods would be unconstitutional. His equal-protection opinion in *Missouri v. Lewis* begged the question by upholding a special court for Saint Louis on the ground that all people in Saint Louis were treated

[5] *See supra* part four.

[6] *Accord*, C. FAIRMAN, MR. JUSTICE MILLER AND THE SUPREME COURT 3-4, 426 (1939). *See also id.* at 248, noting that because of a lack of both formal training and theoretical bent Miller's "strength lay in the wisdom of his judgments rather than in the artistry of their doctrinal elaboration."

alike; his dissent from jurisdiction over a state officer in the *Virginia Coupon Cases* seems clever but erroneous in distinguishing the precedents. Bradley has come down to us as one of the giants of the period,[7] but this assessment does not leap at the reader of his constitutional opinions.

Gray, a comparative latecomer, made an impressive showing although he was not given the opportunity to write many important majority opinions. His dissent from jurisdiction to sue a government officer in *Lee*, while ultimately contrary to precedent, was an able job making excellent use of historical materials. His opinion upholding peacetime legal tender was a model. His opinion on the legality of mill acts was an impressive exercise in scholarship and made a serious effort to rationalize the laws in terms of the assumed meaning of the due process clause. Gray had another fourteen years to sit after Waite died; he promised to be one of the strongest members of the Court under the next Chief Justice.[8]

Another strong Justice with many years of service ahead of him was Harlan, who made a name for himself largely as a dissenter in speaking up strongly in favor of civil rights, contract rights, and the police power.[9] His dissents from the refusals to extend citizenship to assimilated Indians and to apply the grand-jury requirement to the states were thorough and impressive. His principal efforts for the majority reflected the same propensities: he wrote to sustain state power over liquor in *Mugler* and margarine in *Powell*. Both opinions leave much to be desired, though the former has become a leading case; he failed to explain in *Mugler* why he read the police power into the due process clause or in *Powell* why he effectively read it back out. His most notable exercise was his dissent in the *Civil Rights Cases*, a substantial effort by any standard but one in which he seems to have let his heart run away with his head.

Matthews, who served only eight years, was a hard worker who was given significant responsibility. It was he who established the long-lasting test for the incorporation of fundamental procedural rights in the due process clause in a well-constructed opinion in *Hurtado v. California*. It was he who became the Court's spokesman for rationalizing the bewildering precedents involving sovereign immunity, and he did so with great success. He also wrote two major and essentially conflicting commerce-clause decisions that he made no effort to reconcile, allowing states to license railway engineers but not to ban the importation of liquor; and he wrote the famous *Yick Wo* opinion, which unnecessarily appeared to forbid the mere grant of discretion because it might be abused while getting credit for the principle against discriminatory application that Harlan had already established in *Neal v. Delaware*.[10]

Strong carried his weight competently during the few years he continued to sit with Waite; he is most noted during this time for his opinions for the Court in the jury-discrimination cases, where he wrote firmly to enforce the equal protection

---

[7]*See* Fairman, *What Makes a Great Justice? Mr. Justice Bradley and the Supreme Court, 1870-1892*, 30 B.U.L. Rev. 49 (1950).

[8]*See* C. Fairman, Miller, *supra* note 6, at 197, 384, describing the learned Gray and Miller as standing in a relationship similar to that between Story and Marshall.

[9]For an assessment more admiring than analytical, *see* F. Latham, The Great Dissenter: John Marshall Harlan (1970), passim.

[10]For favorable assessments of Matthews, *see* C. Magrath, *supra* note 4, at 269-70; C. Fairman, Miller, *supra* note 6, at 383-84.

clause for the first time in its original racial context. His contribution to the commerce-clause debate in *Railroad Co. v. Husen*, however, only made things worse by reinstating the police-power test that Miller had just gone out of his way to eliminate, without even adverting to the contradiction.

Hunt and Woods were given little of importance to do;[11] Blatchford and Davis were essentially invisible;[12] Lamar served too briefly to make a mark. The opinions of Clifford and Swayne continued to be below standard.[13] The percentage of Justices making significant contributions, however, was greater during the Waite period than at any time since Marshall had abolished the practice of seriatim opinions.

The fourteen closing years of the Court's first century were a time of great cases. It is interesting that, despite the presence of an unusual number of highly talented Justices including Miller, Field, Bradley, Harlan, and Gray,[14] they were also a time of markedly unsatisfying opinions. From the technical standpoint the worst example is the cacophony of commerce-clause decisions. But the most significant failing of the Court under Waite was its omission ever to face squarely the basic questions and assumptions that underlay its seminal fourteenth-amendment decisions; and it managed without explanation to state the law in such a way as to make it easy for its successors to use its own words as support for traveling just as steadily in the opposite direction.

---

[11]*See* C. MAGRATH, *supra* note 4, at 101, concluding that Hunt was "chiefly remembered for holding on to his seat for three years after becoming totally incapacitated."

[12]*See id.* at 271, describing Blatchford as "colorless but conscientious" and reporting Waite's view that he was "a good worker."

[13]*See id.* at 101, terming Swayne Lincoln's weakest appointment; C. FAIRMAN, MILLER, *supra* note 6, at 382, noting the observation of the Reporter Wallace that the Court would be better off (in their later years) without either Swayne or Clifford and his anguished wonder whether there was ever "such a man" as the latter "in such a place"; Currie, *The Most Insignificant Justice: A Preliminary Inquiry*, 50 U. CHI. L. REV. 466, 473-77 (1983).

[14]*See* Fairman, *supra* note 7, 30 B.U.L. REV. at 49: "Even today one would hesitate to say that the Court has ever surpassed the collective strength of the bench of 1882 to '86."

Epilogue

A hundred years, the better part of a thousand cases. From the presidency of George Washington to that of Grover Cleveland; from thirteen states to thirty-eight; from the invention of the cotton gin to the establishment of the Interstate Commerce Commission. The panorama is vast, the landmarks tall. The courts may review the constitutionality of acts of Congress. The national legislature may set up a bank but may not forbid slavery in the territories. The states may neither impair corporate charters nor tax the national bank. State officers may be sued for torts but not for breaking state contracts. Civilians may not be subjected to military trials where civil courts are open. Slaughtering animals is not a privilege of national citizenship, and the fourteenth amendment limits only state action. States may regulate the rates charged for storing grain and outlaw the sale of alcoholic beverages. They may regulate interstate commerce to some extent, but not too much. Admission to the Union, like a diamond, is forever. The history of the land is in the opinions of the Court.

A hundred years, half a hundred Justices. From founding fathers like William Paterson and James Wilson to the rugged frontiersman Field, the railroad lawyers Bradley and Matthews, the reconstructed rebel Lucius Quintus Cincinnatus Lamar; from fleeting shadows like John Blair and Ward Hunt to giants like Marshall and Miller; from dedicated nationalists like Story to extreme states-righters like Peter Daniel. The collection is rich and varied. Here is Samuel Chase, the overbearing Federalist who used the bench as a political platform and was very nearly removed for his impertinence. There is the long-sitting abolitionist John McLean, who spent much of his energy trying to become anybody's candidate for President. There are Marshall's first five Republican brethren, who to a man disappointed Jefferson's expectations by abandoning party considerations upon elevation to the Bench. In this favorable light hangs sturdy old James Wayne of Georgia, who stayed with his country when his state did not, and who cast the deciding vote to sustain Lincoln's blockade of Southern ports. Nearby stands the faithful Bushrod Washington, whose respect for precedent induced him to refrain from giving the last needed voice to strike down a state bankruptcy law he believed unconstitutional. Here is Clifford of Maine, who wrote interminable and incompetent constitutional opinions; and Todd of Kentucky, who in almost twenty years wrote nothing on the subject at all.

Let us not dwell on the weaker Justices;[1] let us only remark that throughout the first hundred years there were a surprising number who left no significant trace upon constitutional history. Of those eclipsed by Marshall's insistence on speaking for the Court we may complain no more than of those whose terms were too short to afford a reasonable opportunity. There remain far too many who ought never to have been appointed to a position whose importance deserves our best legal minds. There is nothing new in the objection that not all Justices are chosen on the basis of ability.

Let us pause to salute a number who labored with admirable skills at a difficult job: the Thompsons, the Iredells, the Strongs, the Campbells, the Grays and Waites and Harlans. Let us raise the cup for the gifted handful who gave the Court its befitting luster throughout the century: for Marshall's eloquence and vision, for Story's learning, for Taney's straightforward technique, for Curtis's awesome analytic powers, for Miller's lucidity and sense for the critical question. Let us not forget their limitations: Marshall's excessive dicta and tendency to equate what is law with what ought to be, Taney's blind spot for blacks, Miller's bouts of lawlessness. But let us be thankful that they were there.

The great opinions? Try Marshall's carefully balanced and comprehensive exposition of the necessary and proper clause in *McCulloch*, his "great poem."[2] Sample the erudition of Story's *Charles River* and *Briscoe* dissents, his effective argument from purpose and balanced use of contemporary understanding in *Martin v. Hunter's Lessee*. Refresh yourself in Taney's simple explanation in the *License Cases* that the commerce clause means what it says, in his liberation of admiralty in the *Genesee Chief* to fulfill its function, in Miller's straightforward objections to the excesses of *Hepburn v. Griswold*. And, whenever things look dark, turn once more to Curtis's *Dred Scott* dissent, the supreme monument of the lawyer's craft in the first century of constitutional adjudication.

The great failures? A whole generation of judges before Story felt little compunction to explain themselves at all. Story himself in *Terrett v. Taylor* and Nelson in *Hays v. Pacific Mail S.S. Co.* struck down state laws without ever saying why. Taney and his four brethren who believed the commerce clause did not limit state power never agreed on a single opinion. Under Chase and Waite the Court issued long trains of unanimous commerce-clause decisions based upon contradictory principles. Substantive due process and the requirement that nonracial classifications be reasonable crept into the law without ever having been discussed. But the capstone again is *Dred Scott*, where five Justices outdid one another in concocting ever more ludicrous excuses for the preconceived and untenable conclusion that Congress lacked authority to ban slavery in the territories.

---

[1]That has been done elsewhere. *See* Currie, *The Most Insignificant Justice: A Preliminary Inquiry*, 50 U. CHI. L. REV. 466 (1983); Easterbrook, *The Most Insignificant Justice: Further Evidence*, 50 U. CHI. L. REV. 481 (1983).

[2]*See* Casper, *The Emerging European Constitution*, in PROCEEDINGS OF THE 72d ANNUAL MEETING OF THE AMERICAN SOCIETY OF INTERNATIONAL LAW 169, 170 (1978).

These are failures of craftsmanship, not always of outcome. In the first century it is not common to find an important decision that clearly distorted the Constitution. I have trouble believing that article III authorized suits against states, that the eleventh amendment did not preclude injunctions against state officers, that the Constitution somewhere forbade state taxation of federal instrumentalities or granted a right to travel, that due process limited substantive legislative powers. I wonder to what extent the Justices themselves believed that some of these conclusions were really consistent with the Constitution. But most even of these are fairly debatable, and their rhetoric is the strongest evidence that by and large the Justices understood that, to the extent possible, they were expected to base their decisions on the law as found in the Constitution.

The exceptions are disturbing. From Samuel Chase in *Calder v. Bull* and William Johnson in *Fletcher v. Peck* to Salmon Chase in *Hepburn* and the Miller of *Kagama* and *Loan Association v. Topeka*, some of the most assertive Justices of the century openly proclaimed their independence from the written Constitution. Fortunately for the rule of law, such instances were rare. One cannot but suspect, however, that similar restiveness may have lain behind other decisions couched in more conventional terms. If this is so, one may readily prefer the candor of a Chase or a Miller; for if a judicial act cannot bear the light of day it were better left undone.

Especially from the smug advantage of a century or two of hindsight, it is easier to find fault than to write a good opinion; an attempt to rewrite *Marbury v. Madison* is sobering even today. Add that the opinions were often prepared by overburdened generalists in as little as a few days, in a time of inferior research tools and an immature tradition of judicial exposition, under the pressure of carrying colleagues with varying views; and it is perhaps inspiring that the Justices did so well. Consider also the unfairness of judging judges by the standards of a much later time, and let us moderate our disapproval. Yet let us take comfort in the fact that Justices like Story, Curtis, Miller, and Gray, who most nearly reflect later conceptions of judicial virtue, were equally respected for these qualities in their own time. For no one since has improved on Story's simple statement of the proper approach to constitutional interpretation:

> And, perhaps, the safest rule of interpretation, after all, will be found to be to look to the nature and objects of the particular powers, duties and rights, with all the lights and aids of contemporary history; and to give to the words of each just such operation and force, consistent with their legitimate meaning, as may fairly secure and attain the ends proposed.[3]

"Wide enough in all conscience," as Cardozo said, "is the field of discretion that remains."[4]

---

[3]Prigg v. Pennsylvania, 41 U.S. (16 Pet.) 539, 610-11 (1842).
[4]B. CARDOZO, THE NATURE OF THE JUDICIAL PROCESS 141 (1921).

Appendix A
Justices of the Supreme Court
1789–1888

JUSTICES OF THE SUPREME COURT, 1789–1888

		1790	1800	10	20	30	40	50	60	70	80	90

*John Jay   (1789–1795)
*John Rutledge   (1789–1791, 1795)
James Wilson   (1789–1798)
John Blair   (1789–1796)
William Cushing   (1789–1810)
James Iredell   (1790–1799)
Thomas Johnson   (1791–1793)
William Paterson   (1793–1806)
*Oliver Ellsworth   (1796–1800)
Samuel Chase   (1796–1811)
Bushrod Washington   (1798–1829)
Alfred Moore   (1799–1804)
*John Marshall   (1801–1835)
William Johnson   (1804–1834)
H. B. Livingston   (1806–1823)
Thomas Todd   (1807–1826)
Gabriel Duvall   (1811–1835)
Joseph Story   (1811–1845)
Smith Thompson   (1823–1843)
Robert Trimble   (1826–1828)
John McLean   (1829–1861)

Henry Baldwin (1830–1844)
James M. Wayne (1835–1867)
Philip Barbour (1836–1841)
*Roger B. Taney (1836–1864)
John Catron (1837–1865)
John McKinley (1837–1852)
Peter V. Daniel (1841–1860)
Samuel Nelson (1845–1872)
Levi Woodbury (1845–1851)
Robert C. Grier (1846–1870)
Benjamin R. Curtis (1851–1857)
John A. Campbell (1853–1861)
Nathan Clifford (1858–1881)
Noah H. Swayne (1862–1881)
Samuel F. Miller (1862–1890)
David Davis (1862–1877)
Stephen Field (1863–1897)
*Salmon P. Chase (1864–1873)
Joseph P. Bradley (1870–1892)
William Strong (1870–1880)
Ward Hunt (1872–1882)
*Morrison R. Waite (1874–1888)
John Marshall Harlan (1877–1911)
William B. Woods (1880–1887)
Stanley Matthews (1881–1889)
Horace Gray (1881–1902)
Samuel Blatchford (1882–1893)
Lucius Q. C. Lamar (1888–1893)

*Denotes Chief Justice.

Appendix B
The Constitution of the
United States

We the People of the United States, in Order to form a more perfect Union, establish Justice, insure domestic Tranquility, provide for the common defence, promote the general Welfare, and secure the Blessings of Liberty to ourselves and our Posterity, do ordain and establish this Constitution for the United States of America.

ARTICLE I

SECTION 1. All legislative Powers herein granted shall be vested in a Congress of the United States, which shall consist of a Senate and House of Representatives.

SECTION 2. The House of Representatives shall be composed of Members chosen every second Year by the People of the several States, and the Electors in each State shall have the Qualifications requisite for Electors of the most numerous Branch of the State Legislature.

No Person shall be a Representative who shall not have attained to the Age of twenty-five Years, and been seven Years a Citizen of the United States, and who shall not, when elected, be an Inhabitant of that State in which he shall be chosen.

Representatives and direct Taxes shall be apportioned among the several States which may be included within this Union, according to their respective Numbers, which shall be determined by adding to the whole Number of free Persons, including those bound to Service for a Term of Years, and excluding Indians not taxed, three fifths of all other Persons. The actual Enumeration shall be made within three Years after the first meeting of the Congress of the United States, and within every subsequent Term of ten Years, in such Manner as they shall by Law direct. The Number of Representatives shall not exceed one for every thirty Thousand, but each State shall have at Least one Representative; and until such enumeration shall be made, the State of New Hampshire shall be entitled to chuse three, Massachusetts eight, Rhode-Island and Providence Plantations one, Connecticut five, New-York six, New Jersey four, Pennsylvania eight, Delaware one, Maryland six, Virginia ten, North Carolina five, South Carolina five, and Georgia three.

When vacancies happen in the Representation from any State, the Executive Authority thereof shall issue Writs of Election to fill such Vacancies.

The House of Representatives shall chuse their Speaker and other Officers; and shall have the sole Power of Impeachment.

SECTION 3. The Senate of the United States shall be composed of two Senators from each State, chosen by the Legislature thereof, for six Years; and each Senator shall have one Vote.

Immediately after they shall be assembled in Consequence of the first Election, they shall be divided as equally as may be into three Classes. The Seats of the Senators of the first Class shall be vacated at the Expiration of the second Year, of the second Class at the Expiration of the fourth Year, and of the third Class at the Expiration of the sixth Year, so that one-third may be chosen every second Year; and if Vacancies happen by Resignation, or otherwise, during the Recess of the Legislature of any State, the Executive thereof may make temporary Appointments until the next Meeting of the Legislature, which shall then fill such Vacancies.

No Person shall be a Senator who shall not have attained to the Age of thirty Years, and been nine Years a Citizen of the United States, and who shall not, when elected, be an Inhabitant of that State for which he shall be chosen.

The Vice President of the United States shall be President of the Senate, but shall have no Vote, unless they be equally divided.

The Senate shall chuse their other Officers, and also a President pro tempore, in the absence of the Vice President, or when he shall exercise the Office of President of the United States.

The Senate shall have the sole Power to try all Impeachments. When sitting for that Purpose, they shall be on Oath or Affirmation. When the President of the United States is tried, the Chief Justice shall preside: And no Person shall be convicted without the Concurrence of two thirds of the Members present.

Judgment in Cases of Impeachment shall not extend further than to removal from Office, and disqualification to hold and enjoy any Office of honor, Trust or Profit under the United States: but the Party convicted shall nevertheless be liable and subject to Indictment, Trial, Judgment and Punishment, according to Law.

SECTION 4. The Times, Places and Manner of holding Elections for Senators and Representatives, shall be prescribed in each State by the Legislature thereof; but the Congress may at any time by Law make or alter such Regulations, except as to the Place of Chusing Senators.

The Congress shall assemble at least once in every Year, and such Meeting shall be on the first Monday in December, unless they shall by Law appoint a different Day.

SECTION 5. Each House shall be the Judge of the Elections, Returns and Qualifications of its own Members, and a Majority of each shall constitute a Quorum to do Business; but a smaller number may adjourn from day to day, and may be authorized to compel the Attendance of absent Members, in such Manner, and under such Penalties as each House may provide.

Each House may determine the Rules of its Proceedings, punish its Members for disorderly Behavior, and, with the Concurrence of two thirds, expel a Member.

Each House shall keep a Journal of its Proceedings, and from time to time publish the same, excepting such Parts as may in their Judgment require Secrecy; and the Yeas and Nays of the Members of either House on any question shall, at the Desire of one fifth of those Present, be entered on the Journal.

Neither House, during the Session of Congress, shall, without the Consent of the other, adjourn for more than three days, nor to any other Place than that in which the two Houses shall be sitting.

SECTION 6. The Senators and Representatives shall receive a Compensation for their Services, to be ascertained by Law, and paid out of the Treasury of the United States. They shall in all Cases, except Treason, Felony and Breach of the Peace, be privileged from Arrest during their Attendance at the Session of their respective Houses, and in going to and returning from the same; and for any Speech or Debate in either House, they shall not be questioned in any other Place.

No Senator or Representative shall, during the Time for which he was elected, be appointed to any civil Office under the Authority of the United States, which shall have been created, or the Emoluments whereof shall have been encreased during such time; and no Person holding any Office under the United States, shall be a Member of either House during his Continuance in Office.

SECTION 7. All Bills for raising Revenue shall originate in the House of Representatives; but the Senate may propose or concur with Amendments as on other Bills.

Every Bill which shall have passed the House of Representatives and the Senate, shall, before it become a Law, be presented to the President of the United States; If he approve he shall sign it, but if not he shall return it, with his Objections to that House in which it shall have originated, who shall enter the Objections at large on their Journal, and proceed to reconsider it. If after such Reconsideration two thirds of that House shall agree to pass the Bill, it shall be sent, together with the Objections, to the other House, by which it shall likewise be reconsidered, and if approved by two thirds of that House, it shall become a Law. But in all such Cases the Votes of both Houses shall be determined by Yeas and Nays, and the Names of the Persons voting for and against the Bill shall be entered on the Journal of each House respectively. If any Bill shall not be returned by the President within ten Days (Sundays excepted) after it shall have been presented to him, the Same shall be a Law, in like Manner as if he had signed it, unless the Congress by their Adjournment prevent its Return, in which Case it shall not be a Law.

Every Order, Resolution, or Vote to which the Concurrence of the Senate and House of Representatives may be necessary (except on a question of Adjournment) shall be presented to the President of the United States; and before the Same shall take Effect, shall be approved by him, or being disapproved by him, shall be repassed by two thirds of the Senate and House of Representatives, according to the Rules and Limitations prescribed in the Case of a Bill.

SECTION 8. The Congress shall have Power To lay and collect Taxes, Duties, Imposts and Excises, to pay the Debts and provide for the common Defence and general Welfare of the United States; but all Duties, Imposts and Excises shall be uniform throughout the United States;

To borrow money on the credit of the United States;

To regulate Commerce with foreign Nations, and among the several States, and with the Indian Tribes;

To establish an uniform Rule of Naturalization, and uniform Laws on the subject of Bankruptcies throughout the United States;

To coin Money, regulate the Value thereof, and of foreign Coin, and fix the Standard of Weights and Measures;

To provide for the Punishment of counterfeiting the Securities and current Coin of the United States;

To establish Post Offices and post Roads;

To promote the Progress of Science and useful Arts, by securing for limited Times to Authors and Inventors the exclusive Right to their respective Writings and Discoveries;

To constitute Tribunals inferior to the supreme Court;

To define and punish Piracies and Felonies committed on the high Seas, and Offenses against the Law of Nations;

To declare War, grant Letters of Marque and Reprisal, and make Rules concerning Captures on Land and Water;

To raise and support Armies, but no Appropriation of Money to that Use shall be for a longer Term than two Years;

To provide and maintain a Navy;

To make Rules for the Government and Regulation of the land and naval Forces;

To provide for calling forth the Militia to execute the Laws of the Union, suppress Insurrections and repel Invasions;

To provide for organizing, arming, and disciplining the Militia, and for governing such Part of them as may be employed in the Service of the United States, reserving to the States respectively, the Appointment of the Officers, and the Authority of training the Militia according to the discipline prescribed by Congress;

To exercise exclusive Legislation in all Cases whatsoever, over such District (not exceeding ten Miles square) as may, by Cession of particular States, and the acceptance of Congress, become the Seat of the Government of the United States, and to exercise like Authority over all Places purchased by the Consent of the Legislature of the State in which the Same shall be, for the Erection of Forts, Magazines, Arsenals, dock-Yards, and other needful Buildings; — And

To make all Laws which shall be necessary and proper for carrying into Execution the foregoing Powers, and all other Powers vested by this Constitution in the Government of the United States, or in any Department or Officer thereof.

SECTION 9. The Migration or Importation of such Persons as any of the States now existing shall think proper to admit, shall not be prohibited by the Congress prior to the Year one thousand eight hundred and eight, but a tax or duty may be imposed on such Importation, not exceeding ten dollars for each Person.

The privilege of the Writ of Habeas Corpus shall not be suspended, unless when in Cases of Rebellion or Invasion the public Safety may require it.

No Bill of Attainder or ex post facto Law shall be passed.

No capitation, or other direct, Tax shall be laid, unless in Proportion to the Census or Enumeration herein before directed to be taken.

No Tax or Duty shall be laid on Articles exported from any State.

No Preference shall be given by any Regulation of Commerce or Revenue to the Ports of one State over those of another; nor shall Vessels bound to, or from, one State, be obliged to enter, clear, or pay Duties in another.

No Money shall be drawn from the Treasury, but in Consequence of Appropriations made by Law; and a regular Statement and Account of the Receipts and Expenditures of all public Money shall be published from time to time.

No Title of Nobility shall be granted by the United States: And no Person holding any Office of Profit or Trust under them, shall, without the Consent of the Congress, accept of any present, Emolument, Office, or Title, of any kind whatever, from any King, Prince, or foreign State.

SECTION 10. No State shall enter into any Treaty, Alliance, or Confederation; grant Letters of Marque and Reprisal; coin Money; emit Bills of Credit; make any Thing but gold and silver Coin a Tender in Payment of Debts; pass any Bill of Attainder, ex post facto Law, or Law impairing the Obligation of Contracts, or grant any Title of Nobility.

No State shall, without the Consent of the Congress, lay any Imposts or Duties on Imports or Exports, except what may be absolutely necessary for executing its inspection Laws: and the net Produce of all Duties and Imposts, laid by any State on Imports or Exports, shall be for the Use of the Treasury of the United States; and all such Laws shall be subject to the Revision and Controul of the Congress.

No State shall, without the Consent of Congress, lay any duty of Tonnage, keep Troops, or Ships of War in time of Peace, enter into any Agreement or Compact with another State, or with a foreign Power, or engage in War, unless actually invaded, or in such imminent Danger as will not admit of delay.

ARTICLE II

SECTION 1. The executive Power shall be vested in a President of the United States of America. He shall hold his Office during the Term of four Years, and, together with the Vice-President, chosen for the same Term, be elected, as follows.

Each State shall appoint, in such Manner as the Legislature thereof may direct, a Number of Electors, equal to the whole Number of Senators and Representatives to which the State may be entitled in the Congress: but no Senator or Representative, or Person holding an Office of Trust or Profit under the United States, shall be appointed an Elector.

The Electors shall meet in their respective States, and vote by Ballot for two persons, of whom one at least shall not be an Inhabitant of the same State with themselves. And they shall make a List of all the Persons voted for, and of the Number of Votes for each; which List they shall sign and certify, and transmit sealed to the Seat of the Government of the United States, directed to the President of the Senate. The President of the Senate shall, in the Presence of the Senate and House of Representatives, open all the Certificates, and the Votes shall then be counted. The Person having the greatest Number of Votes shall be the President, if such Number be a Majority of the whole Number of Electors appointed; and if there be more than one who have such Majority, and have an equal Number of Votes, then the House of Representatives shall immediately chuse by Ballot one of them for President; and if no Person have a Majority, then from the five highest on the List the said House shall in like Manner chuse the President. But in chusing the President, the Votes shall be taken by States, the Representation from each State having one Vote; a quorum for this Purpose shall consist of a Member or Members from two thirds of the States, and a Majority of all the States shall be necessary to a Choice. In every Case, after the Choice of the President, the Person having the greatest Number of Votes of the Electors shall be the Vice President. But if there should remain two or more who have equal Votes, the Senate shall chuse from them by Ballot the Vice-President.

The Congress may determine the Time of chusing the Electors, and the Day on which they shall give their Votes; which Day shall be the same throughout the United States.

No person except a natural born Citizen, or a Citizen of the United States, at the time of the Adoption of this Constitution, shall be eligible to the Office of President; neither shall any Person be eligible to that Office who shall not have attained to the Age of thirty-five Years, and been fourteen Years a Resident within the United States.

In Case of the Removal of the President from Office, or of his Death, Resignation, or Inability to discharge the Powers and Duties of the said Office, the same shall devolve on the Vice President, and the Congress may by Law, provide for the Case of Removal, Death, Resignation or Inability, both of the President and Vice President, declaring what Officer shall then act as President, and such Officer shall act accordingly, until the Disability be removed, or a President shall be elected.

The President shall, at stated Times, receive for his Services, a Compensation, which shall neither be encreased nor diminished during the Period for which he shall have been elected, and he shall not receive within that Period any other Emolument from the United States, or any of them.

Before he enter on the Execution of his Office, he shall take the following Oath or Affirmation: — "I do solemnly swear (or affirm) that I will faithfully execute the Office of President of the United States, and will to the best of my Ability, preserve, protect and defend the Constitution of the United States."

SECTION 2. The President shall be Commander in Chief of the Army and Navy of the United States, and of the Militia of the several States, when called into the actual Service of the United States; he may require the Opinion in writing, of the principal Officer in each of the executive Departments, upon any subject relating to the Duties of their respective Offices, and he shall have Power to Grant Reprieves and Pardons for Offenses against the United States, except in Cases of Impeachment.

He shall have Power, by and with the Advice and Consent of the Senate, to make Treaties, provided two-thirds of the Senators present concur; and he shall nominate, and by and with the Advice and Consent of the Senate, shall appoint Ambassadors, other public Ministers and Consuls, Judges of the supreme Court, and all other Officers of the United States, whose Appointments are not herein otherwise provided for, and which shall be established by Law: but the Congress may by Law vest the Appointment of such inferior Officers, as they think proper, in the President alone, in the Courts of Law, or in the Heads of Departments.

The President shall have Power to fill up all Vacancies that may happen during the Recess of the Senate, by granting Commissions which shall expire at the End of their next Session.

SECTION 3. He shall from time to time give to the Congress Information of the State of the Union, and recommend to their Consideration such Measures as he shall judge necessary and expedient; he may, on extraordinary Occasions, convene both Houses, or either of them, and in Case of Disagreement between them, with Respect to the Time of Adjournment, he may adjourn them to such Time as he shall think proper; he shall receive Ambassadors and other public Ministers; he shall take Care that the Laws be faithfully executed, and shall Commission all the Officers of the United States.

SECTION 4. The President, Vice President and all civil Officers of the United States, shall be removed from Office on Impeachment for, and Conviction of, Treason, Bribery, or other high Crimes and Misdemeanors.

ARTICLE III

SECTION 1. The judicial Power of the United States, shall be vested in one supreme Court, and in such inferior Courts as the Congress may from time to time ordain and establish. The Judges, both of the supreme and inferior Courts, shall hold their Offices during good Behaviour, and shall, at stated Times, receive for their Services, a Compensation, which shall not be diminished during their Continuance in Office.

SECTION 2. The judicial Power shall extend to all Cases, in Law and Equity, arising under this Constitution, the Laws of the United States, and Treaties made, or which shall be made, under their Authority; — to all Cases affecting Ambassadors, other public Ministers and Consuls;—to all Cases of admiralty and maritime Jurisdiction;—to Controversies to which the United States shall be a Party;—to Controversies between two or more States; — between a State and Citizens of another State; — between Citizens of different States; — between Citizens of the same State claiming Lands under Grants of different States, and between a State, or the Citizens thereof, and foreign States, Citizens or Subjects.

In all Cases affecting Ambassadors, other public Ministers and Consuls, and those in which a State shall be Party, the supreme Court shall have original Jurisdiction. In all the other Cases before mentioned, the supreme Court shall have appellate Jurisdiction, both as to Law and Fact, with such Exceptions, and under such Regulations as the Congress shall make.

The trial of all Crimes, except in Cases of Impeachment, shall be by Jury; and such Trial shall be held in the State where the said Crimes shall have been committed; but when not committed within any State, the Trial shall be at such Place or Places as the Congress may by Law have directed.

SECTION 3. Treason against the United States, shall consist only in levying War against them, or in adhering to their Enemies, giving them Aid and Comfort. No Person shall be convicted of Treason unless on the Testimony of two Witnesses to the same overt Act, or on Confession in open Court.

The Congress shall have Power to declare the Punishment of Treason, but no Attainder of Treason shall work Corruption of Blood, or Forfeiture except during the Life of the Person attainted.

ARTICLE IV

SECTION 1. Full Faith and Credit shall be given in each State to the public Acts, Records, and judicial Proceedings of every other State. And the Congress may by general Laws prescribe the Manner in which such Acts, Records and Proceedings shall be proved, and the Effect thereof.

SECTION 2. The Citizens of each State shall be entitled to all Privileges and Immunities of Citizens in the several States.

A Person charged in any State with Treason, Felony, or other Crime, who shall flee from Justice, and be found in another State, shall on demand of the executive Authority of the State from which he fled, be delivered up, to be removed to the State having Jurisdiction of the Crime.

No Person held to Service or Labour in one State, under the Laws thereof, escaping into another, shall, in Consequence of any Law or Regulation therein, be discharged from such Service or Labour, but shall be delivered up on Claim of the Party to whom such Service or Labour may be due.

SECTION 3. New States may be admitted by the Congress into this Union; but no new State shall be formed or erected within the Jurisdiction of any other State; nor any State be formed by the Junction of two or more States, or parts of States, without the Consent of the Legislatures of the States concerned as well as of the Congress.

The Congress shall have Power to dispose of and make all needful Rules and Regulations respecting the Territory or other Property belonging to the United States; and nothing in this Constitution shall be so construed as to Prejudice any Claims of the United states, or of any particular State.

SECTION 4. The United States shall guarantee to every State in this Union a Republican Form of Government, and shall protect each of them against Invasion; and on Application of the Legislature, or of the Executive (when the Legislature cannot be convened) against domestic Violence.

ARTICLE V

The Congress, whenever two-thirds of both Houses shall deem it necessary, shall propose Amendments to this Constitution, or, on the Application of the Legislature of two-thirds of the several States, shall call a Convention for proposing Amendments, which, in either Case, shall be valid to all Intents and Purposes, as part of this Constitution, when ratified by the Legislatures of three-fourths of the several States, or by Conventions in three-fourths thereof, as the one or the other Mode of Ratification may be proposed by the Congress: Provided that no Amendment which may be made prior to the Year One thousand eight hundred and eight shall in any Manner affect the first and fourth Clauses in the Ninth Section of the first Article; and that no State, without its Consent, shall be deprived of its equal Suffrage in the Senate.

ARTICLE VI

All Debts contracted and Engagements entered into, before the Adoption of this Constitution, shall be as valid against the United States under this Constitution, as under the Confederation.

This Constitution, and the Laws of the United States which shall be made in Pursuance thereof; and all Treaties made, or which shall be made, under the Authority of the United States, shall be the supreme Law of the Land; and the

Judges in every State shall be bound thereby, any Thing in the Constitution or Laws of any State to the Contrary notwithstanding.

The Senators and Representatives before mentioned, and the Members of the several State Legislatures, and all executive and judicial Officers, both of the United States and of the several States, shall be bound by Oath or Affirmation, to support this Constitution; but no religious Test shall ever be required as a Qualification to any Office or public Trust under the United States.

ARTICLE VII

The Ratification of the Conventions of nine States shall be sufficient for the Establishment of this Constitution between the States so ratifying the Same.

ARTICLES IN ADDITION TO, AND AMENDMENT OF, THE CONSTITUTION OF THE UNITED STATES OF AMERICA, PROPOSED BY CONGRESS, AND RATIFIED BY THE LEGISLATURES OF THE SEVERAL STATES, PURSUANT TO THE FIFTH ARTICLE OF THE ORIGINAL CONSTITUTION.

AMENDMENT I

(Amendments I–X were ratified 15 December 1791)
Congress shall make no law respecting an establishment of religion, or prohibiting the free exercise thereof; or abridging the freedom of speech, or of the press; or the right of the people peaceably to assemble, and to petition the Government for a redress of grievances.

AMENDMENT II

A well regulated Militia being necessary to the security of a free State, the right of the people to keep and bear Arms shall not be infringed.

AMENDMENT III

No Soldier shall, in time of peace be quartered in any house, without the consent of the Owner, nor in time of war, but in a manner to be prescribed by law.

AMENDMENT IV

The right of the people to be secure in their persons, houses, papers, and effects, against unreasonable searches and seizures, shall not be violated, and no Warrants shall issue, but upon probable cause, supported by Oath or affirmation, and particularly describing the place to be searched, and the persons or things to be seized.

Appendix B

Amendment V

No person shall be held to answer for a capital, or otherwise infamous crime, unless on a presentment or indictment of a Grand Jury, except in cases arising in the land or naval forces, or in the Militia, when in actual service in time of War or public danger; nor shall any person be subject for the same offence to be twice put in jeopardy of life or limb; nor shall be compelled in any criminal case to be a witness against himself, nor be deprived of life, liberty, or property, without due process of law; nor shall private property be taken for public use, without just compensation.

Amendment VI

In all criminal prosecutions, the accused shall enjoy the right to a speedy and public trial, by an impartial jury of the State and district wherein the crime shall have been committed, which district shall have been previously ascertained by law, and to be informed of the nature and cause of the accusation; to be confronted with the witnesses against him; to have compulsory process for obtaining witnesses in his favor, and to have the Assistance of Counsel for his defence.

Amendment VII

In suits at common law, where the value in controversy shall exceed twenty dollars, the right of trial by jury shall be preserved, and no fact tried by a jury, shall be otherwise reexamined in any Court of the United States, than according to the rules of the common law.

Amendment VIII

Excessive bail shall not be required, nor excessive fines imposed, nor cruel and unusual punishments inflicted.

Amendment IX

The enumeration in the Constitution, of certain rights, shall not be construed to deny or disparage others retained by the people.

Amendment X

The powers not delegated to the United States by the Constitution, nor prohibited by it to the States, are reserved to the States respectively, or to the people.

Amendment XI

(Ratified February 7, 1798)

The Judicial power of the United States shall not be construed to extend to any suit in law or equity, commenced or prosecuted against one of the United States by Citizens of another State, or by Citizens or Subjects of any Foreign State.

Amendment XII

(Ratified June 15, 1804)

The Electors shall meet in their respective states and vote by ballot for President and Vice-President, one of whom, at least, shall not be an inhabitant of the same state with themselves; they shall name in their ballots the person voted for as President, and in distinct ballots the person voted for as Vice-President, and they shall make distinct lists of all persons voted for as President, and of all persons voted for as Vice-President, and of the number of votes for each, which lists they shall sign and certify, and transmit sealed to the seat of the government of the United States, directed to the President of the Senate; — The President of the Senate shall, in presence of the Senate and House of Representatives, open all the certificates and the votes shall then be counted; — The person having the greatest number of votes for President, shall be the President, if such number be a majority of the whole number of Electors appointed; and if no person have such majority, then from the persons having the highest numbers not exceeding three on the list of those voted for as President, the House of Representatives shall choose immediately, by ballot, the President. But in choosing the President, the votes shall be taken by states, the representation from each state having one vote; a quorum for this purpose shall consist of a member or members from two-thirds of the states, and a majority of all the states shall be necessary to a choice. And if the House of Representatives shall not choose a President whenever the right of choice shall devolve upon them, before the fourth day of March next following, then the Vice-President shall act as President, as in the case of the death or other constitutional disability of the President. — The person having the greatest number of votes as Vice-President, shall be the Vice-President, if such number be a majority of the whole number of Electors appointed, and if no person have a majority, then from the two highest numbers on the list, the Senate shall choose the Vice-President; a quorum for the purpose shall consist of two-thirds of the whole number of Senators, and a majority of the whole number shall be necessary to a choice. But no person constitutionally ineligible to the office of President shall be eligible to that of Vice-President of the United States.

Amendment XIII

(Ratified December 6, 1865)

Section 1. Neither slavery nor involuntary servitude, except as a punishment for crime whereof the party shall have been duly convicted, shall exist within the United States, or any place subject to their jurisdiction.

SECTION 2. Congress shall have power to enforce this article by appropriate legislation.

AMENDMENT XIV

(Ratified July 9, 1868)

SECTION 1. All persons born or naturalized in the United States, and subject to the jurisdiction thereof, are citizens of the United States and of the State wherein they reside. No State shall make or enforce any law which shall abridge the privileges or immunities of citizens of the United States; nor shall any State deprive any person of life, liberty, or property, without due process of law; nor deny to any person within its jurisdiction the equal protection of the laws.

SECTION 2. Representatives shall be apportioned among the several States according to their respective numbers, counting the whole number of persons in each State, excluding Indians not taxed. But when the right to vote at any election for the choice of electors for President and Vice-President of the United States, Representatives in Congress, the Executive and Judicial officers of a State, or the members of the Legislature thereof, is denied to any of the male inhabitants of such State, being twenty-one years of age, and citizens of the United States, or in any way abridged, except for participation in rebellion, or other crime, the basis of representation therein shall be reduced in the proportion which the number of such male citizens shall bear to the whole number of male citizens twenty-one years of age in such State.

SECTION 3. No person shall be a Senator or Representative in Congress, or elector of President and Vice-President, or hold any office, civil or military, under the United States, or under any State, who, having previously taken an oath, as a member of Congress, or as an officer of the United States, or as a member of any State legislature, or as an executive or judicial officer of any State, to support the Constitution of the United States, shall have engaged in insurrection or rebellion against the same, or given aid or comfort to the enemies thereof. But Congress may by a vote of two-thirds of each House, remove such disability.

SECTION 4. The validity of the public debt of the United States, authorized by law, including debts incurred for payment of pensions and bounties for services in suppressing insurrection or rebellion, shall not be questioned. But neither the United States nor any State shall assume or pay any debt or obligation incurred in aid of insurrection or rebellion against the United States, or any claim for the loss or emancipation of any slave; but all such debts, obligations and claims shall be held illegal and void.

SECTION 5. The Congress shall have power to enforce, by appropriate legislation, the provisions of this article.

AMENDMENT XV

(Ratified February 3, 1870)

SECTION 1. The right of citizens of the United States to vote shall not be denied or abridged by the United States or by any State on account of race, color, or previous condition of servitude.

SECTION 2. The Congress shall have power to enforce this article by appropriate legislation.

AMENDMENT XVI

(Ratified February 3, 1913)
The Congress shall have power to lay and collect taxes on incomes, from whatever source derived, without apportionment among the several States, and without regard to any census or enumeration.

AMENDMENT XVII

(Ratified April 8, 1913)
The Senate of the United States shall be composed of two Senators from each State, elected by the people thereof, for six years; and each Senator shall have one vote. The electors in each State shall have the qualifications requisite for electors of the most numerous branch of the State legislatures.

When vacancies happen in the representation of any State in the Senate, the executive authority of such State shall issue writs of election to fill such vacancies: *Provided*, That the legislature of any State may empower the executive thereof to make temporary appointments until the people fill the vacancies by election as the legislature may direct.

This amendment shall not be so construed as to affect the election or term of any Senator chosen before it becomes valid as part of the Constitution.

AMENDMENT XVIII

(Ratified January 16, 1919)
SECTION 1. After one year from the ratification of this article the manufacture, sale, or transportation of intoxicating liquors within, the importation thereof into, or the exportation thereof from the United States and all territory subject to the jurisdiction thereof for beverage purposes is hereby prohibited.

SECTION 2. The Congress and the several States shall have concurrent power to enforce this article by appropriate legislation.

SECTION 3. This article shall be inoperative unless it shall have been ratified as an amendment to the Constitution by the legislatures of the several States as provided in the Constitution, within seven years from the date of the submission hereof to the States by the Congress.

AMENDMENT XIX

(Ratified August 18, 1920)
SECTION 1. The right of citizens of the United States to vote shall not be denied or abridged by the United States or by any State on account of sex.

SECTION 2. Congress shall have power to enforce this article by appropriate legislation.

Amendment XX

(Ratified January 23, 1933)

Section 1. The terms of the President and Vice President shall end at noon on the 20th day of January, and the terms of Senators and Representatives at noon on the 3d day of January, of the years in which such terms would have ended if this article had not been ratified; and the terms of their successors shall then begin.

Section 2. The Congress shall assemble at least once in every year, and such meeting shall begin at noon on the 3d day of January, unless they shall by law appoint a different day.

Section 3. If, at the time fixed for the beginning of the term of the President, the President elect shall have died, the Vice President shall become President. If a President shall not have been chosen before the time fixed for the beginning of his term, or if the President elect shall have failed to qualify, then the Vice President elect shall act as President until a President shall have qualified; and the Congress may by law provide for the case wherein neither a President elect nor a Vice President elect shall have qualified, declaring who shall then act as President, or the manner in which one who is to act shall be selected, and such person shall act accordingly until a President or Vice President shall have qualified.

Section 4. The Congress may by law provide for the case of the death of any of the persons from whom the House of Representatives may choose a President whenever the right of choice shall have devolved upon them, and for the case of the death of any of the persons from whom the Senate may choose a Vice President whenever the right of choice shall have devolved upon them.

Section 5. Sections 1 and 2 shall take effect on the 15th day of October following the ratification of this article.

Section 6. This article shall be inoperative unless it shall have been ratified as an amendment to the Constitution by the legislatures of three-fourths of the several States within seven years from the date of its submission.

Amendment XXI

(Ratified December 5, 1933)

Section 1. The eighteenth article of amendment to the Constitution of the United States is hereby repealed.

Section 2. The transportation or importation into any State, Territory, or possession of the United States for delivery or use therein of intoxicating liquors, in violation of the laws thereof, is hereby prohibited.

Section 3. This article shall be inoperative unless it shall have been ratified as an amendment to the Constitution by conventions in the several States, as provided in the Constitution, within seven years from the date of the submisison hereof to the States by the Congress.

AMENDMENT XXII

(Ratified February 27, 1951)

SECTION 1. No person shall be elected to the office of the President more than twice, and no person who has held the office of President, or acted as President, for more than two years of a term to which some other person was elected President shall be elected to the office of the President more than once. But this Article shall not apply to any person holding the office of President when this Article was proposed by the Congress, and shall not prevent any person who may be holding the office of President, or acting as President, during the term within which this Article becomes operative from holding the office of President or acting as President during the remainder of such term.

SECTION 2. This article shall be inoperative unless it shall have been ratified as an amendment to the Constitution by the legislatures of three-fourths of the several States within seven years from the date of its submission to the States by the Congress.

AMENDMENT XXIII

(Ratified March 29, 1961)

SECTION 1. The District constituting the seat of Government of the United States shall appoint in such manner as the Congress may direct:

A number of electors of President and Vice President equal to the whole number of Senators and Representatives in Congress to which the District would be entitled if it were a State, but in no event more than the least populous State; they shall be in addition to those appointed by the States, but they shall be considered, for the purposes of the election of President and Vice President, to be electors appointed by a State; and they shall meet in the District and perform such duties as provided by the twelfth article of amendment.

SECTION 2. The Congress shall have power to enforce this article by appropriate legislation.

AMENDMENT XXIV

(Ratified January 23, 1964)

SECTION 1. The right of citizens of the United States to vote in any primary or other election for President or Vice President, for electors for President or Vice President, or for Senator or Representative in Congress, shall not be denied or abridged by the United States or any State by reason of failure to pay any poll tax or other tax.

SECTION 2. The Congress shall have power to enforce this article by appropriate legislation.

Amendment XXV

(Ratified February 10, 1967)

Section 1. In case of the removal of the President from office or of his death or resignation, the Vice President shall become President.

Section 2. Whenever there is a vacancy in the office of the Vice President, the President shall nominate a Vice President who shall take office upon confirmation by a majority vote of both Houses of Congress.

Section 3. Whenever the President transmits to the President pro tempore of the Senate and the Speaker of the House of Representatives his written declaration that he is unable to discharge the powers and duties of his office, and until he transmits to them a written declaration to the contrary, such powers and duties shall be discharged by the Vice President as Acting President.

Section 4. Whenever the Vice President and a majority of either the principal officers of the executive departments or of such other body as Congress may by law provide, transmit to the President pro tempore of the Senate and the Speaker of the House of Representatives their written declaration that the President is unable to discharge the powers and duties of his office, the Vice President shall immediately assume the powers and duties of the office as Acting President.

Thereafter, when the President transmits to the President pro tempore of the Senate and the Speaker of the House of Representatives his written declaration that no inability exists, he shall resume the powers and duties of his office unless the Vice President and a majority of either the principal officers of the executive department or of such other body as Congress may by law provide, transmit within four days to the President pro tempore of the Senate and the Speaker of the House of Representatives their written declaration that the President is unable to discharge the powers and duties of his office. Thereupon Congress shall decide the issue, assembling within forty-eight hours for that purpose if not in session. If the Congress, within twenty-one days after receipt of the latter written declaration, or, if Congress is not in session, within twenty-one days after Congress is required to assemble, determines by two-thirds vote of both Houses that the President is unable to discharge the powers and duties of his office, the Vice President shall continue to discharge the same as Acting President; otherwise, the President shall resume the powers and duties of his office.

Amendment XXVI

(Ratified July 1, 1971)

Section 1. The right of citizens of the United States, who are eighteen years of age or older, to vote shall not be denied or abridged by the United States or by any State on account of age.

Section 2. The Congress shall have power to enforce this article by appropriate legislation.

Table of Cases

Index